D1810598

To Vy-g. kurgh
who is himself a very
intelligent international
lawyer, and excellent,

le chth
13.01.09

INTERNET INTERNATIONAL LAW

International and European
Studies and Comments

International colloquium
19-20 November 2001
Paris

Ministry of Justice
University of Paris I Panthéon - Sorbonne
ARPEJE

Internet
International Law

International and European Studies and Comments

International colloquium
19-20 November 2001
Paris

Ministry of Justice
University of Paris I Pantheon - Sorbonne
ARPEJE

BRUYLANT
BRUXELLES
2 0 0 5

ISBN 2-8027-1743-X

D / 2005 / 0023 / 81

© 2005 Etablissements Emile Bruylant, S.A.
Rue de la Régence 67, 1000 Bruxelles.

Tous droits, même de reproduction d'extraits, de reproduction photomécanique ou de traduction, réservés.

IMPRIMÉ EN BELGIQUE

Forward by Mr. Raymond FORNI
PRESIDENT OF THE NATIONAL ASSEMBLY

All my life I have been committed to the defence of individual freedoms. As President of the National Assembly, this fight continues to be one of my main concerns. The reason is simple : they are the fixed cornerstone of democracy; they form the basis of Republican France and its institutions. However, *the* law is the defence of *our* rights. As a former barrister I shall never tire of repeating it : it is still the best ally in respecting our freedoms. It is the expression of our desire to administer justice and of our genuine, considered rejection of gratuitous violence and the undermining of dignity.

However, advances in new information and communication technology throw down a completely new challenge to lawyers and politicians. Some of our fellow citizens are concerned, others alarmed, eager to denounce the threats of electronic totalitariansm or digital crime. Those fears are legitimate. Nowadays, the keyboard can be transformed into an instrument of fraudulent practices which we must condemn and fight. It has become a weapon that should not be underestimated. Cybercrime is a reality and various urgent questions now arise.

This colloquium will be an opportunity to tackle some of them : for example, how can we ensure that personal data is protected ? How can we conduct judicial investigations on the Internet ? How can we combat fraudulent use of the electronic signature ? How can we prevent the pillage of cultural works and ensure that royalties are paid ? The Internet cannot remain an unregulated area. There are already both national and European laws but we must pursue and broaden our discussions. Together, we must construct the statutory and legal framework that is essential for preserving this new area of freedom.

Because these technologies are an opportunity for our fellow citizens. Let us be wary of hasty condemnations : they are just admissions of powerlessness to which I do not wish to subscribe. The Information Society will be what we decide to make of it. We must create the political vision to make it a fair, harmonious society in which individual rights are respected. We must devise the appropriate legal responses to the problems posed by these technological advances.

Your work will help to provide food for thought and to devise solutions. I thank you for that. Lawyers and legislators, our task promises to be decisive. But I have every confidence in you. I am convinced that your discussions will be equal to the challenge facing us today.

PRESENTATION

**The plan to organise a colloquium
on international Internet law
was not a simple matter
How should the subject be tackled?
How can this colloquium be made truly
international?
Which institutions should organise it?**

The Internet covers all the networks in the world. For Internet users, the journey to the end of the world is transparent. It would appear that there are no borders, no customs officers no oceans to cross or mountains to climb. Click! A computer located in Paris is connected to another computer somewhere in the United States of America. The operation is quite clear and an Internet user who has no legal training cannot imagine that the Internet is an area without rules or that the networks have transparent rules. By contrast, for governments, commercial companies and individuals who want to buy or sell online, the Internet is a kaleidoscope of conflicting rules that clash, and contradict each other : legislation and national case-law; agreements, conventions, charters, international treaties; European and international courts and case-law; arbitration courts and arbitration case-law; law; commercial law; criminal law; international commercial law, international criminal law, public law, copyright, patent law, etc... The national and international laws have governed the relationships of the actors in international life for thousands of years. The customs, needs and legal cultures are very old, different and often heterogeneous. However, from evolution to reform, the law has always found solutions that are often satisfactory, sometimes uncertain but, on the whole, realistic and effective.

So why a colloquium
on international Internet law?

Precisely because the Internet allows hundreds of millions of individuals and companies to exchange data, texts, images, sounds, films, to enter into contracts, download forms, buy and sell, pay, seek teleservices, teach, communicate ideas of all kinds, transfer money, arrange meetings and demonstrations, at the speed of light, for very little cost and, in theory, confidentially.

The Internet has given rise to e-commerce, distance teaching and international forums without anyone having to physically travel, completely new relationships between the public authorities and the ability to download legal texts as soon as they are published. However, a victim of its initial non-regulated, non-secure exchanges, the Internet has also created increasing insecurity, risks of hacking and the most serious computer fraud.

On the one hand, freedom of exchange and trade, on the other, insecurity and risk.

It was therefore necessary to superimpose on the sometimes thousand-year old legal system, new, specific rules that took into account national cultures and sovereignty in an area of global exchanges.

In 1992, President Clinton and Vice-President Al Gore came into office. They decreed the advent of the information society. The major international organisations gradually began to put themselves in a position to negotiate agreements and international treaties. The European Union, the World Trade Organisation, the World Intellectual Property Organisation, the United Nations Commission for Trade and Development, the Organisation for Economic Cooperation and Development, the Economic Commission for Europe, UNESCO are working together and perfecting new rules, adapted to the Internet.

Since the current version of the TCP-IP protocols is not secure, we had to find rules relating to data encryption, electronic signatures for messages, the storage of navigation records, the exchange of online consent, acknowledgements of receipt, the identity and authentication of Internet users (individuals and legal entities), certification of instruments for validating identities, the protection of authors, inventions, software and data.

The usual representatives of the civil society, associations, unions, groups, were not prepared. Their proposals were belated, their reactions timid. Non-specialist legal experts did not take the exponential development of the Internet seriously and the infinite series of new problems caused by this astounding success.

It was therefore the government representatives, international experts and civil servants who did the work.

In 2001, the work carried out by the States and international organisations was almost complete, at least for the major principles and some basic rules : principles of the protection by the law of Internet users' personal data, the original works of authors, the liability of Internet access providers and cooperation with regard to cybercrime; rules relating to the creation of electronic contracts, electronic signatures and certification.

However, it will take time, probably a good ten years before the majority of Internet users observe and comply with these hastily agreed rules. In the meantime, the rules drawn up between 1981 and 2001 will require major revisions and the ensuing new rules will cause further concern.

I. – The programme for the colloquium had to raise the question of determining the law applicable to the Internet

A) Various burning questions are still facing legal theorists, the States, judges and practitioners : how is traditional private international law tested by the networks, how is the law applicable to networks determined, what is the role of the law in technological advances, what influence does the Internet have on the establishment of legal rules? Three university professors, two of them French, (Mrs Bénédicte Fauvarque-Cosson, Professor at Paris-V and Mr Jérôme Huet, Professor at Paris-II), and a Canadian (Mr Pierre Trudel, Professor at the University of Montreal) provide open, new and forward-looking replies to these questions.

Let us quote **Bénédicte Fauvarque-Cosson** : « The development of the networks has generated an increase in situations involving potential sources of conflict and proceedings with an international dimension. In this new borderless area where the navigator can roam freely, the rules and procedures for private international law seem anachronistic whereas the idea of a uniform global law, arising from practice and implemented by cybercourts, is a blinding success. However, far from threatening private international law, the networks reinforce the need for it : the more borders open up and extend the range of possibilities, the more personal rights must be protected. If the rules on conflicts of laws and jurisdictions prove to be unsuitable, it is better to transform them than to do away with them. If the procedure for conflicts of laws appears to be lacking in that it involves applying rules of national origin designed to govern internal relations, it is better to combine it with the procedure for substantive rules rather than to sound its death knell. There are countless legal issues that are likely to arise in relation to use of the networks; no international uniform law will be able to resolve them all. As long as there are variations between national laws, we must define the rules for settling the choice of law ».

Jérôme Huet added : « In order to settle the disputes that can arise, we need to implement the traditional rules of private international law. They provide a tried and tested framework of reference and, most of the time, satisfactory solutions. Those that concern the determination of the applicable law, known as 'conflict of law' rules in space, are nevertheless dependent on the legal system of the judge before whom the action is brought : assuming that it considers that it has jurisdiction, the court determines the law applicable to the dispute in accordance with its own national conflict of law rules. Hence we are obliged to proceed by considering the rules of jurisdiction in the international legal system ».

Pierre Trudel provided a new point of view by sifting through relations between technologies and the techniques for legal argument : « Information technologies challenge the paradigms of law. By redefining the context in which information is exchanged, the Internet affects perceptions with regard to what would seem rational to govern and the changes in the rationale for enacting legislation. The methods of taking action and the techniques for formulating the law have also undergone changes. In addition to the official places where the law is drafted, there are the networks and practices of the actors who help to relay it. The law is increasingly laid down by means of processes that are capable of leaving openings between the various rule-making systems ». Some legal experts cannot tolerate the marriage of genres, the clash between the nature of computer techniques and ideologies that define the law. However, nothing is better suited to the reality of digital technology than the realistic and pragmatic nature of positive law. Pierre Trudel rejects any unnatural association but agrees that a microchip can be the third eye of Justice. In the United States of America, Professor Lessig suggested that legal microchips should be placed in computer processors [Intel and Thémis(?)].

B) Having examined the theory as well as the practice of rules applicable to the Internet and, accordingly, defined the benefits and limitations of the law, it was appropriate to review the methods for drafting international law in order to find out precisely whether these old legal techniques were suitable for the very new issues raised by the internationalisation and globalisation of networks and exchanges on such networks.

Diana Wallis, Member of the European Parliament and **Geoffrey Brigham**, legal advisor to e-Bay explained the relationship between international law and European law. Diana Wallis thus asked the question : « If we are here concerned with the lack of linkage between European and International law we should perhaps pause for a moment to consider that despite celebrating fiftieth birthday of the European Union last year there is still a considerable disparity between the law and legal systems of Europe's present 15 Member States. Disparities which I and colleagues as legislators in the European Parliament, on it's Legal Affairs and Internal Market Committee are increasingly forced to recognise and address almost constantly because of the growth of e-commerce. If Europe has trouble enough linking together its own law, perhaps it is not surprising that there is an even greater problem with international law. However the European Union has its own glue in this respect, it is based; and its members have signed up to the original concept of a common market, and now the Internal Market. Most of Europe's legislation or regulation is designed primarily towards ensuring the proper functioning of the Internal Market and the overall competitiveness of Europe's economy. It is this glue, with its goal of the Internal Market, which binds together the 15 Member States, some with vastly differing legal traditions, into one workable whole. It is this central preoccupation, which has now forced the search for pragmatic solutions to overcoming the differing national legal and regulatory regimes to make a success of e-commerce. However European legislators do have that common cause. What is the common cause or aims that could motivate legislation or agreement at an international level? Does the European approach offer us any pointers or templates for dealing with the quest for linkage between European and International law? »

Geoffrey Brigham, Europe's legal advisor to e-Bay, put forward the idea that « European and international law are united in their goal of promoting increased certainty for consumers and providers of e-commerce services. The chief aim of the European Commission's E-Commerce Directive is to ensure that the Community reaps the full benefits of e-commerce by boosting consumer confidence and giving providers of information society services legal certainty » (1). The « legal framework must be clear and simple, predictable and consistent with the rules applicable at international level so that it does not adversely affect the competitiveness of European industry or impede innovation in that sector. European and international law remain in development, however, with respect to e-commerce, and, as a result, they are not always well linked, leaving unanswered questions for the international corporation doing business within and outside of Europe ».

Professor **Yves Poullet**, Dean of the Law Faculty of Namur, in Belgium, identified the advantages and limitations of European law : « The construction of a European legislative area is certainly taking place through – sometimes tough – dialogue with the other partners in this increasingly global everyday commerce. Indeed the search for common principles or solutions within the national or international organisations, and consequently in particular in the protection of consumers or minors so far as concerns signatures encourages standardisation of the conduct of the parties involved, not to say cooperation (if only police cooperation) between countries. Accordingly, Europe seeks to have a presence within those organisations, including private ones such as ICANN. That involvement shows an awareness of not only the technical (far from it!) issues involved in the decisions concerning the choice of technical

---

(1) Directive 2000/31/EC (8 June 2000) (on certain legal aspects of information society services, in particular electronic commerce, in the Internal Market) [hereinafter « Directive »], Recitals 5, 7.

standards or norms. If a consensus cannot be reached, the European Union, in the name of its sovereignty, points out the choice of values reflected in its legislation. This reminder and the harmful consequences that it may have on e-commerce are the starting point for international negotiations with other countries. No doubt through means that are more in line with their own legal tradition, those countries will find adequate protection in relation to the principles set out by the European Union. The discussions concerning 'Safe Harbour Principles' bear this out. Come on : European Internet law does indeed exist. It has a purpose : to create confidence ».

All the same! The paradigms of neo-Roman law, from para-Germanic law and common law do not simplify matters. Community law is obliged to draw on the creativity of legal experts to find common solutions to so many different cultures. The enlargement from <15 to 27 member countries is a challenge for legal harmonisation.

Valérie Laure Benabou, Professor at the University of Versailles Saint-Quentin en Yvelines discussed the major issue of minimal harmonisation of the law : « At first sight, the question is disconcerting as the reply can seem so obvious. Yes, we need a minimum harmonisation of Internet law, undoubtedly, unquestionably and urgently! Through a common political will, the States need to harmonise their legal systems on the issues concerning the networks. They should agree on a minimum basis of universal values and undertake to ensure that they are actually applied. They must protect individuals against harm to their dignity or image and interference with their property, consent... that can occur via the Internet. However, the time for conjecture is over, it is now time for the demonstration. Why does this deep conviction seem to be so irrefutable and can it not, conversely, be maintained that no, a minimum harmonisation of the law is not necessary ? At least two currents of thought have defended that idea. Their arguments swing between the temptation of leaving it to the network and that of the status quo. »

Maître Eric Caprioli, barrister, Associate Professor at the University of Nice Sophia Antipolis dealt with the international aspects of e-commerce : « Currently, within the information society it is noteworthy that electronic commerce hinges on two central themes connected with temporo-spatial considerations : electronic

communications transcend distance and time between people and
goods and services, numerous people interact with their legal
environment by moving around, with no fixed geographic location.
However, aware of this phenomenon, the States tend to have an
effect on these parameters by localising the liability of the people
who supply electronic services in the information society and by
regulating cross-border transmission of data which takes place in a
relatively short space of time and therefore precludes any physical
supervision. We need to act upstream, to establish a legislative
framework ».

Stéphane Buydens, adminstrator to the Fiscal Affairs Division
at the OECD raised the theoretical and practical problems of the
tax-related issues of e-commerce by describing the contributions of
theoretical works, the practical obstacles and the limitations of the
matter : « Faced with the growth of e-commerce, the potential of
which has remained high despite the recent radical clean-up of the
market, the tax authorities have an important role to play : for
them, it is a matter of independently retaining their ability to
generate the revenue needed by the States to provide their public
services, whilst allowing new economic channels to fully develop.
During the Ottawa International Conference in 1998, the choice was
made between adapting existing tax legislation to e-commerce
rather than amending its basic principles or creating specific rules,
as it must neither be privileged nor discriminated against. Since
Ottawa, these principles have been widely backed on an international level both within the OECD and by numerous non-member
economies or economic communities. So far as concerns consumer
tax, a consensus was achieved on taxing cross-border transactions
in the country in which the consumption takes place, that is to say
where the buyer is normally resident (if it is an individual) or the
registered office (if it is a business), the taxpayer being the buyer
for transactions between companies and the service provider for
transactions intended for individuals (by mechanisms based on new
technologies). So far as concerns direct taxation, the comments
relating to the OECD's model Convention, which serves as a basis
for almost all the conventions in the world to prevent dual taxation, have been amended. The definition of a permanent establishment has been refined to allow a clear distinction to be made
between computer equipment (the server), which, in some cir-

cumstances, may be treated as a permanent establishment, and the information that is stored on it. In addition, the scope of the rules relating to taxable fees in the source country has been better defined in order to identify them in the event that a real intellectual property right is transferred. Finally, so far as concerns fiscal administration, the resources offered by the technologies that underlie e-commerce must be harnessed to provide better identification of the taxpayer, optimise the mechanisms for tax collection and improve the service to the taxpayer. Administrative cooperation must be strengthened both with regard to the legal bases that enable fiscal information to be exchanged and the technologies deployed to improve its efficiency and safety. »

C) Having analysed the contribution of the law to the Internet, highlighted the applicable rules and assessed their limitations, it was appropriate to examine the new forms of regulating the networks made necessary by cybercrime. The international procedures of criminal law, sometimes so slow that they lose their effectiveness, should be revised to take into account the cross-border and global aspect of the Internet.

Guy de Vel, Director General of legal affairs at the Council of Europe, gave a perfect summary of the Convention on cybercrime : « ... the Convention on cybercrime has a threefold objective : to establish common definitions of certain criminal offences, allowing domestic law to be harmonised ; to define the methods of investigations and criminal proceedings adjusted to a computer environment enabling the approximation of national criminal procedures ; to define both traditional and new means and channels for international cooperation to combat cybercrime.... The Council of Europe Convention will become, I hope, a global benchmark law, which will inspire reform of the penal system and criminal procedure in years to come. That will result in providing our legal systems with the means for concerted action against these serious forms of crime, preventing a certain feeling of impunity which seemed to be rife until now in this field and ensuring a precious balance between the requirements of the criminal investigation and the respect for individual rights ».

Jean Wilfried Noël, member of the judiciary, analysed the judicial investigation. He considers that « The Internet can simultaneously paralyse or dynamise judicial investigations, depending on whether it is used by the criminals or the investigators. In addition, the decentralised structure of the Internet network and the volatility of the data that circulates on it can give at every moment the judicial investigation a transnational dimension and therefore require the use of international mutual assistance in criminal matters. The combined influence of the Internet and the recent legal instruments of the Council of Europe and the European Union with regard to mutual assistance in matters of punishment, subjects the judicial investigation to a relative dematerialisation, which finds expression in the dilution of four key concepts of the criminal investigation : meaning, written material, space and time. During the years 2000, the Internet will accordingly enable judicial investigations to free themselves to some extent from the principle of territoriality and will speed up the establishment of the European area of freedom, security and justice announced by the Treaty of Amsterdam ».

Jacques PLAYS, squadron leader, representing management of the national gendarmerie examined the « problems of judicial practice in the context of judicial investigations on the Internet » : « The core logic of the Criminal Investigation Department within its fight against cybercrime is not changed by the nature of the network. However, in addition to the problems of legislative harmonisation at international level and the difficulties connected with establishing police and judicial cooperation, it requires strong technical support and training for all those involved at all its stages. Moreover, the main point is still to establish the conditions for storing data that are essential to discovering the author and, more generally, to the success of the investigation. The nature of offences linked to cybercrime is now well known although there are some important differences of evaluation at international level. However, they are still too infrequently notified to the investigative services in relation to the reality of crime and therefore active supervision of the network is essential. However, having regard to the extent of the area to be covered, effective technical resources must be devoted to this task. Once an offence has been discovered, the main part of the investigator's work is centred on looking for the available traces and evidence. The question of the nature of the data to preserve for the purposes of the investigation and the time they are to be stored has not yet been decided from a legislative point of view. There is still uncertainty for the investigator who, nevertheless, has clearly identified his needs. Moreover, the technical difficulties that can arise either when making seizures, conducting entry and search operations or when setting up computer communications taps, or by the perpetrators of offences using systems that guarantee their anonymity, require support from technicians and experts as close as possible to the investigator who may, however, be trained in a number of reactions with regard to cybercrime. Accordingly, in addition to establishing an adapted legal framework, training for a qualification is needed at all levels in order to exploit all the capabilities of technical and legal investigations. Such training should be vertical, from the investigator in the field to the expert, and horizontally, from the investigator to the judge. It must lead to greater coordination of the various actors, which, moreover, can be encouraged by the administrations involved working as a network. »

D) It was just as important to examine the governance of the Internet with regard to the confidence that Internet users placed in it or not. Governance of the Internet is imperfect. We need to make it an area of civility and develop co-regulation or even self-regulation. The examples from the Internet law, the GBDe and the ISOC give us a better idea of a complex set of issues.

Richard Delmas, Chief Administrator of the European Commission, in the Directorate General for the Information Society demonstrated that « The Internet is a defective governance... Governance of the Internet is presented as an imperfect form of regulation, a 'staircase world' in which each landing would be suspended from its own legitimacy and unique method of organisation, irrespective of any overall coherence or hierarchy. Accordingly, there would be many 'Internet' models, operating in tandem : the new economy, electronic commerce, online democracy, the digital divide, the network infrastructure, free exchanges, protection of data and trade marks, encryption, security, etc. However, it is possible to identify the modes of 'governance' of the Internet from the point of view of its animation and coordinating functions. It would seem to me that recognition of the standard and the law finds a preferred field of application in the phenomenon of the

Internet and the domain names system and that of its management ».

Isabelle Falque Pierrotin, member of the *Conseil d'Etat*, President of the Internet Laws Forum stated that « the Internet Laws Forum is a governing instrument... The Internet Laws Forum is a 1901 law association, created in May 2001 with the support of the State with the aim of bringing together public and private players to construct the regulations and customs of the Internet. It is a unique European initiative which, although very new, is already showing its potential. The current period is decisive : it must enable the Forum to find its identity, its specific field of intervention in relation to the other regulatory agencies. My intention is to find out how much this tool is a response adapted to the question of 'governance' of the Internet environment and how, in this new area of society, it can help to transpose the democratic values we espouse in Europe. Helping to build network courtesy, that, in fact, is the Forum's major ambition... the Forum is underway. It is not only a discussion area but a place of construction, commitment and responsibility. It is tool that is by nature private but its relations with the public sphere are important not in order to establish its legitimacy but rather to make its recommendations effective. In actual fact, it is an aid to governance, in the sense that 'governance' is understood as decision-taking in a complex system : in such systems, a decision can no longer be imposed by a limited number of players whether public or not; it is built step by step, following successive interactions between public players, businesses, representatives from the civil society; it arises from the unstable balance between them. The role of the Forum is to offer a permanent place for managing those interactions, encouraging the expression of this balanced position ».

Bertrand du MARAIS, Legal Advisor at the *Conseil d'État* examined the fundamental question of self-regulation, regulation and co-regulation of networks : « The question of 'regulation' of the Internet has been a topic of heated debate since the network was first opened to the public. In turn or simultaneously this debate took on several dimensions : economic, with the issues surrounding valuation of content disseminated online, in particular artistic content; political, with the identification of the appropriate authority for controlling content, particularly those with violent or pornographic connotations; philosophical, with the clash between the somewhat libertarian paradigm of the American creators of the Internet and the European users' traditions of national intervention. Following the attacks on 11 September, this recurrent debate is now starting up again with discussions over the 'security' control of the network. The purpose of this presentation is to examine which method of regulation, which if not the most efficient, is at least the most justified in the 'cyberworld'. It will be begin by describing the general background to the issues surrounding regulation of the Internet with a view to evaluating the suitability of the institutional methods currently used for such regulation and will end with some proposals with regard to the organisation of the French public authorities in this context ».

Bertrand Cousin, special advisor until 2002 to the Chairman of Vivendi Universal described the advantages and benefits of the Global Business Dialogue on e-commerce, created in 1999 : « At the beginning, the aim was neither philanthropic nor ethical : it was commercial in that it was a matter of making consumers secure, of providing guarantees to potential future customers placing and paying for their orders via the Internet. How has this self-regulation measure overcome several obstacles ? How has it made an effort to settle internal disputes and reduce external objections ? How has it succeeded in presenting reasonable recommendations to the public authorities and the world of business ? »

David Maher, Vice President of the ISOC, spoke from the point of view of non-governmental organisations and users by criticising « the surveillance and control of networks » and made some proposals : « This report shows that, in many respects, the role of the NGOs has been decisive in determining the past development of the Internet and it will play a vital part in the future. As long as governments want to delegate the control of technical administration of the Internet to an NGO (ICANN), the other NGOs will play a key role in protecting human rights in the use of the Internet. Amongst these organisations, ISOC (Internet Society) should occupy the position of leader. The work of ICANN has been a great success in numerous fields, particularly in developing technical standards, allocating IP address and restructuring the domain names system; however, the organisation has not yet been able to establish a viable structure that will allow the direct involvement of its members 'at large'. This is a challenge to be taken up by ICANN and the NGOs concerned with the political issues that ICANN is facing. Although a great many interest groups and commercial entities with solid financial support are active within ICANN, only a very small percentage of individual Internet users are currently involved in its activities. In the near future, the NGOs must therefore assume the main responsibility of representing the interests of the public... Since its creation, ISOC has led debates about the technical and societal challenges of the Internet. As an NGO open to all, it will continue to lend its active support to ICANN, the best hope for non-governmental supervision and control of the technical administration of the Internet. Similarly, it will continue to stand up for the defence of Internet users' civil liberties. Whilst ICANN is developing new institutions to protect the public interest, ISOC will try hard to serve as a model for the involvement of other NGOs in protecting Internet users' rights. »

II. – Having examined and debated the question of identifying the laws applicable to the Internet, the programme for the colloquium then had to raise the question of implementing laws on the Internet. Which laws need to be developed? Who are the actors that must be protected and what are their rights in the context of e-commerce? What rights do creators have and what protection?

A) What is the position of the Internet and e-commerce in the context of multilateral negotiations? Which legal issues need to be resolved to ensure the development of e-commerce? How can we ensure that consumers and S.M.Es are protected? How can we define electronic authenticity so that digital data on the Internet is at least of equal value to paper data? What are the advantages of the model law on electronic signatures?

Alain-Louis Mie, Manager of Institutional and Regulatory Issues at France Télécom and **Mathieu Guennec**, France Télécom, Manager of Regulatory Studies, International Division of External Direction Relations considers that « Although similar, the debates on the Internet and e-commerce within the WTO reveal different legal problems. The arguments that follow will deal mainly with the question of Internet access as this is proving to be crucial for the development of new services. As commercial services, Internet access services, are subject to the *General Agreement of Trade in Services*. However, a debate over the legal system applicable Internet access services arose shortly after the *Basic Telecommunications Agreement* was signed in 1997. Some member countries argue that Internet access services are basic telecommunications services. They draw the conclusion that the obligations arising from the WTO rules that are specific to telecommunications (1994 *Telecommunications Annex* and the 1997 *Basic Telecommunications Reference Paper*) apply to suppliers of Internet access services. By contrast, other member countries consider that Internet access services are value-added telecommunications services and that as such, those services are excluded from the practical scope of application of telecommunications regulations. This lack of consensus, although legitimate, precludes market players from benefiting from a clear, safe legal system. In order to preserve the dynamics of a rapidly expanding market and avoid any risk of 'over regulation', we must return to the spirit and the letter of the 1997 Basic telecommunications Agreement and consider that Internet access cannot be subject to it. »

Jeanne Seyvet, Director General of industry, information technology and the Post Office at the Ministry of Industry asserted that « In order to grasp the new opportunities offered by e-commerce between businesses and consumers, the legal environment must foster their development and, in particular, the establishment of a relationship of trust. That means continuing the processes undertaken both at Community level and at national level to adapt the legislative and regulatory framework for information society services, but also taking into account at multilateral level the delicate issues relating to the methods of dispute resolution in exchanges between actors from different countries. It is a matter precisely of appointing the relevant jurisdictions to examine the disputes and ensuring that the decisions made are recognised and effective and the law established to do so, but also the conditions for out-of-court settlement of disputes. Outside the geographical scope of European legislation (Brussels Regulation, Rome Convention), the rules and case-law of private international law apply, but there are several laws that could claim to be applicable and whose content can be very different. In order to create confidence, it would be necessary to be able to determine beforehand which law will apply. Moreover, we need to look for alternative dispute resolution methods that allow small claims and low value transactions generated by e-commerce with consumers to be settled quickly and cheaply. »

Georges Chatillon observed that the basic digital rights of consumers and S.M.E.s are partially recognised. In fact, the heterogeneous nature of positive laws and case-law on consumer protection precludes the essential effectiveness of protective laws. Can one only imagine drawing up a universal Consumer Charter ? Legal protection within consumer cultures protection is unequal and the emerging countries do not really provide legal protection for their consumers. Moreover, the mechanisms for protecting the fundamental digital rights of consumers and S.M.Es are still in their infancy. Accordingly, we need to provide online prevention by informing consumers and preventing disputes. However, these mechanisms are not sufficient and we must guarantee consumers online protection through protective contractual mechanisms and the introduction of alternative dispute resolution.

Maître Didier Froger, solicitor, representing his profession, took it upon himself to consider the authentic document. He demonstrated that « for the notary profession, the law of 13 March has not changed the legal system of notarial instruments. While it now allows authentic instruments to be drawn up on electronic support, it did not wish to upset the hierarchy of instruments and proof, nor change the factors comprising authenticity. The authentic instrument, the instrument of proof 'par excellence', could not be kept separate from a reform of the law on proof. Nor could it be totally cut off from new technology and the changes that has caused in our environment. On the contrary, authenticity can even bring a security to electronic exchanges which is currently lacking. Society does not need a third party to act as certifier, but a third party to give confidence, who is neutral and impartial and who states the legal position and restores balance in relations between individuals. It is the main role of the notary. The idea of authenticity, even in an age of globalisation and electronics is, in fact, very modern : far from ratifying the rule of impenetrable machinery and anonymous systems, it is reintroducing the human aspect, in this case the witness in the contractual process ».

Renaud Sorieul, Chief Administrator, Department of International Trade Law, Legal Affairs Bureau at UNO made an expert's comment on UNCITRAL's model law on electronic signatures (2001) : « Building on the fundamental principles underlying Article 7 of the UNCITRAL Model Law on Electronic Commerce with respect to the fulfilment of the signature function in an electronic environment, this new Model Law is designed to assist States in establishing a modern, harmonised and fair legislative framework to address more effectively the issues of electronic signatures. In a modest but significant addition to the UNCITRAL Model Law on Electronic Commerce, the new Model Law offers practical standards against which the technical reliability of electronic signatures may be measured. In addition, the Model Law provides a linkage between such technical reliability and the legal effectiveness that may be expected from a given electronic signature. The Model Law adds substantially to the UNCITRAL Model Law on Electronic Commerce by adopting an approach under which the legal effectiveness of a given electronic signature technique may be pre-determined (or assessed prior to being actually used). The Model Law is thus intended to foster the understanding of electronic signatures and the confidence that certain electronic signature techniques can be relied upon in legally significant transactions. Moreover, by establishing with appropriate flexibility a set of basic rules of conduct for the various parties that may become involved in the use of electronic signatures (i.e. signatories, relying parties and third-party certification service providers) the Model Law may assist in shaping more harmonious commercial practices in cyberspace ».

B) The introduction of laws adapted to the Internet with a view to facilitating exchanges of e-commerce, contracts and other documents makes it necessary, at the same time, for Internet users' rights to be preserved and protected. The success of Mp3, Napster or Gnutella triggered the anger of companies that collect royalties. The tactlessness of some companies that gather personal data, without any consent from their owners requires the States to protect their fellow citizens.

Jean Frayssinet, Professor at the University of Aix-Marseille 3, gave a detailed analysis of the reasons for the battles for or against the legal protection of personal data : « In my view, it is obvious that when the operation of the law on the protection of personal data is set back in the context of technology, applications, political, economical and social realities, one is led to reply that at the present time, individual rights and freedoms are not very well protected. Without going so far as to invoke the Orwellian fear of Big Brother which can be fuelled by excessive fantasies, I must admit that based solely on the realities and trends observed, I am one of those anxious people. We must fight the attitude that denies any infringements of rights and freedoms, adopted by those who, often for commercial reasons or on account of public or private authorities, intend to manage personal data without restriction. Because of the individual and collective issues, the importance of managing personal data is underestimated. The Internet needs a suitable set of ethics to prevent it from becoming a tool for subjugating the individual.... Manifestly, new balances must be found between the European model that has plenty of rules for protection but is rarely implemented and complied with because it used too infrequently by societies that are too apathetic, and the North American model which does not offer aware and demanding Internet users a sufficiently developed normative system. One can only hope and encourage a convergence between these two realities to prevent the Internet from being transformed into a freedom destroying spider's web ».

Michel Vivant, Professor at the University of Montpellier I, launched into a knowledgeable debate on the relationship between « French style » *droit d'auteurs* and « American style » copyright, a discussion that was very useful to legal experts on both sides of the Atlantic : « Reasonable : that is no doubt the key to *droit d'auteur* and copyright adapted to the networks and the Internet – by avoiding a war of religion and a war of dogma. Because – as I hope to have shown – neither one is true or false (or conversely), there is no good or bad system. It is what we make of it. Reasonable... *'Reasonable'* is a traditional concept of *Common Law* countries. And the 'good father' of the Code civil is none other, in a more modern and less sexist version, than a 'reasonable person'. That is perhaps the whole problem! Did you say reasonable? Everyone knows that our good father is a fictional being... »

Mads Bryde Andersen, Professor of Law at the University of Copenhagen, shed light from another point of view on the debate over the comparative merits and disadvantages of *droit d'auteur* and copyright : « In the above comments, I have tried to highlight some of the effects that the differences between the *droit d'auteur*s and the copyright gives when copyright legislation is harmonised at a global level. For a number of reasons – cultural, economic and indeed psychological – this particular kind of harmonisation is extremely difficult. The only message that should be sent to legislators is that harmonisation should only take place to the extent it is of *essence* to the world community. Harmonisation in the copyright area should not be a 'nice to have' issue that legislators should be concerned about. In the long run the concepts – also in the area of *droit d'auteur*s and copyright law – have a tendency to develop into similar concepts and results, and indeed so in areas where different cultures meet. The Internet is in itself a meeting place that should trigger case-by-case harmonisation based on a *hands on approach* guided by the common sense that courts throughout the world are well-trained in applying ».

Maître Marc Mossé, Barrister at the Paris Bar set out the now fundamental question of exemption for private copying, the right for Internet users to take credit for a copy of a work that they own, faced with the desire of producers to prevent any copying, at the cost of encryption that is easily deciphered by hackers : « The Internet symbolises the information society without restrictions or borders; it was therefore predictable that it would bear the explicit or implicit challenge to authors' rights. Not only because the idea that technologies make it possible to circulate or reproduce works without control prevails, but also because the user of new information and communication technologies is increasingly less aware of the value of the creation when it is offered in an intangible form and expressed as digital data. The aspiration to maximum freedom triggered by the Internet would thus be destined to a conflict with intellectual property... In the digital era when the transposition of the Directive on copyright is imminent, wisdom seems to dictate that we should consider a new overall system. Keeping to the French situation, no-one will dispute that the system arising from analogue technology must be reviewed in the light of technological developments. Accordingly, the decentralised management of rights could be one of the catalysts for reconciling intellectual property and freedom of access to culture ».

Finally, **Maître Alain Bensoussan**, Barrister at the Paris Bar, gave his point of view by explaining the basic legal argument concerning the patentability of software. *Droit d'auteur* began by protecting the original intellectual works. The inventors of computer programmes obtained copyright protection although some programmes are generated by machines. Computer experts on the other side of the Atlantic wanted to go further and patent software. This protection by a patent is already accepted in North America and in other countries. In Europe, the European Commission is in favour of it. The subject creates a Homeric legal controversy. Alain Bensoussan explained the points of view : « Over 13,000 patents were issued by the European Patent Office (EPO). However, controversy surrounding the patentability of software is still raging. Admittedly, at first sight, the eligibility of software to be patented would appear to be limited since Article 52 (2) and (3) of the Munich convention exclude computer programmes as such from the rules relating to inventions. Under pressure from manufacturers, the EPO made an effort to get round this problem. Taking the view that the exclusion raised in point 2 of Article 52 must be understood restrictively, owing, in particular, to the limit established by point 3 of the same Article, in the condition for industrial application of Article 57 of the Convention, the EPO sought a legislative basis to allow software to be patentable. Without referring to the effect that the ADPIC provisions had on this question or the discussions on the establishment of a Community patent, for its part, the EPO devised the theory known as the technical effect. The technical effect was first understood as being the search for the technical nature of the invention. However, there again, there have been recent changes to this concept that show some dilution. This effect was first assessed through practical measures : that was the case when it concerned a technical effect resulting from an industrial process. The EPO then admitted that the technical effect could be established in an electronic entity, for example, an image created by an electrical signal. For some time, the creation of the technical effect implied that the other conditions for patentability must relate exclusively to it and the EPO returned to a global interpretation of the claims without distinguishing within them the part that had a technical effect from those that had none. Although the technical effect is still one of the EPO's criteria for research, its power is diminished as it can be established by mere technical considerations. Finally, in recent decisions concerning computer programmes the EPO accepted the technical effect merely through its potential or even in the functionality of the information in relation to the recording medium. Although this development does not abandon the technical effect, it opens the way to the patentability of numerous software packages. »

C) Moreover, some permanent aspects of private international law need to be defined : how can we resolve cross-border disputes and conflicts of laws; how can we enforce court rulings?

For Mr Kazunori Ishiguro, Professor at the Faculty of Law of the University of Tokyo, « the most important premise of the traditional system of conflict of laws is the equality of every country's legal system which should be viewed as the most basic prerequisite for negotiations on further liberalisation of trade, too. It is quite understandable that not a few people regard the traditional system of conflict of laws as insufficient and useless, in particular in the context of the Internet or the GII. However, the traditional Savigny-type system of conflict of laws should be viewed as the fruits of scholarly research over centuries, or even a 'crystal' of our historical wisdom, even if it appears to be too fragile at first sight. It seems to be too dangerous for our world to make a sudden jump into the 'virtual darkness' and, in doing so, to abandon such historical wisdom ».

Jean-Sylvestre Bergé, Professor at the University of Paris-X Nanterre, dealt with resolving the conflict of laws, a major problem in Internet law : « The Internet is a fantastic promoter of ubiquity and although ubiquity is not always synonymous with internationality, between the two concepts there is a step which the private internationalist is naturally tempted to take. Accordingly it follows that he seeks solutions to conflicts of laws that are best suited to the reality of digital networks. Essentially, those solutions are in line with the old trends or more contemporary trends of private international law. However, there are two specific fields for which original mechanisms have been introduced. In this respect, two phenomena which have arisen in the field of European Community law deserve examination : the first phenomenon is that of *decompartmentalisation of conflict of laws* which can be found in matters of e-commerce and a second phenomenon of *the inclusion of choice of law clauses in contracts* brought about by the protection of personal data ».

S. Lakshminarayan, Joint Secretary to the Ministry for Information Technology of the Indian Government, considered the appropriate jurisdictions : « Present International Law already provides a base for solutions to problems concerning jurisdiction over crimes committed over the Internet. What is needed is greater co-operation among States and international rules that regulate issues that remain vague or problematic. The rules can be achieved through the establishment of International Conventions or through the development of International Customary law. It is submitted that the former alternative is preferable due to the clarity it brings to issues in a rather quick way (if states can agree to a convention). Customary law has traditionally developed more slowly, but in modern times the concept of 'instant custom' has arisen in areas such as Spacelaw. If State practice concerning a certain matter from the beginning is uniform and consistent and almost all States adhere to it, the usage will develop into binding international customary law rather quickly. However, considering the disparities among States as to technological development and control over Internet it is questionable if customary law is a reliable solution. The Internet's ubiquitous, yet intangible, reach has lead courts to inconsistent conclusions about the Internet's role in the traditional personal jurisdiction framework. These disparate decisions hinder efforts to predict the precise legal consequences a company faces when doing business on the Internet. While inconsistent in result, the court decisions do suggest that the probability of being properly haled into a foreign forum is directly related to the nature and quality of the commercial activity which is conducted over the Internet. Companies wishing to actively engage in e-commerce should anticipate the risk of defending litigation which arises in the markets accessed through the Internet. Companies unwilling to tolerate such a risk may want to consider designing their websites to limit interactivity and take other contractual measures ».

Maître Christiane Féral-Schuhl, barrister at the Paris Bar, dealt with the enforcement of court judgments, a crucial topic for the practical resolution of disputes : « Nowadays, the mechanisms for recognition and enforcement are governed by traditional rules of private international law. The question then arises as to whether such provisions are suitable for the Internet. Would it be more appropriate to draw up a specific international instrument that takes into account the particular characteristics of the Internet ? Are the international attempts at harmonisation that are being developed able to provide an adequate response ? The solutions proposed emphasise the legal problem currently faced by States, which are nevertheless democratic, with regard to the dissemination in their country of unlawful content, from other likewise democratic States in which it is considered to be lawful. Against this background, what avenue of thinking can still be explored ? »

Jean-Jacques Gomez, Judge at the Court of Cassation gave us his experience of the Yahoo case : « We know that in order to cause this search for a democratic regulation of the Internet to fail, some people then thought that by misapplying their purpose and it seems that it was a good idea, they could use the most favourable provisions drawn from the democratic institutions, in particular those relating to freedom of speech by choosing, for example, as a 'home base' the country deemed to be the most open and flexible on the subject. That is to say the United States. That has recently been demonstrated to us in all its 'legal' coolness in the judgment given by the San José Court on the application from Yahoo Inc seeking a ruling that it is impossible to make the decision known in France as the 'Yahoo decision' enforceable in the United States because it would breach the first amendment of the American constitution. Does that mean that we are now completely disarmed and unable to combat infringements against our laws and the rights of those who seek protection from our courts ? A simple reading of the Yahoo decision given in the United States would imply that everyone is afforded wide immunity and accordingly, even those who might transmit messages that breach human rights and offer services that break the laws of other countries, inasmuch as they might invoke the protection of the first amendment of the American Constitution. I do not think so because each national State has an obligation to enforce its laws and to offer its inhabitants the legal protection to which they are entitled. And in the much talked about Yahoo case that legal protection was implemented ».

The report by **Larry M. Smukler**, judge at the Superior Court of New Hampshire in the United States of America, is a case study that illustrates how the use of new information and communication technologies has enabled the State of New Hampshire to bring an action against cigarette manufacturers : « As the world is moving towards electronic document management and Internet data exchange and storage, court systems are lagging. The filing and service of pleadings by the parties and the issuance of orders and notices by the court continues to be accomplished by the printing of paper documents, conventional photocopying and the postal service. The system sags under the weight of heavy dockets. It is particularly unsuitable for multi-district civil litigation involving many parties and complex technical issues. This paper is a case study of how the New Hampshire Court adopted one method of using existing conventional Internet tools to manage several consolidated complex product liability cases. It examines the application of Internet technologies to four consolidated tobacco cases ».

D) Finally, it was essential to consider alternative methods for handling disputes. The problem is new because e-commerce can be interpreted by a multitude of contracts for small purchases and sales, the low value of which could prevent consumers from pursuing abusive vendors. What is the point of incurring lawyers' fees, the costs of proceedings and expert examinations that far exceed the amount of the payments ? Moreover, online mediation can be an appropriate solution for problems arising from electronic contracts and the small disputes between traders and consumers could also be settled online.

Timothy Fenoulhet, from the Directorate General for the Information Society at the European Commission explained the policy and work of the European Union in the field of alternative methods of dispute resolution in the Information Society :

Andrés Moncayo Von Hase, Professor at the University of Buenos Aires examined the legal obstacles and issues for disputes relating to e-commerce and arbitration : « The peculiar context in which private situations and transactions take place in Internet, that is : (i) inherently international in nature, (ii) likely to link individuals, merchants and entities from diverse cultures and distant geographical locations, (iii) frequently involving disputes over small amounts or conditioned by certain technical aspects or peculiarities of the online world that call for quick remedies and enforcement mechanisms, determines the need to promote alternative dispute resolution mechanisms, like online arbitration. Nevertheless, arbitration is currently confronted with a situation in which many legal instruments that are used to promote and facilitate traditional international commercial arbitration are illsuited for the development of online arbitration and the underlying characteristics of transactions made by electronic means through Internet. Legal texts lag behind technology and need to be updated in order to increase merchants and consumers confidence in the use of an open network like Internet to engage in business and settle the disputes that may arise therefrom using the advantages that technological advances offer.

Part I of this report is intended to give an overall picture of the peculiarities of the Internet transactions and the legal environment in which international commercial arbitration shall be resorted to and even promoted. *Part II* focuses specifically on online arbitration, and the legal barriers that may still exist in international arbitration conventions or domestic arbitration regulations for the use of electronic means to settle conflicts through arbitration. A brief mention will be made to experiences in online arbitration. *Part III* includes a reference to the actions that are still needed to foster international commercial arbitration to settle electronic commerce related disputes ».

Maurice Schellekens, Professor at the University of Tilburg in the Netherlands dealt with a new question, that of arbitration boards and e-commerce : « Disputes with an international component are difficult to resolve. Transnational players have long since acknowledged arbitration as an important tool to resolve conflicts because of its accessibility, flexibility, speed and cost advantages. It is only natural to assume that arbitration will also be able to assist in the resolution of conflicts that arise in the e-commerce-context. Moreover, in the e-commerce context, arbitration boards can go a step further and provide for online resolution. Certain arbitration providers have already opened the possibility to perform arbitration procedures online. This report aims to provide an overview of the arbitration initiatives that have geared up to solve disputes online and what legal obstacles might be encountered on the way to online resolution. For the analysis of legal obstacles, the New York Convention of 1958 is taken as a starting point, because of its central position in the recognition and enforcement of foreign arbitration awards... The legal issues that were dealt with here do not constitute insurmountable obstacles to the application of online arbitration within the context of the New York Convention. The rise of providers of online arbitration seems to reflect this. However, some uncertainties remain. Some of them may be easily resolved. They only need 'clarification', certain facts (acceptance of digital signatures as a valid means of authentication) merely need to be placed out of doubt. Other issues are more complicated. I think here mainly of the determination of the seat of arbitration. In arbitration rules that have been adapted to the online environment, a practical solution is found to the problem of determination of the seat of arbitration : the choice of the seat is left to the parties and, absent their choice, to the arbitrator(s). This 'practical' solution might very well work, but some doubts as to the desirability of the solution remain : whether an unconstrained possibility of choice is acceptable, is a complicated matter and difficult to ascertain. Here, lies a question that may not be answered without discussion. Nonetheless, for the time being, I would like to give the practical solution a chance to prove itself. Even more so, because there seems to be no simple legislative answer to the issue either ».

Finally, **Isabelle de Lamberterie**, Director of Research at the C.N.R.S. [Centre National de la Recherche Scientifique – national centre for scientific research] explained the questions raised by the online settlement of small consumer disputes : « Alternative methods of dispute resolution have a place in consumer disputes as in the regulation of the information society. In view of the conceptual and terminological uncertainty, I shall attempt to classify alternative methods taking into account the various meanings of alternative. This classification will take into account the status and role of intervening third parties and will show how the alternative methods contribute both to the preventative and curative treatment of consumer disputes. We shall then examine the principles recommended with regard to the guarantees expected from an alternative method whether or not it is online : information, transparency, effectiveness, fairness... Once again, the Information

Society regulation is in the continuity of that of Society. Use of the Internet medium does not change the balances to be sought and complied with at all. Secondly, to encourage the development of alternative methods is also to help to re-establish the social links. As for the Internet, if access to it becomes more commonplace and is not reserved for the privileged, it also can contribute to this same objective : it can facilitate access to information, help to make exchanges effective, open up new ways of marketing – particularly in emerging countries ».

*

*   *

The University of Paris-I Panthéon-Sorbonne, and more precisely the Post-Graduate School of Public and Tax law, and the Department of Public Law had already organised a colloquium on the Internet and the law on 25-26 September 2000 (2), after the 15th World Congress of the International Academy of Comparative Law (Bristol, July-August 1998) (3).

According to the rapporteurs of these colloquia, it appeared that legal solutions, albeit temporary but solid, were found for the main issues arising from the use of the Internet. However, although these colloquia made an effort to consider a comparative set of issues, according to legal practitioners, researchers and experts, it would appear that the international dimension of legal issues of the Internet had not yet been addressed in any systematic, cross-research or any international debate by practitioners and university experts from France, Europe or the major countries of other continents. There was therefore a *need*, demonstrated both by the university lecturers-researchers and by the representatives of the (IOs) international organisations, the (NGOs) non-governmental organisations and national Ministries (Justice, Foreign Affairs, Commerce, Economy-Finances, Culture, Defence, Information Society, etc.), to ascertain the legal problems of international dimension, to identify

---

(2) International Colloquium « The Internet and the Law – European and comparative Internet law », which was held in Paris in the Great Amphitheatre of the Sorbonne and at the Senate, on 25 and 26 September 2000, for which I was general secretary and the papers for which were published in 2001 by Editions Légipresse.

(3) Georges CHATILLON, rapporteur general for the session devoted to Internet law – Papers published by Editions Bruylant in 2000 : *Droit européen comparé d'Internet*, sous la direction de George CHATILLON, [*Comparative European Internet Law*, under the direction of Georges CHATILLON].

the multi-national or multi-continental issues and to propose responses to deal with the globalised legal state of the Internet.

France, together with its European partners, is resolutely committed to constructing legal areas that are capable of settling the main issues : data protection, copyright, e-commerce, evidence, electronic signatures, teleprocedures, public data. Solutions to these issues can be found both in the European directives and in domestic laws and regulations. Although these solutions take into account positive law and current legal opinions outside Europe, they clash with doctrines and bodies of rules inspired by cultural values that are fundamentally different from those that have been created in Europe. Some forms of legal liberalism conflict with other forms of social protection. North America has a concept of data (goods), authors' rights (copyright) and consumers (freedom not very well protected) that can conflict with the protection of private life, moral law and the commercial protection of individuals in the context of the internal Community market and the global market created by trade on the Internet. The specifically international aspect of the Internet is taken into account at national and Community level but it is primarily debated in international organisations – the Council of Europe, ISO, OECD, WTO, WIPO, UNO, etc. and also in the context of non-governmental or even private organisations, W3C, ICANN, Epic, etc., and by the big private companies, Microsoft, IBM, Intel, Alcatel, etc., and even in the context of world forums such as the Davos forum. Negotiations took place in the G7-G8 but also between the European Union and the United States of America, Japan, Australia, etc.

Whether they are governmental, non-governmental or private, the international arenas are places in which legal values confront each other and even clash so far as concerns the rules that should apply to use of the Internet. Whether it is a question of domain names, the liability of the intermediaries, the underlying rules of e-commerce or of works, there are few topics that naturally find international consensus. The questions of criminal behaviour on the Internet and international police and court proceedings need to be considered in-depth after drawing up a clear inventory. So far as concerns criminal matters, practitioners, experts and academics need to have a meticulous description of current legal practices and forthcoming plans for regulation.

There must be a comparative and proper international study on use of the Internet for the purpose of banking, tax-related issues and circumventing national regulations. The subjects that concern rule-making, standards, protocols and cryptography are just as important as those that relate to the protection of data, software, patents and trade marks at an international level. However, controversies surround all these issues and we need to know the ins and outs of them and grasp the legal consequences of the solutions to them.

The purpose of this colloquium was to take stock of :

- the state of progress of existing or draft conventions and agreements currently being negotiated at inter-continental and global level : standards and rules, telecommunications and convergence, copyright, patents and trade marks, data protection; information society services;
- the state of the main laws and case-law applied in international civil and commercial relations and with regard to the multiple uses of the Internet : commerce, stock-exchange, tax-related issues, public and private data;
- the establishment and implementation of judicial and police measures for the prevention and punishment of Internet crime; plans for constructing an international criminal branch of the law;
- the creation of « international » legal areas designed for the operation of the Internet : domain names, electronic signatures, cryptography, questions of evidence, governance of the Internet, the right to information and freedom of expression.

How could we make
this colloquium truly international?

Rapporteurs from the Member Countries of the European Union, Canada, the United States of America and Japan, the central and eastern European countries and the main international and non-governmental organisations were invited to take stock of the advances of international Internet law and to take part in discussions-debates with experts : academics, parliamentarians, senior international civil servants, managers of international public and private enterprises.

The colloquium's Scientific Committee held many sessions in conjunction with the representatives of the main international organisations concerned with international Internet law : the European Commission, European Parliament, UNCITRAL, Economic Commission for Europe, Council of Europe, OECD, WIPO, ITU, UNESCO.

The representatives of these international organisations well understood the need for such a colloquium and of the usefulness of a dialogue and discussions, specific debates and reports. The list of members (individuals and legal entities) and members of the Scientific Committee, which is published below, illustrates the truly international nature of the colloquium.

Which institutions should organise the colloquium?

The *Ministry of Justice* has a dynamic role together with other ministries [Foreign Affairs, Culture, Economy and Finance, éIndustry, Telecommunications and External Trade è], in the design, drafting, negotiation and creation of new Internet rules.

The University of Paris-I has a great many lecturers-researchers, courses, centres and research networks devoted to the study of Internet law, following the example of other universities.

ARPEJE is a 1901 law association that specialises in holding international seminars on across-the-board questions of law and cooperation. The French Ministries are represented there together with the legal and paralegal professions.

The Ministries of Foreign Affairs, Culture, Economy, Finances and Industry and Justice have appointed representatives to show their keen interest and allow this international colloquium to be organised.

*
* *

I should particularly like to thank Mrs Marilyse LEBRANCHU, Keeper of the Seals, Minister for Justice, Mr Eric WENNERSTRÖM, Swedish Secretary of State for Justice, Mr Michel KAPLAN, Chancellor of the University of Paris-I Panthéon-Sorbonne and Mr

Robert BADINTER, President of the Arpeje Association for the confidence they have shown in me and their unfailing support.

The meetings of the colloquium's Scientific Committee lasted for many months. The main divisions of the Ministry of Justice offered their invaluable help by way of offering their senior managers and experts. I should particularly like to thank Mrs Danièle RAINGEARD DE LA BLETIÈRE, Director of Civil Affairs and Seal, who was so kind as to agree to the idea of the colloquium and seek the help of the Arpeje Association, as well as Mrs Catherine CHADELAT, Deputy Manager, Civil Affairs and Seal Division, Mrs Marie Noëlle TEILLER, Head of the general civil law office, Civil Affairs and Seal Division.

The Department of European and International Affairs played a generous part in preparing this colloquium. Mr Daniel LECRUBIER, Head of the Department of European and International Affairs (SAEI), ensured that preparations for the colloquium were progressing well. Messrs Jean-Baptiste AVEL, Deputy Head of the Department of International and European Affairs and Olivier DE BAYNAST, member of the judiciary, France's representative to Eurojust, attended all the meetings of the Scientific Committee and offered their experience and pragmatism. Their active involvement was an Ariadne's thread for our work.

Messrs Eric RUELLE, Deputy Head of the Office of International and European Criminal Law and Jean Wilfried NOEL, members of the judiciary seconded to SAEI, Mrs Laurence HAGUENAUER, Special advisor at the SAEI, Advisor on Foreign Affairs and Mrs Gwénola DE LA SEIGLIÈRE provided an abundance of pertinent ideas to the Scientific Committee.

Mr Gilles SORBA represented the Criminal Affairs and Pardons Division on the Scientific Committee.

Finally, Mrs Florence SCHMIDT-PARISET, Technical Advisor to the Information Society the Prime Minister's office, with a wealth of international experience kindly provided helpful advice to steer the colloquium in the right direction and make it interesting.

*

* *

The work of the Scientific Committee was rich, imaginative, and thorough. The atmosphere was exceptionally friendly, cordial and respectful. I had planned to hold four meetings at the most. There were nine, at the participants' request. Each meeting lasted three to four hours! The participants got an enormous amount of real pleasure in discussing the issues of an international Internet law, exchanging their ideas and transforming these meetings into fraternal groups.

Mr Didier BUREAU, Deputy Manager, of the Technologies and Information Society Department at the Ministry of Industry showed an amazing clarity of mind, imagination and ability to summarise. Mr Richard DELMAS, Chief Administrator at the European Commission, DG INFSO, contributed his very detailed knowledge of the problems and his exceptional planning skills. Maître Patrick CHABERT, former President of the Bar, Barrister, member of the International Commission of the National Bar Council demonstrated his enduring intellectual powers. Maître Jean Daniel MATHIAS, Administrator at the Higher Council of the Notariat tackled certain debates thanks to his ambitious moderation.

Mr DUCABLE, Manager of External Relations at Alcatel represented some realities of businesses faced with the problems of international Internet law and set some records straight with outstanding diplomacy and courtesy.

Mr Jean-Baptiste AVEL played a big part in the debates with a very strong sense of the balances that need to be respected and with cheerful affability.

And, Mr Olivier DE BAYNAST was true to form with his semi-ironic, semi-respectful sense of humour. His talents as a debater and leader delighted the participants of the Scientific Committee.

Finally, last but not least, without the tireless tenacity of Mr Axel GAMET, it would have been difficult to prepare this colloquium. Let us give him our warm thanks for his efficiency, his tact and keen sense of reality!

*

*   *

The Scientific Committee wanted to stand alongside representatives from the main international organisations concerned with international Internet law. Without the use of email this active involvement could not have been achieved in time. In the Internet, it was possible to set up an international colloquium with very experienced and informed international delegates. I should like to thank Mr Robert BRAY, Chief Administrator, to the Secretariat of the Legal and Internal Market Committee, representing Mrs Ana PALACIO, President of the Legal and Internal Market Committee of the European Parliament; Mr Jernej SEKOLEC, General Secretary of UNCITRAL, represented by Mr Renaud SORIEUL, Chief Administrator at the United Nation's Bureau of Legal Affairs, international contracts department; Mrs Danuta HUBNER, Executive Secretary of the Economic Commission for Europe, represented by Mr David J. MARSH, Vice-Chairman of the Legal Working Group (LWG), United Nations Centre for the Facilitation of Exchanges and Economic Affairs (CEFACT/UN – United Nations Centre for Trade Facilitation and Electronic Business); Mr Walter SCHWIMMER, Secretary General of the Council of Europe, represented by Mr Guy DE VEL, Director-General of Legal Affairs; Mr Donald J. JOHNSTON, General Secretary of the OECD, represented by Mrs Anne CARBLANC, Chief Administrator, PIIC Division, Science, Technology and Industry department; Dr. Kamil IDRIS, Director-General of WIPO, represented by Mr Francis GURRY, Deputy Director-General of WIPO, responsible for legal affairs; Mr Yoshio UTSUMI, Secretary General of the ITU, represented by Mr Arthur LEVIN, Head of Coordination Units, external relations and Communication, Associate Professor of Law at the Franklin Pierce Law Centre; Mr Philippe QUEAU, representative of UNESCO.

I must emphasise that each of these representatives of international organisations contributed a remarkable objectivity and unique knowledge of the problems to the preparations for the colloquium.

*

* *

The Colloquium's organisation committee had to resolve some delicate issues of supply, relations with the institutions, the press, the rapporteurs and the participants. I should like to thank Mrs Laurence HELMLINGER, advisor to the office of Mrs LEBRANCHU, Mrs Agnès DOUVRELEUR, Manager of SICOM – [Service d'Information et de Communication – Information and Communications

Department] at the Ministry of Justice, and her tireless deputy Miss Nolwenn LOPEZ, Mesdames Charlotte FAFART, Irène LACASCADE and, from the Ministry of Foreign Affairs, Mesdames Isabelle GUISNEL, Deputy Manager, Isabelle ESPALIEU, Head of the Translation Department and, from Paris-I, Mrs Yvonne GIRARD, Head of the Computer Science Department, Mrs Paulette TAIEB, webmaster, Professors Bernard Castagnède, Director of the UFR 01, Public Law, Jean-Pierre MASCLET, Director of the UFR 07, Comparative European and International Studies, and Pierre-Yves HENIN, Vice-Chairman of the Scientific Committee. A big thank you to the webmasters of the international organisations who were so kind as to place all the information relating to the colloquium online.

*
*   *

The papers for the colloquium represent a considerable amount of work, a treasury of knowledge, discussions, and intellectual know-how that the reader will appreciate.

The Chairpersons of the Colloquium's sessions, Mr Guy CANIVET, First Chairman from the *Cour de Cassation*, Mr Francis TEITGEN, President of the Order of Barristers at the Appeal Court of Paris, Mr Robert VERRUE, Director-General of the Information Society at the European Commission and Mrs Ana PALACIO VALLELERSUNDI, President of the Legal and Internal Market Commission at the European Parliament led the proceedings in such a way that drew frequent applause from the colloquium's participants!

The general Rapporteurs for the sessions, Mr Herbert BURKERT, Professor at the University of Saint-Augustin in Germany, Mrs Isabelle FALQUE-PIERROTIN, Conseiller d'Etat, Chairman of the Internet Laws Forum, Maître Jean-Paul BRIN, former President of the Pau Bar and Mrs Catherine KESSEDJIAN, Professor at the University of Paris-II, Panthéon-Assas had the daunting task of summarising the proceedings for their session and outlining the main trends of current thinking of experts who have come from all corners of the whole world to present their ideas about international Internet law.

Without them, this colloquium would not have been able to achieve its goals. I am very grateful to them.

GEORGES CHATILLON

Lecturer at the University
of Paris-I Panthéon-Sorbonne
Chairman of the Scientific Committee and
the Colloquium Organisation Committee
Director of the Internet Law –
Administration – Businesses DESS
(Advance studies diploma)

Email : Georges.Chatillon@univ-paris1.fr

Section I

Establishing the law applicable to the networks

A

Standards applicable to the Internet : benefits and limitations

CHAIRMANSHIP

Guy CANIVET

FIRST PRESIDENT
OF THE COURT OF CASSATION, FRANCE

I am sincerely flattered to have been asked to open the first working session of your colloquium on Internet law organised jointly by the Ministry of Justice, the University of Paris I and ARPEJE, the Association for the Renewal and promotion of legal exchanges.

President Badinter, Chairman of Arpeje, who was unable to attend this morning, sends his apologies. He is unavailable today but will be with you tomorrow for the advertised presentation.

Your event brings together legal practitioners, scientists, very eminent academic experts from various fields, all in their different ways, specialists in network law. The aim of the colloquium is to take stock of the international legal issues arising from the development of the Web.

It is interesting to give an account of the numerous initiatives that have recently been taken in this area by the European and international authorities in fields as varied as raising public awareness or international cooperation. The major international organisations and the Council of Europe are obviously looking into the matter. However, ultimately, the places for discussion, reflection and exchanges on the legal aspect of the Internet phenomenon extend to all public and private arenas.

In France, « an Internet rights Forum » was created on 31 May 2001. It takes an active part in the various European and international initiatives. With a specific international committee, it is working to set up a network of correspondents, foreign public or private bodies that want to help bring about a convergence of opinions in a field in which reaching a consensus is not easy. How can we reach agreement on liability, regulation of e-commerce, the protection of works or combating cybercrime ?

During the 23rd international conference of commissioners for the protection of personal data last September, which brought together representatives from fifty countries, the President of the Republic and the Prime Minister emphasised how urgent it was to introduce regulation of the global public area that is the Internet.

Obviously it is essential to encourage convergence of international positions within Europe and beyond. Such a measure must reconcile firstly, the increasing demand from the public for new forms of dialogues and exchanges that are flexible and informal and secondly, the protection of individuals, private life, individual freedom and at the same time, freedom of information and communication.

Admittedly, progress has been made on harmonising guarantees for the protection of personal data. Witness the agreements concluded between the European Commission and the United States with regard to controlling the management of trans-border personal data flow (« *Safe Harbor* »).

However, the international crisis provoked by the dramatic events of 11 September last further induces us to take into account the requirement for collective security. In order to combat cyber-crime, States are having to adopt preventive and investigative measures that must be seen to be effective. Most people wish to do so whilst respecting individual freedom and the confidentiality of personal data. They are thus obviously faced with the classic contradiction between prevention and freedom, exacerbated by the technical complexity of networks.

For example, in its provisions that deal with information technologies, in given circumstances, the law of 15 November last on everyday security allows certain information to be made available to the courts. Accordingly, exceptions have been made to making data anonymous and erasing them. These issues will be at the heart of this afternoon's debate on the new regulations for networks.

No doubt, these same issues will be included in this morning's discussions devoted to determining standards applicable to the Internet which will try to include, in their various aspects, the matter of specific legal treatment for the information society.

Is a *sui generis* law required?

Within what limits and for what purpose?

Subject to some amendments or interpretations, is not ordinary law capable of dealing with the issues raised by the Internet?

Should we adapt it or create new systems?

Having regard to the multiple uses of the Internet, commerce, stock exchange, taxation..., how important and how effective can the traditional legal categories still be : civil law, commercial law, consumer law etc. ?

Does the specific nature of networks mean that the traditional methods of conflict resolution created by international private law will have to disappear ?

In what way does the Internet influence the drafting of law ?

The discussion that will be devoted to methods of drafting international law also promises to be heated. Although the European Union seems to have made progress on the issue of the Internet, its response would appear to be inadequate. The legal problems raised by the development of the web are beyond the scale of the continent. Accordingly, the solutions recommended by the European Union come up against cultural systems that can be substantially different which makes reaching a consensus even more difficult.

Given these circumstances, how can we construct international legal areas on the Internet ?

Is there an international consensus on standard rules ?

Outside the scope of the European Union, do the traditional rules of private international law still allow us to provide effective solutions to cross-border disputes ?

Are we faced with a harmful legal insecurity ?

At the same time, what effect does the development of the information society have on methods of drawing up international law ?

We shall have a better idea, after this discussion, of the progress made in international Internet law and will be able to appreciate the precise extent of the controversies involving different ways of thinking.

I shall now give the floor to the first speaker, Professor Fauvarque-Cosson who will deal with « traditional private international law challenged by the networks ».

1. – STANDARDS
APPLICABLE TO THE INTERNET :
BENEFITS, LIMITATIONS, ISSUES

STANDARD PRIVATE INTERNATIONAL LAW TESTED BY THE NETWORKS

Bénédicte FAUVARQUE-COSSON

PROFESSOR AT THE RENÉ DESCARTES UNIVERSITY, PARIS V

Conceptualisation, location and regulation are characteristic features of private international law; speed, ubiquity and freedom characterise the networks and no doubt also the times in which we live. In the era of information highways, why would one still stray onto the obscure paths of private international law?

Neither the railway, aviation, television or even computer science raised such concerns. Not only had private international law strongly resisted all these technological innovations but the question of amending it never even arose. Because up to that point, the area with which it was concerned had well-defined geographical and legal boundaries. With the Internet, the network of networks, we can subscribe to the idea that these boundaries are blurred, indeed that they are disappearing in favour of a new free, universal area. Hence the idea of a global uniform Internet law (the *lex electronica*) implemented by cybercourts. In reality, far from threatening private international law, the networks reinforce the need for it. Firstly, the development of the Internet sometimes described as « untamed » restores this discipline to its prime function : to guarantee that individuals are protected in all relations in which there is a foreign element. In fact, the more accessible something in a foreign country becomes, the more violations of rights and freedoms proliferate, leading to conflicts of an international dimension. As long as there are differences between national legal systems, choice-of-law rules cannot be avoided. In order to do away with them, it is not merely a *lex electronica* and cyberjudges that we need; all laws would have to be standardised and judges given universal powers and that is inconceivable given the various legal traditions.

From the choice-of-law method to the substantive method : this is rather like a transition from reality, with all its imperfections, into a dream world (I). In order to resolve the numerous international conflicts that are encouraged by the development of networks, we must retain the traditional methods of private international law, but adjust some of its rules (II) and take another look at this discipline which is creating a fever of excitement.

I. – From one method to the other

The choice-of-law method is based on the idea that the law which has the closest links with the situation and not the law of the judge instructed (*lex fori*) should apply. For that, it applies a rule that makes an objective distribution of powers so that each law may govern relations which « fall naturally within its scope, given their location » (1). It can therefore be distinguished from international criminal law, the basic principle of which is the application of French law on French territory (2).

However, the theory according to which judges apply the foreign law when the rules concerning conflict of laws requires them to do so is one thing, the practice of the courts is another matter : for obvious reasons of simplicity and efficiency, they favour the *lex fori*. This discrepancy between theory and practice which is often seen, is particularly highlighted in matters relating to networks where the traditional criteria for location sometimes seem unsuitable. By contrast, the substantive rules method seems to be more attractive as it is truly internationalist. However, by choosing the seemingly modern route of substantive law leading to a global law arising from practical experience we run the risk of succumbing to the mirages of universalism.

---

(1) BATIFFOL and LAGARDE, *Droit international privé (Private international law)*, v. 1, 8ᵗʰ ed., 1993, LGDJ, p. 445.

(2) For an illustration related to the networks, see the *Yahoo!* case (TGI Paris, ord. réf, 20 Nov. 2000), *Com. com. électr.*, Dec. 2000, Comm. n° 132.

A. – The delicate implementation
of the choice-of-law method

Before specifying the applicable law, the judge must satisfy himself that he has the power to deal with an international dispute. Otherwise, the recognition and enforcement of the decision in a foreign country would raise enormous difficulties and that is prejudicial to the interests of the parties and to the overriding principle of good administration of justice. The rules of international jurisdiction are created either by transposing French national rules on jurisdiction or by the new European regulation on jurisdiction and the recognition and enforcement of judgments in civil and commercial matters (3). or by applying Articles 14 and 15 of the Civil Code. In practice, as far as a dispute arising from use of the Internet is concerned, the judge will not inquire whether he is actually designated by one of those rules. He will consider that he has jurisdiction if the Internet site to which the dispute relates can be accessed from the country in which he sits. Admittedly, the judge often hears the matter as an urgent application. His international jurisdiction may then be « deemed to be established once the ordinary conditions – in particular urgency – for bringing proceedings are fulfilled and he would appear to be better placed than his foreign colleagues to rule, and above all, to get the decision he is required to give enforced » (4). Relieved of examining the usual rules of jurisdiction, the judge must nevertheless check that another judge is not better placed than himself. However, for disputes relating to networks, the urgency will almost always justify him having jurisdiction. Accordingly, whether they hear the case on its merits or as an application for interim measures, judges develop a kind of « universal jurisdiction » which is quite unlike the usual spirit of private international law.

However, there is a more serious matter : fortified by this power, French judges generally apply French law without taking the trouble to check whether the rule of conflict of laws designates a foreign law (5). Accordingly, legislative jurisdiction is linked to judi-

---

(3) EC Regulation, n° 44-2001 of 22 December 2000, *OJEC*, L 12, 16 January 2001, p. 1; *D.*, 2001, legislation, p. 440.

(4) P. Mayer, *op. cit.*, n° 285.

(5) See for example, TGI Paris, 1ˢᵗ ch. of 3 May 2000, « Lamy droit de l'informatique » (« Lamy information technology law »), *News bulletin.*, n° 125, May 2000, concerning an online auction service.

cial jurisdiction which is easily established. The solution raises important objections, notably because the applicable law then depends on how quickly the litigant brings the matter before the judge (shopping forum).

Although the simplest and most effective means of applying French law is to combine legislative jurisdiction with judicial jurisdiction, the choice-of-law method offers a whole range of procedures. Another technique is to create a unilateral choice-of-law rule which only determines the scope of application of French law (by giving it a very wide scope), without specifying the situation in which the foreign law has jurisdiction. An extreme solution, (but one that is close to what actually happens in the courts) would be to establish the following choice-of-law rule : if the Internet site to which the dispute refers can be accessed from French territory, French law is applicable (6). Another, more discrete way of favouring *lex fori* is to draw up bilateral choice-of-law rules with several connections (7). These content-oriented choice-of-law rules are primarily designed to favour a certain practical result. In practice, they favour the *lex fori* as there is a good chance that French law will be designated by one of the prescribed connections.

The judges also have two very effective means of reverting to French law : the public policy reservation which allows a designated foreign law to be thrown out when its application leads to a result that is too shocking and international mandatory laws (lois de police). Generally speaking, the legislator does not specify that a particular rule is an international mandatory law; it is for the judges to discover these laws. However there are many fields in which they are likely to apply.

The implementation of the standard rules of private international law, whether from a national or international source, sometimes raises another set of criticisms. In the world of networks, it is not only the predominance of *lex fori* that is perceived to be intolerable but also the fact that private international law prescribes the

---

(6) In favour of this solution, see P.-Y. GAUTIER, « Les aspects internationaux de l'Internet » (« The international aspects of the Internet »), *Proceedings of the French Commission. pr. int. law*, 1997-1998, p. 241.

(7) P.-Y. GAUTIER, using the evocative image of a « raft of laws having virtual jurisdiction » : « Du droit applicable dans le 'village planétaire' au titre de l'usage immatériel des œuvres » (« The law applicable in the 'global village' concerning the non-material use of works »), *D.*, 1996, 131, subsection p. 132.

application of rules of national origin, designed to govern purely internal relations. The objection has already fuelled the myth that arbitration belongs to a transnational legal system that is totally independent from national legal systems; it is currently behind the passion for the substantive method, a rival for the choice-of-law rule with the element of fantasy implicit in the idea of a uniform global Internet law, attached to an international or a-national legal system.

B. – DEFICIENCIES OF THE SUBSTANTIVE METHOD

Lex electronica, cybercourt : these obscure terms are imbued with mystery and have a dreamlike quality. And what if the Internet led to the creation of a uniform global law arising from practical experience, thereby removing all the problems of conflicting laws ? In an ideal world, there would be international substantive rules, drawn up by the authorities who regulate the Internet and enforced by cybercourts (8).

According to popular opinion, the *lex electronica* would be incorporated into the *lex mercatoria* – consequently some authors prefer the statement *lex mercatoria numerica* (9), or it would become identified with a « *neo lex mercatoria* » (10). Once the concept is launched, it is even more important to determine the content but that rarely happens.

In accordance with the rigour of principles, such integration of *lex electronica* with *lex mercatoria* implies the following analogous argument : in the same way that *lex mercatoria* would be this law « produced by the world of international traders and which would govern relations between the members of that society, a law with an essentially traditional base derived from international trade practices but in which arbitration case-law would also play a big

---

(8) For a critical overview, see J.S. BERGÉ, « Droit d'auteur, conflits de lois et réseaux numériques : rétrospective et prospective » (« Royalties, conflicts of laws and digital networks : looking back and forward »), *Crit. rev.*, 2000, 360.

(9) E.A. CAPRIOLI and R. SORIEUL, « Le commerce international électronique : vers l'émergence de règles juridiques transnationales » (« International e-commerce : towards the emergence of transnational legal regulations »), *Clunet*, 2000, 330.

(10) C. KESSEDJIAN, *Summarised report* (p. 149) in *Internet. Which Court Decides ? Which Law Applies ? Quel tribunal décide ? Quel droit s'applique ?*, Kluwer Law International, 1998, ed. K. BOELE-WOEIKI and C. KESSEDJIAN). The author also refers to the « net lex ».

part » (11), the *lex electronica* would arise from network users and would group together « all the informal legal regulations applicable in the context of e-commerce » (12). Such a meaning of *lex electronica* is too restrictive : firstly, because it presupposes limiting the field just to relations between professionals; secondly, because it only concerns this law originating from network users and is identified with self-regulation, a term that is not very forceful, extremely fashionable but too restrictive. If we consider the example of e-commerce, what do we find ? Not so much a plethora of regulations arising from practical experience (codes of good conduct, customary practices and other informal sources of law) as a plethora of transnational legal rules. Although initially they took the form of legal instruments with only contractual value (recommendations, model agreements, standard law) they now include various instruments endowed with the utmost binding force (conventions, European directives and future transposition laws). In actual fact, the *lex electronica* would be more akin to the method of international substantive rules, thus illustrating the need for a real legal pluralism. A global law calls for a globalisation of disputes : supporters of the *lex electronica* are also fervent supporters of cybercourts (13).

However, *lex electronica* and cybercourts must not completely replace national laws and courts. It is still necessary to rely on domestic legal systems and, consequentially, on choice-of-law rules although faced with the dazzle created by globalisation of the law and new technologies, our « bush science » must evolve.

II. – Changing private international law

Changing private international law presupposes amending some existing rules (A); on a more basic level, it implies an overall reflection on the future of a discipline that is deeply affected by the

---

(11) P. MAYER, « Actualité du contrat International » (« International contract news »), *Petites Affiches*, special issue of 5 May 2000 (p. 56).

(12) V. GAUTRAIS, G. LEFEBVRE, K. BENNYEKHLEF, « Droit du commerce électronique et normes applicables : l'émergence de la lex electronica » (« E-commerce law and applicable standards : the emergence of the lex electronica »), *RDAI*, 1997, 548.

(13) Compare E. JAYME, « Le droit international privé du nouveau millénaire : la protection de la personne humaine face à la globalisation » (« Private international law for the new millennium : protection of people in the face of globalisation »), *RCADI*, 2000, book 282, vol. 1, pp. 9-40, subsection 33.

internationalisation of law and conflicts between private individuals (B).

A. – AMENDING EXISTING RULES

Whoever calls for adaptation does not call for a revolution (14). In particular, there would be no point in seeking to establish a vast legal category, covering all the relations between private individuals affected by development of the networks. Issues of private international law relating to use of the network are dispersed amongst existing categories (torts, contracts etc.) that need to be amended but not radically transformed. The general view to which this report subscribes encourages us to consider whether there are some possible common directions both for conflicts of laws and conflicts of jurisdiction. Amongst these, the idea of favouring the law chosen by the parties deserves some consideration. It fits into a general trend of private international law, particularly apparent for contracts and torts, two of the fields most affected by the expansion of networks. As far as contracts are concerned, the Convention of Rome of 18 June 1980 on the law applicable to obligations retains its fundamental role, although it competes with other legislation establishing choice-of-law rules or substantive rules for some special contracts. Article 3 gives the parties freedom of choice as to the law applicable to the substance of a contract. That solution can easily be transposed to electronic contracts. Freedom of the parties to arrange their own affairs could even be strengthened; firstly by a more flexible acceptance of the practice of carving up the contract with some issues specific to the Internet – such as payment or third party content certifiers – calling for separate treatment; secondly and most importantly, by relaxing the ban on contracts without a national law, as the sources relating to network law are of such varied origins.

Everything becomes complicated when the parties have made no choice of law as the choice-of-law rules are based on the location of the contract (Art. 4 of the Convention of Rome). If they are enforced off-line, they remain transposable; on the other hand, if they are enforced online, they are not. For the same reasons, the choice-

---

(14) Comparison of the recommendations of a group of experts meeting at the Geneva discussions on e-commerce and private international law (*Rév. crit.*, 1999, 873).

of-law rules drawn up with a view to protecting consumers are difficult to apply.

In cases of tort, use of the Internet creates completely new situations that warrant extensive amendment of the rules based on the criteria of the place of the tort; how can we punish the huge range of reprehensible behaviour on the network and compensate victims when the loss can be suffered in more than a hundred and fifty countries at the same time? Freedom of contract, although more limited than in contract matters could sometimes provide the solution. More often than not, the parties will reach agreement once the loss has occurred (the choice of the applicable law can then take the form of a procedural agreement during settlement of the dispute). In domestic law as in private international law, another tendency is to place compensation of the loss suffered by the victim at the forefront; it can be seen in the form of choice-of-law rules with multiple connections or connections that are favourable to the victim (such as his place of residence).

For competence of the courts, freedom of contract is expressed in the form of clauses awarding jurisdiction, arbitration agreements or clauses providing for referral to a cybercourt. It is a basic rule for contracts and is also expanding into matters of tort : once the dispute arises, the parties, who are free to exercise their rights, can come to a compromise settlement or rely on arbitration.

B. – THE METAMORPHOSIS OF A DISCIPLINE

Private international law is undergoing a radical change; initially perceptible at the level of the sources of its rules, this transformation also affects its aim.

Although at one time, its aim was international but its origins national, private international law has seen a proliferation of conventions under the influence of the Hague Conference. For a long time that organisation retained the monopoly. For some years now and, in particular, so far as concerns everything relating to the networks, it has faced competition from other international or regional organisations. For example, it has to take into account the model laws of UNCITRAL and the European Union Directive on e-commerce, legislation of the Council of Europe, the OECD and the European Union for the protection of private life, etc.

All these combined efforts will enable choice-of-law rules to be drawn up containing amended criteria for location and, thereby re-establishing some balance between the *lex fori* and the foreign law. However, despite the eminent authority conferred on them by their international origin, those rules can always be overturned by national judges who may rely on the plea of international public order or police laws (15).

For their part, network users are struggling to find their way in this maze of ever changing legislation and draft laws. Paradoxically, this proliferation of rules serves to reinforce the impression that private international law has been eclipsed by practical experience which creates uniform substantive rules. The proliferation of new sources of law, the success of alternative methods of settling disputes make one wonder whether the aim of the discipline – to settle conflicts of laws and conflicts of jurisdiction – has not become too narrow.

At the beginning of the twentieth century, the function of the choice-of-law rule has changed : from being the allocator of sovereignty, it became the regulator of private interests, that is to say designed to allow the national law that best corresponds to the legitimate expectations of the parties (in theory, the law that has the closest links with the situation) to be enforced. Now, at the beginning of the twenty-first century, that function could change again. Indeed, the application of a country's domestic law, even if it is close to the situation, does not necessarily correspond more closely to the legitimate expectation of the parties. In many fields of law the State is increasingly disqualified as a central participant in legislation relating to people and their protection. The institutional sources, even if international, suffer the full brunt of competition from private sources. The role given to intent, which is continually being enlarged, creates an important phenomenon of « contractualisation » of the law. Against that background, notions of national law and foreign law gradually lose their substance; at the same time, notions of conflicts of laws and conflicts of jurisdiction fall from their pedestal and are only one aspect of all the conflicts that may arise.

---

(15) L. GANNAGÉ, *La hiérarchie des normes et les méthodes du droit international privé*, (*The hierarchy of standards and the methods of private international law*), LGDJ, 2001, n° 20.

From conflicts of laws to conflicts of sources of law, from conflicts of jurisdiction to conflicts of decisions : the aim of private international law is broadening. Although the Internet provides the most striking illustration of this phenomenon it is not the only example : international commercial contracts and fundamental rights raise similar problems.

In conclusion, although private international law will actually have to change in order to meet the new challenges of the information society, those challenges have not caused any major upset. The upset, if there were one, would relate to a wider phenomenon in which the networks are only one factor amongst many others. It would be connected with the internationalisation of relationships between private individuals, leading to an increase in conflicts of an international dimension, as well as with national rules being diluted due to the proliferation of new sources of law which are both complementary and rival.

THE LAW
APPLICABLE TO DIGITAL NETWORKS

BY

JÉRÔME HUET

PROFESSOR AT THE UNIVERSITY
OF PARIS II (PANTHÉON-ASSAS), FRANCE
DIRECTOR OF CEJEM
(CENTRE FOR LEGAL AND ECONOMIC MULTIMEDIA STUDIES)

With the Internet standard, electronic means of communication have taken on a global dimension which helps to increase the flow of business and circulation of information from one country to another. These are one of the driving forces behind what is now universally known as « globalisation ». Accordingly, an evolution that began with sea transport in ancient times, the postal service from the 18th century, the telephone in the first half of the 20th century and air transport in the second, each of which, in its own way, contributed to weave the ever closer links around the world.

This ever increasing internationalisation of commercial and intellectual relations between people is fostered by the remarkable potential of digital networks : an electronic letter arrives immediately at the other end of the globe and thus enables a contract to be rapidly sealed; Internet users throughout the world can consult data collected together on an Internet site in real time... Inevitably, at the same time, tensions, not to say conflicts, arise on an international scale more frequently nowadays than before : words or images made public in a country where they are allowed can be consulted in another country where their content is considered to be unlawful; academic works circulate in digital form between Internet users who make copies from one computer to another without their creator having given his consent...

The issues of law applicable to the networks, are therefore of central importance in legal thinking concerning the Internet (see on this subject, N. BRAULT, « Le droit applicable à Internet : de l'abîme aux sommets » (« The law applicable to the Internet : from the depths to the heights »), *Légicom* 1996/2, 1; O. CACHARD, *La régulation internationale du marché électronique*, (*International regulation of the electronic market*), Thèse Paris II, 2001; P.-Y. GAUTIER, « Du droit applicable dans le village planétaire au titre de l'usage immatériel des œuvres » (« The law applicable in the global village concerning the immaterial use of works »), *D.*, 1996, Chron. 131; V. GAUTRAIS, G. LEFEBVRE et K. BENYEKHLEF, « Droit du commerce électronique et normes applicables : l'émergence de la *lex electronica* », (« Electronic commerce law and standards applicable : emergence of the lex electronica »), *RDAI*, 1997, 547; E. CAPRIOLI, « Arbitrage et médiation dans le commerce électronique (L'expérience du CyberTribunal) », (« Arbitration and mediation in electronic commerce (The CyberCourt experiment »), *Rev. de l'arbitrage*, 1999, 224; A. HUET, « Le droit pénal international et Internet » (« International criminal law and the Internet »), *Petites affiches* 1999/224, 39; J. HUET, « Aspects juridiques du commerce électronique : approche internationale » (« Legal aspects of electronic commerce – an international approach »), *Petites affiches* 1997, n° 116, pp. 6 et s.; « Commerce électronique, loi applicable et règlement des litiges, Propositions des grandes entreprises » (« Electronic commerce, the applicable law and settlement of disputes, Proposals from the big companies »), *JCP*, 1999, *Actu.* p. 1761; « Réflexions sur l'arbitrage électronique dans le commerce international » (« Reflections on electronic arbitration in international trade ») *Gaz. Pal.*, 9-11 Jan. 2000, pp. 6 et seq.; P. TRUDEL, *Quel droit pour la cyber-presse*, (*Which law for the cyber-press*) *Légipresse*, March 1996, II, 9. – VAN OVERSTRAETEN, « Droit applicable juridiction compétente sur Internet » (« Applicable law and jurisdiction on the Internet »), *RDAI*, 1998, 373; M. VIVANT, « Cybermonde : droit et droits des réseaux » (« Cyberworld : law and rights on the networks »), *JCP*, 1996, I, 3969).

Moreover, that is not so much due to the extraordinary ease of transmission and therefore of international circulation of information – as it has always been able to cross borders – afforded by digital means of communication, as to the particular features of one of the applications of the Internet network, the « world wide web » or just the « web ». Anyone can set up and operate an « Internet site » on the web, (all the data located at an electronic address) if needs be, by getting it hosted by a server that can be accessed by the whole world, through a domain name that is typed in on a computer keyboard (for example, for my site : <myInternetsite.com>). The procedure means that any information contained on a site *de facto* has an international audience and that anyone who can find fault with it feels that he has grounds for complaining in his country's courts, the place where the information was made accessible to him.

In order to settle the disputes that can arise we need to implement the traditional rules of private international law. They provide a tried and tested framework of reference and, most of the time, satisfactory solutions. Those that concern the determination of the applicable law, known as « conflict of law » rules in space, are nevertheless dependent on the legal system of the judge before whom the action is brought : assuming that it considers that it has jurisdiction, the court determines the law applicable to the dispute in accordance with its own national conflict of law rules. Hence we are obliged to proceed by considering the rules of jurisdiction in the international legal system.

Determining the appropriate jurisdiction

In French law, as in most legal systems, the court that has jurisdiction to rule on an international dispute is, in principle, that in the place in which the defendant lives unless the applicant, if he is French, wishes to rely on the exemption from jurisdiction of Articles 14 and 15 of the Civil Code (the right of a French person to seek justice before a court in his own country). However there is a danger that that would make it impossible to enforce the decision obtained in a foreign country, and, as matters stand, it is prohibited in the European Community by the 1973 Brussels Convention which in 2000 became a regulation « on jurisdiction and the recognition and enforcement of judgments in civil and commercial matters ». However, we must take into account the fact that numerous countries afford their nationals such an exemption from jurisdiction.

Some grounds of special competence can also come into play : accordingly, in contract matters, the court having jurisdiction will be that in the place in which the service was carried out or indeed that named by the parties insofar as that choice is allowed; in relations between professionals and consumers, a consumer may apply to the court of his place of residence if the contract was concluded in the context of a business directed at the country in which he resides (new criterion introduced by Art. 15 of the 2000 regulation, so as to take into account the phenomenon of e-commerce but which will be difficult to implement : it would have been preferable to afford the consumer the right to apply to the court in the place in which he resides, in all circumstances).

So far as concerns intentional offences and technical offences, the court in the place in which the deed causing harm or likely to cause harm also has jurisdiction (Art. 5-3 of the 2000 regulation; and see Com. 7 March 2000, *Légipresse*, 2000, III, 78 : having found that a telematic service whose call directing code is in dispute was accessible in Paris, the Court of Appeal quite rightly decided that since the harm was suffered in that town, the Paris Regional Court had jurisdiction, it mattered little that the act causing harm also took place in the jurisdiction of other courts or even on the whole of the national territory; Paris, 1st March 2000, *Légipresse*, 2000, I, 89 : as the Agency for the protection of programmes revealed the existence of a site that was likely to harm the interests of defendants in Paris, the judge of the Paris court quite rightly held that it had jurisdiction; Paris Regional Court, ref., 22 May 2000, *Yahoo! case* : by allowing people to view Nazi objects in France and potentially allowing an Internet user resident in France to take part in an exhibition-sale of those objects, the site operator, despite the fact that he was established in the United States, is committing an offence on French territory which has resulted in harm to LICRA (the International League against Racism and Anti-semitism) and UEJF (Union of French Jewish Students), both of which are devoted to pursuing any form of trivialisation of Nazism in France, and accordingly, since the harm was suffered in France, a French court has jurisdiction to judge the case; and on the right of the victim, under Art. 5-3 of the Brussels Convention, to choose between the court in the place in which the harm originated and that of the place in which the harm was suffered, see. CJEC, 30 November 1976, *Rec.*, p. 1735, *case of Mines de potasses d'Alsace*; CJEC, 7 March 1995, *case of Fionia Shevill, D.*, 1996, 61, note PARLÉANI, defamation by a press article; 1st Civ., 16 July 1997, *case of Wegman, Journ. dr. internat.* 1998, 136, note A. HUET, counterfeiting).

This last ground for jurisdiction, in particular, allows in many cases a person who has a complaint about what happens on the « web » to take action to seek justice in the courts in his own country.

Having given this information, so far as concerns the determination of the applicable law, I should mention the rules of general scope which must be referred to in the first instance (I), then some special rules that can sometimes override them (II).

I. – The general rules
determining, in principle, the law applicable
to digital networks

Leaving aside the private relations that it enables to be established via email, communication via digital networks performs two main functions : firstly, thanks to Internet sites, it is a medium that allows interactive and widespread access to information distributed by others; moreover, it is a place in which exchanges of products or services take place, the vehicle for what is known as « electronic commerce ». In these two kinds of relations, those involved need to know which legal system they should refer to : in order to develop their business, to cover the contracts they sign, to assess the legality of certain behaviours... The applicable law is designated by what are traditionally known as conflict of law rules.

By contrast, for everything that relates to the organisation of the business of a person who uses the Internet to communicate or trade with someone else, one is bound to apply the rules in force in the place in which he conducts that business : this national law applies as the law of the place of establishment in accordance with Community law (See, in this respect, Art. 3, Internal Market, of the Directive of 8 June 2000 on electronic commerce), or as a police law in accordance with private international law (and on police laws, see, for example, MAYER and HEUZÉ, *Droit international privé*, (*Private International law*) 7th ed., 2001, n°s 120 *et seq.*).

All the same, we must not believe that where there is a dispute, the persons concerned will necessarily go before an official court. They have the right to use arbitration or more simply, mediation, whether by making provision in advance by means of a conctractual clause – an « arbitration clause » in the case of arbitration, which is allowed in relations between all sorts of professionals and not just between traders, since the law of 15 August 2001 on the new economic relations declares it valid in « contracts concluded in relation to a professional activity ». Outside any contractual relationship, one can also envisage using an unofficial means of settlement once a dispute arises. There are arbitration or mediation systems for electronic communication as is illustrated by the dispute resolution process introduced with regard to domain names at international level, particularly under the World Intellectual Property Organisation, which fall more within the scope of mediation (and V. F. GURRY, contribution to the *Second international conference on electronic commerce and intellectual property*, WIPO, Geneva, September 2001). Moreover, the Community Directive of 8 June 2000 on certain legal aspects of electronic commerce encourages the use of this type of procedure.

In any event, the rules to be implemented for determining the applicable law differ according to whether it is a matter of the organisation of the parties' business (A), the contracts they may be induced to sign by electronic means (B) and the offences they are likely to commit (C).

A. – THE LAW APPLICABLE
TO THE ORGANISATION OF THE BUSINESS

In order to use electronic means of communication as a medium or to offer products or services in this way, a person needs to know the legal framework in which he can operate quite legally : he must know in what circumstances the information he wishes to circulate can be published, how the services he is offering can be distributed and to what extent advertising them is allowed... The necessary international dimension of the Internet makes it essential to find out about these matters.

It is true that in principle one can argue that so far as the organisation of his business is concerned, a professional is subject to the law of the country in which he is established, a law which is readily designated as being that of the place from which the information provided or the product or service offered originated. And that solution is likely to give him a considerable degree of security. It is the solution that is imposed, in any event, under the European

Community where the principle of « mutual recognition » (a principle used in the famous 1979 « *Cassis de Dijon* » judgment, and reaffirmed in the 1984 White Paper on completion of the internal market), a principle which gives rise to the principle of application of the law of the country of origin : each Member State allows on its territory that which derives from other Member States and was carried out in accordance with their national law.

And, in order to define what an establishment is, we shall refer to the case-law identified for application of the « Television without frontiers » Directive which is reiterated in the 2000 Directive on Electronic Commerce : is established on a territory « a service provider who effectively pursues an economic activity using a fixed establishment for an indefinite duration » (and adds : « the presence and use of the technical means and technologies required to provide the service do not, in themselves, constitute an establishment of the provider », Art. 2, c of the Directive). It is therefore the location of the organisation's centre and the human resources of the entity in question that are the most important factors.

Indisputable within the European Community (1.), the solution is less certain when outside this framework (2.).

1. – *Within the European Community*

The application of the law of the country of origin is valid for all countries in the European Union. For example, for a trader established in France who is offering products or services on a site accessible to the public, the application of the place of his establishment means that he is deemed to be operating an « audiovisual communication » service within the meaning of the 1986 law on the freedom of communication and that he must comply with the requirements of that legislation, in particular those of the chapter entitled « provisions relating to online communication services other than private correspondence » (Art. 43-7 *et seq*). One of these provides that any professional « whose business is to publish an online communication service » must inform the public of his name, forename and home address, or, if it is a legal entity, of his company name and registered office (Art. 43-10-I), a solution which, moreover, is found in more detail in the 2000 Directive on Electronic Commerce.

Moreover, French legislation requires, *inter alia,* that professionals established on the national territory should present the products or services they are offering in the French language (the law of 4 August 1994 concerning the use of the French language, Art. 2 making it compulsory to use it « in the name, the offer, the presentation, the directions for use, the description of the scope and conditions of guarantee of goods, products or services, as well as on invoices and receipts »; a circular dated 19 March 1996, adopted for the implementation of that law, states that the obligation operates even for « directions for use included in computer software or video games containing on-screen displays »), or even to make a supplier of an online paying service make the user aware of the cost before he is charged anything...

By way of an exception, within the European Community the law of the country in which the information, products or services are received can apply and potentially block their free circulation : that is allowed in fields in which there is no harmonisation of legislation and if the country concerned can invoke arguments of general interest relating in particular, to public health, public order or consumer protection (See SCHAPIRA, LE TALLEC, BLAISE and IDOT, *Droit européen des affaires (European buisness law)*, 1999, T. I, pp. 187 *et seq*, relating to goods)... The argument could be invoked, for example, against sites marketing pharmaceutical products the sale of which is controlled, or against sites with an excessively pornographic content.

2. – *Beyond the European Community*

When one leaves the European Community and looks at it from a wider international viewpoint, the issue becomes more delicate. It is true, that one can continue to maintain that a professional must, above all, comply with the law of the country in which he is established and from which he is offering the information, products or services.

That is the standpoint taken in the ICC's recommendation entitled « The International Chamber of Commerce's Guidelines on Interactive Market Communication », which is designed to lay down « principles that guarantee responsible commercial communication on the Internet, the World Wide Web, online services and electronic networks » (1996, and see this text in the review *Droit de l'informatique et des télécoms*, 1997-1). Whilst recommending compliance with the ICC codes applicable to advertising, sales promotion, direct marketing etc. on modern communication networks and emphasising that « any commercial communication must be legal, decent, honest and truthful », this text points out that the term « legal in the context of interactive, universal media, means that any commercial communication must comply with the laws of the country from which it is circulated (principle of the 'country of origin') ».

However, in this wider context, although compliance with the rules applicable to the place of establishment allows the trader to feel a certain legal security, that security is less than in the Community context. The potential interference of the law of the country where it is received is to be more feared. And it will be feared all the more so because the laws likely to apply include penal sanctions. In that respect, I am thinking of the national laws banning advertising for certain types of products such as alcohol and sometimes the marketing of them.

These observations underline the fact that a certain public order will be imposed on electronic commerce whether we like it or not. It is true that it can be difficult to enforce but it cannot be completely ignored. As regards forbidden or regulated activities, one can mention lotteries or casinos. Numerous countries closely control public games, in particular games for money. However there is a danger that those provisions will be circumvented by the uncontrolled development of casinos or other virtual gaming rooms in countries with relaxed laws.

B. – THE LAW APPLICABLE
TO ELECTRONIC COMMERCE

Nowadays, international contracts are concluded not only by the parties physically travelling, via the post or telephone or fax : they are also concluded by means of computerised data exchanges (CDE) or via the Internet.

To closed networks such as SWIFT for banking, or SITA (State-of-the-art information technologies in the aviation business) for air transport, thanks to which we have been able to carry out computerised exchanges of data for a long time, since the widespread application of the « IP » (« Internet Protocol ») standard, one can add open networks which enable any person to negotiate and enter into contractual relations. Beforehand, electronic means of communication were used by professionals with a regular flow of business and their relations were defined by basic agreements in which provision for dispute resolution was generally laid down in specific clauses. This type of relationship continues to exist but now it is possible for professionals to be in a more or less occasional relationship and they can be contacted in the same way by consumers. In this new context, the stipulations concerning the applicable law, which one of the parties might have taken the precaution of providing and of making it accessible by the other when a contract is concluded, can certainly play a role but there is a danger that their enforceabilty will be disputed on the grounds that there could be doubt that they had really been agreed. More often than not, the parties will not have made any such provision. Hence the particular importance of rules serving to determine the applicable law.

So far as concerns contracts entered into within the framework of electronic commerce, in principle, for Member States of the European Community determination of the applicable law falls within the scope of the principles laid down by the 1980 Convention of Rome on the law applicable to contractual obligations. However, in French law, as far as sales are concerned, account must be taken of the 1955 Hague Convention on the law applicable to the international sale of movable property. Both texts, as it happens, are quite close. The most traditional private international law will therefore be implemented.

Both the Rome Convention and the Hague Convention recognise the role of freedom of contract since it provides that, above all else, the law chosen by the parties (Article 3) shall apply. So far as concerns professionals, the value of this choice will be readily accepted, in a clause in the contract, either because the parties concerned enjoy a lawful relationship or because their mutual agreement on that point can be established. That will cover situations in which a professional client gets supplies from a supplier and that in which a professional includes a number of traders in a portal or virtual shopping mall or even in what is called a « market place ».

By contrast, in relations between professionals and consumers, naturally there will be more hesitation in recognising the existence of confirmed mutual consent as to the choice of applicable law.

Unless a choice is made by the parties, one would need to refer to the solutions provided by the 1955 Hague Convention with regard to the sale of goods and, for other contracts, in particular the provision of services, to those provided by the 1980 Rome Convention : these texts prescribe applying the law of the country in which the seller resides (Art. 3 of The Hague Convention, unless the order was received in the country of the purchaser in which case the law of that country must be applied : however the rule is difficult to enforce when faced with a non-material method of ordering), or that of the country in which the party provides the particular service and therefore, that of the service provider (Art. 4 of the Rome Convention). Between professionals, that will not create any difficulty in situations in which a product or service is provided; by contrast, it will be less easy in situations involving reciprocal services which are also significant, for example in the case of a virtual shopping mall; however the difficulty is the same as in traditional commerce.

In relations with a consumer, the same rules operate (accordingly, the law of the seller of the product or supplier of the service is applied), with this reservation, that so far as concerns the provision of services, the consumer may rely on the protection of his national law if he has replied to a special offer or advertising in his own country and if the documents required to conclude the contract were drawn up there (Art. 5 of the Rome Convention; The Hague Convention does not contain any provision aimed at the consumer but it applies the law of the purchaser where the order was received in the country in which the latter resides, Art. 3 para. 2; however, it is accepted that the consumerist solution of the Rome convention can be extended to a contract for sale governed by The Hague Convention. See O. CACHARD, aforementioned essay, n° 236, quoting a solemn declaration of The Hague Conference). However, the terms in which that solution is worded make it difficult to apply to electronic commerce : one is justified in thinking that the condition of soliciting will be rarely fulfilled as more often than not, the consumer spontaneously visits an Internet site to order a product or service. However, it will be a different matter in cases in which he was solicited, notably through e-mail (« spamming »). As for the requirement that the contract was concluded in the consumer's country, it is ill-suited to electronic commerce : where does the transaction take place from a legal point of view, on the consumer's computer or on the professional's server ? It is a very clever person who can say for certain...

Different again is the situation in which two individuals enter into a contract on an auction site operated by a professional, such as « e-bay » or « i-bazar ». Often it will concern a sale and according to the Hague Convention, the law « of the country in which the exchange is situated or the auction takes place » must be applied (Art. 3, para. 3) and that also raises problems of location which can be very difficult to resolve on digital networks.

C. – THE LAW APPLICABLE
TO ELECTRONIC COMMUNICATION

When digital networks open to the public are used for public communication purposes, for example, for broadcasting an item of news, it can be seen that conflicts often arise from a tortious act – representations that infringe image rights, comments that can be consulted online inciting racial hatred, musical works that are communicated without the author's permission, images of paedophile nature etc. – so that frequently, the individual victim or organisation in charge of defending the scorned interests will bring his action before the court of his place of residence, as the place in which the information is accessible by a computer terminal and, accordingly, where the damage occurred. Then he will seek the application of his national law as being the law of the place in which the offence was committed : generally speaking, the court before which the action is brought declares itself to be competent and thus agrees to apply the law of the defendant's place of residence (in this respect see the aforementioned *Yahoo!* case judged by the Paris District Court on 22 May 2000, Nazi memorabilia; and in the same case, in the criminal division, Regional Court, 26 February 2002, unpublished).

Effectively, the law applicable to extra-contractual liability is that of the country in which the harmful act took place, a place which also extends to both the place of the cause of action and the place in which it occurred; accordingly, in an action for unfair competition arising from an American review containing harmful articles being circulated in France, a decision ruling that the act of extra-contractual liability was in the United States, where the litigious writings had been published and it therefore fell within the jurisdiction of American law, whereas the cause of action, constituted by the circulation of reviews and the place in which the damage occurred, were in France, was quashed (Com. 7 March 2000, *JCP*, 1997, II, 22903, note H. MUIR WATT; adde, Paris Regional Court, 3 May 2000, *case of Nart*, D., 2000, somm. 278, obs. Ch. CARON, *Gaz. Pal.*, 19-20 July 2000, 47 : when all the characteristic features of sales by public auction are present and the offer is addressed to any Internet user, there is interference in the organisation and conduct of auction sales of movable property situated in France, which, by law, can only be conducted by auctioneers).

It is easy to denounce the drawbacks of that solution which makes electronic communication potentially governed by judges and laws of any country, but without any international harmonisation on the matter it is difficult, at the present time, to see any alternative. In any event, so far as concerns cases of infringement of copyright which are often judged in the place in which the liability in tort took place, the solution is backed up by the Berne Convention which states in principle that the law of the country in which protection is sought must be applied (see below II).

II. – The specific rules that sometimes determine the law applicable to digital networks

Counteracting the application of general rules or used in conjunction with them, specific rules can interfere in the determination of the applicable law : this is the case when dealing with artistic and literary property (A), or a criminal offence (B).

A. – THE SPECIAL CASE
OF LITERARY AND ARTISTIC PROPERTY

The international circulation of literary and artistic works is increasing with the growth in world trade (cultural products) and development of electronic means of communication (access to online services), which places special importance on resolving conflicts of law in these matters (see on the subject, in particular, A. LUCAS, *Aspects de droit international privé de la protection d'œuvres et d'objets de droits connexes transmis par les réseaux numériques mondiaux*, WIPO, Geneva 30 and 31 January 2001; J. GINSBURG, *Private international law aspects of the protection of works and objects of related rights transmitted through digital networks*, WIPO, 30 November 1998; J.-S. BERGÉ, « Droit d'auteur, conflits de lois et réseaux numériques : rétrospective et prospective » (« Copyright, conflicts of laws and digital networks : looking to the past and the future »), *Rev. crit. dr. internat. privé*, 2000, 357).

However, it can be seen that at international level there are special rules for this (1.) and these rules do not resolve all the difficulties as the problems are so complex (2.) that it is not easy to identify the desirable solutions (3.).

1. – *Rules peculiar to copyright*

The principal rules of private international law applicable to copyright derive from the Berne Convention and, in particular, Art. 5 (2) which provides that the enjoyment and exercise of rights shall not be subject to any formality, that such enjoyment and such exercise shall be « independent of the existence of protection in the country of origin » and that « the extent of protection as well as the means of redress afforded to the author to protect his rights shall be governed exclusively by the laws of the country where protection is claimed »; one can see there that the application of the law of the country in which the work is received or destination country is upheld, a solution which is quite close to that which is often applied in cases of tort (see above I, C).

In a similar way, to a large extent, Art. 7 (8) of the Convention provides that : « the term shall be governed by the legislation of the country where protection is claimed : however, unless the legislation of that country otherwise provides, the term shall not exceed the term fixed in the country of origin of the work »; here one can see the law of the country of receipt combined with the law of the country of origin. Finally, Art. 14*bis* (2) (a) of the convention provides that « ownership of copyright in a cinematographic work shall be a matter for legislation in the country where protection is claimed ».

Other rules can be found in the 1996 WIPO Treaty, Art. 6 (2) of which mentions the exhaustion of the rights after the first sale (leaving the parties to the contract the right to decide), and in the 2001 European directive on Copyright, recital n° 28 of which states that there is no exhaustion of rights outside the Community (but no article of the Directive confirms it...; Art. 4 (2) provides for the exhaustion of rights where the original or copies of the work are sold within the Community).

The Berne Convention therefore favours the application of the law of the country of receipt – as being the law of the country in which protection is claimed – and it was thought that at Community level the solution ran counter to the principle of application of the law of the country of origin, necessary for the free movement of goods and services, (See p. 41 of the *Green Paper* of 1995 on copyright, drawn up by the Commission), which is undoubtedly incorrect since the two issues of private international law and European law are clearly separate.

2. – *Complexity of the issues*

The specific nature of the issues arises from the fact that despite reference to the principle of the law of the country in which protection is being claimed, contained in Article 5 (2) of the Berne Convention, it is difficult to completely disregard the law of the country of origin of the work (and see in particular, A. Lucas, aforementioned, spé. n°s 37 *et seq*), at least for settling issues that concern the very principle of the law : condition of originality, ownership of the rights (single work, work created as an employee, collective work...), limits and exceptions...

Nevertheless, the law of the country in which protection is claimed undoubtedly takes precedence : favoured by the Berne Convention, one can also observe that it has connections with the law governing liability (law of the place in which the damage took place), that it is often similar to the law applicable to issues of proof and jurisdiction (law of the court before which the action is brought), as well as to criminal law (see below B), and especially that it provides the public with some transparency as to the conditions for protection of works (sanctions for unlawful use).

Moreover, other laws can interfere with the law of the country of origin and that of the country of receipt : that will be the case in particular with the law chosen by the parties to a contract. It may be a contract for audiovisual production, a publishing contract, a contract for access to a database etc.

As for the interests at stake, clearly there are many : besides the interest of authors (who will want the widest protection), there are those of the producers and broadcasters (no doubt concerned about their contractual freedom), not to mention those of the public (for whom there must be transparency and security).

3. – *Aspects of a solution*

In order to overcome the contradictions and divergences inherent in the matter, one cannot rule out that several national laws and, in particular, that of the law of the country of origin and the country of receipt, can be applied in conjunction : the Berne Convention, itself, gives such an example with regard to the term of protection (Art. 7, § 8).

It will be more plausible to do this when there is already some harmonisation of national laws, both at world level (Berne Convention) and regional level (2001 Community Directive), and where *de facto* the major powers that produce works of the mind sometimes harmonise their laws spontaneously (as between Europe and the USA with regard to the duration of rights).

However, when that is not possible, generally speaking one will have to resort to distributing rights by making a distinction between the principle and ownership of the rights on the one hand (law of the country of origin, understood as meaning the country in which the work was first made available to the public), exercise and defence of the rights on the other (law of the country in which protection is claimed, understood as meaning that of the judge before whom the case is brought).

However, in practice, no doubt we will see a certain supremacy of the law of the judge before whom the action is brought as being the law of the place where the damage occurred and potentially as the criminal law applicable to an offence of counterfeiting.

B. – THE SPECIAL CASE
OF PUNITIVE ACTION IN CRIMINAL MATTERS

The solutions that can be provided in the punishing country to issues of the law applicable to digital networks, and in particular the Internet (See especially, A. HUET, « Droit pénal international et Internet » (« International criminal law and the Internet »), *Petites Affiches*, 1999, n° 224, pp. 39 *et seq*), are distinct and rely on three characteristics of international criminal law which exist in French law and often also in the laws of other countries.

The first characteristic, the theory of « ubiquity », enshrined in Art. 113-2 of the New Penal Code, means that whilst in principle, French criminal law is of national scope, it can be applied to offences committed in a foreign country : it is sufficient for only one of the acts constituting that offence to have been committed on French territory. However, this rule is interpreted very widely, to such an extent that the mere finding that it is possible to access from France a site located in a foreign country, which contains content likely to be deemed unlawful, is enough to fulfil this condition (in this respect, A. HUET, « Droit pénal international et Internet » (« International criminal law and the Internet »), *aforementoned*, p. 40; and see the case-law quoted below concerning jurisdiction).

The second characteristic, the cohesion of jurisdictional and legislative competence in international criminal law : the criminal judge necessarily applies his own law, which means that if French law is applicable to an offence that originated in a foreign country, the French judge will declare that he has jurisdiction to hear the court action implementing that law (See Paris Criminal Court, 13 Nov. 1998, *case of Faurisson*, Rev. Lamy dr. aff. 1999, 888 : in matters of the press, it is established that the offence is deemed to have been committed everywhere that the writing has been circulated, the broadcast heard or seen and so the Paris Court has jurisdiction when an offending revisionist text, circulated on the Internet from a foreign site, was received and seen in the territorial jurisdiction of the Paris Court; Paris Regional Court, 12 Feb. 1999, *case of. Chaumet, JCP*, E, 1999, panor. 695 : a court in whose jurisdiction acts of counterfeiting have been committed, particularly when those acts have been committed from an Internet site that is accessible from all points of French territory so that the services offered by a company from its site can be received everywhere in this territory, has jurisdiction to hear an action for counterfeiting). Accordingly, that court is called upon to rule on offences, within the meaning of French law, committed on Internet sites that are located in other countries.

Third characteristic, the absence of an order for enforcement of criminal judgments : in general, no authority is afforded in a foreign country to a punitive decision given in another country. That obviously raises a problem of the effectiveness of the punishment.

However, we must not exaggerate the consequences of this last point as criminal justice can have a certain indirect effectiveness : no one doubts that a person, for example, a company boss, who for professional reasons has to travel frequently all over the world, will not willingly allow himself to be convicted of a criminal offence by a court in a country that is economically important, which would make it difficult to circumvent (and for an example of implication in the criminal field, see in the *Yahoo! case*, Paris Regional Court, 26 February 2002, unpublished, *Amicale des déportés d'Auchwitz (Association of Auchwitz deportees) v. Thimoty K.*). Therefore he will wish to avoid criminal proceedings and, if they are inevitable, will certainly make arrangements to be properly represented. And at worst, if he is fined, he will be committed to paying it so as to avoid any unnecessary inconvenience...

THE INFLUENCE OF THE INTERNET ON ESTABLISHING THE LAW

BY

PIERRE TRUDEL

Centre for research on public law, University of Montreal
pierre.trudel@umontreal.ca

It is reasonable to postulate that the Internet reinforces the characteristic trends of the information society although its own influence remains difficult to evaluate. Similarly, one can put forward a few hypotheses on the way in which the Internet influences the establishment of legal rules.

I. – The internet and its influence

The influence of the Internet can be seen in social perceptions (1). What it enables or facilitates helps to change ways of looking at things. Its deficiencies might appear to be amplified and the rationalities on which the law is based are changing. Those changes are reflected in what forms the basis of the law and the means and processes whereby it is expressed and enforced.

A. – CHANGES

Changes in the conditions for producing and circulating information alter perceptions from which the legal frameworks are conceived. These changes manifest themselves in different ways within the various legal systems. They affect perceptions of what the law is based on, the scope of its application or what appears to be exempt from it. By the changes it causes in the ways that information is produced and circulated, the Internet contains a huge potential for change with regard to the foundations of several legal rules.

---

(1) P. MANNONI, *Les représentations sociales* (*Social perceptions*), Paris, PUF, 1998.

The area created by the network environment cannot be reduced to a physical space : its boundaries are defined in accordance with other criteria. The advent of an area that would appear to be borderless and in which several of the familiar reference points on which the principles and practices of law are based are missing, affects perceptions (2). References to space are changing; interactions are increasingly less sensitive to national borders. When it is a question of establishing the rules of conduct in virtual environments, it can be observed that national law loses some of its relevance, not to say legitimacy. By encouraging the reference areas to be redefined, the Internet contains the seeds of a change in the parameters according to which the legitimacy of the law is understood.

The law is sensible and applied having regard to the communities which established it or consented to it. Modern law is based on the paradigm of the State, the territorial State endowed with sovereignty in order to govern all the behaviour that takes place on the territory it controls. The rules of conduct are generally drawn up in political debates and usually reflect the values of the people. Behaviour, the meaning and scope of the rules are assessed having regard to the cultures and ethics that prevail in the national community. Various value systems coexist in cyberspace. It has the ability to blend expressions of values arising from distant civilisations. By bringing the territories closer together, the Internet blurs the reference frameworks. The communities are increasingly the « users » that are defined in accordance with their interests, the language they speak or the predilections they share. That calls for a rule of law that would be able to meet the concerns of cyberspace communities rather than those of nation States.

The rule of law presupposes a situation that has relatively stable spatio-temporal coordinates. In cyberspace, the spatio-temporal coordinates are a continual problem. Places and roles are redefined there and redistributed in accordance with situations that do not comply with a predictable model. There, messages are ephemeral and that can make it difficult to prove that they were circulated. Networks allow information to be retained for a long time. They

---

(2) D. GILLEROT and A. LEFEBVRE, in collaboration with and under the direction of M. MINON and Y. POULLET, *Internet : la plasticité du droit mise à l'épreuve* (*The Internet : the flexibility of the law put to the test*), Brussels, King Baudouin Foundation, 1998, p. 18.

make it easier to move information to another place and reconstitute it. Information is exchanged at a faster speed than in a paper environment. The speed with which rules are drawn up appears to have changed : practices are developing at a faster pace. There is already talk of codes of practice for online commerce and yet this technology is less than a decade old. The basic categories under which the law controls situations are challenged. The various disciplines such as « public law », « private law », « commercial law » and « international law » are overturned when it is a matter of accounting for interactions on the Internet (3).

The way in which the law is understood and applied depends in part on the medium in which it is communicated. The emphasis placed on precedents in Common Law can be largely explained by the availability of printed texts. Before printed publications of judgments were available, the role of precedents was less obvious (4). The consequences of digitalisation are reinforced by hyperlinks. Accordingly, a potential for synergy between the sources of law is created. Ethan Katsh notes (5) that the move from the world of printed information to a world made up of networks made possible by information technologies gives the law a new environment making it less tangible and more fluid.

B. – MAGNIFICATION

The Internet magnifies problems or contradictions that are already latent. Marie-Anne Frison-Roche notes that the Internet : « causes a kind of hypertrophy of rules (...) » (6). The world of cyberspace affects perceptions with regard to the consequences of circulating information. Circulating an item of public information in the *Official Journal* can be straightforward in the printed environment. One would have hesitations about circulating the same content on the Internet where search engines and other software tools allow it to be retrieved at very little cost. The threats to private life that seemed to be marginal in the world of paper publication take

---

(3) J. REIDENBERG, « Governing Networks and Cyberspace Rule-Making », 45 *Emory L. J.* 911 (1996), http://www.law.emory.edu/ELJ/volumes/sum96/reiden.html

(4) E. KATSH, *The Electronic Media and the Transformation of Law*, New York, Oxford University Press, 1989.

(5) E. KATSH, *Law in a Digital World*, New York, Oxford University Press, 1995, p. 23.

(6) J.-M. CHEVALIER, I. EKELAND, M.-A. FRISON-ROCHE and M. KALIKA, *Internet et nos fondamentaux (The Internet and our fundamentals)*, Paris, PUF, 2000, pp. 41-42.

on new dimensions when it is a question of publishing on the Internet.

This shows how the limits and deficiencies of the law are magnified. Legal systems have developed vague rules for the protection of private life and formulated the principle of the public nature of certain personal information from a context in which the availability of information would remain relatively limited by the research and retrieval capabilities. These facilities for circulation afforded by the research capabilities on the network lead to a reconsideration of the standards of assessment and a strengthening of the protections for private life even at the expense of narrowing the field of information which had hitherto been deemed to be in the public domain.

II. – The establishment of legal rules in an « Internet-enhanced » environment

The law is made wherever it is « conceived ». Governments remain one of the main places where the law is created; it is chiefly here that there is mediation between the values, capabilities and threats of technology. National forums continue to play an important part in creating and enforcing the law. Domestic law often proves to be incapable on its own of adequately controlling the activities that take place in cyberspace. Rules of conduct are also drawn up in other places that either supplant it or relay it (7). The law is laid down having regard to technical rules that we seek to define, produce structures for or harness. It reflects the circumstances prevailing in the places where it is conceived, negotiated and enforced.

A. – THE PLACES
WHERE STANDARDS ARE DRAWN UP

Regulations for the Internet may arise, in part, from technological or legal legislation. There is competition between the places and

---

(7) A.-J. ARNAUD, « De la régulation par le droit à l'heure de la globalisation. Quelques observations critiques » (« From regulation by the law in the era of globalisation. Some critical observations ») (1997) 35 *Droit et société*, 11-35.

networks that have taken it upon themselves to establish regulations for activities taking place on the Internet.

Legal systems are created with a hierarchical, linear and arborescent design. Hierarchical, because the structure of the system is such that each of its organs is either superior or subordinate to the other. Relations between the various hierarchical levels are linear and unidirectional. The system is designed in an arborescent fashion because its various component parts are generated from a single source of creation. The network is increasingly replacing the hierarchical institutions as a place where standards are created and laid down. Legislation of the Internet is tending to replace the hierarchical, linear and arborescent approach. The network circumscribes a virtual space; it is becoming a reference framework, a metaphorical tool, an essential for identifying the *situs* of interactions in cyberspace.

Within the networks, landmark principles are established which must be relayed by other rule-making areas. The law is partly supplanted and partly relayed from international principles to national laws whilst in turn, the latter are relayed by the regulatory rules and standards established by the actors (8). The networks superimpose themselves on the institutional places, that is to say Governments and international authorities (9). They form a process for dialogue and exchange by which the strategies that are capable of dealing with the situations brought about by the dissemination of information through networks are laid down. his results in manifestations of co-regulation that the legal systems are beginning to recognise.

1. – *States*

The official systems express the values, fears, alarms and expectations in whose name rules are demanded. The law established by governments reflects the cultural traits of each society. The fact that the Internet makes it difficult to apply certain rules of law

---

(8) P. TRUDEL, « Quel droit et quelle régulation dans le cyberespace ? » (« Which law and which regulation in cyberspace ? »), *Sociologie et sociétés*, vol. 22, n° 2, Autumn 2000, 189-209, http://www.erudit.org/erudit/socsoc/v32n02/trudel/trudel.pdf

(9) F. OST and M. DE KERCHOVE, « De la pyramide au réseau ? Vers un nouveau mode de production du droit ? » (« From the pyramid to the network ? Towards a new way of establishing the law ? ») (2000) 44 *R.I.E.J*, 1-82.

does not automatically entail the disappearance of their underlying rationale.

When it is applied on the national territory, domestic law frequently fits into a framework for regulation in which it is only one component; it establishes principles, formulates objectives and lays down criteria but increasingly leaves it to other legislative bodies to ensure that it is updated, or indeed relayed. Thus the law begins to look like a constituent of a process within which the other sources of rule-making play a more or less important role.

The new definition of space induced by the Internet seems to influence the effectiveness of state law. When it is applied in relation to an interaction containing an element that is external to the territory, domestic law can run into practical difficulties that undermine its effectiveness. On the Internet, national law is in competition with other rules. It is always possible to get around the rules or quite simply to be excluded from their enforcement.

Faced with the lack of effectiveness of national laws, the automatic reaction will be to seek an international definition of the law. There will be an attempt to make the law broadly similar everywhere. That approach might suit disciplines designed to coordinate behaviour. It will be more difficult so far as concerns rules prescribing behaviour and arising from ethical or moral views or subject to natural cultural referents.

2. – *International forums*

International forums establish universal guidelines defining what is lawful on the Internet. Those rules are designed to be transposed into national legislation and other bodies that have an influence on cyberspace.

The measures taken in the international organisations are based on the traditional premises of international law. The States are considered to be the only subjects of international law and accordingly they alone are able to establish rules of law. Various means are employed to pursue the aim of harmonising national laws such as adopting an international treaty or establishing standard laws.

Both the traditional international authorities and the non-governmental associations present themselves as places for drawing up meta-standards. They are working on identifying the common denominators of national laws. These forums appear to be the most effective place for drawing up meta-standards, expressed in the form of principles designed to be transposed into the national laws and other rules.

3. – *The networks*

Rules are increasingly drawn up in the networks as a result of repeated interactions between people with a common aim. Widespread use of the Internet goes hand in hand with the emergence of networks that unite the decision makers, scientists, regulators and other actors that play a role in creating rules (10). The networks that are involved in creating rules for the Internet are not only made up of lawyers, legislators or government officials of the States. Networks made up primarily of technical experts are taking an active part in regulating the Internet. The Internet Engineering Task Force (IETF) and bodies that preceded it have drawn up sets of rules that play a major role in the conditions of use of the Internet and its resources (11). In addition to these spontaneous combinations, there are several communities that are proposing regulations, ways of behaving or demanding that standards be adopted. Apart from these more or less formal networks there are also bodies comprising decision-makers who form part of the machinery of government (12).

The Internet encourages and increases the effectiveness of some types of networks of experts or decision-makers. However, networks cannot replace the official institutional places. Rather they represent an intermediate level of cooperation between the protagonists of national and international bureaucracies.

4. – *The actors*

The communities are producing trends that are likely to form a set of rules coupled with a degree of constraint that is comparable to the rules of law. These rules arising from the conditions prevail-

---

(10) A.-M. SLAUGHTER, « The Real New World Order », (1997) 76 *Foreign Affairs*, 183-184.

(11) See : M. MAHER, « An Analysis of Internet Standardization », (1998) 3 *Va.J.L.&Tech*, http:vjolt.student.virginia.edu.

(12) M.L. CHEEK, « The Limits of Informal Regulatory Cooperation in international Affairs : A Review of the Global Intellectual Property regime », (2001) 33 *Georges Washington Int. L.R.*, 277, p. 278.

ing in the environment or by repeated behaviour are not necessarily created by the authorities : they result from the repeated and expected behaviour of the actors in cyberspace. These practices show consistent features from which it can be concluded that on the Internet, customs are developing at a different pace from that that prevails in the physical world. Accordingly, it is almost universally accepted that a « click » equates to consent. A custom has spread on the Internet with regard to the conditions for the criteria required for a statement of intent (13).

Often contractual practices are the main source of rules that apply to relations between the protagonists of electronic commerce. The importance of competition between sites from the point of view of regulation explains the crucial role of the contract in cyberspace. The same phenomenon no doubt also explains the key role that self-regulation might play.

The technical environments impose rules that are like back-up provisions when they do not create factual situations preventing a certain kind of behaviour. These rules reflect the conflicting interests and sensibilities but nevertheless have a common basis. Accordingly a back-up corpus is developing, endowed with variable authoritative value and establishing with variable consistency, a regulatory framework into which the contractual agreements made in cyberspace fit and are negotiated (14).

5. – The process of co-regulation

The emergence of networks gives rise to the establishment of a consultation process. This reflects an overriding need to ensure that the principles, rules and policies laid down in the official forums and other rule making places are passed on. It is in order to welcome and encourage such a dialogue that the concept of co-regulation has been highlighted (15). Co-regulation is basically an open process

---

(13) I. DE LAMBERTERIE and M. VIVANT, « Commerce électronique : de nouvelles pratiques contractuelles ? » (« Electronic commerce : new contractual practices ? ») in L'Internet et le droit. Droit français européen et comparé de l'Internet, Paris, Légipresse, 2001, p. 379.

(14) P. TRUDEL, « La Lex Electronica » (« The Lex Electronica ») in Le droit saisi par la mondialisation (The law affected by globalisation), Brussels, Bruylant, 2001, 221-268.

(15) C. PAUL, Du droit et des libertés sur Internet, la corégulation – contribution française pour une régulation mondiale, (Law and freedoms on the Internet, co-regulation – the French contribution to a world regulation) Report to the Prime Minister, Paris, May 2000, http://www.Internet.gouv.fr/francais/.

designed to bring together the various actors in a place of dialogue. That dialogue must allow links between the values to be preserved and the realities experienced by users to emerge. These processes do not necessarily produce rules of law; rather it is a dialogue aimed at identifying trends and consensus and encouraging the adoption of rules of law and practices that are more suited to the characteristics of the Internet.

In a world in which contractual practice is so important, the development of guidelines and standard contracts becomes a means of expressing the law. These tools, designed to establish solutions that facilitate interactions, can reflect the requirements resulting from the values that the national authorities would like to encourage. These trends show to what extent the expression of standards on the Internet is considered to be an aspect of an environment, or indeed of the product or service offered online.

B. – THE EXPRESSION OF STANDARDS

The influence of the Internet can be detected in the forms of rule-making and in the ways in which they are expressed. The rules of law are increasingly expressed as a component of a network in which they are merely a link. So far as concerns its expression, rule-making is often presented as a programmatic package rather than as overriding rules with immediate application. It is often a question of specifying the qualities of the technical tools, processes and conduct that accompany the activities taking place in cyberspace. In order to achieve a sufficient level of adaptability, the opening between the rule-making systems will be sought in order to link national and international ethical, technical and governmental rules.

As regulation is the result of synergy rather than the application of a single provision, laws place great deal of importance on concepts that require enquiries to be made as to what prevails in other legislative systems. Since the law is only a part of a multi-faceted regulation process, it must be drafted in such a way as to leave an opening between other legislative systems. The French law on electronic signatures (16) defers to the regulatory authority in order to determine the qualities required by technical mechanisms designed to produce legal consequences such as electronic signatures. The Quebec law (17) refers to the technical standards drawn up in the international forums. These examples illustrate the tendency to formulate laws by means of generic concepts. In doing so, we are seeking a certain degree of technological neutrality. The legislation must be designed to encompass all equivalent situations regardless of the technical means employed.

From that perspective, the use of standards is a major factor in several legislators' formulation of strategies. Several States have amended their laws so as to afford functional equivalence of documents and their legal value, regardless of medium in which they appear. The laws indicate how legal situations that are familiar in a paper environment are transposed into the world of cyberspace. Rather than seeking to describe the obligations for each area of interaction, the requirements are set out in accordance with the functions performed by the processes of producing and circulating information.

Originally, rule-making for the Internet was mainly driven by processes of dialogue. Discussion groups, using actual situations, debated the best ways of approaching or controlling a certain situation. The results of these exchanges were recorded in FAQ (Frequently Asked Questions) in which the replies given to users' questions were compiled. The establishment of standards also borrowed from the RFCs (Requests for Comments) in order to put forward proposals concerning problems of a technical nature or those perceived as such. This model borrowed from the dialogue process familiar to the scientific communities was then used to organise the deliberations.

On the Internet, the law is also laid down through a process of adapting and transposing models. The model laws have no binding force in themselves. They help to structure the measures taken by the actors, who, in their respective fields of intervention, will intro-

(16) *Law N° 2000-230 of 13 March 2000 on adapting the law of evidence to information technologies and on electronic signatures* http://www.legifrance.gouv.fr/citoyen/jorf-nor.ow?numjo-=JUSX9900020L

(17) *Loi concernant le cadre juridique des technologies de l'information*, L.Q. 2001, c. 32, http://www.autoroute.gouv.qc.ca/loi-en-ligne/index.html

duce provisions modelled on the most widespread models or provisions that differ from them.

Since it is relatively easy for the user to choose the sites and places to visit, several actors have come to consider that the quality of the regulation prevailing there is a competitive advantage for their website. Regulation is becoming competitive : the rules associated with a product or service are part of it. Radin (18) observes that a contract on the Internet is increasingly presented as a product rather than a statement of consent. Everything takes place as if the regulation followed on a given site formed part of the product offered. The French authorities responsible for attributing the national domain name.fr have introduced a strict procedure in order to prevent the registration of domain names that make use of names or brands by people who are not legitimately entitled to use them. For users, the result is an area of relative certainty : it is less risky to trade with a site with the domain name .fr than with sites that have been given a domain name with fewer precautions.

By identifying as closely as possible the risks inherent in the activities taking place on a website, one can then specify the rights and responsibilities of each one. Several self-regulation measures fit into the scheme of risk management. One is also better placed to identify how one complies with the national laws that are likely to apply. Some rules are laid down in accordance with a method based on the circulation of informal information such as in FAQs. Others are established in a guide setting out the rules of conduct. In other situations a formalised text like a code of conduct is drawn up. Often, the drafting of a self-regulatory provision is included in a process designed to explain the rules of and conduct. There again, the law is relayed by instruments that are likely to give it the desired level of effectiveness.

Rule-making can be incorporated in the architecture. The Internet is an area constructed by technology, it is possible to design the very configuration of the area including rules that must be followed. The objects have a regulating effect which has various forms (19). By taking into account the requirements that have to be

---

(18) M.J. RADIN, « Humans, Computers, and Binding Commitment », (2000) 75 *Indiana L.J.*, 1125-1162.

(19) L. LESSIG, « Code and Other Laws of Cyberspace », *Basic Books*, 1999; Joel R. REIDENBERG, « Lex Informatica », (1998) 76 *Texas Law Review* 553-593, http://www.si.umich.edu/%7Epresnick/reidenberg/.

complied with as well as the needs for regulation when the site or
service is designed can help to ensure that the architecture will help
to establish boundaries, making reliance on other regulations less
necessary.

Conclusion

The Internet affects perceptions of the world : many premises on
which the law is based are undergoing transformations. Space, time,
the legal disciplines or even the medium in which the information
is expressed are changing. In the Internet-enhanced world,
standards are established in different places from those that are
usually the crucible of legal rules. The international forums are seeing an increase in their roles of creating universal standards. Governments remain a major place for drawing up and establishing
rules but their role tends to be moving towards one of relaying
international rules and the practices of the actors.

Negotiation and mediation procedures as well as the development
of technical tools are helping to identify the content of rules that
are applied to activities taking place on the Internet. The Internet
encourages the relinquishment of the hierarchical process for laying
down standards. The standards are being established on the
network : they are proposed, debated, applied or remodelled in the
context of informal processes relaying the values and principles and
consensus obtained in official forums or in communities. On the
Internet, the law is the result of a sometimes transient synergy
between interacting rules. In order to get effective rules laid down,
the law must be expressed by leaving openings towards other rule-
making systems. In that way, we can seek a law that is designed
to encompass all situations.

DISCUSSION

Guy Canivet

Mr Chatillon, a question ?

Georges Chatillon

Thank you very much, First Chairman. My question relates essentially to the relationship between the law and technology. The State and business have been set against each other. A whole raft of approaches has been described. An initial question refers, for example, to what fate awaits *peer-to-peer* technology. Should the State make it obligatory for each Internet user to have an identification ? If that were to happen, each Internet user will become his own access provider, obviously, via *peer-to-peer* or rather networks of Internet users. What kind of responsibility ensues ? Is responsibility then individual or collective ? Moreover, if the programmes created by machines can be protected – what one might call the patentability of software – and if one values this protection of programmes thus created, such programmes will inevitably have an effect on the law and, accordingly, in some sense, they will create the law. What is the role of the State then ? Is there not a contradiction with wanting the State to establish rules *a priori* ? They could be general principles ; thus, they would not reach their object. Moreover, how could a law place the whole technology and the law on the patentability of software in abeyance ? It seems to me, therefore, that we should probably look for intermediate solutions, obviously with the option of rethinking a number of legal matters. And since the first chairman is here, I also wonder how judges, apart from experts, can really interpret the application of a rule whose wording cannot be precise enough to tackle technological behaviours which, in practice, as far as contracts are concerned, would prevail over the law.

Guy Canivet

Who is going to reply to this question ?

Joël Reidenberg

I will take the first question concerning *peer-to-peer* – I should say set of problems rather than question – on the identification of each user. I think that it will be essential to individual responsibility which, in my view, is necessary for a democratic society. However, what we must also recognise is that if it becomes compulsory for every user to be identified, naturally, the protection of private life will be affected. In fact, there are ways of having both : technological means that can give access to identification for certain requirements and close it for others. I should also say that leaving aside law, or the law, which also includes case-law, the judge's decision without a law in the strict sense, we arrive precisely at such identification, in any event, because of the current IPV6 proposal. This is the next Internet routing protocol which offers a unique identifying number to each object connected to the network. If IPV6 is not adopted, the commercial goals which seek to target each customer more precisely are, in any event, pushing towards the identification of each user. One can therefore see the pressures, towards such identification that come from both technical and financial objectives. In my view, the only way of achieving a balance between identification and the protection of private life, is a legal intervention which could impose a kind of black box between identification and the use of that identification. It would seem to me therefore, that without any motivation imposed by the law, we will not see this introduced to the network.

Guy Canivet

Please add to this reply, Mr Trudel

Pierre Trudel

Yes. I think that this *peer-to-peer* phenomenon is a good demonstration of how the problem of the intervention of the law is raised today, that is to say that we are faced with technology that is developed literally by chance. By way of an illustration, it is as if a rather imaginative teenager introduced a technology and the consequence of that is to upset the entire balance of the law. Admittedly, that calls for the establishment of national rules, but I very much fear that that will not be enough. These rules need to be properly relayed to the place in which they have to be applied. And that is now the whole challenge. It is relatively easy to draw up a rule in an act. Application on the Internet can sometimes pose considerable challenges and therefore the law no longer suffices; that is why there is so much talk about the co-regulation process because the law can no longer be applied in an authoritarian manner. Even if you manage to identify each of the « *peers* » who pirate music from the Internet, you would also need to find as many police vans to go and arrest them. You can clearly see then that that is not enough. We must find other intermediaries, as Joël Reidenberg pointed out, introduce what is needed to maintain these balances into technology and the technological environment. That having been said, I do not know whether we should be optimistic in this respect because in general, companies are very efficient when it comes to finding ways of improving profitability; they are also very efficient when it comes to proving that it is not possible, from a technical point of view, and that the law is not realistic, that it has been relegated, that there are only bits of information. Accordingly, I am very afraid that it is no longer a question of just adopting laws : we must also act with regard to representations and Internet imaging. That is probably the greatest obstacle today; when we speak of intervening, when States seek to intervene in the Internet, it is generally this whole imagery of the Internet which is presented as incompatible with what is presented as the authority of the freedom-abolishing law, that is going to put an end to this information Eldorado. So, that is the whole challenge and that is why I think that the law is inadequate. We need to go a little further.

Guy Canivet

Thank you. Are there any other questions ? Yes, Sir, Would you be so kind as to state your name for the transcription of the proceedings ?

Macief Lewandowski

Yes. Macief Lewandowski, Minister for Justice in Poland. I have two questions for Mrs Diana Wallis. The first : everyone knows that the decision-making procedures within the European bodies are light years from drafting the law as we are used to drafting it in democratic systems, with precedence given to the executive. The question is therefore how, in these circumstances, can you justify or even claim that the European Union has a right to harmonise these rules which are going to create quite a significant interference with national legal systems. I am not calling into question the need for harmonisation but perhaps the way chosen is not appropriate. The second : the partnership agreements signed between the European Union, the member countries and candidate countries, contain, *inter alia*, the right to services – *freedom of services*. You say that we are going to regulate this right, draft rules relating to the country of origin, the country of destination, etc. At the same time, the candidate countries remain excluded from this discussion; therefore, despite the fact that freedom of services can be used by companies in candidate countries and such a right forms part of Community law, there is no consultation with the candidate countries on the rules that will be applied to enforce that law. Thank you.

Guy Canivet

Can someone reply to this question, Madam, concerning the claims of the candidate countries ?

Diana Wallis

It's difficult with regard to the candidate countries. Candidate countries are exactly that : candidate countries. And therefore, at that stage, you do not have the possibility to participate in Europe's legislative procedures in the same way as everybody else. But I am sure there is every possibility... Me, myself and my colleagues in the Parliament would always welcome discussions with parliamentarians from candidate countries to try and see that your views are represented, but to seek a part in the legislative process before you're members, it is not really, I think, a possibility, even if I look at those countries like Switzerland and Iceland, which are part of the European Economic Area. They have to take all of the Community *acquis* without participating in the legislative process.

Guy Canivet

Thank you Madam. Are there any other questions? Yes?

Catherine Kessedjian

Catherine Kessedjian, Professor at the University of Panthéon-Assas. Since we began this morning, it would seem to me that the speakers have set the law generated by the State, vertically, against the law generated by the operators, let us say horizontally. I think that this is a poor perception of what is currently happening; I believe that we have moved on from this problem of opposition. We are now facing another problem – moreover, some have mentioned it – that of co-regulation. It is a bad translation from the English. French style regulation is not « regulation » in the English sense. However, in my view we should not consider that there is a conflict between what the State does and what the operators do. With regard to international trade law , for many years there have been discussions precisely on the subject of the civil society and on the importance of this impregnation of civil society. What our representatives recently did in Doha is obviously a poor example but I think that e-commerce obliges us to take this civil society / State issue into account, in all fields. In my opinion, e-commerce merely obliges us to do very little more quickly than we would have done it naturally and, in the end, it is indeed this positive interference that I should like to be clearly demonstrated rather than the conflict.

Guy Canivet

Thank you. Mr Trudel, you dealt more thoroughly with this issue.

Pierre Trudel

Yes, indeed. I think that as long as and for as long as commerce is concerned, it is very easy to reach agreement and one can observe that the trend is entirely towards establishing rules that will facilitate e-commerce.

Where it becomes more difficult, in my opinion, is when we deal with rules of law that have, shall I say, arisen from various cultural cloths that coexist throughout the world. Here, it seems to me that coordination is much more difficult. It is a question of values. In my view, the Yahoo case is good illustration of the difficulty, quite apart from all the limits that must be laid down with regard to this case, which, after all, is only one dispute. However, it seems to me that it is a good illustration of the type of problem facing us, much more difficult to coordinate than merely introducing mechanisms to ensure that transactions can take place. I am very afraid that in this case we have more to do than establish the traditional processes of the law, even if, so far, they have been relatively successful in creating ways of facilitating transactions. When it is a question of protecting morality or moralities, in my view, the challenge is much greater.

Guy Canivet

Mr Reidenberg

Joël Reidenberg

Yes. If I may add to that, I think that you are quite right. There is a continual toing-and-froing between technological law and the law of the State because the one influences the other. Accordingly, there is a more complex relationship but nevertheless, I think that this vertical aspect that Pierre has just emphasised will always be there and, in a sense, it is more a question of cohabitation than co-regulation. If you like, to take up the same theme, the Yahoo case demonstrates this cohabitation because Yahoo shows that it is possible for two rules to conflict, the rule of the French State on the expression of racial hatred and the relevant rule of the American State. Technology will allow filtering so that American users will have no difficulty in accessing these comments whereas French users will be blocked by technology. Accordingly, there at the interface, we can see the technology that will allow two regimes of different States to coexist.

Guy Canivet

One question here, another one there. Sir, go ahead

Stéphane Buydens

Thank you Chairman.

Two questions. Firstly a brief question to Mr Reidenberg who just mentioned the possibility, which is apparently within reach, of identifying operators. My name is Stéphane Buydens and I am in charge of fiscal matters at the OECD and for the tax authorities, obviously it is essential to identify the seller and the buyer for taxing the transaction. We have of course, discussed this problem at the OECD. Unfortunately, there are a number of technologies for providing anonymity. As technologies for identification appear, do you not think that, on the other hand, we will see technologies that will allow the contact between the seller and the buyer to be anonymous ? Second question, slightly different, regarding the way in which the standard laws should be drafted. The traditional system includes an elected Parliament which draws up the rules for the nation. The emergence of the Internet obviously calls this model into question because it is no longer an individual, isolated State, an elected Parliament which draws up all the rules. It will therefore be a kind of co-regulation managed by the international bodies such as the OECD, for example. At the moment, we are trying to create rules of law for taxation. In order to counterbalance this lack, this democratic deficiency, we see the arrival of the civil society; for example, in the process of creating these rules, the OECD involves business associations and consumer associations, through consultative statements. How do you see this change, this shift in the way in which the law is created, from a democratic point of view ? Thank you.

Guy Canivet

Mr Reidenberg ?

Joël Reidenberg

Perhaps I can reply, first of all, to the last part about the shift in establishing the law. In my opinion, it is a good thing because the establishment of these rules, whether they be technical or legal, must be based on discussions with all the actors, including the economic civil and political actors. The multiplicity of forums makes such discussions possible and, in my view, it is beneficial. On the first problem that you raised, anonymisation and identification, it is true that there are technologies for anonymisation but at the same time it is rather like during the cold war. At that time there was the arms race : we can see the same thing at a technical level. It is becoming possible to identify, then to use an *anonymiser* to surf the Net anonymously, then to use Web bugs which break the anonymity. We must also acknowledge that there will be – I cannot say always because I am not up-to-date enough with technology – but, generally speaking, it seems to me that there will be someone on the network who is capable of making a link between the person, the anonymised identity and, if you wish, the real identity, even if there is a risk that such a link will have to go through several stages. The necessary tracing will be important but it is an example that has already been seen in the Scandinavian countries about three or four years ago with one of the *anonymisers* : the police came to examine the log files to try and trace the original user. How are we going to supervise that ? It is a legal question. There are others too. It can be seen with the telephone, the caller's number. The American telecommunications companies offer a service for refusing the telephone call if the caller is anonymous. That is to say that if the caller refuses to disclose his number, the telecommunications service puts an end to the call, and informs the caller that his call cannot be taken because he has not identified himself to the person he is calling. It is therefore obvious – since it is a function, an ability – that the same thing can be introduced on the network for certain purposes of e-commerce. On the one hand, the ability to have an anonymiser and on the other, the ability to refuse the communication if it is anonymous. How can we incorporate these functions on the network ? I shall leave technology here and return to the law; I shall return to the beneficial aspect of many actors being involved in a discussion on the « how ».

Guy Canivet

A brief reply from Mr Trudel to this question; we shall then have a break.

Pierre Trudel

On the matter of democracy, I think that in order for the law to be established in a true democratic fashion, we need to maintain this continual dialogue between the various rule-making bodies. Of course, the States continue to be important rule-making bodies but we can observe that they should probably lay greater emphasis on and confine themselves to expressing the fundamental principles and basic values, leaving it, perhaps, for other intermediaries to ensure that such principles and values are adapted to technologies which evolve with a speed that never ceases to surprise us. Accordingly, it would seem to me that consider the democratic nature of drawing up rules in this continual search for opening up this dialogue between the various rule-making poles. There is a problem of lack of democracy, such as in the initial stages of the Internet, when groups which only represent the interests of big businesses or the interests of one group or another, are the only ones to be heard and the only ones to have a voice in the matter, the only ones to be perceived as having the necessary expertise, not to say legitimacy, to draw up these rules. I therefore believe that we should look for this opening rather than postulate that there is only democracy if the State decides everything, which is now – unfortunately or fortunately, depending on your point of view – impossible.

2. – METHODS OF ESTABLISHING INTERNATIONAL LAW

WHAT LINKS EUROPEAN
AND INTERNATIONAL LAW – BEYOND
COUNTRY OF ORIGIN OR DESTINATION

BY

Diana WALLIS

European Parliament, spokeswoman for the ELRD Group
Committee on legal affairs and the internal market

If we are here concerned with the lack of linkage between European and International law we should perhaps pause for a moment to consider that despite celebrating fiftieth birthday of the European Union last year there is still a considerable disparity between the law and legal systems of Europe's present 15 Member States. Disparities which I and colleagues as legislators in the European Parliament, on it's Legal Affairs and Internal Market Committee are increasingly forced to recognise and address almost constantly because of the growth of e-commerce.

If Europe has trouble enough linking together its own law, perhaps it is not surprising that there is an even greater problem with international law. However the European Union has its own glue in this respect, it is based; and its members have signed up to the original concept of a common market, and now the Internal Market. Most of Europe's legislation or regulation is designed primarily towards ensuring the proper functioning of the Internal Market and the overall competitiveness of Europe's economy. It is this glue, with its goal of the Internal Market, which binds together the 15 Member States, some with vastly differing legal traditions, into one workable whole. It is this central preoccupation, which has now forced the search for pragmatic solutions to overcoming the differing national legal and regulatory regimes to make a success of e-commerce. However European legislators do have that common cause. What is the common cause or aims that could motivate legislation or agreement at an international level? Does the European approach offer us any pointers or templates for dealing with the quest for linkage between European and International law ?

The guiding principle in respect of the E-commerce Directive is the so-called – Country of Origin principle. The idea that a business can carry with it wherever it trades its own home country regulation and law. This has become almost a mantra in some quarters of the business and legal community in the EU. Fears are expressed about the compatibility of this approach and what is sometimes perceived as a Country of Destination approach in the Brussels Regulation, which deals with Jurisdiction and the Recognition of Judgments. We have seen an intensifying level of hype in this respect as to what may appear in the long awaited Commission proposal on applicable law relating to non-contractual obligations, known as Rome 11. Along side this we have other developments moving towards a potentially higher level of harmonisation of basic civil law also trying to cut through these arguments and differences; the Commission consultation on Contract Law and on the Green Paper on European Union Consumer Protection – introducing the notion of a general duty to trade fairly. In the light of this debate I think it is high time to consider exactly what the Country of Origin principle is, it's place in community law and indeed some assessment of its effectiveness, in short it needs putting into perspective, rather than being presented as a simplistic answer to all the problems of cross-border e-commerce. Certainly we must proceed with extreme care before there is any attempt to export this approach to an international level.

So where does the Country of Origin principle come from in Europe's legal framework ? We must be aware that Europe's law has grown up in a very piecemeal and incremental fashion, not always entirely logical or coherent, gradually moving its way to a fully functioning Internal Market, whilst at the same time having to respect through the subsidiarity principle the sensitivities and traditions of its Member States. Of course the primary law of the Union is found in the Treaties, the Country of Origin principle is not there, but the principle of having regard to high level of consumer protection is. The nearest the Treaties come to a Country of Origin principle is by following through the logic of Article 28 : prohibition of measures having equivalent affect to tariff barriers and Article 49 : freedom of establishment and freedom to provide services. So under 28 it could be argued that any law or regulation of one Member State that had the effect of a tariff barrier could be attacked, such as the German ban on some kinds of promotional activities which may be open to attack on this basis. Article 49 gives a basic right to provide services but as anyone who is a lawyer will know this in reality becomes hedged about with host country controls as well.

So no Country of Origin principle in the Treaties, so where is it ? The Country of Origin does appear in secondary EU law, in specific sectorial directives. Its first appearance was in the TV without Frontiers Directive (1985), there it was limited to certain areas of TV advertising. The basic principle being that transmission of a TV programme in line with Country of Origin requirements has to be accepted in other Member States. Broadcasting is of course subject to a high level of regulation in all the Member States, yet even within this very limited area of application there have been all sorts of problems that have lead to uncertainty, court cases and confusion. It might seem good for broadcasters to use one regime, – their own, but what about the other side, what about policing or enforcement, say a British broadcaster produces something in Italian, do we really seriously expect the content to be checked by the British regulator ?

Of course the second star appearance of the Country of Origin principle is in the E commerce Directive 2000, it has of course an implementation date of 17 Jan 2002 which is nearly upon us. Article 3 sets out the principle – « *each Member State shall ensure that the information society services provided by a service provider established on its territory comply with the national provisions applicable in the Member State in question which fall within the co-coordinated field* ». So we find that we are talking about merely a specific area – the co-coordinated field. This appears to be areas of public regulation as opposed to private law; we can deduce this from the references to derogations and exceptions within the Directive. Such as *Article (23) this Directive neither aims to establish rules on private international law relating to conflicts of law nor does it deal with the jurisdiction of courts; provisions of the applicable law must not restrict the freedom to provide information society as established in this Directive.* Likewise *Article (55) : « this Directive does not affect the law applicable to contractual obligations relating to consumer con-*

*tracts; accordingly, this Directive cannot have the result of depriving
the consumer of the protection offered to him by the mandatory rules
relating to contractual obligations of the law of the Member State in
which he has his habitual residence ».*

So it should be absolutely clear that the rules of private international law even as applied between Member States are not part of
the co-coordinated field and so are not intended to be subject to the
Country of Origin principle. Perhaps the only caveat is the reinfor-
cement to Article 28 of the Treaty in relation to the content of any
applicable law that might attempt to restrict the freedom to
provide information services. However the exception for consumer
contracts is clear, here we have Country of Destination. Surely this
was inevitable; I have already referred to the high level of consumer protection required by the Treaties. This is arguably one of
the most harmonised areas of EU law. Did anyone really expect
that for instance the contents of the Unfair Contract Terms directive were going to be abandoned or rolled back ? What would any
reduction in the level of EU consumer protection do for confidence
in the e-economy ?

So where does all this leave the Country of Origin principle ? I
hope it shows that whilst it sounds great and simple in theory the
practice and reality are quite another thing. Within the context of
the European Union it sounds so appealing and simple, founded on
the basis of mutual recognition and respecting subsidiarity, as long
as business decisions are made within the legal framework of our
own home state we will be OK. Unfortunately the real world is not
so simple, even within Europe we can still do different things in our
home states which will create potentially a two-tier system – one
for « foreign » service providers, another for « home » service
providers who may find themselves disadvantaged in their own
country. Then what happens to the Internal Market and it's level
playing field ? We could see a flight to those Member States with
lowest/least level of regulation – is this good for consumer confidence ? Is this good for the Internal Market ? So if Country of
Origin actually presents barriers to trade, or fails to remove them –
what is the alternative, the treaties are quite clear then we move
towards more to harmonisation.

I will return to the theme of greater harmonisation, but first it
is worth examining the Country of Destination approach, although

it is questionable whether such a coherent line exists. It is its appearance in those instruments relating to private international law; now within the EU to be comprised in direct community legislation – regulations. Firstly the Brussels Regulation, in connection with which I was the Parliament's rapporteur. This will come into force in March 2002. It deals with the mutual recognition Jurisdiction and Judgments, the question of whose court? Any day now we expect the Commission's proposals on Rome 2 – non-contractual obligation – applicable law, the question of whose law? These instruments have to be seen in context; the context of the EU's long held ambition to make the Internal Market work. The Rome 11 proposal dates back to Council (Member States) Resolution 14th October 1996, it is all part of the Tampere agenda of 1999 to create an area of Freedom Justice and Security. This is borne of a commitment to ensure that businesses and consumers have easy access to cross border justice to enforce contracts and obligations and really make the Internal Market work, this was never particularly conceived as being about e-commerce, which has grown up subsequently and of course needs to be taken into account as another way of doing business that could substantially enhance the Internal Market.

If these EU private law regulations veer towards a Country of Destination approach that allows consumers to use their courts and law at the expense of business having to potentially comply with 15 different regimes why should this be? What are the political imperatives or goals behind this? They are as follows; I have already mentioned the good functioning of Internal Market. This is closely followed by access to justice and a high level of consumer protection. Consumer confidence in the e-economy is essential, recent studies indicate that consumer's greatest worries about Internet trade are privacy, security and access to redress. It is that later concern that Country of Destination seeks to address. Yet it should still be seen as a fall back, there are many other policy tools available other than hard law.

I see this as a hierarchy, firstly business has to be encouraged to have its own well functioning customer service procedures, than there should be access to alternative dispute resolution procedures and lastly if only when all else fails the courts. In the context of the E-commerce Directive and the Brussels Regulation much was done to encourage alternative dispute resolution. I was also the Parliaments rapporteur on the EEJ Net, this is to be commended but it is only a facilitating network, in may lack funding and enforcement mechanisms. It is presently in its infancy and at varying degrees of operation in Member States. Of course it has the possibility to extended outside of Europe. But it can be no alternative to access to the courts. A business group came to see me in Strasbourg last week and they said what they feared was European Consumers having access to a class action, well I'm sorry but what sort of business is likely to be subject to such an action, not I venture to suggest a well run honest one. Consumers have better things to do and there is not an angry army of them out there waiting to take nascent e-businesses to court. So I take the view that many of the concerns being raised in relation to the Rome11 proposals are misguided.

There are ways of limiting the risks for business by targeting and other preventative means. These possibilities find an echo elsewhere in the global legal responses. In presenting the Parliament's proposals on the Brussels Regulation not only did I make much of alternative dispute resolution but also drew on US experience and the Zippo case, this argues for a definition of jurisdiction which is activity based, it is perhaps an easier concept for common lawyers because it involves analysing each case, rather than applying a principle. I was pleased that to some extent the Commission and Council took on these ideas *Art 15 (1) (c) Brussels Regulation refusal to deal with persons in a given jurisdiction* and *reasonable efforts to prevent such dealing.* These ideas have also been carried over into the discussions at the Hague Convention. They may represent one way forward, but we in the EU have to recognise that our solutions are founded in the creation and enhancement of our Internal Market and for that reason we cannot expect them to fit everyone else in the global community.

Indeed Europe's answer to the continuing problem of different laws seems likely to be as I have suggested further harmonisation firstly at the level of basic European contract and commercial law this is foreseen by long discussions in the Parliament on an own initiative report, the Lehne report and the Commission Communication on European Contract Law which we debated last week in

Strasbourg and which goes to the Council before the end of this year.

It is also the thrust of the Commission's Green Paper on European Consumer Law just put before the Parliament, which introduces the notion of a duty to trade fairly.

Again in some quarters this has been greeted with alarm but we have to continue to search for common solutions that also offer our citizens protection and our businesses encouragement; what will not be an option is no regulation at all, I leave you with this quote from the Economist « *The rules governing the Internet will end up like those governing the physical world. That was only to be expected. Though it is inspiring to think of the Internet as a placeless datasphere, the Internet is part of the real world. Like all frontiers, it was wild for a while, but policemen always show up eventually* », *The Economist*, Aug. 2001.

A PRACTICAL PERSPECTIVE
ON SOME E-COMMERCE ISSUES

Geoffrey R. BRIGHAM (1)
Compliance Counsel for eBay Inc.

European and international law are united in their goal of promoting increased certainty for consumers and providers of e-commerce services. The chief aim of the European Commission's E-Commerce Directive is to ensure that the Community reaps the full benefits of e-commerce by boosting consumer confidence and giving providers of information society services legal certainty (2). The « legal framework must be clear and simple, predictable and consistent with the rules applicable at international level so that it does not adversely affect the competitiveness of European industry or impede innovation in that sector » (3).

European and international law remain in development, however, with respect to e-commerce, and, as a result, they are not always well linked, leaving unanswered questions for the international corporation doing business within and outside of Europe. This paper examines one practical perspective of an international e-commerce business; raises a couple of issues that are challenging to those who must deal with the daily application – and occasional uncertainty – of European and international Internet law; and offers some practical solutions in dealing with that uncertainty.

---

(1) Mr. Brigham is based in Paris as the Senior Liaison and Compliance Counsel for eBay Inc. His comments and observations are his own and not necessarily those of the company. He was the former Senior Liaison Legal Advisor between the U.S. Department of Justice and the French Ministry of Justice (1997-1999) and was recently awarded the honour of *Chevalier de l'Ordre National du Mérite* by the President of the Republic of France and the U.S. Attorney General's Award for Distinguished Service by the U.S. Attorney General. Mr. Brigham may be contacted at gbrigham@ebay.com.

(2) Directive 2000/31/EC (8 June 2000) (on certain legal aspects of information society services, in particular electronic commerce, in the Internal Market) [hereinafter « Directive »], Recitals 5, 7.

(3) Directive, Recital 60.

I. – The practical perspective

I work for eBay (www.ebay.com), which provides an online trading platform in more than 17 countries, including France, the
United Kingdom, Italy, Netherlands, Germany, and the United
States. eBay hosts an electronic forum, enabling more than
37 million users to buy and sell goods in diverse markets. On any
given day, there are approximately 7 million listed items, 1 million
new listings, and more than 40,000 new registered users.

A seller on eBay typically lists his product in one of more than
16,000 categories usually with a photograph and a description of
the product. The item remains in the possession of the seller until
the seller ships it directly to a buyer. Buyers and sellers leave feed-
back for each other, allowing subsequent users to evaluate the trading history of those participants. eBay itself is not involved actively
in the listing, sale, or delivery of any item for sale and never possesses the items sold through its site. The company earns its
primary revenues by charging sellers an initial listing fee or a final
value fee (4).

This type of enterprise provides the sort of innovative business,
markets, and trading communities contemplated by the European
Commission when it first embarked on creating the E-Commerce
Directive. eBay is a trading community that gives consumers
expanded choice, granting them access to millions of items. It
affords small – and medium-sized enterprises new markets and
alternatives to the traditional distribution channels controlled by
larger corporations (5).

---

(4) eBay provides a number of services to protect consumers and ensure legal compliance. For
example, on various sites, eBay (a) provides for a fraud protection program, reimbursing users
up to 1500 FF to cover losses due to fraud (http://pages.fr.ebay.com/help/community) ; (b) reim-
burses sellers for their fees when a bidder fails to pay (http://page.fr.ebay.com/help/community/
npb.html); (c) partners with escrow services to eliminate fraud in transactions (http://
pages.ebay.com/help/community/escrow.html) ; (d) invents and develops new technologies to
combat piracy and fraud; (e) oversees its VeRO program to run automated searches for infringing activity and to enlist the active interaction and participation of copyright and trademark
owners (http://pages.ebay.com/help/community/vero-program.html) ; (f) writes and enforces comprehensive policies regarding prohibited and questionable items on its site; (g) provides space on
its service to government agencies (through its « About Me » feature), so that those agencies may
provide relevant information to eBay users to prevent fraud and other illegal use of the service;
and (h) employs an experienced investigative team, including former law enforcement officials,
to work in liaison with governmental and police authorities to reduce risk of fraud and other
illegal activities.

(5) Directive, Recital 2.

II. – Issues that merit further review

A. – Non-Judicial Solutions
to Dispute Resolution

Different views are often expressed in European and international law forums on critical legal questions, as seen recently at the Hague Conference on judicial jurisdiction. European law however envisions practical solutions. Under the European E-Commerce Directive, for example, non-judicial dispute resolution alternatives are available (and indeed essential to) both businesses and consumers, providing cost-effective, rapid alternatives to judicial resolution.

As Article 17(1) of the Directive underscores, Member States « shall ensure that, in the event of disagreement between an information society service provider and the recipient of the service, their legislation does not hamper the use of out-of-court schemes, available under national law, for dispute settlement, including appropriate electronic means ». Such non-judicial methods for resolving disputes must be « genuinely and effectively possible in law and in practice, even across borders » (6). The differences – and inefficiencies – between « national law[s] », however, mandate a dispute resolution policy that seeks a harmonised, simple, cost-reduced policy. This is especially true for a company like mine where the same user is both a consumer and businessperson on an international trading platform. Electronic arbitration must be available, uniform, and flexible to address the needs of the digital community.

Private arbitration services, such as those used by eBay, provide a type of service at a minimal cost, which may be particularly useful when the amounts at stake are not significant. On our U.S. site, electronic dispute resolution without a moderator is without expense to the user (and resolves more than 80 percent of the cases), and the use of a professional mediator costs the user about

---

(6) Directive, Recital 51.

110 FF (with the remaining fees paid by eBay) (7). Codes of conduct – as envisioned in Article 16 of the E-Commerce Directive – may address these non-judicial solutions, but such an approach must include the strong participation of the private sector, whose practical international experience may help promote greater uniformity and certainty. The pilot phase of the « European Extra-Judicial Network » (EEJ-Net) – which helps consumers settle cross-border disputes out-of-court and online – was launched on October 16, 2001, representing an important step.

B. – Disparities in Liability

Like non-European countries, the European Community has recognised that « disparities concerning liability of service providers acting as intermediaries... impair[s] the development of cross-border services and produce[s] distortions of competition » (8). Differences in liability laws threaten effective European and international commerce. With no explicit answer in international law, there are a number of areas where these disparities need to be addressed and limited to satisfy the ongoing need for certainty.

Limitations on Liability for Good Faith Restriction of Objectionable Material. Responsible international service providers have a strong interest in providing a safe and reliable forum in which to offer their services, recognising the individual differences and preferences of users. On both the European and non-European level, the law often requires that service providers remove « blatant » or « apparent » violations or infringements (9). These laws are commendable, but their terms are subjective, often difficult to assess.

---

(7) See http://www.squaretrade.com/spl/jsp/eby/eb.jsp?marketplace—name = ebay&campaign-EBY—OD—7. SquareTrade, a dispute resolution service used by eBay, reports handling more than 150,000 cases to date with users from over 100 countries and in five languages. Direct negotiation, which is an online self-service resolution application linking parties to facilitate communication, has successfully resolved more than 80 percent of the presented cases. Mediation, which allows users the option to obtain assistance from SquareTrade's network of mediators (more than 250 in eight countries), assists parties in obtaining a mutually agreeable settlement, resulting in successful resolution of more than 75 percent of completed cases.

(8) Directive, Recital 40.

(9) *See, e.g.*, Directive, Article 14 (« Member States shall ensure that the service provider is not liable for the information stored at the request of a recipient of the service, on condition that... the provider... is not aware of facts or circumstances from which the illegal activity or information is *apparent...* ») (italics added).

Limitations on liability should cover good faith efforts by Internet service providers to take down « apparent » violations of national laws. A U.S. federal law provides that, in certain situations, « [n]o provider or user of an interactive computer service shall be held liable on account of... any action voluntarily taken in good faith to restrict access to or availability of material that the provider or user considers to be obscene, lewd, lascivious, filthy, excessively violent, harassing, or otherwise objectionable, whether or not such material is constitutionally protected... » (10).

The pending French bill on the Internet Society provides for protection from civil liability if, having actual knowledge of the *manifestly illicit nature* of this content, a hosting provider removes the content (11). Yet, if such a provider believes – albeit mistakenly – that such content is « manifestly illicit » and chooses to remove the item and even suspend the user, a question arises as to whether that provider remains liable to the user who had posted the item in the first place. A conservative hosting provider may hesitate to act, discouraging rapid, confident compliance with the law.

Notice, Take-Down, and Counter-Notice Procedures. The E-Commerce Directive specifically preserves the authority of Member States to « establish[] procedures governing the removal or disabling of access to information » but leaves to national law the decision on how to implement Article 14 (12). Member States should consider implementing practical processes that involve rights owners to protect internationally copyrighted and trademarked materials. Uniform notice and take-down provisions have proven effective in the e-commerce domain, limiting a service provider's liability for infringements of third parties when the infringing party or agent provide explicit notice to the service provider of the infringing item and the service provider acts expeditiously in taking down the specified item (13). The Digital Millennium Copyright Act in the United States includes such legal safeguards for copyright owners,

---

(10) 47 U.S.C. 230(c)(2)(A) (available at http://liiwarwick.warwick.ac.uk/uscode/47/230.html).

(11) *Projet de loi sur la société de l'information*, (*The Information Society Bill*) art. 11 (I) (available at http://www.lsi.industrie.gouv.fr/observat/innov/lsi/index.htm).

(12) Directive, Article 14(3).

(13) eBay has implemented its VeRO program, which details a comprehensive notice and take-down regime that allows copyright and trademark owners to provide explicit notice to facilitate the take-down of infringing items. See http://pages.ebay.com/help/community/vero-program.html.

service providers, and Internet users (14). Similar measures are being considered in Canada, Japan, and Singapore.

Such procedures should envision an active role for the affected party, since, as our practical experience shows, these methods encourage an interactive working relationship with rights owners to overcome differences in law and to find practical solutions (15). Only the copyright, trademark or patent holder – not a service provider – is in a position to know whether a rights owner has authorised use of a copyrighted work or trademark. But, once served with appropriate, explicit notice of the specific infringing item, the service provider has a responsibility to act. Under Article 14(1) of the E-Commerce Directive, such specific notice should give the service provider « aware[ness] of facts or circumstances from which the illegal activity or information [specified in the notice] is apparent ».

Consistent with the need to « expeditiously... remove or disable access » of certain information (16), the law must ensure that a service provider that removes the item or suspends repeat violators in good faith is not legally liable. To prevent misuse by miscreants or business rivals, civil liability should be imposed on those who make a knowingly material misrepresentation to a service provider. And, to encourage prompt take downs and efficient handling of notices, there should be incentives to provide notice to the appropriate point of contact for the service provider trained to respond expeditiously to such notices.

As our experience shows, private parties sometimes overreach in asserting violations of their rights. The law should allow a user to

---

(14) *The U.S. Digital Millennium Copyright Act*, 17 U.S.C. Section 512 (available at http://caselaw.lp.findlaw.com/scripts/ts—search.pl?title = 17&sec = 512).

(15) As part of its VeRO program, eBay works closely with more than 2,500 rights owners worldwide ranging from individuals to large businesses to ensure that items listed for sale do not infringe copyright, trademark, or other intellectual property rights. Rights owners provide input on possible search terms for the take-down of infringing items; eBay offers such owners an automated searching tool called « Favorite Searches » to assist them in searching for and identifying potentially infringing items; eBay enables rights owners to communicate their policies and legal positions directly to eBay users by creating their own home pages (« About Me ») that reside on eBay; eBay works closely with these owners in formulating policy pages, providing specific guidance relating to the offering of potentially infringing items in the music, video games, movies, software and trademarked goods areas (among others); eBay has created special warning messages that service providers may provide space to rights owners to allow them to educate consumers about their product; and eBay works with rights owners by referring « gray area » items to them for their review.

(16) Directive, Article 14(1)(b).

contest a take down by submitting a counter-notification supported by specified indicia of reliability under penalties of law for knowing material misrepresentations (17). Such a counter-notification should constitute agreement by the user to accept a lawsuit from the complaining party in the courts of relevant jurisdiction as a means of resolving the dispute.

A service provider should be protected from liability for taking down material in response to a notice and for restoring the material online in response to a counter-notification. Any other rule would frustrate the goal of the E-Commerce Directive to encourage rapid and reliable takedowns of illegal material (18) and would unfairly expose service providers to liability. This proposed system would provide service providers, private parties, and law enforcement much needed legal certainty and a practical way to deal with infringing conduct online.

Monitoring and Liability. To ensure greater certainty, policy-makers should avoid ambiguous exceptions to limited liability, which discourage service providers from monitoring their sites. Policy-makers understand the need to provide protection for information society services that host third-party content. Article 14 of the E-Commerce Directive decrees that Member States must ensure that a hosting provider is not liable for information stored at the request of a recipient where the provider does not have actual knowledge of the illegal activity or information (among other things) (19).

The same directive underscores, however, that this limitation does not apply « when the recipient of the service is acting under the authority or the control of the provider » (20). Responsible international hosting services should undertake active measures to ensure against illegal activity, including exercising control through independent monitoring and suppression of illicit materials. Such active measures however should not be construed as evidence that a recipient of the service was acting under the « control of the provider » for purposes of Article 14(2) of the E-Commerce Directive. Such a construction would provide a strong disincentive for

---

(17) See 17 U.S.C. Section 512(f) (available at http://caselaw.lp.findlaw.com/scripts /ts— search.pl?title = 17&sec = 512).

(18) Directive, Recital 48.

(19) *See* Directive, Article 14(1)(a).

(20) Directive, Article 14(2); *see also* Recital 42.

hosting services to address the differences in, and compliance with, national laws.

Jurisprudence is evolving on this issue in both the European and non-European forums, even though international law provides no explicit answer. In a recent case brought by a user against eBay for copyright infringement, an American federal court in California held that eBay is entitled to the limitations of liability under the Digital Millennium Copyright Act, holding that the ability to remove infringing material, to close accounts of users who infringe copyright, and to practice selective monitoring does not give eBay « the right or ability to control » infringing activity (21). In an analogous alleged trademark violation case, a German court held that eBay is protected under Section 5(2) of the German Teleservices Act, which deals with provider liability for third party content. The court lifted an injunction against eBay, ruling that the « framework conditions » provided by eBay were « completely neutral where the article in question [was] concerned » and, as a result, the listing in question was third-party content, subject to liability limitation under German legislation (22). Greater certainty however is desired and policy-makers should seek legislative clarification.

C. – COMMUNICATION :
THE KEY TO ADDRESSING PRACTICAL CONCERNS

European and international laws, with their ambiguities, are not theoretical concepts, but concrete rules applied daily to trans-border Internet companies. To improve certainty, the private sector must communicate effectively with oversight institutions. eBay has placed a strong emphasis on working with government agencies and organisations. We have met with data protection authorities of different countries, for example, to air issues frankly and to seek prac-

---

(21) *Hendrickson v. eBay, Inc.*, n° CV 01-0495 RJK, Order Granting Defendants Motion for Summary Judgment or, Alternatively, Motion for Partial Summary Judgment at 20 (C.D. Cal. Sept. 4, 2001) (available at http://news.findlaw.com/cnn/docs/ebay/hendrickson.pdf). The U.S. law at issue was less favorable to service providers than Article 14(2) of the E-Commerce Directive since the U.S. law focused on whether a service provider had the « *right and ability* to control » the user's activity.

(22) *Knirps GmbH v. eBay GmbH*, n° 34 0 27/01 Q (Aug. 22, 2001). Copies of this decision are available (either in original German or translated English) by contacting Mr. Brigham at gbrigham@ebay.com.

tical solutions. e-Bay provides government agencies the opportunity to post sites on its service to educate servers and employ hyperlinks to government sites to educate users about the laws and their requirements. We also work closely with law enforcement agencies and other special-interest organisations to protect against fraud and prohibited items on our sites (which vary according to the culture and laws of each country) and to work out differences in laws of various jurisdictions. These practical approaches help overcome differences, instil certainty, and help serve to identify and develop necessary links between European and international law for the future.

TOWARDS CONFIDENCE : VIEWS FROM BRUSSELS : A EUROPEAN INTERNET LAW? SOME THOUGHTS ON THE SPECIFIC NATURE OF THE EUROPEAN REGULATORY APPROACH TO CYBERSPACE

BY

Yves POULLET

Dean of the faculty of law of the FUNDP
(University faculties of Notre-Dame de la Paix) (Namur)
Director of the C.R.I.D. (Centre for research
on information technology and law) of the FUNDP
Professor at the faculty of law in Liège
YVES.POULLET@FUNDP.AC.BE

The aim is ambitious : a specifically European concept of regulation of the Internet is being considered. It has to be modest : the following thoughts are the result of my own reading of a disparate heap of legislation and official rulings by the European authorities. None of those authorities has indicated the « guiding thread » to understanding them (1). Accordingly, these thoughts are intended merely to provoke debate and probably, to be more precise, to help define a clearly stated European policy.

My first consideration concerns the extent of European intervention. It is not sufficient to state its main features, the specific nature and originality in the various areas of that intervention it must then be described (Section I). Although European legislative measures are increasing, made obligatory by the single market, more impressive still is the concern of the European authorities to establish mechanisms that in addition to common legislation, encourage complete harmonisation of the interpretation and

---

(1) Note, however, some key documents, such as the Communication from the European Commission of 8 December 1999 on an initiative called « e-Europe – An information society for all » repeated to a large extent in the conclusions of the Stockholm European Council on 22 and 23 March 2001.

implementation of those measures. In short, the establishment of a common, comprehensive legal system for the « information society » services. Does that intention of the information society not harm the principle of « subsidiarity » which is nevertheless a pillar in the construction of Europe ? (Section II).

Conversely, the third section considers the way in which Europe is attempting to defend its ideas in relation to non-member countries, especially the United States. That raises the delicate problem of maintaining European « sovereignty » in the context of the global network formed by the Internet.

Finally, the last section deals with the European approach towards self-governance or self-regulation. To what extent, through relevant European legislation, are we going to see the emergence of a strictly regional approach to the normative value of multiple self-governance systems established by practice ?

I. – Some features of european regulatory involvement

European regulatory involvement can be found in the three key areas of development of information society services, that is to say the regulation of e-commerce operators and transactions, the protection of individual freedoms likely to be called into question by that development and finally, the protection of any existing intellectual property and related rights concerning the content of those services (II). It is useful to give an overall description of that regulatory involvement both from a quantitative and qualitative point of view (I).

A. – GENERAL COMMENTS

In that respect, firstly it will be noted that no subject escapes European jurisdiction. Subjects such as electronic signatures, the protection of intellectual investments or the security of electronic methods of payment apparently fall within the jurisdiction of Europe, with the aim of constructing a single European market. European intervention in the protection of freedoms, now widely justified by adoption of the European Charter of individual freedoms (2), would previously only have had indirect justification in that by retaining different legal systems there was a danger of creating barriers to intra-European traffic or it would lead to distortion of the regulations, thereby favouring the establishment of an information society service in one country rather than another.

That indirect justification by the free movement of services or by freedom of establishment led to European intervention, including in matters of computer crime and the protection of minors and human dignity (3), beyond the strict powers conceded by the « 3rd pillar » of the Treaty of Amsterdam (4). In these matters, I would emphasise that without European intervention there would be a danger that different national measures would be adopted, leading to distortions of competition between countries. Consequently, the obligations to set up « hot lines » or systems for filtering or storing data to be used by the services, could be introduced by some countries and not others. That finding explains why European regulations are increasing : in the specific fields of multimedia and e-commerce alone, a consultancy company (5) found no less than 48 initiatives (directives, recommendations and communications) that had been completed or were in the process of being completed, from the famous directive on certain legal aspects of e-commerce to the directive on harmonisation of the rules relating to invoicing for the purposes of VAT including the Communication and outline decision of 28 May 2001 on combating fraud and counterfeit means of non-cash payments or the proposal put forward by the Commission on 12 December 2000 concerning « the use of the generic domain name 'eu' ».

Although the number of interventions is noteworthy, more remarkable still is the rapidity of the adoption procedures followed

---

(2) About this Charter of fundamental rights of the European Union, approved at the Nice European Council in December 2000, read the Reports of the Strasbourg Study Days of 16 and 17 June 2000 published in the universal review of Human rights, 12, 15/9/2000.

(3) Council Recommendation of 24 September 1998 on the development of the competitiveness of the European audiovisual and information services industry by promoting national frameworks aimed at achieving a comparable and effective level of protection of minors and human dignity, *J.O.*, L. 270/48, 7/10/1998.

(4) The provisions of the Treaty of Amsterdam have been in force since 1st May 1999. It should be noted that, accordingly, the recommendation mentioned in the previous note could not even have referred to it.

(5) This is the Cullen International Company in Namur which from this year has been instructed by the European Commission to construct a web site showing all the European legislative initiatives in the fields of multimedia and e-commerce (http:www.cullen-international.com)

by directives and <u>the short transposition times</u> imposed on Member States. When one is aware of the many hazards that litter the obstacle course run when a directive is adopted (6), one might consider that the 18 months required to adopt a directive as important as the one concerning certain aspects of e-commerce are no mean achievement (7). The time-limit for transposing directives on such matters is often 18 months (8) and not the usual three years. I might add that a number of directives make provision for amendment processes, some of which are short-term, in their very wording or in the preamble (9).

The concern to respond quickly to the needs of the market and its development certainly explain the haste of the European authorities, in particular the Commission, which has no hesitation in using processes that are faster and under its sole control when it feels the need. Accordingly, the Commission uses the route of recommendation together with the threat of a directive when the provisions of that recommendation are not followed (10). In any event, it is a question of moving quickly... at the risk of going too

---

(6) In this talk, we cannot analyse the provisions laid down in the Treaty on the European Union concerning the adoption of a directive (see in particular, Article 251 on the co-decision procedure). The reader is referred to the numerous works on European law concerning those provisions.

(7) In this particular case, the proposal for a Commission directive was issued on 18 November 1998; the vote on the first reading of the European Parliament on 6 May 1999; the Commission's amended proposal issued on 1st September 1999 was the subject of a Council policy agreement on 7 December 1999 and a joint position was adopted on 28 February 2000. Parliament's final vote on the second reading took place on 4 May and the directive adopted by the Council and Parliament on 8 June was published in the *Journal Officiel* on 17 July.

(8) The deadline for transposing the e-commerce directive was accordingly fixed for 17 January 2002. The same time-limit for the directive concerning electronic signatures.

(9) See in that respect, the significant example of the so-called E-Commerce Directive which provides for a reassessment of the provisions on the liability of intermediaries and on exceptions in the case of notarial and other instruments; the preamble to the directive known as « copyright and related rights » provides for assessment of the impact of the provisions with regard to changes in new technology and maintenance of the traditional balances between protecting authors and the circulation of ideas.

(10) Two examples :

– recommendation (COM(97)353 of 9 July 1997) on transactions concerning instruments of electronic payment and in particular the relationship between the issuer and the bearer which calls for measures to be taken by issuers before 31 December 1998 with an assessment of its implementation and proposals for a directive if that implementation is insufficient and unsatisfactory. On 20 March of this year, the Commission published the study assessing that implementation (conducted by the CRID of FUNDP and the Centre for Commercial Studies of Queen Mary College London) which found that the European recommendation had not been incorrectly applied.

– recommendation (COM 2001/310/EC) on the « principles for out-of-court bodies involved in the consensual resolution of consumer disputes », published on 4 April 2001.

fast and not weighing up the impacts of the decisions made and the sometimes foreseeable changes in technological contexts (11).

B. – AREAS OF EUROPEAN INVOLVEMENT
AND THEIR SPECIFIC FEATURES

1. – *Concerning e-commerce operators and transactions or how to ensure confidence ?*

a) *The basic directives*

Two directives establish the basic overall principles specific to players and transactions in e-commerce : the Directive of 8 June 2000 (12) on certain legal aspects of e-commerce and that of 13 December 1999 (13) on the legal protection of electronic signatures.

Without claiming to be exhaustive, let us look at some of their principles. It will be noted that so far as concerns players, access to the market by operators of information society services (14) cannot be subject to any additional conditions other than those that already exist for the non-electronic supply of the same services. However, let us note that operators of services that certify electronic signatures may be subject to conditions of interoperability and checks to ensure that they comply with certain conditions if they want the signatures for which they issue certificates to have a particular evidential value. That principle of free access is only tempered by increased obligations for transparency, fair compensation for the fact that supply and demand on the Internet are not « face to face ». Accordingly, a provider of services to the information society will be asked to give details of his identity, his location and means of getting in touch with him and he will be forced to

---

(11) In that respect, we can only reinforce the thoughts of L. LESSIG, *The laws of cyberspace*, available online at the following address : http://cyberlaw.stanford.edu/lessig/content/index.html.

(12) Directive 2000/31/EC of the European Parliament and the Council of 8 June 2000 concerning certain legal aspects of the Information society services, in particular electronic commerce in the internal market (the Directive known as « electronic commerce »).

(13) European Parliament and Council Directive 1999/93/EC of 13 December 1999 on a Community framework for electronic signatures (the Directive known as « electronic signature »).

(14) It will be noted that as far as the basic principles are concerned, the traditional distinction between « traders » and « the professions » and « non-traders » has been abolished.

provide direct and easy access to the terms and conditions, codes of conduct and others by which he agrees to abide.

So far as concerns e-commerce transactions, a major principle is the obligation placed on Member States not to directly or indirectly categorise e-commerce transactions by legal requirements affecting the value, effectiveness or binding force of the use of electronics, at any stage of the transaction (15). That principle of non-categorisation is also valid for electronic signatures and it is even added that in some circumstances an electronic signature can be given the same the legal value as that of a handwritten signature.

That principle is tempered by the requirement to consider an electronic transaction as arising from a multi-stage procedure so as to ensure that the resulting consent is informed, complete and certain. If any peculiarity can be found in electronic transactions, it is in this temporal breakdown of stages resulting in consent, a fair counterbalance for the risks inherent in an instant technology used between « distant » parties to the contract.

How can we fail to see the emergence of a European contract law through these various provisions ? Indeed, the European authorities resist it and emphasise unrestrainedly that their involvement is limited, dictated by the law of subsidiarity (See below, on this principle, n°). However, the Commission recently launched a debate on European contract law (16). According to the discussions, the Commission « wonders, in particular, whether the problems connected with entering into, interpreting and enforcing cross-border contracts might interfere with the smooth operation of the internal market ». Is the reply not already contained in the question ? That is the view of the European Parliament when, in its resolution of 16 March 2000 concerning the Commission's working programme for 2000, it

---

(15) In our view, that principle will not mean abandoning « formality » in contracts but rather seeking functional equivalents of the traditional formalities based on the conventional model of the paper document. See in that respect, D. GOBERT and E. MONTERO, « Les contrats conclus par voie électronique » (« Contracts entered into by electronic means »), in *Le commerce électronique sur les rails*, (e-commerce on the rails) in M. ANTOINE *and others*, *CRID Report*, n° 19, Bruylant 2001, pp. 240 et seq.

(16) Commission communication to the Council and European Parliament concerning the law of contracts, Brussels, 11 July 2001, COM (2001) 398 final. That communication is based, in particular, on the work of the Pavie group which recently published the work : « European Contract Code : Preliminary Draft » (Univ. of Pavie, 2001).

declares : « a more extensive harmonisation in the field of civil law has become essential in the internal market » (17).

b) *Concerning some aspects or specific transactions*

The European Union supplements the framework proposed by the two directives analysed above with provisions that concern consumer protection and so-called electronic money.

With regard to the first, the European conviction that expansion of the information society necessarily requires consumer confidence (18) justified both affirmations of principles, such as Council of Europe Resolution of 19 January 1999 concerning the « consumer » dimension of the information society, a veritable charter of consumer – Internet users' rights (19), and the adoption of legislation with a more direct normative value. In that respect, it will be noted that the Directive of 20 May 1997 concerning distance contracts which extends to the world of electronic commerce a set of obligatory rights asserted for any transaction carried out at a distance and obliges the supplier of services to issue a record of the transactions conducted by electronic means on a « durable medium » (20). Similarly, a directive is shortly expected concerning the distant marketing of financial services (including insurance

---

(17) *J.O.* C 377, 29/12/2000, p. 323. The resolution makes explicit reference to the changes in the technological context to explain this need.

(18) That conviction is forcefully reiterated in the European Commission's comments in its reply dated 21 April 1999 to the request from the American FTC for academic reactions and comments published following the FTC's report : « US perspectives on Consumer Protection in the Global Electronic Marketplace, US Federal Trade Commission Notice requesting academic papers and public comments ».

(19) The Resolution of the Council of Ministers responsible for consumer matters on 19 January 1999 reiterates numerous principles, *inter alia*,

– the principle of transparency and the right to receive sufficient, reliable information before and after the transaction ;

– the principle of non-discrimination in access to products and services and that of protecting vulnerable consumers ;

– the principle of fair distribution of risks and responsibilities ;

– the principle of the involvement of consumer organisations in the protection of consumer interests ;

– the principle of informing and educating consumers, designed to make them capable of developing the appropriate know-how ; ....

(20) On this important concept, read M. DEMOULIN, « La notion de 'support durable' dans les contrats à distance : une contrefaçon de l'écrit ? » (« The concept of 'durable medium' in distance contracts : forgery of the written word ? »), *REDC*, 2000, pp. 361 et seq.

services) aimed *inter alia* at consumers (21) and manifestly broadening the obligations for transparency and information, the time-limits for a period of reflection and withdrawal and making provision for effective and adequate processes for complaining and resolving disputes. Those services include making distance payment services available, which introduces the second subject.

The second subject, which has seen significant normative intervention by the European authorities is, in fact, as we have said, electronic money (22), another essential factor in the development of e-commerce (23). The European Commission's communication and recommendation of 9 July 1997 have already been mentioned (see n° 6 above). In addition to the obligations for information about the method of payment used and its consequences, they introduce clear rules on the apportionment of liability between the issuer and the user of the method of payment, in the case of theft, fraud, loss or error as well as efficient mechanisms for settling disputes. Directives have been adopted or are in the process of being drafted. Two directives dated 18 September 2000 are designed, firstly, to harmonise national legislation relating to credit institutions by extending the number of institutions capable of issuing electronic money (24) and secondly, to check those institutions' transactions. It is a matter of making sure that issuers of payment are stable and robust whilst distinguishing between the various systems according to the risks connected with the type of method of payment issued.

---

(21) Proposal for a Directive from the European Parliament and Council concerning distance marketing of financial services to consumers and amending Directives 90/619/EEC, 97/7/EC and 98/27/EC.

(22) Concept defined as follows by Parliament and Council Directive (2000/28/EC) of 18 September 2000 amending Directive 77/780/EC on the coordination of laws, regulations and administrative provisions relating to the taking up and pursuit of the business of credit institutions. « Monetary value as represented by a claim on the issue which is :
— stored on an electronic device;
— issued on receipt of funds of an amount not less than the monetary value issued;
— accepted as means of payment by undertakings other than the issue ».

(23) See Communication from the Commission on electronic commerce of 16 April 1997 (COM(97) 157) : « A European initiative on electronic commerce ». The Commission noted that electronic commerce would not develop « without robust, user-friendly, efficient and safe methods of electronic payment ».

(24) One might consider telephone network operators, or indeed more widely, distributors of goods or services. I would add that in the communication on electronic commerce of 1st April 1997 already referred to, the European Commission had emphasised the importance of ensuring full competition between traditional issuers and the newcomers.

Besides those initiatives, I would add the European authorities intention to combat fraud and counterfeit means of non-cash payment, particularly by preventative measures (25).

2. – *Concerning human rights and fundamental freedoms : a difficult balance between « freedoms » and « security » of the network*

Both Europe and the United States recognise freedom of expression as one of the Internet's fundamental values. However, these two areas of the world are faced with the need to set some limits to that freedom when it is abused through illegal or harmful content that harms others. It is important to emphasise some nuances amongst the responses proposed by these two regions.

This difference in approach is even more discernible when one considers the problem of protecting personal data. As borne out by the Directive of 24 October 1995, the European Union considers this issue to be crucially important whereas, subject to some specific laws, the United States refuses to provide the appropriate legislation. The increase in risks that harm private life caused by the use of modern communication networks has led the European courts to propose new legislative measures. As various recent declarations show, Europe has repeated that it considers the protection of personal data to be « the key issue in the development of the information society » (26). Accordingly, the second point examines the specificity of the European approach both with regard to freedom of expression (a) and the issue of protecting personal data (b).

---

(25) In that respect, see the following 3 documents :
– Communication from the European Commission of 1ˢᵗ July 1998 : « A framework measure to combat fraud and counterfeiting of non-cash means of payment ».
– Outline decision of the European Council of 28 May 2001 bearing the same title as the first document cited.
– Commission communication (COM (2001)11) of 9 February 2001 : « Preventing fraud and counterfeiting of non-cash methods of payment ».
(26) It noteworthy that American surveys broadly confirm the European authorities' feelings. Accordingly, the Americans questioned affirm that the risks connected with the use of their personal data are the major obstacle to wider use of Internet services.

a) *The delicate balance between freedom of expression and other fundamental values in European legislation*

The introduction of any form of censure of the Internet is one of Europe's main concerns. As shown in Articles 14 and 15 of the Directive on certain legal aspects of electronic commerce, which, following the American model, (27) strictly limit the responsibility of intermediaries in relation to the content they host and exonerate them from any obligation to carry out preventative checks on that content.

Although the principle of freedom of expression is clearly laid down, the need to combat illegal or harmful content, particularly child pornography, led the European Union to define how it balanced freedom of expression with the other values mentioned in Article 10 of the European Human Rights Convention.

That balance is achieved through various pieces of legislation (28) : the 1996 Green Paper followed by Council Recommendation of 24 September 1998 on the development of competition in the audiovisual and information services industry by promoting national systems aimed at achieving comparable and effective protection of minors and human dignity, a recommendation which has recently been assessed (29); then the communication of 16 October 1996 on illegal and harmful content on the Internet followed by a Council and Parliament decision on 25 January 1999 « adopting a multiannual action plan to promote safe use of the Internet by combating illegal and harmful content on the global networks »; finally, Council decision of 29 May 2000 concerning the fight against child pornography on the Internet.

The European position can be summarised as follows. Certainly the first provisions adopted in the aftermath of the American decisions following the declaration that the Decency Act was unconstitutional refer exclusively to self-regulation and technologi-

(27) With regard to the American origin of the European provision and a comparison of the two texts, read R. Julia BARCELO, R. and KOELMAN, K.J., « Intermediary Liability in the e-commerce directive : so far so good but it's not enough », *Computer Law and Security Report*, 16, n° 4, 2000, 213-239.

(28) For a commentary on these provisions and a discussion on regulation of Internet content, read M. D'UDEKEM-GEVERS and Y. POULLET, *Concerns from a European User Empowerment Perspective in Internet Content Regulation, Communications and Strategies*, Montpellier, 2001, not yet published.

(29) On 27 February of this year, the European Commission adopted the evaluation report which proposed a heterogeneous implementation of the 1998 recommendation.

cal developments to ensure the development of a « secure network ». Gradually, and subject to what will be said later (see below, n°s 41 et seq.), the State's involvement is more insistent, firstly, by a framework of self-regulation (30), secondly, by introducing maximum cooperation between Internet operators and public authorities insofar as the legislation imposes on the former the obligation to keep a record of each person's use as a precaution (31) and finally, by the obligation placed on intermediaries to set up their own control system for child pornography at least (32).

The recent discussions that have taken place in Europe (33) following the Council of Europe's adoption of a draft convention on cybercrime in 2000, show that the trend observed with regard to messages relating to child pornography, that is to say a freedom of expression under a control that takes place *a posteriori* resulting from the cooperation imposed between public and private authorities, will henceforth be aimed at all computer crime (infringement of data protection, economic crimes such as sabotage, unauthorised access, infringement of copyright, cybersquatting, defamatory, racist or xenophobic messages.

b) *The protection of personal data*

The Green Paper on the convergence of the telecommunications, media and information technology sectors, better known as the « 99 Review » highlighted the absolute necessity to review Directive 97/66/EC of 15 December 1997 on the processing of personal data and protection of private life in the telecommunications sector, in view of the additional risks created by technological advances.

---

(30) Accordingly, in an appendix, the recommendation of 24 September 1998 already referred to sets out « guidelines for the development of national self-regulation systems ».

(31) This obligation to keep a record is explicit in Council Decision of 29 May 2000. The Council of Europe Convention on cybercrime adopted... gives a legal basis for this requirement for information services operators to keep a record of traffic data and allow the police and judicial authorities to access it.

(32) See, in that respect, Council Decision of 29 May 2000 to combat child pornography on the Internet, which, let us note, contradicts Article 15 of the directive on some legal aspects of electronic commerce which exonerate intermediaries from the obligation to introduce surveillance measures.

(33) See, in that respect, the Commission's communication of 26 January 2001 on the creation of a more secure information society by improving the security of information below structures and combating computer crime, followed by a *public hearing* (7 March 2001), a discussion in the Council of Ministers (16 March 2001) and taken up by the European Parliament in the « Freedoms and rights of citizens » (19 June 2001) and Legal Affairs Committee (26 June 2001).

For Europe it was a question of maintaining the requirement for a « high degree of protection of personal data », considered to be an absolute necessity to guarantee the confidence of users in relation to development of the information society (34).

The Commission's proposal (35) broadened the special protection afforded not only to telephone networks but also to all mobile, satellite or cable networks. It imposes heavier duties on all service providers of electronic communications offered to the public, particularly security and confidentiality. So far as concerns the processing of details about traffic and location, it significantly limits the right of service providers to process them without the user's consent, requires the latter to provide information and, finally, introduces an opt-in system for unsolicited e-mail communications (36). Finally, the Commission reserves the right to impose technical standards with regard to the terminal equipment if it were to find « invasion of privacy » practices, notably through the use of invisible processing (37).

3. – *On intellectual property*
and related rights : from affirmation to doubts

An analysis of the relevant European trends shows a hesitation between two desires : on the one hand, to ensure maximum protection of the investment, beyond the traditional area protected by intellectual property law; on the other, to maintain a legal system for protection which is consistent with the way in which the traditional paradigms of intellectual property law guarantee a fair

---

(34) In that respect, the opinion of the Economic and Social Committee on the effects of electronic commerce on the single market (OMU – Single Market Watchdog) (Doc. 2001/C 123/01, J.O., 25.4.2001) : « The Community must give absolute priority to data protection ».

(35) Commission proposal (COM (2000)385) of 12 July 2000 for a Parliament and Council directive on the processing of personal data and protection of private life in the electronic communications sector.

That proposal was the subject of an initial European Parliament report dated 19 June 2001.

(36) This point highly controversial. A study of the impacts of such a choice is underway.

(37) The so-called Article 29 Group made a recommendation concerning the risks connected with invisible processing (a group made up of representatives of data protection authorities set up by Article 29 of Directive 95/47/EC already mentioned) « Invisible and automate processing of personal data on the Internet performed by software and hardware » (Recommendation 1/99 on Invisible and Automatic Processing of Personal Data on the Internet Performed by Software and Hardware, 23 February 1999, W.P. 17, available on the web site http://europa.eu.int/comm/internal—market/en/dataprot/wp.does/wp.does—99/htm.

balance between the interests of the « authors » or their « heirs » and users of the work or indeed the community in general.

Directive 96/9/EC of 11 March 1996 on the legal protection of databases certainly fits into the first trend. It creates a « *sui generis* » law for protecting databases which it is acknowledged, are not covered by copyright laws. We know how much American literature has been up in arms against this European departure which clearly protects the investment and no longer protects the intellectual creation.

The same tendency is shown in Directive 98/84/EC of 20 November 1998 on the legal protection of conditional access services such as pay-for-view television but also any multimedia service that is accessible on the basis of an individual licence for which access is protected by technical devices such as encryption. Independently from any legal protection of such private content, the Directive provides that the technical measures for protection are in themselves a subject worthy of protection. Accordingly, technical protection becomes the source of legal protection of a work which in itself cannot necessarily be protected by law and guarantees controlled access to the work (38).

Unlike this tendency which admittedly satisfies information society service providers' lobbies and, more widely, promoters of the electronic publishing market, other provisions prove to be more concerned with improving the circulation of works and programmes. Accordingly, European Parliament Resolution of 22 October 1998 clearly advocates supporting free software and open, interoperable platforms (39). More recently, it has been pointed out that the Parliament and Council directive, adopted on 9 April 2001 (40) after lengthy and difficult debates, a directive on copyright and related rights in the Information Society, finally sets out the right of Member States to prescribe exceptions to authors' monopolies (the right to reproduce or communicate to the public). Those exceptions which, admittedly, were proposed as an option, can be

---

(38) In that respect, the reader is referred to the results of the workshop on this topic during the 25th anniversary of Crid in November 1999 and published under the direction of Séverine DUSOLLIER, « Towards a law of access to works », *CRID Report*, n° 18, Bruylant, Brussels, 100 pages.

(39) That resolution follows on from the Commission's Green Paper (COM (97)263) of 3 December 1997 concerning the convergence of the telecommunications, media and information technology sectors and its implications for the regulation.

(40) Published on 22 June 2001 in the *Official Journal*.

justified by private use, the benefit to public educational institutions, use for research purposes, quotation, journalism, etc. Similarly, the directive limits the protection that might be afforded by technical measures (41).

Admittedly, it is for each country to incorporate those reservations into its national legislation thereby ensuring the traditional balance that copyright legislation provides between the legitimate interests of the creators (or their heirs) and those of society, to the advantage of some players such as research, education, the press, etc.

Having thus defined the limits of protection of Internet content, the European authorities are quite legitimately adopting the necessary measures for more effective legal protection by improving cooperation between the government authorities responsible for detecting and punishing acts of piracy or counterfeiting (42).

II. – The mechanisms introduced for Europe to ensure the closest possible unification in national legal systems and their implementation

It is trivial to set the global nature of the Internet against the existence of multiple national legal systems. This multiplicity of legal systems is harmful to the development of the information society. For the service provider whose service can be accessed from several points of the globe, it creates uncertainty as to the legislation likely to be relied on by the Internet user-consumer or simply contracting party; for the latter, it increases the administrative difficulties of a claim and reduces the chances of rapid, effective enforcement of any judgements made.

Those findings led the European courts to simultaneously develop a vigorous unification policy presented in Section I as well as proce-

---

(41) On the limits to be imposed on the protection provided by technical measures, read S. DUSOLLIER, Y. POULLET, M. BUYDENS, *Report to the UNESCO's third « Infoethics » colloquium* available on the CRID's website; http://www.

(42) See, in that respect, Parliament resolution of 4 May 2000 following on from the Commission's Green Paper of 15 October 1998 « Combating counterfeiting and piracy in the single market » and this same Commission's communication dated 30 November setting out practical measures for combating them and a proposal for a directive for the harmonisation of national measures.

dures designed to prevent disparities of content between legal systems. It is a matter of controlling national legislation in a preventative manner and limiting the national margin for manœuvre. That subject will be analysed in point I of this section.

To this policy, which is directed at the reference legal framework, one must add (this will be point II of this section), the European initiatives designed to encourage the creation of a single area of jurisdiction which guarantees that compliance with the established rules. Three points will be highlighted in that respect :

— the recognition of foreign judgements;
— administrative cooperation between Member States;
— finally, the promotion of out-of-court systems for resolving disputes.

A. – From the « Cassis de Dijon » judgement to the « Transparency » and « Electronic Commerce » directives (43)

Since the famous *Cassis de Dijon* judgement (44), the traditional case-law of the Court of Justice of the European Communities with regard to concerns divergences between the regulations of Member States and the creation of a single market, can be summed up as follows :

— The Court takes a positive view of the existence of divergent legal systems, considering them to be an aspect of competition necessary to the dynamics of a single European market; in particular, using the so-called « equivalence » principle, the Court identified from the Treaty, in a number of judgements relating to more or less analogous facts (the ban by a Member State on importing any service or product because it does not comply with the regulations of the country of importation or non-approval of those products or services in accordance with that country's rules of law) a principle that can also be applied to trading in goods, the supply of services or carrying out paid work in a Member State other than the country of origin. That principle prohibits

---

(43) This part of the report is based on the excellent article by M. van Huffel, « Protection du consommateur et commerce électronique : quelques réflexions au départ du droit de la concurrence » (« Consumer protection and electronic commerce : some thoughts based on competition law »), *Revue Ubiquité*, n° 5, 2000, pp. 119 et seq.

(44) C.J.E.C., 20 February 1979, *Digest* 1979, p. 649.

the national authorities from imposing material requirements or measures for control whose effect is equivalent to that of the measure already deployed by the Member State from whence the goods, person or service in question originates.

- However, limits (45) are set on the variations accepted by application of the so-called rule « of reason ». Accordingly, Member States can intervene and restrict importation or subject it to conditions when the legislative requirements imposed by the country of importation fulfil the conditions of necessity, causality and proportionality (46) in relation to the objectives which, in some cases, are already specified in the Cassis de Dijon judgement and supplemented thereafter by other decisions : the effectiveness of fiscal controls, the protection of public health, fair trading and consumer protection.

Accordingly it is in view of the obstacles conceded in the abovementioned circumstances that European action for harmonisation is justified. That European harmonisation may be achieved by mechanisms for mutual recognition, be minimal (encouraging stricter national measures), optional (leaving the Member States various options) or total.

The various measures for harmonisation referred to in Section I show that as far as legislation for information society services is concerned, the European Union took the view that there were numerous possibilities for obstacles liable to be justified by the rule of reason whereas it considers that it is absolutely necessary to create a market for information society or electronic communication services operating on rules that are more or less identical. That conjunction of arguments explains the increase in European actions and accordingly, it will be understood that although some of the

---

(45) M. VAN HUFFEL, art. quoted, p. 20 and the numerous references referred to therein.

(46) « The national measures liable to hinder or make less attractive the exercise of a fundamental freedom guaranteed by the Treaty must fulfil four conditions : they must be applied in a non-discriminatory manner, they must be justified by imperative requirements in the general interest, they must be suitable for securing the attainment of the objective which they pursue and they must not go beyond what is necessary in order to attain it », CJEC, 30 November 1995, case C-55/94, *Gebhard, Rec.* 1995, p. 14165.

measures for harmonisation mentioned refer to minimal (47) or optional measures (48), the majority are total (49).

Apart from this increase in so-called harmonisation legislation, Europe is introducing mechanisms aimed at preventing variations in legal systems when new regulations are adopted in Member Countries. It is a question of preventing national legislative measures for information society services that would run the risk of creating impediments but also by that preventative analysis, of detecting, where appropriate, areas where harmonisation is necessary and taking action if needs be.

In that respect, Directive 98/48/EC of 20 July 1998 on transparency (50) is noteworthy. Taking the view that the harmonisation of rules concerning information society services decreed *a priori* by the Community authorities is too risky not to say premature, the directive introduces a Community level system of control and coordination of any relevant national measure. That prevents fragmentation of the internal market, legislative inconsistencies or a frenzy of legislation which would slow down the development of the information society.

Accordingly, the directive obliges Member States to subject any draft legislation relating to an information society service, a concept with a very broad definition, to a procedure for notifying the Commission. The notification suspends the national procedure for three months. That period allows the Commission and other Member States to issue comments or indeed « detailed opinions » (the latter being binding in relation to the Member State that took the initiative) on any aspect of the initiative taken that might have an effect on the free movement of services or the freedom of establishment of operators of those services.

---

(47) Accordingly, Directive 97/7/EC on distance contracts introducing minimum rules, authorises Member States to regulate distance contracts beyond the minimum threshold set by the directive.

(48) Accordingly, the directive on the harmonisation of certain aspects of copyright and related law in the information society leaves it for each Member State to lay down the exceptions to the law of reproduction or communication from a list specified by the directive.

(49) Accordingly, directive 99/93/EC on electronic signatures is a directive for total harmonisation. In addition, it includes an « internal market » clause which prohibits restrictions on the provision of certification services originating from another Member State.

(50) This is a directive that amends for the third time directive 83/89/EC laying down a procedure for the supply of information in the field of technical standards and regulation. It is to be noted that at the outset, Directive 83/89/EC was only concerned with technical standards. Directive 98/48 broadens the field to all the regulations.

Issuing such « opinions » extends the suspension. The Commission is also entitled to extend the suspension by invoking the existence of a proposal for Community legislation.

The so-called « Electronic Commerce » Directive goes even further. Article 3 thereof affirms the principle whereby operators of information society services are subject to the legislation and control of the countries in which they are established (51). Their compliance with that legislation entitles them to offer the service throughout the whole of the European Union.

The other Member States may only object to such an offer for reasons of public order as specified in the directive (52) using proportionate measures (53). The directive adds that those measures may only be taken after establishing that there is no prompt reaction from the country of origin and after notifying the Commission which may take specific legislative measures to resolve the issue.

Thus, not only is the European Union gradually standardising the rules but more importantly, through mechanisms that oblige Member States to notify it of their draft legislation, it reserves the right to intervene if needs be when it finds that an existing or draft national piece of legislation, not to say the threat of implementing

---

(51) However, as noted in the recommendations for the second reading (European Parliament, 12 April 2000, Final A5-0106/2000, p. 11), this Article 3 of the directive cannot be interpreted as a rule of private international law. However, note the same passage : « As Parliament requested, the common position now leaves no doubt as to the supremacy of the directive on international private law since it provides that, even though that directive does not in itself constitute an additional rule of private international law, the implementation of that law must not have the effect of restricting the free movement of information society services as laid down in the directive ». With the exception of some particular fields, for which explicit derogation is provided, the directive will state that the information society services are normally subject to the national law of the Member State in which the service provider is established and that the other Member States in which these services may be received shall not restrict the free supply of information society services. Accordingly the directive will apply the principle of « mutual recognition » of national legislation in the « relevant field », that is to say « the requirements applicable to information society service providers or to information society services ». The proposed directive will establish specific harmonised rules in the fields in which it is necessary for businesses and citizens to be able to supply and receive information society services throughout the whole European Union, regardless of borders. Accordingly, the proposal strives to remove the barriers caused by the obstacles to the supply of online services by concentrating on five key areas.

(52) In fact the text of the directive gives a restrictive list of these reasons of public order.

(53) On Article 3 and its interpretation, read A. CRUQUENAIRE, « La clause de marché intérieur : clef de voûte de la directive sur le commerce électronique » (« The internal market clause : keystone of the E-commerce directive »), in *Le commerce électronique européen sur les rails ? (European electronic commerce on the rails ?), Analysis and proposals for implementing the e-commerce directive, CRID Report*, n° 19, Bruylant, Brussels, pp. 41 et seq.

it, runs the risk of creating an obstacle to the creation of a single European market for information society services.

In that respect, it will be noted that these possibilities for preventative intervention will endow the European Commission with powers which hitherto were only granted to the European authorities within the framework of a claim that was *a posteriori* based, as we said (see n° 24 above) on the rule of reason.

That intervention, which the European authorities will say is legitimised by the very characteristics of the supply of *on line* services, in particular their ubiquity and ability to easily be freed from the constraints of locality, nevertheless raises the question of the limits of European intervention. The principle of subsidiarity (54) of European involvement in those fields that do not fall within its sole jurisdiction was affirmed by the recent European Union treaties (55). Although it is clear that in that respect it is for the European authorities, particularly the Commission, to prove the need for a specific action at Community level rather than at national, regional or local level, in matters of information society services, such proof would appear to be quickly established and the suitability of the methods of Community intervention to the aim pursued immediately affirmed (56). The intrinsic « transnational »

---

(54) « Generally speaking, applied to the institutional field, the principle of subsidiarity means that in a given entity (Country or federation of States), the higher level of the political corps only acts when the action being considered can be taken more effectively at that level than at a lower level, having regard to its dimension or its effects. That principle based on common sense is designed to ensure that judgements are made as close as possible to citizens. It would appear that there is a need to place the methods of intervention in hierarchical order : local, regional, national, European, not forgetting international. The principle of subsidiarity can thus be understood as a 'multilevel' principle ». (S. VAN RAEPENBUSCH, *Droit Institutionnel de l'Union et des Communautés européennes* (*Institutional Law of the Union an its European Communities*), 3th ed., 2001, de Boeck ed., p. 128). On that principle, amongst others, M.A. GAUDISSART, « La subsidiarité : facteur de désintégration européenne ? » (« Subsidiarity : a factor in European disintegration ? »), *J.T.*, 1993, 173-182 ; K. LENAERTS, « The principle of subsidiarity and the Environment in the E.U. : Keeping the Balance of Federation », *Fordham International Law Journal*, 1994, pp. 846 et seq., etc.

(55) In particular by Article 5, par. 2 and 3 of the European Community Treaty : In areas that do not fall within its sole jurisdiction, the Community, in accordance with the principle of subsidiarity, only acts, if and to the extent that the aims of the envisaged action cannot be achieved sufficiently by the Member States and therefore, because of the dimensions or effects of the envisaged action, can be better achieved at Community level. « The Community's action does not go beyond what is necessary to achieve the objectives of this treaty ».

(56) Accordingly, the least binding methods of intervention must be favoured : e.g.. « minimal » harmonisation in preference to mutual recognition or total harmonisation.

aspect of activities concerning such services would indeed seem to be an indication of this Community added value (57).

Is this harmonisation thus legitimised and justified, effective? The Commission increases its observations and recommendations to Member States during the difficult exercise of transposing Community legislation. Will this European monitoring of transpositions prevent the work of European integration being destroyed in the future?

B. – Towards
a single European « judicial » area

Apart from the standardisation of substantive law, covered in point I, the introduction to the section mentioned three areas of involvement in which Europe intended to contribute to a common legal area and beyond that a common judicial area. Initially, it is a question of making it easier to bring an action before the courts of appeal and courts of other countries in the European Union and making the judgements made by those courts easier to enforce. It is true that European action in such cases cannot only be explained by the development of *on line* transactions, however we need to recognise that the development of electronic commerce and the resulting increase in cross-border transactions has precipitated discussions on the subject, both at European (58) and international level (59).

Council Regulation of 22 December 2000 (60) on the jurisdiction and enforcement of judgements in civil and commercial cases proposes some amendments to the 1968 Brussels Convention. Accor-

---

(57) ... and this even if it means overturning, as the « transparency » and « e-commerce » directives do, the presumption of sufficient capacity to act at national level.

(58) In particular, the conclusions of the Tampere European Council of 15 and 16 October 1999 emphasised the need for judicial co-operation in civil matters, based on Section IV, so as to create an area of « freedom, safety and justice » (SI (1999) 800.

(59) See, in that regard, the proceedings of the Hague convention on international jurisdiction and foreign judgements in civil and commercial matters which expressly mention the importance of e-commerce (see in that respect, preliminary document n° 12 « Electronic Commerce and International Jurisdiction », Ottawa, 28 Feb.-1er March 2000) (proceedings and documents available at the address http:www.hech.net/e/workprog/jdgm.html)

(60) This regulation (published in the *J.O.* of 16 January 2001) follows on in particular from a European Parliament resolution (European Parliament legislative resolution on the proposal for a Council regulation on jurisdiction and the recognition and enforcement of judgements in civil and commercial matters (COM(1999) 348-C5-0169/1999 – 1999/0154(CNS)). Parliament having been consulted on the regulation had proposed some amendments which were not accepted.

dingly, it sets out the hypothetical situations in which the consumer might benefit from derogations to the principle of jurisdiction of the court in the place where the defendant is resident and, above all, makes the procedures for enforcing the foreign judgement in the country of the party seeking enforcement easier.

The two other areas of intervention deserve to be examined more closely in that the European regulations are directly aimed at e-commerce transactions.

1. – Alternative methods of settling disputes : fashionable trend or real benefit?

« Europe keen to promote consumer confidence and thereby develop electronic commerce, emphasises the need for consumers to be able to settle their disputes effectively and adequately by means of out-of-court or other similar procedures ».

Europe has been concerned with the establishment of alternative methods of resolving disputes in consumer matters for about ten years. That concern was highlighted notably by the following documents :

– the Green Paper on consumer access to justice and the settlement of consumer disputes in the single market (1993);
– European Parliament Resolution on the Commission's communication « action plan on consumer access to justice and dispute resolution » (1996);
– the Communication from the Commission concerning the principles applicable to bodies responsible for the out-of-court resolution of consumer disputes (1998);
– Commission recommendation on the principles applicable to the bodies responsible for the out-of-court resolution of consumer disputes (1998).

In order to encourage the development of e-commerce and make it effective whilst ensuring a high level of consumer protection, the so-called E-commerce Directive is designed to guarantee the best means of redress by the online use of out-of-court systems for settling disputes (61). On this view, its Article 17, § 1, obliges Member

---

(61) Alternative Dispute Resolution Mechanisms according to the English expression. So far as concerns bodies that operate in a totally electronic manner (receipt of complaints, instructions

States to remove or amend any obstacles to that use in their legislation (62).

Apart from this first requirement which imposes an obligation on Member States to achieve a certain result, relating to all A.D.Rs, the rest of Article 17 imposes an obligation to use best endeavours and for Member States to encourage the bodies responsible for the out-of-court settlement of consumer disputes to apply the principles of independence, transparency, the participation of both parties, effectiveness of the procedure, legality of the decision, freedom of the parties and representation, in complying with Community law. These principles are the ones mentioned in Commission Recommendation 98/257/EC of 30 March 1998 concerning the principles applicable to the bodies responsible for the out-of-court settlement of consumer disputes.

The Commission's non-obligatory recommendation of 4 April 2001 supplements this first recommendation. It specifies the principle of independence of the body and that of transparency of the procedure. It dwells on the effectiveness of the procedure, which, must provide a rapid, genuine solution to the difficulties encountered by consumers, at a reduced cost (63). Finally, it dwells on the need to inform consumers of the possibilities of redress before the judicial courts and their right to terminate the out-of-court procedure at any time.

Finally, it will be noted that the Commission's idea is to create a network of out-of-court settlement bodies in order to make it easier for consumers to make cross-border claims (64).

---

in the case, issuing the sentence) we then speak of O.D.R. (On line Dispute Resolution Mechanisms).

(62) P. DE LOCHT, in *Les modes de règlement extrajudiciaire des disputes (Out-of-court methods of dispute resolution), Le Commerce électronique européen sur les rails ? (E-commerce on the rails ?)*, M. ANTOINE *and others*, under the direction of E. MONTERO, *CRID Report*, n° 19, Brussels, Bruylant, 2001, pp. 327 et seq. Article 17 of the e-commerce directive states : « Member States must ensure that where there is a disagreement between an information society service provider and the recipient of the service, their legislation does not hinder the use of out-of-court mechanisms for settling disputes that are available under the national law, including by appropriate electronic means ».

(63) In that respect, the recommendations of the e-confidence Forum (http://www.confidence. jrc.it/default/htm) created on 30 March 2000 by the European Commission. In that respect, the web site of the SANCO DG, Out-of-court bodies responsible for drafting consumer disputes, http://europa.eu.int/comm/policy/developments/aacec—just/acec—just04—fr.html.

(64) On 5 May 2000, the European Commissioner David Byrne announced the launch of such a network : EEJ Net which since 1st February 2001 has been supplemented by a FIN-NET network, specialising in financial services.

Moreover, those initiatives which sit alongside all those traditionally classed as self-regulation (see below Section IV, n°s 41 et seq.) are the subject of experiments financed by the European authorities (65) and have received the often enthusiastic support of the various forums (66).

2. – *Administrative cooperation*

A number of European provisions call for better coordination of the actions taken by the national authorities (exchange of information, passing on complaints etc.). In a way, these national authorities play the role of a one-stop shop for their citizens when they have some wrangles with operators or providers of services that are located in another country in the European Union. Beyond that, this cooperation between national authorities will hopefully lead to a more uniform application of national legislation under a Community directive and will reinforce the harmonisation of legal systems. In addition, the coordination will take place under the aegis of the Commission which highlights its role and the development of a specifically European policy in the various fields concerned.

The directive known as « E-commerce » is a fine example of that European policy. Article 24 prescribes cooperation between Member States (with the help of the Commission) by establishing points of contact for the authorities where the recipients and providers of information society services can get information about their contractual rights, the mechanisms for claims and the authorities to contact if necessary.

The same initiative for combating fraud and counterfeiting of non-cash methods of payment : the outline decision of 28 May 2001

---

(65) Accordingly, ECODIR, a project launched in 2000 and run by a consortium made up of universities (CNRS SNational Centre for Scientific Research, CRID-CITA SInterfaculty Committee for Technology Assessment), Univ. of Namur, Univ. of Munster and Dublin) and an ODR operator (e-resolution).

(66) Accordingly research by the :

– Transatlantic Consumer Dialogue (T.A.C.D.) : Alternative Dispute Resolution in the context of the Electronic Commerce, February 2000, http://www.tacd.org/papers/ecommerce/Ecom-12-00.rtf.

– Consumer International : Consumer International, « Disputes in Cyberspace Online Dispute Resolution of Consumers in cross-border disputes – an international survey », http://www.con sumersinternational.org/campaigns/electronic/electronic/sumadr-final.html, p. 3.

– of the GBDE (Global Business Dialog) : Alternative Dispute Resolution and e-Confidence, Recommendations, 24 August 2000.

prescribes cooperation between authorities and national points of contact so as to combat fraudsters or counterfeiters more effectively (67).

The « Electronic Signature » Directive provides for the creation of an « Electronic signature » Committee made up of representatives from the various Member States, which will help the Commission to define the standards and criteria for conformity to be applied in such cases. Similarly, the « Copyright in the Information Society » Directive establishes a contact committee between representatives of the national authorities (68).

I should also mention the recent communication of 6 June 2001 concerning the « Security of information and networks – Proposal for a European policy approach » which would like to set up a European information and warning system based on national intermediaries.

Finally, effectively combating illegal and illicit messages calls for the creation of a European network of national *hot lines* with an exchange of information and « best practices », designed to promote the coordination of national measures (69).

III. – Relations with non-community countries : a policy of sovereignty : from a defensive policy to a more active policy

If the European authorities are seeking to create a uniform legislative framework within the Union in order ensure the smooth running of a single European e-commerce market, what is their attitude towards the existing situation, beyond European borders ?

No doubt, and it is a leitmotiv of their discussions, the European authorities are convinced of the need to create a framework for e-

---

(67) Same type of initiatives proposed by the Commission on 30 November 2000 following its Green Paper. Combating counterfeiting and piracy in the single market (15 October 1998, COM(98)569 final) and a draft directive concerning specifically a general framework for cooperation between authorities on such matters (expected for the beginning of 2002).

(68) This contact committee is presided over by the Commission. Its aim is to encourage the exchange of information, to analyse the impact of the directive and to organise consultations on any relevant issue.

(69) See, in this respect, Council and European Parliament decision of 25 January 1999 adopting a multiannual Community action plan to promote safer use of the Internet by combating illegal and harmful content on the global networks.

commerce that is not only European but global. The idea of the « Global charter » for the Internet advocated by Commissioner Bangemann in September 1997 at the ITU's « Interactive Telecom 97 » forum (70) was expanded on in numerous discussions, resolutions and debates held within various European bodies (71).

Although this « global » coordination is sought and justifies the action of the Union bodies within public international authorities such as the OECD, the ITU, G.8., etc., that intention should not be understood as meaning that Europe will denounce the values it espouses and thus make national rather than European « sovereignty » take precedence.

No doubt, we need to reconsider the concept of sovereignty in the cyberspace era in view of the global dimension of the networks, the players and, accordingly, the issues, a dimension which further encourages technology ? Sovereignty is a manifestation of freedom and independence through which the State imposes a rule on its nationals and requires other countries to comply with it. The fact that a person belongs to a State gives that person the right to benefit from that country's protection through legislation of the constitutional guarantees and freedoms granted to him whilst at the same time imposing some limits dictated by the consideration that the State might have for the essential values it seeks to enforce. Those guarantees and freedoms, just like their limits, cannot be challenged merely because information and communication technologies are breaking down the physical barriers.

In the context of those technologies, sovereignty must then be viewed as a positive obligation on the State ant its judges to get compliance with those values in their relations with people residing on its territory, including in relation to foreign countries and operators. If there is a risk of invasion, it will no longer be physical

---

(70) Mr Bangemann's speech gave rise to a European Commission Communication on 4 February 1998 : « Globalisation and the Information society : the need for reinforced international coordination ».

(71) Accordingly, the resolution adopted on 14 January 1999 by the European Parliament on the Commission's communication, the debate held within the Council of Telecom Ministers, on 30 November 1999 : « The I.S. of the future, responding to the challenges of global electronic commerce ». That resolution follows on from the recommendations made by the Global Business Dialogue (G.B.D.) on the future framework for the legislative policy. More recently, within the European Parliament or to be more precise the legal and internal Market Commission, the opinion on the Commission communication to the Council and European Parliament. Organisation and management of the Internet – International and European issues (COM(2000)202 – C5-0263/2000-2000/2140(COS)).

but it will operate through networks as was recently shown by the debate in Europe on the Echelon network's practices of listening to satellite messages.

That defence of European sovereignty operates in various ways :
— the first attitude is no doubt defensive : notably, it is that of the French judge in the Yahoo case and of the European Parliament in the Echelon case. It is a question of prohibiting certain extraterritorial practices or at least limiting their effects in relation to European citizens, and this in the name of social values which a particular country considers to be vital;
— the second possible attitude is more open : without renouncing European values, it is a question of seeking adequate protection of the freedoms and values that Europe extols, without extreme imperialism and whilst complying with other countries' systems. Article 25 of European Directive 95/46 on the protection of personal data and more importantly its recent application in negotiations between the European Union and the United States illustrate this second approach;
— finally, a third approach is that of entry of the European authorities to the self-regulation bodies. This third approach is the one adopted by the European authorities in relation to « the organisation and management of the Internet », in other words entry of the European Commission as such to ICANN which manages the attribution of domain names at global level.

A. – THE NEGATIVE ATTITUDE :
THE YAHOO AND ECHELON CASES

1. – *The Yahoo case*

Without further analysing the decision and discussing its validity (72), let us simply observe that the Vice-President of the *Tribunal de Grande Instance* in Paris ordered an American company to take the necessary steps to prevent French Internet users from accessing the pages of an auction web site hosted by that company and offering Nazi memorabilia for sale.

---

(72) On that decision, the reader is referred to the debate organised by L. THOUMYRE on his web site Juriscom (http://www.juriscom.net/uni/doc/yahoo.htm) (Jan.-Feb. 2001) in which P. TRUDEL, J. REIDENBERG, M. GEIST, and the author himself took part.

By doing so, the French judgement made the national rule on the prohibition of racist and xenophobic messages prevail on the principle of freedom of expression, affirmed by the first amendment to the American Constitution. In other words, cyberspace is not an area without laws. It is the role of the national laws and judges who enforce those laws to remind, in the name of values that the State considers essential, that there are narrow but real limits to freedom of expression.

In the case in question, it will be remembered that the judge's call for an examination by an expert of the actual technical possibilities of blocking French citizens' access to the offensive site had highlighted the virtues of the IP address which, in the majority of cases, enabled the origin of an Internet user's request to be established. Accordingly, the « sovereign » ruling of a State may even find an ally in technology ensuring its effectiveness. No doubt that effectiveness is not absolute but isn't that always the case with any rule of law!

Moreover, Yahoo was well aware of the automatic use of the IP address to reveal the provenance of an Internet user, who, on that basis, automatically selected the language used for the web pages and some advertising. The fact that the judge then condemned Yahoo for having benefited from this system of addressing without simultaneously having suffered the consequences with regard to the selection of pages made accessible, challenges the irresponsibility of hosts with regard to the content to which they provide access. It is their duty, when they use the new media of the Internet, to promote their products or services in a national market other than their own, to ensure that they set up or simply use the existing technological tools that guarantee that the basic values of that country are not challenged.

2. – The Echelon case

In 1998, A European Parliament report published by the STOA (73) alerted European opinion to the existence of a network

(73) The STOA (Scientific and Technological Options Assessment) is a department of the general research division of the European Parliament. The STOA's report « Appraisal of Technologies Control » is based in particular on the works of D. CAMPBELL (Working Document for Stoa Panel « Development of Surveillance Technology and Risk of Abuse of Economic Information », Part 4/4 : The State of the Art in communication intelligence of automated processing

called ECHELON, run by the English, American, Canadian, New Zealand and Australian secret services, capable of capturing not to say analysing, all or at least some of the messages passing through geostationary satellites, both telephone and fax messages as well as telexes or Internet type messages.

The ensuing anxiety related both to a breach of confidentiality of private messages originating or received by European citizens and to financial messages from businesses.

European reaction was kept on hold since the United Kingdom belonged to the network and other countries were developing similar practices. No doubt, the economic concerns and the fight against industrial espionage against European businesses by foreign powers also determined this reaction but the greatest concern of Members of Parliament was a reminder of the principles of the Council of Europe convention on the right of countries to interfere with the private life of citizens.

That protest led the European Parliament (74) to call for an independent, absolute European policy on cryptography, an area in which European dependence on the United States is obvious (75) and also for a European system to control the activities of information services.

B. – More open attitude :
the « adequate » protection of Article 25
of European Directive 95/46
on the protection of personal data

Under Article 25.1 of Directive 95/46, « The Member States shall provide that the transfer to a third country of personal data which are undergoing processing or are intended for processing after transfer may take place only if, without prejudice to compliance with the national provisions adopted pursuant to the other provisions of this

---

for intelligence purposes of intercepted broadband multi-language leased or common carrier http://www.europarl.int/stoa/publi/pdf/98-14-01-2en.pdf).

(74) See the report presented by G. Schmidt on the existence of a global surveillance system to intercept private and commercial communications (Echelon Interception System) to the temporary committee on the Echelon interception system dated 18 May 2001 (PE 305.391).

(75) See Resolution n° 15 proposed in the Schmidt report mentioned in the previous note : « Urges the Commission and member States to develop appropriate measures to promote, develop and manufacture European encryption technology and software and above all to support projects aimed at developing user-friendly open-source encryption software ».

Directive, the third country in question ensures an adequate level of protection ». The principle is therefore the prohibition of the transfer of personal data unless it can be shown that the protection afforded in the other country is adequate.

In Article 25.2, the directive goes on to state that the assessment of whether a third country's protection is adequate must take into account « all the circumstances surrounding a data transfer or set of data transfer operations » and, in particular, of various factors, some of which are a function of the transfer in question, such as the nature of the data, the purpose and duration of the proposed processing operation, the country of origin and country of final destination, and others relating to the level of protection in the third country, such as « the rules of law, both general and sectoral, in force in the third country in question and the professional rules and security measures which are complied with in that country ».

In particular, the wording of Article 25 presupposes a functional approach, that is to say that the protection is evaluated both in relation to the risks of a breach of the data protection, risks caused by the flow in question, and in relation to the specific or general measures introduced to counter those risks by the person in charge of the data in the third country.

The concept of « adequate protection » leads to a comparison of the requirements the directive imposes for protection with the responses of the third countries. It is a question of inquiring whether there is a « functional similarity ». This means examining not merely whether the European principles and protection systems have been transposed in the third country, but rather whether there is any element that fulfils the functions sought, even if those elements are different in nature from those we have in Europe. It probably leads to better compliance with the local legal structures and characteristics than a request for equivalent protection, which calls for fully comparable legislation (76).

In particular, so far as concerns the instruments for protection established in the third country, Article 25 refers not only to the

---

(76) On « adequate » protection or how a state legal system may flexibly impose values on third countries in the global information society, see Y. POULLET and B. HAVELANGE, « Preparation of a methodology for evaluating the adequacy of the level of protection of individuals with regard to the processing of personal data », *Office of Publication of the European Communities*, 1998, Annex to the Annual Report 1998 (XVD/5047/98) of the WG Art 29 of Dir. 95/46/EC.

rules made by the State, whether they be general or sectoral, but also to codes of conduct and indeed technical measures, provided that those instruments are « complied with ». Accordingly, the person responsible for evaluating another country's protection will pay more attention to the effectiveness of an instrument than to its nature : what is important is that those in charge of the files and the beneficiaries of that instrument should have a broad awareness of the instrument and its content, even if it is merely a « Company Privacy Policy »; similarly, one will be mindful of the possibility of a claim from private individuals against those responsible for the files where the instruments in question have not been complied with. Finally, he will carefully assess the status of the authority in charge of the claim, how accessible it is and whether it operates with transparency (77).

This policy that Europe has introduced relating to third countries' data protection systems is interesting in more than one respect :

- It formed the basis of Europe's acknowledgement of « Safe Harbour Principles » established in the United States, at the instigation of the Department of Commerce (78);
- it shows – and we shall return more fully to this point (see below n° 41) – a positive attitude by the Commission towards self-regulation (79);
- finally, one might think that the open attitude afforded by the concept of adequate protection might be extended to fields other

(77) See, on these criteria, the documents published and approved by the Group for the protection of people in respect of the processing of personal data, known as the « Article 29 » group, and WP 4 (5020/97) « Premières orientations » (June 97) and WP 12 (5025/98) « Applying articles 25 and 26 » (July 98).

(78) The reader will find the principles on the web site : http://www.ita.doc.gov/safeHarbour.htm.

78 organisations which on 1ˢᵗ July stated that they followed the Safe Harbour principles.

On the American approach v. the European approach, read C.H. MANNY, *European and American Privacy : Commerce, Rights and Justice*, a paper presented at the annual conference of the Academy of Legal Studies in Business, 11 August 2001, Albuquerque. For a more detailed analysis of the provisions of the Safe Harbour Principles and whether they are adequate or not, Y. POULLET, « Les Safe Harbour Principles : une protection adéquate » (« Safe Harbour Principles : adequate protection or not »), available on the CRID's web site (http://www.droit-.fundp.ac.be/crid.htm.).

(79) ... in the case of the Safe Harbour, one wonders : is this pure self-regulation or co-regulation ? The reply is not easy in that the Department of Commerce played a role in establishing the Safe Harbour Principles and plays a role in implementing them by keeping a register of companies which have declared to abide by them, the effectiveness of the rules derives, *inter alia*, but certainly from the right to claim before an official jurisdiction (the Federal Trade Commission).

than the protection of personal data. I am thinking in particular of consumer protection.

C. – A « PARTICIPATORY » ATTITUDE :
EUROPEAN POLICY IN RELATION TO THE ICANN

The importance of the « non profit » association ICANN (Internet Corporation for Assigned Names and Numbers) is well known, not only in the organisation and management of I.P. addresses and domain names but also more generally, in view of the requirements for convergence, on the questions of numbering and addressing in the entire electronic communications sector.

These questions of attribution of names and numbers are strategic (80). The structuring of the network depends on their response. It will be remembered that at the outset, it was the American government which, in 1998 (81), decided to entrust the organisation and management of the Internet to this private organisation.

In July 1998 (82), the European authorities reacted to those decisions which kept such strategic issues for development of the

---

(80) « What is the issue, for example, of the new IPv6 protocol ? In that respect it is useful to know that version 4, currently being drafted, was developed to support 4 billion (410^9) addresses, two thirds of which are now reserved for North America, that is to say around 5 % of the world population. The new protocol was to support $3,410^{38}$ addresses (340 trillion, trillion, trillions) and authorise the convergence of all communication technologies (current IP addresses, generalisation of an IP telephony, electronic directories, ...). However, underlying this purely technical aspect, there are unresolved private life issues for which the IETF now seems to be putting forward proposals; there are also political decisions on future ways of living, notably an increasingly invasive information technology, taken outside the national and international authorities. There are only 13 routing servers in the world : 10 in the USA, 2 in Europe (London and Stockholm) and 1 in Asia. Does not this state of affairs contravene the international nature of the Internet ? What legitimacy do organisations that have given themselves the right to technical regulation without any acknowledged supervision by the state or by public international bodies have ? What will happen when China calls for the standards it has developed to be taken into consideration by the virtually strictly American bodies that lay down technical standards ? Etc. » (J. BERLEUR and Y. POULLET, « Les régulations pour l'Internet », *Etudes*, (« Regulations for the Internet ») 2001, not yet published.)

(81) See the « White Paper » in this connection published by the US Department of Commerce in June 1998. The structure of this private organisation was changed by the association's Board on 10 March 2000 (Cairo Assembly) and the election of 5 directors from 18 candidates was closed on 10 October 2000.

(82) On 24 July 1998, the Commission adopted a communication entitled : « Internet Governance – Management of Internet from the E.C. of the U.S. Department of Commerce ». On all these points and a re-reading of European policy in this respect, read R. DELMAS, « L'Internet et les chantiers législatifs européens » (« The Internet and the European legislative platforms ») in *Internet and the Law*, Records of the Colloquium organised by the Post Graduate School of public law and tax law of the University of Paris I, on 25 and 26 September 2000, Coll.

network of networks under American influence by calling for a more geographically balanced representation in the bodies of ICANN. However, European demands did not stop at that stance. It is true that Europe campaigned for the attribution of domain names to fall within the scope of the World Organisation for Intellectual Property (OMPI/WIPO) (83), an international public organisation, and played an important role in WIPO's adoption of rules in this connection. Also, fortified by the creation of the generic domain name : « eu » (84) which gave the European authorities legitimacy to act in such matters, they called for « a leading role in the administration of the Internet, notably with regard to defining the future organisation and policies of ICANN » (85) and the joint establishment by Europe and ICANN of codes of conduct in areas as sensitive as the allocation and protection of domain names, combating fraud and cybersquatting, access to and protection of personal data in the context of the attribution and management of addresses and domain names (86).

It is clear that although such stances, do not challenge the « self-regulatory basis of ICANN's activities » they call for a system of co-regulation (87).

IV. – The european approach
to self-regulation : a « yes, but »

The famous « 99 Review » or European Commission communication of 10 November 1999 considered that public regulation must be

---

Legipresse, Paris, 2001, pp. 70 et seq. See the letter dated 4 November 1998 from Commissioner Bangemann to the American Secretary of Trade which notes the progress made.

(83) Some people (in particular L.R. HELFER and G. DINWOODIE, *Hybrid anational Lowmaking*, not yet published, pp. 33-42) have criticised WIPO's intervention for being too strong, by noting that the issues connected with the attribution of domain names raise other questions such as copyright, freedom of expression, competition etc.

(84) See the Commission's communication of 5 July 2000 (COM(2000)421) on the system of Internet domain names – « Towards the creation of a generic domain name EU » and draft regulation of 12 December 2000 on the implementation of that domain name.

(85) European Parliament Resolution of 15 March 2001 following the Commission's Communication (COM(2000)202, 7 April 2000) on the organisation and management of the Internet – European and international policy issues, 1998-2000).

(86) This is a good illustration that the protection of freedoms even in such technical matters is one of Europe's main concerns (see. n° 18 above).

(87) As when one reads that « ICANN's neutrality must be reinforced by a strong presence from the European Union, in collaboration with the United States and other governments, via the governments' consultative Committee ».

limited « to the minimum required to attain clearly defined objectives » (88). That desire to limit public regulatory intervention can be explained by the fact that some form of subsidiarity of public rules in relation to private rules can be called for : « whatever can be best and more effectively achieved by self-regulation must be done so in this way » (89). Self-governance or self-regulation is defined by P.Trudel (90) as « reliance on rules that are voluntarily established and accepted by those who take part in an activity ». If « as envisaged in most environments, the law is based on a paradigm of the State, the territorial state having sovereignty (91) in order to govern all the behaviours in the territory it controls... » (92), the link between national sovereignty, territoriality and law seems to lose its relevance not to say its legitimacy in an open, borderless area such as cyberspace where there are multiple value systems. Accordingly, some people wonder : is the flourishing self-governance on the Internet not, in the end, a more rapid, expert, international and effective response to the challenges of the Internet than international public regulation which is difficult to define and *a fortiori* establish, than national public regulation (93). A number of public international authorities such as the OECD, G.8 or the WTO have strongly advocated self-regulation, dispensing and dispensed by various lobbies in the business world, including, *inter*

---

(88) Those objectives being moreover defined : promotion of an open, competitive European market of communication services ; benefit for the European citizen ; consolidation of the internal market in an environment of convergence ; safeguarding European interests in international negotiations.

(89) The principle of subsidiarity is affirmed in Article 5 of the Treaty establishing the European Community : « In areas which do not fall within its exclusive competence, the Community shall take action in accordance with the principle of subsidiarity, only if and insofar as the objectives of the proposed action cannot be sufficiently achieved by the Member States and can therefore, by reason of the scale or effects of the proposed action, be better achieved by the Community » and its application to self-governance, read Y. POULLET, « Les diverses techniques de réglementations d'Internet, l'autorèglement et le rôle du droit étatique », *Ubiquité*, n° 5, June 2000, pp. 55 et seq.

(90) P. TRUDEL, « Les effets juridiques de l'autoréglementation » (« The legal effects of self-governance »), *the University of Sherbrooke's Law Review*, 1989, vol. 19, n° 2, 251.

(91) See our earlier comments on this context in the Echelon debate, above, n° 37.

(92) P. TRUDEL, « Quel droit et quelles régulations pour le cyberespace ? » (« Which law and which regulations for cyberspace »), *Sociologie et sociétés*, Vol. XXXII, 2.

(93) According to L. LESSIG's famous expression (Talk to the New York Media Association, on 10 June 1998, reproduced in *Code and other Laws of cyberspace*, Basic Books, New York, 1999) : « We have no problem of governance in cyberspace. We have problem with governance ».

alia, « Global Business Dialog » (GBDe) (94) created at the initiative of the European Commissioner Mr Bangemann to increase international cooperation and the development of e-commerce.

It is in that context that the European position can be understood. Numerous documents issued both by the Council and Parliament attest to the clear support of the European self-regulation authorities (95). They will be analysed in the first point. However, the second point will show that this « promotion » of self-regulation is far from being a document signed in blank but is surrounded by conditions. It is a matter of finding the « right balance between self-regulation and regulation » (96).

A. – The promotion of self-regulation

It is noteworthy that the majority of areas tackled by European legislation contain provisions that clearly promote self-regulation. So far as concerns the protection of personal data, Article 27, § 1 of the directive known as « Data Protection » affirms that Member States and the Commission should « encourage » the drafting of codes of conduct which, in accordance with the specificity of the sectors, are designed to assist in the enforcement of national provisions. Those who draft such codes will be able to subject them to the controlling bodies who will check that they comply with the legislation.

The directive also provides for the drafting of Community codes which themselves may be submitted to a European data protection group that will check, in particular, whether they comply with national provisions.

---

(94) See this organisation's web site illustrated by works of remarkable quality on the various instruments of self-regulation, http://www.gbde.org. Note the presentation by Associated press of the formation of the group : « Global Companies form group to curb government regulation of Internet ».

(95) In particular, in the documents following on from the European Commission's Green Paper on convergence (COM(97)263) of 3 December 1997, already mentioned, and the opinion expressed by the European Parliament on 27 January 2000 and the adoption by the Council of Ministers for Culture on 28 June 1998 of the conclusions expressed by the Commission in the context of the follow-up to its « Green Paper ».

(96) In any event it is the request expressed by the Council of Ministers for Telecommunications on 30 November 1999 to the COREPER (Committee of Permanent Representatives). That request followed the debate organised by the Council on « The I.S. of the future : responding to the challenges of global electronic commerce ».

The principle of the directive is simple : both self-regulation and certification, downstream of the directive's principles, are effective tools for implementing those principles. They help to improve the brand image of anyone who abides by them and increase the Internet user's confidence. Their flexibility and specificity make them capable of providing progressive solutions adapted to the specific features of each sector. Finally, the fact that they are European guarantees equivalent protection in relation to processing carried out anywhere in Europe.

The European Council recommendation of 24 September 1998 (98/560/EC), concerning the development of competition in the audiovisual and information services sector by the promotion of national frameworks capable of ensuring a comparable and effective level of protection of minors and human dignity, goes further still in that its appendix lays down « indicative » guidelines designed to promote self-governance.

Similarly, the draft directive on certain aspects of e-commerce, provides that for issues relating to users, the relevant codes of conduct must have been drafted with the help of consumer representatives, contain measures designed to make them accessible by all and ensure that their implementation is evaluated.

That promotion does not stop at the private sector's right to define the content of regulations, Europe also encourages the settlement of disputes by mediation or arbitration systems outside the official courts and courts of appeal (97). Accordingly, as already mentioned, Article 17 of the so-called « E-Commerce » Directive obliges Member States to encourage the use of alternative dispute resolution systems and in response, two provisions establish the principles applicable to the bodies in charge of those alternative systems. (98) It also encourages the creation of a Community network for the alternative resolution of consumer disputes (99).

---

(97) Note, in connection with these systems known as O.D.R. (on line Dispute Resolution), the reflections of the ECODIR (CNRS-CRDP-CRID) consortium created under a European project of the same name aimed at establishing a system for settling B to C disputes (http://www.ecodir.org).

(98) See the recommendation of 30 March 1999 on the principles applicable to the bodies responsible for the out-of-court settlement of consumer disputes and more recently Commission recommendation of 4 April 2001 (2001/310/EC) on « Principles for the bodies working towards the consensual settlement of consumer disputes », J.O., 19.4.01.

(99) See Council resolution of 13 April 2000 on the creation of a Community network for the alternative resolution of consumer disputes.

B. – THE CONDITIONS
FOR RECOGNITION OF SELF-REGULATION

Under a working group called « e-confidence », the European Commission's SANCO DG established a number of principles and recommendations for the drafting and effectiveness of codes of conduct (100). Accordingly, codes of conduct, « best practice » systems, quality labels and other self-governance measures must operate on the principles of « fairness », « transparency », « added value » non-discrimination, global dimension and social responsibility and guarantee that the solutions comply with existing law and provide accessible mechanisms for security and data protection.

In addition to those principles, it is in the legislation itself promoting self-governance referred to earlier that some conditions for European recognition of self-governance can be inferred. Those conditions hinge on three aspects : the first concerns the « legitimacy » of the authors of self-governance; the second, compliance with the rules laid down in the relevant public legislation; the third and final, the effectiveness of those rules, that is to say the guarantee that they are complied with.

The need for legitimacy of those involved can be understood as the need, to the largest possible extent, to get all the « interested » parties directly or indirectly involved in issues of self-regulation. That involvement should be understood as meaning involvement in the establishment, control and assessment of the system. Accordingly, as we have said, the so-called « E-Commerce » Directive provides for the involvement of professional organisations and consumer representatives in drafting codes of conduct relating to B to C transactions; the guidelines aimed at combating illicit and harmful content refer to a much wider involvement and the Commission's evaluation report dated 27 February 2001 on monitoring the guidelines laments the lack of involvement of some groups in drafting the instruments of self-regulation; finally, so far as concerns alternative systems of settling B to C disputes, in the Resolution of 13 April 2000 already mentioned, the Council calls on Member States to encourage cooperation between professional and consumer organisations in setting up such systems.

---

(100) Available at the following address : http://www.econfidence.jrc.it/default/htm.

The compliance of private rules with statutory rules is another concern. It can be found in the principle whereby self-governance adds value affirmed by the aforementioned « e-confidence forum » (101). In several documents the European authorities dwell on the fact that self-regulation must supplement the legislation of Member States (102).

This control of compliance of the instruments of self-regulation operates through flexible mechanisms : the procedure whereby codes of conduct for data protection are approved by national or European protection authorities is set out in Article 27 of Directive 95/46/EC referred to above (103). The directive known as « E-commerce » provides for codes of conduct to be communicated to the Commission (104).

The effectiveness of a rule is achieved through various measures specifically designed to ensure that the rule is actually complied with. The need to inform the relevant people of the existence of a code of conduct and its content is affirmed by the conclusions of the « e-confidence forum » and by the directive known as E-commerce. The first of these documents adds the need to establish both procedures for complaint and dispute resolution and procedures that allow a genuine control of compliance with the requirements arising from self-governance before a quality label or certification is issued; Article 22 of the second document asks Member States to ensure that there are proportionate and at the same time sufficiently dissuasive punishments for any breach of a public or private rule.

Accordingly, the European legal approach to the other methods of regulation (technical regulation and the various forms of self-regulation) deserves to be emphasised. Although technical regulation and self-regulation are promoted, in any event this is within the context of legal rules that are under the control – the word is

---

(101) See n° 41 above.

(102) See the declaration of the Council of Ministers for Culture on 28 June 1999, concerning the Commission's Green Paper on convergence (COM(97)263) already referred to. The same declaration from the Council of Ministers for Telecommunications of which on 30 November 1999 during the debate : « The information Society of the future : responding to the challenge of global electronic commerce » emphasises the complementary nature of self-regulation and public regulation, and this in response to the recommendations of the Global Business Dialog, more in favour of self-regulation.

(103) This system of voluntary approval could be extended to other fields : accordingly, one might foresee that the quality label bodies might get their services « accredited » by a private, public or mixed organisation.

(104) The same procedure laid down in the Green Paper on commercial communications.

perhaps a little too strong – of the State. The recent European actions taken in the field of « governance » of the Internet, and in particular in the ICANN, are a good illustration of that tendency (see above n° 39).

The Commission's proposal to be able to take action in the field of technical standardisation in order to ensure that the principles for protecting personal data are complied with when using the Internet also reveals that tendency. Obviously the state cannot be left out of the technical debate in that the choices arising from it have an important impact on the rights and freedoms of users of these technologies.

Next, through the wording of directives, all self-regulation is subject to certain conditions. The importance of the involvement of all the interested parties has already been stressed and a number of European provisions highlight this. Far from being a substitute for legislation, self-regulation appears to complement it instead, offering real added value. Accordingly, the more or less voluntary systems of official approval that have been introduced to give a « legal » quality label to self-governance measures are increasing. Finally, although self-regulation can be applied by judges or private mediators, certain procedural rules have to be complied with and certain conditions fulfilled insofar as concerns the judges or mediators (see above n°ˢ 29 et seq.).

Finally, to the American players and governments who advocate that laws are not necessary to regulate cyberspace, the European authorities retort that the Americans were the first to legislate intensively in the field of protection of intellectual property and new technologies and that only some issues such as the protection of private life or the limits of freedom of expression remain subject to self-regulation alone.

Conclusion

As an epigraph to these reflections, we shall ask ourselves : is there a European policy for Internet law ?

It cannot be denied that every day Europe asserts its presence in Internet legislation. Europe is increasing the number of directives, recommendations, White Papers, communications, etc.

How can this phenomenon be explained ? In one word which we have already said : confidence. It is clear that the difficulties that are increasingly felt by the e-commerce sector, for example, can be explained by Internet users' lack of confidence both with regard to security of the network and transactions that take place there and, where there are disputes, the opportunity to be able to clearly identify the relevant legal framework in order to provide a solution and enforce the decisions made (105).

It is obvious that in that respect the law has a reassuring function. It creates a clear, relevant framework, subjects those involved to requirements that will guarantee fairness and the successful outcome of the transactions. Furthermore, it lends the weight of public force to claims from those who venture onto the net. No doubt its territorial limits are being questioned in the era of the global nature of the network of networks, but the construction of regional legal areas such as the European Union and the ever growing number of discussions within official supranational organisations such as the OECD, WIPO the OMC, the Council of Europe, etc. allow an appropriate legislative consensus to be gradually established (106).

That said, it is perhaps useful to consider the areas where the legislator might act and examine the aims of those areas. It is said that it is a question of creating confidence but in what and for whom ? We shall limit our analysis to a comparison of European and American actions.

The first area of legislative action is unquestionably intellectual property and related rights. As already noted in the Bangemann report, it is a question of protecting the investments granted by those who will become the future suppliers of information society services. That political will to protect the investment takes the form of laws which very often prescribe taking into consideration balances that form the core of traditional copyright legislation.

Protecting investors ensures that there is content on the Internet. Transactions then have to be developed, whether they are between professionals (B to B) or consumers (B to C). In order to do this,

(105) See the particularly instructive opinion of the European Parliament's Economic and Social Committee on « Effects of e-commerce on the single market (OMU) » of 2 March 2000, *J.O.* of 25 April 2001, C 123/1.

(106) On the activities of these various authorities, read P. TRUDEL (ed.), *Le droit du cyberspace* (*The law of cyberspace*), Thémis, 1995.

there must be reassurance as to the identity of the partners, messages must be authenticated and their confidentiality assured. Legislation on electronic signatures on both sides of the Atlantic affording them the same validity as handwritten signatures and electronic documents the validity of written ones, satisfies this first concern. The failure of B to C e-commerce led Europe to respond to Internet users' concerns with legislative measures. The E-Commerce Directive adopted in June 2000 had two aims : firstly, to promote e-commerce by obliging Member States to revamp their arsenals of legislation by withdrawing any legal provision that could deprive electronic transactions of validity or effectiveness and by imposing new obligations for transparency on service providers and breaking the transaction down into various stages so as to ensure the full, informed consent of the Internet user.

Protecting the investment and Internet transactions also calls for the ability to detect unlawful activities on the Internet and to effectively punish the perpetrators. Highlighting paedophile offences on the Internet and other misconduct that offends human dignity, such as xenophobic or racist messages, rapidly led the national legislator, with the support of public opinion, to give a broad definition of computer crime (in some countries the mere act of accessing a site, even without any fraudulent intent, is punishable), to significantly broaden the police authorities' grounds for investigation by giving them the right to search using the networks, by obliging private service providers (for example, access providers) to store the data concerning the use of their services and to cooperate with those authorities, and finally, by promoting international police cooperation. Under pressure from America, in December 2000 the Council of Europe adopted an international convention on cybercrime which reflects all those tendencies and allows efficient cybersurveillance of everyone's activities on the net (107). In this field, the principles of freedom of expression and protection of private life might be all too soon forgotten. In its founding convention, the same Council of Europe had sought almost absolute protection of those principles, to the great displeasure of the European authorities.

---

(107) The text is available on the Council of Europe's web site (http://conventions.coe.int/Treaty/FR/cadreprojets.htm). On this problem of computer crime, read D. MARTIN, *La criminalité informatique* (*Computer crime*), Paris, PUF, 1997.

Indeed, it is in relation to this latter subject, the protection of freedoms, that legislative intervention must be analysed. Freedom of expression is certainly one of the fundamental dogma of the Internet. Some people would even say that self-regulation would be a compromise in order to maintain the Internet's spirit of freedom. The issue of abuse of that freedom (unlawful or harmful messages) has been considered, apart from the question of penal sanctions against the perpetrators, via a system of exoneration of liability of intermediaries with regard to the supervision of the information to which they provide access (108).

The issue of protection of personal data seems to be the one that most deeply divides the United States and Europe. Even if it must be conceded that the sensitivity of American Internet users is much greater than that of their European counterparts, the United States refuses to take any action in this regard, whereas Europe has every intention of further adapting its legislative requirements to meet the challenges posed by new technologies.

Balanced between these various interests to be protected, does Europe speak with one voice ? The distribution of powers and budgets between the European Commission's many « Directorate Generals » explains why the intentions are not always convergent, some give more weight to the trade lobbies or, conversely, to consumers, others invariably extol the virtues of the single market by setting out or disregarding, as appropriate, the need for an original European policy in relation to those of other regional blocks.

Through the impressive mass of European provisions, the desire to construct a common legal, judicial, indeed, jurisdictional and administrative platform shines through. No doubt, subsidiarity gets nothing out of it but rather the « requirements » of e-commerce. Europe and, especially the Commission within it, appears to be a place of preventative control of national measures. It coordinates the work of the administrations and establishes more effective methods of judicial and jurisdictional remedies, at the same seeking to make it easier to enforce judgements. The Commission's audacity on these points seems genuine : establishing a European contract

---

(108) These are the famous Articles 14 and 15 of the European directive on certain legal aspects of e-commerce and their American counterparts found in the aforementioned Digital Millenium Copyright Act of 18 Nov. 1998 (on these provisions, read E. MONTERO, « La responsabilité des prestataires intermédiaires de l'Internet », Ubiquité, (« Liability of intermediary Internet service providers »), Ubiquité, June 2000, n° 5, p. 114).

law, desire to create an original European system of mediation and/or conciliation. On these various points, e-commerce and the desire to promote it would seem to legitimise these innovative measures which go far beyond this single field of economic activities.

The construction of a European legislative area is certainly taking place through – sometimes tough – dialogue with the other partners in this increasingly global everyday commerce.

Indeed the search for common principles or solutions within the national or international organisations, and consequently in particular in the protection of consumers or minors so far as concerns signatures encourages standardisation of the conduct of the parties involved, not to say cooperation (if only police cooperation) between countries. Accordingly, Europe seeks to have a presence within those organisations, including private ones such as ICANN. That involvement shows an awareness of not only the technical (far from it!) issues involved in the decisions concerning the choice of technical standards or norms.

If a consensus cannot be reached, the European Union, in the name of its sovereignty, points out the choice of values reflected in its legislation. This reminder and the harmful consequences that it may have on e-commerce are the starting point for international negotiations with other countries. No doubt through means that are more in line with their own legal tradition, those countries will find adequate protection in relation to the principles set out by the European Union. The discussions concerning « Safe Harbour Principles » bear this out.

The European authorities seek to tie this dialogue on standards not only to the outside in international bodies but also internally with the private players. A number of principles are driving the European legislator in this dialogue. Firstly, it is a question of recognising the value of these so-called self-governance rules. It is better to encourage them in order to draw inspiration from their content to establish new rules of law.

This movement towards confidence is not total. Secondly, we must remember that private creation operates within a legislative framework set by the European authorities themselves, going as far as defining the conditions of such a creation. Accordingly, from the point of view of their content, private measures must provide added value to the national legislation. From the point of view of their creation and implementation, the mechanisms for perfecting these techniques for regulation and the application of the content of those private rules must be transparent and take into account the interests of the various players.

Come on : European Internet law does indeed exist. It has a purpose : to create confidence.

SHOULD THERE BE
A MINIMUM HARMONISATION
OF THE LAW?

BY

VALÉRIE LAURE BENABOU

PROFESSOR AT THE UNIVERSITY OF LYONS 2

At first sight, the question is disconcerting as the reply can seem so obvious. Yes, we need a minimum harmonisation of Internet law, undoubtedly, unquestionably and urgently! Through a common political will, the States need to harmonise their legal systems on the issues concerning the networks. They should agree on a minimum basis of universal values and undertake to ensure that they are actually applied. They must protect individuals against harm to their dignity or image and interference with their property, consent etc. that can occur via the Internet.

However, the time for conjecture is over, it is now time for the demonstration. Why does this deep conviction seem to be so irrefutable and can it not, conversely, be maintained that no, a minimum harmonisation of the law is not necessary? At least two currents of thought have defended that idea. Their arguments swing between the temptation to leave it to the network and to maintain the status quo.

Some of the Internet pioneers are developing the « endogenous » approach whereby the network is best placed to govern the behaviours it relays and the States must abandon any temptation to introduce self-regulation or Netiquette, codes of ethics, moral values, technical protective devices, etc. This libertarian debate is gradually becoming a cross between an embryonic allocator of responsibility and the current approach, rather than advocating total freedom, leads to highlighting instances of contractualisation and « modelling » (1), a kind of *de facto* harmonisation by the operators themselves.

The temptation of the status quo is more the prerogative of the sovereigntists. It is now unanimously accepted that the Internet is not an unregulated area but rather an area of accrued laws. The argument is based on the premise that the Internet must not be regarded as a separate area. Accordingly, what holds for traditional society is equally valid for the Internet (2). Besides, producing autonomous rules for the networks would be dangerous in that it would lead to competition between the rules applicable within the same legal system, a major source of insecurity for the rules in the « real » environment. One of the logical consequences of that approach leads to a unilateral application of domestic laws, and more particularly, of their overriding provisions without considering the connecting factor with the national territory. Since the Internet can be received at any point on the planet, it is sufficient for that connection to exist in order to provide proof of jurisdiction, both *ratione loci* and *ratione materiae*.

None of these solutions is inherently bad and no doubt we must retain some aspects of them, according to a principle of effectiveness. To rely on modelling, to use technical protection, to reinforce the law, to consider interchangeable standards, not to preclude the application of the domestic law when there are no real extraneous factors. Nevertheless, none of these solutions on its own is satisfactory as is demonstrated by two decisions that reveal the limits of these respective approaches.

In the *FRONT 14* case, concerning the hosting of an openly racist and anti-Semitic website, in interlocutory proceedings on 30 October 2001, the Paris Regional Court, held (3) « that there is no point in expecting even a minimum self-regulation of the Inter-

---

(1) On the concept of modelling, see A. MARTIN-SERF, « La modélisation des instruments juridiques » (« Modelling legal instruments »), in *La mondialisation du droit* (*The globalisation of law*), under the direction of E. LOQUIN and C. KESSEDJIAN, CREDIMI (Centre for research on international markets and investment law), Litec, 2000, p. 178 : « modelling, a means of standardisation that comes from the bottom, that is to say, consumers of economic law, is opposed by its origin and nature to harmonisation, which is an approximation of legal systems based on a common political will and it is also opposed to the unification of the various legal systems, the aim of which pursued by political authorities is to adopt identical rules », p. 180.

(2) « Internet et les réseaux numériques » (« The Internet and digital networks »), *Report by the Conseil d'Etat*, La Documentation Française, 1998, p. 14 : « There is no specific law for the Internet and networks and there is no need for one ».

(3) Http://www.foruminternet.org.

net, a network increasingly given over to excesses, to the all-powerful 'I want' and which has 'become the last refuge of all forms of excess and provocation' ».

In the Yahoo case, on 7 November 2001 (4) the judge in San José gave a judgment denying any power of enforcement on American territory of the French decision ordering the company to prevent French Internet users from gaining access to a revisionist website. The reasons for his judgment were as follows : « What makes this case uniquely challenging is that the Internet in effect allows one to speak in more than one place at the same time. Although France has the sovereign right to regulate what speech is permissible in France, this Court may not enforce a foreign order that violates the protections of the United States Constitution by chilling protected speech that occurs simultaneously within our borders ».

Both cases denounce the obstacles to the envisaged means of regulation, underlining the need for harmonisation. Harmonisation that coordinates the extensive responses from national legislative systems which, owing to the international nature of the network clash with each other, harmonisation that lays down minimum rules of behaviour by restoring the exogenous function of the rule of law. Harmonisation is therefore a remedy for the abundance of laws and a support to the influence of the law.

Accordingly, the question of the need for harmonisation shifts to the method of implementation : what ? who ? when ? how ? to what extent ? Should harmonisation be only minimal ?

Without using the term « harmonisation » in its Community dimension, we shall nevertheless refer to the principles for action identified by the Union in order to outline a reply to these questions. When the Community legislator considers harmonisation, he must first ask himself two questions which will guide the principle and intensity of his intervention. Two successive principles direct the steps he takes : the principle of subsidiarity and the principle of proportionality. We shall rely on these two linchpins in our attempt to answer this two-stage question. Do we need harmonisation ? Must it be minimal ?

---

(4) US District Court, District of California, 7 November 2001; http://www.foruminternet.org.

I. – Subsidiarity in relation to harmonisation

A. – WHAT ?

Naturally, the what is a pre-requisite, the starting point for the action. The need for harmonisation relies on finding the existing rules to be ineffective, deficient or contradictory (5). In that respect, both the lack of rules and abundance of rules can be indicators of the potential usefulness of the action. However, the lack of a national rule is not *per se* a reason for intervention and an abundance of rules can be quite smoothly fitted into the hierarchy of rules of law (6). Simple symptoms, no rules and an abundance of rules must not be confused with the cause. The catalyst for action must be the conflict, inaction or the ineffectiveness of legal systems.

Accordingly, there is no need for action in fields in which unanimity is based on common values, other than to provide the means for implementing them, and that is important. Admittedly, the process of harmonisation would be easier in consensual situations but it would also be useless. That is not to say that there is no point, but it would be more procedural (7) and less substantive (8).

By contrast, the trigger for action presupposes a strong political will to harmonise laws, without which any attempt is doomed to failure. So, although in some respects it would seem to be useful, there is no point in seriously considering harmonising systems relating to freedom of expression on the Internet, given the fundamental conceptual differences of States. Accordingly, it would be an illusion to consider harmonisation on points on which national sensitivity is exacerbated, other than to have means of coercion against recalcitrant elements. The effectiveness of harmonisation therefore depends in part on the authority from which it arises, which leads quite naturally to considering the who.

---

(5) On the current course of action, see in particular the work of UNCITRAL, Doc. A/CN.9/484, 24 April 2001, *Report of the Working Group on electronic commerce on the proceedings of its thirty-eighth session*, New York, 12-23 March 2001.

(6) L. GANNAGÉ, *La hiérarchie des normes et les méthodes du droit international privé (The hierarchy of standards and the methods of private international law)*, LGDJ, 2001.

(7) C. KESSEDJIAN, « La modélisation procédurale » (« Procedural modelling »), in *La mondialisation du droit, op. cit.*, p. 237.

(8) H. VAN HOUTTE, « La modélisation substantielle » (« Substantial modelling »), in *La mondialisation du droit, op. cit.*, p. 207.

B. – Who ? When ?

The logic of the principle of subsidiarity (9) means favouring the body that is best qualified to achieve the aim pursued by harmonisation, being able to match the body with the required level of effectiveness. However, the Internet is inherently global. Does that mean that the body responsible for harmonisation must necessarily proceed on a global level ? It is also full of technical constraints, does that mean that the response presupposes the involvement of a specialist body ?

Admittedly, the effectiveness of harmonisation would appear to be influenced by the size of the international organisation. A global organisation for a global network. However that equation must not be applied too stringently because an increase in the number of those involved in the negotiation necessarily contributes to slowing down and watering down the rule. It is sometimes more appropriate to start with a smaller circle of States who will adopt a rule, which, by its virtue will be copied as a model. Accordingly, Community harmonisation can be an alternative system to the American system, carrying its own ideology that can spread and be passed on beyond the European sphere, that is by extension a concentric system.

However, we must not understate the disadvantages of competition between international organisations in this field. Accordingly, in a few years, in addition to the Community actions, we have seen the development of initiatives from the Council of Europe, the OECD, UNCITRAL, the ICC, WIPO, the ITU, ICANN etc. Admittedly, the principle of specialisation could lead to an efficient distribution of jurisdictions but some overlapping and incompatibilities are likely to be revealed. The legal *mille-feuille* is a difficult object to handle and heavy to digest. One of the characteristic features of producing rules for the Internet is precisely to envisage *ab initio* cooperation between international initiatives through the cross-participation of actors.

The manager of the harmonisation project must have an effective system to guarantee that the rule is enforced, which is not always the case with private sources of harmonisation. By contrast, the

---

(9) J.-L. CLERGERIE, « Le principe de subsidiarité » (« The principle of subsidiarity »), *Ellipses*, coll. Le droit en questions, 1997.

WTO, both by the number of its members and through cross-retaliation mechanisms would appear to have a reasonably adequate structure to meet the challenges of the Internet in the commercial sector. One can also consider those organisations that have some powers of technical constraint over the network.

However, there then arises the problem of the legitimacy of this action. It is important that the organisation should comply with a principle of democratic representativeness. One remembers the American government's power grab on the issue of naming and the turmoil caused by that ultimatum in the other States (10). ICANN relied on the WIPO (11) to organise, *inter alia,* the resolution of disputes, thereby gaining this legitimacy which had been strongly disputed. Accordingly, the appropriate response to the needs to regulate the network does not necessarily come from an authority that has technical powers over the network, even if the support of such an organisation may be helpful in the harmonisation process as a guarantor that the rule will be enforced.

C. – WHEN ?

The last condition for the principle of action, the right moment for harmonisation. The rapidity of transmissions and the ever-changing technical systems tend to favour accelerating the legal response. However, we must be careful to distinguish between the law and its purpose. It is not because the purpose of the regulation contains concepts of a-territoriality, rapidity, continual technical advances that the law must model its response on those characteristics.

The race between law and technology can therefore be rejected. Two extreme temptations threaten the quality of harmonisation :

---

(10) See, in that respect, Internet et les réseaux numériques, *op. cit.*, p. 116 : « (...), the principle of a reform decided unilaterally by the United States is not acceptable to European countries. In fact, the structure of the future regulatory authority destined to replace the IANA is not sufficiently international. This is an American private law body, which is therefore exposed to any amendment of the legislation decided unilaterally by the American authorities. Furthermore, it does not include representatives from the other States or from intergovernmental organisations such as the ITU or WIPO. Accordingly, such a body has no real international legitimacy ».

(11) V.-L. BENABOU, « Les défis de la mondialisation pour l'OMPI : les noms de domaine » (« The challenges of globalisation for WIPO : domain names »), in *La mondialisation du droit, op. cit.*, 2000, p. 297.

the normative response in real time to the technological challenge and abandoning the law to technology.

The first leads to rushed legislation because it is drafted in a hurry and without consultation, inaccurate because it is shrouded in an abstruse technical discussion (one cannot filter). Above all it produces inappropriate solutions (12), drafted in a specific temporal and spatial state of technology which proves to be outmoded when the new legislation is adopted. The legal response in real time is an illusion.

The second way, that of abandoning the law to technology is no less dangerous. It leads to an actual transfer of the legislator's power to the expert who does not have the same legitimacy. *The answer for the machine is not in the machine* : technology is neutral, it is for the law to direct it. The media examples of breaking the software protection systems show how technology fails to guarantee protection. Without State intervention, market forces will steer technology in a direction which is not necessarily consistent with the general interest.

Accordingly the requirement contained in the WIPO treaties of December 1996 on copyright and related rights to provide adequate legal protection for the technological safeguards gives the full measure of the limits of the mechanical response. Protected by the law, the technical device must also comply with it. And the sole purpose of the convoluted Article 6, paragraph 4 of the Directive of 22 May 2001 (13) is to protect the copyright system itself, not only from pirates but also from temptations of excess reservation arising from rightowner systems. Paradoxically, by affording legal protection to a technical measure, the law here serves the cause of general interest by curbing any excesses stemming from technology.

The time for harmonisation will be well-judged. Neither too late nor too early. Maturity of the political project and time for democratic consultation must combine to provide an appropriate

---

(12) See the vicissitudes of the provisions concerning the liability of access providers in French law in the law on audiovisual communication of 1ˢᵗ August 2000 (*J.O.*, n° 177, 2 August 2000, p. 11903), invalidated by the Constitutional Council.

(13) Directive n° 2001/29 on the harmonisation of certain aspects of copyright and related rights in the information society, *OJEC*, n° L 167, 22 June 2001, p. 10. On this text, see special number of the periodical *Propriétés Intellectuelles*, n° 2, January 2002.

response (14). This necessary distancing of the law from the object of its application nevertheless has consequences on the quality of the legal rule. It leads to rules that are « cut off » from the technical reality : the generality and timelessness of the rule presuppose this degree of abstraction : localised responses will be made by the judge, arbitrator or mediator referring to a body of rules that govern his decision.

II. – Proportionality
in relation to harmonisation

Having accepted the principle of specific harmonisation by the competent authority, we must now determine the methods and extent of intervention. These two questions of « how » and « to what extent » are intimately linked. The intention to take action directs the choice of certain instruments for harmonisation which, in turn, influence the extent of penetration of the harmonised rule of law.

A. – To what extent ?

The extent of the action depends not only on the deficiency found but also on the overriding nature of the legal rule. By adopting the nuclear metaphor, one can consider that at the heart of the law is a hard core of provisions that provide the bedrock for social stability – public policy – and other laws less directly concerned with this fundamental objective and those at whom they are directed have some room for manœuvre in enforcing them.

Harmonisation of Internet law will no doubt be more exacting when it sets itself the goal of countering breaches of these basic social rules : combating the circulation of pornographic, racist or terrorist messages, protecting private life, combating piracy of works and methods of payment. These areas must not put up with optional harmonisation but in theory, there is nothing to prevent the harmonisation from being minimal, in that it authorises the

---

(14) The tribulations of the Communications Decency Act, invalidated by the Supreme Court because of the fact that it is contrary to freedom of expression, as shown by D. Lessig, leads to inaccurate representation of an unchanging technical data. D. LESSIG, *The Laws of Cyberspace*, Stanford site. See also for a new attempt to regulate pornographic messages in relation to children, *New York Times*, 29 and 30 November 2001, more particularly on the issues relating to « Community Standards ».

States to maintain or lay down more binding rules. Insofar as my public policy is assured, it matters little that my neighbour has a more draconian approach on his territory. On the other hand, the issue will be tricky if two public policies clash. In this field, harmonisation has therefore been assigned the difficult task of approximating the fundamental viewpoints of the State's role, which can only be achieved on the basis of common values. Furthermore, substantive harmonisation must be accompanied by harmonisation of the means of enforcing the penalty in order to make the rule as effective as possible.

When the purpose of the rule is to foster legal or economic relations on the network, harmonisation can be more flexible. Thus the e-commerce regulation, the introduction of new ways of electronic addressing do not automatically necessitate an « authoritative », maximum harmonisation. Some leeway for action can be afforded to the various States and within them, to the actors on the network. Accordingly, there is nothing here to prevent the method of functional equivalents being adopted for electronic signature which gives it the binding force required for the security of transactions but which nevertheless does not result in a unified decision (15).

However, this classic dichotomy combines with the specific nature of the Internet which leads to repercussions on the normative methods of production (16). In fact, the scale of action and the prudence required with regard to technical developments naturally lead to favouring the drafting of a general rule of law, laying down more standards than specific rules (17). Consequently, harmonisation can only become exhaustive by adopting new methods.

Accordingly, it is based on the « flexible response » method by containing within it the means for adapting it. Harmonisation therefore comes with a measure of uncertainty. The caution surrounding the creation of the rule leads to the inclusion of « amend-

---

(15) Art. 3 of UNCITRAL's model law on electronic signatures adopted on 5 July 2001, Equality of treatment of signature techniques, No provision in the present Law, (...) is applied in such a way as to exclude, restrict or deprive of legal effects any method of creating an electronic signature that meets the requirements mentioned in paragraph 1 of Article 6 or otherwise meets the requirements of the applicable law.

(16) See the contribution of P. Trudel in this work.

(17) Y. POULLET, *Quelques considérations sur le droit du Cyberspace* (*Some considerations on Cyberspace law*), CRID's website.

ment » clauses, application reports, the organisation of contact committees, all the stigmata of a law on trial. It belongs to the same
spirit that might be classified as « graduated » normativity : the harmonised rule comes with a timetable for implementation breaking
down the various stages of the action.

Finally and most importantly, the specific nature of the Internet
determines a multi-polar creation of rules. The dose of law to be
instilled will therefore be measured in accordance with the
possibility of combining it with staged rules. From cooperation
between international organisations there might emerge a
graduated set of rules, each referring to the other, lightening or
strengthening the weight of such an initiative in a coordinated
framework. The completeness of harmonisation will not necessarily
be sought within a single text but in the simultaneous application
of several bodies of rules of varying importance and from varying
sources (18). The content of harmonisation will no longer therefore
be determined in an autarchical manner having regard to a single
text but in accordance with a ratio of complementarity (19). Harmonisation is combined *inter alia* with self-regulation, being given
the role of correcting its divergences

B. – How ?

There is a wide choice of tools : international conventions,
whether substantive or on conflicts, model laws, scholarly harmonisation, etc. And it is not a question of theoretically anticipat-
ing the suitability of one instrument or another for regulating the
Internet as they depend so much on the particular sector harmonisation. For example, the system of model laws would appear
to lend itself particularly well to the field of electronic commerce
and electronic signature as shown by UNCITRAL's initiatives in
this field. Simply harmonising methods of dispute resolution as
effective as it may be from a technical point of view, does not seem

---

(18) V. J.-S. BERGÉ, *La résolution des conflits de lois* (*Resolving conflicts of law*), in this work,
especially on the protection of personal data which leads to delegating some points of harmonisation to self-regulation.

(19) The example of giving brand names to sites is quite edifying in that respect. The objective of legal security for the Internet user is achieved by a system that ensures that the actions
he is likely to take on a website are « legally correct ». In theory, the mechanism can free itself
of any reference to a national or international rule, which is not without danger : who will ensure
the quality of the brand, who will guarantee its permanence ? a satisfactory level of competition ?

to be an adequate response to the problems raised by the Internet (20).

Nevertheless, it is possible to establish some of the main thrusts of harmonisation. Accordingly, the uselessness of a practicable universal response leads imperceptibly to mutual recognition systems. Rather than demanding an exhaustive international convention, the States are now content with a system of equivalence. The aims set out broadly in the harmonisation text can be achieved well enough by the application of the domestic law of another State. There is only an obligation to achieve a reasonable result leaving each one free to choose the means, assuming, of course, that the system sought is guaranteed *a priori* to be sufficiently effective. This system of adequate protection can be found in the *Safe Harbor Principles* concerning the protection of personal data, albeit with limited success (21). The principle of a conflict of laws is not denied but the *a priori* knowledge of the result eradicates its uncertain dimension (22).

The new challenges of the Internet show the uselessness of a traditional legal response based on the dogma of the all-powerful State. The peculiarities of the network lead to getting back in touch with humility and pragmatism. These feelings must inspire any viable attempt at harmonisation which from now on will be achieved through a multiplicity of initiatives. The State's perception of its own limitations in the application of its law must not result in it abandoning any regulation in this field, rather it must induce it to reach a compromise with these characteristics.

The regulators must match the rapidity of the network with the necessary inertia of the Law by producing general rules that are able to evolve, by not hesitating, where necessary, to adjust their application in time using suitable techniques. To match the complexity of the network, States must use the democratic function of

---

(20) Thus from ICANN's system of dispute resolution which does not resolve the problem of parallel application of domestic laws, see, for example, C. MANARA, *Observation de l'évolution des noms de domaine* (*Observation of the evolution of domain names*), Dalloz, 2001, chron, p. 2958.

(21) In view of the low number of signatory businesses...

(22) This system of approbation of the law can even be transposed to the sensitive area of police laws. Accordingly, it has been suggested that a mechanism of police laws with a lesser effect authorising an interstitial application of the overriding rule within the foreign law, should be introduced. The main function of the police law would then be one of complementarity and its secondary role would be to get rid of just that part of the law that is in conflict. V. X. BOUCOBZA, « Le contrat et l'espace » (« Contracts and space »), in *La relativité du contrat* (*The relativity of contracts*), *Journées* H. Capitant, Volume IV, Nantes/1999, LGDJ, 2000, p. 97.

regulation by the public authorities, the need for monitoring of the technical systems and contractual practices, whilst still leaving it to the most suitable authority to resolve the problems that it is in a position to handle. Finally, to match the ubiquity of the network, States must, respond with increased solidarity when enforcing the law of other States. More than ever, the emphasis will be placed on the similarities of legal systems, a natural basis for mutual recognition. Harmonisation then seeks to ensure that legal systems are interoperable (23).

Professors of law can make a decisive contribution to this latter undertaking : it is for them to rediscover the « *jus commune* » (24).

---

(23) According to the words of P. SIRINELLI.

(24) B. OPPETIT, « Droit commun et droit européen » (« Common laws and European law »), in *Mél. Loussouarn*, Litec, 1994, 311.

INTERNATIONAL ASPECTS
OF ELECTRONIC COMMERCE

Eric A. CAPRIOLI

BARRISTER AT THE NICE BAR
PROFESSOR AT EDHEC (SCHOOL OF ADVANCED BUSINESS STUDIES)
ADVISOR TO THE UNITED NATIONS
CAPRIOLI@DIAL-UP.COM

For many years now modern legal experts have been concerned with the phenomenon of globalisation of the economy (1). Accordingly, the globalisation of physical exchanges saw unprecedented growth during the 20th century owing to advances in transport, logistics and means of communication. That surely heralded the recent upheaval we have seen with automated information processing during the seventies, followed by computerised data exchange in the nineties (2), and finally, more recently, the digital networks such as the Internet which contribute to the globalisation of exchanges and communications (3). Whereas the first networks were closed and reserved for those involved in a particular business sector (banking, maritime transports, automobiles, mass distribution, ...), with electronic transactions in an open environment, the legal issues are taking another turn, assuming other forms : the States do not intend to lose one iota of their sovereignty and a substantive

---

(1) See, in particular : « Le droit des relations économiques internationales », *Etudes offertes à Berthold Goldman*, (« The law of international economic relations », *Studies offered to Berthold Goldman*), Litec, 1987; « L'internationalisation du droit », *Mélanges en l'honneur de Yvon Loussouran*, (« The internationalisation of the law », *Compilation of writings in honour of Yvon Loussouran*) Dalloz, 1994; « L'internationalité dans les institutions et le droit », *Etudes offertes à Alain Plantey*, (« Internationality in institutions and the law », *Studies offered to Alain Plantey*), Pedone, 1995; « Souveraineté étatique et marchés internationaux à la fin du 20ᵉ siècle », *Mélanges en l'honneur de Philippe Kahn* (« National sovreignty and international markets at the end of the 20th century », *Compilation of writings in honour of Philippe Kahn*), Litec, 2000.

(2) E. CAPRIOLI, *Le crédit documentaire : évolution et perspectives* (*Documentary credit : developments and prospects*), Paris, Litec, Coll. Dr. de l'entr., t. 27, 1992, see n° 555 et seq.

(3) *La mondialisation du droit* (*The globalisation of law*) under the direction of E. LOQUIN and C. KESSEDJIAN, *Travaux du Crédimi*, Litec, 2000; *le droit saisi par la mondialisation* (*The law in the grip of globalisation*), under the direction of C.-A. MORAND, Bruylant, Brussels, 2001.

law on electronic international trade is gradually being sketched out (4). However, the principles of free exchange and freedom of establishment are also to be found in the European internal market, based on freedom of movement (people, goods, services and capital), and in the context of the OECD and the WTO which promote free exchange and the prohibition of customs barriers or other quantitative restrictions to entering markets (5). Our modern societies are in the process of drawing up international rules for relationships which are being formed using new media, the digital networks. Accordingly, new methods of establishing standards that combine the legal, technical and security aspects are appearing.

Currently, within the information society it is noteworthy that electronic commerce hinges on two central themes connected with temporo-spatial considerations : electronic communications transcend distance and time between people and goods and services, numerous people interact with their legal environment by moving around, with no fixed geographic location. However, aware of this phenomenon, the States tend to have an effect on these parameters by localising the liability of the people who supply electronic services in the information society and by regulating cross-border transmission of data which takes place in a relatively short space of time and therefore precludes any physical supervision. We need to act upstream, to establish a legislative framework. However, in addition to the fact that information society service providers (providers of access and hosts) are able to move around, nevertheless, people themselves become nomadic due to the portability of communication terminals (mobile telephones, lap-top computers) (6). It is now possible to trade from any part of the world and at any time (24 hours a day 7 days a week). However, the nub of my arguments will focus on methods for establishing international rules to govern the activities of electronic com-

---

(4) E. Caprioli and R. Sorieul, « Le commerce électronique international : vers l'émergence de règles juridiques transnationales » (« International electronic commerce : towards the emergence of transnational legal rules »), *JDI*, 1997, pp. 323 et seq. and E. Caprioli, « Aperçu sur le droit du commerce électronique (international) » (« An outline of Sinternational electronic commerce law »), in *Mélanges en l'honneur de Philippe Kahn*, Litec, 2000, pp. 248 et seq.

(5) M. Rainelli, *L'organisation mondiale du commerce (The global organisation of trade)*, 5th ed., Paris, La découverte, 2000, pp. 97 et seq.

(6) J. Huet, « Eléments pour une définition du droit de la communication » (« Elements for a definition of communication law »), in *Clés pour le siècle*, University Panthéon-Assas/Paris II, Dalloz, pp. 483 et seq.

merce (7), but I shall only touch on issues of private international law indirectly (conflicts of laws and jurisdictions) (8).

Together with the principles of freedom of establishment, access, pursuing an activity and free movement of information society services in the internal market, the European directives (electronic signature and e-commerce) (9) include the principle of subjecting the service provider to the domestic legislation of the State in which he is established : the law of the place of establishment (I). The same idea can be found indirectly in the laws and proposed laws drawn up at international level in the United Nations Commission on International Trade law (UNCITRAL). Moreover, it is true that in fiscal matters, stable establishment is the key concept which serves as a basis for the taxation of electronic commerce (VAT). According to the ECJ, stable establishment is characterised by a « permanent combination of human and technical resources required to provide given services » (10). The fiscal dimension will be left out of the analysis.

Furthermore, data are governed by the principle of free movement but it must be pointed out that so far as concerns recognition of foreign electronic signatures and certificates, equivalence is either fixed *a priori* under the alternative system of the electronic signatures directive, or in relation to a level of reliability in the

---

(7) J. HUET, « La problématique juridique du commerce électronique » (« The legal problems of electronic commerce »), *R.J. com.*, 2001, special n°, pp. 17 et seq.

(8) See the contributions of R. DE BOTTINI (on conflicts of jurisdiction), and J.-M. JACQUET (on the applicable law) in *Les premières journées internationales du droit du commerce électronique* (*The first international days of electronic commerce law*), Litec, Actu. Dr. de l'entr., 2001 and C. KESSEDJIAN, *Rapport de synthèse* (*Summary report*), in *Internet, Which Court Decides? Which Law Applies? Quel tribunal decide? Quel droit s'applique?*, ed. K. BOELE-WOELKI and C. KESSEDJIAN, Kluwer Law International, 1998, pp. 143 et seq.

(9) Directive n° 1999/93/EC of 13 December 1999 on a Community framework for electronic signatures, *JOEC*, L 13, of 19 January 2000, pp. 12 et seq.; E.xxCAPRIOLI, « La directive européenne n° 1999/93/CE du 13 décembre 1999 sur un cadre communautaire pour les signatures électroniques » (« European Directive n° 1999/93/EC of 13 December 1999 on a Community framework for electronic signatures »), *Gaz. Pal.*, 29-31 October 2000, pp. 5 et seq. Directive 2000/31/EC of the European Parliament and of the Council of 8 June 2000 on certain legal aspects of the information society, in particular electronic commerce in the internal market, *OJEC*, L 178/1 of 17 July 2000.

(10) Case of *Gunther Berkholz v Fimanzamt Hamburg*, 4 July 1985, J.-L. BILON, *Fiscalité du numérique* (*Digital fiscality*), Litec, 2000, p. 65 and L. BOCHURBERG, *Internet et commerce électronique* (*The Internet and electronic commerce*), Delmas, 2nd edition, 2001, p. 179. According to the Conseil d'Etat any operation characterised by « *the personal and permanent disposition of a facility containing the necessary human and technical resources to carry out the taxpayer's service* » (EC 31 January 1997, n° 170164). Egal. X. LE CERF, « L'Internet, accélérateur de l'harmonisation européenne de la fiscalité » (« The Internet, a catalyst for European harmonisation on tax matters »), *Common Market Rev.*, n° 451, September 2001, see pp. 560 et seq.

approach adopted by UNCITRAL (II). However, there is another area that includes international aspects and which will not be dealt with either, that is to say, the cross-border flow of personal data outside the European Community. In this context, an adequate level of protection is required; it can be expressed in « safe harbor » principles or in standard contracts provided for that purpose (11).

I. – The service provider's place of establishment

The two European laws on electronic signature and electronic commerce exclude private international law from their scope of application, but each, in its own way, prescribes the law of the place in which the service provider is established as a rule of jurisdiction, firstly for the liability of certification services providers (CSP) (12) (A) and secondly, for services in the related field supplied by Internet service providers (B). This location of service providers in the place in which they carry out their business is the counterpart of the principles of freedom of establishment and freedom to carry out their business which underpin the free movement of services. Let us remember that from another point of view, so far as tax is concerned, the States apply the traditional principle of territorial jurisdiction based on the no less traditional concept of « stable establishment », but it can be evaluated differently from that which appears in the « electronic commerce » directive.

UNCITRAL's proposed draft agreement on electronic contracts also refers to the concept of establishment in terms that are vir-

---

(11) Y. POULLET, *Les Safe Harbour Principles – Une protection adéquate?* (*Safe Harbour Principles – Do they provide adequate protection?*), www.chez.com/lthoumyre/uni/doc/20000617.htm, quotation from Juriscom.net, 17 June 2000; J. HUET, « Etude relative aux contrats de données personnelles entre les parties à la convention 108 et les pays tiers n'offrant pas un niveau de protection adéquat » (« Study concerning contracts of personal data between parties to the 108 convention and non-member countries that do not offer an adequate level of protection »), *Report for the Council of Europe*, Strasbourg, 7-9 February 2001 and *Comm. Com. electr.*, May 2001; J. FRAYSSINET, « Le transfert et la protection des données personnelles en provenance de l'Union européenne vers les Etats-Unis : l'accord dit 'sphère de sécurité' » (« The transfer and protection of personal data from the European Union to the United States : the agreement known as 'safe harbour' »), *Comm. Com. electr.*, March 2001, p. 10; A. LUCAS, J. DEVÈZE, J. FRAYSSINET, *Droit de l'informatique et de l'Internet* (*Computer and Internet Law*), Paris, P.U.F., 2001, see n°s 338 et seq.

(12) Under the Decree of 30 March 2001, it is called « *electronic certification service provider* » so as not to compare it with the certification processes laid down in the provisions of consumer law.

tually identical to those used in the electronic commerce directive (13). Some convergences herald a definite harmonisation

A. – SUBJECTION OF THE CSP
TO ITS NATIONAL LAW SO FAR AS CONCERNS LIABILITY

CSPs have freedom of establishment within the Member States. The latter are not entitled to establish a prior authorisation scheme for pursuing these activities (Article 3 of Directive 1999/93/EC).

So far as concerns private international law, it would first appear that recitals n° 17 and n° 22 are contradictory. In fact, according to the first, the directive does not interfere with the rules determining the place in which a contract is entered into. According to the second « certification-service-providers providing certification-services to the public are subject to national rules regarding liability ». One can take the view that the directive does not lay down any choice-of-law rule determining the law applicable to electronic signatures and certificates or *a fortiori* to contracts signed; so far as concerns contractual obligations, this issue remains subject to the rules laid down by the Rome Convention of 19 June 1980 and for extra-contractual obligations to the choice-of-law rules of the forum court, pending adoption of the Rome Convention II on the matter. However, the fact that, as regards liability, the CSP is subject to the national law of the territory on which it is established, can be explained by the fact that CSPs are supervised by the State which must introduce an « adequate system ». Supervision relates to the qualified certificates and it takes place under a national accreditation scheme (14) and obligations to provide declarations and information to the relevant authorities and bodies. Under Article 11, Member States must notify the Commission of information relating to voluntary accreditation schemes, national bodies responsible for accreditation and accredited CSPs. This obligation to pass on information originating from the States to the Community authorities is the counterpart for setting the standards applicable to electronic signatures where private actors are in a privileged position. The

---

(13) UNCITRAL, Secretariat's note, Doc. A/CN.9/WG/WP.95, of 20 September 2001, see article 7 consultable on the website : http://www.uncitral.org.

(14) See Article 9-II of the Decree of 30 March 2001, which refers to a judgment. In practice, this supervision will be carried out by the DCSSI of the SGDN (Central Division for the Security of Information Systems of the French Ministry of Defence).

entire provisions of the directive thus pursue a dual aim : competition and consumption, serving the harmonisation of rules and
standards (15).

This provision is practical and logical and will prevent any conflicts of laws which undoubtedly would arise without such a provision. The law of the State in which the CSP is based is a rule which
provides a guarantee of legal security to users of the services of
these providers. Moreover, it prevents the system of liability of the
CSP from being divided up in the European Community. However,
what would happen when a certificate holder (contractually bound
to the CSP), or an even more tricky situation, when one party who
relies on the certificate (a third party to the contract with the CSP)
is in a State that is not a member of the Community and intends
to hold the CSP liable before a court situated outside the Union ?
Will the CSP be able to rely on a presumed exemption from
jurisdiction and/or refuse the application of other rules of substantive law applicable to liability ? One might also wonder about the
meaning of the term liability. No doubt, one might consider
without too much risk of being mistaken, that it covers both the
CSP's contractual liability and liability in tort. But one can also say
that it is its rules of operation as a legal structure and those relating
to its supervision (those of the Member State in which it is based)
which prevail. Users, whether they be the signatory or the party
that relies on the signature, should be sure from the outset that in
this State, the CSP has adequate financial guarantees and insurance
to cover the risks inherent in its business (16).

Articles 8 and 9 of UNCITRAL's model law go as far as the directive. They establish an identical principle, albeit not explicit,
whereby the signatory and the CSP « bear the consequences of their
failure » to satisfy their obligations; and for implementation of the

---

(15) V. LANDES, « Normes techniques et certifications » (« Technical standards and certification »), *J-Cl. Europe, fasc. 530.*

(16) See Annexe II, h) of the directive : « *have sufficient financial resources to operate in accordance with the requirements laid down in this directive, in particular to assume responsibility for
damage, for example, by taking out appropriate the insurance* ».

liability of these parties to an electronic signature it refers to national laws (17).

B. – LOCATION
OF THE INTERNET SERVICE PROVIDER

The e-commerce directive is based on the principle of freedom of establishment of information society service providers. Access to those services and pursuit of the activity cannot be restricted or subject to prior authorisation (article 4).

Article 3 is designed to ensure the free provision of services in the information society (Article 49 of the Treaty of Rome). However, these services must be supervised at the source of the service provider's activity. Who is better placed than the Member State, the country of origin, to carry out this supervision? In exchange, the other Member States, for reasons falling within the coordinated field, are not allowed to « restrict the freedom to provide information society services from another Member State » (article 3-2).

That explains why Article 3-1 of the directive states : « Each Member State shall ensure that the information society services provided by a service provider established on its territory comply with the national provisions applicable in the Member State in question which fall within the coordinated field ». In other words, it is the law of the State in which the service provider is established, the law of the country of origin of the service. Furthermore, it would seem that the reference to the « national provisions applicable » only relates to the rules of national substantive law and that it is likely to exclude the choice-of-law rules of the legal system concerned. That interpretation has led some legal experts to conclude that there can be no transfer to the country of origin (18).

According to the terms defined in Article 2-c, an « **established service provider** » is a person « who effectively pursues an

---

(17) E. CAPRIOLI, « Le projet de règles uniformes de la CNUDCI sur les signatures électroniques : ébauche d'une harmonisation internationale », (« UNCITRAL's draft standard rules on electronic signatures : outline for international harmonisation »), in *Droit et nouvelle économie du savoir, Journées Maximilien-Caron 2000*, Montreal, Thémis, 2001, v. p. On the model law adopted in July 2001, see our article in *Comm. Com. Electr.*, 2001, December.

(18) S. MUÑOZ, « La loi applicable aux contrats 'on line' au regard de la directive 'commerce électronique' : la tentative d'une approche pragmatique » (« The law applicable to online contracts having regard to the e-commerce directive : an attempt at a pragmatic approach »), *Petites affiches*, 12 December 2000, see p. 18.

economic activity using a fixed establishment for an indefinite period. The presence and use of the technical means and technologies required to provide the service do not, in themselves, constitute an establishment of the provider ». The directive excludes purely formal (domiciliation/letter boxes) and technical criteria and only uses criteria of effectiveness connected with the economic activity of a stable establishment. Accordingly, the place where the service's web pages are hosted cannot be used on its own. The place (the establishment) where the service provider supplies the service in question must be determined. Difficulties will certainly arise when the service provider has several places of establishment (19). That definition is directly based on the case-law of the European Court of Justice : « the concept of establishment within the meaning of Article 52 et seq. of the Treaty, covers the actual pursuit of an economic activity by means of a stable establishment in a Member State for an indefinite period » (20). It is this same concept which prevails in fiscal matters for applying the principle of territoriality of the tax. Sovereignty is expressed by the connection with a territory through a rule of location.

The « coordinated field » is defined in Article 2, h) and i) and ii) of the « e-commerce » directive. This Article relates to information society services, which is broader than merely providers of those services, as follows :

« coordinated field » : the requirements laid down in Member States' legal systems applicable to information society service providers or information society services, regardless of whether they are of a general nature or specifically designed for them.

i) The coordinated field concerns requirements with which the service provider has to comply in respect of :

- the taking up of the activity of an information society service, such as requirements concerning qualifications, authorisation or notification;
- *the pursuit of the activity of an information society service, such as requirements concerning the behaviour of the service provider,*

---

(19) A. STROWEL, N. IDEET, F. VERHOOGSTRAETE, « La directive du 8 juin 2000 sur le commerce électronique : un cadre juridique pour l'Internet » (« The directive of 8 June 2000 on electronic commerce : a legal framework for the Internet »), *Journal des Tribunaux* (Brussels), 17 February 2001, n° 6000, see n° 7, p. 136.

(20) ECJ 25 July 1991, case C-221/89, *Digest* 1991, p. 1-3905, pt. 20.

*requirements regarding the quality or content of the service including
those applicable to advertising and contracts, or requirements concerning
the liability of the service provider.*

ii) The coordinated field does not cover requirements such as :

— requirements applicable to goods as such,
— requirements applicable to the delivery of goods,
— requirements applicable to services not provided by electronic
  means.

So far as concerns ascertaining the place of establishment, it
should be remembered that Article 5 obliges service providers to
communicate certain information : name of service provider,
geographic address at which he is established, trade registration n°,
VAT n°, ...

However, the scope of the principle of the place of establishment
must not be underestimated since some fields are not covered by it :
either because they are excluded from the scope of application of
the directive, or because of derogations from Article 3 shown in the
Annex (21), or because of the possibility of exclusion by Member
States (Article 3-4). Moreover, this principle is deemed not to establish additional principles of private international law nor to deal
with jurisdiction of the Courts (Article 1-4) (22).

Under Article 7-1 relating to the « location of the parties » of
UNCITRAL's draft convention on electronic contracting (23), « for
the purposes of this convention, a party is presumed to have its
place of business in the geographical location indicated by it in
accordance with Article 4 » (24). However, draft Article 4 establishes the principle freedom of contract of the parties who may
exclude or derogate from the provisions of the convention, and
modify its effects, which would appear to create additional
problems.

---

(21) Eg : the contractual obligations with regard to contracts entered into with consumers.

(22) For more details on the internal market, see R. DE BOTTINI, « La directive 'commerce
électronique' du 8 juin 2000 » (« The 'electronic commerce' directive of 8 June 2000 »), *Common
Market and EU Rev.*, n° 449, June 2001, pp. 368 et seq. ; *Cahiers du CRID, Le commerce électronique européen sur les rails? (European electronic commerce on the rails)* under the direction of
E. MONTERO, Brussels, Bruylant, 2001, spec. pp. 41 et seq.

(23) UNCITRAL, *Legal aspects of electronic commerce. Electronic contracting : provisions for a
draft convention)*, Doc. : A/CN.9/WG.IV/WP.95 of 20 September 2001, see p. 30.

(24) Shown in brackets after the draft article : « *[..., unless it is manifest and clear that the
party does not have a place of business at such location and that such indication is made solely to
trigger or avoid the application of this Convention]* ».

In truth, it seems clear that both directives, since they set out the principle of the law of the place in which the service provider is established for some legal issues – the fields of which vary according to each of the directives – go so far as to establish the applicable law, even if they are not, *stricto sensu*, choice-of-law rules.

II. – Mutual recognition of foreign electronic signatures and certificates

What happens when a European supplier of goods or services receives an order from a customer established in the United States of America signed electronically using a device for creating electronic signatures in accordance with an American market standard (the licence for the signature software or the option given in the navigator) who relies on a certificate issued by a CSP established in Canada ? What validity would the signature have in France ? Which legal system will apply ? Will it benefit from the presumption of reliability laid down by Article 1316-4, par. 2 c. civ. and Article 2 of the decree of 30 March 2001 ? (25) In the European context, it will be observed that the provisions relate just to the certificate, as Article 5-2 of the directive – applying to other electronic signatures which do not meet the criteria for advanced electronic signatures – lays down a principle of non-discrimination : « *Member States shall ensure that an electronic signature is not denied legal effectiveness and admissibility as evidence in legal proceedings solely on the grounds that it is in electronic form or not based upon a qualified certificate, or not based upon a qualified certificate issued by an accredited certification service provider, or not created by a secure signature-creation device* ». *The use of these electronic signature processes means that the judge is*

---

(25) Law n° 2000-230 of 13 March 2000, *JO* of 14 March 2000, see E. CAPRIOLI, « Sécurité et confiance dans le commerce électronique » (« Security and confidence in electronic commerce ») *JCP*, 1998, ed. G, I, 123 ; « La loi française sur la preuve et la signature électroniques dans la perspective européenne » (« The French law on electronic evidence and signatures from a European point of view »), *JCP* 2000, G, I, 224. In Belgian law, see D. GOBERT and A. MONTÉRO, « L'ouverture de la preuve littérale aux écrits sous forme électronique » (« Opening up documentary evidence to writing in electronic form »), *Journal des Tribunaux (Belgium)*, 17 February 2001, pp. 113 et seq. For Decree n° 2001-272 of 30 March 2001, *JO* 31 March 2001, pp. 5070 et seq. ; C. CHARBONNEAU and F.-J. PANSIER, « La signature électronique, signature sous surveillance (à propos du décret n° 2001-272 du 30 mars 2001) » (« Electronic signatures, a signature under supervision (with regard to decree n° 2001-272 of 30 March 2001 ») , *Les Petites affiches*, 6 April 2001, pp. 3 et seq. ; E. CAPRIOLI, « Commentaires du décret » (« Comments on the decree »), *Rev. dr. banc. fin.*, 2001, May-June, pp. 155 et seq. ; L. JACQUES, « Aperçu rapide » (« Brief overview »), *JCP* 2001, ed. G, Actualités of 5 September 2001.

provided with evidence of their technical reliability. By contrast, for a certificate which is « an electronic attestation which links the data relating to signature verification (the public key) to a person and confirms the identity of that person », the situation is different for CSP established outside the European Community because if it is electronic data that is to be circulated and used in the internal market, they must comply with the requirements of annexes I and II of the directive in order to be recognised as equivalent to the qualified certificates issued by a CSP established within the Community (26).

Under Article 12 of UNCITRAL's model law on electronic signatures :

« 1. In determining whether, or to what extent, a certificate or an electronic signature is legally effective, no regard shall be had to :

a) the geographic location where the certificate is issued or the electronic signature created or used; or

b) The geographic location of the place of business of the issuer or signatory.

2. A certificate issued outside (the enacting State) shall have the same legal effect in (the enacting state) as a certificate issued in (the enacting State) if it offers a substantially equivalent level of reliability ».

According to this brief analysis, one might take the view that the new methods of establishing international and European rules meet the requirements of electronic commerce and express a wise measure based on globalisation and localisation.

---

(26) According to Article 2-1 of the directive, « *'electronic signature' means data in electronic form which are attached to or logically associated with other electronic data and which serve as a method of authentication* ».

TAXATION
OF ELECTRONIC COMMERCE :
INITIAL RESULTS (1)

Stéphane BUYDENS

OECD
Administrator of the tax affairs division
Responsible for e-commerce

Global networks contain an extraordinary potential in terms of economic growth, job creation, expansion of world trade and improvement in living conditions. The OECD continues to regard e-commerce as a central factor in that potential. E-commerce is intrinsically international and its successful development relies to a great extent on devising coherent solutions, drawing not only on co-ordination between national policies but also on all the other actors in the virtual world. The difficulties involved in drawing up a global, cohesive policy require a wide-scale examination and an in-depth dialogue between the public and private sectors, activities for which the OECD is particularly well suited.

E-commerce is still crucial to the development of the world economy even though some of the wilder dreams have not been realised. In a rapidly changing world, e-commerce is already beginning to reach maturity. After less than five years of a tormented life, consisting of dazzling successes and equally rapid failures, it has returned to the basic principles of good financial administration : not spending more than you can earn, learning from your mistakes, accepting that developing a business takes time. The fact remains that e-commerce has already changed the way in which many businesses work, opening up the international market to many private or professional consumers who did not have access to it before.

---

(1) All the documents and reports referred to in this text are available on the OECD's web site. http://www.oecd.org/taxation/

Accordingly, e-commerce does not develop in abstraction but in a very real economic and institutional environment.

I. – The role of the tax authorities

The tax authorities have a role to play in realising the potential of e-commerce, through establishing a fiscal context that will allow it to fully develop whilst ensuring that it does not interfere with their ability to obtain the tax revenue needed to finance the public services that their citizens demand.

In order to achieve those objectives, governments have recognised two major forms of e-commerce : business to business commerce and private consumer commerce.

Whilst the political debate tends to focus on commerce directed at private consumers, it is business to business commerce which plays and in the foreseeable future will play a dominant part in e-commerce. In fact, if one excludes the transactions made by public bodies, almost 90 % of e-commerce takes place between businesses. Even within this sector there is a great diversity. For example, the multinational companies have used Internet technologies to develop global networks with their subsidiaries. The small and medium enterprises (SME) were quick to exploit the means that the Internet offered them to access global markets. Businesses that provide services to professionals in such diverse fields as architecture or finance, already use the Internet to develop and promote their services to other businesses.

The attitude of governments towards the taxation of e-commerce in such a complex environment has resulted in considerable speculation. At one extreme, there were those who thought that e-commerce should develop in a tax-free environment whereas at the other extreme, some envisaged the creation of new taxes specifically affecting this form of commerce, such as a byte tax for example. None of these extreme solutions was accepted by the governments : the first, because apart from the distortions of competition that it would create, it would make the governments incapable of meeting the legitimate demands of their citizens with regard to public services, the second, because it would curb the development of e-commerce and technological development would be distorted by tax issues.

It is true that e-commerce is a promising new tool for development but neither its nature nor the desire to see it expand justify excluding it from the normal taxation system. Transactions conducted in the cyberworld are no different from those conducted in traditional commerce so far as concerns justifying the principles for exemption from taxation.

Nowadays, agreement has been reached on the concept that the most appropriate way of achieving this dual objective (to keep the tax revenue without curbing the development of e-commerce) is to establish an international consensus on the method of adapting the existing rules to e-commerce rather than creating completely new tax systems.

The greatest challenge facing the tax authorities today is adapting the existing legislation, procedures and practices in order to overcome their weaknesses in the face of the emergence of new means of communication and supply of products and services. To do nothing would lead firstly to exempting a high proportion of e-commerce directed at private consumers from the payment of consumption tax and secondly, to growing uncertainty as to the tax rules to be applied. It is with an adaptive view of the tax issue that the OECD, in co-operation with the economies of non-members of the OECD, has undertaken to try to find an international consensus on taxation and e-commerce matters (2).

In drafting those principles, the tax authorities intended to pursue two parallel aims :

– To strengthen the growth of e-commerce by establishing a welcoming fiscal environment that offers a truly competitive environment and prevents tax-related distortions.
– To preserve the independence and tax revenue of the States.

The crux of the matter is knowing how to achieve these two objectives in a practical way, and that is precisely the task to which the OECD has committed itself, using these two essential principles as a starting point. Firstly, it has been acknowledged that e-commerce must not be subject to specific treatment that is either more favourable or less favourable than the other forms of commerce : it is the principle of neutrality of treatment. Secondly, an interna-

---

(2) The economies that are not members of the OECD took part in the OECD's work carried out on the application of the principles of taxation to e-commerce since 1997 and they have been increasingly involved since then.

tional consensus must be reached on adapting the existing tax rules
without changing their basic elements.

II. – The major tax principles
that apply to e-commerce

These principles were expressed in 1998 by the OECD in the
Framework Conditions for the taxation of e-commerce. This
framework was defined in collaboration with a number of countries
that are not members of the OECD and international and professional organisations. (3) It was favourably received by the Ministers
at the Ottawa Conference in October 1998, adopted by the member
countries of APEC (Asia-Pacific Economic Cooperation) at the
OECD-APEC conference in November 1998 and approved by
APEC's Ministers for Finance in May 1999.

These framework Conditions which served as a basis for the work
that the OECD has carried out over the last three years also
highlighted two essential points for the taxation of e-commerce :

– The technologies which underpin e-commerce offer governments
  new opportunities to improve their service to the tax payer.
– The same tax principles which guide governments so far as concerns traditional commerce must also be applied to e-commerce.
  And here, the opportunity was seized to refer to the principles of
  good tax legislation : neutrality, efficiency, certainty, simplicity,
  effectiveness, fairness and flexibility.

Obviously, those principles do not mean that we can be content
with treating e-commerce as we would treat traditional commerce
in the last century. On the contrary, we must seize the opportunity
offered by the electronic revolution to improve the whole of the
taxation process.

The Ottawa Conference also confirmed the importance of the distinction between customs duties and consumption tax : the
proposal whereby services provided by means of e-commerce should
be exempt from customs duty received wide support. However, that
does not mean that the whole of e-commerce should be free from

---

(3) Argentina, Brazil, Chile, China, Chinese Taipei, Hong Kong (China) Israel, Malaysia, the
Russian Federation, Singapore, the Slovakian Republic, South Africa, *Centre for Inter-American
Tax Administrators* (CIAT), *the Commonwealth Association of Tax Administrators* (CATA), the
European Union, the World Customs Organisation and business federations.

tax as that would be contrary to the principle of neutrality set out in the Ottawa Framework Conditions.

Since Ottawa, the Framework Conditions have been widely adopted and generally speaking, they are acknowledged to be a good reference for drawing up a common position on the treatment of the taxation aspects of e-commerce.

III. – Implementation of the Ottawa principles

As in other fields, such as the protection of intellectual property, consumer protection or security of networks, all the actors in e-commerce have a common interest in constructing a stable, balanced legal environment.

In order to do this, for some issues of common interest, the OECD's Fiscal Affairs Committee has worked with other organisations such as the European Commission for taxation or consumer issues and the World Customs Organisation for customs duties. It has also continued to make a contribution to the debates which took place within the Member countries (for example, the work of the OECD on tax issues was submitted to the e-commerce consultative committee – the United States ACEC). It has also organised a consultation on precise topics with representatives from business, governments of the member countries and non-member economies through Technical Advisory Groups.

In essence, adapting the existing taxation rules to comply with the Ottawa principles poses two challenges to the administrations, essentially in four areas :

– Tax on consumption;
– International taxation agreements;
– Transfer prices;
– Tax administration;

A. – TAX ON CONSUMPTION

The principle of the place of the service is important for systems of tax on consumption such as Value Added Tax and Taxes on Goods and Services. Generally speaking, there are two major categories of rules :

– Those which are based on identification of the appropriate establishment (in some cases the seller in others the purchaser), and

– Those that are based on the place of the service or use.

Since e-commerce has made the links between the place of the service, the place where the business is situated and the place where the service is used or consumed more complex, the authorities responsible for ensuring compliance with tax obligations are faced with new problems.

In response, a three-pronged approach was accepted :

1. To tax cross-border transactions in the country where the consumption took place;

2. To treat the provision of a digitised product as a provision of services for tax purposes;

3. To use the reverse charge as a means of processing cross-border transactions between business so far as concerns digitised services and products.

To transpose the principle of « the place of consumption » into concrete rules requires agreement on the way in which that place should be defined, similarly on the way in which the relevant taxation rules should operate. Furthermore, we need to work out the methods for ensuring effective recovery and administration of tax, which means, *inter alia*, a re-examination of how the European Union's VAT systems fit in with non-European taxes on consumption and systems of sales tax.

So far as concerns customs duties and tax on consumption levied on the importation of tangible goods, governments must ensure that the customs procedures do not curb the development of e-commerce. The best way of achieving that objective lies in establishing simplified customs procedures and revising the rules of exemption from excise duty on imports. The World Customs Organisation is currently working on that problem.

As for taxation of services, there is already a very wide consensus on the definition of the jurisdiction for consumption and the guiding principles were approved by the OECD's Fiscal Affairs Committee in June 2001, following public consultation. Their scope of application covers services likely to be provided at a distance, such as, for example, downloading software of sounds or images but also access to games or databases.

With regard to the place of taxation, for practical reasons, business to business commerce was distinguished from commerce directed at private consumers :

- For business to business commerce, the services must be taxed in the area of jurisdiction in which the buyer is commercially established, that is to say the company's registered office or branch at which the service is actually provided. A « safety net » has been provided for cases where some operators try to take advantage of the flexibility of this rule to avoid tax, for example, where it concerns services that do not give full entitlement to deduction such as financial or insurance services (the buyers might then be tempted to artificially locate these services in areas of jurisdiction where the VAT rate is very low or even nil). Further work is currently being carried out on the precise definition of cases in which such a « safety net » should be used.

- For commerce directed at private consumers, the place of taxation has been defined as being the place where the purchaser has his usual residence.

With regard to mechanisms for taxing those services, the Fiscal Affairs Committee recommended a number of methods :

- For business to business commerce (which represents around 95 % of the value of international e-commerce), the reverse charge method has been accepted because of its recognised practical aspect : it allows the seller not to have any administrative obligation with regard to the consumer's jurisdiction. Comments from businesses were unanimously in favour of this mechanism.

- For commerce directed at individuals (who nevertheless represent less than 5 % of the value of international e-commerce) there were long discussions, mainly due to its symbolic value. Insofar as it is extremely difficult to make the consumer liable to tax in the jurisdiction where he is resident, we have to seek ways of allowing the seller who is not established in that jurisdiction to pay the tax. The method that would appear to be the most promising is based on the use of the very technologies that underpin e-commerce and its new intermediaries to achieve taxation by automated means.

Based on these main guidelines, the second stage of the work would be to define the practical methods for making taxation in the place of consumption effective.

Firstly, we must provide businesses and tax administrations with a set of clear guidelines that will enable the vendor to know in which jurisdiction his buyer can be found (for example, by using numerical certificates, technical indexes or declarations from the buyer) or what his tax status is (VAT registered or not).

Next, we must lay down the conditions and requirements that these new mechanisms for tax collection must meet so as to offer both the best guarantees for the governments and the best chances of succeeding in the market.

B. – REDEFINING TAX CONVENTIONS

For direct tax on businesses, unlike VAT for which there is no international standard or agreement, (except for the scheme in force in the European Union) there is an OECD model Convention which serves as a basis for almost all conventions in the world for preventing double taxation.

Here, the Internet poses delicate problems of interpretation for the negotiators of these fiscal conventions. Can concepts such as those of permanent establishment and charges be adapted to cover transactions conducted on the Internet or must the tax authorities undertake a more fundamental reform ? At this stage, the OECD has not entered into discussions on the modification of the concepts which underpin the model convention but only on its comments regarding interpretation. So far as concerns e-commerce, the discussions centred mainly on two areas : adapting the definition of a permanent establishment and the characteristics of some payments.

A primordial factor in establishing taxation laws in the fiscal conventions is the permanent establishment used to establish whether there is sufficient commercial presence in a country to justify taxation. The question of whether an establishment situated in a country is of sufficient size to amount to a permanent establishment is mainly a question of fact. The Model Convention defines it as « a fixed place of business through which the business of an enterprise is wholly or partly carried on ». The question arose as to whether when the commercial activities carried out by electronic means could constitute such a permanent establishment. In particular, when the presence of a business in a country is merely a web site located on a piece of computer equipment.

During its meeting in January 2001, the Fiscal Affairs Committee approved the wide consensus that had been reached on the clear distinction that should be made between a piece of computer equipment (the server) and the information and software which are used or stored on that equipment in order to make it operate. It decided that a web site in itself cannot constitute a fixed place of business. On the other hand, the server, which is described as a piece of computer equipment with a physical location, may constitute such an establishment. However, it is only when the web site operator is the owner or lessee of that equipment for a sufficient period of time that it may constitute a permanent establishment. The question here is not whether the server can be removed, but whether in fact it does move. Furthermore, it was decided that a piece of automatic equipment alone, without any human presence, may be considered as a permanent establishment. Finally, a third condition is required for the server to constitute a permanent establishment in a given jurisdiction : the company must conduct its core business via that server. That will be the case, for example, when this business consists of selling software and those sales are carried out through a server from which they are downloaded. On the other hand the server will not constitute a permanent establishment if it is only used to carry out preparatory or ancillary activities (such as advertising, storing or collecting information for example). The reply to that question depends on an examination of individual cases.

The second stage of the work will now consist of evaluating the rules for allocating the profits to permanent establishments as they have just been defined and which are used for e-commerce. The question relates to the distribution of taxing rights between the jurisdiction under which the business falls and that of the permanent establishment, initially by examining a specific case : a business that distributes products on the Internet via a site hosted on a server which constitutes a permanent establishment in another country and which sells to the end consumer within the context of electronic retail commerce.

The second stage of our work on redefining the fiscal conventions relates to the issue of characteristics of payments and principally, the definition of **royalties** in the context of e-commerce as well as the characterisation of a number of other transactions in the Model Convention.

It is important to note here that the debate was not limited only to the provisions of the OECD's Model Tax Convention but also dealt with some provisions which are not part of the model but which appear in a number of bilateral conventions.

For example, whereas the processing of royalties and profits from businesses is similar in the Model Convention, there are numerous bilateral conventions which, in the case of payment for a royalty, make provision for deduction at source even if the beneficiary does not have a registered office or permanent establishment in the payer's country.

The same applies to a number of other provisions in conventions that provide for taxation at source, especially, for example, with regard to remuneration for know-how or payments for the use or concession for use of a piece of industrial equipment.

By way of an example, let us see which solutions were adopted for two very recent transactions (out of the 28 examined so far).

With regard to payment for downloading a digital product that the buyer intends for his personal use (whether it is a business or a private individual) that payment must be considered as a profit and not a royalty. In fact, the buyer's right to make a copy on his hard disk (or on any other permanent medium) is only a secondary part of the transaction. The transaction relates more to the use of the product than to a copyright.

On the other hand, if the transaction actually relates to an intellectual property right over the product, as for example the right to reproduce to sell multiple copies of it, naturally the concept of royalty could apply with deduction at source where appropriate.

As for remuneration for know-how, which may give rise to a royalty, a number of criteria were highlighted to define it more precisely.

Accordingly, only payment for the provision of a set of technical information, not disclosed to the public, required for the industrial reproduction of a product or procedure will not amount to a royalty. For example, payment for technical assistance or for an after-sales service will not fall within this category.

In conclusion, one can summarise the method used to define the nature of a transaction as an analysis of its dominant elements, leaving aside the incidental aspects or the way in which the product is transferred.

C. – IMPLICATIONS FOR THE TRANSFER PRICES

In principle, e-commerce does not pose any problems that are radically new or completely different as regards transfer prices (that is to say the prices paid for transactions that take place between different parts of a multinational business). However, it is likely to make an analysis of transfer prices more complex. The development of private internal networks (Intranets) within multinational groups exerts heavy pressure on the traditional application of the principle of full competition (« arm's length principle ») (4) by stimulating the complete integration of multinationals, particularly with regard to the provision of services. For the tax authorities, that situation makes it even more difficult to determine the nature of a given transaction and examination of a transaction between independent businesses which may be considered to be comparable to that which is conducted between connected businesses. The OECD's guiding principles on transfer prices specify that a functional analysis is needed to establish such comparability but with e-commerce and the use of private internal networks it could be difficult to find out who does what.

A deeper integration can also generate profits from synergies which exceed the directly measured contributions from the participants. That situation poses the difficult question of how those profits should be shared between the related businesses. Clearly, defining transfer prices is going to get more complicated.

D. – TAX ADMINISTRATION

A number of observers had predicted that e-commerce would force governments to change the composition of their tax base. They quoted the mobility of web sites and the apparent lack of tools to identify the place and the parties to electronic transactions as good reasons to transfer the tax expenses to less mobile bases, such as immovable property or work. However, these arguments

---

(4) For example, the principle whereby transactions between businesses linked to a multinational must be treated as if they had taken place between independent companies.

would only have been valid if governments had done nothing to adjust their methods for identifying those liable for tax or for collecting information and tax in an environment in which money is earned by e-commerce.

That adjustment will probably require significant changes in the way in which businesses and administrations work, the most important thing being that the new methods implemented should be internationally cohesive and well suited to e-commerce.

In particular, a number of issues are now arising for tax administrations. These are : identifying the taxpayer, obtaining reliable information about his business and collecting the tax in an effective manner.

1. – *Identifying the taxpayer*

In the conventional commercial world, tax administrations were able to identify those liable for tax, have access to verifiable information on their taxable activities and had proven tax collection systems. Nowadays, a company that is involved in e-commerce on the Internet could only be identified by its domain name but the connection between that name and the place in which it is actually established is rather tenuous. The connection between a domain name and the true address is made through data it provides when it is incorporated (available on http://www.allwhois.com). Unfortunately, that data is not always reliable and similarly the information that businesses spontaneously offer on their web site is often very sparse.

Nevertheless, numerous actors have a common interest in improving the identification of businesses on the Internet : consumer associations, the bodies responsible for the domain name registration and the companies themselves who want guarantees as to the protection of their intellectual property or improving consumer confidence. The cost of managing that information will be even lower if it is collected and used in an internationally cohesive manner.

2. – Collecting fiscal information

In addition to the problems of identification, e-commerce poses the question of the ability of the tax authorities to collect information. In a conventional commercial environment, those liable for tax keep accounting documents and provide the tax authorities with the necessary information for establishing the basis of assessment. When they feel the need to check that information, they can rely on information provided by third parties such as financial institutions or intermediaries. However, in the electronic environment, the accounting documents can be easily stored in a foreign jurisdiction. In addition, cryptography which is legitimately used to protect trade secrets can also be used to prevent the tax authorities from gaining access to accounting records. The traditional sources of information which came from third parties can also be reduced in that the Internet encourages the process of disintermediation. Finally, the methods of electronic payment can also pose significant problems to the tax administrations.

Professional accounting bodies are also faced with similar challenges when they have to conduct commercial audits. The tax administrations must seize the opportunity of working in collaboration with those bodies in order to jointly devise the means of tackling these common concerns.

If a number of requirements in this field are covered by a solid, globally cohesive agreement, the mechanisms designed to provide better information to all the partners of e-commerce can be included in the accounting software used by businesses and in the transaction process, for little expense.

3. – Collecting tax

An effective tax collection system is essential to the management of any tax system. Such systems cannot be introduced into the e-commerce environment without posing new challenges, especially with regard to tax on consumption.

A very large portion of tax revenue is collected by intermediaries, but in some cases, e-commerce can remove those intermediaries (for example, when a producer deals directly with the consumer rather than using a retailer) so that the tax authorities are then obliged to collect small amounts from a great number of taxpayers situated in a foreign country. That situation could place an unbearable administrative burden on taxpayers and result in higher administrative costs for the tax authorities although it is likely that e-commerce will also develop some new points of intermediation.

The technologies that underpin e-commerce can open up new channels for tax collection. Many countries already accept tax payments and declarations electronically. Furthermore, companies are already experimenting with the functions of incorporating tax into their commercial transactions.

The OECD's Fiscal Affairs Committee has taken into account the international dimension of these problems. Four regional fiscal organisations (CATA – the Commonwealth Association of Tax Administrators, CIAT – the Inter-American Centre of Tax Administrators, CREDAF – the conference and study centre for tax administration executives (*Centre de Rencontres et d'Études des Dirigeants des Administrations Fiscales*) – and IOTA – the Intra-European Organisation of Tax Administrations – in conjunction with the OECD have organised the first world tax conference on the subject : Tax Administrations in an Electronic World. This meeting was organised by Canada in June 2001 and included 106 countries. This new type of conference, which is the first gathering of tax administrations on such a scale, enabled tax administrators to share their experiences on the ways of applying taxation issues to e-commerce. The work will of course be continued in that respect.

IV. – International administrative co-operation

The spectacular progression of e-commerce as well as the increasing globalisation of economies and companies' strategies have made strengthening administrative co-operation a key aspect of the work of tax administrations.

Of course, the new methods devised for reliably collecting and exchanging information must not be used as a pretext for changing the existing rules concerning protection of private life. Those rules exist and we must continue to obey them.

V. – New opportunities
for service to the taxpayer

The technologies of e-commerce provide tax administrations with new ways of improving the management and quality of tax legislation as well as efficiency in collecting revenue and interaction with a wider community. The following can be mentioned as opportunities offered by the new technologies :

– Communications between administrations and taxpayers can be revolutionised and access to information improved significantly so as to help taxpayers fulfil their tax obligations;
– The registration of taxpayers and the administrative obligations can be simplified;
– Electronic management and collection of tax can become the norm rather than the exception;
– Faster, easier and safer ways of paying tax or getting refunds can be devised.

In this new environment, the tax administrations of both small and large countries are facing the same challenges. All can benefit, for very little expense, from leading-edge technologies which can offer the taxpayer a better service whilst reducing the costs of collection and administrative expenses. A number of administrations have already started to implement these new technologies and can share their experience with other countries.

DISCUSSION

Guy Canivet

Thank you, Sir, for having expounded on the principle of legal security from the operator's point of view. It was very interesting. The debate is now open; would anyone like to ask a question? Yes? Please state your name.

Olivier Cachard

Olivier Cachard; I wrote a thesis at Paris II on international regulation of the electronic market and my question is addressed to Professor Benabou who spoke to us about minimum harmonisation as a desirable or commendable method. In fact, from a global point of view, it is quite certain. Nevertheless, from a Community point of view, minimum harmonisation raises major difficulties because in the end it authorises the States, or some States, to adopt a higher level of protection, so that we find quite considerable divergences between the Common Market countries. These considerable divergences are extended and might produce their harmful effects in private international law because minimum harmonisation presupposes mutual recognition and no doubt the application of the law of the country of origin. But to what extent could I, as a consumer, rely on the law of the country of destination, my own, with which I am familiar and which I can legitimately expect to protect me?

Valérie-Laure Benabou

I am not sure that I am the best person to reply to your question, as the links between private international law and Community law do not fall within my field of activity. On the other hand, it seems to me that the question of harmonisation was put to me on a more global scale than Community harmonisation, but I should like to return to one of the observations I made, that is to say, the risk of contradiction in envisaging various levels of harmonisation, as we could end up with solutions that are not all in line with each other. The problem of minimal harmonisation is, naturally, as its name suggests, that a minimum of common elements will be laid down, which Member States are at liberty to surpass, reinforcing the protection where necessary. We have the same problems with copyright. I do not have a solution to the question you are asking me; you can see it is difficult for me to answer. I have no solution in that harmonisation cannot be standardisation. It is a challenge, an illusion – I think we are all agreed on that – to seek a standardisation of solutions at the present time. We are looking at the last resort scenario, but it is not a bad thing in itself to meet the challenges facing us, in that we at least have this common basis from which we cannot depart. Minimal protection is therefore at least a guarantee in these cases, even if we cannot necessarily rely on the maximum protection sought. There was already an almost identical approach, so far as concerns copyright, on the, Satellite / Cable directive, which, whilst being relatively respectful, in inverted commas, of the system of choice-of-law, enabled overriding rules to be established that would be common to the Member States and which could not be overstepped, by quite complicated connecting factor systems, the details of which I shall spare you. Perhaps these system approaches can be found in the theory put forward by some people, of police laws with a lesser effect, where the idea is that although the police law must protect the consumer's interests, for example, it will only be incorporated in really sensitive legislation, the rest of the foreign law being designed to do its job in full and correction being only partially achieved. However, I am merely giving you some rather unbridled avenues for thought; I am not sure that I have replied to your question, but perhaps there are some people here who...

Guy Canivet

Mr le Doyen could perhaps...

Yves Poullet

Yes, just two comments. Firstly, you are right to emphasise that at European level, the mechanisms for harmonisation are not always total harmonisation mechanisms and it is difficult for them to be so. I should simply like to say – it is all in my text – that one only has to see the recent directives : we are seeing an increasing number of so-called directives for total harmonisation. Minimal harmonisation and optional harmonisation are becoming increasingly rare. That is my first comment. Second comment. I presume that there are a number of people here who must have had the same experience : because of the Transparency Directive, there is an obligation to negotiate with the Commission, to provide the Commission with the first draft of the national law so as to check whether or not it really creates an obstacle to cross-border trade. Against that background, the Commission, (and I do not think that I am the only one to have experienced it), exerts some pressure in order to get it amended. Therefore, I believe that increasingly, both with legislation and in practice, we are managing to create mechanisms for harmonisation. Third point. An increasing number of directives establish mechanisms for administrative cooperation. That can be seen in the Electronic Signatures Directive and in measures for combating paedophile messages and harmful content. There are mechanisms that are mechanisms for administrative cooperation under the aegis of the Commission, which ensures that an attempt is made to harmonise the implementation of regulations.

Guy Canivet

Thank you Mr le Doyen. Are there any other questions ? If there are no more questions, I shall give the floor to our rapporteur. I shall now leave you. I should first like to thank the speakers for their addresses in which I have taken as much interest as the delegates. Your interest has been constant and, accordingly, I should also like to thank you for paying close attention to these speeches.

GENERAL REPORT
STANDARDS APPLICABLE
TO THE INTERNET :
BENEFITS AND LIMITATIONS

« Internet and the Law –
Disturbances and Early Sorrow »

BY

HERBERT BURKERT

PRESIDENT OF THE « INFORMATION LAW »
RESEARCH CENTRE AND DIRECTOR OF THE CENTRE
OF EXPERTISE ON « NETWORK POLICIES »
FHG – INSTITUTE FOR MEDIA AND COMMUNICATION
SAINT AUGUSTIN, GERMANY

I. – Changes in law

It is the privilege of the reporter to misunderstand those he is reporting on in order to be better understood himself. But for the time being I regard myself mainly as an access provider to the contents of my colleagues.

The general impression of this session is that there are, of course, legal problems of the Internet – but most of all there are what may be called « Internet problems of Law ».

Let me be more precise : If we take « Internet » as representation for communication *technology*, i.e. technical changes absorbed by the cultural, political and social life of a society then we will have to realise that this absorption process is accompanied – against the background of this session's papers – by disturbing changes in law.

I say « *accompanied* » because I suspect that there are complex relationships of causation which by themselves would be the worthy object for further attention : How much of these changes are caused by law providing the ground for technical change; where and how does technical change influence law; do these changes work directly on each other or are they mediated by changes in the economy, in our ways of cultural perception ? Here and at this stage, however, my intention is simply to make some phenomena more visible so I speak of *parallelism* rather than of causation.

To talk of change in law may sound surprising. Law – as *Benedicte Fauvarque-Cosson* and *Jerôme Huet* have shown with examples from private international law – is well prepared to meet the challenges of the new and in particular the challenges of internationalisation. I use the term « internationalisation » with intent – I am reluctant to use the much more fashionable term « globalisation » because of our pre-occupation with the European – American-Asian triangle, and – as we may remember from geometry – a triangle is not a globe.

Law seems well prepared to meet the future : Laws passed are passed to apply to future events and courts apply past laws and decisions to those future events which have become present at the moment of decision.

Law, at the latest since the understanding of how to navigate the seas, and more recently and more specifically, as shown by *Jerôme Huet*, since the key communication inventions of modernity, has developed and refined its mechanisms to deal with the laws of those others who also have laws.

Law has many ways to deal with « internationalism » :
– by hegemony like Roman law,
– by attempts at hegemony, throwing out the hook of reciprocity like Washington law (remembering the Semiconductor Chip Protection Act) (1) and Brussels law (everybody remembering the database directive) (2),
– through bilateral and multilateral treaties and conventions, through Geneva, Paris, Warsaw and Strasbourg law,
– by mutual recognition and harmonisation again through Brussels and Luxembourg law,
– by the highly flexible and grandiose invention of individual contract law as *Valerie-Laure Benabou* has reminded us.

Certainly during the last decades European Law – with all its imperfections – has given us excellent examples of how to meet the challenges of our neighbours' laws. And there *are* opportunities and

---

(1) US Code, Title 17, Chapter 9, Sec. 914.
(2) Article 11 of Directive 96/9.

mechanisms to balance international market freedoms with the control power of states, as *Eric Caprioli* has outlined.

There are, of course, remaining tasks. *Yves Poullet* has pointed to them :

- creating, maintaining and managing trust and common expectancies,
- risk management and risk allocation, and providing,
- adequate compensation arrangements.

And, as we have heard from the various contributions either explicitly or implicitly law is very well prepared to meet these tasks, even if this view may not always be shared by those unfortunate outsiders, the « muggles », who do not understand the magic of law.

II. – The real challenges of law

And yet, like a « leitmotiv » going through the contributions of this morning, there seem to be disturbance and sorrows, early sorrows about the implications of the new : The network of networks seems to pose a challenge that goes well beyond other technological challenges we have met before. There seems to be – as *Pierre Trudel* has suggested – a deep change, or at least beginning mutations in law. We see affected :

- law's disciplinarity,
- its understanding of technology,
- its understanding of time,
- its symbolism and rituals,
- and last but not least some of its essential paradigms.

A. – DISCIPLINARITY

The Internet is like the nasty examiner we may remember from our legal exams who is always asking that question that demands an in depth answer from just the other area of law which we had not prepared, and then goes on to ask us about the close interrelations between that and yet another area of law which we had regarded as marginal so far. The Internet is questioning in depth our current responses, in tax law e.g. – as outlined by *Stéphane Buydens* – as well as our horizontal understanding of interrelations between e.g. intellectual property rights and fundamental freedoms. It requires us to return to essential values and functionalities of the genotype of law in order to master the new phenotype of law (3).

B. – TECHNOLOGY

The Internet is finally discarding a myth we should have discarded long ago : The myth of technology neutral law. While the myth may reflect a deep wish, there is no law that remains neutral towards a technology. There is certainly – as *Joel Reidenberg* has described so vividly – « technological negationism ». This negationism, however, does not affect technology in general; rather it seeks to avoid a particular technology of the day. Each regulator still has a particular technology in her or his mind when setting out to regulate, patterns of usage, a cultural understanding of devices and processes which influences the understanding of the world and how regulation will work on this world : Data protection regulation was introduced precisely because the new technologies of information handling had made us aware that the limitations on old procedures of information handling (complexity, quantity, time, distance) which had been, unconsciously almost, on our mind when we had regulated in the old world, were no longer valid. And – it is always with a particular technology in mind that a disturbed electorate requires reaction from its regulators. Regulators who seem to serve anything else, something more abstract or more basic, have their offers usually rejected as premature, not answering the practical needs, or simply politically foolish.

C. – PLACE

Benedicte Fauvarque-Cosson and *Stephane Buydens* have shown us the perceptual necessity of place and location in law, even if it must be admitted that these notions are increasingly turning into legal fiction, i.e. consciously made assumptions for legal purposes only. But legal fiction, of course, can and does transform reality. After all, legal persons are a vivid example of the viability of legal fiction.

---

(3) « An observed trait is referred to as phenotype; the genetic information defining the phenotype is called the genotype »– JAEMSON, J. Larry; KOPP, Peter, « Principles of Human Genetics », in BRAUNWALD, Eugene *et al.* (eds.), *Harrison's Principles of Internal Medicine*, 5th ed., McGraw Hill : New York etc. 2001, 375-396, 387.

But to remain viable legal fictions have to remain functional, and it also seems from these presentations that location has become like Paris, a « moveable feast ».

D. – Time

The half-life time of regulations is getting considerably shorter. *Eric Caprioli* and *Yves Poullet* have both been making this point : More regulations at shorter intervals for a shorter period of time. Laws do not conceal this change any longer. Once made for eternity (or at least the life time of a political regime) now explicitly state that they will only last for two years and that then there will be a review. Other laws now simply fade away if they are not explicitly renewed.

E. – Paradigms

Some basic paradigms of law are in disarray : Reference has already been made to the notion of « property » as in « intellectual property »; other examples could be given like data protection where non-negotiable liberty rights are slowly and quietly being transformed into marketable property rights.

F. – Symbols

Pierre Trudel has made allusions to this issue : Law is changing its symbolic appearances. Or rather, law is struggling with its symbols : There is, of course, a basic difference between the traditional signature and the electronic signature, both in appearance and in process, even if electronic signatures claim to meet the same demands of functionality. But there is uneasiness as to whether these functionalities are adequately reflected by what electronic signature procedures *show* to us. How else can a recent prototype of an electronic signature card be explained : The card, in smart card format, carries the secret key of its owner in a chip, but it can only be activated if the card, which also carries a miniature needle, identifies the DNA pattern of the blood sample it takes from its holder as being identical to the DNA pattern of the rightful owner which is also stored in that same chip. So the electronic signature brings back the truly archaic symbol of signing contracts with your own blood.

It almost seems as if – while law is screening the Internet for problems – law itself turns into something like the Internet : It becomes less hierarchical, it is turning into a multiplayer-multilevel affair with international bodies competing to become the new hubs of regulation.

III. – European Law as an Example for the Law of the Networks?

This « state of the art » description invites several responses : A more passive one, with a social scientist attitude, would speculate on probabilities and chances for the survival of law in the Internet environment. As lawyers, however, we are faced with normative expectations and are invited to address law in a more active manner, to shape the face of Internet law, to overcome our early sorrows, to clarify our objectives, to choose priorities and to set examples :

Geoffrey Brigham has shown the main objective : The networks remind us that we do need to bring European Law and international law together without compromising our value system and to provide for legal certainty.

The priorities have been stated clearly – among others by *Yves Poullet* :

– safeguarding the role of individual rights in this period of change, ranging from privacy and access to property rights;
– safeguarding interoperable communication as such – as exemplified by the resources of the network of networks, the Internet, – as a common international public good;
– paying particular attention to the current carriers of change : the service providers.

I also tend to agree with *Yves Poullet* that one could point to the whole of European Law and its development as an example – at least as a methodological example – as *Valérie-Laure Benabou* has called it – to get from regional levels to higher levels of integration however global they may be. But even this – basically optimistic example shows as – as exemplified by *Diane Wallis* – how much more there is left to be done even in such apparently innocent areas like European contract law not to mention European criminal law.

Geoffrey Brigham has pointed to the possibilities of good, if not best, practices and has hinted to the advantages e.g. of a one-stop shopping place for International Consumer Law.

But the European example also reminds us that in law the physics of politics match centripedal forces with their centrifugal counterparts. Law is not an innocent sand-box for building conceptual sand-castles (if there ever were innocent sand-boxes – my childhood memory and current observations show quite a competitive environment there); law is about interests, power, money, lobbying for influence.

We live in a time of new players gaining importance, to thaw out the political compromises frozen into our old laws by the old players and keepers of the bank, new players like the service providers who are so desperately needed to bring products and users together and whose functions and achievements *Geoffrey Brigham* has described so well. We live in a time of fragile alliances like between hardware producers and rightholders today, and hardware producers and end-users tomorrow; or alliances between software producers and the defenders of free use of cryptography which at least for a period in time had created remarkable consequences.

In short we have seen the relationship between law and the Internet to be like in Einstein's relativity tale : while law is invited to judge the speed of a running train it is sitting in a running train itself.

IV. – Times of Change

At times of change – and French history in particular is rich with examples – you never know exactly whether you are at the brink of a revolution or whether you are witnessing a restoration.

At this stage then it seems appropriate to change the role of the rapporteur, the access provider, to the role of the contents provider and assume full responsibility :

- In these changes in law alluded to is there not at play what Brian Wilson in his book « Misunderstanding Media » (4) has called the « the 'law' of the suppression of radical potential » ?
- Are there not signs of what Christian Vandendorpe has very recently called in Le Débat « the new feudalism » ? (5)
- Is it not alarming – as Stephane Buydens has shown us with the example of tax law – that network law is focusing on the target that is the least able to move just like the Westphalian Treaty forced religion on the least mobile, the poor peasants who could not leave their toil ?
- Is the special view on access service providers and their limited liability just an innocent clarification of the law of the land or is it the introduction of privileges to gatekeepers of the promised land ?
- Do not the latest developments at the Internet Corporation for Assigned Names and Numbers, proposing voting rights only to the holders of domain names, show us that this is again the time of the owners of land, this time in « cyberspace » ?
- Do we not observe in the ever more important area of international law making a return to the « Système Metternich ». Is there sufficient national debate preparing such law making; is there sufficient transparency ? Is there sufficient influence on modifying such proposals for international law making if you do not have an internationally organised lobbying group ?
- Is the chain of legitimacy from the elected parliamentarian to the government elected by parliament to the delegate chosen by that government for international negotiations not a bit too long ? What choices have national parliaments for modification when international agreements come back for ratification, not to mention cases of intentional « policy laundering » where governments force regulations on their parliaments as an international necessity which they had been unable to obtain from those parliaments nationally.
- Should we not – against such pressures of internationalisation – seek to reconsider – as suggested by *Yves Poullet* – the notion of sovereignty – redefining sovereignty in the age of the networks

---

(4) Harvard University Press : Cambridge, Massachusetts 1986, 23 ff.

(5) Christian VANDENDORPE, « Pour une bibliothèque virtuelle universelle », in *Le débat*, n° 117, November-December 2001, pp. 31 et suiq.

e.g. as the duty of states to make binding agreements only if and when these agreements have been made sufficiently transparent to their citizens, their citizens having had the opportunity of directly influencing these agreements. For this, too, there is a European model : European Parliament's painful way to empowerment and – as a very long road still to be travelled : the European Referendum.

We tend to associate certain values with the Internet, and law we should not forget is not only a social technology for confidence building it is also about values – if this is the way we want it to continue to be.

Technologies, their architecture and encoding are not law, as some make want us to believe. But technologies, their architecture and encodings tend to make the law's realisation of some values more probable than that of others.

This insight provides us with a double task : At a very early stage of a technology, we indeed do have to make value judgments, and we have to make them consciously and explicitly. By making value choices we do set the genetic traits for our societies which will come to depend on these technologies and we should be aware of that and make this transparent and not hide behind « technology ». And, moreover, these early choices (not early sorrows) do not free us from watching and safeguarding at each and every step the environmental value factors for this technology so that it can continue to develop to our wishes.

B

New forms of regulating networks : issues and prospects

CHAIRMANSHIP

Francis TEITGEN

CHAIRMAN OF THE BAR COUNSIL AT THE PARIS COURT OF APPEAL

1. – Cybercrime and networks

THE CONVENTION ON CYBERCRIME

BY

Guy DE VEL

DIRECTOR GENERAL OF LEGAL AFFAIRS
AT THE COUNCIL OF EUROPE

Introduction

Allow me first of all to express my gratitude and compliments to the French Ministry of Justice, the University of Paris I and the ARPEJE association for having organised this colloquium on Internet law – a fast-developing subject of the utmost international relevance. I am especially grateful to them as it seems to me that the time is particularly apposite so far as concerns the Council of Europe, which I have the honour to represent today before you. In fact, this very week, our Organisation is on the verge of signing the first international treaty on cybercrime. The presence of the Minister for Justice, scheduled for tomorrow morning, bears witness to the importance and urgency of the topic we are tackling as well as the issues at stake : can the law designed for the physical world be applied to the virtual world ? Can legislation safeguard individual rights, the fundamental values and principles embraced by our societies, when human beings are changing – expressing themselves, trading, selling and enjoying themselves – in cyberspace ? Can the Internet remain an unregulated area, an area of absolute freedom as millions of Internet users suddenly converted to anarchy would seem to wish ?

If you will allow me, before tackling the heart of the matter, I should like to personally express my warmest thanks to Mr George Chatillon, Chairman of the Scientific Committee and the Colloquium organisation Committee for having involved the Council of Europe in this important event.

I was asked to give you a brief presentation of the objectives and content of the Council of Europe's Convention on cybercrime. This international treaty was adopted on 8 November last by the Committee of Ministers of the Council of Europe during a meeting of Ministers of Foreign Affairs of our 43 Member States. The Convention will be open to signature on 23 November next in Budapest, that is to say in four days' time. We expect a great number of ministers to sign during the ceremony which will take place next Friday on the banks of the Danube, in the prestigious building used as the headquarters for the Hungarian Parliament.

This ceremony and the rapid entry into force of this Convention will be the culmination of five long years of work and tough, difficult negotiations within the Council of Europe to clear an obstacle-strewn and legally uncharted path. It is therefore a pioneer legal instrument destined to become the essential benchmark law in the matter. This law is impatiently awaited by the whole international community as proven, for example, by the fact that the European Union or the G8 suspended their work on the subject pending the outcome of ongoing negotiations in the Council of Europe.

In spite of that, I have to tell you that drafting it was not a « smooth ride ». In fact, after it was declassified in April 2000, some associations and representatives from certain sectors of industry vehemently criticised the draft, accusing it of having the worst evils and intentions. On reading the text of the Convention, I still find it difficult to understand the reason for these accusations. It is possible that unfortunately, the true purposes of the draft law were not properly understood.

In any event, the time has now come to resolutely enter the battle against cybercrime; the Council of Europe Convention is particularly important for several reasons :

1) firstly, because information technology and the telecommunications networks have transformed the world into a global information society which no longer has any borders in cyberspace either for legitimate or criminal activities;

2) secondly, because any information has become accessible to any user, anywhere in the world; it is now possible to gain unimpeded access from a distance, whether lawful or unlawful, to vast quantities of computer data;

3) the networks carry the inherent promise of a new era of « online trade », conveying services and goods whose value could soon exceed hundreds of billion Euros.

However, this virtual world full of promises is threatened by new types of crimes. Nowadays, computer networks enable illegal content such as child pornography, computer viruses or coded instructions from terrorist organisations, to be distributed to an unlimited number of users at phenomenal speed. The networks are used for spying or stealing confidential information, often with a high financial value or for attacking the computer systems of governments or private companies from a distance and in complete anonymity, causing tremendous damage.

This is not all done by young computer whizzkids who are testing the limits of their knowledge : they are often deliberate acts by pirates, cyber-terrorists or professional cyber-spies, acting on behalf of other people, companies or even governments, for remuneration. It follows that the benefits offered by a global information network can soon disappear if impunity is the only response to these criminal attacks.

Accordingly, the Convention on cybercrime has a threefold objective :

– to establish common definitions of certain criminal offences, allowing domestic law to be harmonised;
– to define the methods of investigations and criminal proceedings adjusted to a computer environment enabling the approximation of national criminal procedures;
– to define both traditional and new means and channels for international cooperation to combat cybercrime.

I. – The offences

Accordingly, first of all the Convention is designed to harmonise the definition of criminal offences committed against the computer networks. That should eliminate the problems connected with dual criminal liability. These offences, some of which have already been the subject of the Council of Europe's Recommendation N° R (89) 9, can be divided into four categories :

1. breaches of confidentiality, integrity and availability of data or computer systems;
2. computer-related offences;
3. offences relating to content;
4. offences connected with breaches of copyright and related rights.

The offences in the first category concern interference with computer systems or data. Their specific offence is based on a clear choice of criminal policy, that of protecting the networks, and the communications and data within them. In fact, the damage caused by these attacks should not be under-estimated : penetrating a computer system, placing a virus in it, can easily trigger the destruction of data or entire systems with colossal value owing to the interconnection of networks (do you remember « I LOVE YOU »).

I should point out that in order to be liable for these offences, the attacks must be committed deliberately and unlawfully, that is to say without authorisation. Properly authorised actions carried out by government authorities or generally accepted as lawful commercial practices, are not covered by the Convention. This expressly exempts software design and trials designed to protect the security of computer systems from any criminal liability or legal consequences.

The offences in the second category cover the commission of offences in a computer environment (fraud and forgery) hitherto committed in the physical world. However, the draft covers « virtual » acts of fraud and forgery committed through or due to the networks. It is necessary to make them offences as in the majority of legal systems, the traditional criminal definitions do not cover acts committed via the networks. Furthermore, the number of victims of this type of computer crime is often very high.

The third category of offences, those relating to content, define a number of actions connected with child pornography, a real scourge in today's society and the subject of international traffic, the punishment of which has become one of the Council of Europe's top priorities. The Convention makes a whole range of acts offences, from possession to intentional distribution of child pornography.

Many people in Europe have spoken out in favour of making some other unlawful content an offence such as racist propaganda. The President of the French Republic and the Minister for Justice have adopted a particularly firm stance on the matter. Accordingly, although the Convention has not tackled this problem – transatlantic dialogue demands it –, a mandate has quickly been given to a special Committee of experts to draft a Protocol to supplement the Convention within a year, making racist propaganda and xenophobia via the networks a crime.

Similarly, following the tragic events of 11 September, the Council of Europe Parliamentary Assembly asked for the Convention to be reinforced by provisions concerning the transmission and deciphering of terrorist messages via the Internet. The Committee of Ministers could therefore soon decide to extend the mandate of the Committee of experts to cover this extremely topical issue.

Finally, the fourth category includes breaches of copyright and related rights committed via the networks – for example, by the large-scale distribution of illegal copies of works protected by intellectual property rights. In fact, the draft law makes what other conventions (WIPO) had already defined as « piracy » an offence but by extending its scope to other fields.

II. – Procedural measures

The procedural part of the Convention draws inspiration from the work previously carried out by the Council of Europe (Recommendation N° R (95) 13 on the problems of criminal procedure connected with information technology) and is designed to facilitate the conduct of criminal investigations in the computer environment. In fact, there are some remaining, often insurmountable problems in applying to the virtual world the means of investigation designed for the physical world. Moreover, the lack of clear rules on the collection, preservation and submission to the courts of reliable electronic evidence is a major obstacle. The legislation therefore establishes basic rules on certain procedural measures (data conservation, computer searches and seizures, collection of traffic data, interception of communications) the use of which enables electronic evidence relating both to the offences specified in the Convention itself (such as child pornography) and other offences (for example terrorism or money laundering) to be found and gathered. It follows that the scope of application of the procedural part of the Convention is wider than that of the substantive part.

The legislation only covers specific criminal investigations and does not advocate setting up an Orwellian type of general electronic surveillance system. Let it be clear : the Convention in no way authorises and should not be used as a legal excuse to create « *Big Brother* ». It is true that it will allow data to be seized or oblige the possessor to communicate it or preserve it for the purposes of the investigation. However, unless a criminal investigation has been opened, this legislation does not allow communications or connections to be monitored, either by suppliers or by law-enforcement agencies.

Moreover, there are many procedural guarantees that will prevent any abuse. Firstly, the introduction, implementation and enforcement of the powers and procedures in the legislation will be subject to conditions and safeguards provided for by the domestic law of each contracting Party, so as to ensure compliance with human rights, as defined by the applicable international instruments, in particular the European Human Rights Convention. Secondly, the legislation requires the application of the test of proportionality, taking into account both the nature and circumstances of the offence under investigation. Lastly, each procedural measure will be covered by existing safeguards, including the prior authorisation off a judge depending on the legal system of the country.

III. – International cooperation

By definition, cybercrime treats barriers with disdain and no investigation could progress without effective, rapid international cooperation. Therefore, where it is a question of electronic evidence which is by nature very volatile, it is essential that the law enforcement agencies of a State can carry out investigations on behalf of another State and pass it on with the necessary haste. Accordingly, in addition to the traditional forms of international cooperation on criminal matters (mutual judicial assistance and extradition), the Convention provides that the new procedural measures to which I referred earlier, are also implemented as new forms of mutual judicial assistance (for example, seizing or conserving data on behalf of another Party.)

Although at this stage, the Convention does not provide for real cross-border computer searches, because the States that negotiated the draft law were unable to agree on this point, by contrast it does include the idea of rapid cooperation by establishing a network of points of contact that are available 24 hours a day, 7 days a week. The rapid involvement of these points of contact will enable investigative measures to be taken and information to be communicated instantaneously. This network of contacts will not replace the more traditional communication channels but will supplement them.

Conclusions

This Convention which will be open for signature in a few days time represents a large-scale legal pioneering effort, capable of meeting the challenges that Europe and the world are facing from computer crime or cybercrime. It should be emphasised that Non-Member States – in particular the United States, Canada, Japan and South Africa – have taken an active part in the negotiations and have made a vital contribution to their outcome. I am certain that they will all be signatories.

In this connection, I should also like to remind you that the European Union expressed its support for the drafts under negotiation, especially by adopting a common position of the Fifteen and that the European Commission took an active part in the proceedings. Furthermore, there were regular consultations with the G8, which have been working in this field for several years.

It was time to legislate the matter. The Council of Europe Convention will become, I hope, a global benchmark law, which will inspire reform of the penal system and criminal procedure in years to come. That will result in providing our legal systems with the means for concerted action against these serious forms of crime, preventing a certain feeling of impunity which seemed to be rife until now in this field and ensuring a precious balance between the requirements of the criminal investigation and the respect of individual rights

INTERNET AND JUDICIAL INVESTIGATION

BY

JEAN-WILFRID NOËL

JUDGE, TRIBUNAL D'INSTANCE, VANVES
JEAN-WILFRID.NOEL@WANADOO.FR

The applicability of the rule of law to the Internet is no longer disputed. We now need to be able to ensure that it is effectively enforced : in that respect, the conceptual and practical adjustment of criminal procedure to the networks would seem to be a vital factor in the success of investigations related to the Internet.

There are several conflicting ideas which tend to present the State alternatively as the opponent of freedoms and the private life of citizens or as the only true defender of individual freedoms against illegal content.

Protection of the Internet user against the State or protection of the Internet user by the State ? In reality, the Internet is presented simultaneously as restricting and enhancing police enquiries, depending on the circumstances of its use. In the final analysis, the Internet paralyses judicial investigation but it also makes it more dynamic.

The introduction of another distinguishing feature would appear to be essential : the potential existence of several extraneous factors. In fact, the cross-border dimension of the investigation generally means having recourse to mutual judicial assistance in criminal proceedings.

I. – Judicial investigations paralysed by the Internet

A. – INVESTIGATIONS WITH NO EXTRANEOUS FACTORS

1. – *The legal obstacles*

The apprehension of illegal content by the investigative authorities arises necessarily from the express authorisation of the court.

Electronic data produced in evidence by the prosecution must be reliable in order to convince the court judging the matter and to form the basis of a guilty decision. The criteria for evaluating that reliability vary according to the States, where there is not necessarily a legal system for adducing evidence.

The Internet calls into question the principle of territorial jurisdiction of the investigative authorities. According to Article 18 of the Code of Penal Procedure, « *criminal investigation officers have jurisdiction within the territorial limits in which they perform their usual duties* ». The question therefore arises of determining to what extent a criminal investigation officer may recover data via the Internet which is helpful to the investigation but which is situated outside his own district. If one analyses the recovery of Internet data which took place in these circumstances as exceeding the territorial jurisdiction of the criminal investigation officer, it must in any event comply with the specific requirements of Article 18 of the Code of Penal Procedure which only allows extensions of territorial jurisdiction in a limited, express manner.

In on-the-spot investigations as in preliminary enquiries, the coercive powers invested in the law-enforcement agencies allow them to call for any qualified persons, where appropriate, in order to obtain evidence or carry out technical examinations. Nevertheless, no specific law imposes any real obligation on Internet service providers to cooperate with the police.

2. – *The practical obstacles*

Cultural reserve and the lack of special training for the criminal investigation officers help to restrict the effectiveness of their enquiries, although efforts to train staff have been made, in accordance with the wish expressed by the Prime Minister in 1997 under the Government Action Plan for the Information Society.

Constant changes in new technologies also pose a problem for the investigative agencies. For example, the development of *peer to peer* (P2P), based on the principle of sharing data between several servers without the intermediation of a service provider makes the work of the investigation services even more difficult. With the disappearance of the client/server architecture, the police authorities will no longer even be able to try and trace the illegal data with the guaranteed cooperation of the service providers, since those are by-passed towards by a client/client architecture. The situation would appear to be even more worrying as the next version of the Internet protocol, IPv6, should result in an important *peer to peer* development.

B. – INVESTIGATIONS INCLUDING
ONE OR SEVERAL EXTRANEOUS FACTORS

The international nature of the Internet naturally leads to a consideration of the situation in which an offence can be connected to two or even more sovereign powers.

1. – *The legal obstacles : the obligation*
to use mutual assistance in criminal matters

The requirement of dual criminal liability serves as a legal basis for refusing mutual assistance, when the facts at the origin of the request from the applicant State are not punishable by the criminal law in the requested State. Respectful of the sovereignty of the requested State, that circumstance amounts on the contrary to an insurmountable handicap to the investigation.

The State can also simply object to a request for mutual assistance : Article 2 (b) of the Convention of 20 April 1959 provides the requested State with that right when it « *considers that execution of the request is likely to prejudice the sovereignty, security, ordre public or other essential interests of its country* ». Moreover, Article 30 of the Council of Europe's Convention on cyberspace repeats this statement almost word for word. One cannot rule out a risk that mutual judicial assistance will be used as a device for purposes which in fact are related to economic, political or military information.

2. – *The practical obstacles*

The traceability of packages of information on the Internet depends on complex criminalistic techniques, even though state of the art and expensive software packages sometimes enable the pathway followed by the digital data to be recovered and hence their source and/or destination to be located.

Obviously, cryptography is also a challenge for the investigation authorities since the use of heavy encoding measures makes it very difficult for the forces of law and order to access the plain text.

The same observation can be made with regard to steganography, which consists of blending sound, text or image data into another file so as to hide sensitive information.

II. – Judicial investigations made more dynamic by the internet

A. – INVESTIGATIONS
THAT DO NOT CONTAIN ANY EXTRANEOUS FACTORS

A draft law on everyday security (*Loi sur la Sécurité Quotidienne* – LSQ), currently being discussed in Parliament, contains numerous innovative features which help to change the face of judicial investigations by dematerialising it somewhat. In this instance, this dematerialisation takes the form of a dilution of space, time, meaning and the written word.

1. – *Dilution of space : videoconferencing and searches using communications technology*

The LSQ project provides for the use of videoconferencing in order to successfully handle hearings and confrontations, which will allow the investigators to extend their enquiries towards remote areas of the national territory. In practice, it is more than likely that *webcams* will be the preferred means of conducting the hearing by *videolink*.

Searches using communications technology also allow the investigators to free themselves from the spatial borders of the enquiry and recover data situated outside their area of territorial jurisdiction. At the present time they are not mentioned in the draft law on everyday security but are naturally designed to be transposed into French law. In fact, Article 19 of the Council of Europe's Convention on cybercrime makes express provision for them with no possibility of reservation.

2. – *Dilution of time :*
conservation of connection data

The concept of investigation time is put into perspective by the right of the police authorities to gain access to data that hypothetically precedes the beginning of the enquiry. France has followed the way opened up by Belgium by applying the principle of compulsory retention of connection data by telecommunications operators and service providers.

a) *Examination of the provisions for the compulsory retention of data*

The principle of deleting data relating to a communication or making it anonymous as soon as it is over is laid down, which is in accordance with Article 6 of Directive 97/66/EC of 15 December 1997 concerning the processing of personal data and the protection of privacy in the telecommunications sector.

Operators can be forced to retain that data when it is a question of investigating, recording and prosecuting criminal offences and for the purpose of making information available to the courts where necessary.

b) *Criticism of the provisions on the compulsory retention of data*

It is up to the State to construct the legal bases needed to resolve investigations connected with new technologies. The principle of an obligation for retention seems all the less shocking as it is compatible with the principle of the end purpose of the data collected laid down by the Council of Europe's Convention of 28 January 1981 on the automatic processing of personal data. Article 9, § 2 of that convention affirms that « *derogation from the provisions of Articles 5, 6 and 8 of this convention shall be allowed when such derogation is provided for by the law of the Party and constitutes a necessary measure in a democratic society in the interests of protecting State security, public safety, the monetary interests of the State or the suppression of criminal offences* ».

The duration of such an obligation is desirable : it is not feasible to successfully conduct in a very short time investigations that are somewhat complex – if only because of the length of time it takes to get replies from the operators who have a legal requirement to provide them.

Finally, there are criminal sanctions for non-compliance with that obligation in order to guarantee its effectiveness. The draft LSQ imposes one year's imprisonment and a fine of 75,000 Euros on an operator who fails to delete data when he is bound to do so and also an operator who deletes connection data that he should have retained. The pressure applied to telecommunications operators and service providers is even stronger as the law expressly provides for the right to find legal entities criminally liable.

Nevertheless, the content of the obligation for retention as it appears in the draft LSQ would appear to be very vague : « *connection data relate solely to the identification of people who use the services provided by the operators and to the technical characteristics of the communications provided by those operators [...]; in no circumstance must they relate to the content of correspondence exchanged or information consulted, in any form whatsoever, within the context of those communications* ». Accordingly, it would seem that the concept that connection data includes URLs can be ruled out insofar as they are likely to betray the nature of the content offered by the site. However, the draft law does not give a strict definition of connection data. It refers to a later definition of such data by a *Conseil d'État* decree, after getting an opinion from the CNIL (the French national commission for information technology and civil rights.

In any event, it would seem to be desirable that in future the definition of data should include not only the sender's IP address but also that of the intended recipient of the communication. Obtaining those IP addresses does not in itself betray the content of the communications exchanged and accordingly respects the private life of Internet users. By contrast, it enables the link in the transmission of information to be reconstructed and points the investigators' enquiries in the right direction.

3. – *Dilution of meaning :*
access to plaintext and to keys

The diffusion of cryptography will oblige courts to break encoded illegal content. The difficulty of accessing plaintext and keys interferes with the intelligibility of the data obtained : from now on, judicial investigation will sometimes consist less of obtaining data than of giving meaning to it. The draft LSQ covers three hypothetical working situations, the last of which raises a number of difficulties.

a) *Access to plaintext and to keys by the courts*

Whatever the maximum penalty incurred, the court may call for any qualified person to obtain access to plaintext and/or the secret decryption convention. The qualified person must give an account of his endeavours to the requesting court. In order to access the plaintext without the key, where appropriate, the qualified person may use cryptoanalysis.

b) *Access to plaintext and to keys by the administrative authority*

So far as concerns so-called security interception for the purposes of « *seeking information affecting national security, safeguarding essential aspects of France's scientific and economic potential or the prevention of terrorism, crime and organised crime* », the Prime Minister has grounds for sending an order directly to the person who provides cryptology services designed to ensure confidentiality, to provide the key or indeed the plaintext.

c) *Access to plaintext without the key by the court*

When the maximum penalty incurred is two years' imprisonment or more the court « *may order the use of the State's resources subject to the confidentiality of National defence* » by addressing its order in this case to the Central Office to Combat crime connected with new information and communication technologies, which passes the order to a technical department subject to National Defence confidentiality and appointed by decree. The technical service that receives the order is not subject to any obligation to report to the requesting court.

Here we have a fundamental contradiction between the end and the means, in that the concern for the effectiveness of the investigation and the protection of national defence harms the rights of defence period! In fact, if the prosecution uses the plaintext as part of the evidence against the accused, the latter must be able to dispute the circumstances in which those items of evidence were obtained, which is impossible if the means of uncoded access are not submitted to the proceedings. It cannot be ruled out that the court in question might only analyse the plaintext as the as a clue or anonymous piece of information, which would limit the scope of the law.

4. – *Dilution of the written word : videoconferencing via the Internet and electronic mail*

Videoconferencing via the Internet allows the traditional requirement of the written word to be placed in perspective since the digitisation of enquiry reports is a new medium for investigative measures.

In the long term, electronic mail should also become a favoured real time medium for communication between the courts and the police authorities, to the detriment of the traditional paper mail. However, that situation presupposes that the issue of security and authentication of exchanges of computer information between units has been resolved.

B. – INVESTIGATIONS
CONTAINING ONE OR MORE EXTRANEOUS FACTORS

Like judicial investigations, mutual assistance in criminal matters also appears to be marked by a trend towards dematerialisation. The second major trend, in Europe at least, is the development of judicial cooperation towards further European integration.

1. – *Dematerialisation of mutual assistance*

When a cross-border investigation takes place on the networks, the investigating authority is sometimes technically in a position to recover from its own territory data that is situated in another country without the need to have recourse to mutual assistance in criminal matters. In the long term, no doubt there will be a shift in the very concept of mutual assistance which will no longer necessarily correspond to an investigative action taken by the requested State at the request of the applicant State but rather to the simple authorisation by the requested State to the applicant State to carry out the envisaged action itself.

a) *Searches using communications technology*

Article 32 of the Council of Europe Convention governs *a minima* searches using communications technology, by reiterating the compromise reached by the G8 countries within the Lyons group. In fact, searches are only allowed when they relate to data available from an open source or when they are handed over with the legal, voluntary consent of its owner.

b) *Videoconferencing*

Provided for by Article 10 of the European Union Convention on mutual assistance in criminal matters of 29 May 2000, videoconferencing will probably be implemented thanks to the Internet. Accordingly, States will be able to substitute traditional requests for mutual judicial assistance with requests for hearings by *webcams*. Italy and Austria already have this facility and France has just included it in the draft LSQ.

c) *Mutual recognition*

Point 33 of the conclusions of the Tampere European Council (15-16 October 1999) calls on the States to allow court rulings made by Member States to be effective outside the territory. In other words, a ruling made in a State whose legal system satisfies the fundamental rules in Human Rights issues should be able to be enforced in another State which meets the same criteria. The implementation of the principle of mutual recognition could be a partial answer to the difficulties surrounding the freezing of computer-held data threatened with destruction on the territory of a State other than that to which the investigation relates.

In a communication dated 26 January 2001, the Commission announced normative plans concerning mutual recognition applied to the networks. However, it would appear that that plan has been postponed *sine die*.

2. – *European integration of mutual assistance*

a) *The legal bases for judicial cooperation*

Article 15, paragraph 2 of the Council of Europe Convention on mutual assistance of 20 April 1959 authorises the direct court to court transmission of rogatory commissions in urgent cases. That transfer may take place by electronic means of communication, subject to the introduction of reliable security and authentication measures.

Furthermore, the wording of Article 29 and following of the Council of Europe Convention on cybercrime provides for the obligation of each Party State to be able to expedite the retention of data stored on its territory or indeed to simply seize it.

b) *The operational instruments of judicial cooperation*

Within the European Union, Eurojust and the European Judicial Network should speed up requests and enforcement documents in cases of mutual assistance. Europol, whose mandate is shortly to be extended to computer crime could also be helpful in supporting common investigation teams which Member States of the European Union may create when faced with offences of a cross-border dimension (Article 13 of the Convention of 29 May 2000).

Moreover, Article 35 of the Council of Europe Convention provides for the establishment of a permanently operational network of points of contact, so as to be able to issue, receive and transmit information originating from or destined for another country. Directly inspired by the network of points of contact set up within the G8 at the Washington summit in December 1997, this network may not however substitute for the appropriate central and/or local authorities for mutual judicial assistance.

Three proposals can be put forward by way of a conclusion :

The Internet, a technical revolution, will radically change the way in which judicial investigations are conducted by contributing to their relative dematerialisation.

That technical revolution will facilitate the introduction of the new investigative techniques prescribed by the recent European instruments for judicial cooperation in criminal matters.

During the years 2000, the Internet will accordingly enable judicial investigations to free themselves to some extent from the principle of territoriality and will speed up the establishment of the European area of freedom, security and justice announced by the Treaty of Amsterdam.

INTERNET
AND JUDICIAL INVESTIGATION :
DIFFICULTIES IN JUDICIAL PRACTICE

Jacques PLAYS

Squadron leader
General Headquarters of the national Gendarmerie

The development of the Internet opens up a new field of action for the criminal investigation department and without altering its intrinsic nature, poses specific problems.

Since the criminal investigation department is responsible for establishing breaches against criminal law, gathering evidence and seeking out those responsible, we shall concentrate on these stages to demonstrate the need both to adapt resources and for the specific training of those involved.

I. – Establishing offences

A. – Offences discovered

1. – *The Internet, is it just a medium or the main vehicle for offences*

Traditionally, two categories of offences can be distinguished : those that use the Internet as a medium for traditional criminal offences and those that are specific offences and include all misconduct against information systems.

The simplicity of that division and the proper adjustment of French law to the various types of criminal behaviour does little to conceal the lack of harmony of criminal law within the most industrialised countries. In fact, the transnational nature of the network is still a problem when enforcing criminal law. Since 1997, the most industrialised States have sought solutions within the G8 proceedings. An action plan decided by the Ministers for Justice and Ministers for the Interior was approved during the Birmingham summit in 1998, whilst the Council of Europe initiated a plan to draw up an international convention on cybercrime.

The diversity of national situations with regard to criminal offences is partially illustrated by the example below taken from the G8 States.

2. – *Unauthorised access to or penetration of a system*

Access is unauthorised when it is gained by a person who is not entitled to access the system whatever the means employed. That lack of authority may arise from failure to comply with a protocol or from an access profile that is non-existent or insufficient to take account of a level of secrecy imposed by national legislation. However, that action does not necessarily constitute an offence in all the industrialised States. Accordingly, Russia does not punish unauthorised access to a computer.

When that behaviour constitutes an offence, there can be differences in assessment.

Accordingly, a charge of fraudulent access may relate to a public or private network without distinction. That is the case in Italy and Germany. By contrast, the United-States only consider it to be an offence if the fraudulent access concerns a government website.

In the Canadian Penal Code (Art. 342.1) the intention to cause harm must be established in order to institute proceedings. That is not the case, for example, with French law which points out that the access must merely be intentional.

Finally, some States (British 1990 Computer Misuse Act) expressly state that there is no need for the system to be protected in order to define the offence.

B. – SEEKING OUT OFFENCES

1. – *The low number of complaints*

Although for some offences that directly target individuals or businesses, proceedings are traditionally instituted by lodging a complaint, an increasing number of direct reports from user-witnesses can be observed. In that respect, it should be noted that where illegal content is detected, the effectiveness of spontaneous testimonies will depend on the effort made to promote information about the available possibilities for reporting the offence.

However, it may be in the victims' interests not to declare the damage they have suffered. In fact, cybercrimes frequently go unreported, either through ignorance, lack of confidence in the solutions offered or the desire to avoid bad publicity.

In the United-States, an FBI Computer Crime and Security Survey highlighted the reluctance of the security services of the main public or private bodies to account for the number and nature of computer related attacks they had suffered. Accordingly, three out of four times the fear of bad publicity and the admission of weakness with regard to the competition are cited. Hence the search for ever stronger passive protection (firewall) and the failure to report the offences to the law-enforcement agencies who are deprived of experience.

2. – *Proactive searching*

The law-enforcement agencies cannot just give a reactive response but must actively seek out offences and introduce effective monitoring of the network.

In an open environment, the need to obtain relevant information that is buried amongst general data makes that search difficult and tedious. The use of search engines is essential but human intervention is still vital in order to frustrate attempts conceal it. Effective monitoring of the network must therefore be carried out by staff who are qualified and dedicated to that task. Apart from the role reserved for the central office for the fight against crime connected with information technologies and communication (1), in 1998, within its *service technique de recherches judiciaires et de documentation (STRJD)* (technical department for judicial and documentation searches) the gendarmerie created the national centre for monitoring the Internet. Acting on its own initiative or at the

---

(1) The role of the office is the subject of a presentation by Commissioner Mrs Chambon; it will therefore not be examined here.

request of units, it is responsible for implementing measures to combat offences against property and harm caused to persons or the interests of the State by the circulation of messages of an illegal nature. The centre also coordinates the actions of regional monitoring units set up within the thirty research sections. The national centre and the regional centres are responsible for :

– checking that a site exists, following information provided by an Internet user;
– looking for information for the purposes of analysing relevant phenomena for specific classes of offences (paedophilia, etc.);
– identifying servers;
– capturing sites in order to preserve information or technical evidence;
– monitoring a site's activity (they also have the power to monitor forums or chat rooms).

They carry out targeted searches or random monitoring of the network in order to detect suspect sites in a preventative manner.

The offences detected are reported to the investigation units by sending a technical file listing the facts that constitute the offences discovered and the legislation relating to them. The investigation, designed to identify the perpetrator of the deeds, is conducted by the unit that has territorial jurisdiction in accordance with the appropriate judicial procedure. However, often the courts ask the investigators to reiterate the findings, which poses problems when in the meantime the site in question has migrated or ceased operating. That difficulty can be resolved by awarding national jurisdiction to the personnel in charge of monitoring the network.

Finally, only offences committed on French territory or by a French person in a foreign country, or those that involve an accomplice are taken into account (2). For the rest, the information is passed on to Interpol to be forwarded to the countries in question.

---

(2) In 2000, the gendarmerie's national monitoring centre handled 155 cases proactively, including 95 commercial forgeries and infringements of copyright, 13 incidences of decoder piracy, 11 breaches of drugs legislation, 8 cases relating too child pornography and 4 to racism as well as 24 miscellaneous.

II. – Gathering evidence
and identifying the person responsible

A. – FREEZING DATA
AND THE SEARCH FOR DIGITAL EVIDENCE

1. – *Clearly identified needs*

When the investigator arrives at the scene of a crime, as the first person to get involved, he is responsible for sealing off the scene and preserving the evidence. On the Internet, the data is the only available trace. It is even more necessary to preserve it because :

– it is potentially very fleeting whereas the complaint could take a long time;
– international police or judicial cooperation will never be immediate and in some countries where there are innumerable problems, it will be difficult and slow;
– the data could be used as evidence related to another crime and the relevance of their use might become apparent belatedly;

A minimum of data, relating either to the user or to the communication itself must therefore be retained :

– the user's company identity (name and forename), if it is a question of commercial data permanently held by the access provider;
– the login;
– the e-mail address, where one exists;
– the physical identifier of the origin of the communication (depending on the type of apparatus, telephone number of the caller, modem number, ADSL number etc.);
– the date and GMT time of the beginning and end of the connection;
– the IP source address or any other information that enables a connection to be linked to a user.

Content data is not retained but in specific cases there may be targeted retention following letters rogatory.

2. – *Continuing difficulties*

The debate on the nature and duration of retention of this data has not been settled : the law on everyday security imposes an obligation on access providers to retain technical data for the requirements of the criminal investigation department but leaves the details of it to a forthcoming decree by the *Conseil d'Etat* after an opinion from the CNIL (the French national committee for IT freedoms). The one-year retention period, announced as a maximum, is considered to be essential by all the investigation authorities.

Moreover, since the issue of computer eavesdropping is settled by analogy to telephone tapping devices (3), we must simply acquire adequate technical resources. This is all the more important since the concept of a remote search was rejected for legitimate reasons connected with the protection of personal freedoms. Admittedly, such an investigative procedure also raises technical problems for « breaking » any protection as well as problems of discretion. However, a recent case concerning child pornography showed the savings of time and resources that the investigators would have been able to make from such a possibility when 71 simultaneous home searches had to be carried out by staff who were specially trained in this type of computer manipulation.

Finally, any legislative progress must be modulated because of the international nature of the network and the lack of global coordination. In particular, since the periods for data retention are often short, sometimes only a few weeks, for financial reasons, a number of items of evidence will no doubt escape the investigator. Inevitably, that will adversely affect investigations relating to money laundering criminal organisations for example.

B. – SEEKING OUT THE PERPETRATOR

1. – *Anonymity made easy*

Technical identification may not lead to incriminating someone. In fact, even though one comes across cases of fraudulent use of IPs the investigators come up against the problems connected with new methods of accessing the Internet (mobile telephone, public terminals) which make it more complicated to identify the person responsible. Moreover, we are still faced with the problem of

---

(3) In fact, the current position confirms the application of Article 100 of the Code of Penal Procedure on computer eavesdropping.

anonymity both through the appearance of services that provide anonymity and the use of proxy sites.

The existence of servers that guarantee total anonymity, possibly including deletion of data likely to identify the Internet user, is a real stumbling block for law enforcement. Only harmonisation of national legislation would put an end to the problem once and for all.

Furthermore, the use of proxy sites by access providers in order to make transactions more fluid could have the same effect as the anonymity providers since the data are only retained for a few hours.

2. – *The increased use of cryptography*

For two years there has been a sharp increase in the use of cryptography which makes it more difficult to access data stored or exchanged on the Internet. On this point, the law provides investigators with guarantees, firstly, by imposing punishment for failing to hand over deciphering keys of the plaintext document to the relevant authorities, and secondly, when the sentence exceeds two years' imprisonment, the right to call on the specialist resources of the State which is covered by national defence confidentiality. This latter possibility guarantees investigators access to the best specialists, especially when the fact that the holder of the decoding keys is outside the territory raises problems.

III. – Technicality and training : a dual essential requirement

A. – THE NEED FOR CONTINUAL TECHNICAL SUPPORT

The handling of digital evidence raises problems at all levels. Incorrect handling of a computer can alter a potential item of evidence. A badly conducted police operation can make the available digital evidence unusable. That is why the work must be carried out by experts, or alternatively, by well informed staff.

The technical resources deployed determine the success of the operation. Therefore a gendarmerie unit may have the technical support and expertise of a specialist department within the *institut*

de recherches criminelles de la gendarmerie (IRCGN) – the gendarmerie's institute of criminal research (4) – and the technical support
of the central office acting as an expert.

The IRCGN's most common tasks are to :

– determine the origin of a message or illegal publication;
– detail the use that has been made of software specific to the
  Internet (recovery of e-mails, proof of exchanges of files...);
– pinpoint the perpetrator of a computer offence;
– arrange for eavesdropping on a computer network.

The problem linked to this need for technical support is a question of human and financial resources in view of the sharp rise in
this type of offence.

B. – ESSENTIAL TRAINING AT ALL LEVELS

The first people to arrive at the scene of a home search need to
know simple manipulation techniques. To that end, several guides
have been drawn up by various police agencies but they must be
more widely circulated and better promoted. It is a considerable
training programme to achieve, especially since the rapidity with
which techniques and technologies evolve requires it to be
monitored and updated.

The digital evidence collected is transferred to a specialist
investigator who might want to have rapid access to information
stored in order to evaluate its relevance to the enquiry without
relying on laboratory work. However, in some cases it is possible to
read the information recorded on a digital medium using simple
equipment without altering the original evidence. The investigator
must therefore be in a position to rapidly establish both the potential usefulness of the data and the complexity of extracting it with
a view to deciding whether it is necessary to call in an expert. That
is why the gendarmerie has created « new technology » training
courses aimed at its detectives from investigation units and the
national police are training *enquêteurs spécialisés en criminalité
informatique* (ESCI) – investigators who are specialists in computer
crime. However, it is vital that their knowledge is updated in order
to guarantee the effectiveness of their work. This concern is com-

---

(4) This department also has powers for memory cards and telephony.

mon to all European police forces. Accordingly, in Germany, specific twelve-week training courses have just been created.

We shall not dwell on the training of laboratory forensic specialists as it is so obvious that it must be effective and kept up to date.

Having thus provided training for specialists and technical experts, the issue is not quite settled. In order to meet the expectations of the public, individuals and businesses (5), it is essential to have a large number of staff who are able to deal with complaints. However this is not provided as some investigators who have little awareness of computers as a new vehicle for crime are so reticent and apprehensive. Similarly, other categories of staff involved in judicial investigations and, first and foremost, the judges, must be taught about the opportunities for committing offences on the network and the legal and technical resources at their disposal. A common training for the criminal investigation department and judges is therefore essential in order to establish a common methodology and language for Internet investigations.

Moreover, that cooperation can be fostered by the administrations concerned operating as a network. Encouraging transparency of inter-departmental exchanges and, therefore, mutual confidence and knowledge, must improve the partnership that is vital to criminal investigation work.

Apart from the obstacles to the smooth running of the investigation that can be created by the international aspect of the Internet and the problems connected with international police and judicial cooperation, a criminal investigation enquiry relating to cybercrime mainly causes difficulties of a technical nature, requiring a specific know-how on the part of the investigators and considerable support from the expert. The issue of staff training is therefore vital in order to guarantee the success of operations. Nevertheless, the decisive issue is still that of data retention without which nothing can be done in view of the paramountcy of digital evidence.

---

(5) Companies that do not have computer security departments must be able to call on the police and gendarmerie services who are able to advise them as an « expert ».

DISCUSSION

Francis Teitgen

Thank you.

Thank you Madam Commissioner.

The floor is open to the hall for any questions or comments.

The first is the most complicated. There are requests to speak, here and there. Yes, be so kind as to introduce yourself.

Yves Poullet

My name is Yves Poullet. I should like to ask Mr de Vel a question. It is an observation I made whilst listening to the various addresses, especially with regard to the storage of traffic data. You said at the beginning that the Council of Europe's convention was extremely clear : no anticipatory monitoring, no exploratory monitoring and that monitoring would only be triggered when an offence is discovered. I then listened to Mr Noël who began to talk about potential data storage. Mr Jacques Plays went much further since he spoke about the needs for investigation which made it necessary to store data for a certain period of time – we know the period proposed in France, one year; since I am Belgian, I can simply say that we preceded you because at home it is a minimum period of one year – and he spoke about storing all connection data saying that, in any event, the access providers already did so for invoicing purposes. I presume that you aware of the scope of the discussion that is currently taking place within Europe on the problem of storing traffic data. Therefore, it seems to me – I am expressing my point of view, although I acknowledge that it is a complex problem – that the problem of the security aspect has perhaps been exaggerated after September 11. Obviously, we know that what happened was terrible but also that it happened independently of any computer crime. So therefore, all of a sudden, taking advantage of the security aspect which is currently being debated, we are rushing towards what really seems to be the best way of tracing the behaviour of every individual, that is to say computer tracing. Everyone knows that the use of the Internet leaves information at various levels and that no doubt it is the easiest way of recovering such information. So, for how long and for what type of offence? Naturally, you spoke about paedophilia; that is the example that everyone chooses, or, possibly, money laundering. You should know that the most important research that is decided on the subject has nothing to do with these issues, it concerns problems of intellectual property, and that the lobbies are there in the background to try and obtain the necessary information. Accordingly, for what type of offence and in what context? You spoke about international coopeation but everyone is familiar with the events and action of Europol on the subject. I should like to think that when this international cooperation takes place, certain people will provide the same guarantees as those that exist at national level – that is to say the fact that it is based on a judicial decision and external supervision by an independent body – particularly in the context of relations with the United States where we are not sure that these guarantees exist in the same way. There you are, Mr de Vel, I do not have much idea what the Council of Europe thinks; it was the champion of human rights and data protection, now it has become the champion of security, perhaps rather in spite of itself. So I should be very interested in your reaction in this respect.

Guy de Vel

Thank you very much, Mr le Doyen. First of all I should like to say that, generally speaking, the questions of data protection and the prevention and fight against crime are all heading in the same direction. I can tell you that those who are responsible for this Cybercrime convention are experienced people, either from the registry of the Court of Human Rights or from the Human Rights division, like myself, or the Human Rights Commission. So I do not think that you can suspect us of suddenly abandoning human rights. I should also like to say that so far as concerns the events of September 11, the Convention was formally adopted on 8 November, after the events of September 11, but it is clear that the wording was finalised well before, and nothing was changed after September 11 although this legislation has arrived at the right moment. I should also like to say, so far as concerns human rights and guarantees, that to begin with, the preamble to the Convention makes ample reference – reference not only to European legislation, such as the European Human Rights Convention, the Data Protection Convention, but also to the United Nations Protocol, because we must not lose sight of the fact that non-European States are invited to become parties and that they are not all necessarily bound by European legislation. So, with regard to guarantees, I should like to refer you to Article 15 of the Convention – no doubt you will be familiar with it – which recommends very precise guarantees and which, in addition, refers to the guarantees that must exist in national laws and which, in turn, must comply with the European Human Rights Convention, it is absolutely clear in all our Member States. All Member States, except for two, have ratified the Convention and these two Member States will no doubt ratify it shortly.

So, so far as concerns the time-limit for storing data, I should like to refer you to Article 29 of the Convention, which provides that any storage shall be valid for a period of at least 60 days to enable the requesting party to submit an entry and search application or access by a similar means, seizure or access by a similar means, or disclosure of the data. The maximum period for storing such data is 90 days, that is to say, three months.

Mr Noël was involved in drafting the Convention.

Jean-Wilfried Noël

No, I would just like to add something to Mr Poullet's address. It should be remembered that the Council of Europe includes more than 40 States and accordingly, during negotiations, this results in many sensibilities being expressed. In relation to the very sensitive question of data storage, I think that matters can be summarised as follows : some States were in favour of creating a legal obligation in proper form, for storing connection data, the responsibility for which lies with operators. France was one of these States. From another point of view, some States, whilst agreeing to the desirability of accessing these famous connection data, because they enable criminal information to be identified and therefore traced, preferred to act on a more consensual basis, shall we say, by developing partnerships : a kind of informal cooperation with providers, at the risk, « but that only concerns France », in my view, of clouding the issue somewhat and exposing the police services to some difficulties, in that the requesting police services could possibly have been faced with a different connection time depending on the access supplier to whom they made the application. Be that as it may, the Council of Europe very wisely, took formal note of this divergence of the means of implementing the storage of data, and, as Article 17 of the Convention shows, the Council of Europe was keen to finalise wording that would not make anything compulsory but which, at the same time, would enable each State to impose this obligation in its domestic law. Accordingly, on that basis, there is no incompatibility between the letter and the spirit of the Strasbourg wording and the letter and the spirit of the LSQ – *Loi sur la sécurité quotidienne* – (French everyday security Act), which I shall say in passing, is confined to reiterating the provisions for criminal matters which appeared in a draft known as LSI – *Loi sur la société de l'information* (the French Information Society Act) – which was completed well before the events of September 11. Therefore, as far as France is concerned, I would say that the attacks on September 11 modified the content, in that criminal provisions were transferred into a specifically criminal piece of legislation, and, in any event, those provisions had been designed to be incorporated into the general law on the information society which contains numerous other non-criminal provisions. Just a word to add that, of course, (and that can also be seen in the Everyday Security Act in France), the rights afforded to the law-enforcement agencies must, in any event, comply with principles, and, in particular, the principle of purpose which is expressed in the Council of Europe Convention of 28 January 1981, under which data collected and processed by one department cannot be used for purposes other than those that had initially justified their collection. This type of provision can also be found in EU Directive 97/66.

Francis Teitgen

I am going to take advantage, however, of my position as chairman because I very much agree with what you have just said, Judge, but when you say that to remove a text from the LSI and insert it in the LSQ has no kind of consequence, I cannot agree with you. For the uninitiated : the Information Society Act : a completed draft in which there are a number of provisions that are criminal provisions. This legislation is under discussion. The Everyday Security Act : the debate has been very much accelerated since September 11. Three criminal provisions have been taken from the

LSI – Information Society – and placed in the LSQ which contains only penal provisions. Personally speaking, admittedly, the wording has not been amended, but two things : firstly, parliamentary debate has been seriously shortened; secondly, for a judge, the interpretation of the legislator's intention also depends on the environment in which the legislation is placed. The LSQ environment does not have much in common with the LSI environment. And finally, it is the example I always give : with regard to the Everyday Security Act, we recently heard the president of a police officer's union say : « I am in favour of the fact that, in the context of the anti-terrorist law, the opening of car boots is authorised ». Be that as it may. And he added « In fact, that will help us to fight everyday crime ». Well there it is. All the same, I think that one should not cut short the debate over the way in which this country legislates, clearly under pressure after September 11, as it can appear to be more of a pretext than an overriding necessity to combat crime. Because all the same, it does not seem to me that computer safety was the very centre or vehicle for the crimes of September 11. I don't have that impression. In any event, the proof had not been provided for the time being. Apologies for having taken the floor. Madam, I believe you asked to speak.

Catherine Kessedjian

President of the Bar Association, my contribution is very tentative after what you have just said. Catherine Kessedjian, Professor at Panthéon-Assas. Indeed, I should like both to pick up on what my colleague Mr Poullet said and make a comment on cross-border crime, particularly on international cooperation between the authorities responsible for combating that crime. On the storage of traffic data, I am a little concerned that no mention was made this afternoon of a tool that seems to me to be available to criminals and perhaps less available to others, which is called the erasure of any trace on the net. However, nowadays, the companies that specialise in producing extremely refined software that erases any trace of activity on the net are companies that have no difficulty in finding the necessary capital to provide finance. I have in mind the example of a Canadian firm which is on its third financial package for millions and millions of dollars. Therefore, it seems to me that there is a problem there and I should very much like those who spoke at the beginning of this afternoon to explain what our authorities are doing to counter this ability to erase all traces on the net. I am well aware that this morning we were told that that it was not 100 %, possible but the information that I have reveals that after all, it is possible. So that is a debate for technical experts but nevertheless it also creates an anxiety, in any case for a citizen like myself : I am concerned when I hear that in fact any trace of a message on the net can be erased. Secondly, and in fact it was my initial observation, on international cooperation : this is not a new problem. One can see enormous difficulties, and there again I am speaking as a concerned citizen, about what our authorities are doing with regard to international cooperation. In 1996, I had the opportunity to take part in research conducted by the University of Bourgogne research centre. That resulted in a book on unlawful behaviour in international relations. There was a discussion between the World Customs Council, Interpol, Europol and other organisations that are so-called organisations that will facilitate this international cooperation. However, these institutions have publicly admitted that they were not talking to each other. That they were not talking to each other! I therefore think that there is a problem; In reality, the Internet does not create a new problem, it has existed for a long time. The Internet simply requires that we react differently as it creates extra complicating factors : the potential number of victims that is increased by use of the Internet. Ubiquity, since the Internet is everywhere. I am rather surprised that the Judge told us this afternoon that it was nowhere. No, it is not nowhere. And the rules of territoriality that we have with regard to jurisdiction mean that each State has such jurisdiction; therefore it is not nowhere, it is everywhere. I must emphasise this point because I think it is rather a pity to allow it to be said that it is nowhere. And the time factor : it is very fast. Remember what we used to say about mafias who used very fast cars at the time when cars were the burning issue and the authorities did not have the necessary tools.

Francis Teitgen

Perhaps Mrs Chambon's would like to reply.

Catherine Chambon

Gladly, thank you Chairman. Well, I am delighted to hear these questions... By way of history I shall quote Georges Clémenceau who created the Tiger Brigades and equipped them with vehicles that replaced their bicycles because the criminals were already mobile. Therefore, let us now imagine that we are on the information highways; not only do the criminals have high speed trains to get around, but what is more they have the means to make them disappear immediately, without ever being able to be found again. So far as concerns erasure, we are faced ever more frequently and markedly with anonymisation. What we call anonymisation, is an entire relatively simple or complex circuit, depending on the case, which helps traces to disappear and therefore the chance of identifying the perpetrators. That having been said and placed in parallel with the concept of the time-limit for storage, it is obvious that it complicates matters. I would point out, however, in reply to the Chairman of the session, that the LSQ, reiterating the LSI, establishes the principle of erasure of data, except for invoicing and security requirements. It is these terms that are currently being decided in order to be inserted in decrees. However, despite everything, just like the provisions of the Telecoms Directive, the principle is erasure. That is to say that the obligation to erase data in a number of cases is added to the natural erasure that occurs on the net. We have an almost ideal combination which can be extremely favourable to criminals, even if these provisions are, of course, clearly necessarily protective of freedoms in a number of cases. So far as concerns the need for investigators to have appropriate measures, in fact, we cannot – I think I said so – be content with the principle of dematerialisation. The investigations are necessarily objective, the people we arrest are physically recognisable human beings and we cannot be content with virtual evidence which, moreover, is extremely impermanent. Therefore, the tools are legal : a maximum legislative harmony, that is important and technical measures as well, so that we have a capability without being harmful to a number of things, a right to have information that will guarantee that security. The third and last point is international cooperation. You are right to emphasise the appearance of a multitude of partners responsible for providing such cooperation, or in any case, for implementing it. However you make reference to bodies which, admittedly, do not necessarily speak to each other but which are nevertheless each involved in the debate and invite each other when it is a matter of moving certain topics forward, in particular cybercrime. It is not completely untrue to say that they are regularly, whether it be G8, Europol or Interpol, involved in the debate. I think that it is more a problem of principle. Nevertheless, these institutions exist. Interpol has been around for a very long time. It is seasoned and despite everything it guarantees the effectiveness of information transfer; of course, it then clashes with domestic law but it is a fantastic communication tool. Its use is very widespread and of course it is well known to the police and justice departments. So far as concerns Europol, this is a more restrictive area, since it is confined to Europe – Europol. This is more a case of making the analytical tools available to a number of investigators; accordingly, it does not have the same operational documentation function as Interpol can have. Although they do not compete with each other, one can say that nevertheless, they sometimes work in parallel.

Jacques Plays

Yes, I should just like to add something. From the point of view of international cooperation, it is true that it is not new, there are problems. Neither should we exaggerate the difficulties as Mrs Chambon has just pointed out. However, for your first comment regarding the technical possibilities of anonymisation that I mentioned very briefly, I think that we can turn your comment regarding the second question around : this is not new either. In the entire history of the investigative police, criminals have always been ahead, when they use their brain a little, and I think that the law-enforcement agencies are also equipped with a brain. If the problem remains solely technical, I am very confident that it will be resolved. In my view, the problems facing us are more difficult to resolve when they are legal rather than technical. We have already introduced both in the office and in the gendarmerie's institution for criminal research, highly effective tools to counter all the technologies used by the criminals, at least for the few years of observation that we have. It is clear that we will monitor the technology as the criminals are monitoring it. It is an everyday race but for that one at least, I am confident. Thank you.

Francis Teitgen

I suggest that we adjourn the proceedings and return at 4pm precisely; during the break, you could discuss the respective merits of the pursuing authorities' brains and those of the criminals!

2. – GOVERNANCE
OF THE INTERNET AND TRUST

THE INTERNET, A DEFECTIVE GOVERNANCE

BY

Richard DELMAS

Principle administrator (*) European commission,
Information society, Directorate general

> « *Names must be carefully balanced with the spirit
> of the language for which they are created* » (**).

Guyton de Morveau, 1774

The Internet is now at the crossroads of the information and financial spheres, at the juncture between private and public areas. From the outset, the *network of networks* has been engaged in ontological ambiguity : the need of government agencies for isolation, secrecy and security but also inclusiveness, freedom and concern for autonomy for researchers and universities. Since the nineties, with the widespread use of the *web* and the domain name system as a universal identifier, a commercial, merchant mind-set has been adopted, *e-commerce*, without weighing up the regulatory adjustments required for this transformation. However, denomination, the power to name, also includes a societal and ethical dimension. And the sudden emergence of the market into the Internet environment has upset the balances that have been established since the 1970s. Even today, there is no specific regulatory framework for the Internet.

Governance of the Internet is presented as an imperfect form of regulation, a « staircase world » in which each landing would be suspended from its own legitimacy and unique method of organisation, irrespective of any overall coherence or hierarchy. Accordingly, there would be many « Internet » models, operating in tandem : the new economy, electronic commerce, online democracy, the digital

---

(*) The opinions expressed in this text are those of the author and do not necessarily reflect the position of the European Commission.
(**) Unofficial translation

divide, the network infrastructure, free exchanges, protection of data and trade marks, encryption, security, etc.

However, it is possible to identify the modes of « governance » of the Internet from the point of view of its animation and coordinating functions. It would seem to me that recognition of the standard and the law finds a preferred field of application in the phenomenon of the Internet and the domain names system and that of its management

I. – Governance and consensus

It should be remembered that at an international level, recognition of the Internet has been achieved by the regulation of a technology. It consisted of specifying and stabilising, through an organisation, the IETF (Internet Engineering Task force), assisted by the IAB (Internet Architecture Board), the series of Internet technical protocols established in the 1960s by the ARPANET network, at the instigation of the American agencies concerned, DARPA (Defence Advanced Research Projects Agency) and NSF (National Science Foundation).

This process took place outside the traditional information technology standardisation and harnessed the consensus of the world community of researchers and developers with the financial support of the industries concerned. The system is still operational and functions effectively.

In reality, the process has not given rise to any specific legislation : the IP protocols, which became *de facto* standards and PAS (*Public Available Specifications*) have been swallowed up in a general movement towards open standardisation.

At the same time, the physical infrastructure of the networks, initially borne by the American agencies, universities and research centres such as CERN in Europe, has been taken up by the computer and telecommunications industry.

A. – THE EMERGENCE
OF REGULATION CHALLENGES

In 1997, the Clinton administration wanted to transfer the management of the DNS system to the private sector. The main reason for this was the need to put an end to a *de facto* monopoly, particularly as regards the management of generic domain names (.com), which appeared to contradict the aims of transparency and openness to competition. But also, with the widespread use and commercial success of the *web,* the American authorities thought it would be opportune to obtain consensus on the detailed rules of the phenomenon from all interested parties.

The approach was based on two principles : 1) recognition of the function of switching the Internet to a global scale and ii) the need to ensure enduring stability of the system. These two requirements, still provided by the supervision of the American administration, rely on a three-pronged mechanism : 1) the domain names system (DNS), 2) the allocation of IP addresses by regional registers, 3) the consortium of the 13 route servers which are still administrated and financed on a voluntary basis, essentially by American agencies or universities (there are two route servers in Europe, in London and Stockholm).

The discussions which opened in 1998 at the time of the American government's Green Paper, followed by the White Paper, enabled the European Union to have an influence on the process of creating ICANN at the time it was launched.

Thanks to the action taken by the Commission and Member States, general principles – this time of a legal and not technical nature – were put forward : the applicability of international law – internationalisation of the system – opening up the DNS system to competition. Moreover, a consultative committee of governments (GAC) was appointed to ICANN to highlight the objectives of public policy and those of the international community of states.

In actual fact, the entire system is still a project led by the American authorities, in particular by the Department of Commerce, which exercises direct supervision over ICANN and the route servers' system. Accordingly, at the end of 1998, ICANN entered into a series of agreements with the American authorities and the NSI/Verisign company which had a monopoly over generic domain names. Responsibility for the technical management and the transfer of technical functions that were previously operated by the ANA is gradually being devolved (1).

---

(1) The documents are available at : http://www.icann.org

ICANN's legal set-up must be put into perspective. It is now subject to a review process which should find a new balance between now and the end of 2002. It is really a matter of granting delegated powers rather than truly decentralised powers. The applicable law and appropriate jurisdictions are essentially under a North American system. The agreements and contracts are concluded by an organisation under Californian jurisdiction, responsible for managing a public resource and for services of general interest to the international community. In particular, the legal system of contracts to be concluded with national domain name registers (ccTLDs) raises problems that the international arbitration procedures will not always be able to resolve. Moreover, trade mark and intellectual property law is applicable to many disputes with domain name holders.

B. – The Community approach

Although the European Union and the Commission took part in the negotiation process, they are not contractually bound by the current undertakings. There is no agreement or international treaty relating to management of the Internet.

The communication from the Commission to the Council and to the European Parliament of 11 April 2000 on the organisation and management of the Internet enabled a preliminary assessment to be made. The communication emphasises that the Internet calls for light regulation, but one that is strong enough to fully encourage its potential in terms of creating businesses and jobs.

The Commission's basic recommendations are as follows :

– to elect members of the ICANN council by means of procedures that are transparent and globally representative;
– to register gTLDs and higher level domain names by country code (ccTLD) in accordance with the principles concerning intellectual property and the protection of personal data;
– to ensure that the financing of ICANN by the « registers » and « registration bureaux » is transparent and safe for domain names and IP addresses.

A Council resolution was approved during the Telecommunications Council of 3 October 2000. The wording provides that Member States and the Commission must continue their work with a view to achieving a real internationalisation of the management of the Internet, whilst complying with the requirements of public policy and international agreements.

II. – Tension between unity and plurality

A. – PLACING THE TECHNICAL STANDARD IN A SOCIAL CONTEXT

It should be pointed out that the procedure for creating and running ICANN shows a loss of the traditional reference points of political science and economic regulation. Since the 1998 White Paper, an artificial « consensus » culture has been promoted, which is presented as giving incontrovertible legitimacy to a particular mode of governance. In accordance with a consistent process in the Internet communities, the search for an impossible consensus leads to favouring the dynamics of judgment and persuasion of the actors. Here, for the DNS and ICANN, the system has been introduced to the advantage of some industries and not with the aim of encouraging the management of a common good for the benefit of the greatest number. Gradually, ICANN has allowed the establishment of a speculative and uncontrolled market for domain names and IP addresses, reflecting the economic value of what needs to be treated as a resource that is necessarily scarce and of public interest.

B. – TOWARDS A HYBRID INTERNET LAW

Recently, the Vice-President of the *Conseil d'Etat*, Renaud Denoix de Saint Marc (2), identifying an inexorable progression of common law compared to civil law, invited us to transcend the confrontation of these two families of law. It could be useful, so far as concerns the Internet, to examine the possibilities of creating a hybrid, with a view to a mixed law which would guarantee the concept of an asset forming part of the community, which has always underpinned the establishment of the major infrastructure networks, whilst leaving the public and private actors free to innovate and take the and initiative. That is the price for creating

---

(2) Renaud DENOIX DE SAINT MARC, in *Le débat*, n° 1115, Gallimard, May-August 2001.

a Europe of digital networks, based on social and cultural cohesion. The concepts of services with a general economic interest, of a universal service upholding the basic rights of the European Union are Community achievements which should be implemented in order to construct the integrated city state of the Internet.

INTERNET RIGHTS FORUM : AN INSTRUMENT OF GOVERNANCE

Isabelle FALQUE-PIERROTIN

Legal advisor to the Conseil d'Etat
President of the Forum of the Internet rights

The Internet Rights Forum is a 1901 law association, created in May 2001 with the support of the State with the aim of bringing together public and private players to construct the regulations and customs of the Internet. It is a unique European initiative which, although very new, is already showing its potential. The current period is decisive : it must enable the Forum to find its identity, its specific field of intervention in relation to the other regulatory agencies. My intention is to find out how much this tool is a response adapted to the question of « governance » of the Internet environment and how, in this new area of society, it can help to transpose the democratic values we espouse in Europe. Helping to build network courtesy, that, in fact, is the Forum's major ambition.

I. – Historical

Firstly, it is necessary to understand the path which led to the Forum, to put it in context from the point of view of French legal thinking on the Internet since 1996.

In fact, the Forum has not arisen by chance or from the thinking of a single person; it is the culmination of the collective thinking on regulation of the networks conducted in France since 1996 which was marked by the *Conseil d'Etat* report in 1998 and the report by Christian Paul in July 2000.

In 1996, France discovered the Internet through the scandal of the book written by Dr Gubler, President Mitterrand's doctor who, without authorisation, placed confidential information relating to the Head of State's illness online. The political world realised with horror that this technological innovation can leave the world of specialists and affect the public arena. This was the time of fear of an unregulated area, of a territory without any law in which only the principle of freedom prevailed.

In its July 98 report the *Conseil d'Etat* put an end to this fantasy once and for all : the Internet is an area in which the law applies and we must ensure that our major principles are transposed to this area : respect for private life, preservation of public policy and intellectual property... At the same time, self-regulation made its appearance : it is the spearhead of the Americans who, through Vice-President Al Gore and Bill Clinton's advisor, Ira Magaziner, claimed a determining if not exclusive role for businesses in laying down the rules of the Net. Events that showed the limits of self-regulation very soon gave the lie to that extreme position which was contradicted by a very determined government intervention regulation when the USA's major interests could be threatened. In the *Conseil d'Etat*'s report, self-regulation is considered not as a tool to replace regulation but as a means of implementing it in the new world of the Internet. This pragmatic approach to self-regulation, which fits in between gaps in the law and enables its practical application, is the approach that prevails today.

The last stage of the reflective thinking is co-regulation : it is that which is behind the creation of the Forum.

Let us concentrate for a moment on this term : it has had a great deal of success and sparked off many debates. It was mentioned only recently, when the key witnesses were being heard by judge Gomez in the *Front 14* case.

It is not a Crimea Conference between governments, businesses and civil society for power sharing : they are not equal and retain their respective responsibilities for regulation, that is to say, issuing legal rules. The essential issue now is to manage their constant interactions and articulate their effects. In fact, co-regulation, is taking into account the complex environment in which we live and the interdependency of the players. Accordingly, the world of the Internet invites a multilevel system of regulation.

Obviously it is quite complicated, perhaps even more complicated than inventing new regulations, but this is our world.

The Forum subscribes to that analysis and aims to give practical expression to it.

II. – The Forum's missions

There are three :

A. – CONSULTATION

This first mission gives a practical illustration of what co-regulation can be. For the Forum it is a question of working on the legal and social issues of the Internet, of getting public and private players together round a table and encouraging dialogue between them so that, where appropriate, they can reach a consensus. Businesses, administrations, associations and users will therefore meet with the aim of creating something together. In many cases, the questions raised do not offer obvious solutions; we must go beyond the sectorial approaches and find a balance between the divergent rights and freedoms. The Forum's contribution is to offer an authoritative process for dealing with these issues enabling everyone to have a better understanding of the others' point of view and a better appreciation of the areas of convergence and divergence. The aim of the Forum is to make decision-making easier by clarifying its parameters and, possibly, by making a recommendation.

Obviously, this activity is purely consultative. The Forum does not have any binding power. The major strength of its recommendations lies in the way in which they are drawn up and in the Socratic approach between the players which is reflected in them.

All this is new but not revolutionary! When the issues of medically assisted procreation, the sale of organs, experiments on embryos appeared at the beginning of the 90s the National Consultative Committee for Health and Life Sciences was created. It is true that its legal status is very different from that of the Forum but the spirit is the same : to offer a permanent, authoritative process for reaching a consensus on complex issues.

An interesting question is that of the positions of minority groups who at the end of the consultation process refuse to abide by the consensus reached. This does not pose any problem as long as the

Forum is not a deciding body and is not bound by any kind of majority rule. In this case, the Forum will make a note of these irreconcilable positions and the reasons behind them. However it will have played its role of facilitator, allowing everyone to express themselves fully and calmly and referring the final decision to both the public and private regulators.

We began to implement this consultation mission in June : three topics are now being considered : the Internet and labour relations, alternative methods of dispute resolution and hypertext links.

They have given rise to the creation of five working parties which have set a programme and timetable and are conducting their enquiries. Each group has placed a file online gathering together the textual references needed to understand the issues. You will find full information about these groups on the Forum's website : www.forumInternet.org.

I would draw your attention to the fact that the hypertext links group was created following public consultation which we launched on our website on 31 May and which showed this subject to be very important in the eyes of Internet users. Accordingly, at their suggestion, the Forum decided to address this subject.

B. – INFORMING THE GENERAL PUBLIC AND RAISING THEIR AWARENESS

This second dimension is essential because the first player of civility is the Internet user himself : he uses the network and is not always aware of his rights and obligations. On a more fundamental level, often he does not realise, (especially the younger ones), that he is faced with a new area of socialisation that needs to be tamed and mastered. It is even more harmful since the Internet user himself is a key influencer of developments on the Internet. The aim of the Forum is therefore to make the Internet user and more generally the public at large, aware of the specific nature of the Internet and to inform him of the regulations and customs that now apply to it. Today, that objective has been implemented by Forum's website which provides the Internet user with a database on the law and customs of the Internet, from a national and international point of view. In addition to this base there are questions-replies and practical forms offering very pragmatic replies to legal issues or customs that Internet users wonder about. Tomorrow, that introduction to Internet manners will manifest itself in action in schools, at *collège* level, and by the Forum having a presence in all public points of access. This groundwork, directed at Internet users and non-Internet users, is the condition for a collective appropriation of the Forum by citizens.

However the relationship with Internet users is not only vertical or just for information. The Forum would also like to include them in the collective construction process and seek their opinion on the subjects it is tackling. Although the Forum is an association of legal entities and does not take individuals as members, its objective is not to exclude them from consultation in the name of some kind of supremacy of experts especially as on the Internet, the individual is an important key influencer. Accordingly, each working party regularly places a progress report of its work online and can make use of a public discussion forum. An Internet user who visits the website is therefore invited not only to consume information but also to contribute and publicly express his point of view to the working party to which a summary of contributions is regularly presented. The Forum aims to create a « citizen's reaction » around its website. You are all invited to take part in these forums, to seize the opportunity they present for fuelling the debate.

The Internet and labour relations group has therefore opened a discussion forum designed to gather the experiences of Internet users at work in order to pick out and discuss with them the major issues arising from the introduction of the NICT (New Information and Communications Technologies) in businesses.

C. – INTERNATIONAL COOPERATION

The fact on which this third mission is based is simple : the legal issues of the networks are international. And yet, international organisations are relatively unsuited to deal with these issues for a number of reasons : they are slow, the major players of the Internet or the civil society are not members of them and finally they are specialists whereas the questions raised by the world of the network require a transverse approach. We therefore need to encourage a more informal, flexible and horizontal international dialogue on these issues, between public and private players and that will help to harmonise positions. The objective is to create a global community of sensibilities, a base for common understanding which can be decisive in the case of more traditional imposing initiatives. In order to implement that objective, the Forum wants to set up a network of foreign correspondents, public or private bodies who are concerned by its issues. These bodies are legally heterogeneous but they are all key influencers in their country.

The Forum has begun to weave this cloth, particularly at European level. Some, such as the Canadians are ready to join it but the most important work is yet to be done. In the very short-term, the website is in English so as to encourage the participation of foreign contributors.

III. – The organisation
of the Forum and its operating principles

In an organisation such as the Forum, its organisation and operating principles are essential in order to establish the identity and legitimacy of the tool.

Several characteristics can be mentioned :

– Firstly, the Forum is an association, therefore a private body, separate from the government authorities. This choice was made in 1998 by the *Conseil d'Etat* in order give a very clear affirmation of a non-governmental approach and one that is different from an independent regulatory authority. It is not a matter of involving the State in another form, or creating an add-on to the civil service. It is a question of introducing, with the financial assistance of the State, a mechanism whereby players can work together, facilitating the subsequent decisions of public and private regulators. Accordingly, the State is not a member of the Forum and that is justified by the fact that as public regulator, it may have to make a decision whereas the Forum makes recommendations. Similarly, and for the same reasons, the independent government authorities are not members of the Forum.

However, autonomy does not mean total separation : the Forum is not a private foundation on Internet law, neither is it a lobbying association for a limited number of particular interests. It is part of a process of general interest designed to draw common solutions from public and private players. This general interest is essential to ensure the legitimacy of the Forum and the positions it adopts. Apart from a mainly public means of financing, that objective is achieved by the participation of representatives of governments or regulatory authorities to the working parties' meetings. It is also achieved having transparent procedures and opening up the association to a wide variety of players : businesses, associations, public bodies, trade federations, local authorities...

In short, relations between the Forum and the public sphere fall somewhere between independence and proximity. It is this delicate balance which makes the Forum more attractive and guarantees that its recommendations will be at least listened to if not followed.

– Secondly, the Forum is based on a process of participatory democracy :

It is important that the work of the Forum can be open to all the players in order to gather the most varied points of view; it is also necessary to reconcile that objective with a concern that the working parties should be productive. In order to achieve that, two internal consultation committees have been set up which group together members in two separate colleges and which are consulted electronically before the Forum gives any recommendation or opinion. This mechanism allows a member who has not participated in the specific work of a working party to get his voice heard. Furthermore, from an external point of view, discussion forums with Internet users are open in liaison with the working parties. This allows a process for collective construction between Forum members and non-members to be set up.

– Thirdly, the Forum wishes to operate like the Internet itself : its light structure of six people prohibits it from acting as a substitute for the existing bodies and encourages it towards partnership and cooperation. In addition, the Forum seeks to handle issues in a transversal rather than sectorial manner since most of the questions raised by the Internet break down conceptual borders. Finally, the Forum is a continually developing and not a structure whose activities and way of operating are set in stone. It must form itself step by step and offer flexible and innovative responses to the issues raised by the Internet. It proceeds by experimentation rather than a theoretical conceptual approach.

Conclusion

The Forum is underway. It is not only a discussion area but a place of construction, commitment and responsibility.

It is tool that is by nature private but its relations with the public sphere are important not in order to establish its legitimacy but rather to make its recommendations effective.

In actual fact, it is an aid to governance, in the sense that « governance » is understood as decision-taking in a complex system : in such systems, a decision can no longer be imposed by a limited number of players whether public or not; it is built step by step, following successive interactions between public players, businesses, representatives from the civil society; it arises from the unstable balance between them. The role of the Forum is to offer a permanent place for managing those interactions, encouraging the expression of this balanced position.

SELF-REGULATION, REGULATION
AND CO-REGULATION OF NETWORKS

BY

Bertrand DU MARAIS

LEGAL ADVISOR AT THE *CONSEIL D'ETAT* (1)

The question of « regulation » of the Internet has been a topic of heated debate since the network was first opened to the public. In turn or simultaneously this debate took on several dimensions : economic, with the issues surrounding valuation of content disseminated online, in particular artistic content; political, with the identification of the appropriate authority for controlling content, particularly those with violent or pornographic connotations; philosophical, with the clash between the somewhat libertarian paradigm of the American creators of the Internet and the European users' traditions of national intervention. Following the attacks on 11 September, this recurrent debate is now starting up again with discussions over the « security » control of the network.

The purpose of this presentation is to examine which method of regulation, which if not the most efficient, is at least the most justified in the « cyberworld ». It will be begin by describing the general background to the issues surrounding regulation of the Internet with a view to evaluating the suitability of the institutional methods currently used for such regulation and will end with some proposals with regard to the organisation of the French public authorities in this context.

Firstly, I should draw attention to the commonly accepted definitions of the concept of regulation and the various forms in which it can be found (I). Secondly, a reminder of some teachings of the economical analysis of information will complete the overall picture of the background against which the Internet is developing and identify the conditions for regulating it (II). Similarly, it is impor-

---

(1) The content of this article is only binding on its author and not on the institutions to which he belongs.

tant to draw attention to the authorities which already have responsibility for all or part of the « management » of the network and which, in practice, therefore provide a regulatory function (III). We must then get to the heart of the matter. In this economic climate, conflicts of objectives arise from the day to day operation of the network. In view of its characteristics, we will find that the necessary procedures require mechanisms for coordination that are both legitimate and hierarchical (IV). Armed with this diagnosis, we can then test the French mechanism for being involved in regulating the Internet and find that it is not necessarily very appropriate (V). Finally, it will « remain » to establish the objectives and methods of regulation. It must be a question (nothing less) of establishing a rule of law on the network via what might be called « protocols for market launching » (VI).

I. – Some definitions (2)

A. – REGULATION

Perhaps because it is increasingly used, the concept of regulation is ambiguous. It covers at least three meanings.

Firstly, there is a traditional definition, derived from cybernetics. According to Larousse, regulation is « *all the mechanisms that help it to maintain the constancy of a function* ».

Then there is an economic definition, which is more relevant to our subject. According to this definition, regulation refers to the micro-economic analysis and Anglo-Saxon administrative practice. Regulation is therefore *all the techniques that help to establish and maintain an optimum economic balance required by a market which is itself incapable of providing it*. The purpose of regulation is therefore *to establish or preserve competition*. In fact, economic theory teaches that the optimum economic balance of a market is achieved in a purely and completely competitive market. It is then a question of encouraging the entrance of new competitors, of combating distortions in competition, especially abuses of a dominant position, or even of limiting monopolies. The favourite place of economic regula-

---

(2) B. DU MARAIS, « Réglementation ou autodiscipline : quelle regulation pour Internet ? » [« Regulation or self-discipline : what regulation for the Internet ? »], *Les Cahiers Français*, n° 295, La Documentation Française, Paris, March-April 2000, pp. 65-73.

tion can generally be found in « public service » markets or rather collective services. As it is, nowadays these markets have the specific characteristic of being structured around physical networks, which is not accidental.

However, in a third, social or even societal sense, the term regulation takes on a more general meaning, used by public opinion. In this case, regulation means all the rules and institutions that allow life in society and that guarantee a certain degree of public order and industrial harmony. Regulation is therefore *all the operations that consist of devising rules, supervising their application as well as giving instructions to those involved and settling disputes between them when the system of rules is incomplete or ill-defined* (3).

B. – SELF-REGULATION

Self-regulation *is the drafting and compliance, by the actors themselves, of rules that they have drawn up (for example, in the form of good conduct or best practice codes) and which they themselves enforce.* This system therefore appears to be *decentralised and non-hierarchical and* makes its rules *self-enforceable.*

According to its disciples, self-regulation offers greater effectiveness. Firstly, it allows a good match between the scope of the regulation and the geographical scope of the network. The operators themselves are transnational and some of them control final access to the public. Secondly, compliance with charters should be made easier by the fact that they have arisen from negotiations between the same people who have to apply them. Finally, the methods for adopting and revising them are faster and more flexible than the legislative process.

However, the « topical » experiments with self-regulation have special characteristics. Accordingly, for the British financial markets, whose *Take Over Panel* offered the archetypal self-regulation, the following particular constituent elements could be found :
– Very strict, upstream regulation, operators allowed to be involved in the market and therefore to take part in the regulatory body;

---

(3) « Internet et les networks numériques » [« The Internet and digital networks »], *EDCE*, Paris, La Documentation Française, 1998.

– Closed « club » feature, which offers the advantages indicated previously but produces two types of major disadvantages. In the
hushed atmosphere of a club, the members doze off. Membership
of a closed club provides a comparative benefit to the existing
operators who can regulate the market to the detriment of new
entrants.

It should be noted that after decades of supervision of the London stock exchange by the « *Take Over Panel* », this system was
replaced by a more hierarchical means of regulation. In 2000, the
British law created an independent Authority, the *Financial Services Authority*.

C. – CO-REGULATION

Co-regulation (or, a more explicit term in English, the *cooperation
policy* mentioned here by Bertrand Cousin) *can be interpreted as a
place of exchange and negotiation between the « stakeholders » and the
owners of the legitimate constraint and in which good practices are compared in order to entrench them as recommendations. This place can
also serve as a mediation authority.*

In view of Isabelle Falque-Pierrotin's speech at this same Colloquium, there is no need to dwell on the definition of this term,
which in France was penned for the first time in the field of the
Internet by the Report and Surveys Division of the *Conseil
d'État* (4).

II. – Some non-legal reminders

In order to assess the relevance of the various possible methods
of regulating the network, we can borrow from the economic
analysis in order to give a preliminary summary of the very specific
characteristics of the property that is disseminated there : information.

---

(4) For an economic analysis of these issues of regulation of the Internet see : E. BROUSSEAU,
« Régulation de l'Internet : l'autoregulation nécessite-telle un cadre institutionnel ? » [« Regulation
of the Internet : does self-regulation require an institutional framework ? »], *Economie de l'Internet, Revue économique*, special issue, 52, September 2001.

A. – INFORMATION IS A MIXED, COLLECTIVE PIECE OF PROPERTY

Economic theory teaches that information is a specific property that has most of the characteristics of collective property or « public property » but which also has some features which any regulation of the Internet must take into account (5). In normal circumstances, firstly, information has the two characteristic features of a collective asset or « public property » according to economic theory : it is non competing and non-excludable.

The consumption of information is considered to be « non-competing ». It is an asset whose consumption is fixed and stable, regardless of the number of consumers. In this case, consumption by an agent does not reduce the quantity that can be consumed by the other agents. However, so far as concerns information, this condition is not completely fulfilled as is shown by the concept of a « scoop ». The first revelation of an exclusive piece of information obviously reduces the interest of that information and, accordingly, its very value, for all the other users since the information has entered the public domain. Nevertheless, once this initial revelation has been made, consumption of the same information remains non-competing since its use by some people does not interfere with its use by others.

Moreover, it would be difficult for the supplier of this asset to exclude a certain group of consumers on a discretionary basis, for example, by charging such a high price for information that only a few consumers could have access to the asset. There again, the initial supplier may at best decide on the initial recipients of the information – by confidential means of publication, etc. – but he may not then himself object to that same information being disseminated to an increasingly wide circle.

Information also has other very specific characteristics.

Firstly, the difficulty of regulating access to information increases with the number of agents who are aware of it. Common sense shows that the greater the number of agents who are aware of it, the more difficult it is to keep a piece of information secret.

---

(5) E. BROUSSEAU, « Economie des données publiques » [« The economy of public data »], *Le Communicateur*, special n° 32, winter 1996, p. 35.

Secondly, the information in itself produces numerous positive external uses. This justifies the existence of public information services, for example to announce disasters or storms or even simply to broadcast the weather forecast (6).

From the economic theory point of view, all the characteristics result in making information a collective or public asset, admittedly impure or « mixed » but one which does indeed contain both constituents. Accordingly, information is an asset, the wide dissemination of which is both : virtually *inevitable* because of the condition of non-exclusion; and, secondly, *without any negative effect*, in particular on consumers of information, because of the second so-called non-competing condition, indeed it can be *favourable* to the whole community.

B. – THE DIGITAL ECONOMY :
EXPLOSIVE RETURNS ON SCALE

Extending the use of the economic analysis, we find that the use of digital techniques causes a profound upset to the information economy. In fact, the digitalisation of information enables it to be disseminated very easily and cheaply.

In short, the economy of the producers and disseminators of information is therefore characterised by high fixed costs – for example when setting up an Internet server – but conversely, nil marginal costs. In fact, the cost of servicing an extra user by a website is extremely low compared to the initial cost of the investment which represents the creation of the site. Accordingly, the « returns on scale » increase rapidly not to say, to some extent, explosively. To put it more clearly, in the normal operational stage of a website and therefore, before it becomes saturated, any additional paying user will create extra revenue which will result in an extremely high extra profit since the additional cost of servicing this user is virtually nil. However, economic analysis shows that in these types of situations, the creation of increasing returns on scale constitute so many barriers to entry. In some circumstances, these economies of scale lead to the appearance of so-called « natural » monopolies. You

---

(6) Cf. D. MANDELKERN, B. DU MARAIS, *Diffusion des données publiques et révolution numérique* [*The circulation of public data and the digital revolution*], Paris, La Documentation française, 1999, p. 44. Naturally, this approach must be combined with determining the necessary remuneration of the producer of the information.

will see straightaway that the need for regulation, in the economic sense of the word, can make itself felt. However, we also need to include the additional economic characteristics that govern the Internet like any other network.

C. – THE INTERNET COMBINES THE ECONOMIC CHARACTERISTICS OF EVERY NETWORK

The development of all networks is connected to the combination of two types of effect.

Firstly, the operation of the network creates *scope economies*. The wider the network from a geographic or demographic point of view, the greater the use each actor derives, quantitatively, from his involvement in the network. Moreover, within every network there are *club effects*.

Membership of the network has positive effects that are not only quantitative but also qualitative. Each actor gains from contact with others and conversely, the whole community also gains from the involvement of each individual. Accordingly, the issue of *rules of interoperability* within a network is crucial. The ability of various individuals to communicate with each other with common rules or standards guarantees the efficiency and regulation of a network.

These characteristics that are common to the majority of networks then create two consequences which, in the context of the Internet, would seem to be very important. Firstly, a network cannot tolerate a proprietary mentality for any length of time (« *Lock in* »). A network then loses all its benefit, which is to increase the scope of dissemination of the asset circulating on it – in this case, information – but also to increase the individual ability of each participant to process information which, by its nature, is very varied, because its origins are very diverse. Secondly, and taking into account all these conditions, economic and technical regulation are closely linked on the Internet.

On the one hand, there are external factors that are strictly technological. Such technological external factors can develop between technologies themselves : one technology encourages the use of other technologies which, however, do not appear to be directly connected. In that respect, it is difficult not to see a relationship between the increased use of the Internet by the public and the circulation of certain software applications, whether they be proprietary, such as those of Microsoft or « free » like Linux. On the other hand, there are external technological factors created by regulation itself : some prescriptive devices facilitate the introduction or retention of purely technical solutions.

Technology, services and content are therefore closely interwoven in the Internet. This complicates the task of regulation since there cannot be a single point of application of this regulation unlike some information industries which are not connected to an open network such as the Internet.

In Hertzian television for example, legislation on content, applied to a small number of broadcasters, is relatively easy to implement (7). Finally, in order to conclude this brief presentation of the economical analysis of the Internet, I must also emphasise that the structure of a network without any identifiable physical infrastructure therefore relies on the addressing function and, accordingly, in the case of the Internet, on ICANN (Internet Corporation for Assigned Names and Numbers).

III. – The Internet is already regulated

However, these various criteria for analysing the regulation of a network cannot be fully applied to the Internet as if it were virgin territory. It should be remembered that for at least a decade the Internet has already had some form of regulation which has primarily developed in a technical form.

Accordingly, several international authorities are responsible for technical standardisation, and, in particular :

– IETF (Internet Engineering Task Force) is the body responsible for standardising protocols for interoperability ;
– W3C (World Wide Web Consortium) is the authority responsible for standardising the computer languages used on the Internet ;
– ISOC (Internet Society) is a knowledge society association that works towards the expansion of the Internet and under whose aegis the IETF, in particular, is developing.

---

(7) Obviously, subject to and so long as there were no alternative methods of broadcasting on the Hertzian channel...

Finally, I should mention the authorities that are in the process of being created and which are designed to regulate the circulation of content by an exclusively technical regulation, via the DRM (Digital Rights Management) projects. Accordingly, at least two consortiums bringing together software manufacturers, content providers and telecommunications companies are each seeking to introduce a world standard for managing copyright and monitoring the circulation of content.

It is important to emphasise the following characteristics of these various technical standardisation authorities, All these bodies originated in North America, which is consistent with the birth of the Internet. More interesting is the fact that only the W3C has a specific legal existence. The other authorities, in particular the IETF, seem to be like open forums with no legal personality, governed only by procedures for smooth running.

The downside of this very flexible method of regulation is *the lack of a system for representation and delegation*. Involvement in these forums cannot be subject to mediation by a representative appointed in accordance with a standard, transparent procedure that was laid down beforehand. As B. Cousin has very honestly just shown us using the example of « *Global Business Dialog* », this mutuality of involvement is particularly difficult for operators that might be competitors.

Accordingly, defending one's point of view in these informal regulation forums *requires a physical presence* on a regular, if not permanent basis and that represents a real financial investment.

Finally, and this is significant for international regulation of the Internet, all these organisations have developed alongside the traditional international organisations (ITU and ISO in particular). In the latter, under public international law, each Member State is represented by its government and has one vote. Accordingly, ICANN is a non-profit-making organisation under Californian law, the composition of which is independent from the States.

IV. – Conflicts
of aims, instruments or duties?

These characteristics, both physical and economic, which concern both the information itself and the network on which it circulates, determine a complexity of multiple and contradictory aims which need to be identified in order to establish the objectives and methods for regulating the Internet.

A. – Multiple conflicts of aims

The first type of problems that arise are linked to the conflict between the ease of implementing the rule and the transaction costs that such rules entail. Although this opposition can be found in the whole of regulation in its widest sense, we must nevertheless take into account in this problem the fact that the Internet is open and decentralised.

However, any decentralised system of regulation, and, more generally, any decentralised system for managing the rules – that is to say enacting them, implementing them and monitoring them – means higher set-up costs than in a centralised system. These costs can however be avoided if the rules themselves are « self-enforceable ». In this case, the rules are implemented by themselves as may be the case, for example, with regulation of a solely technological type in which the software itself or the technique more generally, can order its use and prohibit criminal behaviour. The attractiveness of a purely technical regulation method, such as DRM, is therefore very strong.

However, a second type of conflict, which is apparently exclusively economic but in actual fact of a political nature, opposes competition on the one hand and the fair remuneration of productive investments on the other. This conflict is as valid for the content sector as it is for the technical infrastructure sector.

In the first case, content is governed by *intellectual property and artistic property rights* (*droit d'auteur* or copyright, depending on the respective importance attributed by each legal culture to the economic value of the work and the protection of the author as a person). These rights must produce a balance between preserving a certain degree of competition on the one hand and remuneration of the producer of original ideas on the other. With that in mind, the question of proprietary technological concepts is therefore crucial. Similarly, the competitive intensity in certain technological equipment markets is also crucial for managing other aspects of the network : social aspects – dissemination, access, etc. – or for managing other markets – upstream or downstream – in which the network is involved. However, in some relevant markets which contribute to the smooth running of the Internet, some operators hold dominant positions. In software, the proceedings brought by the American government against Microsoft showed, *inter alia,* the abusive nature of such positions. So far as concerns servers, some manufacturers (CISCO in particular) occupy a privileged position. As if by coincidence, one can observe that some of these operators are particularly active in the technical standardisation forums. Finally, a third type of conflict, very specifically of a political kind, sets transparency of the operation of the network against the necessary security of that operation, both at the level of the network itself and that of its users.

Accordingly, there are many objectives that are often contradictory but concomitant. To be more direct and precise, the aim of regulation must therefore be to resolve these contradictions. They impose themselves harshly on a daily basis on the actors of the network and their political representatives, as the numerous disputes referred to throughout this Colloquium readily demonstrate.

B. – THE NEED FOR A HIERARCHICAL AND LEGITIMATE COORDINATION

All these conflicts, and, in particular, their coexistence, therefore show the need for an arbitration function between these various imperatives.

However, at this stage I must issue a warning : the existence of positive external factors, as identified earlier, does not necessarily mean that any method of private or indeed commercial regulation is impossible. The work of Ronald Coase has shown that external factors can be managed by a system of commercial transactions. However, such a system must then satisfy two conditions. Firstly, the rights of ownership must be properly established. Secondly, the transaction costs – in this case the cost of allocating rights (*adjudication*) and implementing them (*enforcement*) – must be nil. However, owing to its very structure, the Internet makes it difficult to fulfil this type of condition.

Accordingly, there is a need for coordination which finds expression in two aspects. Firstly, coordination presupposes the existence of a quick and cheap method of arbitrating between the preferences. However, since Condorcet we know that the preferences are not transitive : accordingly, there needs to be a practical method of choosing between the preferences that cannot only arise from a logical construction. This encourages establishing a hierarchical type of coordination.

In order to ensure that this coordination role is effective, its incumbent must also have some legitimacy. This is even more essential when coordination becomes hierarchical and not merely charismatic. We need to ensure that it accepts, *inter alia,* the measure of constraint that any coordination necessarily entails.

These truisms then bring us back to the process of identifying and selecting the legitimate coordinator. There then appears, as if by chance, the need for a function such as that traditionally performed by a particular social individual in a democratic society : the State.

V. – How shall we assess the french method of taking part in international debate?

Armed with all this information, the question then arises as to the relevance and effectiveness of the French method for taking part in the international debate on regulating the Internet.

A. – The salience of « French values »

Our society possesses a number of specific characteristics which derive in some way from the salience of the concept of « value » in our institutional system and which influences – not to say hampers – our relations with regard to the Internet.

Compared to many other regimes, our society would seem to express numerous claims. Firstly, it has a deep-rooted attachment to a centralised method for protecting individual freedoms, which are strongly linked to a tradition that goes back at least as far as the 1789 Declaration of Human Rights. In the field of the Internet, as beforehand in the computer environment, this manifests itself by a well developed arsenal of rules with regard to the protection of personal data. Moreover, our country also expresses claims in terms of cultural value. Our regulatory device thus forged the concept of « cultural exception ». Accordingly, France's representatives find themselves in a special position in the international debates concerning regulation of the Internet : undoubtedly they have more « values » to defend than a number of their other partners.

The alternative with which we are then faced, either to abandon some of these values in order to comply with the decisions of regulation bodies, or to create an effective device for taking part in debates which are necessarily international.

B. – GOVERNMENT AUTHORITIES DISPERSED
IN A MULTIPOLAR INTERNATIONAL NEGOTIATION

Despite these issues that are specific to our country, the government authorities responsible for representing it are dispersed. This creates a handicap which is all the more restrictive because these international negotiations are multipolar and, as we have seen, involve bodies that are not international organisations. The representatives or negotiators are not necessarily the representatives of political institutions but rather « stakeholders » belonging to the private sector, whether profit-making or not.

Accordingly, the issues surrounding international regulation of the Internet demonstrate the need to establish a system in France which both concentrates the appropriate government powers and, something completely new in our administrative system, establishes a *stronger coordination with our private operators* on an international scale. This system is that which is adopted in the Anglo-Saxon countries : in the United States, in the form of a « CZAR », or in Great Britain with the « e-Envoy ».

In these two countries these institutions concentrate all the powers held in France by authorities as varied as :

– the Ministry of Economy and Finance's Mission for the digital economy,
– the relevant divisions of the Ministry of Foreign Affairs,

- independent government agencies of which there at least two : CSA [*Conseil supérieur de l'audiovisuel* – Higher audiovisual council], ART [*Autorité de régulation des Télécom* – national telecoms regulatory authority] or even ANF [*Agence nationale des fréquences* – national frequency agency];
- the specialist agencies that come under the Prime Minister such as ATICA [Agence pour les technologies de l'information *et de la communication dans l'administration* – Agency for the information and communication technologies in the Civil Service] or MAPI [*Mission interministérielle* pour *l'accès public à la micro-informatique, à l'Internet et au multimédia* – Interministerial department for public access to computers, the Internet and multimedia];
- public technological research bodies that are independent from central government agencies, such as INRIA [Institut National de la Recherche en Informatique et en Automatique – National institute for computer science control];
- and even associations, such as AFNIC [*Association française pour le nommage Internet en Coopération* – French association for the fr. domain names].

In view of our institutional culture, such a concentration of powers of negotiation, enforcement and coordination with the private sector can only exist in our country, through the establishment of a « Minister for the Internet »...

VI. – Conclusion : towards « protocols for market launching » ?

It remains for me to raise the fundamental question which we should obviously have tackled at the outset : that of the ultimate political aim of regulation, beyond the establishment of a mechanism for resolving the tensions that we identified earlier.

A. – Naming or « homage » ?

The plethora of informal Internet regulation bodies and the fact that they take very different organic forms, from traditional international organisations like the IUT to the informal forum like the IETF, constitutes a structure for managing international relations that is both atypical and contains a number of negative ripple effects.

In particular, this organisation creates the risk of a feudal type of structure based on serf and overlord relationship in accordance with criteria that are in turn technological, economic, political, philosophical etc. Such relationships can be established at various levels between the different economic actors : between companies; between companies and their subsidiaries; between competitors; between purveyors in an upstream market and users in a downstream market, of a resource that is essential to any transformation activity. These relations also appear between companies and States as we can see on both sides of the Atlantic. On the one hand, the proceedings brought by the American Ministry of Justice against Microsoft give a good demonstration of the complexity of interests between a very big national company and a State, whose room for manœuvre is ultimately limited. On the other side of the Atlantic, the same can be said for the relationship between France Telecom and the French government. The telecommunications operator, which is partly private, is subject to competition which might appear to derive from ordinary law. Conversely, France Telecom's status as a public enterprise guarantees it a certain financial security and a more favourable environment for risk-taking since it is immune from takeover bids. Finally, these serf/overlord relationships also apply between States as in the traditional game of international relations.

Are we going to reach a situation in which in some *ad hoc* Internet regulation forums serf/overlord and man to man relationships would develop as a result of promises of allegiance and exchanges of services ? In some way, naming would lead to « homage » in the feudal sense of the term.

B. – PROTOCOLS FOR LAUNCHING NEW TECHNOLOGIES ON THE MARKET

The governance applicable to the Internet is specific owing to the very characteristics of the development of the network. According to Jean-François Abramatic, the development of the Internet simultaneously combines two very different stages : reaching its full size and the creation of prototypes.

Accordingly, owing to the fact that their technological innovations are launched on the market very quickly, the technological advances of some operators, concentrated in a given country, gives them a competitive advantage and therefore a dominant economic position, which is reflected in a third stage in a standardisation of the operating rules of this market, and, accordingly, of the law.

This development therefore carries risks so far as concerns a feudal-type institutional order. Somewhat paradoxically, this new « geo-technological » order does not mean the disappearance of States as actors. On the contrary, it leads to giving the States an *arbitrary* like power. For all the Internet actors, and, in particular, for the economic operators, no doubt it would be preferable to confer on them a certain *discretionary* power, that is to say one that is regulated by jointly pre-defined rules.

If the economic actors want to guarantee the security of their transaction, it is undeniably in their interests to develop the network and preserve its openness and stability, and therefore to ensure that the technologies that they deliver very rapidly to consumers are first assessed in terms of legal risks and social consequences. It is therefore in the interests of all actors, whether they be private or public, manufacturers, sellers or even users, on both sides of the Atlantic, to establish some kind of « protocols » for launching new technologies on the market. Such an objective could be assigned to the international regulatory authorities.

GBDE, SELF REGULATION, TRUST, GOVERNANCE

BY

Bertrand COUSIN

Special adviser to the chairman of Vivendi Universal

Since the World Wide Web is an area of permissive, non-interventionist freedom, any form of regulation would be vain and ineffective...

It would be <u>vain</u>, (apart from minimum technical regulations such as the publication of technical standards and the administration of URL names and numbers' assignment), for several reasons :

- Where resources are abundant (particularly once broadband access will be freely available), there is no need for a body in charge of distributing scarce resources, such as radio spectrum and cable distribution.
- Nor will there longer be any need to regulate competition, as it will be impossible to acquire a monopoly or dominant position on the Web, since new operators can open new sites as and when they wish.
- Web users are entirely free and responsible to personalise their options thanks to technical tools, which should prevent any public authority from regulating content.

It would be <u>ineffective</u>, unless a Soviet-style system were introduced, to control Internet services providers, because :

- The pace at which national legislators make decisions is not the same as that of the Internet's development. One need only think of the painfully slow progress of the French bill on the Information Society that will be partly obsolete as soon as it is voted.
- Also, by definition, the various national laws are patchy and unequal, and hardly provide a harmonised framework for the development of the Internet, and in particular, of global electronic commerce.

– Lastly, the fact that sites may be created in every corner of the world, and that private individuals may exchange the content of their computers directly, without going through an Internet service provider (the « peer to peer » system) would, in any event, make laws and regulations illusory.

This was the point of view that prevailed in early 1999 when the major global companies met in New York, upon the initiative of Commissioner Bangemann, to find a flexible self-regulation framework that would be globally oriented from the outset and run by themselves. This meeting gave rise to the Global Business Dialogue on e-commerce (GBDe).

Originally, its objectives were neither philanthropic nor ethical. Rather they were business oriented, aiming at reassuring consumers and at providing guarantees to potential clients that order and pay online.

How did this self-regulation approach overcome the obstacles in its path ?

How did it settle internal conflicts and minimise external opposition ?

How did it succeed in drawing up reasonable recommendations for public authorities and the business world ?

I. – The obstacles

A. – DIFFERENCES
BETWEEN INTERNET-RELATED BUSINESS

The advantage of this exercise was that it brought to the same table, representatives from all the electronic commerce-related professions covering all the links in the Internet « chain of value ».

– Hardware manufacturers, such as Alcatel, Hewlett Packard, IBM, Nokia, Siemens, Sharp, Toshiba, NEC, Fujitsu, Acer in Taiwan...

– Service providers in telecommunications, such as Bell Canada, Cable&Wireless, Deutsche Telekom, France Telecom, Korea Telecom, NTT, Telefonica...

– Media groups such as Disney, Bertelsmann, AOL Time Warner, MIH (Richemont group from South Africa), Vivendi Universal.

– Financial and consulting services such as ABN Amro, Deutsche Bank, Bank of Tokyo, Banco Bilbao of Viscaya Argentaria, EDS, Accenture, Nomura Research.

In all, almost 60 companies (including a few SMEs), some of which being keen competitors, others, conversely, having first little or no idea of the aims and constraints of the various industrial sectors.

B. – CULTURAL
AND METHODOLOGICAL DIFFERENCES

– Many books have been published on the variety of *styles of management* from one country or one continent to another, of consultation and decision-making channels within firms, and of methods of collaboration with employers' organisations or administrative bodies. This diversity was reflected in the different negotiating methods of GBDe members, and often the alliances forged to defend a given position bore no relation to geographical frontiers or professional categories.

– Also, initially, the companies sent *teams from completely different sectors*. They ranged from traditional legal departments with virtually no knowledge of the Internet, to marketing departments specialising in mass marketing techniques, or public policy, government relations and lobbying departments.

– National administrative bodies were not the only ones for which new procedures had to be set up and *ad hoc* « missions » created to circumvent the incomprehension and attendant resistance of traditional bureaucracies with regard to the Internet. In fact, the companies also had to *reorganise their teams*, though happily they did it more rapidly so far, leaving only competent and motivated people to work together on these highly complicated topics. The professional sociology of the Internet is rather unusual – it has nothing to do with age, but is more a matter of vision.

– These people faced an extraordinary challenge : to collaborate in tackling thorny issues at a global level and to reach a *consensus between completely different companies*. If we take as a benchmark the time needed by intergovernmental conferences and international organisations to obtain concrete results, the task could have taken several years, instead of a few months.

I must admit I was sceptical, and for me the success of GBDe is nothing short of a miracle. This success was facilitated by :

– The systematic use of e-mail through the automatic distribution lists (listservs) and specialised web-sites.

– Regular conference calls at continent level (the companies were grouped in three regions : Asia-Oceania, Europe-Africa and the Americas) and at the global level for the Executive Committee and certain working groups.

– Face to face meetings approximately once a quarter alternatively in each continent at sherpa level, and twice a year at CEO level. Last year, for instance, meetings were held in Mexico City, Madrid, Korea and Tokyo.

Incidentally, the sociology of organisations in the digital era would be an interesting subject for a thesis on the GBDe. It could tackle the use of Internet technologies, the internal mobilisation of appropriate resources, reactivity when dealing with new or related subjects, and the rapidity of the decisions finally taken by CEOs despite their extremely heavy schedules...

All this while bearing in mind that the GBDe relies on a secretariat of two people to administer its web-sites and draft the minutes of telephone conferences.

And also bearing in mind that the cost to each major group is 30,000 US $, and 5,000 US $ for SMEs.

II. – Conflicts

There were evidently a few stumbling blocks on which several companies confronted each other, by profession or by region, before reaching a consensus of opinion. They may be classified in two categories :

A. – TRADITIONAL AREAS OF CONFLICT

– Regarding *taxation*, American corporations have a clear advantage over their European competitors with respect to VAT since, for example, a company selling online content or services in France is liable to VAT if it is established in France, but not if it is set up in the USA.

– An agreement was finally reached to back the European e-VAT draft directive that aims at taxing non-European countries in the same way.

– Concerning the *responsibility of hosting providers* with respect to the content providers protected by intellectual property laws, a consensus was laboriously reached by recommending the extension to all countries of the « notice and take down » procedure for infringing content, adapted from the American procedure set forth in the Digital Millennium Copyright Act. The telcos finally understood that it was in their long-term interest to protect intellectual property if they did not want to see the dissemination of works on the Internet – a major source of traffic – gradually petering out over time.

– Regarding *technical protection* against the illegal copying of works, web-sites and services, the Japanese business community has accepted the principle of banning devices which copy content illicitly and circumvent protection measures, even though they designed and sold such equipment.

B. – However, there were
also major « theoretical » conflicts
that gave rise to heated discussions

1. – *The debate around co-regulation,*
or « policy co-operation »

(policy cooperation should be rather used, as co-regulation may mean partnerships in the elaboration of policies and regulation).

– The predominant feeling at the first GBDe meetings was grounded in two axioms : « free flow of information » and « free trade ». By definition, government intervention was considered detrimental, particularly regarding the Internet. Companies felt capable of dictating their own codes of conduct in order to make the Internet secure and develop e-commerce and considered that it was merely a matter of « self-regulation ».

– The other premise, which was the one finally adopted, recognises the inevitable role of governments which cannot remain indifferent to public safety, in particular, crimes on and through the Internet (paedophilia, piracy, attacks on information systems), consumer protection in a virtual environment, the taxation of electronic commerce services, and notably the defence of languages and cultural identities.

– However, « policy cooperation » is simply a specific dialogue at expert level, then at senior level, between the private sector and public authorities to try to define together the least disruptive rules to endorse as a framework for electronic commerce. Everyone then adopts the appropriate measures in his area of competence. This kind of dialogue may be held within an institutional framework such as the *Internet Rights Forum* (French organisation launched in May 2001 whose purpose is to set up a policy cooperation process on e-commerce regulatory and policy issues). It can also take the form of regular expert meetings, like those between the GBDe and the European Commission or between the GBDe and Japanese administrative bodies.

In summary, the aim is to bring together free market values and the ones that are fundamental to our democratic societies.

2. – *The debate on cultural diversity*

Cultural Diversity has found a highly relevant meaning in the current world situation. Globalisation of communication groups does not inevitably lead to standardisation of content. In the contrary, the different actors need to realise that the Internet can be an effective means of encouraging cultural diversity, for two reasons :

First, in the interests of good marketing, the major groups have to adjust their commercial ranges to the tastes, habits, languages and all the other factors making up a community's identity. Such profiling and variety of products and services is possible on the Internet.

Secondly, creators can exhibit their works, be they musical or audiovisual (thanks to digital video) under previously impossible conditions. Local cultural industries will be stimulated and the catalogues of major companies will benefit.

3. – *The debate on Cyber Ethics*

Private companies do not feel particularly concerned by morals, leaving the choice up to individuals and the government when certain deviancies threaten public safety.

However, bearing in mind the « elusive » aspect of the network, some companies, in particular Bertelsmann, considered it desirable that the private sector should take every step to ban paedophilic or xenophobic content from their web-sites and use filtering software in order to protect children, and rating systems as used in traditional television in France. A declaration to that effect was endorsed in Tokyo in September.

III. – The sucesses

After three years, the GBDe may be considered a success, though with the comment « could do better ».

A. – A REAL SUCCESS REGARDING ITS IMAGE

The development of the Internet has led to the creation of several new organisations and the inclusion of information society issues on the agenda of existing organisations. The list is long : TABD, GIIC, GIPI, International Chamber of Commerce, Global Cities Dialogue, etc...

The efficacity of the GBDe, demonstrated by the personal commitment of the CEOs of major groups and the relevance of its recommendations, has induced several organisations to collaborate formally with the GBDe. Agreements have also been signed with regional organisations such as the e-Asean and APEC. Collaboration on the digital divide is currently underway with the World Economic Forum.

The GBDe is therefore credible.

B. – The mitigated success
of the implementation by the GBDe
of its own recommendations

Certainly, we are far from the cosmetic commitments made by certain companies to appease governments and reassure consumers but which were rarely followed up in practice. Adopting strict personal data protection rules, non-intrusive commercial communication, Alternative Dispute Resolution (ADR) procedures, and active policy co-operation with judicial and police authorities complicates the daily lives of web-site editors, reduces sales efficiency and means extra costs.

On the other hand, there is no GBDe charter with its own trustmarks monitored across the world by a GBDe bureaucracy. There are no plans to set up a cumbersome and restricting organisation that to a certain extent would be « closed ». The aim of the GBDe is that its recommendations gradually spread throughout the private sector. Strict, monitored commitments would be dissuasive for companies operating in emerging or developing countries. And we must also be aware that by wanting to do too much we might defeat the object.

C. – Consolidation of the success regarding
the consistency of its recommendations

I do not intend to weigh this presentation down with details of the recommendations issued by the GBDe over the last three years that form a solid basis for the prosperity of electronic commerce. The recommendations concern cyber security, electronic signatures, jurisdiction and applicable law with regard to online disputes, e-government, Internet payments, the regulatory framework for the convergence of media and services in the digital area while avoiding discriminatory practices, the classification of products and services with respect to GATS and GATT, intellectual property and, above all, the means of promoting consumer confidence through the protection of personal data, the implementation of fair trading practices, the introduction of ADR mechanisms and the membership of independent trustmarks. The GBDe is also taking an active part in a digital bridges working group.

All these recommendations may be consulted on the GBDe.org web-site.

Conclusion

We must be aware that the Internet is in the throes of adolescence, like in a Jurassic period in the view of forthcoming developments. The widespread access to broadband, the increasing number of efficient search engines, the matching of services to the various local clienteles, and effective consumer protection (personal data, payments, rapid dispute settlement), shall, in the next five years, make the Internet a more user-friendly medium that will be increasingly used by the younger generations.

It is through constant, confident work between the private sector and the public sector that the information society will be able to emerge into the Higher Cretaceous.

STATEMENT
OF THE INTERNET SOCIETY
SUPERVISION AND CONTROL
OF THE NETWORK : NON-GOVERNMENTAL
ORGANISATIONS AND USERS

BY

David W. MAHER

ISOC, Vice President, Public Policy, USA

AND

Marc ROTENBERG

Lawyer, EPIC, USA

I. – Introduction

A. – The Internet Society

1. The Internet Society (ISOC) is a professional membership society – a non-governmental organisation – with more than 150 organisational and 6,000 individual members in over 100 countries. It provides leadership in addressing issues that confront the future of the Internet, and is the organisation home for the groups responsible for Internet infrastructure standards, including the Internet Engineering Task Force (IETF) and the Internet Architecture Board (IAB).

2. The Society's individual and organisational members are bound by a common stake in maintaining the viability and global scaling of the Internet. They comprise the companies, government agencies and foundations that have created the Internet and its technologies as well as innovative new entrepreneurial organisations that help to maintain that dynamic. The Society is governed by its Board of Trustees elected by its membership around the world.

3. Since 1992, ISOC has served as the international organisation for global coordination and cooperation on the Internet, promoting

and maintaining a broad spectrum of activities focused on the Internet's development, availability, and associated technologies.

4. As a non-governmental organisation, ISOC is directly involved in many aspects of Internet administration. For example, ISOC played a key role in the creation of the Internet Corporation for Assigned Names and Numbers (ICANN), and is a member of the Non-commercial Constituency of ICANN's Domain Name Supporting Organisation.

B. – Internet Society Position

ISOC strongly supports the concept of non-governmental supervision and control of the technical administration of the Internet. In particular, ISOC supports ICANN in its efforts to succeed as the « global consensus entity to coordinate the technical management of the Internet's domain name system, the allocation of IP address space, the assignment of protocol parameters and the management of the root server system ». (http://www.icann.org/general/factsheet.htm). ISOC further supports the role of non-governmental organisations as key players in assisting ICANN to achieve consensus among its conflicting interest groups.

II. – Issues of supervision and control of the Internet

A. – An Overview

The issues of supervision and control of the Internet, as it pertains to technical administration, may best be understood by reviewing a number of perspectives, namely, historical, technical, trademark, governmental, country code top-level domains and users. This overview omits certain important perspectives of other significant interest groups, including the general commercial interests, the telecoms and the service providers, but these are not so directly involved in the current debates over supervision and control. Also, this overview will not consider those aspects of supervision and control that are purely matters of national and local law. It must be recognised that there are some areas, such as privacy and security, where both legal issues and technical management issues intersect.

B. – Historical Perspective

From the mid-1980's, the Internet Assigned Numbers Authority (« IANA »), under the leadership of Professor Jonathan Postel, had *de facto* control of the technical administration of the Internet. Professor Postel, Director of the Information Sciences Institute (« ISI ») of the University of Southern California, operated IANA as a function of the ISI pursuant to a contract between ISI and an agency that is part of the United States Department of Defense. (U.S. government involvement and funding of Internet research is primarily a consequence of the earliest history of the Internet, when much of the research was supported by government grants.)

Under the IANA contract with the U.S. government, the domain name system (« DNS ») was clearly part of the functions of IANA. Professor Postel led the consensus process to develop the DNS, based on the structure originated by another Internet pioneer, Paul Mockapetris. In the early 1990's, Professor Postel recognised that the availability to the public of only three generic top-level domains (.com, .net and .org – the generic top-level domains or « gTLDs ») created an artificial shortage of choices for domain name registrants. In August, 1996, he circulated a draft proposal recommending the creation of 150 new top level domains. (Draft-postel-iana-itld-admin-02.txt) This proposal was not universally welcomed, especially by trademark owners who saw the creation of new domains as an increased opportunity for the infringement of trademarks by so-called « cybersquatters ».

In September, 1996, Professor Postel and ISOC created the International Ad Hoc Committee (« IAHC ») to make recommendations for an orderly transition to an expanded generic top-level domain name system, with due regard for legal considerations, including the interests of trademark owners. The IAHC was formed with the cooperation of the International Telecommunications Union (ITU), the International Trademark Association (INTA), the United States Federal Networking Council, and the World Intellectual Property Organisation (WIPO), as well as IANA and the Internet Architecture Board. The IAHC published a report in February, 1997, which proposed the creation of seven new generic top level domains initially and more later. The report also proposed the establishment of a non-governmental administrative structure consisting of a not-for-profit corporation to act as the registry for new domains, supported financially by for-profit and competitive registrars that would register the second level names.

In May, 1997, the report of the IAHC became the basis for the « Generic Top Level Domain Memorandum of Understanding » (the « gTLD-MoU »), which was ultimately signed by more than 200 parties, including major Internet and telecommunications enterprises. (http://www.gtld-mou.org/gTLD-MoU.htm)   The   gTLD-MoU immediately became the subject of global controversy, and was never implemented.

Several governments, including the United States of America, then concluded, for a variety of reasons, that they would not support the gTLD-MoU, and a process was initiated by the United States government to establish a new organisation that would take control of the technical administration of the Internet. The process culminated in the so-called « White Paper », issued by the U.S. Department of Commerce in 1998. (http://www.ntia.doc.gov/ntiahome/domainname/6-5-98dns.htm) In that document, the Department called for the creation of a « new corporation » (which became ICANN).

The structure of ICANN is complex. It is the result of strong lobbying of the U.S. Department of Commerce by conflicting interest groups wanting to insure that their interests would be represented in the new corporation. ICANN is chartered in the state of California as a not-for-profit corporation. The charter provides for a Board of Directors of eighteen persons plus a president, who serves *ex officio* as the nineteenth Board member. Of the eighteen directors, three each are selected by each of three « Supporting Organisations », one concerned with technical protocols, one concerned with IP address allocation, and one concerned with domain names. The remaining nine directors are supposed to be elected « at-large ». In fact, the only election held for « at-large » directors was limited to the election of five directors, one from each of five major regions of the world. They currently hold office together with the nine elected by the three supporting organisations plus four who are holdovers from the initial board approved by the U.S. Department of Commerce.

ICANN has achieved considerable success in its short life. It has gained worldwide support for its efforts in the more technical aspects of coordinating « the technical management of the Internet's domain name system, the allocation of IP address space, the assignment of protocol parameters, and the management of the root server system ». These activities have clearly reflected a global consensus supporting the concept of a non-governmental organisation to manage these activities. The addition of new generic top-level domains and the introduction of competition in the provision of registrar services have been welcomed by all participants. The Uniform Domain Name Dispute Resolution Policy (UDRP), although criticised – particularly in academic circles – has provided an efficient and economical means of resolving thousands of disputes between trademark owners and domain name holders.

C. – TECHNICAL PERSPECTIVE

If proof were needed of the importance of non-governmental organisations in the Internet, the Internet Engineering Task Force (IETF) and its related body, the Internet Architecture Board (IAB), provide shining examples of achievement by NGOs. The IETF is a consensus based, unincorporated, voluntary association that is the ultimate authority on the technical protocols of the Internet. The Economist magazine recognised this in an article on April 14, 2001 (« Survey Software », p. 26) : « ... it is the Internet's institutions – such as the...IETF – that offer a possible solution » to the regulatory issues of the Internet.

There remain serious regulatory issues – involving both technology and public policy – that must be resolved if ICANN is to succeed. The Internet is a hierarchy of networks, with an authoritative set of thirteen synchronised « root servers » at the peak of the hierarchy. Ten of these are physically located in the United States. The dominant server – the « A server » – is under the legal control of the United States Department of Commerce, and no change can me made to the authoritative root zone file without the consent of the Department. In other words, the United States government effectively controls the delegation of authority over all top level domains, even including those allocated to other nations, including, e.g.,.fr for France, .uk for the United Kingdom and so on. Three other root servers are located in the United Kingdom, Sweden and Japan, respectively. All thirteen root servers accept the authority of the A server, but there is no written agreement, law or international treaty that obligates any of them to do so.

Without clear legal authority to regulate the root servers, ICANN cannot claim to have succeeded in becoming the « global consensus entity » of the Internet. The situation is further complicated by the growing number of « alternative root servers » that have sprung up in the United States and elsewhere. The IAB has clearly spelled out the risks these pose to the Internet :

> « To remain a global network, the Internet requires the existence of a globally unique public name space. The DNS name space is a hierarchical name space derived from a single, globally unique root. This is a technical constraint inherent in the design of the DNS. Therefore it is not technically feasible for there to be more than one root in the public DNS. That one root must be supported by a set of coordinated root servers administered by a unique naming authority » (RFC 2826).

D. – TRADEMARK PERSPECTIVE

The principal issues of supervision and control of the technical administration of the Internet, including the protection of personal and property rights, have become inextricably intertwined with the question of what to do about domain names. A seemingly peripheral matter in the larger technological scheme of things has become one of the dominating issues of Internet governance.

The character of the Internet as a medium of telecommunications changed radically in the early 1990's with the development of the World Wide Web and the explosive growth in the number of users. With this growth came an unforeseen and unexpected interest in the subject of domain names. Domain names, after a simple start as a useful mnemonic device to avoid the use of awkward number strings, became themselves trademarks and brand names of enormous value. This has coloured all of the legal and public policy debates ever since.

The interests of trademark owners have been well represented in the development of the Internet since 1996, when Professor Postel first publicly suggested expanding the universe of domain names. Trademark owners in general have opposed the addition of new domain names on the grounds that each new domain only adds to the number of possibilities of trademark infringement. The development of the UDRP has helped to assuage the concerns of the trademark interests, but each new domain offers new challenges and significantly adds to the expense of trademark administration and policing. As a result, trademark owners and their international organisations, both governmental (*e.g.*, WIPO) and non-governmental (*e.g.*, INTA), have played a prominent role in the creation and structuring of ICANN. Even though the Trademark Constituency is only one of several in the Domain Name Supporting Organisation, it is better financed and better organised. As a result, it has been more influential than most of the other constituencies.

E. – Governmental Perspective

Shortly after ICANN was formed, a Governmental Advisory Committee (GAC) was created to provide a formal structure for advice and counsel from governments of the world. In general, the GAC has been strongly supportive of ICANN, reflecting a realisation that the alternative to ICANN is most likely a governmental organisation, requiring a global treaty or delegation to one of several existing global organisations. At least for the time being, nearly every government appears to have a commitment to the concept of non-governmental control of the technical administration of the Internet. In the United States, however, some members of the Congress do not necessarily subscribe to the goals set forth in the White Paper. Legislation has been introduced which would prevent the Department of Commerce from proceeding to transfer control of the root zone file to ICANN.

Also, serious conflicts in national law have already arisen on the Internet. For example, the French interest in controlling material on an American web site that contravenes French law has led to litigation that is still unresolved. These issues involving both national law and technical administration will undoubtedly grow in importance over time.

F. – The Perspective of the Country Code Top Level Domains (ccTLDs)

When Professor Postel and his colleagues established the Domain Name System, the decision was made to allocate a top-level domain to every nation in the world. Not wishing to become involved in political decisions, Professor Postel used a United Nations official designation, ISO 3166, to determine the two letters to be allocated to each nation. ISO 3166 takes an expansive view of nationhood. For example, Puerto Rico, officially a territory of the United States, has its own designation, .pr; there are many other comparable examples.

The delegation of control over each ccTLD was made with the same informality that coloured all of the early decisions made regarding technical administration of the Internet. Professor Postel simply assigned control in each nation to a network information centre controlled by fellow engineers whom he knew and trusted. As a result, the governments of the nations involved were normally not consulted and had no voice in the selection of these administrative centres. Subsequently, many governments have successfully asserted control, but many have not, and the ccTLDs now represent an interest group distinct from the GAC. Attempts by ICANN to reach agreement with the ccTLDs have not been successful.

G. – The Internet Users' Perspective

Caught in the snares of conflicts among powerful and well-financed interest groups, the unorganised user community has not had a strong voice in the issues of Internet governance and control. This is especially true with regard to mixed questions of policy and technology, where ICANN decisions have not always been supported by a consensus of those participating in its meetings and deliberations.

There is currently a bitter dispute over the procedures for election of at-large directors. An ICANN sponsored committee, the At-Large Membership Study Committee (ALSC) has proposed a change in the corporate charter so that six at-large directors will be elected to represent an At-Large Supporting Organisation (ALSO), one from each of six major regions of the world. Only domain name holders would be eligible to vote for these directors. Presumably, there would be a further corporate restructuring so that the six directors would represent one third of the total of eighteen directors. A conflicting study has been prepared by the NGO and Academic ICANN Study (NAIS) which calls for preserving the original number of nine directors to be elected at-large, with less restrictions on eligibility to vote.

The dispute over the definition of at-large membership illustrates the importance of non-governmental organisations in representing the interests of the user community. It appears highly unlikely that a truly global democratic administrative structure for the Internet can be developed in the near future. Even the NAIS study concedes that much work has to be done to get more users involved. Esther Dyson, the first chairperson of ICANN, recently commented : « the real problem is making this mostly technical group and its issues interesting to anyone but a small number of people ». In this context, the non-governmental organisations must take a leading role in the protection of civil rights – the protection of privacy of individuals, respect for property rights, and assuring security for personal and private commercial transactions.

Conclusion

Since its founding, ISOC has played a leadership role in both technical and societal issues facing the Internet. As a non-governmental organisation with an open membership, it will continue to be active in support of ICANN as the best hope for non-governmental supervision and control of the technical administration of the Internet. As well, it will continue to provide a strong voice for the protection of civil liberties of Internet users. During the current period of ICANN's development of new institutions to protect the public interest, ISOC will endeavour to serve as a model for the participation of other non-governmental organisations in the protection of the rights of individual users.

DISCUSSION

Georges Chatillon

Would someone like to take part in the debate ? M. Reidenberg ?

Joël Reidenberg

I'll pose this in English because it's a question particularly for Mr Rotenberg and particularly for Mr Maher. I would be interested in Mr Rotenberg's comment on the role of the US government in regulating it because I know that EPIC has made submissions to the US Congress to say stop ICANN from doing something and, I could be wrong, but it seems to me that sometime in the spring of this year, EPIC or one of the other organisations that you cited, but I think it was EPIC itself, was asking the US Congress to intervene to stop ICANN from doing something that ICANN wanted. And I'm wondering whether you think any port in a storm, any tool in a construction or whether there is a legitimate rule for the US Congress to continue to have, in the longer term, in running the Internet. Thank you.

Georges Chatillon

Could you please identify yourself ?

John D. Gregory

John Gregory from the government of Ontario in Canada, not speaking for the government.

Georges Chatillon

Thank you very much.

John D. Gregory

Well my brief answer is that we've largely stayed away from the fireworks that have constituted the relationship between the US government and ICANN. My own view is that ICANN should follow a narrow technical function and I respect that function, in fact I think it's an important function and I don't see that its mission should be significantly expanded. But, to the extent that ICANN chooses to expand its mission and by the architecture make decisions that affect the privacy rights not only of citizens in the US but also in Europe and around the world, then I think we will have to play a very active role because I simply don't believe you can hide your policy making behind your technological veil.

Marc Rotenberg

As the identified ISOC public enemy, I couldn't resist noticing an irony in David Maher's remarks in that you used the ITU as an example of something positive in network management and the ITU, unlike ISOC and unlike ICANN, is an intergovernmental organisation, it's not a private organisation. And I think one of the consequences of that struck me in the comments on the IETF and its policy position with respect to IPV6 specifically, that wiretap capability should not exist in IPV6, that IETF was taking a policy position on what the technology should make available as a private non governmental organisation. And since I think it's always useful as a public enemy to try to enlist some assistance, I wanted to ask Mr Delmas what his response is to that type of position from IETF and ISOC.

Richard Delmas

Yes, in fact, but I believe that we need to understand how decisions made by ICANN fit in. As David Maher said, ICANN's Articles of Association include the supervision of domain names, the allocation of IP addresses and the establishment of IP protocols. Therefore, theoretically, its powers include decisions on the development of IPV6 and, potentially, on the means of allocating IPV6. Until now, one can say that with regard to the role of supervising domain names in conjunction with WIPO, ICANN has done an excellent job which is now showing its limitations, particularly with regard to the question of ccTLD, the same was said for management. For the allocation of IP addresses and the establishment of protocols, the work of the IETF and regional bodies for allocating IP addresses, that is to say RIPE, ARIN and APNIC, has been carried out without any very close interaction with ICANN : they have continued to work in their sector and to make their decisions. It is true that now, probably in the next few months, ICANN, the IETF and the regional bodies will be faced with relatively important decisions which might exceed ICANN's original mandate as a technical body : IPV6 and not only technical specifications, that is to say methods of allocating IPV6 using transparent procedures. It is a question that should be settled shortly. The other major question is apparently that of ENUM, that is to say what method of regulation for convergence not only between telecommunications and domain names but also probably access to media and the major content on the Internet via a domain names platform. I would simply add that, despite everything, the mechanism lacks one element of regulation : that of competition law. Although the European Commission has been active so far and is still active in relation to the development of the Internet and the major actors of the Internet – Microsoft is one of them and Verisign another – one does not get the feeling that the competition authorities beyond the Atlantic or other world players have had the same concern for regulating and supervising the system. Accordingly, in this structure which must be regulated on the basis of competition law, which, in the end, is the major economic law, there is a certain imbalance and perhaps a difficulty that will have to be resolved. Thank you.

Igor Chovan

My name is Igor Chovan and I'm from the Council on Broadcasting and Retransmission of the Slovak Republic and I have two questions for Mr Maher. I would like to ask him to give us a brief history of both Internet Society and ICANN, and the second question is : could you clarify for us the legal position or the legal standing of both these organisations ? I mean are they companies or are they non-governmental organisations and what is their internal structure, if it's not a secret ? Thank you.

David Maher

It is certainly not a secret. I will be very brief. The Internet Society was founded, I believe, about 12 years ago by the fathers of the Internet, Vince Cerf, Jonathan Postel, Dave Farber, Bob Kahn and other great names, and it was founded specifically to be a legal umbrella for these unincorporated voluntary associations like the IETF to provide, among other things, liability insurance for the chairs of the various committees. The Internet Society is open to anyone who wants to join. There is a sliding scale of fees :

Alcatel, Microsoft and AT&T pay a lot of money, individuals in the US can join for 35 $, in the third world you can join for a lot less than that. It is semi-democratic : the board of trustees is elected, it's a staggered board elected globally. Most of the trustees of the Internet Society are not US citizens. Turning to ICANN, ICANN is a California not-for-profit organisation. It was founded by Ira Magaziner and the US department of commerce, specifically to take over the operations of what was called IANA, the Internet Assigned Numbers Authority, which was not really an organisation. It was in the good old days when Jon Postel ran the Internet out of his hip pocket. IANA was is research project at the University of Southern California Marina Del Rey. ICANN is specifically organised as a California corporation not-for-profit. Its bylaws currently provide for 18 directors : 3 from the domain name supporting organisation, 3 from the protocol supporting organisation and 3 from the address supporting organisation, and then 9 to be elected at large. As many of you may know, there is a war going on as to whether it should be 9 or 6 of the at-large members. Five of them were elected in an election that really did not work very well. There is great debate going on as to how these additional directors will be elected. In very brief compass I hope it answers the question.

Georges Chatillon

Thank you very much Mr Maher. I think that without being impatient, a while ago Mr Cousin wanted to ask Marc Rotenberg a question himself and therefore, if you will permit me, he may take the floor.

Bertrand Cousin

Thank you. Mr Rotenberg raised a problem that is a bit of a stereotype – I do not know the English translation, dog's breakfast or something similar – of the democratic control of the co-regulation process. So my question : would he like it to be the general assembly of the United Nations that regulates the Internet – effectiveness guaranteed ? Secondly, does he think that the civil society of which he speaks, the NGOs, have themselves arisen from a democratic process ? What I am saying very simply, because that is what I experience, is that co-regulation is a positive thing and that we must include the NGOs in the dialogue. The GBD in particular has had very in-depth discussions with Consumer International and other organisations that represent civil society. However, I believe that this general criticism of co-regulation is not a relevant criticism.

Marc Rotenberg

You may not agree with my criticism but I think it's constructive. I don't think it's an argument that the United Nations should govern the Internet and I suspect I have as much Internet experience as anyone else in the room. I was teaching computer science more than 20 years ago, I was member of the Internet Society the year when it started, I had dinner in my home with Vince Cerf. I don't feel a great need to establish my credentials on that particular point but I think you need also to appreciate that there is a genuine problem in the policy making right now with regard to the Internet, and that is that those organisations and those companies with the greatest interest in the outcome are exerting the greatest influence. Now maybe this shouldn't surprise us, and it's quite rational in many respects, but it's not democratic, and it is not taking us in the direction that we need to go if we're going to sustain this new type of economy and this new type of interconnected world. I don't have a problem with the GBD, we actually work with you through Scott Cooper quite a bit. I think you play a very important role, but I think you have an interest and GBD's members have an interest in establishing stable democratic institutions, so that when we confront large policy challenges, which we will confront, we will have solutions which feel legitimate and valid; and I don't think that ICANN's experiment right now is giving us comfort. So I think we're flexible, we're not looking to the United Nations but we need to take very seriously the need to actively involve civil society and to build democratic institutions if this is going to be a sustainable environment in the future.

Georges Chatillon

Thank you very much. Are there any other questions in the room? We still have five minutes left to devote to questions since Mrs Falque-Pierrotin has very willingly agreed to reduce her speech as rapporteur general to about ten minutes.

Diana Wallis

It's not so much a question. I'd like to come to the support of Mr Rotenberg. As a parliamentarian and especially in a parliament which brings together a number of countries and is, in that sense, supranational, certainly within the European Parliament I think a number of my colleagues, as democratically elected politicians, feel slightly threatened and uneasy by the emergence of co-regulation. That's not to say we're against it but it does lack the direct democratic legitimacy that we've become used to. And I think if we are to have co-regulation, there need to be very clear guidelines about who has access, how that access is paid for and the whole system needs to be incredibly transparent, and I think that's what I would certainly ask for and I know a number of my colleagues would. Thank you.

Isabelle Falque-Pierrotin

I am taking the liberty of saying a word about the origin of this word co-regulation which first appeared in the 1998 *Conseil d'État* report. I think that in actual fact, your fears show that you do not understand this word correctly. It does not mean that the respective liabilities of the various parties will be called into question. The States and parliament will retain their role of drafting and passing laws. The term co-regulation simply means that there are now other actors who must be allowed to take part in the debate on behalf of the civil society – in particular, consumer associations and businesses. Accordingly, the bodies that refer to the term co-regulation are not going to replace Parliament or the government, they are simply going to take part in the decision-making process and clarify it by involving all the powers that exist in the debate. I therefore think that there should be no fear about the primary roles : they will not be challenged; by contrast, the decision will be taken in an environment that allows all actors, whether public or private, to express themselves.

Georges Chatillon

Mrs Kessedjian would like to speak.

Catherine Kessedjian

Just to continue, I do not think that there is any contradiction between what Isabelle Falque-Pierrotin and Mrs Wallis have just said. What I personally find difficult and tricky is that in actual fact, we are witnessing a relationship of unequal forces in international negotiations and the emergence of this civil society. The non-governmental organisations such as those that are represented by Mr Rotenberg or the GBDe have nothing to do with the power that is both organisational and financial and the power of direct relations with the people who have the power within governments, parliaments, etc. That is what I believe we should be very aware of and I think that we should confront it. We must not hide the reality from ourselves. And if you will permit me, Chairman, I have a question for Mr Cousin : if I have understood correctly and followed the work of the GBDe properly, you said a moment ago that you now had a code of ethics which contained this obligation for filtering, especially for « hate speeches ». Is not Yahoo a member of the GBDe ?

Bertrand Cousin

No.

Catherine Kessedjian

Really. That is strange because I have seen lists on which Yahoo is a member of the GBDe, in which case it would be in breach of this code of ethics.

Bertrand Cousin

France Télécom is a member of the GBDe but not Yahoo as such. What I wanted to say, is that the best is the enemy of the good. For example, after the Tokyo recommendations, I shall give you a practical example, Vivendi Universal decided to introduce an out-of-court system for settling online disputes. We therefore make contact with a « Global Alliance » which consists of BBB On Line, the FENMA, their equivalents in Asia, so that we people who trade globally have an independent third-party system for out-of-court dispute resolution. Accordingly, it is already a good thing that we have available an organisation that tends to be global. Secondly, when you contact the managers of the subsidiaries and the managers of the sites to tell them, « after the traditional method of handling disputes with consumers, we need to establish an out-of-court resolution system », they drag their feet because that makes life complicated for them, it costs money, it burdens the costs account. It is a process in which general management must bang their fist on the table so that all this is actually introduced, and it will not be overnight. So you see that when a global company, and we are all affected – there is Hitachi, EDS, Nokia etc. – decides to introduce a self-regulationsystem, after consultation with consumer organisations, with people who are in charge of it at the Commission, with Commissioner Byrne, it really takes time to implement it. We must be on the alert. And what I say and repeat to my colleagues at the GBD : your credibility with regard to consumers and the government will be judged on the basis of your effective, actual and secure implementation of these recommendations. And so I clearly ask consumer associations and the NGOs to monitor this implementation and criticise it if it does not keep to a satisfactory pace.

Georges Chatillon

There we have some perhaps promising commitments. Are there any more questions ? Madam ? If you will allow me, it will be the last question because in a few minutes time the Chairman Kaplan from the University of Paris I is to address us.

Meryem Marzouki

It will not even be a question but a brief comment. I am Meryem Marzouki I speak both as a member of the Paris VI computer laboratory and president of the IRIS association – *Imaginons un Réseau Internet Solidaire* (Let's imagine a joint Internet network). I should like to return to the issue of co-regulation, not to rush to the aid of my friend Marc Rotenberg, who I do not think has any need of it, but to repeat that the problem of co-regulation, in any event such as it is applied in experiments such as the Internet laws Forum in France, is, firstly, that it perpetuates the relationship of unequal powers that Mrs Kessedjian spoke of – we are even, to use a rather dated expression, in the context of an illegal exchange –

and, secondly, it puts private actors, and accordingly, businesses, private actors in the civil society and the State, on the same level. And Mrs Falque-Pierrotin used this formula : the Forum of laws sees itself as a « midwife for consensus ». On the one hand, I would point out that it always a good thing to limit the number of births, but joking aside, this formula presupposes that there is necessarily consensus, which is not always the case as experience shows. There, that is all I wanted to add.

Georges Chatillon

And now perhaps, in the wake of her reply, we shall let her speak so that she can summarise this afternoon's proceedings.

Isabelle Falque-Pierrotin

It is a rather tricky balancing exercise. Yes, just a word about consensus. In fact, as far as possible, the aim of the forum, is to encourage convergence of the actors' positions and therefore to reach a consensus. However, having said that, we are not bound by this consensus; there is no dictatorship concerning consensus within the forum and for an extremely simple reason, which is that the forum has no decision-making power. Which means that if there is no consensus on an issue – and this happens frequently – the forum will also take account of minority positions and will nevertheless have played its role as clarifier of the debate. I shall pass over these matters of consensus.

GENERAL REPORT

Isabelle FALQUE-PIERROTIN

Legal advisor at the *Conseil d'Etat*
Chairperson of the Internet Law Forum

I am going to embark on the delicate task of summarising this afternoon's two round tables which were extremely productive : the first on cybercrime and the second on co-regulation.

Cybercrime :

This is a subject that is of particular topical interest following the events of 11 September. It is a subject on which a number of countries have legislated, in many cases as a matter of urgency. It is a topic that is the subject of an international Council of Europe convention to be adopted shortly.

The whole focus of this issue, which was widely debated during the round table, is to find a balance between the concerns for security and the legitimate concerns for respect for public freedoms.

So, if I try to sum up what was said by all the speakers, I think that these observations can be grouped together in several points :

- firstly, the characteristics of cybercrime and the specific nature of the investigation. Both Jacques Plays and Jean-Wilfried Noël laid great emphasis on making us understand that cybercrime on the Internet is elusive, therefore it disappears just as quickly as it appeared. It is transnational, largely due to technological developments (peer to peer) and, finally, it can be resolved through cooperation between the law-enforcement agencies and access providers.

All these factors mean that cybercrime has specific features and, accordingly, criminal investigation is specific.

- secondly, we discussed the point of harmonising legislation and adapting the procedure to these specific characteristics of cybercrime, that is the aim of the Council of Europe's Convention. This

Convention is an instrument that is not completely finalised but it is an absolutely essential stage which pursues three objectives :

- To harmonise positive law, that is to say to get all the signatory States to agree on a joint definition of an offence. It is virtually complete, with the exception of the additional protocol which should be relevant to issues of racism and terrorism.
- To create new criminal investigation methods, new procedures that allow virtual reality to be taken into account.
- To give international cooperation new resources in order to be more effective : remote access to foreign data, the concept of a point of contact.

– The third point of this round table is the presentation of the Office by Mrs Catherine Chambon. There was mention of the French experiment with the Office which was created in May 2000. It is a real means of centralising crime relating to new technologies so far as France is concerned.

So, faced with all that, what are the findings ? Is the organisational and legislative system appropriate for taking into account this new type of crime ?

There remain a number of questions which were raised either by the speakers or during the discussions with the participants.

The problem of data storage was not included in the Council of Europe Convention, through lack of consensus. By contrast, this issue is tackled in the law on day to day security in France but with many debates concerning this legislation.

Has the Council of Europe exhausted the mechanisms for international cooperation. Can we, nevertheless, make further progress ?

We can also question the methodology because many laws were adopted with urgency, and such circumstances precluded any public debate. They are presented as temporary legislation. Can we really legislate on subjects as important as these in such circumstances ? Can we actually believe that this legislation is temporary ?

Commander Jacques Plays mentioned issues of training. Given the specific nature of this crime, it is important to raise the awareness of all the investigation services and judges and train them on the problems of cybercrime.

That, Chairman, is what I have to say about this first round table.

The second round table related to issues of regulation. My overall impression was that there was an extraordinary profusion of experiences and organisms. So, are we, as Bertrand Cousin said, in the Jurassic age of the Internet? I have no idea. In any event, it is certain that we are faced with a gigantic global laboratory with a very diverse range of experiments.

First of all, there was mention of ICANN which is a very interesting regulation experiment as it concerns international cooperation on a non-national basis. It is a unique practice, the finding that Richard Delmas made is that it is a relative failure, that is to say that ICANN was able to resolve a number of issues but the second version of ICANN does not appear to be completely ready. This is deplored by the Vice-President of ISOC in whose eyes ICANN is essential to ensure the technical stability of the Internet. ICANN must evolve in order to survive.

We heard a second presentation that I would describe more as self-regulation than co-regulation, as I think that the Gbde is an experiment that is conducted by private actors and has their voice. So is it a legal UFO?

I do not know. In an event, the Gbde already exists and according to the address given by Bertrand Cousin « it is experiment that was difficult to achieve as within this structure there are cultural differences and sensitivity differences which have been surmounted in order to allow the Gbde to exist today ».

The third type of experiment is that of the NGOs, ISOC and EPIC together. I think that this emergence of civil society in the debate on drawing up rules and practices is something quite new. In my view, it is eminently positive. Marc Rotenberg stated that it was important that these NGOs should henceforth be a voice in the decision and be able to enter the room in which these decision are made, and this for a fundamental reason which is that these NGOs take into account the defence of human rights. I believe that we are all keen on the defence of human rights.

To conclude this second round table, I would like to use Bertrand Du Marais's analysis model which gave a simultaneous general and prospective presentation of the issues surrounding regulation that are outlined through these various experiments and through him and echoing the debate, I would ask a number of questions, which apply to all the regulation experiments presented here :

How representative are these bodies ?

How are we going to manage the increasing internationalisation of the Internet ? Whereas the USA still believes that it owns the Internet, as Richard Delmas said. I think this issue is very simple but very real today.

How can we ensure a democratic control of decision-making in an environment such as the Internet in which public and private actors who have different responsibilities, confront each other and are connected ?

Finally, how can we link the methods for regulation that are beginning to emerge with technological developments ?

That is all, thank you.

ADDRESS BY MICHEL KAPLAN

BY

Michel KAPLAN

Vice-Chancellor
of the University of Paris I Panthéon-Sorbonne

President,

Ladies and Gentlemen,

At the end of this first day, the theme of which was to determine the law applicable to the networks, we were able to listen to the analyses of a great number of experts from various continents.

The rules applicable to the networks are somewhat difficult to determine and even more difficult to put into practice. In fact, we are living in a multi-layered period as computer experts say. The first, the fruit of our modern (I was going to say traditional) heritage, was formed at the time of the second world war with the development of the consumer goods and service industries. That is the visible, material, tangible, layer, the reality of appearances. The second is recent, barely fifteen years' old. It is in competition with this new forty-year old world, produced by the giant factories and the unbridled exploitation of raw materials. The second layer is that of the globalised Internet networks.

The unimaginable speed of the development of the Internet relied on an irrepressible energy, the need to communicate, to exchange information, ideas, plans, images, films and songs. Driven by this speed and irrepressible energy, the investors invested enormous amounts of capital to develop the networks and make them places for trade and speculation. Tens of billions of dollars were invested and sometimes vanished in Stock Market misfortunes or got lost in plans that were conceived too hastily.

This haste on the part of investors to jump over the barriers of the new forty-year old world did not shake the legal experts. Once the surprise was over and with the help of understanding, they did their work, which consists of finding rules that are adapted to the contradictions, the departures and the innovations.

You have been able to find the necessary explanations to show how the post-war legal order had evolved, how the new international order imposed by the networks coexists with the old one and what new rules need to be devised, weighed up and perfected.

Some of the morning's speakers demonstrated that technology had a profound influence on the law and also on some of its concepts and some of its methods. Until now, the law could be applied if there was material evidence. Electronics, networks and the Internet have led legal experts to accept the undoubted existence of digital evidence. We are now obliged to accept that two layers coexist, the visible and the invisible layer, the external and the internal aspect. Nevertheless, the two worlds remain completely material. The Internet does not lead us into schizophrenic situation of superimposing a material world onto another immaterial world. No, there is still only one world. The Internet induces us to use other instruments of vision that are more powerful than our eyes.

The digital evidence of an electronic deed is revealed using a microscope that explores a hare disk. The traces are then visible.

Another phenomenon has troubled the calm minds of some legal experts : the speed at which information is spread and disseminated, assisted by the new facility to duplicate data very cheaply.

It has been said that the Internet had a cross-border nature. It is true. But it is also a nomad, a migrant, an illegal immigrant. Every day billions of dollars go through the accounting paths of bank accounts and stockbrokers' accounts without the purpose of such exchanges being apparent. Dummy companies, tax havens, it cannot be denied that the Internet and the networks facilitate globalised transactions, whether they are clean or dirty. The States and international organisations had to react to arm themselves against cybercrime. That is what you demonstrated aptly. One can also identify from your reports an idea drawn from the cross-border and nomadic nature of the Internet : the fight against cyber-criminals has also brought together the police and judges and has led them to coordinate their forces in order to combat worldwide organised networks.

The networks oblige political, industrial, cultural and commercial decision-makers to review governance procedures and to raise questions of the trust that must exist between the people and all forms of the new technical means of exchanges.

The Internet reforms and changes procedures for management, advertising and providing information. There is a danger that the Internet will upset the traditional structures of commerce and distribution.

The Internet requires the fastest solutions to be found for resolving disputes. Your work tomorrow is to discuss these three aspects.

These are cultural issues. They cannot be resolved in a few years because they affect old, tested, sound systems : commerce, administration, justice, dissemination of leisure industry products, songs, films, art in all its forms.

The Internet raises questions that are often new. Depending on their temperaments, people respond to them by illustrating a new quarrel between the old and the modern. As the legal experts that you are, you have been able to create new balances and delicate rules for transition.

These findings augur well for the wisdom of tomorrow's talks.

The University, of which I am proud to be Chairman, is happy to be a co-organiser of these two invaluable days. I hope that your discussions tomorrow will be as heated as today's.

President,

Ladies and Gentlemen,

Thank you.

Section II

The implementation
of Internet laws

A

E-commerce :
what protections?

Robert BADINTER
PRESIDENT OF ARPEJE

As soon as this plan for a colloquium was submitted to me, I had no hesitation in endorsing the suggestion of making it one of ARPEJE's major events this year.

In fact, ARPEJE has set itself the objective of re-exploring the themes of legal cooperation and reflecting on the most modern of them. New technologies are a matter of considerable interest for legal experts and for modern society as a whole. Minister for Justice, I have made modernisation of the legal system *a priority*. Information technology was only just beginning to change the lives of legal experts.

Now the sometimes daunting developments are taking place faster than ever, shaking hierarchies, working practices, greatly increasing the circulation of information but at the same time, sometimes causing the legal security that the paper-based environment afforded us or gave us the illusion of having, to be called into question. Another of ARPEJE'S purposes : to bring together all the actors from the legal and judicial world to provide a place of contact for exchanges and cooperation, particularly at European level, between the applicant countries whose representatives here I especially welcome. This gathering held in Paris – our old world must also excel in new subjects – has a universal dimension that is perfectly suited to ARPEJE; it will not end there and its participants will be able to continue the dialogue that has taken place over these two days and which will be documented, as after each ARPEJE colloquium.

It is the contribution of legal experts to an accepted, controlled globalisation, an area of freedom, security and justice, according to the fine expression of the Amsterdam Treaty, which we must extend to the world by discarding our fears whilst keeping our creativity alive.

First of all, I should like to talk about the legal relationship between man and machines.

In all cultures, the law is a set of social rules designed to regulate human behaviour. It should be the expression of the wisdom of governments. It can also be the expression of their abusive practices.

Until now, no culture had recognised that the operation of a machine can create valid rights for entire societies. That would mean making Internet law, whose eminent specialists from throughout the world are gathered here today in this National Assembly room, a very specific case.

Can a computer, that is to say, as far as legal experts are concerned, a machine, a thing, and its software that is also categorised as a thing, create laws?

This is obviously a burning question for legal experts from the traditional schools. It is natural for defenders of the patentability of software who believe that works created by a machine must be protected in the same way as works created by the human mind. It is fundamental for the creators of computer works that make their machines operate in order to produce images, sounds, and, if one is to believe some groundbreaking experts on the mind, soon legal texts and, why not, lawyers' pleadings.

The legal differences between man and machines created by man have always influenced positive law. Does not Article 1384 of the Civil Code say that we are responsible for the things that are under our control?

A priori, the Internet is a thing which begins to operate when there is a connection between two or more computers linked together and its work ceases when that connection is broken.

However, there is a great temptation to give an almost human dimension to its creations, but it is true that machines that are considered by legal experts to be things, are also an extension of the human mind, an adjunct to the body. Some surgeons operate on patients from thousands of kilometres away, thanks to the Internet and robots. Some patients owe their lives to microprocessors grafted inside their bodies and regulated by software.

Some software, known as « intelligent agents » can make calculations that could not be made without them.

We are told that in the future there will be « intelligent » cars « intelligent » houses and all this intelligence is due to machines that are linked together by the Internet.

Accordingly our technical culture increasingly combines body and machine, mind and software.

It is becoming ever more necessary to question the legal classification of so-called « intelligent » things and their role in creating rules.

I should now like to refer to the use that can be made of the Internet and the relations of trust or mistrust arising from that use.

So far, the Internet has been presented as a panacea by its enthusiasts. The Internet was to link the most isolated people and educate the most disadvantaged. The Internet was to be a permanent, universal trade fair allowing buyers and sellers throughout the world to exchange any goods or services.

The dot.com crash dashed some over enthusiastic expectations.

And, suddenly, the Internet clearly revealed our traditional mistrust of new communication tools.

More than ever, the hour of the law, that is to say the security of intellectual and commercial exchanges, chimed.

In order to give Internet users confidence, legislators would need to provide legal solutions to fundamental problems.

For example, States must GUARANTEE :
– The protection of personal and commercial data;
– The rights of electronic commerce consumers;
– Secure methods of payment over the Internet;
– Alternative solutions to dispute resolution;
– The right to freedom of expression, whilst complying with the fundamental values of European and universal human rights Charters.

Drawing up principles for protecting and guaranteeing the rights and freedoms applicable to the Internet was a good start.

The terrorism that struck the United States of America on 11 September resulted in a declaration of war on terrorists and suspended continuation of the work.

The Internet, which has already been reviled as a vehicle for money laundering and all kinds of depravity, from the expression of racism to paedophilia and the sale of human bodies, is now suspected of being a means of communication for terrorists.

Legal experts must keep in mind a sense of proportion and consider that the Internet machine is mainly used by people, the great majority of whom are neither Utopians nor criminals.

That does not mean that judicial procedures and police investigations cannot be adapted to the technical subtleties of the tool.

Must we restrict or even prohibit encryption because some people would make their messages invisible by using steganography ? That would leave the Internet open to all kinds of espionage, including government espionage.

Must we encourage police investigations, handing over encryption keys and searches without consent on the basis of mere presumptions ? That would lead to ruses such as removing sensitive files to electronic safes.

Should these exceptions target the whole of society whereas they are aimed at a few people ?

Criminal acts that are the exception require appropriate responses. The laws of war, well known to international law experts, contain exceptional provisions which cease to have effect when peace is made.

The new judicial and police measures that governments now wish to apply to the Internet should not lead to potential confusion between instruments applicable in periods of conflict and those that are applicable in normal times.

Yesterday, Mrs Chambon, Chief Superintendent of the Criminal Investigation Department, and Mr Plays, Squadron Leader of the Gendarmerie Nationale set out the key points of the new measures and the reasons for their legitimacy.

In tandem with the legal definitions of the new measures to combat terrorism through the Internet, the Parliaments of the information society passed laws on electronic commerce, electronic signatures, distance contracts and the protection of personal data.

These directives and laws are designed to establish relations of trust towards the Internet tool so that exchanges of a legal nature can develop by having capabilities that should be safer than those of a paper-based environment.

The international relations brought about by the globalisation of the Internet are the subject of two movements with wide scope and contradictory objectives : on the one hand, we want the Internet to inspire confidence; on the other, we affirm that it can give rise to mistrust.

Is there not a danger that these two forces, one positive, the other negative, might trigger an aversion for a tool that we don't know which end to hold?

There again, we must remain rational. All revolutionary communication tools gave rise to passion and aversion.

Legislators' efforts must concentrate on making computer tools as secure as possible, on the freedom of their use and on the guarantee of inviolability of data.

Finally, I should like to mention the European and international approaches to Internet law.

The stage is now a global one. The Internet, a universal tool par excellence has been adopted by that globalisation. The reality of Internet law is far behind the globalisation of international relations.

Can that change?

Rivalries between nation States appear to increase in accordance with competition between the major global businesses.

The international sectored organisations reflect the struggles between pressure groups with conflicting and antagonistic interests.

Non governmental organisations pursue specialist aims.

A global government, the hope of the 1950s, seems as Utopian as ever.

However, the differences between the major industrialised countries and the others and between the major global businesses and the others are too great to leave it solely to the most powerful and minority bodies to establish an international Internet law.

The current rules of operation and the missions of nation States, inter-governmental organisations and global businesses preclude the establishment of rules that are sufficiently fair, balanced and proportional to satisfy far too conflicting interests.

One of the aims of this colloquium is to seek solutions that will allow an Internet law to be established and applied with a maximum consensus, at least within the rich industrialised countries.

We will need another colloquium to examine the similarities and differences between the law of rich countries and those of poor countries; and yet another to look at the international conditions for a universal harmonisation of rules.

Legal experts have been invited to work in this vast area, the ARPEJE association quite rightly wanted to help them. Thank you for having taken part in the discussions.

1. – THE IMPLEMENTATION
OF INTERNET LAWS

EUROPEAN UNION INITIATIVES
IN THE FIELD OF INTERNET LAW

BY

Robert VERRUE

DIRECTOR GENERAL FOR THE INFORMATION SOCIETY
EUROPEAN COMMISSION

The last five years have seen a dramatic change in the use of the Internet which has penetrated all areas of life : economic, social, cultural, educational or governmental.

Five years ago, the legislative framework in Europe and elsewhere was in a serious need of adaptation to the online environment. There was, of course, the legislative framework of liberalisation of telecommunications services which was established in the 1990s. This framework has contributed significantly to the creation of the e-economy as we know it today. It is today being revised to take into account both market and technology developments, including the dramatic increase in Internet usage.

As regards more specifically e-commerce, the first model law at international level was adopted by UNCITRAL in 1996. In 1997, the European Commission adopted a policy document – the Communication on a European Initiative in electronic commerce – which aimed at mobilising the resources and launching the actions to move Europe towards the Global Network Economy. It outlined the key directives that would pave the way for an enabling legal framework in Europe. Some directives were already in place and others have been adopted since : *i*) the 1995 directive on personal data protection, establishing the conditions for the lawful processing of personal data, the rights of the individuals concerned, the security and confidentiality obligations of data controllers, the conditions for transfers to third countries and the role of independent supervisory authorities; *ii*) the 1997 telecommunications data protection directive, applying the privacy principles to personal data created by the use of telecommunications services; *iii*) the three intellectual property directives, concerning computer programs (1991), databases (1996) and certain aspects of the information society (2001); *iv*) the directive on electronic signatures (1999), facilitating the use and the legal recognition of e-signatures in an internal market, mutual recognition context; and the directive on e-commerce (2000), helping the establishment of a single market for electronic commerce by providing for conditions concerning information, transparency, commercial communications, contracts and liability which should encourage consumers and suppliers to establish trusted electronic commercial relationships.

In addition to legislation, the potential of the Internet should be exploited through initiatives in the area of practical technology applications. The *e-Europe* initiative endorsed at the Lisbon European Summit in March 2000 and the Action Plan endorsed at the European Council in Feira in June 2000 aims at accelerating the development of the information society in Europe. The *e-Europe* Action Plan aims at stimulating the use of Internet in major areas such as transport, healthcare, schools, technological research, development of e-content, promotion of e-government. The intention is to speed Europe's transition to the new economy by exploiting the full potential of the Internet.

There are a number of additional burning issues which have been raised while the main pillars of the information society legal framework are being put in place :

– issues of jurisdiction and applicable law, the first one being addressed at European level with a Regulation of December 2000 but being still discussed internationally; the main debate has concerned the country of origin (provider) or country of destination (consumer) dilemma;

– the adaptation of the taxation and fiscal requirements to e-commerce, including the possibilities for electronic invoicing; the main question being what e-services should be subject to value added tax and where should this be paid;

– the issuing of electronic money and the guarantees that are required to do so;

– the challenges to trademarks raised by abusive registration of domain names;

– the challenge of cybercrime, requiring the striking of right balances between very important societal interests.

The speed with which new business models emerge, change and disappear calls for new flexible approaches to deal with some of the legal challenges. Most of the new information society directives include review clauses. Soft law can also be very useful, e.g. online dispute settlement mechanisms and codes of conduct complementing legislation. Technical means are being put in place to protect privacy, minors and human dignity, intellectual and other property. The European Commission has launched initiatives in all these areas. The main objective is to provide flexible tools that will complement the law and can be easily adapted as technology develops, new challenges appear and the needs and priorities of our societies evolve.

THE PLACE OF THE INTERNET
AND E-COMMERCE
IN MULTILATERAL NEGOTIATIONS

BY

ALAIN-LOUIS MIE

FRANCE TÉLÉCOM
MANAGER OF MULTILATERAL EXTERNAL RELATIONS
MEMBER OF THE *GLOBAL BUSINESS DIALOGUE* ON E-COMMERCE

WITH THE COLLABORATION OF

MATHIEU GUENNEC

FRANCE TÉLÉCOM, HEAD OF LEGISLATIVE STUDIES,
INTERNATIONAL DIVISION OF EXTERNAL RELATIONS

Nowadays, most of the big global operators provide Internet access services both on their own national territory and abroad. The question of the place of the Internet in multilateral negotiations is therefore of particular concern to telecommunications operators and more widely the service industry. Before outlining the current state of this problem in more detail, two observations deserve consideration :

– firstly, there are no WTO administered commercial agreements specific to the Internet or to e-commerce as there are for agriculture or textiles; however, these two fields are included in commercial agreements negotiated within the WTO;

– secondly, so far as concerns debates on the Internet within the WTO, these are mainly centred on Internet access services.

The business of providing Internet access services can be divided into two separate markets involving two categories of *Internet Access Providers* (IAP) with a hierarchical structure. The first, commonly known as « *Internet Service Providers* » (ISP) provide end users with access to the Internet, that is to say individuals, businesses, suppliers of online services, and governments. The « ISPs » provide « *retail Internet access services* ».

The second, commonly known by the English name, « *Internet Backbone Providers* » (IBP) are at the top of the hierarchy. They also provide Internet access services but these are « *wholesale Internet access services* ». The « IBPs » provide these services to the « ISPs » in exchange for payment of a charge fixed by a « *transit agreement* ». « *Internet Access Providers* » (IAP) of the same level (two IBPs for example), can rely on other forms of agreements called « *exchange of traffic agreements* » (*peering agreement*). No financial compensation is paid in this type of agreement and each IAP routes the other's traffic using its own transmission capabilities.

Unlike the access and interconnection agreements between telecommunications service operators, to date, agreements between IAP's have never been subject to any sectoral regulation. That does not mean that the Internet access service sector is excluded from the law but that competition rules are the only form of regulation in this area at the present time (1). It is interesting to note that compared to telecommunications regulation, so far, IAP's have had rights rather than obligations.

Having provided these details, the place of the Internet and e-commerce in unilateral negotiations must be considered taking into account, respectively :

– the legal system of the Internet access services, a legal system based on the 1994 General Agreement on Trade in Services (GATS) and the 1997 Basic Telecommunications Agreement;
– factors that are an obstacle to the acknowledgement of this legal system by all the Members of the WTO.

In the following arguments, the analysis will focus more on the issue of the Internet, since the problems raised by e-commerce are certainly financially linked but legally separate. However, in view of their importance, they will be mentioned in the conclusion of these arguments in order to put forward the concerns and expectations of the NTIC industry in multilateral negotiations.

---

(1) See, for example, the Worldcom/MCI ruling : « Commission Decision 99/287/EC of 8 July 1998 declaring a concentration to be compatible with the common market and the functioning of the EEA agreement » [Case n° IV/M.1069, *WorldCom/MCI*], *OJEC*, L 116 of 04/05/1999, pp. 0001-0035.

I. – A Legal system
for Internet Access Services based
on the 1994 GATS and the 1997
Basic Telecommunications Agreement

At the close of the Uruguay Round at the end of 1994, the Internet was not directly concerned by the practical scope of the WTO agreements as it was not a proper commercial sector. It only became one in April 1995 (2) with the commercial advent of Internet access services. From that date, Internet access services quite logically became subject to the General Agreement on Trade in Services as « *commercial services* ».

However, those services are only subject to all the GATS rules where a Member country has adopted « *specific commitments* » for such services. In fact, it should be remembered that GATS is made up of two types of rules of law. The first apply, without limitation, to all commercial services (3) whereas the second only apply if a Member has adopted specific commitments (4) for a particular category of services. Accordingly, each Member of the WTO adopts a schedule of commitments in which it states the services it wishes to liberalise and the restrictions it wishes to apply with regard to access to a particular market.

During the Uruguay Round, many WTO Members adopted specific commitments with regard to telecommunications services with added value (5), most of which came into force in 1995 :

– electronic mail,
– voice mail,

---

(2) In fact, until 30 April 1995, the Internet was administered by an independent American federal agency, the National Science Foundation (NSF).

(3) For example, Article 2, § 1 of GATS on the treatment of the most favoured nation states that « *With respect to any measure covered by this Agreement, each Member shall accord immediately and unconditionally to service suppliers of any other Member treatment no less favourable than that it accords to like services and service suppliers of any other country* ».

(4) For example, Article 6, § 3 of GATS on internal regulation states that « *Where authorisation is required for the supply of a service on which a specific commitment has been made, the competent authorities of a Member shall, within a reasonable period of time after submission of an application considered complete under domestic laws and regulations, inform the applicant of the decision concerning the application* ».

(5) Value-added services are defined as « *services offered by means of facilities for the transmission of public telecommunications transport, which use computer processing applications, acting on the format, content, protocol or other similar aspects of the information transmitted to the subscriber; which provide the subscriber with additional, different or restructured information or which involve an interaction between the subscriber and the information stored* ».

- online information and database retrieval,
- electronic data interchange,
- enhanced/value-added facsimile services,
- code and protocol conversion,
- online information or data processing.

Some Members (6), such as the United States, did not stop at the above examples and stated that all telecommunications services corresponding to their definition of added-value telecommunications services were covered by their schedule (7). In that respect, some time after the commercialisation of Internet access services in 1995, under their domestic legislation the United States likened them to value-added services. The Internet access services were then excluded from the scope of application of the basic telecommunications services regulations (8). Accordingly, it is not incorrect to consider that at the present time there are specific American commitments with regard to Internet access services (9).

In order to guarantee the effectiveness of the specific commitments with regard to value-added services, the WTO Members adopted an « Annex on telecommunications » which is one of the eight GATS Annexes. This guarantees providers of added value services access to the networks or basic telecommunications services (10). The Annex on telecommunications uses the expression « public telecommunications transport networks and services ». Nevertheless, the « decision on the negotiations on basic telecommunications » expressly treats basic telecommunications as networks or services for conveying telecommunications (11).

---

(6) This is Mexico, Norway, Poland, the Czech Republic and Slovakia.

(7) In their 1994 specific commitments, the United States included in the column on value-added telecommunication services, the heading « others » which makes their schedule non-exhaustive.

(8) See « In the Matter o Federal-State Joint Board on Universal Service », CC Docket n° 96-45, Report to Congress on Universal Service, 13 FCC Rcd at 11511, April 10, 1998, p. 30.

(9) In order to establish whether there are specific commitments with regard to access to the Internet, each WTO Member's schedule should be examined.

(10) Article 5-a of the Annex on Telecommunications states that « a) Each Member shall ensure that any service supplier of any other Member is accorded access to and use of public telecommunications transport networks and services on reasonable and non-discriminatory terms and conditions, for the supply of a service included in its Schedule. This obligation shall be applied, inter alia, through paragraphs (b) through (f) ».

(11) Accordingly that decision states that « negotiations shall be entered into on a voluntary basis with a view to the progressive liberalisation of trade in telecommunications transport networks and systems (hereinafter referred to as 'basic telecommunications') within the framework of the General Agreement on Trade in Services ».

However, although on the basis of the 1994 acts, providers of added-value services had a right of access to the public telecommunications transport networks or services, by contrast, at the time, due to a lack of competition in that sector, they did not have any choice with regard to the leasing of lines from basic telecommunications operators who were traditionally covered by special or exclusive rights.

For the Internet access sector, that is precisely the benefit of the « Basic Telecommunications Agreement » adopted in Geneva on 15 February 1997 by 69 Member countries. Under that Agreement, Member countries included in their schedule of specific commitments, under the heading « additional commitments », a text called « Reference Paper ». This contained, inter alia, provisions relating to interconnection and obliged those Members who had adopted it to introduce competitive safeguards and to establish an independent regulatory authority for those countries which did not have one. The Reference Paper also tackles the question of licences, universal service and scarce resources. It should be remembered that the statutory obligations arising from this text can only be imposed on major suppliers of basic telecommunications (12).

In the Reference Paper, telecommunications suppliers are treated as suppliers of public telecommunications transport networks and services so far as concerns the provisions relating to interconnection. The Annex on telecommunications and the Reference Paper therefore impose statutory obligations on basic telecommunications suppliers (13).

By thus imposing, firstly, the establishment of a « sectoral regulation » applicable to suppliers of basic telecommunication services and, secondly, the adoption of commitments aimed at liberalising – so far as concerns access to the Internet – the market of packet switched data transmission, the Basic Telecommunications Agreement helps to reduce the price of leased lines needed to provide Internet access services.

---

(12) The Reference paper states that a « major supplier is a supplier which has the ability to materially affect the terms of participation having regard to price and supply) in the relevant market for basic telecommunications services as a result of :

  a) control over essential facilities; or

  b) Use of its position in the market ».

(13) In the case of the Reference Paper, subject to being classified as major suppliers.

As described, the international legal rules for Internet access services would appear to be coherent both from a historical and financial point of view. However, alongside the economic growth of the NTIC industry, over the last few years there have been objections within the WTO to the rules governing Internet access services. Differences in sensitivity to the subject are obviously legitimate. However, they have created a real feeling of legal insecurity within the Internet access industry. It is vital that WTO Members do not call into question a process which began in 1994, whilst applying themselves to obeying the spirit and letter of the 1997 Basic Telecommunications Agreement.

II. – A legal system for Internet Access Services which is now faced with divergent assessment within the WTO

In their 1997 schedules of specific commitments, Members adopted, in varying degrees (14), measures for liberalisation relating to most national and international basic telecommunications markets, such as :
– fixed telephone services,
– mobile telephone services,
– telex services,
– telegraph services,
– private leased circuit services,
– facsimile services,
– circuit-switched data transmission services,
– and above all packet-switched data transmission services.

It is important to understand that packet-switched data transmission services and basic telecommunications services within the meaning of the 1997 agreement are vital but not sufficient for the provision of Internet access services, whether they are provided by « ISPs » or « IBPs ». The « IAPs » do not provide basic telecommunications services as defined in the Annex on telecommunications.

---

(14) In their schedules of specific commitments, developing countries have kept many more restrictions to access to their markets than the industrialised countries.

According to that Annex, the public telecommunications transport service (15) means « *any telecommunications transport service required, explicitly or in effect, by a Member to be offered to the public generally. Such services may include, inter alia, telegraph, telephone, telex and data transmission typically involving the real-time transmission of customer-supplied information between two or more points without any end-to-end change in the form of content of the customer's information* » (16). Internet access does not correspond to the technological criteria used in this definition of basic telecommunication services.

Internet access services provided by « ISPs » are, in fact, a combination of the functions of computer processing, data storage, protocol conversions and routing with transmission capabilities allowing users to access Internet content and services. These different functions prevent the transmission from taking place in real-time (data storage) and change the content of the information (conversion of protocols, routing tables, computer processing).

The same is true for Internet access services provided by « IBPs ». They use the infrastructures of telecommunications operators reserved for packet-switched data transmission services but do not offer this transmission capability themselves. In reality, when they are not vertically integrated, « IBPs » lease transmission capabilities from long distance telecommunications operators. They use these leased capabilities (17) but provide added value to the data transmitted on the leased lines. Accordingly, « IBPs » « *use routing tables which act on the information contained in the packets* » (18). « IBPs » also use « *protocol conversions so as to ensure that information using different communications protocols can cross disparate networks* » (19).

However, on this vital point, there are differences of opinion between some members of the WTO, the issue being whether or not to include Internet access services in the scope of application of the

---

(15) It is useful to remember that the decision on the negotiations on basic telecommunications likens the service of transporting telecommunications to the basic telecommunications service.

(16) See Article 3b of the Annex on Telecommunications.

(17) It should be noted the fact that an IBP is the owner of a basic telecommunications network does not change the legal classification of the services it provides. These are still value-added services as routers are still involved which act on the format of the transmitted data.

(18) See KENDE M., OXMAN J., « *the information interchange : interconnection on the Internet* », 11/12/99, p. 27.

(19) *Ibidem.*

basic telecommunications regulations. Although this debate could prove to be technical, it is nevertheless fundamental from a financial point of view. The introduction of *ex ante* regulations can have a real negative impact on technological investment and innovation in an emerging sector such as that of Internet access.

The debate over the legal classification of Internet access providers arose within the WTO in 1999. It is unfortunate that this objection is often compartmentalised in the field of affirmations of principles (20) with no real legal or technical arguments. Moreover, during the 1997 basic telecommunications negotiations, the insertion by some Members of explicit specific commitments concerning access to the Internet caused some confusion. However, that does not mean that Internet access services are basic services. In fact, during these same negotiations, some Members adopted explicit specific commitments relating to value-added telecommunications services. In other words, the mere inclusion of a category of telecommunications services in the 1997 schedules does not prejudice the legal classification of a telecommunications service.

Finally, there are two opposing arguments on the legal classification of Internet access services :

— according to the first, Internet access services are basic telecommunications services and the obligations for access, both under the Annex on telecommunications and the provisions relating to interconnection in the Reference Paper, apply to « IAPs » (21);
— according to the second, Internet access services (22) are value-added telecommunications services. In this case « IAPs » have no obligation under the Annex on Telecommunications and the Reference Paper. By contrast, the Annex on Telecommunications entitles them to access to public telecommunications transport services.

At the present time, the international legal system for Internet access services has therefore not reached a consensus which is vital in an area where national sovereignty still carries real weight and

---

(20) That is especially true for those who favour likening Internet access services to basic telecommunications services.

(21) See, in particular, « *Council for trade in services – communication from Australia – proposal for negotiations for telecommunications services* », S/CSS/W/17, 5 December 2000, p. 4.

(22) See the position of the United States on the legal classification of Internet access services « In the Matter o Federal-State Joint Board on Universal Service, Report to Congress on Universal Service », *op. cit.*, p. 30.

unfortunately this opposition has not been settled by a WTO body with normative or interpretive power. The issue of the legal classification of Internet access services could be raised by the Dispute Settlement Body or at the end of the Doha cycle, by Members taking part in the negotiations.

Conclusion : The concerns and expectations of industry in multilateral commercial negotiations on the internet and e-commerce

For any global operator, the results of the WTO's multilateral negotiations have a real impact on the implementation of their international strategy. At the conclusion of the « *1997 Basic Telecommunications Agreement* », the majority of market players welcomed the step taken by Members who were parties to the negotiations. By allowing access to the markets of a large number of countries and by requiring some regulatory barriers to be lifted, there is no doubt that that agreement helped the telecommunications services' growth in world trade. In 1997 the world telecommunications services market increased to 698 thousand million $. In 2000, it was 969.5 thousand million $ and forecasts for 2004 are around 1334 thousand million $. However, despite these very encouraging results, the work begun at the WTO is far from complete. There is much progress to be made and debates to be settled, whether on telecommunications or e-commerce.

A. – THE POSITION OF THE GLOBAL OPERATORS IN NEGOTIATIONS CONCERNING TELECOMMUNICATIONS

The 1994 GATS agreement and especially the 1997 basic telecommunications agreement, marked a breach in the international telecommunications world. These achievements are fundamental to the telecommunications industry and the development of the Information Society. Accordingly, it is important to :

– ensure compliance with the 1994 commitments on Value-added Telecommunications Services (enforcement of the provisions of the Annex on telecommunications);

– ensure full implementation of the 1997 commitments on basic
telecommunications (enforcement of the provisions of the
Reference Paper);
– improve the level of specific commitments (increase the « critical
mass », harmonise the dates for liberalisation of the existing
specific commitments).

Attention will naturally turn to the direction that the arguments
in the regulatory debate on the legal classification of Internet access
services take :

– firstly, this debate must not be a pretext for calling into question
the balance of agreements;
– secondly, it would be desirable for Members of the WTO to
expressly acknowledge that Internet access services are indeed
value-added services, moreover IAPs must be free from any
obligation under the Annex on telecommunications and the
Reference Paper on basic telecommunications. That express
acknowledgement would appear to be essential in order to establish a clear, reliable international legal system for Internet access
services.

On this last point, the legal system for Internet access services
must not be a carbon copy of that for basic telecommunications
services. It is not appropriate to regulate an emerging dynamic sector whilst the general tendency is towards lightening the sectoral
regulation in favour of the increasing application of existing competition law. In that respect, the reworking of Community legislation on telecommunications is moving in that direction. The
industry will pay close attention to the work undertaken under the
aegis of the WTO to establish a multilateral framework for competition matters.

B. – THE POSITION OF INDUSTRY
IN NEGOTIATIONS CONCERNING E-COMMERCE

E-commerce, together with telecommunications services and the
work concerning competition, is one of the three areas of interest
covered by the WTO that is of direct concern to the NTIC industry.
The measures taken for e-commerce under the aegis of the WTO
were introduced in 1998. These are respectively :

- the Members of the WTO Declaration on global e-commerce (23) of 20 May 1998, an important initiative designed to keep electronic transmissions exempt from customs duties;
- the e-commerce work programme launched on 25 September 1998, the aim of which is to examine all the issues connected with the development of e-commerce on a global scale. This programme involved the Councils of traders in goods, traders in services and those of the TRIPS (24) and commerce and development.

Numerous informal agreements were reached following the meetings held in Geneva but several points still have to be clarified. The issue of the classification of electronically delivered goods (application of GATT or GATS) is a good example of an issue raising a number of questions. In that respect, we need to ensure that the political considerations do not take precedence over the technical and legal considerations. Globally, the majority of the major operators believe that the Members of the WTO should make e-commerce more dynamic by removing the barriers to access to markets in all the sectors concerned (horizontal approach, « cluster »). Accordingly, in future negotiations we must ensure that the basic telecommunications services, Internet access services and e-commerce do not become a bargaining point between sectors, to their detriment.

---

(23) It was adopted on 20 May 1998 during the WTO Ministerial Conference which took place in Geneva on 18 and 20 May 1998.

(24) Agreement on the Trade-Related Aspects of Intellectual Property Rights.

THE INTERNATIONAL LEGAL FRAMEWORK FOR ELECTRONIC COMMERCE : THE ISSUES TO BE CONSIDERED TO ENSURE ITS DEVELOPMENT

BY

JEANNE SEYVET

SECRETARY OF STATE FOR INDUSTRY
DIRECTOR GENERAL FOR INDUSTRY
INFORMATION TECHNOLOGY AND POSTAL SERVICES, FRANCE

Electronic commerce affects all sectors of economic activity : manufacturing, retail trade, publishing, entertainment, financial services etc. The new opportunities are there to be exploited. It is very likely that in the long term they will create jobs, particularly in areas of high added value. In order to seize these opportunities, the legal environment must be conducive to their development. That means continuing the processes begun both at Community and at national levels to adapt the legislative and regulatory framework of information society services. On a more global geographical level, for many years now, adjustments have been made to the international rules that govern trade, made necessary by the dematerialisation of exchanges and the cross-border nature of networks.

The development of electronic commerce is based on a relationship of confidence between a buyer and a seller and that confidence can only exist if the international legal framework is safe, according to the various meanings of this word : known or predictable, stable and readily enforceable.

I shall concentrate my talk on electronic commerce with consumers (B2C), for which the legal framework is the most difficult to implement and yet the most necessary.

[*The lack of confidence on the part of actors : a constraint to the development of B2C electronic commerce :*]

There have been numerous studies and forecasts concerning the issues and prospects offered by electronic commerce. However, some indicators show that performance falls short of forecasts. In France, electronic commerce with consumers only represents a small part of the retail trade (apart from Minitel (1), admittedly). The reasons most often given (2) are fear and lack of confidence on the part of actors, as to the risks of electronic commerce, whether real or imagined. This is confirmed by a recent SESSI – *Service des Etudes et des Statistiques Industrielles* (surveys and industrial statistics service) survey, a service for which I am responsible.

[*The state of affairs with regard to international regulation*].

It is now widely recognised that it is important that self-regulation by the actors themselves (codes of good conduct, alternative methods of dispute resolution) should be fully available, but also that the States should define a set of basic rules that allow the fundamental principles which, moreover, are essential to the development of economic activities, to prevail. This balance refers back to the concept of co-regulation. As cross-border transactions increase, the actors in the information society expect harmonised laws from the governments, or at the very least, legislative cooperation that will allow sellers to trade and consumers to order outside their national market.

There have already been *numerous international studies* concerning the legal framework for electronic commerce, in various official bodies and within the European Union.

Accordingly, within the official bodies, issues such as taxation (OECD, WTO), the protection of personal data (OECD, Council of Europe), intellectual property (WIPO, WTO), security and authentication (UNCITRAL, OECD) and commercial aspects (WTO). These studies are important and their results encouraging. They are not designed to create a specific legal framework for electronic commerce but to adapt the existing framework to this new form of trading in its international dimension. In that respect, in accordance with the principle of technological neutrality, equal treatment

---

(1) In 1999, Internet purchases by consumers in France reached 0.2 thousand million euros (between 20 and 36 thousand million euros in the United States) and 1.3 thousand million euros for purchases via Minitel.

(2) A survey conducted by PriceWaterhouseCoopers and American Express at the end of 2000 showed that European consumers were still mistrustful of online commerce; the English were the least prepared to make online purchases or even to use online banking services.

should be given to the various types of commerce and, in particular, international commerce.

The European Union has established a coherent legislative framework applicable to electronic commerce. Directive 2000/31/EC (3) known as the « E-commerce Directive » harmonises the laws of the Member States as far as the regulation of advertising, transparency and fairness in transactions, and promoting codes of conduct is concerned. Similarly, the Community studies are designed to promote Community networks of bodies for the out-of-court settlement of consumer disputes covering the entire Union and designed to help Internet consumers settle their disputes without going to court. Outside this geographical area, there are major differences in approaches to legislation (time-limit for withdrawal, access to the courts, non compliance with public policy etc). Without a legal framework for exchanges with other countries, this gap damages the confidence of actors in the information society. However, when a basic principle is under threat, Europe introduced a specific and truly outstanding device : the directive on the protection of personal data (4), which addresses the transfer of data to other countries (and which gave rise to the « Safe Harbor » with the United States).

[*There are still some important issues to be resolved :*]

However, although the work carried out within international circles has led to an examination of issues such as the protection of personal data or the security of transactions, no organisation has got to grips with electronic commerce in its entirety, and in my view, some issues have no global discussion forum in which to address them. These problems, which all concern the methods of dispute resolution in exchanges between actors in different countries concern :

1. The appropriate jurisdiction for settling them and ensuring that the decisions made are recognised and enforced and the law applied to do so.

---

(3) Directive 2000/31/EC of the European Parliament and of the Council of 8 June 2000 on certain legal aspects of information society services, in particular electronic commerce, in the internal market (« the e-commerce directive »).

(4) Directive 95/46/EC of the European Parliament and of the Council of 24 October 1995, on the protection of individuals with regard to the processing of personal data and on the free movement of such data. Chapter IV of the directive concerns the transfer of personal data to third countries.

2. The terms and conditions for the out-of-court settlement of disputes.

I. – The appropriate jurisdiction for settling them and ensuring that the decisions made are recognised and enforced and the law applied to do so

There will be an increase in cases in which the outcome of a dispute requires issues to be resolved concerning the *determination of the appropriate jurisdiction and applicable legislation but also and above all, the recognition and enforcement of judgments given in a foreign country and/or on the basis of a foreign law.*

Indeed *the selection of an appropriate jurisdiction* is the subject of a draft worldwide convention on the jurisdiction of courts and on facilitating the recognition and enforcement of decisions in civil and commercial matters between States (The Hague conference on private international law). This project is promising.

Within Europe, these issues are settled by the Brussels Convention of 27 September 1968 which binds all Member States of the Community and Member States of the ex-EFTA and Poland under the Lugano Convention of 16 September 1988 which contains similar provisions. The Brussels Convention is replaced by Regulation (EC) n° 44/2001 of the Council known as [« Brussels 1 »], which will enter into force as from 1st March 2002. For European countries, the draft global convention of The Hague Conference, which addresses this same issue, represents a decisive challenge for relations with non-member countries.

Selection of the applicable law is the other major challenge for the legal framework applicable to online commercial exchanges. When cross-border disputes arise and several laws conflict with each other, it can be particularly difficult to select the applicable law. In the field of electronic commerce, this issue is even more complex in that it is difficult to determine the place of the dispute, particularly in cases of cross-border exchanges, not to mention cases in which there is a problem of precisely locating the actors involved.

In the context of intra-Community exchanges, the Convention of Rome designates the law applicable to contractual obligations and the E-Commerce Directive does the same for extra-contractual obligations.

Outside the geographical scope of these legislative provisions, the rules and jurisprudence of private international law apply but we are then faced with several laws which could claim to apply and whose content can be very different. In order to establish confidence, it would first be necessary to determine amicably which law applies.

The current legal framework for electronic is therefore characterised by what I shall call a legal « insecurity » in cross-border relations. The insecurity relates to the legal basis of the measures a consumer can take in relation to services of a service provider who is established in another country. The consumer, and more generally, the recipient of the services, is dissuaded from entering into an online contract and taking advantage of the new opportunities if he believes that he is in an environment that is unclear and has few guarantees as to the protection afforded to him. An international study must be undertaken before inextricable situations arise from cross-border disputes.

II. – The terms and conditions
for the out-of-court settlement of disputes

We must seek *alternative methods of dispute resolution*, which allow small claims and low-value transactions generated by online commerce with consumers to be settled quickly and cheaply. There is a common ground of understanding on the general principles that should govern the methods of alternative dispute resolution : transparency, accessibility, free of charge or low cost, quick decisions, confidentiality, impartiality, independence etc., but there again, there are numerous difficulties to be overcome and widely differing points of view. And yet, the diversity or even the divergence of systems or principles implemented in the various States does not create serious problems for electronic commerce that takes place within the same country. By contrast, this disparity causes great difficulties for cross-border exchanges, especially with regard to the problems I have just set out concerning selection of the applicable law and the authority which will be responsible for settling disputes. The binding nature of alternative methods of dispute resolution, their scope, their relationship with legal proceedings and the role of the courts of last instance are the main questions which so far remain unanswered.

Finally, one must bear in mind that both consumers and businesses must help to create confidence which is essential for the development of electronic commerce. And the debate over the selection of the applicable law illustrates the difficulties in reconciling the legitimate interests of both actors.

Moreover, the question arises as to whether the aim of « effective protection of actors in international exchanges » should not be achieved to some extent by a minimum harmonisation of rules. For example, one might imagine that an agreement should be sought that covers the greatest number of countries and establishes a legal basis for consumer protection (similar to the OECD's guidelines) by also encouraging the convergence of practices when selecting the applicable law, or failing that, that an agreement should be drawn up with fewer signatories and more ambitious rules, possibly drawing inspiration from European law. The two approaches can be complementary.

Conclusion

This outline of a state of affairs which would obviously require a more methodical examination of the issues raised by electronic commerce with consumers at an international level and on the work currently being undertaken within existing forums and of the options for action available to the authorities concerned therefore indicates that important results are either attained or expected. Our concern relates to the matters over which there is neither international consensus nor even discussion in an appropriate forum.

During a discussion at the beginning of the year led by the Ministry for the Economy, Finance and Industry, several key themes were identified : consumer protection, selection of the applicable law, alternative methods of dispute resolution etc.,

Insofar as they seek to establish a reliable legal framework and effective protection for consumers, in my view, the expectations of the actors of electronic commerce would appear to centre on these major themes.

CONSUMER PROTECTION AND S.M.ES

BY

GEORGES CHATILLON

LECTURER,
UNIVERSITY OF PARIS-I, PANTHÉON-SORBONNE

Introduction

Since the 18th century, philosophers and politicians have been concerned with Human Rights. Numerous charters and declarations have been drawn up, reviled and worshiped.

Twentieth century culture which was clearly geared towards mass production, to the benefit of manufacturers, has only just begun to be directed towards the protection of consumer rights.

The universal charter of Human Rights does not contain any explicit provisions in favour of consumers. The constitutions and fundamental laws of the industrialised nations are hardly verbose in this regard.

After the second world war, the general principles of contract law were deemed to be sufficient to settle very unequal conflicts between consumers and sellers, wholesalers, manufactures and builders.

The economy of the industrialised countries, based on mass consumption had a duty not to discourage consumers. Legal experts, asked by producers of consumer goods had to leave aside the traditional principles of civil law and forge new rules which, over time, proved to be generously protective of the rights of average consumers.

We have even come to take into legal consideration the sometimes huge phenomenon of over-indebtedness, regardless of the absolute rights of creditors and expected fulfilment of the proper right of ownership.

In this field also, the Internet imposes changes which upset the usual rules.

Traditional law had assimilated and settled unusual questions of distance selling which takes place via a purchase order set out on standard documents and which, as legal improvements are introduced, is subject to rules that prevent consumers from causing misunderstandings that might lead to financial disasters that involve the entire assets of some.

However consumers could, and still can, buy recommended goods in recommended shops.

With the Internet, the relationship to the physical world disappears. The only material presence is that of the consumer's screen. The beloved salespersons have disappeared. The desired goods are small format images. Selling propositions and offers become the text and images that the unknown and unreachable individuals and traders have communicated to anyone who wants to download them. Mistrust replaces the customary prudence.

The alarming news are increasing : bank card numbers would circulate on the net, bank accounts would be pillaged, some goods offered would be illicit, one would not be able to trace the swindlers, personal information disclosed to Internet companies would be passed on.

In these circumstances, careful consumers prefer not to get involved.

Amongst other causes, the low growth in e-commerce is due to the mistrust, the lack of protection, to the opacity of commercial and bank transactions that have very little security and, to say the least, lack transparency.

Governments must react. Legal experts must work. Consumer protection associations must intervene.

Until now, the problems of the liability of Internet access providers and that of hosts, issues relating to copyright, the definition of unlawful content on the Internet and the means of pursuing the criminals have received a great deal of attention from the public authorities and legal experts in general. Criminal Internet law and the legal measures for punishing offences have grown to the same extent.

So far as concerns the Internet, the attack on the Twin Towers in New York and the murder of 6,000 of its inhabitants triggered the fight against cyberterrorism. Everywhere, or almost everywhere, the powers of investigation of the courts and the police were significantly increased. The new laws, created for the exceptional situation will also do for the common situation. Certain boundaries have been crossed.

It is appropriate to pose the global question of the legal protection of consumers and S.M.Es on the Internet.

Within the incredible labyrinth of global networks of the commercial Internet, the average consumer is definitely the weakest link, the most vulnerable, the most lacking in ammunition when confronted with commercial offers for desirable goods and services.

What economists call ophelimity, the desire to purchase, finds, its most extensive expression in the Internet : a consumer alone in front of his screen, transported by a few magic clicks into the most gigantic market stalls since the beginning of history. The good Aladdin's genie is no longer in the oil lamp but in the belly of a computer mouse.

It would be mistaken to treat consumers as individuals, artisans, small traders and consumers as small and medium enterprises with fewer than ten people and which do not specialise in computers, the networks and online trade and services, differently. Accordingly, in this report, the word consumer will mean both individuals and small enterprises that do not specialise in computers, networks or online trade.

The predictions relating to online trade, each one more marvellous than the next, until the net-economy crash in 2000, have given governments of nations and the heads of specialist international organisations a strong impetus to lay down the foundations for regulations for e-commerce.

It was quickly understood that the Internet must be a place of commercial trust and that the rules of the game for traders and customers needed to be established.

These objectives found responses within the European Union which has proved to be fruitful so far as concerns legal innovations.

The European E-commerce Directive (1) is a piece of legislation that protects consumer rights relatively well. However an analysis

---

(1) EC Directive n° 2000-31 of 8 June 2000, on certain legal aspects of information society services and in particular e-commerce, in the internal market (e-commerce directive).

of its application has yet to be conducted. The 15 member countries of the Union must transpose it.

Will the raft of national legal divergences make this directive the founding legislation of the European Union of consumers, specific to a single market?

Faced with a legally divided Europe, the American commercial regulations do not really seem to protect consumer rights, in any event any more safely on the Internet than elsewhere. However, the customers of the biggest commercial nation in the world are naturally the rest of the world's consumers.

China has just entered the World Trade Organisation. Using online trade, it intends to export products and services made with one of the cheapest labour forces in the world. What legal protection will there be for e-commerce with China?

It would appear that the fundamental digital rights of consumers and S.M.Es are partially recognised (1st part), whereas the mechanisms for protecting the fundamental digital rights of consumers and S.M.Es are still in their infancy (2nd part).

I. – The fundamental digital rights of consumers and S.M.Es are partially recognised

Since the Internet creates a global market, the rules of that market must find harmonious, if not similar legal solutions. At the moment, that is not the case at all.

The very issue of fundamental digital rights remains in abeyance. What are they? Where do they begin? Where do they end?

Also, no list of the fundamental digital rights of consumers who are Internet users has been established by any international authority.

On a global scale, the fundamental digital rights of consumers are entirely different, unequal, not to say non-existent (A).

Legal protection is unequal within industrialised countries and all the more so between industrialised countries and emerging countries (B).

A. – The fundamental digital rights of consumers and S.M.Es

The European Union's legislation roughly covers most of the issues relating to online transactions : 1995 : Directive 95/46/EC on the Protection of Individuals with regard to the Processing of Personal Data and the Free Movement of such Data; 1996 : Directive 96/9/EC on the Legal Protection of Databases; 1997 : Directive 97/66/EC on the Processing of Personal Data and the Protection of Privacy in the Telecommunications Sector; 1999 : Directive 1999/93/EC on a Community Framework for Electronic Signatures; 2000 : Directive EC n° 2000-31 on certain Legal Aspects of Information Society Services, and in particular E-Commerce, in the Internal Market (the E-commerce Directive); 2001 : Regulation (EC) of 28 May 2001 on Cooperation between the Courts of Member States in the taking of Evidence in Civil or Commercial Matters.

In seven years, the representatives of the States and Community institutions have updated the rules, which are often new, adapted to the European legal culture. It is a tour de force.

There is one directive missing on consumer rights in the European information society.

The efforts of European nations have not always been taken up by the other countries.

However, the sequence of transactions on the Internet, the irrepressible links between the reliability of data, their integrity, their necessary protection, questions of identification of individuals, authentication of signatures and the security of transactions, require the law to take into account the whole process whilst simultaneously and systematically taking into consideration the legal links between the transactions, as much as the classification and legal fate of each of these functions : authentication, integrity, durability, data protection, evidence, reciprocal information, exchanges of consent, secure payments, after-sales service, management of contracts and returns of products and services.

The heterogeneous nature of positive laws and case-law relating to consumer rights faced with globalisation of the Internet (1) inclines towards establishing a Universal Charter of consumer rights (2).

1. – *The heterogeneous nature*
of positive laws and case-law

The general principles of various national consumer protection laws are not fundamentally different when the systems of positive law take account of them. However, in such matters, it is all a question of details. A European consumer can legitimately expect that his rights are reasonably protected in the United States. For example, no-one will take the decision to issue legal proceedings before an American court for the fistful of dollars that the purchase of a CD, a piece of software, or a work, etc. represents. Especially as the national authorities do not often provide any help where there is a dispute with a foreign trader.

The American commercial Internet sites are in English and consumer rights are not explicitly set out. In fact, they are not shown. If they were, Internet users who are consumers would have to understand the rules of a foreign law and provide for their practical implementation.

The matter is too often resolved by refraining from a purchase where there is a risk of not recovering the money paid. However, a number of consumers take this financial risk.

The American example is not the only one. In fact, it is risky to buy on the Internet anywhere in the world, even on domestic sites.

In the age of globalisation and the omnipresent Internet, at least in the « rich » countries, the main hindrance to trade is undoubtedly the legal protection of consumers. It would be reasonable to draw up a universal charter of Internet users' consumer rights.

2. – *Towards a Universal Charter*
of Internet user's consumer rights?

A great many international legal instruments have been drawn up for a century and a half in order to improve relations between States, and, through them, between individuals and legal entities : a Universal Charter of Human Rights, the European Convention on Human Rights, international treaties and agreements on trade, tax, transport, etc... A great number of human activities have been the subject of international pacts.

There is little chance of a Universal Charter of Internet users' consumer rights being created in the near future. However, because of the Internet, it would be of immediate benefit. A preparatory conference would probably take about ten years of all manner of negotiations between States, consumer associations, trade federations and a great many non-governmental organisations. Presuming that the principle of such a charter is discussed, many member States of the United Nations, including those that enjoy a right of veto, would be inclined to refuse its creation in the name of liberalism, poverty or the necessary supervision of activities by the State.

The typical example is that of Microsoft, a world power that dominates computer operating systems, software, office automation, navigators and soon, servers. Despite many complaints from a number of federate States of the United States of America, the American giant is about to be let off with regard to its commercial practices. However, its extreme domination of the world market is legally presented as harming the interests and rights of consumers.

The World Trade Organisation could create rules to protect consumers at the same time as inter-State commercial exchanges. However, its statutes would need to be revised and the objectives of negotiations reviewed. There again, the practices adopted create as many obstacles.

The American desire for a minimum regulation of the Internet in order to leave room for market forces does not leave much hope that consumer rights will be better protected at international level. However, the American authorities are aware that market regulation by businesses alone, not to say self-regulation, is not sufficient.

Accordingly, the « legal paradox of the Internet » remains almost in its pure state, since the Internet is a virtually global network whereas the rules of law are still established by each State.

Admittedly, there are blocks of rules in the United States of America, in Canada and in Western Europe. However these rules are not always harmonised and in some regions of the world, the States are not yet considering consulting each other (Africa, South America, Asia, Middle East).

In time, the application of the new rules on signatures and e-commerce by the States of the European Union and those of North America, should generate exchanges of best practice around 2005-

2010. However, these dates are too far ahead to make reasonable diagnoses.

We must hope that the continental consumer associations will pay attention to the problems encountered by e-commerce customers and will want to consult each other to put forward propositions for harmonisation, or in any case cooperation.

In fact, the needs for legal protection of Internet users who are consumers are equal.

B. – Unequal measures for legal protection

The globalisation of the economy should lead to a globalisation of legal systems, or in any case, a better harmonisation of laws. That is what has happened to the advantage of the offer, that is to say sellers, in the context of e-commerce, thanks to the work of the UNCITRAL, WIPO, UNCTAD, the International Chamber of Commerce, the ITU, contractual bases, electronic signatures and the basic principles for protecting data have found solutions. Those who have been left out are consumers without whom markets do not exist.

In any event, there are fundamental differences between the legal systems for protecting consumers in rich countries and those in poor countries.

1. – *Legal protection within consumerist cultures*

The consumerist cultures of the rich countries find expression in aggressive promotion and sales policies. Faced with the ingenuity of sellers, consumers have had to organise themselves and claim rights to protect them. Legal and para-legal measures have been introduced by means of laws or clear legal precedents : regulation of advertising and promotional offers; regulation of credit and financial products; regulation of contractual clauses and consumers' right to cancel; innovations with regard to online and offline mediation; the right of consumer associations to get involved in legal proceedings as the party claiming damages; public policies for information, prevention and assistance. The panoply of legal instruments for protection is vast, complex and often effective.

Before making any purchase, consumers can consult guides and receive advice. The obligation for sellers to inform and advise purchasers is a general basic principle of legal systems in rich countries as is the clarity of contractual clauses. These are two important reasons why the courts declare sales contracts void. The right for consumers to reflect, for a short time, is itself, an effective protection against impulse buying without thought or the sometimes improper persuasive powers of salesmen and their procession of promotional arguments.

2. – The lack of legal protection in emerging countries

By contrast, on the whole, purchasers in emerging countries find themselves doubly disadvantaged by a lack of money and real shortcomings on the part of the public authorities with regard to laws that protect consumers. Admittedly, the rules of law in force on the popular markets are nothing like those in rich countries and the more fortunate consumers in the emerging countries have means available that are often effective. It is also true that the penetration rate of the Internet is very low if not non-existent in entire areas whose inhabitants do not even have a telephone because there are no lines.

However, use of the Internet is another matter and more often than not it takes place through cybercafes. That does not stop the ever-increasing number of mobile phones and double click to accept a contract can be made via the telephone.

The States and businesses in rich countries were able to prepare for the advent of e-commerce and establish rules with wide application. It is essential that the States and business in emerging countries do the same. Cooperation in that respect should be established and developed. We are a long way from it. Purchasers in poor countries do not have real access to the courts or to wise advice. In the future they will have access to purchasing via the Internet or by telephone with UMTS technology without any real protection.

It can bee seen that globalisation is not yet legal. There are some commercial islands in which the comparable legal systems are attempting to regulate relations between sellers and buyers. However, apart from North America, Western Europe, Japan, Australia and New Zealand, the rest of the world is too deficient in protective rules, especially as their political and social systems are far from being transparent and controllable by the law.

II. – Mechanisms for protecting the fundamental digital rights of consumers and S.M.Es are still in their infancy

The longstanding existence of contracts by postal correspondence, that is to say the development of distance selling, has given legislators enough time and judges enough experience for them to arrange for consumers' rights to be protected.

By contrast, the fact that online sales contracts are still in their infancy, the lack of hindsight of the judges, the unsuitability of traditional procedures for current consumer contracts have not yet allowed the emergence of a justice suited to the instantaneous nature of the exchange of consent.

We must reckon with consumers' legal inexperience and establish an online prevention policy (A) at the same time as an online legal protection policy (B).

A. – ONLINE PREVENTION

Various legal mechanisms have been provided by the E-commerce Directive and, for example, the French draft law on the information society designed to provide some kind of prevention and *a priori* protection of consumers. Let us quote the general principle of the law of the double click, the display of the contract, the right of consumers to check the data in the contract which goes hand in hand with a right to examine the vendors' files and the right to withdraw.

These provisions appear to be minimal having regard to the right to sell on the Internet. They do not take into account the technical subtlety of the language of lawyers and therefore its esotericism for consumers who are not legal experts, that is to say almost everyone.

We need to provide mechanisms for providing legal information online which would ensure that information is secure and reliable (1).

However the right information does not prevent disputes arising. We therefore need to provide mechanisms for preventing disputes so that they do not arise (2).

1. – *Information concerning consumers' rights*

There is a danger that consumers' gradual mastery of Internet tools will bring about two complementary situations. The first can be caused by the development of e-commerce and the rapid selection by consumers of « good » commercial sites and « honest » sellers, the buyers increasingly acting as selectors. The second is the use of the Internet to protest against unethical sites and sellers with a speed and cohesive force that is impossible in the world of traditional commerce.

Consumers' associations can present online comparative tables of the methods used by the sellers, model contracts offered and possible guarantees. There is therefore nothing to prevent consumers from consulting this information prior to any purchase. It is even foreseeable that the sellers can pride themselves on the number of stars or ranking they have on the consumer associations' files. There is no rule of law to prevent comparing sales methods or clauses of contracts online. The public authorities could not risk legislating to prohibit such comparisons. Consumers will be warned fairly quickly about the existence of unfair or perverse clauses and should make a difference.

2. – *The prevention of online disputes*

We must prevent disputes from arising by every means. The economical, social and commercial cost of proceedings is largely offset by the expense required to establish online mediators whose role would be to give an opinion on the legal clarity of contracts and commercial procedures. It is fair to envisage that the use of an online mediator would entail costs. It is legitimate to suggest that such costs should be borne by the seller if the mediator's opinion is unfavourable to him. Otherwise, the consumer will have to pay, the cost of mediation being set off against the risks of suffering unfavourable contractual clauses or wasting time an money and losing the benefit of the purchase.

B. – Online protection of consumers' rights

The law of contracts is based, more or less, on the principle the autonomy of parties' will and the freedom of rules of evidence.

The autonomy of parties' will may have as its corollary a situation of inequality between the contracting parties. The famous ophelimity triggers impulse buying with clauses that can be unfair.

Freedom of the rules of evidence is radically limited with the use of the certified electronic signature.

E-commerce or traditional commerce, adjusted or discretionary evidence, ultimately, the interpretation of contractual clauses remains under the control of the judge and procedural rules.

The great heterogeneity of rules applicable to contracts is definitely not a unifying factor for rules for the commercial Internet (1).

Especially as the time taken and the cost of court proceedings are antinomic to the instantaneous nature of Internet procedures. We must therefore create new rules for resolving online disputes (2).

1. – *The contractual mechanisms*

Apart from the European directives on electronic commerce and electronic signatures, an attempt to harmonise the contractual rules applicable to contracts entered into online on a continental scale, the rules relating to contracts vary from one country to another. Moreover, the jurisdiction clauses, drawn up in accordance with national rules of the seller's country are hardly favourable to consumers residing in another country.

2. – *Alternative dispute resolution*

There again, the mechanisms for alternative dispute resolution that are in force within the European Union are a model that should be widespread and which can only be disseminated.

Conclusion

It would appear that only the first part of the work of the legal experts has been done. It is now possible to enter into contracts online, to make them secure and to pay for them. The basic rules have therefore been established.

These rules are not sufficient to establish consumer confidence. They must be given sufficient information online to prevent them from becoming the victims of online legal pitfalls : clauses that cannot be understood, poorly identified objects and services, legal consequences of their actions not appreciated or ill-perceived, commercial and legal strategies that are possibly perverse and promoted by the sellers.

The contracting parties also need to be able to prevent disputes from arising and the mechanisms for mediation must clarify the misunderstandings and resolve them. It is a question of interpreting the proposals of offer and acceptance based on the fact that sellers wish to sell and not litigate and that the buyers wish to buy and not assert their rights before the courts.

Finally, once disputes have arisen, they need to be resolved quickly, as inexpensively as possible and with the minimum subsequent court intervention.

Above all, the question of consumers' fundamental rights must become a founding issue of Internet law for consumer associations, States and international organisations.

The creation of a Universal Charter of fundamental rights of consumers is a necessary project.

ELECTRONIC AUTHENTICITY

Maître Didier FROGER
Notaire

The law of 13 March 2000 « amending the law on proof and concerning the electronic signature » changed the articles in the Civil Code on documentary evidence and gave the written document in electronic form conclusive force equal to that of the written document on paper.

Neither the preparatory work, nor the European directives, dealt with the authentic instrument (*acte authentique*) (1). But the legislator logically reintroduced the concept of authenticity in electronic written matter, and the law states that the authentic instrument can be drawn up on electronic support.

As it is the instrument of proof « par excellence », the legislator therefore showed consistency and we can only congratulate him for doing so. However, the implementing decree which lays down the conditions for drafting and preserving the electronic authentic instrument has not yet appeared and we may wonder what the nature and methods for the application of electronic authenticity will be.

I shall try to dispel these doubts in two ways :

– firstly, by comparing the difficulties and looking at the differences between the authentic instrument and the private uncertified document (*acte sous seing privé*). I will point out that the system set in place by the decree of 30 March 2001 to validate the electronic private document is very complex and the reliability it attempts to instil is only an assumption and does not provide any security.

---

(1) *Translator's note* : « acte authentique » – I have translated this term as « authentic instrument » to retain the link in the text with « authenticity », in the sense of « officially attested ».

– then, by examining how we can adapt the authentic instrument to electronic support, concentrating particularly on the notarial act.

I. – The authentic instrument

A. – WHAT IS THE DIFFERENCE
BETWEEN THE AUTHENTIC INSTRUMENT
AND THE PRIVATE UNCERTIFIED DOCUMENT ?

The private uncertified document is a written deed drawn up directly between private individuals or professionals in law, but signed by the parties themselves without the intervention of a public officer.

The authentic instrument is accepted by a public officer, a member of the court for court decisions, prefect or minister for administrative measures, registrar for civil status certificates, or notary for notarial acts. In all those situations, apart from a certain solemnity in the formalities, the physical presence of the public officer and the appending of his written signature are compulsory. The signature is of critical importance :

1°) It gives the document a particularly vigorous conclusive force, much greater than that of private uncertified documents : the authentic instrument is presumed to state the truth and can only be disputed by civil proceedings to challenge its authenticity, a particularly cumbersome legal procedure. Moreover authentic means « self-sufficient », etymologically. The authentic instrument thus guarantees the content of a contract at least in its main provisions. It is proof of its existence and date. It is equivalent to a final judgment.

2°) The notary, a public officer, signs and thus commits himself on the truth and perfection of his document. He commits his civil liability, but also his disciplinary liability. The sanctions are considerable : a forgery by a notary is subject to the Assize Court and leads to dismissal.

Therefore, the main features of the authentic instrument are as follows : it is written, obviously on paper at present, in a legible and indelible manner. The notary must retain and file the original; he will provide a copy at the request of the signatories in unlimited numbers as all copies signed by the notary and certified as true copies have the same value as the original.

B. – Is it unrealistic to adapt this document
with all its virtues to electronic support?

It is wrong to think primarily that drawing up an electronic authentic instrument will be complicated. Nothing is less certain :

The essence of the private uncertified document is that the two contracting parties append their signatures and nothing more. With the electronic signature, there are some difficulties : the signatory and author of the document has to be identified, the link between the document and the signatory must be made, a third party has to intervene to certify that link and a higher authority has to intervene to validate the certificate. It is far from being simple, and the decree of 30 March 2001 has increased the requirements to attempt to make the electronic signature secure.

The essence of the authentic instrument lies in the presence of a person, a public officer, or notary, who accepts the consent of the parties, witnesses it and draws up the document. Therefore, the important signature is not the contracting party's, but the notary's.

Consequently, there is no longer any need to worry about the way in which the contracting parties will show their consent, whether it is electronic or not, or certified or not. They can simply click on an icon, the main point is that it takes place before the notary, in his presence.

C. – Will drawing up
an authentic instrument on electronic
support weaken authenticity ?

There has been a dispute since the vote on the law of 13 March 2000. Some people have said that from the moment the notary accepted electronic instruments, he lost his role as a privileged witness, which deprives the authentic instrument of its essence. Some have even gone as far as to predict the fall or decline of the authentic instrument!

A second idea was immediately added to the first : the authentic instrument is now useless as the electronic signature and its system of certification (even the term authentication is used) will give the private uncertified document indisputable security in terms of proof, security which would be even better than with a paper document!

Such statements fail to understand the role of the notary and confuse certification and authenticity. The task of the notary is not to certify the process of identifying the sender of an electronic message. The instrument is authentic because after making sure of the identity of the contracting parties the notary has checked whether their consent was sincere and well-informed, because he drew up the document and the contracting parties signed it with his explanations and advice.

Contracting parties can resort to the authentic instrument, either by a personal approach or by legal obligation, to benefit from its conclusive force, enforceability, definite date, in short its security. Those virtues are nothing to do with the support used to draft and preserve it. A document is authentic because it is accepted by the notary and signed by him, and not because it is drawn up on paper.

The rules for paper support must nevertheless be adapted to the new electronic support.

II. – Electronic authenticity

What could be more different than the universe of authenticity and the electronic world?

The former has the physical meeting of people, the real and solemn presence of the public officer, the territorial regulations, the material nature of the seal and the formalities, continuity.

The latter has speed, evanescence, an ephemeral nature, informal, virtual and instantaneous transmission, the abolition of frontiers and time, the dematerialization of paper flows and written documents.

How can we combine the rules of authenticity with new technology?

That is the whole question :

The definition of the authentic instrument has not changed since 1804 : « *The authentic instrument is the instrument which is accepted by public officers who have the right to draw up deeds in the place where the document has been drawn up and with the required solemnities* » (Art. 1317 of the Civil Code).

Three fundamental requirements are contained in that text and thus influence the existence and validity of the authentic instrument :

- the document must be accepted by a public officer acting in fulfilment of his duties; that is acceptance,
- the public officer must have the right to draw up a deed, which implies that he has the power and capability,
- formalities (« solemnities ») must be complied with.

The criteria of power and capability are not affected by the new law. However, the advent of an instrument of communication which transcends borders will perhaps one day raise the problem of cross-border recognition of the power of a public officer. We are not yet at that stage.

What about the other conditions of authenticity : acceptance and solemnities ? Are they changed by electronic support ?

A. – Acceptance

The document must be accepted by the notary himself. Why ? Because the task of the notary is to be a witness, he witnesses the exchange of consents in order to give proof of it; it is a task of public service and he alone has the confidence of the State to carry it out.

This rule has two consequences :

- firstly, the requirement of the physical presence of the notary during the exchange of consents and particularly when the signatures which demonstrate that exchange are appended. If the notary is not present when these signatures are appended, he is not a witness and the document would not be authentic;
- secondly, the notary cannot delegate his powers, in principle. This rule has been changed with the authorisation of clerks. But it is clear that the authorisation does not involve important contracts and that the notary does not delegate the power to grant authenticity, as it is always his signature on the document;
- thirdly, the uniqueness of the notary : one notary is present at all stages of the document and collects all the signatures. It is only

in this way that he can witness the sincerity of all the consents and their meeting.

The « real » physical presence of the notary at the time of acceptance thus constitutes a substantial element of the authenticity and cannot be dissociated from it.

We can see the difficulty straight away, as one of the features of electronic support is to be able to make exchanges at a distance. It is clear that because of distance, the notary could not be present with the signatory parties when they are on the network, if they are geographically distant from one another; if he is with one, he is not with the other.

A solution would be to allow different notaries to be at each end of the chain and collect the consent of the parties on separate documents. Thus, the need for the physical presence of the notary as a witness will be preserved and the notaries each legalise one document, the intervening notary a document of power of attorney or proposal, the *instrumentary* notary, the final document.

B. – 2ND CONDITION
OF AUTHENTICITY : SOLEMNITIES

There are two kinds :

a) the first is part of the substance of the authenticity : the intervention of the public officer can be seen in his signature on the contract and legislation specifically sanctions the absence of the notary's signature by making the document null and void.

The importance of that signature was confirmed by the law of 13 March 2000.The new article 1316-4 which defines it states : « When it is appended by a public officer, it gives the document authenticity ».

As it concerns the electronic signature of the notary, the signature process which the notary will use must therefore comply with article 1316-4.

Thus, its reliability will lie in the use of an electronic certificate which is issued by a certification service provider.

Can the service provider be one of the accredited operators who will come on to the market ? That is not easy to reconcile with the status of the notary who is a public officer and grants authenticity in the name of the Republic and under the State seal. A public operator or a system of self-certification within the profession should be used.

b) There are also other formalities. For example, the purely material instructions for drafting the document such as the prohibition of too much text and spaces, the approval of words struck out, initials at the foot of pages. All these formalities are laid down by the Ventôse law and the decree of 26 November 1971 « on the form of notarial acts ».

Article 7 of that decree provides that « *notarial acts are drawn up in a legible and indelible way on paper of a quality which guarantees preservation* ». That article will have to be amended to be adapted to electronic support.

That is what the notary profession proposed when they requested that the decree of 1971 should be updated. The decree should no doubt be supplemented by orders setting standards for encoding to be used and also procedures for electronic storage.

In conclusion, for the notary profession, the law of 13 March has not changed the legal system of notarial instruments. While it now allows authentic instruments to be drawn up on electronic support, it did not wish to upset the hierarchy of instruments and proof, nor change the factors comprising authenticity.

The authentic instrument, the instrument of proof « par excellence », could not be kept separate from a reform of the law on proof.

Nor could it be totally cut off from new technology and the changes that has caused in our environment.

On the contrary, authenticity can even bring a security to electronic exchanges which is currently lacking.

Society does not need a third party to act as certifier, rather a third party to give confidence, who is neutral and impartial and who states the legal position and restores balance in relations between individuals.

It is the main role of the notary. The idea of authenticity, even in an age of globalisation and electronics is, in fact, very modern : far from ratifying the rule of impenetrable machinery and anonymous systems, it is reintroducing the human aspect, in this case the witness in the contractual process.

THE UNCITRAL'S MODEL LAW
ON ELECTRONIC SIGNATURES

BY

RENAUD SORIEUL

CHIEF ADMINISTRATOR,
DEPARTMENT OF INTERNATIONAL TRADE LAW
THE UN'S LEGAL AFFAIRS OFFICE (*)

Introduction : the role of UNCITRAL

The United Nations Commission for international trade law
(UNCITRAL) is an intergovernmental organisation created in 1966
to promote the « progressive harmonisation and unification of international trade law ». Sitting at the highest level of the UN system,
as it directly responsible to the General Assembly, this discreet
organisation has undergone rapid expansion over the last few years,
since it is increasingly called upon to provide models for international private trade law, sometimes with the aim of regulating it.
It distinguished itself in particular through the work that has had
major repercussions in the field of international sale of goods law
(1990 United Nations Vienna Convention on Contracts for International Sales of Goods) and international commercial arbitration
(1976 UNCITRAL arbitration rules and the 1985 UNCITRAL
Model Law on International Commercial Arbitration). It was not
particularly prepared to deal with such a new subject as electronic
commerce. A pioneering spirit is rarely the dominant feature in circles that are concerned with harmonising the law, whether it be
trade law, for the basic reason that the costly and relatively complex process of harmonisation is only usually implemented in fields
in which the diversity of legal systems applicable throughout the
world is such that it demonstrates the very harm that needs to be

---

(*) The author, secretary of the working group set up by the United Nations for international
trade law (UNCITRAL) in order to draw up UNCITRAL's model law on e-commerce (1996) and
UNCITRAL's model law on electronic signatures (2001), sometimes expresses here his own ideas.
They do not necessarily reflect the opinions of the United Nations Organisation.

remedied. It can already be observed that the involvement of an organisation such as UNCITRAL in certain fields of e-commerce will have had the effect of illustrating a theory of preventative harmonisation in which the establishment of a uniform international system goes hand in hand, or even precedes, the creation of various domestic laws on which it is normally based.

In 1983, the working group on the facilitation of international trade procedures (WP.4), placed under the joint aegis of the United Nations European Economic Commission (EEC/UN) and the United Nations Conference on Trade and Development (UNCTAD), had noticed legal issues raised during the work carried out for the development of UN/EDIFACT standard messages. To the extent that those issues fell within the scope of international trade law, it seemed natural to focus UNCITRAL's attention, (the main body responsible for matters of international trade law within the UN system), on the need to « finalise and coordinate the measures to be taken ». It was by means of that initiative that almost twenty years later, UNCITRAL finds itself amongst those international organisations that have been conducting research on the legal problems connected with the dematerialisation of information media, automated data processing, the computerised exchange of data and e-commerce for the longest time. One might hope that the mountains of paper produced by this collective think tank on the ins and outs of paperless exchanges will also have led to the acquisition of a minimum, essential know-how.

The results of this work (the 1996 Model Law on Electronic-Commerce and its 2001 extension on electronic signatures) are determined by the constraints of UNCITRAL's composition and nature. In its composition, UNCITRAL tends to the universal in that the States that are members are elected to represent all the regions as well as the main legal systems in the world and the various degrees of economic development, while all the non-member States are also invited to participate in its work as observers. This universality, which is one of the most striking and positive features of UNCITRAL's work, nevertheless means that in numerous situations, the normative legislation resulting from its work cannot claim to be as complete and detailed as might be expected from a uniform law arising out of a more homogeneous group, for example in some projects for regional harmonisation such as those undertaken by the

European Union or the Organisation for harmonisation of business law in Africa (OHADA). The only way to overcome the heterogeneity of a group is sometimes to increase the degree of abstraction of the rules proposed to it, in a text which is more akin to a digest of general principles than a provision of positive law. However, to express such general principles in a language that helps them to be introduced into positive law is one of the constant concerns of UNCITRAL's law drafters. In addition to this tendency towards abstraction, UNCITRAL's texts are also marked by the nature of the institution in that, unlike many regional organisations, UNCITRAL is not in a position to impose the implementation of its texts. Neither regulations nor directives, UNCITRAL's « models » are left to be interpreted freely by the States which alone can decide to follow them, draw inspiration from them more or less freely or ignore them. Obliged to convince on their own merits, these texts must be drafted in such a way as to uphold their reputation which is at the same time their raison d'être : to represent as perfect an expression as possible of a state of international consensus, of a type of universally acceptable legal rule.

In describing the purpose of the Model Law on Electronic Signatures, in the *Guide* that accompanies the text in UNCITRAL's publication we had the opportunity to write the following :

« Building on the fundamental principles underlying Article 7 of the UNCITRAL Model Law on Electronic Commerce with respect to the fulfilment of the signature function in an electronic environment, this new Model Law is designed to assist States in establishing a modern, harmonised and fair legislative framework to address more effectively the issues of electronic signatures. In a modest but significant addition to the UNCITRAL Model Law on Electronic Commerce, the new Model Law offers practical standards against which the technical reliability of electronic signatures may be measured. In addition, the Model Law provides a linkage between such technical reliability and the legal effectiveness that may be expected from a given electronic signature. The Model Law adds substantially to the UNCITRAL Model Law on Electronic Commerce by adopting an approach under which the legal effectiveness of a given electronic signature technique may be pre-determined (or assessed prior to being actually used). The Model Law is thus intended to foster the understanding of electronic signatures and the confidence that certain electronic signature techniques can be relied upon in legally significant transactions. Moreover, by establishing with appropriate flexibility a set of basic rules of conduct for the various parties that may become involved in the use of electronic signatures (i.e. signatories, relying parties and third-party certification service providers) the Model Law may assist in shaping more harmonious commercial practices in cyberspace ».

Let us hope that a study of this text will verify the aforementioned assertions. We shall attempt to show that UNCITRAL's Model Law on Electronic Signatures, designed (I) to combine flexibility and legal security (A) in the interest of preserving the necessary technological neutrality (B), is especially innovative (II) by outlining the establishment of a system of liability that is applicable to the various parties concerned (A) and the general principles of cross-border recognition of electronic signatures (B).

I. – A text designed to introduce extra legal security

A. – ORIGIN OF THE NEW MODEL LAW AND ADDED VALUE

Article 7, paragraph 1 of UNCITRAL's Model Law on Electronic-Commerce, reiterated in Articles 2(a) and 6 of the Model Law on Electronic Signatures states :

1. Where the law requires a signature of a person, that requirement is met in relation to a data message if :

a) a method is used to identify that person and to indicate that person's approval of the information contained in the data message; and

b) that method is as reliable as was appropriate for the purpose for which the data message was generated or communicated, in the light of all the circumstances, including any relevant agreement.

This text is based on the recognition of the functions performed by the signature in a paper-based environment. During the preparatory work on this law, the Working Group examined the following functions traditionally performed by handwritten signatures : to identify a person; to provide certainty as to the personal involvement of that person in the act of signing; to associate that person with the content of a document. It was noted that, in addition, the signature could perform a variety of functions, depending on the nature of the document that was signed. For example, a signature might attest to the intent of a person to be bound by the content of a contract signed; a person's intention to endorse authorship of a text (thus showing that he is aware of the fact that the act of signing may have potential legal consequences);

a person's intention to associate himself with the content of a document written by someone else; the fact that, and the time when, a person had been at a given place. The purpose of the various techniques currently available on the market or being developed is to create the technical means whereby a number or all the functions deemed to be characteristics of a handwritten signature can be performed in an electronic context. These techniques can be grouped together under the generic term of « electronic signatures ».

In order to guarantee that a message that has to be authenticated cannot be denied legal value simply because it has not been authenticated in the desired manner for paper documents, a general wording has been chosen in Article 7. This Article lays down the general circumstances in which data messages are deemed to be authenticated with sufficient credibility and are enforceable in view of the requirements for the signature of documents. Article 7 is concerned with the two main functions of a signature, that is to say identifying the author of a document and confirming that the author approves the content of that document (at least sufficiently to want to associate his name with it). Paragraph 1 a) sets out the principle whereby, in an electronic environment, the main legal functions of a signature are performed by a method which allows the sender of a data message to be identified and confirms that the sender approves the content of that data message.

Paragraph 1 b) establishes a flexible approach to the level of security to be achieved by the method of identification. It should be as reliable as is appropriate for the purpose for which the data message is generated or communicated, in the light of all the circumstances, including any agreement between the originator and the addressee of the data message. In determining whether the method used under paragraph 1 is appropriate, the *Guide for enactment of the model law on electronic commerce* into domestic law suggests that the following factors should be taken into account : 1) the sophistication of the material used by each of the parties; 2) the nature of their trade activity; 3) the frequency at which commercial transactions take place between the parties; 4) the kind and size of the transaction; 5) the function of signature requirements in a given statutory and regulatory environment; 6) the capability of communication systems; 7) compliance with authentication procedures set forth by intermediaries; 8) the range of authentication procedures made available by any intermediary; 9) compliance with trade customs and practice; 10) the existence of insurance coverage mechanisms against unauthorised messages; 11) the importance and value of the information contained in the data message; 12) the availability of alternative methods of identification and the cost of implementation; 13) the degree of acceptance or non-acceptance of the method of identification in the relevant industry or field both at the time the method was agreed upon and the time when the data message was communicated; and 14) any other relevant factor.

Accordingly, the effect of Article 7 of UNCITRAL's Model Law on Electronic Commerce is to open the way to a broad validation of any « method » that can be used to meet a legal requirement for handwritten signatures. However, the legal effectiveness of that « method » depends on proving its « reliability » to a judge or any other authority such as a state authority invested with the power to make decisions in that respect. That is a considerable limitation of the legal security and predictability that their users could expect from electronic signature techniques.

Articles 6 and 7 of the new model law establish a mechanism whereby electronic signatures which meet the objective criteria for technical reliability may benefit from a timely assessment as to their legal effectiveness. The new model law establishes two distinct regimes systems depending on the time at which certainty is achieved as to the recognition of an electronic signature as functionally equivalent to a handwritten signature. The first, and broadest regime is that described above. The second, is narrower and provides for methods of electronic signature that can be recognised by a public authority, an accredited private entity or the parties themselves as meeting the requirements for technical reliability as set out in the model law (see A/CN.9/484, par. 49). The advantage of that recognition is the security it gives to users of these electronic signature techniques before they actually use them.

B. – PRESERVATION
OF TECHNOLOGICAL NEUTRALITY

Technological neutrality is the dual concern to avoid affording a monopoly to a given technology or commercial product, and also to prevent the law being frozen whilst the technique is in a transitory state.

In view of the rapidity of technological progress, the Model Law lays down criteria for the legal recognition of electronic signatures regardless of the technology used (digital signatures based on asymmetrical cryptography; biometric devices; (enabling the identification of individuals by their physical characteristics, whether by hand or face geometry, fingerprint reading, voice recognition or retina scan, etc.); symmetrical cryptography; use of personal identification numbers (PIN codes); use of « tokens » to authenticate the data messages through a smart card or other device held by the signatory; digital versions of handwritten signatures; signature dynamics and other methods such as that of clicking on the « select » box. These various techniques can be used in combination to reduce systemic risk.

II. – Other innovative features : rules of conduct applicable to the parties concerned and regognition of signatures created abroad

A. – LIABILITY OF THE MAIN PARTIES INVOLVED

The model law does not deal with the details of questions of liability which might affect the various parties taking part in the operation of electronic signature systems. Those questions fall within the scope of the law applicable outside the model law. However, the model law lays down criteria to enable the conduct of those parties to be assessed, that is to say the signatory, the party relying on the signature and the certification service provider.

So far as concerns the signatory, the model law is based on the principle that he must take reasonable precautions with regard to any data and any device through which he creates electronic signatures, in particular to avoid any unauthorised use of that data. When he knows or should have known that the data related to the creation of his electronic signature have been compromised, the signatory must immediately inform any person who might reasonably be thought to rely on the signature or who might offer services supporting that signature. Where a certificate is used to support the electronic signature, the signatory must exercise reasonable care to ensure that all material representations made by the signatory in connection with the certificate are correct and exhaustive.

A party who wishes to rely on an electronic signature must take reasonable steps to verify the reliability of that signature. Where the signature is supported by a certificate, the party relying on the signature must take reasonable steps to verify the validity, suspension or revocation of the certificate and observe any limitation with respect to the certificate.

As a general rule, it is for a certification service provider to use trustworthy systems, procedures and human resources and to act in accordance with the representations it makes concerning its policy and practices. Furthermore, a certification service provider must exercise reasonable care to ensure the accuracy and completeness of all the material representations he makes in connection with the certificate. He must provide the essential information in this document to allow the party relying on the signature to identify it. It must also declare : 1) that at the time when the certificate was issued, the signatory identified in it had control of the data relating to the signature creation; and 2) that the data relating to the signature creation were valid at or before the time when the certificate was issued. In the interests of the party relying on the signature, it must provide further information concerning : 1) the method used to identify the signatory; 2) any limitation on the purpose or value for which the data relating to the signature creation or the certificate may be used; 3) the validity of the data relating to the signature creation; 4) any limitation on the scope or extent of liability stipulated by the certification service provider; 5) if he knows whether the signatory has or does not have the means to notify that the data relating to the creation of the signature have been compromised; and 6) that he knows whether or not a timely revocation service is offered.

In order to facilitate the assessment of whether systems, procedures and human resources used by the certification service provider are trustworthy, the model law provides a non-exhaustive list of indicative factors.

B. – Non-discrimination
against foreign electronic signatures

The model law establishes the fundamental principle whereby the place of origin must never in itself be a determining factor as to whether and to what extent foreign certificates or electronic signatures can have legal effect in an enacting State. That determination must not depend on the place in which the certificate or electronic signature was issued but on its technical reliability which is assessed in accordance with the usual principle of functional equivalence.

CANADIAN AND AMERICAN LEGISLATION ON ELECTRONIC SIGNATURES WITH REFLECTIONS ON THE EUROPEAN UNION DIRECTIVE

BY

JOHN D. GREGORY

GENERAL COUNSEL, POLICY BRANCH
MINISTRY OF THE ATTORNEY GENERAL, ONTARIO – CANADA

I. – Approaches to electronic signature legislation

This article considers first the general nature of law reform in electronic commerce, then the nature of signatures, then how laws in Canada and the United States have handled the question of signatures in paperless transactions, with an eye on European Union parallels.

Two approaches have been taken to supporting the reliability of electronic documents so they can be accepted in law. The first is to indicate only the general nature of the results to be achieved in using electronic documents, leaving the details to the parties and the circumstances. The second is to spell out in detail the technology or at least how the technology is to work to create legal effects. Both approaches have been tried in electronic signature legislation, and indeed some such legislation has combined both for different kinds of signature (1).

---

(1) Some governments have used two other techniques. The first is to abolish the need for signatures entirely. The second is to « close the system », usually by contract, so the participants are known to each other by other means than signatures. Both have been used in electronic filing systems in Ontario. See John D. GREGORY, *Legal Situation of Electronic Signatures : Ontario Perspective* (1999), http://www.euclid.ca/ontsig.html.

A. – MINIMALIST LEGISLATION

1. – *Reasons for minimalism*

Both Canada and the United States have generally preferred a minimalist response to the quest for certainty about the legal status of electronic communications. First, the existing law is capable of resolving a good number of questions on its own. Next, the technology underlying electronic records is changing rapidly, so attempts to prescribe specifically how to conduct legally effective communications risk becoming quickly obsolescent. The uses to which electronic communications are put vary so widely that no single technology would suit all of them. Finally, e-commerce is global in scope and neither country wants to take a seriously different approach from its major partners. The international consensus today is arguably in favour of minimalism, as shown by the success of the U.N. Model Law on Electronic Commerce (2).

Minimalism has been particularly attractive in Canada and the United States for dealing with signatures. The basic function of a signature is to link a person with a text or document. Thus a signature must identify or permit the identification of (3) a person (4). It is important to note that nothing in the form of the signature itself shows the intent with which it was made or the purpose for which it appears. The intent or purpose may be inferred only from the context, i.e. from the signed document. The context for the signature is more important to its legal effect than the physical characteristics of the signature itself.

2. – *The American and Canadian uniform legislation*

The American uniform statute that deals with electronic signatures is the Uniform Electronic Transactions Act (UETA),

---

(2) *Official Records of the General Assembly*, Fortieth Session, Supplement n° 17 (A/40/17) (1996). The text and the very useful Guide to Enactment are at http://www.uncitral.org/english/texts/electcom/ml-ecomm.htm.

(3) A signature does not necessarily identify a person ; manual signatures are often illegible and require other evidence to show who created them. The signature permits the identification in any event.

(4) One may have to answer separately the formal question « is it signed ? » – which the uniform statutes discussed here allow to be answered positively by an electronic signature – and the practical question « who signed it ? ». See J.D. GREGORY, « The Authentication of Electronic Legal Documents », (1999), 6 *The E.D.I. Law Rev.* 277.

adopted in July, 1999 (5). The Uniform Law Conference of Canada adopted the Uniform Electronic Commerce Act (UECA) as of September 30, 1999 (6). Both statutes affect more than commerce; the UETA covers « transactions » and the UECA « information » and « documents », subject to express exclusions (7).

The two uniform statutes intend to make the law media neutral, equally applicable to paper and to electronic documents. The treatment of electronic signatures therefore does not create a new legal « thing » with this name. The Canadian definition reads, « 'Electronic signature' means information in electronic form that a person has created or adopted in order to sign a document and that is in, attached to or associated with the document » (8). The American definition is, « an electronic sound, symbol or process attached to or logically associated with a record and executed or adopted by a person with the intent to sign the record » (9). The legal essence of a signature is the intention with which it was made, rather than its form or medium. The intention in both statutes is « to sign ». The use of the word « sign » was deliberate. The existing law about the appropriate intention for an effective signature, and how one proves it, continues in effect (10). (The definition in the EU Directive is about the same, except that it uses the more obscure synonym « authenticate » for « sign »).

The purpose of defining electronic signature is to make clear that the electronic version does not have to look like a handwritten

---

(5) Over half the states have adopted the UETA. The texts are online at : http://www.law.upenn.edu/bll/ulc/ulc.htm#ueccta for the drafts and the final version, and at : http://www.uetaonline.com for a record of the discussions leading up to its adoption and a list of states that have adopted it, with links to electronic versions of their legislation. For the relation between international and domestic (U.S.) commercial law, see A.H. Boss, « Electronic Commerce and the Symbiotic Relationship between International and Domestic Law Reform », 72 *Tulane L.R.* 1931(1998), and « The Uniform Electronic Transactions Act in a Global Environment », 37 *Idaho L.R.* 275 (2001).

(6) [1999] Proceedings of the Uniform Law Conference of Canada 380, online at : http://www.ulcc.ca/en/us/index.cfm?sec = 1&sub = 1u1. Seven provinces and one territory have adopted the UECA and another province has introduced implementing legislation. A status chart with citations and URLs of all the statutes appears online at http://www.ulcc.ca/en/cs/index.cfm?sec-=4&sub = 4b. A couple have varied the signature provisions slightly; those wishing a detailed view should look at the statutes in Manitoba (a reliability requirement) and Prince Edward Island (a more restrictive definition of electronic signature).

(7) For exclusions, see UECA s. 2 and UETA s. 3.

(8) UECA s. 1(b).

(9) UETA s. 2(8).

(10) C. REED, « What is a Signature ? », [2000 (3)] *Journal of Information, Law and Technology* (*JILT*), online at : http://elj.warwick.ac.uk/jilt/00-3/reed.html.

signature when it is displayed (11). Likewise, an electronic signature may travel apart from the document it signs if its association with the document is clear (12).

The UECA and the UETA provide that a signature requirement can be met by an electronic signature (13). Unlike the U.N. Model Law (14), they do not go on to require that the electronic signature must be as reliable as is appropriate in the circumstances. At common law, and arguably in the civil law of Quebec as well (15), a method of signature on paper does not have to meet any test of reliability. If the association with a person is demonstrated and the intent to sign is demonstrated, the signature will meet the signature requirement. The EU Directive discussed below also imposes no general requirement of reliability but leaves proof to the parties.

However, it is possible that the authority that imposed a particular signature requirement did have some degree of reliability in mind. In that case, the UECA allows that authority to make a regulation imposing the reliability standards of the U.N. Model Law (16).

3. – *Non-uniform minimalist statutes*

a) *E-Sign*

Besides the UETA, made for the states, the United States has the federal Electronic Signatures in Global and National Commerce Act, known popularly as « E-Sign » (17). E-Sign was inspired by the 1996 Model Law and by UETA, but was intended to harmonise the

---

(11) Just as an electronic record under the statutes may be a record of oral speech, so in principle an electronic recording of speech could constitute a signature, if the intent were clear.

(12) The American expression « logically associated » suggests a mathematical logic rather than simply sound reasoning, but it could mean either. To avoid such questions the Canadian statute omitted the adverb.

(13) UECA s. 10. UETA s. 7(a). The Canadian statute follows the Model Law in giving a broad reading to « requirement », to cover negatively-phrased rules (e.g. « an unsigned document is not enforceable ») and permissions (e.g. « a signed document is admissible »). See UECA s. 4.

(14) *U.N. Model Law, supra*, n° 25, art. 7(1).

(15) The Quebec Civil Code defines signature in Article 2827 as follows : « A signature is the affixing by a person, on a writing, of his name or the distinctive mark which he regularly uses to signify his intention ».

(16) UECA s. 10(2). The UETA has no such provision. E-SIGN permits states to enact such provisions only for limited purposes, generally in communications with the state government. E-SIGN s. 104.

(17) E-Sign, *Public Law* 106-229, June 30, 2000, can be found online at : http://frwebgate.ac cess.gpo.gov/cgibin/getdoc.cgi?dbname = 106–cong–public–laws&docid + f:publ229.106.pdf.

law across the country for interstate commerce. While UETA accepts any electronic signature, E-Sign limits its application in respect of some consumer transactions. Otherwise E-Sign prohibits state legislatures from enacting any rules for electronic signatures that would be more onerous or more technology-specific than the rules of the UETA, the adoption of which E-Sign encourages (18).

b) *Quebec's legislation*

The main non-uniform minimalist Canadian legislation is Quebec's Act to provide a legal framework for information technology (19). It aims to make the law almost completely media-neutral and spells out ways by which rules of law can be met by intangible information. The stability of the content of the document is a primary concern of the Act.

While the statute is technology neutral, it spells out in more detail than the UECA the requirements for attribution of what it calls « technology-based documents ». Signatures are just one form of evidence of attribution in this statute, a point in which it joins the analysis made earlier for the common law. The Act says that a link between a person and a technology-based document may be established by any process that allows the identity of the person to be confirmed and the link with the document to be confirmed, and, of course, the document itself to be identified (s.38). A signature may be used to establish this link (s.39); the section refers back to article 2827 of the Civil Code for what constitutes a signature. In short, the Act, though in different language, has the same effect as the UECA : it allows new technology to create a signature but leaves the essence of a signature in law the same as it was for a signature on paper.

4. – *Prudence and Consent*

There is always a distinction between basic legal requirements – what is good enough in law – and prudent business practices. The

---

(18) More on the complex relation of the US federal and state laws can be found online at : http://www.uetaonline.com and in S. MEEHAN and B. BEARD, « What Hath Congress Wrought ? E-Sign, the UETA and the Question of Pre-emption », (2001), 37 *Idaho L.R.* 389.

(19) S.Q.2001 c. 32, in force November 1, 2001. A very full description of the Act and its background may be found in French at http://www.autoroute.gouv.qc.ca/loi–en–ligne/index.html.

elements of reliability of attribution of a document are many and the technical aspects of the signature, on paper or electronic, are only a part of the « threat/risk analysis ». The need for the parties to decide what they should have for their own purposes makes the consent rule absolutely fundamental in both these technology-neutral statutes (20). Only the proposed user can make that judgment accurately. The power to say No is the power to say Yes if the signature is secure enough or satisfies other concerns of the recipient (21).

As a result of the consent provision, an electronic signature that satisfies the legal requirement for a signature is not necessarily effective against someone who does not want to deal electronically at all. Since most electronic communications, and certainly most commercial transactions, will be on consent, this will not usually be a problem. Both statutes state clearly that consent to use electronic documents may be inferred from conduct, moreover; an express agreement is not needed. Otherwise there is too much risk of bad faith refusal.

5. – *Attribution of documents and signatures*

Article 13 of the U.N. Model Law on Electronic Commerce provides that data messages may be attributed to those who create them or who authorise their creation. This is of course the general law in Canada and the United States. The UETA (22) has a similar provision. The Canadian Conference thought this went without saying, so did not say it.

The 1996 U.N. Model Law goes on to provide a rule of attribution (23) where certain agreed security procedures are used on data messages. The Americans attempted to devise similar rules, but they fell under severe criticism based partly on the fluidity of the technology available and partly on the likely lack of sophistication

---

(20) The consent rule is in UECA s. 6 (« Nothing in this Act requires any person to use or accept information in electronic form... ») and UETA s. 5 (« This Act applies only to transactions between parties each of which has agreed to conduct transactions by electronic means »).

(21) The UETA provides in subs. 5(c) that a party who consents to conduct a transaction electronically may refuse to conduct other transactions by electronic means. Comment 5 to that section notes some limits to this right of refusal. The UECA is silent on the point, but the policy is not likely to be held to differ.

(22) UETA s. 9(a).

(23) U.N. Model Law art. 13(3)(4). The *Guide to Enactment* calls it a presumption at par. 83.

of its users (24). The Canadian Conference did not try to follow the Model Law on this point in the Uniform Act but the federal government has reflected parts of it in its legislation (25). UNCITRAL's working group on electronic signatures aimed to give more substance to the provisions of Article 13 but there too, efforts to draft clear attribution rules ended up much narrower than originally hoped (26).

As a result of the silence of the UECA and the near-silence of the UETA, parties to electronic transactions will have to satisfy themselves of the origin of electronic documents and signatures. A technology-neutral statute can do little more without hampering parties who are capable of making their own decisions (27).

B. – NON-MINIMALIST STATUTES

1. – *Reasons for a more detailed approach*

The other major approach to electronic signature legislation is to spell out the requirements for such signatures in more detail. There are two main reasons for taking this approach. Firstly, people are concerned about the reliability of electronic documents, including signatures. It is easy to amend many electronic documents and the amendments may be very hard to detect. Accordingly, more rules are thought to be needed to ensure appropriate security.

The second reason for a more detailed legislative approach is that the creation of electronic signatures is often different from that of signatures on paper. A signature on paper involves two people or classes of people : the signer and the person or persons who rely on it. While an electronic signature may also involve only the same

---

(24) Reports of the Drafting Committee meetings at the ETA Forum (the predecessor to the UETA Online site) can provide details. Online at : http://www.webcom.com/legaled/ETAForum/ mtgrpts.html, notably the meetings of September 1997 and January 1998.

(25) See below, section II.3.b.

(26) See the reports of the meetings of UNCITRAL's Working Group on Electronic Commerce, notably for July 1998 (A/CN.9/454, par. 40-53); for February 1999 (A/CN.9/457, par. 99-107, and Working Paper WP.79 par. 31-33); for September 1999 (A/CN.9/465, par. 68-77); and for February 2000 (A/CN.9/467, par. 44-71). All are online at : http://www.uncitral.org/english/ workinggroups/wg–ec/index.htm.

(27) Quebec's statute (s. 39) says that a person's signature on a technology-based document may be « set up against » the person if the integrity of the document is ensured and the link between the signature and the document was established at the time of signing and has since been maintained. This may not come to anything more than saying that you can rely on attribution if you can prove it.

two classes, it may also involve a third person, someone who acts as an intermediary to establish the relying party's trust in the signature itself. Many people believe that e-signatures will inspire more confidence if a trusted third party certifies to the relying party that the signature is, in fact, that of a particular person. Legislation has thus been devised to ensure that such certification authorities (CAs) are trustworthy. Some of them offer limitation of liability for mistakes of identity if the proper procedures are followed, to encourage CAs, and some offer to the relying party reinforced credibility of the identification in such certificates by way of a presumption of attribution (28).

2. – *Technology-specific legislation*

Much of the early conceptual work about such a system was carried out by the American Bar Association, whose Digital Signature Guidelines were influential (29). The first legislation to this effect was the Utah Digital Signature Act of 1995 (30). It dealt expressly with public key cryptography as signature. It regulated CAs and exempted them from liability if they followed the rules. It also provides a presumption of attribution for duly certified signatures. The Utah Act was followed in three other states (31).

However, this approach was severely criticised. Firstly, the statutes were said to allocate risk by law differently from how the real risk fell. This was « legislating market winners », which was thought inappropriate in a free market (32). Secondly, as technology evolved there were many different implementations of digital signatures, with different degrees of engagement by CAs and relying parties and thus, different risks. Thirdly, digital signature legislation was thought to impede the free development of signature technology as it gave an unfair legal advantage to the technology

---

(28) When such signatures are created by asymmetric or public-key cryptography, they are called digital signatures, and the system of hardware, software and rules that govern the signature, certification and reliance processes is a public key infrastructure (PKI).

(29) The Guidelines are available at http://www.abanet.org/scitech/ec/isc/digital–signature.html.

(30) Utah Act, Utah Code Annotated, Title 46-3, http://www.le.state.ut.us/öode/TITLE46/46–02.htm.

(31) Washington, Minnesota and Missouri. See sources cited in footnote 4 above.

(32) B. BIDDLE, *Legislating Market Winners* (1997), http://www.acusd.edu/~biddle/LMW.htm.

of public key cryptography. No further states have followed the Utah example (33).

3. – *Technology-neutral hybrid statutes*

a) *American hybrid legislation*

As the Utah model fell into question, attempts were made to find technology-neutral statutes that would recognise that some kinds of e-signatures were more reliable than others. The main such statute was the Illinois Electronic Commerce and Security Act of 1998 (34). Illinois provided that parties might agree that an electronic signature would satisfy a legal signature requirement. In addition, particularly reliable e-signatures were described as « secure electronic signatures ». These had characteristics first described in the United States by the National Institute of Science and Technology (NIST) in the early 1990s.

These characteristics were, in the words of the Illinois Act :

– The signature is unique to signer in the context in which it is used;
– It can be used to objectively identify the person signing the electronic record;
– It was reliably created by such identified person (e.g. because some aspect of the procedure involves the use of a signature device or other means or method that is within the sole control of such person) and cannot be readily duplicated or compromised;
– It is created and linked to the electronic record to which it relates, in such a manner that if the record or signature is intentionally or unintentionally changed after signing then the electronic signature is invalidated.

Illinois allowed the Secretary of State to designate electronic signature systems that met these criteria, so that litigants would not have to prove compliance with them in every case. Where the

---

(33) One should note as well the role of E-Sign in pre-empting state rules for signatures in interstate commerce where they were inconsistent with the minimalist approach of the federal and uniform statutes. However, the steam was out of the Utah model well before E-Sign was passed.

(34) See the resources noted at n.4 to locate the text of the Illinois statute. The relevant section is 10-110.

criteria were present, the Act provided a presumption of attribution, i.e. that the signature actually came from the person who apparently made it. It also set out criteria for evaluating the reliability of certificates.

The Illinois model has influenced many others, including California (35) in the US, Singapore (the first nation to implement the U.N. Model Law on Electronic Commerce) (36), the UNCITRAL Model Law on Electronic Signatures (37) and the European Directive (38) on that subject.

b) *Canadian hybrid legislation*

In Canada, the federal government has adopted its own form of legislation : the Personal Information Protection and Electronic Documents Act (PIPEDA), Part 2 of which deals with electronic documents. It is a hybrid statute as well. Some of the signature provisions simply allow signature requirements to be satisfied electronically by use of an e-signature in the form to be prescribed by regulation. However, several sections contemplate the use of a « secure electronic signature ». For example, one can use a secure electronic signature to create a certificate signed by a minister or public official that is proof of a fact or admissible in evidence (39). A secure electronic signature may serve as a seal, if the seal requirement has been designated under the Act (40). Affidavits may be made electronically if both deponent and commissioner of the oath sign with a secure electronic signature (41). Declarations of truth may be made with such signatures (42), and witnesses may sign under similar conditions (43). Unlike the Illinois hybrid or the EU Directive, the federal statute gives no choice about whether to use a secure electronic signature. To sign electronically and validly

---

(35) The California Digital Signature Regulations are online at : http://www.ss.ca.gov/digsig/regulations.htm.

(36) *Singapore, Electronic Transactions Act* 1998.

(37) The January 1998 draft of the Model Law is very clearly influenced by Illinois. See http://www.uncitral.org/english/workinggroups/wg–ec/wp73.htm, article 1.

(38) Directive 99/93/EC, December 1999, http://europa.eu.int/comm/internal–market/en/media/sign/Dir99-93-ecEN.pdf. This is discussed in section c. below.

(39) *Ibid.*, s. 36.

(40) *Ibid.*, s. 39.

(41) *Ibid.*, s. 44.

(42) *Ibid.*, s. 45.

(43) *Ibid.*, s. 46.

within the meaning of the provisions named, people must use the secure electronic signature.

A « secure electronic signature » is not defined in the Bill, except as « an electronic signature that results from the application of a technology or process prescribed by regulation » (44). The Act sets out the usual provisions for signatures of this type, in language reminiscent of Illinois (45). The only technology to be designated in the short term will be that of digital signatures certified by the Government of Canada, or those from systems cross-certified with that system. To date, no regulations have been made on secure electronic signatures.

The Quebec statute mentioned in the first section as a technology-neutral statute nevertheless makes rules for persons who certify the identity of signatories of technology-based documents and it sets up a voluntary accreditation scheme. It also outlines how to establish recognised standards for reliable technology in this area. It is not a hybrid statute because it gives no special status to certified signatures.

c) *International hybrid legislation*

The UNCITRAL Model Law on Electronic Signatures aims to help the parties determine in advance whether the reliability standard of the 1996 Model Law has been met (46). The new Model Law also avoids detailed descriptions of the technology to be used, however, for the reasons that support minimalism in the first place. Earlier drafts talked of « secure » or « enhanced » electronic signatures. The terms have been dropped but the criteria of identification, sole control and detection of alteration remain in the criteria for reliability of an electronic signature (47).

The European Union's Directive on Electronic Signatures is another hybrid (48). It ensures that electronic signatures can be valid despite their electronic form and despite not meeting the more

---

(44) *Ibid.*, s. 31.

(45) *Ibid.*, s. 48.

(46) See the final text at http://www.unictral.org/english/texts/electcom/ml-elecsig-e.pdf. For a Canadian viewpoint on the nearly-final text, see Department of Justice (Canada), « UNCITRAL Working Group on Electronic Commerce : Report on the Meeting of September, 2000 », online at : http://canada.justice.gc.ca/en/ps/ec/UN2000rep.html.

(47) UNCITRAL Model Law on Electronic Signatures, final text, art. 6.

(48) Above n° 38.

demanding standards described in the rest of the Directive. It goes on to prescribe in considerable detail a regime for « advanced electronic signatures » created by « secure-signature-creation devices » and supported by « qualified certificates ». One recognises the NIST/ Illinois language in these provisions, although the appendices on technical requirements for qualification (some borrowed from the UNCITRAL work) are more detailed than in those texts. If one uses an advanced electronic signature, member states must give it the legal effect of a handwritten signature. There are no presumptions of attribution. This may strike some as a weak result for what is supposed to be a strong technology.

These detailed requirements will not be easy to meet, judging from the difficulties in setting up public key infrastructures in Canada and the United States. In any event, as noted in the earlier discussion of the nature of a signature, the fact of a signature is less valuable in a commercial transaction than evidence of attribution. (Indeed the identity of the other party is often less important than its solvency or the quality of its goods or services (49)). Business parties may in practice choose to satisfy themselves about attribution through procedures that do not qualify as a signature at all, and certainly not as an advanced signature.

The Directive also contains provisions on the liability of parties to signatures, on recognition of foreign signatures and certificates and on respect of privacy rights. The first two items were clearly inspired by the parallel discussions on these topics at UNCITRAL. Of the U.S. legislation, only Utah and its followers dealt with liability, and then it was to exempt regulated certification authorities from liability if they followed the rules. In Canada, Quebec's statute has provided rules on liability and data protection similar to those of the Directive. Otherwise the minimalist statutes leave these topics for another day.

---

(49) For this reason one distinguishes sometimes between identification – who is this person ? – and authentication – is this the person I want it to be ? The latter is often a more important function of a signature, because one uses other means to determine who one wants to deal with.

II. – Related topics

A. – EVIDENCE

In general, the common law does not give signatures or signed documents any special status as evidence, except for documents signed by public officials which may be « self-authenticating », i.e. admitted without proof of origin beyond that signature. As a result, most of the U.S. and Canadian statutes discussed here say very little or nothing about matters of evidence.

The UECA is silent on evidence. The Uniform Law Conference has adopted a separate statute on electronic evidence (50) but it too says nothing about signatures. The UETA says only that evidence of a record or signature may not be excluded solely because it is in electronic form (51). E-Sign is also silent on evidence. Many of the uses of secure electronic signatures in the Canadian federal legislation support an evidentiary use, however. That statute also amended the Canada Evidence Act (52) to allow the creation by regulation of presumptions of the association of secure electronic signatures with persons and of the integrity of information in documents where a secure electronic signature is used. No such regulations have been made to date.

In Quebec, as noted earlier, an electronic signature is approved where made « by means of any process that meets the requirements of article 2827 of the Civil Code », which is part of Book VII of the Code on evidence. No special rule of admissibility is provided. The Quebec statute did amend one article of the Civil Code on the use of electronic documents as evidence (53), without mentioning signatures in particular.

By contrast, the EU Directive on Electronic Signatures provides that advanced electronic signatures must be admissible in evidence, and that other electronic signatures may not be denied admissibility on grounds of their electronic form or because they are

---

(50) The Uniform Electronic Evidence Act, [1998] Proceedings of the Uniform Law Conference of Canada 164, http://www.ulcc.ca/en/us/index.cfm?sec = 1&sub = 1u2.

(51) UETA s. 13.

(52) R.S.C. 1985 c. C-5, new section 31.4.

(53) Article 2837 is repealed and replaced by a new provision pursuant to s. 77 of the information technology statute.

not qualified in one element or another (54). To the extent that documents are more readily admissible when signed, and that in practice, courts will be hard to satisfy with less than an advanced signature, compliance with the requirements for an advanced signature would be more important in European law than in Canadian or American jurisdictions.

B. – STANDARDS

The choices for private parties and public parties may be made easier by the development of technical standards for the use and admissibility of electronic signatures. Such standards are being worked on domestically and by international organisations like the International Standards Organisation, and within Europe by the European Electronic Signature Standard Initiative (55). This could be compared to the work of the American Bar Association on evaluating public key infrastructure programs, recently published for consultation (56). General conformity with compatible technical standards may help generalise the use of signatures on both sides of the Atlantic that would qualify as « advanced » or « secure ». Such technical standards are the likely underpinning for mutual recognition of certificates and thus electronic signatures.

Conclusion

The main legislative approach to electronic signatures in the United States and Canada is minimalist and technology neutral. This approach places a lot of responsibility on the parties to a signature, particularly on the relying party, to decide what kinds of electronic signatures they will accept for what purposes. The relying party still bears the risk of loss from a fraudulent signature as it does for signatures on paper.

The major exception to this approach is essentially public sector electronic signatures. Many levels of government are developing digital signature systems supported by certificates to be used in dealings between citizens and the government. To date, only the

---

(54) EU Directive art. 5.
(55) See http://www.etsi.org/T–news/0005–ESI.htm.
(56) Http://www.abanet.org/scitech/ec/isc/pag/pag.html.

Canadian Federal Government has legislated expressly on that front. Other jurisdictions are contemplating whether to support the reliability of their public key infrastructures by law, or to set out the duties and liabilities of the parties to certified electronic signatures. The UNCITRAL Model Law on Electronic Signatures and the EU Directive contribute to that process of reflection.

DISCUSSION

Georges Papapavlou

Any questions? I see a hand raised. Madam.

Ewa Kozlowska

Thank you. My name is Ewa Kozlowska. I am Polish; I work for the Ministry of European Integration in Poland. I have a question, probably for Mr Papapavlou, because it relates to the legislative method applied by the Commission, particularly with regard to electronic signatures and e-commerce. You said that it is an approach that is quite new in Community school of thought, therefore a « light and flexible approach ». I wonder what that means exactly but also, because I have the impression that because it is new, the directive created numerous questions when it was transposed in the member countries. So, has the Commission had the opportunity and the time to draw up the initial report on the effectiveness of this method? Is it a favourable method in the context of e-commerce? Finally, with regard to the institutional environment and the certification associations, as the directive seems to be the minimal harmonisation, domestic law still tends to regulate beyond what the directive prescribes.

Georges Papapavlou

I am going to try and give a very quick reply. Firstly, it is clear that a European directive is the result of discussions between the member countries, the European Commission and Parliament; therefore, the result is never a perfect solution. It is always a compromise that has been found between the interests on the table. There are always things that could be improved but they have to be tested, as you said, in transposition. For the E-Commerce and Electronic Signature Directives, there is a detail : there is a review clause – I think over two or three years – and that will enable us to see exactly to what extent they have achieved their goal or whether we need to revise them to make them either more strict or more flexible. However, we are not there yet : for the E – Commerce Directive this period has not even begun and for the Electronic Signature Directive it has just started. Therefore, there are still two or three years in which to revise these Directives. There you have it. Another question. Mr Cachard.

Olivier Cachard

A brief observation and then a question. A brief observation on consumer protection. You mentioned a timetable, Mr Chatillon, if I might say, with, on the one hand, prevention and on the other, or subsequently, protection. It seems to me that prevention, especially by pre-contractual information, has already driven consumer law for some time with this particular difficulty for the Internet : if we provide even more information, we are in danger of drowning the consumer. Therefore, we should perhaps select the information but even so, I am thinking of labels : faced with an ever-increasing number of labels, there is also an increase in mechanisms for selecting information. Accordingly, is information really the most appropriate mechanism for protection ? And next, a very quick question for Mr Froger on acceptance of the authentic electronic document. How will it work in practice when the parties are distant from one another because in the end, that is the question. When the parties are present in the office and when the solicitor draws up the document on a computer there are few problems but what do we do when the parties are at a distance ? Thank you.

Georges Chatillon

Thank you, Mr Cachard, but it seems to me that, in any event, we do not have a choice because when you look at what the directive is proposing and, then, of course, the Bill, you find that after the exchange of consent and therefore, after the contract has been drawn up, the consumer has the right to review the clauses in the contract, if only by looking at them again on the server at the vendor's company. At that time, he will obviously notice, after the event, that he doesn't understand what he has signed or agreed to and that in his mind, he has interpreted it badly or, in any event, his interpretation is not the same as that of the vendors. Therefore, he will obviously want to prevent the contract from being performed and in these circumstances we will be back to square one. Accordingly, in my view, since this right to review the clauses after the contract has been drawn up has been established, it would obviously be better to go back a little bit further upstream and prevent all these consequences of transactions which would only impede the smooth progress of commercial transactions. After all, the vendor wants to a quick sale and certainly doesn't want the customer to escape from him. Similarly, the customer wants a quick purchase and he wants the product or service to arrive. It would therefore be better to give the consumer the opportunity to completely resolve in his mind the pre-contractual problems that you mentioned, as he will have seven days in which to do so. As it happens, online computer transactions make it possible. It is merely a question of the mechanism and naturally, the mechanism can only exist if there are obligations to do this. There would be nothing to prevent the consumer from being able to go and consult, for information purposes, an authority which subsequently could become a mediation or conciliation body if a dispute should arise. In any case, it would enable a consumer association and representatives of such institutions to be consulted, so that the customers are satisfied with entering into a contract and do not have the impression that it is incomprehensible, that there will be subsequent pitfalls and that « in any case, what does this online mediation and conciliation mean if people speak to me in a jargon that I don't understand ? And then, I would have been bound by the contract and now I need to get myself out of it and people around me, my family and others, are totally dissatisfied. I seem to have caused a dispute within the family and now I need to get out of it with my head held high ». Obviously, all this creates conflicts, not only legal but also commercial and therefore psychological kinds of conflicts. It seems to me, therefore, that by way of an experiment, it is in our greatest interest, because once again, the Bill and the Directive already contain this chain of mechanisms for preventing the slightest objective kind of dispute from arising, with regard to the interpretation of the wording, the payment procedure, the interpretation of the contractual clauses and even the interpretation of the mechanisms themselves. Of course, that does not mean that all consumers would use such mechanisms. As soon as they have online replies following a set of questions known nowadays as « frequently asked questions », I think that most of them will be content, especially if authorised replies are given to these questions, that is to say that they themselves would have been the subject of a kind of mediation between consumer associations, mediation bodies and legislative bodies.

Georges Papapavlou

Thank you. Maître Froger, please could you be a little more brief.

Maître Didier Froger

In two words : I usually say that we merely need to transpose the rules that apply to written material to electronic material. Therefore, the state of our discussions is as follows : there will be two solicitors and two witness solicitors. One will receive an electronic document by way of a power of attorney, as currently we have a solicitor who draws up powers of attorney, and that solicitor will transfer said power of attorney electronically to the solicitor who will prepare the officially recorded document. On the other hand, there will only be one solicitor who will witness the exchange of consent. Consideration is being given to this. Moreover, a certification structure and policy has been established which is beginning to take shape and which, in the context of secure exchanges, will allow such transfer of documents between solicitors. However, in my opinion, we must not begin to work on the basis of two documents and two solicitors. We are no longer dealing with the rules that govern acceptance of paper-based documents. We must simply have a transposition from the paper document to the electronic document.

Georges Papapavlou

Thank you very much. We will now have a break and reconvene at 11 am precisely.

2. – WHAT PROTECTION?
WHICH LAWS?

IS PROTECTION OF PERSONAL DATA GUARANTEED ON THE INTERNET?

BY

JEAN FRAYSSINET

PROFESSOR AT THE UNIVERSITY OF AIX-MARSEILLE III

In the history of information technology law, the subject of the protection of personal rights and freedoms, in particular of private life, was the first to appear at the end of the 70s and beginning of the 80s. In Europe it resulted in a wave of specific legislation on the protection of personal data in order to cover the management of such data using computer systems and files of any size. The advent of the networks and, in particular, the Internet, upset the existing problem areas by exacerbating the old problems surrounding the collection, storage, processing and circulation of personal data by accentuating new problems such as the profiling and traceability of individuals, collecting data without their knowledge, making data management secure, encryption and circulating information without regard for national borders.

Surveys conducted both in Europe and the United States show a high level of anxiety and mistrust on the part of Internet users, fuelled by several high profile cases concerning respect for their rights and freedoms; that is a handicap to the introduction of several applications connected with health or electronic commerce sites, for example. Admittedly, through its technology, services and uses, the Internet focuses all its problems arising from the protection of personal data by acting as a pointer and catalyst, by raising the question of adapting existing legal protection systems. So far as the protection of personal data is concerned, one might say that the Internet has a before and after, which explains the renewed interest in the subject.

I shall try to reply to the direct question raised with equal directness. In my view, it is obvious that when the operation of the law on the protection of personal data is set back in the context of technology, applications, political, economical and social realities, it follows that one has to reply that at the present time, individual rights and freedoms are not very well protected. Without going so far as to invoke the Orwellian fear of Big Brother which can be fuelled by excessive fantasies, I must admit that based solely on the realities and trends observed, I am one of those anxious people. We must fight the attitude that denies any infringements of rights and freedoms, adopted by those who, often for commercial reasons or on account of public or private authorities, intend to manage personal data without restriction. Because of the individual and collective issues, the importance of managing personal data is underestimated. The Internet needs a suitable set of ethics to prevent it from becoming a tool for subjugating the individual.

I. – The illusion of protection

By being connected with the protection of individuals, the protection of personal data forms part of the benchmark of values defended by democratic countries. That can be clearly seen in the views of all the actors on the Internet stage : politicians, international organisations (in particular the European Union, the Council of Europe and the OECD), access providers and hosts, electronic traders and site managers, Internet users.etc. This fine theoretical unanimity highlights the necessary defence of individual rights and freedoms, particularly in relation to private life and it is fuelled by the anxiety caused by the wide media coverage of many harmful practices that take place on the network.

The law's response to society's demand for protection is inconsistent, alternating between the application of a common law to protect the individual (where one exists!) and/or the implementation of a specific law for the protection of private data, found in around fifty States, mainly European. Against this simplified background, two models appear to emerge : the European one and that of the United States.

The fifteen States of the European Union have Directive 95/46/ EC of 24 October 1995 on the protection of individuals with regard to the processing of personal data and on the free movement of such data, which was transposed into the national legislation of almost all the Member States (but not yet in France where the 1978 law on Information Technology, files and freedoms continues to be applied pending amendment, a draft law having been submitted to the National Assembly in September 2001). There is no doubt that the Internet is covered by the scope of that directive even though the word is not mentioned once. There is also Directive 97/66/EC of 15 December 1997 on the processing of personal data and the protection of privacy in the telecommunications sector, which is already being amended to include some aspects relating to the Internet such as spamming.

European legislation would appear to provide proper protection for the personal data of Internet users who have been granted the right to access their data and dispute the quality or use thereof, the right to know whether data concerning them is being processed, the right to object to processing for legitimate reasons at any time, etc. The person in charge of processing must comply with several obligations : the individual's consent (subject to certain exceptions), restriction on the management of sensitive data, forewarning the individual in question, compliance with confidentiality and security of processing, notification of processing to an independent national authority, for protection and regulation with wide powers to act and the power of the judge to impose sanctions, including penal sanctions.

No-one disputes that the prescribed obligations apply to all Internet or telecommunications operators. However, clearly both the 1995 directive and its national implementing legislation include the Internet in a roundabout way, without considering it specifically either from its technical aspect or from the point of view of services or the specific forms of infringements of individual fundamental rights and freedoms. Accordingly, European law applies the principle of technological neutrality which means that the same basic rules must apply without making a distinction between fast evolving technological tools. This can be seen in the provisions of Chapter VI of the directive on the transfer of personal data originating in the European Union to third countries, with the requirement for adequate protection imposed on them; the Internet is therefore particularly affected.

As for the United States model, that relies on pragmatic and sectorial self-regulation by the private actors, the federal or federated State only intervening in cases of extreme necessity or deficiency.

The emphasis is placed on protecting the consumer or children, on the judge's ability to identify new balances that are suited to the Internet using ordinary laws or very casual legislation.

II. – Inappropriate and ineffective protection

If one observes the operation of the law that protects the individual in the context of the Internet, one might think that the guarantees offered are still largely illusory; positive law is still poorly understood and little used against an increasing number of unlawful acts that interfere with rights and freedoms. Already, outside the Internet, the right to information, the right to access and dispute data, the right to object to it being processed etc. is rarely exercised although the methods for implementing them are simple. These methods will be more complicated for a distant site that is difficult to identify and has no nationality.

The current law relies on concepts that are ill-suited to the realities of the Internet : the harm is not only to private life (a too narrow concept which, moreover, differs from American privacy) but to all aspects of personal life; must we afford new rights such as the right to anonymity (greatly reduced by police laws) and the right to be left in peace (spamming)? The concept of personal data is not suited to the new identifiers such as the IP number that applies directly to a machine and not to a person although it will be used to « identify », profile and score a user, (hence the appearance of the personalised anonymous ID!), the identifiers integrated into electronic components and software. Can the law take into account identification features contained in the future IPV6 standard? What is the status of spamming and cookies and how can their legality be regulated? On these points, national legislative distortions that can already be seen are just breaches in the protection system. The necessary international coherence comes up against different cultures, political, economical and technological interests as well as different legal systems. For example, on a practical level, the application of the 1995 directive to the transfer of personal data originating in the European Union proves to be very difficult, if not impossible; otherwise one would have to ban (and how?) transfers to countries without adequate protection, starting with the United States; the 2000 « Safe Harbour » agreement has made its appearance only to prove ineffective and be disputed by the new American executive power. As a matter of fact, this deficiency in the law of protection of data on the Internet favours the interests of those who consider that the protection of the rights and freedoms of Internet users is a pointless restriction. The failure of American self-regulation is manifest.

The existing law appears to be too far removed from some technical realities such as the traceability of individuals, the use of connection and navigation data, the difficulty of making processing secure.

It would appear to be ill-suited to embracing the technological convergence between the Internet and the mobile telephone for example, which will favour the services that are based on the geographic location of the user or the development of biometric and cybersurveillance techniques, particularly at the workplace. None of these new aspects are tackled head on by a law on the protection of personal data that was designed essentially for techniques and services that existed before the Internet. Such failure to adapt the rules harms its credibility whereas a move to make it more specific and to adjust it would give suitable results; however, we also need individuals and society to actively demonstrate their will to defend individual rights and freedoms on the Internet as elsewhere.

III. – The paradoxical role of the Internet

Because legal systems for protecting personal data, where they exist, now show their limits and deficiencies, we must take the defence of individual rights to new fields otherwise there is a danger that we will have an ineffective law that goes round in a closed circuit, serving as an alibi and smokescreen by leading people to believe that there is protection which, in actual fact, is very partial. Sleep in peace good people, the law is protecting you...

That is why I say, with deliberate provocation : long live the many and very varied excesses and abuses that can be found on the Internet! Let interference with the rights and freedoms of individuals be serious and frequent, let the « cases » multiply, let them be highlighted in the media, let them affect us seriously, individually and collectively. They will then change our behaviour by rousing us from our pervading torpor, by raising our awareness of the risks involved; then the protective law will become a useful resource.

It is not enough to have a theoretical protective law : we also must be motivated to use it to defend our rights and freedoms and it must serve as a lever to change the current balance of power, to move from mistrust to passive and active opposition.

The United States example speaks for itself. The debate on the protection of personal data and respect for rights and freedoms remained lifeless until the proliferation of failures of security of computer systems involving access and the illegal disclosure of personal data, transfers of connection data by access suppliers, the introduction of commercialisation of user and consumer profiles, the excesses of spamming and cookies, abuses in the collection of data about the family through children who can also access paedophile, pornographic, violent, hateful and racist sites (which is excessive despite the very liberal and acceptable interpretation of the first amendment to the American Constitution in favour of the freedom of communication and expression), the circulation and sale of sensitive data about health, the criminal records of individuals etc. Many e-commerce start-ups that went bankrupt sold personal data on customer profiles and prospective customers to former competitors, discovering that it was their only remaining valuable asset, without complying with the rights of individuals or the undertakings made.

For the federal state and the federated states alike, these excesses that received wide media coverage resulted in numerous draft laws being submitted in order to prohibit or control the abuses within the framework of a rather incoherent sectorial approach; many disputes arose. Although legislation is under discussion, not many laws have yet been passed except for the protection of minors; however, the legal political and legislative debate continues with some people seeking the enactment of new and specific federal laws.

Having gained awareness, public opinion is exerting increasing pressure on the public authorities to provide suitable responses. Today there is a real social demand for the protection of individuals on the Internet. This is another feature of the American experience, raised, controlled and expressed by powerful organisations that defend personal rights and freedoms such as EPIC (Electronic privacy information centre), ACLU (American civil liberties union).

One only has to visit EPIC's website for example (www.epic.org) to become aware of the liveliness of the debate, actions and reactions, the reality of social control. It is thanks to the existence of such active and well-informed pressure groups that a better balance has been established between those who defend individual rights and freedoms and those who seek to interfere with them. One cannot help but regret that there are no such opposition movements in Europe, and especially in France, although some tentative progress has been made towards creating defence groups or bodies such as the Internet Rights Forum. In order to be effective, the protective law needs intermediaries and sounding boards for public opinion.

The opposition by Internet users and the influence of these bodies that defend the rights of individuals on the Internet are taken into account by operators, those in charge of public and private sites, and especially by businesses. Accordingly, there is an increase in undertakings that might serve to incur liability, to respect individual rights and freedoms, to discipline the collection, processing and circulation of personal data through posting charters and labelling sites. However, there again, the American experience shows that this self-regulation is often lacking in seriousness, gives the Internet user confidence without preventing abuses, is tantamount to self-promotion not to say deception. (As in the Double click or E-Toys cases in which the Federal Trade Commission threatened to take legal proceedings). About fifty major companies, including IBM, American Express and ATT created their own « corporate privacy officer » reporting to management and having a certain amount of functional autonomy; this officer is responsible for auditing the sites and files to detect anomalies, define good practices and handle complaints. That is in response to the anxiety of the American government, which, following a survey, estimated that only 20 % of Internet sites guarantee Internet users protection against the abusive use of their personal data.

The most effective strategy for changing the behaviour of those who fail to respect individual rights and freedoms on the Internet is to hit businesses' weak spot, that is to say their « wallet », with the law serving to support and legitimise the action. When the excesses lose customers and potential customers who have lost confidence and seeking redress, when word goes round to boycott the site or products and services offered as a reprisal, when well-orchestrated media campaigns harm the brand image of the public or private institution, when far-reaching and costly court proceedings are instituted, the results are immediate and spectacular. No public or private organisation can withstand justified, public denunciation; examples abound in the United States and European Internet users who are much more passive and unorganised would do well to draw inspiration from them to support the measures taken by the regulating authorities. It is then that one discovers the interest in being virtuous (and why not highlight it on the Internet to reinforce a positive brand image and inspire confidence) by respecting individual rights; the protective law is then perceived as a good investment. In that respect, the financial analysis of laws is pertinent : the American firms, with the support of the federal government, refuse protective legislation which is always presented as being a pointless and costly restriction; their behaviour will change under pressure from Internet users when they realise that the lack of trust, the active opposition, the loss of image, can prove more costly. The United States, which presents itself on the global stage as a universally worthy example in matters of protecting individual freedoms and regulating the Internet, has difficulty in realising that these freedoms also have an incalculable value on the Internet, albeit a fluctuating one. It can be seen clearly in the recent legislation passed in the United States (Patriot Act), in France (the law on everyday security), in Great Britain, in Germany etc. in the name of combating terrorism, or through the Budapest Council of Europe's Convention on cybercrime. In the context of security, there are loopholes in the protection of personal data, with the retention of and access to connecting traces and message decoding (not to mention Carnivore and Magic Lantern...) which some public administrations are taking advantage of for suspicious motives, with the backing of a manipulative political power which itself is partially manipulated.

In fact, the Internet has a paradoxical effect : it increases the real risks and dangers for individual rights and freedoms and at the same time encourages progress in the law for protecting personal data by making it more necessary and firmly established in the national, Community or international context, by provoking debate and raising awareness of public opinion, by changing behaviour and the legal and technical approaches to deal with new realities.

Obviously, new balances must be found between the European model that has a wealth of protective rules but which is rarely implemented and complied with because it is used too infrequently by societies that are too apathetic, and the North American model which fails to offer aware and demanding Internet users a sufficiently developed system of rules. One can only hope and encourage a convergence between these two realities to prevent the Internet from being transformed into a freedom destroying spider's web.

DROIT D'AUTEUR AND COPYRIGHT :
WHAT IS THE RELATIONSHIP?

BY

MICHEL VIVANT

PROFESSOR AT THE UNIVERSITY OF MONTPELLIER I
DIRECTOR OF THE RESEARCH TEAM
« INTANGIBLE CREATIVE WORKS AND LAW »
ADVISOR TO FRENCH AND EUROPEAN GOVERNMENTS
PARTNER IN THE FIRM OF GILLES VERCKEN, PARIS

1. *Droit d'auteur* and copyright : Alain Strowell devoted a brilliant 722 page (1) essay to this subject. Admittedly, it includes the bibliography and index, but nevertheless, it naturally calls for the utmost modesty from anyone who is going to tackle this issue! There is a danger of being superficial in having to deal with the same subject in a few minutes or a few lines! On a positive note, no doubt it will provide some incentive to summarise...

2. However, even the choice must be radically summarised, *what*? What to mention? What to select in these two areas of *droit d'auteur* and copyright, which are increasingly confronted with this other world, that of the networks?

It is always possible, of course, to stick to age-old platitudes. And it will be said that *copyright* protects the investment or primarily the investment whereas *droit d'auteur*, as its name already suggests since it gives prominence to the author, focuses on the persons (those who create, of course).

One can also reiterate the accepted views, the platitudes that the debate between intellectual property and the networks inevitably gives rise to. However, the snag is that the accepted views differ depending on who holds them. According to « *high tech* » common parlance, that is to say avoiding, as one might expect, any in-depth examination, we should sing the praises of copyright, available to

---

(1) *Droit d'auteur et copyright, Divergences et convergences* (*Droit d'auteur and copyright, Differences and similarities*), LGDJ, 1993.

an investor who will only be present on the networks provided that
he can be guaranteed the best possible legal security. And, I shall
not forget to mention here, through the filter of the *Huston* case,
the difference between copyright which allows « studios » to use a
film as they wish in order to serve their best interests and, in particular, authorises them to colourise it, and *droit d'auteur* which
keeps this film under the author's power, thereby preventing any
change even when it would appear to be financially beneficial (2).
However, indeed, the example can be turned around : this
copyright allows or would allow anything and would thus condone
any distortion of the work... such as colourising (colouring) a film.
The other accepted view emerges : *droit d'auteur* is essential to
ensure that a work is really protected, and it alone is capable of
doing so. There can be no doubt that, from this point of view, *droit
d'auteur* offers more protection than copyright. However, we must
look at what actually happens in everyday practice and also in the
light of any specific rules for audiovisual (3) or software (4) for
example.

Let us therefore leave accepted ideas... (« Music subdues
behaviour; example : the Marseillaise » wrote Flaubert) (5).

3. And let us start with the basics – in the sense of fundamentals.
Let us start with the « fundamentals ».

Droit d'auteur or copyright : they both give rights over a piece of
work to someone or other. To whom ? For what ? To do what ?
These are the « leading questions ». What is the situation, therefore,
based on these fundamental questions, with regard to the relationship between *droit d'auteur* and copyright in the light of
networks and the Internet ?

And yet, having posed the question, it seems to me that the differences one might like to make between these two systems prove
to be less marked than people say. Insofar as the function creates

(2) Cass. civ. 1ˢᵗ, 28 May 1991, *JCP* 1991, II, 21731, note FRANÇON, and *JCP* 1991, ed. E,
II, 220, note SIRINELLI and GINSBURG, *D.* 1993, 197, note RAYNARD, *RIDA* 1991, n° 149, p. 161,
obs. KÉRÉVER, *Rev. crit. DIP* 1991, 752, note GAUTIER.

(3) When the French intellectual property Code requires, for example, the exclusive rights to
use an audiovisual work to be transferred to the producer (Art. L.132-24).

(4) Of which it has been said that it was virtually an industrial property right (see,
symptomatic, the work of Mrs J. SCHMIDT-SZALEWSKI and Mr J.-L. PIERRE, *Droit de la propriété
industrielle (Industrial property law)*, Litec, 2ⁿᵈ ed., 2001, which deals with the protection of
software under « rights related to patents »).

(5) *Dictionary of received ideas.*

the right, provided that, in a given context, the challenges are the same, it is not surprising that the responses given should be similar, whether it is a question of *droit d'auteur* or copyright.

We shall try to verify this – quickly – using the three questions mentioned, put more academically. Which leads me to consider : purpose(I), ownership (II), content (III).

I. – Purpose

4. Firstly, in considering what purpose *droit d'auteur* or copyright might serve in the « information society » and networks environment, one cannot help but note that everything... and anything is deemed to be capable of being copyrighted.

It is good form to say that copyright is infinitely more permissive. However, should we be reminded that with the *Feist* judgment the United States Supreme Court refused to protect a telephone directory (6), whereas the French courts did not shrink from protecting such directories ? (7)

It would seem to be very difficult nowadays to claim that we have discovered a sort of « ontological » difference between the systems.

In fact, the influence of *droit d'auteur* is identical « in the field » to that of copyright and the common danger is that everything will be covered : anything that is conveyed by a network (a piece of music, a text, a website itself... but also the faintest graphics) everything such as that which « constitutes » the networks (languages, links...). Of course, certain questions are carefully avoided... in order to avoid having to provide replies that we don't want to get. That is the case for the status of languages we referred to a moment ago. There is nothing which clearly impels them to be excluded from contemporary copyright or *droit d'auteur* (revisited).

---

(6) *Feist Publications Inc. vs Rural Telephone Service Co. Inc.*, 111 S. Ct. 1282, 18 U.S.P.Q. 2d 1275 (1991).

(7) Accordingly, Paris, 18 Dec.1924, *DH* 1925, 30, concerning a classic directory ; or again Paris, 4th Ch., 27 Nov. 1976, *Juris-Data* n° 028715, concerning a medical and pharmaceutical directory listing all the public and private laboratories.

However, honesty must lead to specifying that a mere « work of compiling information » must be deemed not copyrightable (Cass. civ. 1ᵉʳ, 2 May 1989, *JCP* 1990, II, 21392, note Lucas, concerning company organisation charts – and also on the same subject Paris, 4ᵗʰ Ch., 16 Jan. 1995, *D.* 95, somm. comm. 286, obs. Colombet).

There is substance. There is certainly this minimalist originality which has become the (almost) universal common law. But what would we do, in practical terms, if rights were claimed over these languages? Would this routine line of enquiry also be disallowed?

In my view, that is where the real current questions lie (8) and they are common to both *droit d'auteur* and copyright.

II. – Ownership

5. Investor versus author? Here is yet another point over which we must be careful not to lapse into caricature. There is no question that in the French system, the author takes precedence and accordingly, in a very remarkable way, the author (usually) remains the holder of the *droits d'auteur* even when he creates his work as an employee (9).

However, it would be a mistake to transform French *droit d'auteur* into a universal model of *droit d'auteur*. In a country which also has *droit d'auteur* and is culturally similar to France, such as Italy, for example, the rule is that where something was created as an employee, the employer has *droit d'auteur*.

The fact remains – and it is undeniable – that the author is notably absent from copyright (10).

However, rather than emphasise the differences, it seems to me that the important thing is to recognise that, in one way or another, we must ensure the author's *presence* and he must not be excluded from his field of creation by the law. There is nothing to force him to occupy centre stage (11). On the other hand, he must not be absent from the stage. Firstly, as an author, recognised as

---

(8) In this unbridled increase in the strength of intellectual properties; see on this subject M. VIVANT, « L'irrésistible *ascension des propriétés intellectuelles?* » (« *The unstoppable rise of intellectual properties* »), *Mélanges Mouly*, Litec, 1998, p. 441.

(9) The Court of Cassation forcefully affirms this (settled case-law – thus Cass. civ. 1st, 16 Dec. 1992, *JCP* 1993, ed. E, I, 246, n° 4, obs. VIVANT and LUCAS, *RIDA* 1993, n° 156, p. 193, obs. KÉRÉVER and note SIRINELLI, *Rev. dr. propr. intell.* 1993, n° 50, 48, *Dossiers Brevets* 1992, V, 2 : « The existence of an employment contract entered into by the author of a work of the intellect » it says, « does not override any derogation from the enjoyment of his intangible property rights, the transfer of which is subject to the condition that the extent, destination, place and duration of the sphere of use of the transferred rights should be defined »).

(10) Everyone knows the name of Walt Disney. But who can cite the name of Mickey's (real) « father »?

(11) Apart from a philosophical position of principle presented as not open to discussion.

such (12), but also financially speaking. From this latter point of view, the important thing is that the author should benefit from the use of his work. But in my view, the way chosen to do so is not the main issue to be fought over (13).

However, an examination of the position of the author naturally extends to casting an eye over the content of *droits d'auteur* or copyright.

III. – Content

6. A marked difference emerges here, because although economic rights are common to both systems (A), moral rights, awarded to the author (and to him alone as such), are peculiar to the system of *droit d'auteur* (B).

A. – ECONOMIC RIGHTS

7. Economic rights are present in both systems. Nevertheless the traditions are different. In that respect, the most immediately noticeable difference is the one that soon becomes apparent between the analytical approach of *copyright* and the global approach of *droit d'auteur*. But the truth is that on a deeper level, that is only one manifestation of the difference between practices in *Common*

---

(12) Where Mickey would find his father again.

(13) For a (more extensive) development of this idea, see M. VIVANT, « Pour une épure de la propriété intellectuelle » (« For a working diagram of intellectual property »), *Mélanges Françon*, Dalloz, 1996, p. 416.

On the specific point of financial profit that an author might expect from the use of his work, see n° 13 of that article : « Once again without *a priori* being dogmatic, there is no obligation to award him ownership of a creation that was designed by agreement, for a particular purpose, incorporated in a policy decided without him : is the case of one of its employees abstracting a court decision for a legal review so different from an invention commissioned whilst working as an employee of a pharmaceutical company ?

On the other hand, we must undoubtedly ensure that the creator designer, inventor or author is not deprived of any profit when his creation, in whatever form, can result in added value. However, a very simple reply to that can be found in the solutions offered by a number of national patent laws which consist of offering an exceptional payment to an employed inventor. With the option of considering, if it is deemed appropriate, a formula for sharing in the profits based on existing methods of proportional remuneration of *droit d'auteurs* and introducing procedures for arbitration between the parties. A complicated system, might one say ? No more, in truth, than that which is prevalent today in trial and error, bit by bit and contradictions. *The important thing is that when his creation generates profit, the creator can somehow derive profit from it himself* ». And n° 14 : « the creation must generate profit for all those connected with it but there are various ways of creating this profit and, all things considered, doing so with a realism that does not sacrifice fairness, rather than dogmatically, is a good thing ».

Law countries and those in countries with a Romano-Germanic tradition. Dare I say, that bearing in mind that nowadays the dominant copyright is that of the United States, empire for empire, I prefer the Roman spirit ?

However, that said, the pressure of identical challenges that I referred to earlier, clearly encourages similar developments. The network environment is particularly favourable to that. A good example is that necessary reproductions which are « transient or incidental reproductions » and form « an integral and essential part of a technological process », whose purpose is to be transmitted via networks that the European Community – and therefore countries based on the two traditions of *droit d'auteur* or copyright – are made lawful by Directive 2001/29/EC of 22 May 2001 « on certain aspects of copyright and related rights in the information society » (14). And we can also mention the definition of « right of communication to the public » afforded by this same directive (15) and also the WIPO Copyright Treaty of 20 December 1996 (16), which, in the latter case, brings together countries with different traditions but this time on a global scale (17). Other examples could also be given.

But that is not the most delicate issue.

B. – MORAL RIGHTS

8. *Last but not least* : the recognition of moral rights is not only a real, but a significant difference between the *droit d'auteur* system and the copyright system (18).

And it is there that the process of *droit d'auteur* is generally appraised : this moral right would be a hindrance, especially in the context of networks and the Internet, since the author would still be in a position to undo what has been done. A hindrance ? Let us leave caricatures aside. Let me simply observe that moral rights can

---

(14) Art. 5.1.

(15) Art. 3.

(16) Art. 8 on which, moreover, the identical wording of the directive was based.

(17) Right to communicate to the public which – must we be reminded ? – had to be redefined for some national laws that are ill-suited to the phenomenon of the Internet and the related practice of consultation on demand.

(18) Even if theoretically, by signing the Berne Convention, all Member States are obliged to recognise a minimum of moral rights. Many remain close to this minimum. And one might ask oneself whether, sometimes, it is not interpreted in such a way that it approaches zero.

be considered just as much a hindrance as a right that has to be respected. Certainly, the conquest of the West can be better achieved by violating the rights of Indian populations. It is not certain that the Internet must be a Far-West.

Having said that, I shall make just three observations.

First observation : if one accepts the idea that it is fair that the author should be present in the creation, whether one calls it *droit d'auteur* or copyright (19), it is also fair that a moral right, which reflects the deep link between the author and his work, should be recognised. And in that respect – we must not be afraid to affirm it – *droit d'auteur* can serve as a model for copyright.

Moreover, does not the fact that most countries, including the United States, have signed the Berne convention, mean some kind of recognition of the validity of the framework ? As for the fact that the reality might be different, and particularly in the United States, is that not merely a demonstration that the rule of law only exists insofar as one wants it to, and in fact, does not exist for the mighty ?

Second observation : as fair as this moral right may be, in my view, we must certainly take the opposite view in terms of the influence that *droit d'auteur* actually has. Can it be seriously maintained that home pages and hypertext links command the same respect as the work of Marguerite Yourcenar ?

That calls for a fundamental examination which also leads us back to our first question on how much importance to place on *droit d'auteur* and copyright (20).

Third and final observation : as an extension of the previous one, we must certainly argue for a reasonable use of moral rights in the network environment (and, in truth, outside networks too). In my view, it would be absurd to liken – as sometimes happens – *droit au respect* (respect due to the work) and intangibility, for example. Moral rights must prevent the work from being distorted and even from being « rewritten » against the author's will. Their aim is not to prevent a normal use of the work, which takes account of its

(19) See n° 5 above.
(20) See n° 4 above.

specific context and, in particular, in the case of the *net*, an inevitable change brought about by the effect of interactivity (21).

It will be observed that such a *reasonable* (22) concept of moral rights precludes claiming that it would be unduly restrictive.

In conclusion

9. Reasonable : that is no doubt the key to *droit d'auteur* and copyright adapted to the networks and the Internet – by avoiding a war of religion and a war of dogma. Because – as I hope to have shown – neither one is true or false (or conversely), there is no good or bad system. It is what we make of it.

Reasonable... « *Reasonable* » is a traditional concept of *Common Law* countries. And the « good father » of the Code civil is none other, in a more modern and less sexist version (23), than a « reasonable person ».

That is perhaps the whole problem! Did you say reasonable? Everyone knows that our good father is a fictional being...

---

(21) Unless, of course, we make the author, like an image from an other era, an almost divine, extraordinary being, who is not accountable to anyone...

(22) On this concept, see M. VIVANT, « Raison et Réseaux, De l'usage du raisonnable dans la régulation de l'Internet » (« Reason and Networks, On the use of what is reasonable in regulating the Internet »), *Mélanges Mehl*, Doc. fr. 1999, p. 153.

(23) As in Quebec, for example.

COPYRIGHT AND DROIT D'AUTEURS

A note on differences in legal culture and practical implications – today and tomorrow

BY

MADS BRYDE ANDERSEN

PROFESSOR OF LAW, UNIVERSITY OF COPENHAGEN,
INSTITUTE OF LEGAL SCIENCE
MADS.BRYDE.ANDERSEN@JUR.KU.DK

I. – The problem defined

Seen from a global perspective, the legal protection of literary and artistic works follow two paths that are different in principle. Legislation in continental Europe is based on the so-called continental *droit d'auteurs* approach by which copyright protection is seen as a « natural right » that basically « belongs to » the author – partly because it originates from his or her personality. Common law countries like the U.K. and USA, are based on a *copyright system* by which the exclusive right is seen as a privilege that is given to the right-holder by the State.

As explained in par. 3, the two systems may not only lead to different views on a number of copyright issues (including the issues' originality and of *droit moral* and *droit de paternité*), but also to different political perspectives on the need to legislate, and how. These differences have to do with the origin of both systems, cf. the short outline in par. 2, and they are confronted when attempts are made to merge copyright and *droit d'auteurs* systems when attempts for global unification are made, cf. par. 4.

The paper argues that the differences in copyright and *droit d'auteurs* systems spring from differences in legal culture that should not be ignored. It therefore argues that one should not try to erode those differences even though global legal unification may be seen as necessary to facilitate world trade. Differences in law will always exist and the difficulties that these differences imply are not insurmountable.

II. – Origin of differences

Telecommunication and shipping have one thing in common : Throughout the history of civilisation they both have served as media for communication over distances and led to *globalisation* of legal rules. When different cultures met in earlier ages (during the Roman Empire, in the renaissance period and subsequently) a merge of cultures occurred. In some cases, this led to wars – in others in the merge of legal cultures.

Roughly speaking there are two ways in which one legal system can merge into another : The one is by the force of *laws* (e.g. according to the will of an emperor or legislator). The other is by common sense as applied by the *courts*. In a rough picture, those two paths have led to the basic difference between the *civil law system* (which usually originates from the force of an emperor), and the *common law system* (according to which legal rules develop case by case and under the guidance of courts).

Although rather new in the history of law, both the copyright and the *droit d'auteurs* systems can be explained by such developments. In a *droit d'auteur* system, every little aspect of the exclusive rights that the right holder owns is described with precision in the law, whereas under a common law *copyright system*, the legal basis is more fuzzy. Furthermore, under a common law copyright system, the scope of copyright will usually be established in a court of law (assisted by barristers!), whereas under a civil law system legislators (assisted by lobbyists!) play a much more predominant role.

There are also other implications of the said distinction and those indicated above : Under a copyright system, the exclusive rights of the right holder are envisaged as purely economic, whereas under a *droit d'auteurs* system, the exclusive rights are regarded more as an extension of the personal rights of the right holder.

III. – Some practical implications

Apart from those consequences of the basic distinction, some practical implications occur when the legal cultures of copyright collide in the networked world of computer and communications technology. Among them are the following :

1. Ownership : There is a basic difference between copyright and *droit d'auteur* systems when it comes to the *ownership* of the exclusive rights. In a copyright system the « property » analogy leads to a total transfer of the exclusive rights (including the right to be named as the author of the work). In a *droit d'auteur*s system, the author may even find himself in a position to object to the transfer of his rights. This may have consequences when rights are being transferred in bulk (e.g. as a part of business mergers or acquisitions).

2. Paternity rights : The property analogy in a *copyright system* indicates that the right of the author to be named as such when the work is being displayed to the public is much weaker than in a *droit d'auteur system*. This again may have implications on the practice by which works are being displayed to the public on Internet sites.

3. Exemptions : When it comes to exemptions and modifications to the exclusive right, there are fundamental differences in how you explain (if possible) that such exemptions exist. Under a *droit d'auteur* system each exemption to the exclusive right will be written into the law, whereas under a copyright system, general exemptions as to the « fair use » of/or « fair dealing » in regard to the work would apply and be interpreted by courts on a case-by-case basis. One example of this is the legality of copies (including the temporary copies) that the user will have to make when he reads) the information from an Internet site (or saves it to a disc).

One could claim that differences of the said nature have always occurred and that the Internet as such does not fundamentally change the legal culture. After all, the global copyright system has had to live with numerous changes of attitude since the 1886 Berne Convention (which, on the other hand was not adhered to by the United States until the 1990s). Still, there is a difference. In a networked world where every IT-user is in control of a reproductive machinery of immense proportions (in the form of a PC with state-of-the-art capabilities), this conflict has become much more immense. Furthermore, the widespread agreement that world e-commerce should be supported on the interest provides a substantial argument for harmonisation of rules that might otherwise be seen as trade obstacles. In other areas of the law, e.g. personal data protection law, such differences have been envisaged as threats to global trade. Furthermore, the frequency and speed by which loopholes in the legal protection could be exploited has led legislators to introduce numerous rules that basically work as « digital speed limitations ».

For these – and indeed other – reasons, there seems to be general agreement on the need for global harmonisation (at least to some extent) of the copyright and *droit d'auteur*s systems in relation to the use and transmission of works in a digital format. The question is then what prospects there really are for such harmonisation and how – in such case – it should take place.

IV. – Prospects for global unification

With a starting point in the above distinction between the law-making by courts or legislators, the prospects for globalisation of the law of copyright/*droit d'auteur*s depends on whether you rely on the courts or the legislators to do the job. In this decision, a fundamental question occurs : Who do you trust most – legislators or courts ? And secondly, is it possible at all to achieve unification in due time if you put the job of harmonisation in the hands of the court or the legislator ?

There is no absolute answer to these questions since they depend on the legal culture you feel most familiar and comfortable with : A person familiar and comfortable with a legal culture that « trusts » *legislators* will favour a legislative approach and expect the legislator – working within the framework of international conventions – to do the job. However, if you favour a *court-based* legal tradition, you would expect the landmark cases to provide the relevant answers.

When copyright legislation is being harmonised within the European Union, the legislator (i.e, the Commission, the Council and the Parliament) will tend to look for clear answers to the questions that come up in public copyright discussions. However, since the EU comprises jurisdictions that belong to both the *droit d'auteur* civil law approach, the EU legislator finds itself in a difficult position : If legislators are asked to « harmonise » copyright laws, you may very well end up in extremely complicated discussions as those that occurred during the legislative process that led to the 1991 Software Directive and the 2001 Infosoc-Directive. In both cases extremely difficult political situations occurred with a lot of lobbying. The legislative end result that followed is widely seen as problematic in a number of respects.

If, on the other hand, you prefer a court-based legal tradition, the answer to the emerging issues in the area of copyright law (as those described above at 3) may not be within reach in a short term perspective : When it comes to the areas of law that have not been subject to EU harmonisation, it is hardly likely that the courts in the various jurisdictions will come to the same conclusions, since their backgrounds are basically different. However, when it comes to the areas that have been subject to harmonisation, the situation is not much better : the troublesome hazes will have to be brought before the national courts first, and thereafter – in form of a preliminary question – towards the European Court of Justice in Luxembourg.

Concluding remarks

In the above comments, I have tried to highlight some of the effects produced by the differences between *droit d'auteur*s and copyrightwhen copyright legislation is harmonised at a global level. For a number of reasons – cultural, economic and indeed psychological – this particular kind of harmonisation is extremely difficult. The only message that should be sent to legislators is that harmonisation should only take place to the extent it is of *essence* to the world community. Harmonisation in the copyright area should not be a « nice to have » issue that legislators should be concerned about.

In the long run, the concepts – also in the area of *droit d'auteur*s and copyright law – have a tendency to develop into similar concepts and results, and indeed so in areas where different cultures

meet. The Internet is in itself a meeting place that should trigger
case-by-case harmonisation based on a *hands on approach* guided by
the common sense that courts throughout the world are well-
trained in applying.

AUTHORS' RIGHTS AND EXCEPTIONS FOR PRIVATE COPYING IN THE AGE OF THE INTERNET

BY

Marc MOSSÉ

MEMBER OF THE PARIS BAR, AUGUST & DEBOUZY

One of the great strengths of the Internet is its ability to invite the most diverse imaginations to the modernity ball. Occasionally, it even operates like a machine for going back in time, noting sometimes transient schools of political thought or philosophies on its dance card. Accordingly, Proudhon's theories are restored to favour, since some claim that « *property is theft* ». The libertarian and, some would say, at times, ultra-liberal culture which has grown up around the « net » proposes the sanctioning of absolute freedom of circulation of information and knowledge. To the extent that circulating cultural creations via the Internet is often portrayed as being free from laws. In that respect, the « *Napster* » *incident* would have been the time to affirm the dogma. Accordingly, *Wired* magazine asserted that « *the future will prevail, there will be no ownership in cyberspace* ». The idea has the merit of being both simple and frank. The claim of an uncompromising utopia in whose name we will be called upon to become successively or simultaneously, governors and governed, actors and spectators, producers and consumers, naturally challenges some values that we believed to be well established and for which national, regional or international laws seemed to be the guarantors, taking sometimes different approaches.

The Internet symbolises the information society without restrictions or borders; it was therefore predictable that it would bear the explicit or implicit challenge to authors' rights. Not only because the idea that technologies make it possible to circulate or reproduce works without control prevails, but also because the user of new information and communication technologies is increasingly less aware of the value of the creation when it is offered in an intangible form and expressed as digital data. The aspiration to maximum freedom triggered by the Internet would thus be destined to conflict with intellectual property.

Indeed, what is at stake is to avoid a grotesque confrontation between these two standards and, on the contrary, to seek to effectively reconcile them. This connection is all the more necessary as it would be an opportunity to reaffirm the value of intellectual property and its relevance as set out in Article 17-2 of the European Union's Charter of Fundamental Rights. The relationship with human rights is beyond question. The recognition in French law of an intellectual property right that is exclusive and enforceable against everyone arose directly from revolutionary legislation, as echoed in the Universal Declaration of Human Rights. The value of a fundamental right attached to intellectual property would enable a defence of *droit d'auteur*s to be predicated, perceived not as an attack on individual freedoms but rather as *one of the criteria for a cultured society*.

At the heart of this reconciliation between intellectual property and freedom of access to culture imposed by the digital world, lies the central, not to say symptomatic issue, of private copying. In fact, in French law, *private copying is defined as the creation of a copy or reproduction of a work strictly for the copier's private use and not intended for general use*. It is not so much a right as an *exception to the author's exclusive right*. In 1985, the French legislator decided to introduce a compulsory levy on media that allowed such copying : the « *payment for private copying* ». It was a question of remunerating creators by offsetting the losses arising from the use of products devoted to copying and the profit made by the sellers of those media. That took place in the age of analogue technology. Today, we are promised, everyone is a budding copyist monk.

Now, digital technologies allow perfect copies to be made, that is to say of a quality that is identical to the original and in infinite numbers. Private copying intended as an exception then takes on another dimension and seems to be able to free itself from its initial field. The risk is then twofold : firstly, the distinction between a legal copy and an illegal copy could become so blurred that pirating works becomes socially acceptable and lawful and secondly, the multiplication of copies could have a significant negative impact on the economy of culture and creation.

In other words, it is important to prevent entitlement to private copying from being transformed into a right to copy.

The Member States of the European Union do not all share the same view of private copying. This heterogeneous situation could be improved when the Directive on copyright and related rights in the information society [hereinafter : the Directive], is transposed, even though this law contains several options. So far as concerns France, the situation is complex inasmuch as firstly, the « commission on private copying » has already decided to extend remuneration to some removable digital media and is pursuing its work on media that are not dedicated to copying without waiting for the national law to be adapted, and secondly, the legislator recently extended the scope of remuneration for digital private copying.

At this moment in time, without claiming to have settled such a complex issue here, I shall take the liberty of emphasising that although firstly, technologies offer the opportunity to refocus the concept of private copying on its essence (I), secondly, they offer solutions for making the exception of private copying a catalyst for a new dialogue between creators and citizens (II).

I. – Technology necessitates reconsidering the sources of exception for private copying

Digital technologies have made it possible to copy works that analogue technology precluded. It is therefore essential to define the spectrum of what must remain an exception to an exclusive right (A) made clearer, in the digital age, by new methods of circulation (B).

A. – REMUNERATION FOR PRIVATE COPYING IN THE DIGITAL AGE OR THE TEMPTATION TO EXTEND

Sound and audiovisual works are no longer the only ones at issue (1) but software, whether for business or pleasure, remains excluded from this system of legal licensing (2).

1. – Works concerned by private copying
in the digital age can no longer be confined
to music and film : methods of copying allow
what analogue technology precluded

The French Parliament has therefore amended Article L. 311-1 of the Intellectual Property Code which concerns remuneration for private copying, by adding a second paragraph providing that such remuneration is *also due* :

« *to the authors and editors of works fixed on any medium other than phonograms and videograms, for reproducing them in the circumstances set out in paragraph 2 of Article 122-5 of the Intellectual Property Code, on a digital recording medium* ».

That legislation which arises from an amendment derives from a proposal for a law from the senate, taking up the idea that « *these media can be used to reproduce written, graphic, photographic works and some plastic works as well as musical or audiovisual works* ».

However, its application will not be without problems since the legislator has « forgotten » to amend the criterion for the duration of recording required to calculate the remuneration. And yet, it has to be said that the duration of recording, of a photograph, for example, is not the easiest of things to ascertain. Admittedly, it is always possible to convert that criterion into a compression rate and calculate in bytes rather than minutes. But such a shift is unconvincing. The duration that serves as a legal basis for defining this levy begins as from the initial duration of the work and not from an initial conversion into compressed data.

Be that as it may, one thing is certain : software is excluded from the scope of private copying and from remuneration for it.

2. – Taking advantage of the legislator's action,
some people claimed that software
and in particular, so-called leisure software,
is also eligible for remuneration for private copying

That approach does not appear to be justified.

As indicated earlier, the new second paragraph of Article L. 311-1 of the IPC states that private copying that gives entitlement to remuneration   concerns   works   such   as   those   included   in

Article L. 122-5 of the IPC. And yet, that article expressly excludes software from the scope of private copying.

It has to be said that Community law restricts any enterprise in that respect since the Directive of 14 May 1991 on the legal protection of computer programmes makes no provision for an exception for private copying for software, a law to which the Directive refers. That is the interpretation which the recommendations of the CSPLA (Higher Council of Copyright) seem to apply.

The particular fate reserved for software can be explained, *inter alia* by the fact that this was the first digital creation and because infinite numbers of exact copies can be made, there was a danger that the floodgates to unlimited copying would be opened, posing a major risk to the sector's economy. The principle of preventing any private copying of software could have been extended to all digital works. However a return to the right that citizens had long held weakens such an interpretation of the Directive, at least from a political point of view. That is why the boundaries between copying for private use and pirating works need to be re-established.

B. – Methods of circulation via the Internet or the essential distinction between entitlement to a copy and the right to copy

There is a great temptation to want to apply a broad interpretation to private use when navigating on the Internet. On the contrary, I think it is important to interpret it strictly (1.), in particular because nowadays methods of circulation enable this need for private copying to be managed differently (2.).

1. – *One might have wondered at what moment reproducing something on the Internet without the author's permission becomes collective, and therefore unlawful*

Returning briefly to the famous « *Napster* » case, it can be seen, by being unfortunately simplistic, that the Court held that downloading MP3 musical files, could not be likened to private use within the meaning of the concept of « *making use* ». This assessment, brings us close to the definition used by the directive that is aimed at copying carried out by « *a natural person for private use and for ends that are neither directly nor indirectly commercial* ». A concept which nevertheless falls far short of the more restrictive French definition which will be preferred. One will therefore be tempted to *demand a personal identity between the copyist and the user*, and to consider that a work sent to a recipient in the form of an attached file is not a private copy, especially as there can be many recipients. The same argument must prevail in the situation of an Intranet since it is a community and therefore a collective space.

Like the TRIPS (Trade Related Aspects of Intellectual Property Rights) agreement and WIPO treaties, the Directive emphasises *the exceptional nature of any exception* to the rightholder's monopoly and Article 5-5 thereof, directly echoing Article 7 of the 1996 December WIPO treaty, sets the *triple test* according to which *exceptions are restricted to special cases which do not conflict with the normal exploitation of the work or cause prejudice to the legitimate interests of the author.*

This is perfectly logical.

In 1996, a French Court held « *that by allowing third parties connected to the Internet to visit their private web pages and potentially to take copies, the defendants encouraged the collective use of their reproductions* ».

The Directive leaves it for the Member States to decide whether or not to apply the exception of private copying. Let us suppose that in France it will be retained. Let us hope that when it is transposed, it will be interpreted strictly. Once again, the issue is not to hide behind a tolerance because we are disarmed by technical considerations and practices but to see how technology makes it possible to create mutual respect between the author and the consumer.

2. – *Behaviour connected with changes in the way that works are distributed is difficult to detect and all those involved in culture wonder about these changes*

It is still possible to propose the legal frameworks open to the new ways of implementing authors' exclusive rights as a course for reflection. In fact, the Directive provides that rightholders can make their works and services available to the public so that everyone may *access them from a place and at a time individually chosen by them*. No doubt this is the influence of technology : apart from allowing reprehensible acts, it also allows interactivity. Downloading is both the simplest and the most obvious example.

One is then tempted to wonder whether exploitation is going to be increasingly direct and immediate in the digital world. The connection between the rightholder and the consumer will be made-to-measure, making any downloading an act of authorised copying.

Accordingly, online music is based entirely on the idea of copying a file. This results in two options : either downloading is authorised, in accordance with a pre-set scale of remuneration, and therefore lawful; or it is an act that is not authorised by the rightholder and is unlawful.

This interactive relationship between the author and his work might result in citizens having a better understanding of intellectual property. Technology has the impetus to encourage it : that is the role of technical protective measures. Far from being the bolt in a an environment of monitoring, they can become the catalyst for a new dialogue between creators and their audience.

II. – Private copying as a catalyst for a new dialogue between creators and « *consumers* »

Awareness of the need to protect intellectual property in the world of digital technologies is reflected in the development of tools for monitoring the circulation and use of works. Their inclusion in legal instruments shows the expectation placed on these technical measures for guaranteeing the rights of creators without interfering with citizens' freedom (A). That approach encourages the dynamic management of rights to the detriment of centralised procedures (B).

A. – TECHNICAL PROTECTION
MEASURES PROTECT WORKS WITHOUT
DISREGARDING THE FREEDOM OF CITIZENS

Following the example of the WIPO Treaty, the Directive considers these technical protection measures to be one of the cornerstones for safeguarding intellectual property (1) whilst respecting the freedom of citizens and, in particular, their private life (2).

1. In 1985, the French legislator anticipated this change. In his report, Senator Charles Jolibois, having noted the loss suffered by authors due to copies made on cassette, emphasised that « *failing something better, the only answer would appear to be to establish compensation designed to ease the loss suffered by holders of exclusive rights arising from the fact that they find it impossible to exercise those rights* ».

Since then, technology has certainly made copying easier whilst at the same time offering ways of restricting it or even preventing it. The « *best* » that could be expected in 1985 by the French Parliament is looming on the technological horizon.

According to the Directive, these technical measures mean any technologies which, in their normal context of use, are designed to prevent or restrict actions that are not authorised by the rightholder. They could help to eradicate the right to make private copies. In France, it would seem that we are moving towards upholding this exception. The necessary supervision will be provided by the implementation of these technical measures and it will be an offence to try and circumvent them.

Work has been carried out on these technical devices since the middle of the 1980s. There are three main types of technical procedures and, where appropriate, they can be used in conjunction :

– encryption of the content which guarantees the integrity of the works and control of access solely to authorised users and encryption of systems that restrict the communication and circulation of content between the different hardware systems that are likely to exploit it;

– watermarking, which identifies the rightholder or the origin of the work;

– digital right management (DRM) systems which allow the circulation and distribution of works to be managed as far as use by the end consumer.

We must not overlook the current work on the MPEG 21 standard.

However, any technological control procedure leads to questions about the potential risks to the private lives of users who are confronted with it.

2. Achieving the protection of intellectual property at the expense of what citizens would see as an interference with their freedom would be detrimental. It is therefore crucial that these technical measures are not likely to call into question the protection of personal data and private life.

Of special concern are the means of identifying users, fuelling the suspicion that any data gathered will be used for purposes other than to protect the work. It is a pity that the Directive has nothing to say on this point. However, one suspects that the rules drawn from the 1995 directive on the protection of personal data, and, so far as France is concerned, the 1978 law that is currently being amended, will be enough to deal with any deviations.

The argument is not only academic. *The development towards technological measures for protecting works must be socially acceptable.* Public opinion, therefore every potential consumer, must see it as progress for the circulation of culture and not as an additional restrictive measure or indeed a social control. That is not the least important issue. We must definitely take up this challenge so that intellectual property does not become a mockery.

This need for confidence which is at the heart of the development of new information and communication technologies requires simultaneously rigour and transparency in the methods of remuneration linked to private copying.

B. – Technical protection measures
to encourage transparency of methods
of remuneration connected with private copying

In the light of technical protection measures, the existing procedures for setting the remuneration for private copying seem dated

(1) and must ultimately give way to a dynamic rights management (2).

1. The French example is quite typical of this situation. We know that remuneration for private copying is decided by a commission which takes administrative decisions. This compulsory levy thus decreed gives rise to a lively legal discussion. The « official » argument considers it as a private law remuneration. The opposite proposal equates it to a tax and is not short of serious arguments. In the background, there is a debate on the lack of transparency of the existing procedure and its lack of democratic legitimacy.

Incidentally, very recently, that led the general rapporteur of the National Assembly's Finance Commission to devote a study to it, demonstrating the institutionally unsuitability of the current scheme where tools that are not specifically dedicated to copying are concerned.

Admittedly, since 1985 the situation has changed radically, at least from three aspects.

Firstly, the fact that the Article L. 311-5 of the IPC commission envisages making any recording medium that allows a work to be fixed subject to a levy, and therefore, where appropriate, digital decoders or computers and tomorrow – why not – mobile telephones, changes the perspective.

In fact, the possible extension of this levy to media that are not dedicated to copying works poses a problem. By keeping solely to the example of the computer, clearly a number of its purchasers will never use it to make copies of works in the sense of private copying. In any event, it seems difficult to accept that people should be asked to pay something to offset a loss in which they have no involvement. The wishful thinking to extend it to so-called hybrid media reveals this stumbling block.

Secondly, such a compulsory fixed levy would not be suited to the practices of « *time-shifting* » for example, or downloading in exchange for payment. Recital n° 35 of the Directive favours this.

Thirdly, by introducing a fixed levy at a time of decentralised practices and network operations accentuates the image of a tax with no democratic basis. And it makes intellectual property something that is binding but poorly understood. Its effect can only be pernicious, not to say paradoxical, by giving to those who had never thought of it the desire to copy : « I am paying therefore I shall make copies... ».

The current French system is less than satisfactory and would seem not to be in line with the idea of fair compensation as envisaged by the Directive.

In fact, any centralised taxation procedure in a profoundly decentralised world can only result in disproportionate levies.

2. The dynamic management of rights offers a way of meeting rightholders' expectations.

Firstly, as shown in the Directive's statement of reasons « *the level of fair compensation should take full account of the degree of use of technological protection measures* ».

Secondly, it would prevent consumers from paying twice : once, for example, in respect of an act of electronic commerce and secondly via a levy on the recording medium. Finally, it will oblige a genuine link to be established between the loss suffered by the rightholder and the act of copying.

Furthermore, these technical measures will give the creator better control over his work, to the extent that he himself can control the number of copies he authorises, receiving a remuneration exactly in proportion to his authorisation. This true price of the work will be at the heart of the link between the consumer and the author and would help to raise awareness of the value of intellectual property.

Obviously, that presupposes establishing mechanisms for managing these rights. Far from disputing the role of collective management companies, these decentralised procedures would restore to them the role that history had initially granted them : that of a dynamic interface. The whole would gain in rigour and transparency, restoring to the author and the citizen a status that appears to be diminished in the modern cultural world.

In the digital era, when the transposition of the Directive on copyright is imminent, wisdom would seem to dictate that we should consider a new overall system. Keeping to the French situation, no-one will dispute that the system arising from analogue technology must be reviewed in the light of technological developments. Accordingly, the decentralised management of rights could be one of the catalysts for reconciling intellectual property and freedom of access to culture.

THE PATENTABILITY OF SOFTWARE

BY

Alain BENSOUSSAN

Barrister at the Paris Bar

Over 13,000 patents were issued by the European Patent Office (EPO). However, controversy surrounding the patentability of software is still raging. Admittedly, at first sight, the eligibility of software to be patented would appear to be limited since Article 52 (2) and (3) of the Munich convention exclude computer programmes as such from the rules relating to inventions.

Under the twin pressures of advances in information technology, which is now a real economic sector, and the industrial world, which affords software an increasingly significant position in manufacturing processes, the EPO has made every effort to get round this problem.

Taking the view that the exclusion established in point 2 of Article 52 should be understood restrictively, especially on account of the limit established in point 3 of the same Article, in the condition for the industrial application of Article 57 of the convention, the EPO sought a legislative basis to enable software to be eligible for patentability.

Without making reference to the effect that the TRIPS provisions might have on this issue or the discussion on the introduction of a Community patent, for its part, the EPO devised the so-called technical effect theory.

At first, the technical effect was understood as meaning an inquiry as to the technical nature of the invention. However, there again, there have been recent changes to that concept which reveal some dilution.

I. – The technical effect expresses the technical nature of the invention

Since the EPO understands exclusion from patentability of software established by Article 52 as being limited on account of point 3 of that Article, a piece of software could constitute an invention eligible for patentability provided that it fulfils the characteristic of industrial application of Article 57 of the Convention.

As it still has to take into account the exclusion of Article 52, the EPO strove to seek a concrete expression of the technical effect.

Was the interest of such technical effect with regard to the patentability of software going to induce the EPO to favour the place of this technical effect in order to evaluate the other criteria for patentability and, more particularly, the condition for inventive activity ?

A. – THE CONCRETE EXPRESSION OF THE TECHNICAL EFFECT

The technical effect was first given concrete expression in industrial processes. Subsequently, the EPO reduced the weight of the concrete expression of the technical effect by holding that such effect could be produced on an electronic entity.

1. – *The technical effect derives from an industrial process*

It should be remembered that the argument concerning the patentability of industrial processes in which software plays a part, was settled positively in the 1980s.

« *Whereas the process claimed comprises six successive stages, some of which indisputably involve the application of computer programmes, but the whole description of the patent is not reduced to information processing by computers; whereas the claim also includes concrete measures found in the reference drillings and development drillings and obtaining a result, which is the practical measurement of physical characteristics, reflected by obtaining curves giving measurements at the various depths of the development drillings* » (Court of Appeal of Paris 15 June 1981, *Schlumberger case, Ann. Prop. Indu.* 1982, p. 24).

In this judgment, the Court had emphasised the economic importance of not excluding software from patentability.

« *Whereas a process cannot be excluded from patentability for the sole reason that one or several of its stages are carried out by a computer that must be operated by a programme : whereas such a solution would lead to excluding from patentability the majority of recent important inventions which require the involvement of a computer programme and from a practical point of view, such a solution would only lead to aberrant results* ».

For its part, in 1986 the EPO also accepted the technical character deriving from a technical process, holding that it contributed to the prior art.

« *Generally, claims which can be considered as being directed to a computer set up to operate in accordance with a specified programme (whether by means of hardware or software) for controlling or carrying out a technical process cannot be regarded as relating to a computer programme as such and thus are not objectionable under Article 52 (2c) and (3) EPC)* » (*Case of Vicom* T 208/84, Technical Board of Appeal 15 July 1986, *OJ EPO* 1987/014).

Moreover, in that decision, the EPO Board reiterated the position expressed by the Court of Appeal of Paris in 1981 :

« *Generally speaking, an invention which could be patentable in accordance with conventional patentability criteria should not be excluded from protection by the mere fact that for its implementation modern technical means in the form of a computer programme are used* » (*Case of Vicom* T 208/84, Technical Board of Appeal 15 July 1986, *OJ EPO* 1987/014).

2. – *The technical effect can be expressed in an electronic entity*

The entity which expresses the technical nature of the invention can be constituted not only by a material object, which is intellectually understandable, but also by an image created using an electric signal.

In the Vicom case which related to a patent application for the processing of images by a calculator, the EPO's Technical Board of

Appeal held : « *Clearly a method for obtaining and/or reproducing an image of a physical object or even an image of a simulated object (as in computer-aided design/computer-aided manufacturing CAD/ CAM), may be used eg. in investigating properties of the object or designing an industrial article and is therefore susceptible of industrial application. Similarly, a method for enhancing or restoring such an image, without adding to its informational content, has to be considered as susceptible of industrial application within the meaning of Article 57 EPC* » (*Case of Vicom* T208/84, Technical Board of Appeal 15 July 1986, 1987/014).

B. – THE SEAT OF THE INVENTIVE ACTIVITY
IS NOT NECESSARILY AND EXCLUSIVELY LIMITED
TO THE PLACE OF THE INVENTION'S TECHNICAL EFFECT

In its decision of 14 February 1989 (Case of IBM T38/86 Technical Board of Appeal OJ EPO 1990/384), the Technical Board of Appeal tried to demand that the criteria for patentability should be assessed on the basis of the invention's technical contribution.

« *(...) according to Claim 1 of the present application does not contribute to the art anything involving an inventive step within the meaning of Article 56 EPC in a field not excluded from patentability by Article 52 (2)(c)* ».

This position of the Technical Board of Appeal appeared all the stronger as it referred to previous decisions :

« *In decision T208/84 the claimed method is patentable, even though it could be carried out by known hardware suitably programmed, because it makes a contribution in a field not excluded from patentability, namely a more efficient restoration or enhancement of the technical quality of an image. Similarly, in T26/86 the claimed apparatus is patentable, even though the x-ray apparatus without the computer programme was known, because it makes a contribution in a field not excluded from patentability, namely, controlling the X-ray tubes so that optimum exposure is obtained with adequate protection against overloading the X-ray tubes* ».

If that position had been maintained, it would have caused the EPO to segment and fragment claims in order to concentrate its examination of the other criteria for patentability solely on the part constituting the place of the technical effect.

However, that measure was not upheld by the EPO. Moreover, it would appear that in the *Koch Strezel case* (Technical Board of Appeal 21 May 1987, *OJ EPO* 1988/19 T26/86) the Board had already expressed a different opinion.

« *When the technical effect occurs is irrelevant to the question of whether the subject-matter claimed constitutes an invention under Article 52 (1) EPC. The only fact of importance is that it occurs at all* ».

In this decision of 21 May 1987, the Technical Board of Appeal held that « *The European Patent Convention does not ask that a patentable invention be exclusively or largely of a technical nature* » in other words, it did not exclude from patentability inventions that rely on a set of components, some technical and others non-technical.

In rejecting the application of the theory of an essential element, the board stated « *the Board fails to find any legal basis in the European Patent Convention for the theory of the Federal Court of Justice concerning the essence of inventions, it also sees practical objections to a need to give a weighting to technical and non-technical aspects because according to the Federal Court of Justice the criterion to be applied is which aspect makes the essential contribution to the invention's success. Not only is such a decision fraught with difficulties in practice; it also has the effect of making the teaching unpatentable in its entirety if the greater part is non-technical and even though the technical aspect which is found to be subordinate is in fact judged to be novel and to involve an inventive step* » (*Case of Loch & Sterzel*, Technical Board of Appeal, 21 May 1987, *OJ EPO* 1988/19).

Accordingly, we must conclude from the EPO's practice that the European Patent Convention does not require a patentable invention to be exclusively and largely of a technical nature, in other words, it does not exclude from patentability inventions that rely on a set of components, some technical and others non-technical.

In other words, the EPO accepts an overall assessment of the claim in order to examine whether it is patentable or not. Since the technical effect is not necessarily expressed in a material entity and is not an exclusive requirement for assessing the novelty and the inventive step of the invention, this criteria is also being somewhat diluted, having regard to recent decisions by the EPO.

II. – Dilution of the technical effect

The pertinence of the technical effect is undermined when the EPO concedes that this criterion is satisfied by technical considerations. Although recent EPO decisions do not deprive that criterion of any substance, in considering that a technical effect can be potential or even occurs by a functionality of the data having regard to their recording medium, they have certainly made the patentability of numerous software packages possible.

A. – THE TECHNICAL EFFECT
ESTABLISHED BY CONSIDERATIONS

The decision of 31 May 1994 in the *Sohei case* (T769/92 Technical Board of Appeal, *OJ EPO* 1995/525) shows a change in the requirement for a technical character. The patent application related to a financial and stock management system. Having drawn attention to the purpose of the claims which related to a combination of computer equipment (technical characteristic) and processing (functional characteristic), the Board pointed out that « *such a mix may or may not be patentable* ». There again, reference should be made to the arguments given by the Technical Board of Appeal.

« *If, for instance, a non-patentable (e.g. mathematical, mental or business) method is implemented by running a programme on a general-purpose computer, the fact alone that the computer consists of hardware does not render the method patentable if said hardware is purely conventional and no technical contribution to that computer (art) is made by the implementation. However, if a contribution to that art can be found either in a technical problem (to be) solved or in a technical effect achieved by the solution, said mix may not be excluded from patentability, [...]* ».

Having expressed these hesitations, the Technical Board of Appeal – and that is the contribution of that decision to case-law theory of the technical effect – considers that « *the non-exclusion from patentability also applies to inventions, where technical considerations are to be made concerning the particulars of their implementation* ».

Accordingly, the technical character is no longer examined through the technical effect expected of the invention but on technical considerations, that is to say through a more general and, accordingly, less precise concept.

Moreover, in this decision, the Technical Board of Appeal states that when assessing technical considerations they may refer to the technical problem or to its solution.

« The very need for such technical considerations implies the occurrence of an (at least implicit) technical problem to be solved [...] and (at least implicit) technical features [...] solving that technical problem ». Reference to the implicit nature of the technical problem or its solution further strengthens the generality of the criterion.

B. – THE TECHNICAL EFFECT POTENTIALLY ACHIEVED BY THE INTERACTION OF THE SOFTWARE AND ITS MEDIUM

1. – *The potential nature of the technical effect*

The decision of the Technical Board of Appeal on 1 July 1998 (Case of IBM T1173/97 Technical Board of Appeal OJ EPO 1999/ 609) has become famous since it afforded patent protection to a computer programme.

However, the impact of that decision does not mean that mere programming is patentable.

It should be remembered that in the decision of 31 May 1994, the Sohei case (T769/92), the Board considered that *« mere programming as such would, in the Board's view, also be excluded from patentability by virtue of the fact that is an activity, which essentially involves mental acts excluded and, in addition only results in computer programmes which are also excluded from patentability ».*

Subject to that reservation, the IBM case is particularly interesting because of the definition it gives of the technical effect.

« a technical effect which goes beyond the 'normal' physical interactions between the progamme (software) and the computer (hardware) on which it is run ».

Previous EPO decisions had already paved the way, as they set out to show that the technical effect could be produced by introducing software to an external device such as a central unit.

This decision of 1 July 1998 contributes to the theory of the technical effect by stating that it might be potential. The Board pointed out that « *physical modifications of the hardware (causing, for instance, electrical currents) deriving from the execution of the instructions given by programmes for computers cannot per se constitute the technical character required for avoiding the exclusion of those programmes* ».

The Board's illustration also deserves to be noted : « *Although such modifications may be considered to be technical they are a common feature of all those programmes for computers which have been made suitable for being run on a computer, and therefore cannot be used to distinguish programmes for computers with a technical character from programmes for computers as such* ».

The technical nature in the sense that it is meant above must therefore be sought elsewhere : it could relate to effects resulting from the performance (by the hardware) of instructions given by the computer programme.

When these other effects have a technical character or when they result in the software resolving a technical problem, it can be considered that, in principle, an invention producing such effect is patentable.

After this analysis, which seemed to be quite conventional, the Board developed the concept of potential technical effect using arguments containing various points which also deserve to be mentioned.

« *Every computer programme product produces an effect when the programme concerned is made to run on a computer. The effect only shows in physical reality when the programme is being run. Thus the computer programme product itself does not directly disclose the said effect in physical reality, It only discloses the effect when being run and consequently only possesses the 'potential' to produce said effect* ».

Accordingly, this decision introduced the concept of a potential technical effect.

The Board immediately drew the inference from it « *Once it has been clearly established that a specific computer programme product, when run on a computer, brings about a technical effect in the above sense, the Board sees no good reason for distinguishing between a direct technical effect on the one hand and the potential to produce a technical effect, which may be considered as an indirect technical effect, on the other hand* ».

There remained only one more step for the Board to take to accept that a computer programme could be patentable, and it took it. The Board took the view that consequently « *a computer programme product having the potential to cause a predetermined further technical effect is, in principle, not excluded from patentability under Article 52(-2) and (3)* ».

Accordingly, since a technical effect could be merely potential, this decision made it possible for numerous software packages to be patented.

2. – *The interaction between the information and its recording medium creates the required technical effect*

The IBM decision of 1 July 1998 (T1173/97 Technical Board of Appeal OJ EPO 1999/609) had accepted that the recording medium could constitute the hardware « *if, for instance, the computer programme product comprises a computer-readable medium on which the programme is stored, this medium only constitutes the physical support on which the programme is saved and thus constitutes hardware* ».

The interest of that finding was to be widely developed in the decision of 15 March 2000 (*Case of Philips Electronic* T1194/97, Technical Board of Appeal *OJ EPO* 2000/525).

This case related to a patent application for a picture retrieval system comprising a recording medium and a reading device. The Board held that the structure of the data intrinsically contained the technical characteristics of the system (in this case, the reading device and the recording medium). Accordingly the medium for these functional data was not excluded from patentability.

Moreover, the Board stated : « *clearly this was a technical field, because the storage was realised in physical properties of the recording medium which properties were to be detected by a technical device and to be decoded and displayed by electronic means* ».

It is indeed the interaction between the information and its medium that establishes the technical effect required to be eligible for patentability. In other words, the functionality of the information with regard to the recording or reading medium can be the seat of the technical effect.

In this decision, the Technical Board of Appeal was keen to also point out the nature of such a functionality.

Reiterating the arguments of the applicant who drew a distinction between « *presentation, which means 'bring into the presence of someone, bring before the public '* and representation, which means *'to serve as a symbol of something '* », finding support for its approach, the Board, in reiterating the wording of the debate, stated that « *the features of the storage retrieval system were technical in that the retrieval could not be performed by a human and stored pictures could not be accessed directly via his senses* ». In conclusion « *in the Board's opinion, this is subject-matter* [the presentation of information] *which merely conveys cognitive or aesthetic content directly to a human* » (point 3.7.3).

Should we conclude that as far as software is concerned, the technical effect required can be constituted even by a potential function between the information and its medium other than that which is perceptible by human senses ?

GENERAL RAPPORTEUR

BY

Jean-Paul BRIN

Barrister at the Pau Court of Appeal
Former Chairman of the Bar

The protective role of the law as regards technology

In his opening speech to the proceedings, Chairman Robert BADINTER placed the debate firmly in the field of humanism which must be the aim of establishing Internet laws and not secondary to it.

This technology must not be an excuse for legal experts to lose control of it in its relationship with the law. The tool, which promises unlimited scope for exploring knowledge, must be accompanied by control of its concept, which can only be achieved through international regulation. That is the dimension of the law today, particularly in this field.

Respect for the individual, basic rights, the rule of law, so many areas of regulation that this discipline must provide, regardless of the difficulty of the task. Indeed, from an economic point of view, the stakes are enormous in the globalisation era. All the same, countries must offer concerted judicial reaction to the anomalies of the Internet, such as discrimination or injury to the person.

We must measure the exact limits between freedom of expression and respect for the individual : legal thinking has rarely faced such a challenge. It is this initial question and the search for a response to this fundamental expectation that must inspire the debate.

*

Against this background, Chairman Georges PAPAPAVLOV, representative of the European Commission, firstly pointed out the importance of the changes caused by the development of the Internet over the last five years, in all areas : government, economy, education etc.

Of course, there were already telecommunications rules but they only provided very incomplete answers to the new issues. UNCITRAL's e-commerce law paved the way for an adapted legislation; the aim of the first European directives on the subject, in 1995 and 1997, was to protect personal data and regulate exchanges with foreign countries.

The purpose of the directive on electronic signatures, in December 1999, was to ensure circulation whilst at the same time avoiding any discrimination as regards the accreditation of certification authorities, to guarantee that those authorities, created according to each country's domestic rules, are recognised by others.

At the same time, the European Community introduced regulations on copyrights, the protection of databases, electronic commerce etc.

Apart from the legislative aspect with regard to technologies, we must remember the e-Europe directive on transport, health, education etc., the purpose of which is to ensure that within the Community, activity in these fields is open.

However, there are still many issues to be settled such as :

– jurisdiction and the applicable law,
– adaptation of taxation,
– electronic currency (issuance, guarantees),
– domain names, trade marks,
– cybercrime.

We need to develop original measures for dealing with the requirements of the Internet.

I. – The introduction of Internet laws

Paradoxically, the economic and political issues caused by the development of the Internet both accelerate and restrain this introduction which is first and foremost conditional on the right of access to the networks.

A. – The Internet and electronic commerce in multilateral negotiations

Alain-Louis Mie observed that the WTO has no specific provision relating to the Internet or to electronic commerce, since these two areas are included in trade agreements it negotiated and in which the debate centres on access services.

1. – *The legal system for access to the Internet*

By becoming a commercial service in April 1995, the Internet was subject to a number of rules under the General Agreement on Trade and Services established during the Uruguay Round of the WTO in 1994. That agreement establishes two types of standards, the first applying to all commercial services and the others to Members who have adopted specific undertakings relating to the services they want to liberalise and those to whose market they intend to restrict access.

Value added telecommunications services include electronic mail, voice messaging, searching for information online and from databases, the electronic exchange of data, advanced fax services, online code and protocol, online information or data processing; and in order to guarantee that they are effective, members of the WTO adopted a telecommunications annex. Some members, such as the United States, have adopted a broad position, declaring that all the services that correspond to their own definition of value added telecommunications were covered.

Although operators of value added services were therefore given a right of access, they had no real choice because of lack of competition and in 1997, 69 Members signed a basic telecommunications agreement, with a view to regulating interconnection and the right to competition within the sector, which enabled the price of lines rented by these Internet access suppliers to be reduced. However, the growth of the ITC industry was accompanied by political tensions creating a legal insecurity which discouraged its development.

2. – *Variations in the legal system*
for Internet access services

Liberalisation which arose from the 1997 agreement concerned a number of basic services and, in particular, data transmission by packet switches, essential for access to the Internet and the issue is whether they should be included, a fundamental question from an economical point of view.

For some, Internet access services would be basic services subject to the obligations of access and interconnection under the aforementioned agreements. For others, they fall within the scope of added value and are outside these restrictions and at the same time have a right of access to the public telecommunications transport networks or services.

3. – *The ITC's industry's concerns and expectations*
as regards multilateral commercial negotiations

So far as concerns telecommunications, the 1994 and 1997 agreements are fundamental and the regulatory debate on the legal classification of Internet access services must not serve as a pretext for challenging them. The WTO should regard them as being value added, with no obligation under the telecommunications annex and reference document. Faced with a lightening of the sectorial framework in favour of common competition law, we must avoid over-regulating this emerging, dynamic sector.

So far as concerns electronic commerce, the WTO set out the practice for its members in a declaration on 20 May 1998, which consisted of not imposing customs dues on electronic transmissions. Then, in September 1998, it launched a working plan on electronic commerce.

The WTO now needs to give an impetus to electronic commerce by removing the barriers to accessing the markets.

B. – AN INTERNATIONAL LEGAL FRAMEWORK
FOR THE DEVELOPMENT OF E-COMMERCE

Mrs Jeanne SEYVET's view is based on seeking the factors that encourage the development of electronic commerce with regard to all its actors and in all the sectors of economic activity. First and foremost, that requires a reliable legal environment that is likely to establish the relationship of confidence which is essential to such progress, especially in B to C where this legal framework is more difficult to establish, albeit more essential.

Confidence of the actors derives both from self-regulation that they are introducing and the basic principles that are inseparable from any economic activity, laid down by the States, in a harmonised manner. In this respect, significant progress has been made by the international organisations with regard to taxation, protection of personal data, intellectual property, security and authentication.

In addition, the E-Commerce Directive of June 2000 regulated the rights of Member States with regard to advertising, transparency, fairness of transactions and codes of conduct.

There remain two major issues on which development of the system depends :

– determination of the appropriate jurisdictions to settle disputes and ensure that their decisions are enforced, remembering that from May 2002 the Brussels convention makes way for the so-called Brussels regulation,

– Selection of the law applicable to online commercial exchanges, remembering that although within the Community the Rome Convention designates the law applicable to contractual obligations and the E-Commerce Directive regulates the extra-contractual field, at an international level, there is still uncertainty.

That means continuing the processes begun to adapt the legislative and regulatory framework of information society services but also, at a multilateral level, taking into account delicate issues concerning the means of dispute resolution in exchanges between actors in different countries. To be precise, it is a matter of ensuring that decisions made are recognised and enforced and which law to apply in order to achieve this; creating confidence therefore presupposes the ability to determine the applicable legislation *beforehand*.

Moreover, we must emphasise the need to seek alternative methods of dispute resolution, that provide a rapid and cheap solution to small consumer claims relating to low value transactions generated by online commerce.

C. – PROTECTING THE WEAK LINKS IN THE CHAIN

Having been exclusively directed towards mass production, the 20th century culture has only just begun to concern itself with consumer law.

On that basis, Georges CHATILLON observes that legal experts have had to throw away the traditional rules of civil law in order to create specific laws, especially with regard to contracts; one can cite, amongst others, over-indebtedness, the right to retract in sales or credit matters etc.

In addition, the Internet has further upset the most common application of traditional law, for example, online sales which remove the material link between the buyer, the product and the seller.

Mistrust is growing with regard to the process : giving out a card number on the network, the fact that it is impossible to locate unscrupulous traders, the uncertain quality and compliance of products.

Legal experts had to react, in particular by giving themselves resources that are adapted to cyberterrorism and all types of related crime.

This means that the consumer remains the weakest link in the chain of the new economy, not forgetting small businesses that are not familiar with the networks or online commerce, who can be included in this category.

The E-Commerce Directive tackled the response within Europe, but outside, there are still some more or less significant problems. The fundamental digital rights of consumers and micro-businesses remain in abeyance, if only because they have not been specified and, as I have said, this situation is a hindrance to the expansion of this method of marketing.

In practical terms, the possible substitutes for court action that have been mentioned could be :

– *online prevention*, at the time the contract is entered into, obliging the seller and buyer to specify the terms and conditions of the transaction,
– *online protection* by alternative methods of dispute resolution, as no-one wishes to go before the courts for such matters.

In all cases, it is certain that drawing up a charter of the cyber consumer's rights is inevitable.

D. – THE GUARANTEE AFFORDED
BY THE AUTHENTIC ELECTRONIC DOCUMENT

According to article 1316-4 of the Civil Code, when an electronic signature is affixed by a professional officer, it gives the document authenticity. However, although this is the most conclusive form of an electronic document, Maître Didier FROGET first of all defines what makes the document authentic.

In a paper document, it is not really the status of the signatory that gives it its authenticity but rather the physical presence of the professional officer when that document is being drawn up. Accordingly, affixing the signature can appear to be contradictory to the electronic treatment of evidence.

In fact, the same logic underpins both situations :

– the signature of the parties, by digital means, does not cause a problem when it takes place in the presence of the professional officer,
– the document is authentic because it is received by the solicitor himself and not because it is on paper, it is authentic because the public official is a witness to the exchange of consent and the fact that it is clear; his presence is therefore inseparable from the authenticity.

The guarantee of such a document derives from the fact that it is drawn up in the most indisputable way.

E. – ELECTRONIC SIGNATURE :
CONFIDENCE IN DIGITAL WRITING

Apart from authenticity, the development of the electronic signature is a major step forward in the area of the evidential value of all kinds of documents. That is why, within Europe, the directive of 13 December 1999 and the French Act of 13 March 2000 rapidly introduced it in order to strengthen the confidence of users.

The resulting reform of the Civil Code with regard to evidence places electronic written material on the same level as written material on paper, provided that the author and the conditions in which it was created and kept can be identified so as to be able to assess it as a whole.

The difference in the type of documents is no longer the distinguishing criterion for assessing their evidential value : it is the level of the technologies used that enables the reliability of virtual written material to be established by linking its content and its author's identifier.

In the European model, it is therefore compliance with the procedure and regulation laid down by legislation concerning certification which determines the level of the evidential value of electronic written material; in another way, one can say that assessment of the evidence is essentially formal.

Although the use of technology is similar in the United States and Canada, the basic approach is different. The model law of 1996 on electronic commerce defined the function of the signature : to link a person to a document, but beyond that, it is merely the means of establishing the source of that document.

According to John D. GREGORY the signature has a mythical effect compared to reality and focuses the attention; however, the legal scope of the signature does not depend on its form but on the content of the document and the signatory's intent in that document, regardless of the medium.

The United Nations Commission on International Commercial Law (UNCITRAL) drafted a model law on the subject, which provides that :

– where a signature is required, an electronic signature fulfils that role,
– the signature is linked to the document and must both identify its author and confirm that he approves the content,
– the method of signature must be sufficiently reliable, taking into account the circumstances and content of the document.

The person relying on it must demonstrate this, remembering that in the United States and Canada, it constitutes a contractual agreement between the parties and not a legal provision as in Europe.

Quebec has adopted a law on information technologies, the signature being only one piece of evidence amongst others; on this point, the European directive has the same approach in that it prohibits refusal of an electronic signature because it is electronic and thus refers to the intention of the parties to which it bears witness.

However, with reference to the Community, it has tried to place the intrinsic force of the signature in hierarchical order (see the concept of the advanced signature) whereas the criteria applied by UNCITRAL are flexible and pragmatic : the degree of security is a function of the circumstances, of the purpose of the message and its content, of practices, of the normal relations between the parties and the frequency thereof, of authentication procedures etc.

That measure is therefore more concerned with seeking the true intention of the parties than its formal proof through the signature process, an essential difference which cannot be disregarded by Community law where international contracts are concerned. Nevertheless, according to the model law, the risk of the signature is referred back to the user and it is for each person to ascertain its reliability. This government opting-out places consumer security in the balance.

*

From access to the networks to the security of data circulating on them, the establishment of Internet laws therefore provides users with a security which, although not perfect, makes the conditions for using the digital arena acceptable and often more satisfying than those of the traditional routes whose requirements would appear to be singularly less exacting.

However, some problems are specific to the use of ITCs and require an adapted approach both with regard to the drafting of rules and the introduction of protective measures.

II. – What protection? Which laws?

The accessibility of the network and the traces left there by Internet users, duplication, sampling, copying, as many sources as there are risks for personal data, ownership of works or software. The protective measures must be tailored to the particular context of ITCs, again, in order to encourage and extend their use by the ensuing confidence.

A. – The protection of personal data

The diversity of methods for gathering information on individuals, together with the potential to cross-check files, are real causes for anxiety, accentuated by the development of high throughput.

However, one must not lose sight of the fact that it is essentially a western concern (North America and Europe) and, as Professor Jean FRAYSSINET points out :

1. *there is only an appearance of protection,* although there is a positive view from a political standpoint (that of the operators) and the legal standpoint (50 States have adapted their laws). In fact, although the Internet falls within the scope of this legislation and is the subject of attention from the regulatory authorities (CNIL) (1) or self-regulation (United States), nevertheless the protection is not adequate or really established ;

2. *the protection is inappropriate* because the concept of private life is poorly defined and inconsistent and it merges with the concept of personal life ; let us take the simple example of the IP address : how can it be traced (connection and navigation data, addresses, java, cookies, etc.) ? In fact, the Internet is not really honest ;

3. *The Internet has a provocative role* since the protection of personal data is not really guaranteed ; paradoxically abuses and excesses have a regulating effect.

They enrich discussions and cause Internet users to be wary and operators to be concerned. One only has to see what happens in the United States where mistrust has been replaced by opposition.

Accordingly, the risk of economic penalties resulting from their customers' loss of confidence and this loss of brand image (boycott and others) is causing the operators to react.

It is not a question of legislative regulation but one of market regulation.

In fact, the clash between the two systems shows that the European model has regulation that is very adapted but ineffective as society has not taken it on board, whereas the American model,

---

(1) *Commission Nationale de l'Informatique et des Libertés* – an organisation dedicated to information technology and civil rights in France.

constructed around a powerful organisation for defending people, lacks this legal framework.

B. – DROIT D'AUTEUR AND COPYRIGHT

Copyright is superior to *droit d'auteur* in that it allows the work to be kept by the investor, but *droit d'auteur* is essential to protect the creative act.

For Professor Michel VIVANT, there is less of a contradiction between these two legal systems than there appears to be; whether it is *droit d'auteur* or copyright, the purpose is to award someone rights over a work. In the light of the networks and the Internet, each one can be examined in accordance with the purpose, title and content.

1. *the purpose* : it is a *work*, a vague notion that covers both concepts, which is conveyed by the networks (photo or text, graphics...), but it is also *what constitutes the networks* (the protectable nature of languages and the nature of hypertext links).

2. *title* : where the two systems are in opposition between the investor and the author, the latter must not only be at the forefront stage but also have a presence from a financial point of view.

3. *the content* : pecuniary rights and non-pecuniary rights are facing identical challenges and the same solutions should be found, although non-pecuniary rights are different in nature and that has consequences on the issue of transferability.

Copyright should draw inspiration from the author's non-pecuniary rights but although this expansion is desirable, one has to question the relevance of invoking it in all circumstances because it must be used sparingly and with good reason.

For Professor Mads BRYDE ANDERSEN, the American approach to copyright and *droit d'auteur* is basically financial in one case and cultural in the other.

The way in which legislation and the courts deal with the subject is quite different, remembering that in the Anglo-Saxon context, the content of the protection is defined by what is worth protecting, without consideration for the creativity of the author.

So far as concerns the European Union, in 1991 it initiated the concept of *originality* halfway between copyright and *droit d'auteur*.

In fact, non-pecuniary rights are a French creation that the Americans have had to adapt in relation to copyright which allows the ownership of rights to be transferred.

Moreover, the Anglo-Saxon system includes broad exceptions whereas in Europe they are very specific and limited (right to private copy etc.) and were the subject of a directive on the matter.

In the Community context, the protection of databases was laid down in a strange directive making use of the concept of copyright and providing that *sui generis* rights of databases presuppose fair use that does not harm the author.

The legislators having expressed themselves, it is now up to the courts to implement the laws and, where necessary, to interpret them.

C. – DROIT D'AUTEUR
AND EXCEPTION FOR PRIVATE COPYING

As creative works are increasingly immaterial, do they have an ever decreasing value? Maître Marc MOSSÉ quite rightly believes that this would be a ridiculous approach to intellectual property.

Between intellectual property and freedom of access to culture, private copying, strictly reserved for the use of the copyist, is an exception to the exclusive right of the author.

However, digital technology is in danger of moving from lawful copying to mass reproduction, or even cloning with the financial consequences that one can imagine.

This exception constitutes a right to a copy and not a right to make copies, and indeed that is its limit which must be precisely defined so that we can then envisage the new type of exchange between creators and the public as a result of the Internet.

1. – *Technology obliges us to reduce the proposed copy to its essence, to its source*

For the works in question, in the digital age we have gone further than in the analogue age (literary works, graphics, photographs, music, images). The legislator believed that it fell within the context of the *duration* of the recording of a work, a solution that is highly disputable and relative and which leads to having a *restric-*

tive view of private copying and sticking to the idea of the copier making copies for use within the family circle (a French concept). Moreover, the copy must be legitimate and not harm the interests of the author nor exploitation of the work.

2. – *Private copying, the impetus for a new dialogue between creators and consumers*

The technological evolution allows works to be protected and controlled (tattooing, encryption) when they are recorded and when they are circulated.

These measures for protection and control must be taken with the consumer's support, as their effectiveness depends on it.

The compensation for *droit d'auteur* must be transparent : otherwise, the remuneration risks being based on supports that have nothing to do with private copying; for example, a tax on computers penalises users who don't make copies (which, moreover, can encourage them to do so). Without criticising fair compensation, the future lies in the dynamic management of the protection of rights, preventing the consumer having to pay twice both for the medium and the use.

D. – THE PATENTABILITY OF SOFTWARE PACKAGES

The very nature of software packages creates differences relating to the protection of their designers' rights.

Chairman Alain GIRARDET points out that unlike what happens in the United States and Japan, in Europe, software packages are excluded from the scope of patents and their protection lies in the field of *droits d'auteur*.

The fact that disputes in this area are rare implies that such protection is inappropriate. In Europe, we are witnessing a detour to arrive at the same result in that although software is not patentable, its applications are.

Accordingly, the main problem lies in the coexistence of different kinds of rights over the same object : the patent system and that of *droits d'auteur* cannot be used together; where is the border between the two so far as software is concerned ?

– patents protect an invention that is likely to have industrial application,
– *droit d'auteur* protects the intellectual idea.

Moreover, it can be observed that, from a technical point of view, the fast pace of software developments means that the time and cost of the procedure for applying for patents makes it inappropriate.

To that extent, no solution really offers itself that would make the simple transposition of the protection of patents to software seem satisfactory.

*

Maître Alain BENSOUSSAN favours such a solution, pointing out that in the entire world, more than 13,000 patents for software were issued by the EPO (European Patent Office) despite this controversy.

It is true that on the face of it, giving software access to patentability would appear to be limited since Article 52 (2) and (3) of the Munich convention excludes computer programmes per se from the inventions system.

Under pressure from the manufacturers, the EPO got round this problem considering that the exclusion arising from this legislation should be understood restrictively; accordingly, in the condition for industrial application in Article 57 of the convention, the EOP sought a legislative basis to allow software access to patentability by devising the so-called technical effect theory.

First of all, the technical effect corresponded to identifying the technical nature of the invention, assessed in a rather concrete way, for example as resulting from an industrial process. The EPO then acknowledged that the technical effect could be established on an electronic entity, for example an image created using an electrical signal.

Accordingly, for some time, development of the technical effect implied that the other conditions for patentability must relate exclusively to it and the EPO fell back on a general interpretation of applications without making a distinction within them between the part that had a technical effect and those that did not.

In any event, this situation can no longer endure as it is not democratic and there cannot be so many uncertainties for such a poor result; we need to return to the form : the patentability of software.

*

Note : At the beginning of 2002, the European Commission proposed a directive in support of this in which the existence of a « technical contribution » in the software would be the criterion for its patentability, remembering that this should be understood as meaning « a contribution to the state of the technique in a technical field », *which is not obvious to someone in the business*. This latter part of the definition for the criterion refers to a relative, if not subjective assessment which does not appear to provide the total legal security required and deserves to be specified.

III. – A new legal system ?

The issue of use of the Internet is not without a paradox : everyone aspires to ensure that it continually develops, ever wider and ever faster, and this is achieved by confidence in the tool, provided in part by the introduction of specific laws. However, this progress in itself brings new problems which also call for original solutions. In other words, this interactive competition between technology and the law leads to seeking original solutions to deal with a situation in which the States' traditional system of regulation in a given geographical area proves to be somewhat inappropriate.

The deconstruction of space and time, due to increasingly efficient technical facilities, balanced against the essential requirements for legal security based on rules that are universal and permanent, that is what it takes to square the circle.

Although this debate over the introduction of Internet laws is testament to these problems, nevertheless they show that there are often too many questions raised about the subject and that the replies are not merely palliative but are quite capable of providing real legal control of the system.

B

How to resolve transnational conflicts?

CHAIRMANSHIP

Ana PALACIO VALLELERSUNDI

PRESIDENT OF THE COMMITTEE ON LEGAL AFFAIRS
AND THE INTERNAL MARKET, EUROPEAN PARLIAMENT

Introduction

BY

ANA PALACIO VALLERERSUNDI

This afternoon's subject is « how to resolve transnational disputes ? » This is a huge issue and I therefore take great comfort from the fact that my role is limited to presiding over this session rather than having to provide answers!

At the risk of making the task of the speakers even more difficult, I shall confine my introduction to making four methodological observations instead.

I. – The first is that in my view, it is essential to distinguish between the community level and international level when examining the question of dispute resolution

In fact, in the numerous debates that have taken place on the legal aspects of the information society. I am always surprised to see that all too often, the specific characteristics of the Community legal system are not taken into account. The Community aspects lumped together with the « international aspects » as if the only difference was one of geographical scale and not of nature between the Community level and international level.

However, the development of the Internet highlights all the potentialities afforded by Community law as an instrument of regulation capable of responding to the complexity of the changes we are undergoing today. The level of Community integration now reached means that member countries can have real confidence in each other. It is that specific aspect that has led to the adoption of the E-Commerce Directive, which rejects the application of traditional choice-of-law rules to Private International Law by establishing the principle that the law of the country in which the e-com-

merce activities originated should apply. That principle enables
activities to be controlled at their very source and thus reduces the
risks that any unlawful activity might cause wide-scale damage.

The problem of settling disputes at international level is more
complex because it must take into account the diversity of the legal
systems of the countries concerned. Settling a dispute between a
French company and a customer in Singapore must be handled in
a different way from a dispute between a French company and a
German customer.

II. – My second observation is that we must avoid establishing legal mechanisms that would lead to a « re-territorialisation » of the internet

A good system for settling disputes must afford protection to victims and encourage the development of cross-border business. For
example, there is no point in introducing rules awarding jurisdiction
which appear to be very protective of the consumer or the victims
if they have the effect of dissuading companies, in particular Small
and Medium Businesses, from selling to consumers living in other
countries.

At Community level, the application of the law of the country of
origin under the E-Commerce Directive limits the risks of « re-
territorialising » the virtual world. However, the issue of jurisdiction
is not covered by this directive. It falls within the scope of the settlement of jurisdiction adopted in December 2000 which, unfortunately, has been unable to find a solution that is suited to the
opportunities afforded by the Internet.

At an international level, the situation is no doubt even more
complicated, both on the issue of the applicable law and of jurisdiction. The only way in which to deal with the differences in legal
systems is not to hide behind technical or legal barriers but to confront the real problems of substance by drawing up international
conventions. In that respect, the legal framework established at
Community level is a pilot experiment and the European Union
must play the role of leader in international negotiations.

III. – The third observation is that it seems to me just as essential to take into consideration the specific nature of activities on the internet

The law and dispute resolution systems must deal with the reality of the risks arising from the activities in question. There is no doubt that online activities are not the same as off-line activities. For example, the mere accessibility of a Web page throughout the world, the fact that a customer has no direct contact with a seller or that he can ask for written information or have access to a competitor in a few seconds, creates a different legal situation compared to other forms of commerce. The argument of the so-called « technological neutrality » seems to me to totally ignore the reality of the Internet and can only lead to poor quality legal solutions.

The question of whether we should envisage a special system for the Internet has been widely discussed in the European Parliament in relation to the proposal for settlement on the basis of jurisdiction. The discussion triggered by the European Parliament on the possibility of providing, under certain conditions, jurisdiction clauses in contracts entered into by a consumer has shown how difficult it is to get away from clichés and stereotypes in this field. However, it is a crucial issue if we want to convince European SMEs to sell outside their own country. The Council simply refused to examine the solutions considered by Parliament, preferring to retain the old system that had been introduced in 1968 which bans any prior clauses awarding jurisdiction in contracts entered into by consumers.

IV. – Finally, my last observation concerns the need to devise new practical systems for regulating activities on the Internet

The Internet is a marvellous means of evaluating and testing the effectiveness or hypocrisy, of our legal systems. By allowing small enterprises or individual consumers to cross borders in a virtual world, the Internet shows that we certainly need to adapt and modernise some aspects of our legal systems that were designed at a time when cross-border trade was the province of large enterprises.

Against that background, it seems to me that we need to give alternative methods of regulation a chance. Two types of initiatives should attract the attention of the legal expert : codes of conduct and out-of-court dispute resolution.

Codes of conduct, self-regulation and « co-regulation ». Beyond a mere description of method, all these expressions reveal a need to devise different regulation systems from those that consist of drafting formal legal texts in the form of laws, regulations, decrees etc. At Community level, codes of conduct can be a useful supplement to Community or national laws on some issues. In that respect, the E-Commerce Directive recognises their legitimacy and seeks to promote them in some fields, in particular *notice and take down* procedures concerning the liability of intermediary service providers and unsolicited commercial e-mails.

– *procedures for out-of-court dispute resolution* also offer very interesting prospects which we shall talk about in a moment. There again, the E-Commerce Directive sets the example by laying down the legal conditions in which it is possible to use *online* mechanisms for out-of-court settlement of disputes such as arbitration, conciliation, mediation and other « ADRs ». The requirements of form which might limit the use of online ADRs will have to be abolished (sentence on paper, requirement of the physical presence of the parties, etc.).

However, these initiatives must fulfil two conditions : firstly, codes of conduct must be *drawn up at Community level*. What would be the use of abolishing the legal barriers between Member States if they could be reintroduced through national codes of conduct ? Secondly, codes of conduct must comply with Community law and, in particular, with the principles of the Internal Market. In that respect, it is essential, particularly for SMEs, that codes of conduct are based on the principle of the country of origin.

In addition, so far as concerns ADRs, we must ensure that they are not used to justify unbalanced legal systems. During discussions on this settlement, we have all too often heard the argument that says that there would be no problem in establishing a system that discourages cross-border trade because, in any event, consumers will use ADRs rather than go to court.

We must give these initiatives a chance. They can solve a great number of problems, in particular, limiting the need for legislative action and one of the biggest benefits is that it can compete with the national formal method and therefore encourage the quality of legislation or the quality of the way in which legal institutions operate. Giving these alternative methods of resolution a chance means that we must avoid « short-circuiting » them by adopting laws that would make all these measures useless. We must also avoid any attempt at recovery by the public authorities, in particular they must not substitute for the parties involved in drawing up codes of conduct.

In conclusion, I can guarantee that the European Parliament intends to play a key role in this exercise of devising better legal solutions, not only for resolving disputes but also and especially for preventing them. In the short term, the European Parliament will ensure that the European Commission rigorously monitors the transposition of the E-Commerce Directive into the national legal systems, especially with regard to the key provisions which are the principle of the country of origin and the question of liability of intermediaries. Apart from monitoring the transposition of the E-Commerce Directive, Parliament will also ensure that existing Community law is not called into question by new initiatives, particularly under the draft directive on the sale of distant financial services which is currently being discussed in the Council.

I must now leave the floor to our speakers who, I am sure, will demonstrate that the legal expert is very capable of showing imagination in finding effective solutions to encourage both the development of cross-border online activities and afford a high level of protection to consumers.

1. – HOW TO RESOLVE THE CONFLICTS?

HOW TO RESOLVE
TRANSNATIONAL CONFLICTS?

BY

KAZUNORI ISHIGURO

PROFESSOR, THE UNIVERSITY OF TOKYO, FACULTY OF LAW

Introduction

Transnational conflicts occur not only in private law areas, but also in other areas of law. Sometimes people say that the situation completely free from any regulation or measures is the best for further developments of the Internet, and that networks of international contracts are sufficient to resolve transnational conflicts regarding the Internet. However, on one hand, one must analyse the real intention of the people who push such arguments, and, on the other hand, one must realise what is happening on the Internet (1).

I. – Private interests vs. public interests

A. – THE « PLAYMEN » CASE
VS. THE CASE OF « YAHOO! »?

To begin with, it seems to be important to make a comparison between the U.S. « Playmen » case (2) and the recent French case of « Yahoo! ». There is an understanding that « [t]he decision of the French court represents one of the greatest threats to the promise of the Internet » (3). However, rather the « Playmen » case may be viewed as a real threat for the future of the Internet. The case of « Yahoo! » was focused on the specific, well-targeted public (social)

---

(1) This paper is a shortened version of the paper submitted by the present author to this colloquium. For further discussions see the latter paper.

(2) 1996 U.S. Dist. LEXIS 8435, Filed on June 19, 1996.

(3) See Michael MAHONEY, « Yahoo! Gets Backing in Nazi Memorabilia Case », *E-Commerce Times*, Sept. 7, 2001.

interest, but the « Playmen » case was concentrated on the interest
of maintaining the dignity of the U.S. judicial system itself. In the
solution of the « Playmen » case, the U.S. court relied on « contempt
of court » and automatically bypassed the problems of conflict of
laws (4), and ordered the Italian site to be shut down as one of the
alternative remedies.

People who criticise the case of « Yahoo! » should compare these
two cases carefully before referring to the so-called « chilling
effects », and should realise the grave impact of the Internet on
society. At least, only relying on private transactions is not enough,
and under the present situations, it is unreasonable to introduce in
this area the simple « standstill » and/or « rollback » approach often
taken in trade and investment negotiations.

B. – THE TREND OF STICKING
TO THE PRIVATE LAW APPROACH IN RESOLVING
TRANSNATIONAL CONFLICTS REGARDING
THE INTERNET : THE CASE OF AN « ITU » MEETING

The ITU's « High-Level Experts Meeting on Electronic
Signatures and Certification Authorities » was held in Geneva in
December 1999. However, curiously enough, the secretariat of the
ITU seemed to favour the system of closed CA networks guarded
by contracts, and rather hostile to governmental regulations which
overrode such contracts, and even to setting international *de jure*
standards regarding CAs for keeping security at the global level (5).
The actual aim of the « Briefing Paper » issued for the said Meeting
is similar to that of the GBDe referred to later in this paper. It was
regrettable that the outcome of the said ITU Meeting (6) could not
pay due attention to public interests, including those in consumer
protection and « interoperability ».

---

(4) See ISHIGURO, « Appendix ? of paper submitted to the ILPF International Symposium :
'Jurisdiction : Building Confidence in A Borderless Medium' », held in Montreal (July 26-27,
1999). On the web site see : http://www.ilpf.org/events/jurisdiction/presentations/ishiguro–
a1.htm.

(5) See Stewart BAKER and Mattew YEO of the law firm Steptoe & Johnson, Washington,
D.C., in collaboration with the secretariat of the ITU, « Briefing Paper : Background and Issues
Concerning Authentication and the ITU ». On the web site see : http://www.itu.int/osg/spu/ni/
esca/meetingdec9-101999/.

(6) See also paper submitted by the present author to the ITU Meeting referred to in note 5,
supra.

C. – To what extent can treaties resolve
transnational conflicts ? : prerequisites
for harmonisation

I dare say that superficial harmonisation would be the cause of numerous misunderstandings, and even harmful. One must be realistic (7). For example, in the U.S. legal system, there are remedies of distinctive features such as punitive or multiple damages, disgorgement in security regulations, *parens patriae*, etc. (8). They will surely survive any attempt of international harmonisation, because they are so deeply embedded in the U.S. legal system.

We must analyse the reality, namely the « differences », the real features of each legal system of our world as deeply as possible. « Supply-side voices » would regard such differences as too dangerous, or even as unfair « trade barriers », for everyday business activities, as stated later in this paper.

However, we may already have too many treaties which sometimes contradict each other. In such cases, those who worried about the divergence of each legal system now worry about the so-called « conflict of conventions », a very complicated problem at the level of public international law (9).

On top of that, first, suppose a case, as an example, where without the official consent of the Japanese government, an official of a foreign government or his nominee has actually removed from the Japanese territory, over the telecommunication networks or by using other means, a decryption key deposited within the Japanese territory. That should be viewed as a clear infringement of the Japanese sovereignty. Although this sort of problem can be solved by concluding international treaties, constitutional problems on

---

(7) Also the Japanese MITI's « eQuality Paper » (*infra* note 21) pays attention, in the context of the next WTO negotiations, to the activities of the « Hague Conference on Private International Law » regarding the future Convention on Jurisdiction and Foreign Judgments in Civil and Commercial Matters (see on the web site : http://www.hcch.net/e/workprog/jdgm.html). However, from the beginning, the present author has been quite sceptical about the outcome of the activities of the said Conference.

(8) In details see Ishiguro, *Borderless Economy heno Houteki Shiza* [A Warning Concerning The Emerging Borderless Economy Vol. ?], at 155 sqq [1992 Chuuou Keizai-sha].

(9) See Kokusai Shihou, *Conflict of Laws*, at 103 ff. (1994 Shinsei-sha).

fundamental human rights may remain, at least in some countries, including Japan (10).

Secondly, the « exclusiveness » of treaty routes depends on the constitutional system of each country and the actual practice which reflects such a background (11). Even if a treaty is concluded among countries, there remains room for « imbalance », or even « free riding », among the relevant countries. This point is serious, especially in cases where a country agrees to use unilateral measures which might contradict its treaty obligations. If unilateral measures survive all attempts at harmonisation, one must reconsider the very notion of « equal footing » before one devotes oneself to such attempts.

II. – Various instutions into the traditional system of conflict of laws regarding the Internet

A. – PROPOSALS FOR CYBER LAWS AND THE INFLUENCE OF THE U.S. REVOLUTIONARY THEORIES ON CONFLICT OF LAWS : THE CASE OF TRANSNATIONAL COPYRIGHT INFRINGEMENTS

There has been a trend, though the peak seems to be over, that people say that traditional legal frameworks, including that of « conflict of laws », and even the « principle of territoriality » based on international copyright conventions, should give way to the new system of cyber laws (12). In doing so, such people, especially some of the U.S. authors, actually intend to « export » the U.S. revolutionary theories on conflict of laws to other countries through the « cyber-route » of the Internet, taking the examples of transnational copyright infringements in cyberspace.

---

(10) See paper submitted by the present author to Concurrent Session C.B.2 [« Communications Content, Security, Privacy and other Legal Issues »] of the APEC/OECD/PECC Symposium on the Information Infrastructure : « Building the Foundation for the 21st Century », held in Vancouver, Canada (February 19-21, 1995).

(11) An unfortunate example is « Société National Industrielle Aérospatiale v. U.S. District Court » (107 S. Ct. 2542 [1987]).

(12) As a typical example see P.E. GELLER, « Conflict of Laws in Cyberspace : Rethinking International Copyright », 44 Journal of the Copyright Society of the U.S.A., at p. 104 (1997).

However, such « legal impressionism » will end in an impasse. Indeed, the U.S. revolutions on conflict of laws themselves seem to have been in a great impasse. The use of prisoner's dilemma in this context is not so helpful (13).

B. – THE « COUNTRY OF ORIGIN » RULE
AND THE ONE-SIDED SUPPLY-SIDE VOICES :
THE CASE OF « GBDe » (1999)

The GBDe was, especially in 1999, very eager to introduce the « country of origin » rule in order to guard the private interests of major companies active in e-commerce, and tried to push the governments to follow such a suggestion (14). However, such arguments were based on typical « supply-side voices » which remind the present author of the OECD activities on the MAI collapsed, with good reason, in 1998 (15). They even said that compliance with all legal regimes of all jurisdictions, based on the location of each consumer, would create insurmountable « trade barriers » (16).

However, intermingling of trade issues and those of conflict of laws is not acceptable. According to such a proposal, for example, Article 120 (2) of the 1989 Swiss Code on Private International Law which clearly rejects the party autonomy (17) for consumer contracts will become the target of negotiations aiming at reducing « trade barriers ». Further development in consumer protection at the level of conflict of laws should be recalled here.

C. – THE NEXT « WTO » NEGOTIATIONS
AND THE INTERNET

Although problems on e-commerce or the Internet are now going to be covered by the world trade regime, the fundamental and ultimate object of further liberalisation of trade (and investment) is

---

(13) See ISHIGURO, *supra,* note 9, at 61 ff.

(14) See, *Additional Paper* of paper submitted to the ILPF Symposium, referred to in note 4, supra. On the web site see : http://www.ilpf.org/events/jurisdiction/presentations/ishiguro–addl.htm.

(15) In this respect see, « The WTO NEW Round and Japan's Role », *Japan Review of International Affairs* Vol. 13, n° 4, at 235 f (2000).

(16) See note 14, *supra.*

(17) See Anton HEINI *et al., IPRG Kommentar,* at 990 ff (KELLER/KOSTKIEWICZ) [1993 Schulthess]; ISHIGURO, *supra,* note 9, at 271.

to realise « the betterment of all people and all nations ». According
to the most basic economic theory, the liberalisation itself is not the
purpose but only a means for the betterment of all people and all
nations (18). If such means is conceived as if it were the only purpose for every trade (and investment) negotiation and the
« regulatory reform » (19), various social, cultural and even economic
problems and turmoil would occur, as seen in the recent crises in
Asian countries and in east European countries, also even in New
Zealand, a country once viewed as a world leader of « regulatory
reform » (20).

That is the reason why the Japanese MITI (now METI) proposed
the « eQuality Paper » regarding the treatment of e-commerce at the
level of the WTO (21). Needless to say, « eQuality » in the title of
the Paper is based on the firm belief in the importance of
« equality » and the « quality of life » of every person in the information society. The Paper's fundamental policy is stated as follows :
« Background and Purpose : This draft proposal reflects our firm
belief that the future of the Internet and E-Commerce shall be for
the betterment of all people and all nations. ... ».

One should be aware of the fact that the very notion of
« equality », not « efficiency », which forms the firm basis of the
« eQuality Paper » is one of the most important premises of the
traditional « Savigny-type conflict of laws ».

Conclusion

There is nothing new in my conclusion. However, the most
important premise of the traditional system of conflict of laws is the
equality of every country's legal system which should be viewed as
the most basic prerequisite for negotiations on further liberalisation
of trade, too.

---

(18) In this respect see ISHIGURO, *Hou to Keizai* [*Law vs. Economics*], at pp. 129-236 (1998
Iwanami Shoten).

(19) OECD, C/MIN(97) 10; C/MIN(97)10/ADD.

(20) See Joseph STIGLITZ, *Whither Socialism?* (1994 MIT Press); Jane KELSEY, *The New
Zealand Experiments : A World Model for Structural Adjustment?* (New Edition : 1997 Auckland
University Press : Bridget Williams Books).

(21) « Towards eQuality : Global E-commerce Presents Digital Opportunity to Close the
Divide Between Developed and Developing Countries : MITI's Proposal for WTO E-Commerce
Initiative » (2nd Draft, dated June 2, 2001). On the web site see : http://www.meti.go.jp/english/
information/data/cw001019e.html.

It is quite understandable that not a few people regard the traditional system of conflict of laws as insufficient and useless, in particular in the context of the Internet or the GII. However, the traditional Savigny-type system of conflict of laws should be viewed as the fruits of scholarly research over centuries, or even a « crystal » of our historical wisdom, even if it appears to be too fragile at first sight. It seems to be too dangerous for our world to make a sudden jump into the « virtual darkness » and, in doing so, to abandon such historical wisdom.

RESOLVING CONFLICTS OF LAWS

BY

JEAN-SYLVESTRE BERGÉ

PROFESSOR AT THE UNIVERSITY OF PARIS X-NANTERRE

Introduction

The complexity of certain issues, whether real or presumed, is a reason for returning to them, several times if need be. That, apparently, is the fate reserved for private international law by the organisers of this colloquium since at least four reports are devoted to it (1). We shall not complain. The Internet is a fantastic promoter of ubiquity and although ubiquity is not necessarily synonymous with internationality, between the two concepts there is a step that one might be tempted to take. For the private internationalist, the definition of « an Internet law » thus comes quite naturally through what we are being asked to tackle : *resolving conflicts of laws.*

Considered from an abstract and general point of view, the quest for solutions to disputes that are suited to digital networks is a considerable task. Just like the excesses of the world wide web, an innumerable different situations are likely to call for the application of a particular national law under a particular rule of conflict. There is no point in expecting a summary from me. At the very most, in opening my talk, I shall try to generalise.

That generality is based on a finding that was made by most of those involved in positive law when the information society emerged around ten years ago. The existing rules, including the rules of conflict, are able to define solutions to the issues raised by the development of the Internet. There is no more room here for a legal vacuum than elsewhere.

---

(1) Apart from the various general reports and this analysis, see the work of Mrs Fauvarque-Cosson and Messrs Huet and Ishiguor.

Since it is a question of resolving conflicts of laws, legal opinion made a considerable effort to consider the implementation of existing rules (2). On that occasion, suggestions were made to change the positive law in a more or less radical way. These issues were also referred to the courts which made an effort to resolve them, with great difficulty (3).

Two kinds of lessons can be drawn from this implementation of the existing rules and the various proposals that were put forward on that occasion. The first relates to the fact that in the majority of hypothetical situations, the Internet does not upset the old or more contemporary trends of private international law, although sometimes it accentuates its characteristics. Without being allowed to go into details of an illustration, the following phenomena can be observed :

– confirmation of the predominant role of the rules concerning conflict of jurisdiction, rules of conflict often playing a secondary role, sometimes coming close to being relegated;
– a desire on the part of a civil judge ruling in tort cases to apply, as in criminal cases, a strict principle of territoriality resulting more or less in the systematic jurisdiction of the defendant's place of residence;
– a desire on the part of law makers to improve the predictability of solutions by extending the scope of freedom of the parties to make their own arrangements beyond its favourite field : contracts;

---

(2) For an overall examination of the aspects of private international law of the Internet, see, in particular, (in alphabetical order) : S. BARIATTI, « Internet : aspects relatifs aux conflits de lois » (« The Internet : aspects concerning choice of law ») in *Le droit au défi de l'Internet*, Libraire Droz, 1997, p. 61; K. BOELE-WOELKI and C. KESSEDJAN (eds.), *Internet, Which Court Decides? Which Law Applies?*, Kluwer, 1998; Conseil d'Etat, *Internet et les réseaux numériques (Internet and the digital networks)*, Report, La Documentation française, 1998; P.-Y. GAUTIER, « Les aspects internationaux de l'Internet » (« The international aspects of the Internet »), Work of the CFDIP 1997-1998, Pedone, 2000, p. 241; P.E. GELLER, « Les conflits de lois dans le cyberespace » (« Conflicts of laws in cyberspace »), *Bull. dr.auteur*, January-March 1997, p. 3; J. HUET, « Aspects juridiques du commerce électronique : approche internationale » (« Legal aspects of e-commerce : an international approach »), *Petites Affiches* 26 Sept. 1997, n° 116, p. 6; E. JAYME, « Le droit international privé du nouveau millénaire : la protection de la personne humaine face à la globalisation » (« Private international law for the new millennium : protection of persons in the face of globalisation »), *RCADI*, 2000, T. 282, p. 9; P. SCHONNIG, « Applicable Law in transfrontier Online Transmissions », *RIDA*, Oct. 1996, n° 170, p. 21; M. VIVANT, « Cybermonde : Droit et droits des réseaux » (« Cyberworld : Network law and rights »), *JCP* 1996, I, 3969.

(3) Indeed more often than not without argument on the question of the law applicable in space, a question that is rarely raised by the litigants or completely absorbed by the establishment of jurisdiction.

– a withdrawal of the connecting factors based on the location of the goods and services (place where situated or from which business is carried out) and, at the same time, a strengthening of the criteria for location of the main Internet players (place of residence, home address or establishment), whether they be professionals or consumers.

A second type of lesson, which we shall examine in more detail, can also be identified. It would appear that the development of digital networks has caused deeper upsets, especially in the environment of European Community law. Two phenomena in particular deserve examination :

– firstly, the phenomenon of *decompartmentalisation of conflict of laws* which can be found in connection with e-commerce (I);
– secondly, the phenomenon of *inclusion of choice-of-law clauses in contracts* brought about by the protection of personal data (II).

I. – The decompartmentalisation of the conflict of laws : the example of e-commerce

A. – THE PHENOMENON OF DECOMPARTMENTALISATION OF THE CONFLICT OF LAWS

1. – *Double compartmentalisation of private international law*

Private international law is the subject of what might be called a double compartmentalisation. The first results from the distinction between the rules of private international law on the one hand and the rules of criminal or public law on the other. The latter are applied without consideration for the connecting factors usually specified by private international law. In fact they have a potentially disturbing effect on the normal set of rules of conflict (for example, the immediate application of a rule of public law considered to be a police law). However, for all that, of course private international law is not disappearing. It continues to follow its own mechanisms and remains – (quite naturally) – somewhat isolated in its own preferred field : private law.

The second compartmentalisation phenomenon is internal to private international law. The science of conflict of laws is beginning to divide up the various subjects of private law. Each subject belongs to what is called an applicability category, which in turn specifies one or several connecting factors. For example, contract law is subject to the principle whereby the parties are free to arrange their own affairs, under which the contract is governed by the law chosen by the parties. For liability in tort, the law of the place in which the crime was committed must be applied. For succession to movables, one will be inclined more towards the law of the deceased's last place of residence whereas the law of property is subject to the law of the place in which it is situated, etc.

2. – Decompartmentalisation connected with the establishment of a single applicable law

The development of digital networks has upset this basic pattern somewhat. In particular, the question was posed as to whether it was possible to avoid the pitfall of the ubiquity of the Internet by declaring the law of a single country to be applicable, independently, or almost, from the nature of the rule applied. For example, there was uncertainty as to whether a host and/or content provider could be subject to the regulations in the country in which he is established for all his business, if those rules related to questions of public or private law (circumstances in which the business is carried out, monitoring authority, rules governing advertising, rules governing contracts, competition, protection of consumers, minors, liability, etc.)

An affirmative reply to such an enquiry would have particularly significant consequences both in practice and theoretically. From a practical point of view, the jurisdiction of a single national law is sought by those professionals who fear that the laws in all the countries from which their website can be visited will be applied in a cumulative fashion. However, that can also be feared. It has been said time and again that there is a real danger that service providers will relocate their business so as to benefit from a certain aspect of a more favourable legal system. For example, the protection of consumers, minors and intellectual property rights would, on the other hand, justify the application of the national law for each country.

From a theoretical point of view, the advent of such a solution would be a real revolution. Digital networks are tantamount to a specific, autonomous category of application, obliterating the different rules of conflict established for a particular matter of private law. Better still, we should be considering a total decompartmentalisation of the conflict of laws since the competence of a single law (for example that of the country in which the service provider is established) would be overriding both in private and in public law.

B. – ILLUSTRATION IN MATTERS OF E-COMMERCE

This scenario of a total decompartmentalisation of the conflict of laws is like a strange dream. And yet, to a certain extent, fiction has combined with fact, especially in the field of European Community law. In that area, the principles of e-commerce and free exchange have had to be reconciled, which has not been without repercussions on the conflict of laws.

1. – *E-commerce and the Community principle of free-exchange*

As everyone knows, the Community legal system is based on the principle of free exchange, involving *inter alia* the free circulation of goods and free provision of services (Art. 28 et seq. and 49 et seq. of the EC Treaty). Those freedoms allow a person who is resident or established in a Member State to freely carry out his business in the other Member States. However, exceptions are specified. *Pressing or compelling requirements*, such as public order, public health, the protection of intellectual property rights or consumers (etc.) justify restrictions being placed on the principle of free exchange.

Various Community directives have sought to retranscribe that EC Treaty rule. Accordingly they contain what is known as an « internal market principle ». There are various more or less explicit examples, especially on matters concerning insurance, radio broadcasting and above all, e-commerce (4).

---

(4) See Art. 3 of European Parliament and Council Directive 2000/31/EC of 8 June 2000, *OJEC* L 178/1 of 17 July 2000 : http://europa.eu.int/comm/internal–market/fr/ecommerce ; compare the *French draft law on the in formation society* (especially Art. 17 to 19, reproduced in the appendix) which was adopted in the Council of Ministers and submitted before the National Assembly in June 2001 (document n° 3143 : http://www.legifrance.gouv.fr/htm/actualite/actualite–legislative/).

2. – *Effect on the applicable law*

The issue in question is to determine what effect the internal market principle might have on resolving the conflict of laws. By sticking to the letter of the Community directive on e-commerce (motive n° 23), the reply is not absolutely clear. On the one hand, it states that the aim of the directive is not to lay down *additional* rules of private international law (it has to be said that there are already several in Community law : law of contracts, consumer protection, etc.). On the other hand, it is explained that the law duly designated by the rules of private international law must not interfere with the principle of freedom of exchange, except in the cases provided for by the directive.

In my view, that formula, unquestionably of political origin, no doubt designed to set minds at rest, does not remove any effect the internal market rule might have on private international law.

This is how we might try to understand matters. The principle of the internal market is not allied to a traditional choice-of-law rule in that its scope is far too wide. It is imperative that the hindrance to exchanges should arise from the application of rules of private or public law, or, that it results from rulings in administrative, civil or criminal matters. However, that does not mean to say that there is no effect on private international law, on the contrary. Since the internal market principle is not limited to any particular field of law and its scope is very wide it imposes itself in all areas, including private international law.

In that respect, e-commerce law provides an interesting illustration of this inevitable influence of the principle of the internal market on the conflict of laws. Various documents can be cited as evidence, including the French draft law on the information society on which I shall rely (aforementioned especially Articles 17 to 19, reproduced in the appendix, see below) (5). Transposing the rules laid down by the directive, the draft law provides that :

---

(5) See also « the official legal opinion » of the European Commission (http://europa.eu.int/comm/internal–market/fr/ecommerce/2k-442.htm) and of the French government (http://www.internet.gouv.fr/français/textesref/pags12/lsi.htm) or the « personal opinion » expressed by some European officials in papers (see for example : E. CRABIT, « La directive sur le commerce électronique. Le projet 'Méditerranée' » (« The e-commerce directive. The Mediterranean Project »), *Revue du droit de l'Union européenne*, n° 4/2000, pp. 749 et seq.).

— any professional who carries out business by electronic means is, in principle, subject to the law of his country of establishment within the Community; country of establishment is understood as meaning the place (actual and genuine) where the business is actually carried out, on the understanding that « *the location of the technical resources needed to carry out the business are not the only criteria for the principal place of business* » (Art. 17 of the aforementioned draft law).

— that law of the country in which the professional is established – we speak readily of « law of the country of origin » – governs contracts for the supply of goods or services, unless the parties want to choose another law;

— however, that law of the country of origin must not frustrate firstly, certain overriding French provisions that protect consumers residing on the national territory or secondly, those relating to the form of contracts creating or transferring rights over an immovable property situated in the national territory.

That range of solutions is striking. On the one hand, the jurisdiction of the law of the professional service provider's country of origin is mooted as the necessary reflection of the internal market principle. That jurisdiction operates whatever the nature of the rule applied (private or public law), obviously within the limits of the directive's scope of application. So, for example, the criminal rules are not affected by the legislation (see paragraph n° 26 of the directive which expressly advocates the application of penal rules). On the other hand, one might think that the important question of civil liability of the service providers which is governed by Articles 12 to 15 of the directive is normally subject to the law of the professional's country of origin.

On the other hand, the directive advocates the application of specific rules of private international law, either in the areas that are already governed by private international law originating from the Community (law applicable to contractual obligations, consumer protection) or on issues where the applicability of the law of the service provider's country of origin was not deemed to be appropriate (in matters of real estate).

That is to say that although we are far from complete decompartmentalisation of the conflict of laws, which is obviously neither desirable nor thinkable, the principle of the internal market has managed to take its place alongside some traditional rules of private international law. No doubt the definition of its precise role deserves to be set out. As far as I am concerned here, I shall simply say that the development of the Internet sometimes calls for solutions that shake up the barriers usually erected between legal disciplines or subjects.

II. – The contractualisation of the conflict of laws : the example of the protection of personal data

A. – PROTECTION OF PERSONAL DATA IN RELATIONS BETWEEN THE EUROPEAN COMMUNITY AND NON-MEMBER COUNTRIES

The first illustration we have given for resolving conflicts of laws might set us thinking. We are entitled to wonder about the effectiveness of a rule whose scope is limited to internal relations in the Community. The E-commerce Directive and the French draft law for implementing it only provide for the jurisdiction of the law of the service provider's country of origin if he is established in a Member State. No solution is given for service providers established in non-member countries.

This attitude, although understandable (it is normal for Community law to seek primarily to govern domestic situations), can very soon prove untenable, especially within the context of the Internet. By definition, digital networks have a global dimension which the law, whether it be Community law, cannot ignore. That is why, in certain fields, it has proved necessary to grasp the issue of the applicable law in relations with third parties. From that point of view, the protection of personal data provides a particularly interesting illustration.

Briefly, let us remember that since data protection falls within the area of private law (in France, we speak readily about *personal information*) has long been one of Europe's priorities, especially the Council of Europe. The Community legal system has also taken an interest in the subject to the extent that significant disparities between national legislation in matters of protection of private life could constitute an obstacle to exchanges. The development of the information society, which makes it considerably easier to collect and circulate personal data, has unquestionably highlighted the need for Community legislation. As positive law stands at the moment, numerous Community provisions have been adopted or are about to be so. I would mention principally the existence of a directive (6) which the Member States are striving to implement with great difficulty (7).

In intra-Community relations, the rules laid down by the directive are similar to those we have seen in e-commerce matters. Alongside substantive rules designed to guarantee a certain level of protection, one can find a mechanism quite similar to designation of the applicable law (Art. 4 of the directive read in conjunction with Art. 1.2 and Art. 1 of the aforementioned draft law). Jurisdiction is accordingly awarded to the law in the place where the « *person in charge of processing the data* » is established, provided that that person is established within the Community. Specific rules have also been introduced in the situation where the person in charge has several establishments within the Community and in the situation where, although established in a non-member country, he uses resources located in the Community.

Conversely, in relations between non-member countries and the European Community things are very different from what we have seen in e-commerce law. A complex mechanism has been introduced, establishing a framework for the exportation of personal data to non-member countries whilst achieving a sufficiently high level of protection in those countries (Art. 25 and 26 of the aforementioned Directive 95/46/EC state « adequate »).

---

(6) Directive 95/46/EC of the European Parliament and of the Council of 24 October 1995 on the protection of individuals with regard to the processing of personal data and on the free movement of such data, *OJEC* L 281/31 of 23 Nov. 1995, supplemented by European Parliament and Council Directive 97/66/EC of 15 December 1997, *OJEC*, n° L 24/1 of 30 January 1998. On all the provisions applicable in Community law, see the website of the Internal Market DG : http://europa.eu.int/comm/internal–market/fr/dataprot/law/index.htm.

(7) On the latest legislation underway in France, see the draft law on the protection of individuals with regard to the processing of personal data adopted in the Council of Ministers and submitted to the National Assembly in July 2001 (document n° 3250) http://www.legifrance.gouv.fr/html/frame.html.

B. – THE PHENOMENON
OF CONTRACTUALISATION OF CONFLICTS OF LAWS

A priori, the rule set out by the directive for the exportation of personal data to a non-member country does not directly concern the conflict of laws. It falls more within the scope of material reciprocity and, where appropriate, results in decisions from the European Commission authorising and/or laying down the conditions in which the data may be exported.

Accordingly, to date, two types of decision have been taken by the Commission. The first concerns non-member countries which it considers guarantee a satisfactory level of protection of personal data. Three decisions have thus been taken with regard to Switzerland, Hungary and more atypically but also more controversial, the United States of America (8).

The second type of decision from the Commission is of more interest to us. It concerns drawing up *standard clauses* designed to be inserted into contracts between an exporter of data established in the Community and an importer established in a non-member country which does not necessarily provide adequate protection. Numerous organisations both governmental and non-governmental have worked on drafting standard clauses (9). The Commission has recently taken part by adopting a decision approving a number of standard clauses (10).

In the main, the formula for standard clauses has been accepted insofar as it allows a number of principles that are very dear to Community law to be contractualised. In the absence of an international treaty or a uniform law between the member countries of the Community and third parties, the technique of the contract is used to « export » rules and impose them on those who would like to

---

(8) Decisions of 26 July 2000 (*OJEC*, L 214 of 25 August 2000). On the famous and controversial « safe harbour » for « area of security » established with the United States : see, in particular, the information available on the EC Commission's website (Internal Market DG) : http:// europa.eu.int/comm/internal–market/fr/dataprot/news/safeharbor.htm

(9) I am thinking, in particular, about the work of the Council of Europe or the International Chamber of Commerce. For an analysis of these numerous difficulties raised by these clauses, especially in contract law, see : J. HUET, « Les contrats encadrant les transferts de données personnelles » (« Contracts incorporating the transfer of personal data »), *Communication Commerce électronique*, May 2001, chron. n° 11.

(10) Commission Decision n° 2001/97/EC concerning standard contractual clauses for the transfer of personal data to non-member countries pursuant to Directive 95/46/EC, *OJEC*, L 181/ 19 of 4 July 2001.

import personal data into a country which does not always provide sufficient guarantees of adequate protection of personal data.

However, that does not mean that the role of the national laws totally disappears. In accordance with the tradition of private international law, a contract including standard clauses is not *a contract without a law*. On the contrary, it is expressly subject to *the law of the Member State in which the exporter of data is established* (paragraph 17 and clause n° 10 of the aforementioned decision n° 2001/97/EC).

We are witnessing here what could be called a *contractualisation of the conflict of laws*. A choice-of-law rule is imposed on operators established both within the Community and in non-member countries. Nothing obliges the operators to enter into such a contract. However, from the moment they decide to exchange data, they must subject themselves to the law of the Member State in which the exporter of data is established. The clause designating the applicable law is accordingly formulated in a compelling manner, damaging the principle of freedom of contract, which is dear to private international contract law.

Of course, the jurisdiction of the law of the Member State in which the exporter of data is established is not absolute. An importer of data, established in a country other than the Community, can definitely not escape its legal system, which potentially structures compelling rules and awards jurisdiction to public authorities. Moreover, application of the law concerning importers of data is expressly provided for by the Commission (The aforementioned Decision n° 2011/97/EC : Art 3.1a, clause 5a). However it is strictly defined. For example, it is specified that in the situation where an importer of data were to find himself obliged to breach the standard clauses by application of his national law, power is given to the national authorities of the Member States to suspend or ban the exportation of data.

*

* *

In conclusion, one might say that the two illustrations chosen in the fields of e-commerce and protection of personal data show that the Internet is perhaps not only this technical revolution that the traditional legal rule is striving to tame and quieten down. In the field of resolution of conflicts of laws, it undeniably provides some originality, even if we have to recognise that in order to do so, it is greatly assisted by Community law. However, that is another issue altogether.

APPENDIX
Draft law on the information society (extracts)

FRENCH REPUBLIC – NATIONAL ASSEMBLY

Draft law on the information society

Registered at the Presidency of the National Assembly on 14 June 2001 (Document N°3143)

Article 17

Any activity whereby persons established in France and acting as a professional, offer or provide services to supply goods or services at a distance and by electronic means, is subject to the provisions of this section, with the exclusion of :

- legally authorised games played for money, betting and lotteries;
- activities of representation and assistance in court;
- activities of solicitors carried out for the application of the provisions of Article 1 of Order n° 45-2590 of 2 November 1945 concerning the status of the profession of solicitor.

A person is considered as being established in France within the meaning of this section when he is established there in a stable and durable manner in order to conduct his business, whatever it may be, and if it concerns a legal entity, the place in which its registered office is located. The location of the technical resources needed to carry out the business does not constitute the only criteria for establishment.

Article 18

When the activity defined in Article 12 is carried out by persons who are established in a Member State of the European Community other than France it shall be carried out freely on the national territory, subject to compliance with Articles L 181-1 to L 183-2 and L 361-1 to L 364-1 of the Insurance Code, Article L 214-12 of the Monetary and Financial Code, Book IV of the Commercial Code, the laws and regulations relating to unsolicited advertising sent by electronic mail, the laws governed by the Intellectual Property Code and the provisions of the General Tax Code.

The supply of goods or services referred to in Article 17 shall be subject to the law of the Member State in which the person who offers or provides them is established, subject to the common intention of that person and the person to whom those goods or services are directed.

The application of the previous paragraph may not have the effect of :

a) Depriving a consumer whose usual place of residence is in the national territory from the protection afforded by the overriding provisions of the French law relating to contractual obligations. Within the meaning of this article, the provisions relating to contractual obligations include the provisions applicable to the elements of the contract, including those which define the consumer's rights or have a determining influence on his decision to enter into the contract;

b) creating an exemption from the overriding rules of form laid down by French contract law that create or transfer rights over an immovable located in the national territory.

Article 19

In the circumstances laid down by decree in the Council of State, the administrative authority may take measures to restrict the persons mentioned in Article 17 from freely exercising their business when they are necessary to maintain public order and safety, to protect the interests of national defence or to protect consumers and investors other than those mentioned in Article L 411-2 of the Monetary and Financial Code.

JURISDICTION AND THE INTERNET

BY

S. LAKSHMINARAYAN

MINISTRY OF INFORMATION TECHNOLOGY
GOVERNMENT OF INDIA

The Internet has evolved to become an extremely important medium for communication. It has touched all aspects of life including education, health, entertainment, business and governance. However, existing laws did not specifically address many of the new aspects opened up by the Internet. In any case, due to inherent special features of the Internet, some of these aspects do not lend themselves easily to the application of traditional legal mechanisms. As a result, a number of countries have enacted special legislation to deal with legal issues pertaining to the widespread use of the Internet.

However, most of these national legislations, can only be effective within the boundaries of the nation in which they are enacted, even though the law could provide for applicability to any offence or contravention committed outside the national boundaries.

The legal consequences which accompany an Internet presence are emerging as courts struggle to apply conventional legal concepts to e-Commerce. A company's e-Commerce strategy not only helps attract customers in new markets but also may expose companies to the *jurisdiction* and laws of these new markets. The term *jurisdiction* refers to a court's ability to hear a particular case. While courts continue to grapple with the question of whether a company has a duty to defend against litigation arising in distant forums where its only contact is through its website, companies will want to consider these risks when formulating their e-commerce strategies.

The ubiquitous nature of Internet activity has caused courts to reach differing conclusions on whether websites subject a company to the jurisdiction of a foreign forum. These differing conclusions have caused uncertainty in the business community. Companies

which until now have avoided the duty to litigate in distant states
by limiting operations to their home state, should be aware of these
jurisdiction rulings.

Internet communications know no geographical boundaries,
whereas jurisdiction under traditional legislation incorporates a
notion of territoriality. The very origin of an e-mail message may
be unknown. It may have traversed through a number of sovereign
nations. Information on websites is not to be confined to a target
audience but is disseminated simultaneously to a global audience,
thus affecting individuals and organisations in a number of jurisdictions, all of which have their own particular local laws.

Different laws are applicable under different jurisdictions. Different courts provide different advantages and disadvantages for
the parties involved. Accordingly, this gives rise to a number of
questions which are vital to the legality of commerce in cyberspace.

– Who has the authority to prescribe the law in a given area, for
  example e-commerce ?
– Where can the action commence and the entity be subjected to
  legal proceedings ?
– How and when will a court judgment or arbitration award rendered in one jurisdiction be enforced in another ?

While court decisions do not specify definitively when a corporation's Internet activity will subject it to the jurisdiction of a distant
forum, a few guidelines have emerged. Personal jurisdiction will
likely exist when a company clearly conducts business over the
Internet with persons in a foreign jurisdiction. Thus, use of the
Internet to enter into contracts, to transmit computer files or to
accept purchase orders from a distant venue may subject the defendant to jurisdiction in foreign states. Conversely, where a corporation hosts a passive website which simply posts information
accessible to residents of a foreign jurisdiction, a finding of
necessary minimum contacts based solely upon the website is
unlikely. In the middle, the more difficult cases involve interactive
websites where a user can exchange information with the host computer. In these cases, « the level of interactivity and commercial
nature of the exchange of information that occurs on the website »
determines the validity of personal jurisdiction.

Under this approach, which has been increasingly adopted by the
courts, the likelihood of being compelled to defend litigation in a

distant venue based upon an Internet presence is directly proportionate to the nature and quality of the commercial activity that is conducted over the Internet. Companies can use this approach to predict the exposure they face so that their websites may be designed in accordance with their risk tolerance. Unfortunately, for most businesses with an ambitious Internet strategy, the risk of subjecting themselves to litigation in a distant venue directly corresponds with the utility of the website. Companies unwilling to bear the risk of distant litigation may minimise their exposure by limiting the interactivity – and perhaps the usefulness – of their websites.

Some companies have added to their website terms and conditions requiring that any dispute must be brought in a certain venue. While the enforceability of these provisions varies, based upon the facts and jurisdiction, several companies have successfully invoked such clauses when defending cases brought in foreign jurisdictions.

Europe

In the area of cross-border transactions, jurisdictional issues have traditionally been decided by nation states within the framework of international law. In Europe during the last half-century, such issues have increasingly become subject to international conventions and treaties. The nation-states have increasingly realised the need for conformity. Thus, there are conventions in various fields, such as Family law and Commercial law. However, in other fields such as criminal law, conventions are lacking and each country has to be examined individually.

In order to determine whether a party is domiciled in a contracting state, a court can apply its internal law. The seat of a company shall be treated as its domicile; however, in order to determine that seat, the court shall apply its rules of private international law. According to the Brussels Convention the parties to a contract have the right to make an agreement as to which court is to have jurisdiction to adjudicate a dispute. This agreement will hinder a trial in another court but only if one of the parties raises an objection with regard to the court's jurisdiction. There are, however, certain formal requirements that must be fulfilled for such prorogation to be accepted under the Brussels Convention. In the context of which jurisdiction to prescribe, the Rome Convention provides that the law chosen by the parties shall govern a contract.

In the European environment, issues concerning jurisdiction still have to be examined in a national context, i.e. in relation to a certain nation-state's legal rules. However, so far as concerns commercial matters, conventions such as the Brussels Convention cover a number of European states. These international rules will be essential in the interpretation of jurisdictional issues on the Internet. When examining the conventions, it becomes clear that they are not updated and adjusted to the specific aspects of electronic commerce. For example, in the case of electronic commerce, especially in cases where products are delivered over the Internet, i.e. digital products. However, conventions such as the Brussels Convention are the best starting points for helping to evolve the framework for jurisdiction in cyberspace.

USA

USA courts have been among the first to address issues of jurisdiction raised by Internet transactions and US cases determining such issues may serve as indicators of the direction other countries may take.

According to the US Supreme Court, a person may be subject to a court's « long-arm » jurisdiction if « he [has] certain minimum contacts with [the territory of the forum] such that the maintenance of the suit does not offend traditional notions of fair play and substantial justice ». US courts require that a « defendant's conduct and connection with the forum State are such that he should reasonably anticipate being haled into court there ».

A number of cases have held that the maintenance of a web-site accessible from within the USA, but based elsewhere, may constitute sufficient « presence within the jurisdiction » to give rise to such « long-arm » jurisdiction. This is also referred to as the « place of download » test. Essentially, the place from which information is downloaded will be regarded in some courts as the place where the alleged wrong has been committed, thus again giving rise to the court's exercise of « long-arm » jurisdiction.

While in some early cases jurisdiction was exercised merely on the basis that the material or web-site in question was accessible in the USA, more recently a stricter standard has been adopted. A distinction has now been drawn between active and inactive or passive web-sites. The American approach can be summarised as follows :

« Firstly, jurisdiction is almost certain to be exercised where the defendant has engaged in active business on the Internet. Secondly, jurisdiction is possible where there is an exchange of information between computers and the website is interactive. This will depend upon the degree of interactivity and the nature of the information exchanged, including whether it is commercial and whether the website is directed at local residents. Thirdly, jurisdiction is unlikely to be exercised where the website is passive and does little more than provide information » (GARNETT, Richard, « Are Foreign Internet Infringers Beyond the Reach of the Law ? », *University of NSW Law Journal* 23(1), 2000, 105-126).

Efforts have also been underway by the Cyberspace Law Committee of the American Bar Association Section of Business Law to analyse jurisdictional problems that affect global e-commerce (www.abanet.org/buslaw/cyber/initiatives). This Project proposes to examine how these problems are addressed in various countries' legal systems and under applicable treaties, and to begin to articulate, for the global dimensions of cyberspace, controlling principles that can be applied in commerce, government, and the administration of justice. The goals of the Project are threefold. Firstly, it would produce a continuing resource for practitioners on what the law currently is (encompassing national laws and international conventions) and what trends can be observed. Secondly, it would consider the impact of various rules of national and international law in the sense of fairness to the parties involved and whether electronic commerce is encouraged or discouraged, in order to provide policy guidance to lawmakers in the future. Thirdly, the Project will serve as a meeting ground for the increased global collaboration of the legal community in defining the law of cyberspace, resulting in such proposals as suggestions for revision of current international conventions so that they might provide a proper and safe framework for electronic commerce or other proposals for international solutions to the issues.

The Project will focus on the following broad areas :

A. – Jurisdiction to Prescribe

The rules that will govern conduct, persons, or things which are entirely or partially extraterritorial? Even if it may, when should it refrain from doing so?

B. – Jurisdiction of Courts to Adjudicate

Generally, the jurisdiction of the courts of a nation state to adjudicate with respect to a person or thing is based on some link between the forum and the person or thing over which jurisdiction is to exercised. For example, the person or thing may be present in the state, may have conducted business in the state, or may have carried on activity outside the state that has an effect within the state. How are these principles applied in the area of electronic commerce? What electronic links will be sufficient to permit the exercise of jurisdiction over a person or thing whose connection to the forum consists of some combination of voice, video, or data transmissions over wires or radio waves? When more than one court has jurisdiction, which one should actually hear the matter?

C. – Arbitration of International Disputes

In the contractual environment, some uncertainty may be avoided by specifying that disputes will be arbitrated in a given forum. Article II of the United Nations Convention on the Recognition and Enforcement of Foreign Arbitration Awards provides for contracting states to recognise agreements in writing to arbitrate.

D. – Enforcement

The category of enforcement breaks down into two separate issues. The first is jurisdiction of a state to enforce its laws. The second is enforcement of judgments and arbitration awards. Both of these issues of enforcement may raise special questions in the realm of commerce in cyberspace.

Conclusion

Present International Law already provides a basis for solutions to problems concerning jurisdiction over crimes committed over the Internet. What is needed is greater co-operation among States and international rules that regulate issues that remain vague or problematic.

The rules can be achieved through the establishment of International Conventions or through the development of International Customary law. It is submitted that the former alternative is preferable due to the clarity it brings to issues quite quickly (if states can agree to a convention). Customary law has traditionally developed more slowly but in modern times the concept of « instant custom » has arisen in areas such as Spacelaw. If State practice concerning a certain matter is uniform and consistent from the outset and almost all States adhere to it, the usage will soon develop into binding international customary law. However, considering the disparities among States as to technological development and control over the Internet it is questionable if customary law is a reliable solution.

The Internet's ubiquitous yet intangible reach has led courts to inconsistent conclusions about the Internet's role in the traditional personal jurisdiction framework. These disparate decisions hinder efforts to predict the precise legal consequences a company faces when doing business on the Internet. While inconsistent in result, the court decisions do suggest that the probability of being properly haled into a foreign forum is directly related to the nature and quality of the commercial activity which is conducted over the Internet. Companies wishing to actively engage in e-commerce should anticipate the risk of defending litigation which arises in the markets accessed through the Internet. Companies unwilling to tolerate such a risk may want to consider designing their websites to limit interactivity and take other contractual measures.

THE IMPLEMENTATION
OF COURT RULINGS

Partner
Legal Office Salans, Hertzfeld & Heilbronn

Introduction

Nowadays, the mechanisms for recognition and enforcement are
governed by traditional rules of private international law (I). The
question then arises as to whether such provisions are suitable for
the Internet. Would it be more appropriate to draw up a specific
international instrument that takes into account the specific
characteristics of the Internet? Are the international attempts at
harmonisation that are being developed able to provide an adequate response? (II). The solutions proposed emphasise the legal
problem currently faced by States, which are nevertheless
democratic, with regard to the dissemination in their country of
unlawful content, from other likewise democratic States in which it
is considered to be lawful. Against this background, what avenue of
thinking can still be explored? (III).

I. – The use of traditional mechanisms
for the recognition and enforcement
of foreign judgments : a qualified assessment

It is appropriate to briefly summarise the conditions laid down
by the French, Community and American legal systems on the subject (A), and then consider the most significant problems encountered in connection with the circulation of judgments between
Europe and the United States (B).

A. – The conditions
for recognition and enforcement

1. – *In French law*

Unless there is a specific provision deriving from bilateral agreements, according to which a judgment made by a Member State of the European Union is or is not challenged, the rules of ordinary law (1) or those arising from the Brussels Convention (2) will apply.

a) *Ordinary law*

Having for a long time been a supporter of the strict control of foreign judgments by authorising the French judge to review the substance of a case, in the *Munzer* judgment, the civil division of the Court of Cassation maintained that verification of the legality of the foreign judgment « *is sufficient to protect the French legal system and its interests* » and « *in all matters constitutes both the expression and the limit of the power of control* » of the enforcement judge « *without him having to review the substance of the decision* ».

A list of the combination of conditions laid down by the *Munzer* (1) judgment was somewhat changed by the *Bachir* (2) judgment from the same court but it reduced the five conditions initially laid down by the *Munzer* judgment to four. This reduction in the number of conditions derives from the fact that the condition for checking the legality of the procedure followed by the foreign judge no longer appeared to be a separate condition but was included in the condition for complying with public procedural policy, which is now enriched by decisions of the European Court of Human Rights.

Accordingly, henceforth, checking the legality of a foreign judgment is based on :
- the jurisdiction of the foreign court, known as verification of the general and special jurisdiction of the court;
- the law applied to the substance of the case, known as verification of the legislative authority;

---

(1) 1ˢᵗ Civ., 7 January 1964, *Rev. Crit.*, 1964, 344, note BATIFFOL.
(2) 1ˢᵗ Civ., 4 October 1968, *Rev. Crit.*, 1968, 98, note LAGARDE.

– compliance with public policy, within the meaning of private international law, split between procedural public policy and substantive public policy which we know has a weakened effect since the question does not arise at the stage of creation of individual rights but rather their international effectiveness. Moreover, this requirement is common to the various systems of private international law and, in my view, must not be abolished because it is the necessary safety valve;

– the absence of fraudulent evasion of the law.

Careful observers will have noticed that unlike other legal systems, French law does not require the condition of reciprocity, which, in my view, seems to be a wise choice as it is so difficult for the enforcement judge to assess that condition.

In order to illustrate the application of these rules in the field of e-commerce, let us take as an example a French company that sells goods on its website, which are bought by a Canadian consumer resident in the province of Quebec. When they are delivered, the goods prove to be faulty and the purchaser takes action against the French seller in the Quebec courts. The seller is properly notified of the summons, appoints a lawyer and presents his defence on the merits of the case properly. The judge in the Quebec court applying *lex fori*, orders the French defendant to reimburse to the consumer the price of the faulty goods as well as his expenses and costs. In order to obtain payment of these sums, the Quebec consumer then seeks an order to enforce this decision before the French courts.

In order to obtain enforcement of the Canadian judgment, the applicant must provide the French judge with all the relevant facts to prove that the foreign judgment is legal, having regard to the conditions mentioned above. Accordingly, he must establish that :

– the Quebec judge was competent in that (a) there is no rule awarding exclusive (3) jurisdiction to the French courts since the matter concerns a Canadian consumer, (b) the disputed sale which took place in Quebec is clearly related to that province and (c) referral to the court that made the decision is not fraudulent, since it concerns a court located in the place in which the purchaser/consumer is resident;

_____

(3) Subject, of course, to the exemption from jurisdiction established by Article 15 of the French Civil Code.

— the applicant has indeed benefited from the main principles of procedural justice;

— since it concerns a consumer, application of the Quebec law is compatible with the French rules governing choice of law on the subject;

— the judgment ordering the French vendor to reimburse the defective goods does not conflict with French public policy;

— the applicant has not conferred jurisdiction on the Quebec court with the sole aim of placing himself beyond the influence of French law.

If the applicant for enforcement of the judgment is unable to prove these various conditions, his case will be rejected. If he can satisfy them, where the French seller contests the application for enforcement (the defendant of the application for enforcement must prove that his interests have been harmed by the failure to comply with one of these conditions), the French judge will decide. By contrast, if no objection is raised, he will base his judgment on the applicant's allegations and will grant the order for enforcement (4).

b) *The Brussels Convention of 27 September 1968* (5)

The recognition and enforcement of a judgment given by the authorities of a contracting State (nowadays all the Member States of the European Union with the exception of Denmark so far as concerns the Regulation) before another contracting State, forms the subject of Title III of the Convention which is due to enter into force on 1st March 2002 (article 32 *et seq.* of Regulation 44/2001, former Articles 25 *et seq* of the Convention (6)). The Convention applies to any civil or commercial (7) judgment, of whatsoever nature : whether or not it is final, preparatory, interlocutory, for provisional enforcement, in non contentious matters (8), in contentious

---

(4) 1st Civ. Cass., 3 June 1969, *Rev. Crit.*, 1971, 743.

(5) This convention, signed on 27 September 1968, only entered into force on 1st February 1973 (*OJEC*, L 299 of 31 December 1972). It has been amended on several occasions. Today it has been replaced by Council Regulation (EC) n° 44/2001 of 22 December 2000 on jurisdiction and the recognition and enforcement of judgments in civil and commercial proceedings, *OJEC*, L 012 of 16/01/2001, p. 1.

(6) Here we will use the new numbering of articles as provided in Regulation n° 44/2001.

(7) On this point, see H. GAUDEMET-TALLON, *Les Conventions de Bruxelles et de Lugano (The Brussels and Lugano Conventions)*, 2nd ed., LGDJ, 1987, n°s 323 *et seq.* (hereinafter : *Gaudemet-Tallon*).

(8) However, purely « responsive » acts are excluded, such as court transactions.

proceedings, given after hearing the arguments of all parties or in default etc.

Only decisions that are « lawful » within the meaning of the Convention are recognised automatically and authorised to be enforced. Nevertheless, it must be emphasised that the procedure to check whether it is lawful is much lighter here than in ordinary law and takes place downstream by means of grounds of refusal to recognise, a restrictive list of which is provided in the Convention, rather than an *a priori* verification of the conditions.

The alternative grounds of refusal of recognition are :

— an obvious conflict with public policy;
— failure to notify or serve the originating writ to the defaulter within the proper time, unless an appeal has been lodged against the decision whilst he was able to do so;
— the decision in question conflicts with a previous judgment given in the Member State addressed or in another Member State or third country by the same parties involved and having the same purpose if that judgment fulfils the conditions for being recognised in the Member State addressed;
— or the control of exclusive jurisdiction (in particular, that which protects the consumer and the insured).

It can be emphasised here that there are considerably fewer grounds for refusing recognition than in French ordinary law (only substantive public policy and procedural public policy are mentioned) and that judgments made by Member States and even third countries which have *res judicata* authority prohibiting the courts of Member States from ruling on the same case, are taken into consideration.

2. – *In American law*

As a preliminary point, it is appropriate to draw attention to the problems arising from shared jurisdiction between the Federal law and the various national laws.

In principle, the law of each separate State is designed to govern the rules of indirect jurisdiction of that State. In practice, it often happens that a foreign judgment can be recognised in one State but not in another.

However, federal jurisdiction holds sway in some situations, in particular, when the foreign judgment is used as a ground of defence in a federal appeal.

Similarly, when the foreign judgment is used in connection with an appeal based on a federal law or an international Treaty, the recognition and enforcement of that judgment will be subject to the federal law (9).

Accordingly, despite the fact that the majority of States have adopted the *Uniform Foreign Money-Judgments Recognition Act* (hereinafter, the UFMJA) there are still significant differences in interpretation which leave a foreign lawyer who wishes to get a foreign judgment recognised or enforced in the United States somewhat perplexed.

In principle, it is accepted that foreign pecuniary judgments are recognised and enforceable when they are final and enforceable in their countries of origin.

If the defendant objects to such recognition or order for enforcement, he must rely on one of the grounds accepted by the UFMJA (and by the 3rd *Restatement*). These are :

The lack of jurisdiction of the foreign judge (10) : the foreign judge will be recognised within the meaning of these two provisions if one of the events occurs in the territory of his State (11) : (a) notification of the document instituting proceedings, (b) voluntary appearance of the defendant, (c) clause awarding jurisdiction to this State, (d) residence of a natural person or main business centre of a legal entity, (e) motor vehicle or aeroplane accident, (f) the defendant's business connected with his company is located in this forum ;

i) A breach of international public policy (12);

---

(9) L.J. SILBERMANN & A.F. LOWENFELD, « A Different Challenge for the ALI : Herein of Foreign Judgments, an International Treaty, and an American Statute », 75 *Indiana L.J.* 635 (hereinafter : *A Different Challenge for the ALI*).

(10) *Restatement 3rd of the foreign relations law of the United States*, § 482(1)(b) (hereinafter *Restatement 3rd*); *Unif. Money-Judgments Recognition Act* § 4.

(11) It should be noted that these criteria are not exhaustive, the judge may find new ones.

(12) The intransigence of American law with regard to the limits to freedom of speech is also illustrated from a domestic point of view. Judges are able to invalidate a law that has been passed and published, when it is contrary to the Constitution. Accordingly, the *American Civil Liberties Union* used those grounds to successfully attack the 1996 *Telecom Act* which was held to be unconstitutional by the Supreme Court on 26 June 1997 (Case of *ACLU v. Reno*, 924 F Supp 1, US Sup.Ct 1997). Nowadays, this same association relies on the *Child Online Protection*

ii) Fraudulent evasion of the judgment;

iii) A breach of public procedural order : impartiality and « *due process of law* » (13);

iv) The existence of a final conflicting judgment;

v) A breach of an agreement between the parties establishing an alternative way of resolving the dispute (an arbitration, conciliation, or mediation clause etc.);

vi) *Forum non conveniens* (14).

It should be noted that the various domestic laws generally exclude the criterion arising from reciprocity – even though some countries continue to ask for this factor (15).

B. – RECOGNITION
AND ENFORCEMENT OUTSIDE THE BRUSSELS
CONVENTION : THE DIFFICULTIES ENCOUNTERED

So far as concerns monetary judgments, recognition and enforcement in the United States generally takes place smoothly via the *Uniform Foreign Money-Judgments Recognition Act* (UFMJA).

In the context of the European Union, the circulation of judgments in civil and commercial proceedings does not create major problems either, thanks to the instruments established by (the Brussels Convention of 1968 amended by Regulation n° 44/2001).

By contrast, there are numerous obstacles to recognition where judgments have to circulate between Europe and the United States, relating, for example, to freedom of speech, since such judgments are not covered by the Brussels Convention.

The First Amendment of the American Constitution is used as a means of creating an obstacle to foreign judgments that restricts that freedom, notably by convictions for defamation or unlawful content (16).

Act which makes the communication of content that is dangerous for minors for commercial purposes a punishable offence and imposes heavy sanctions (Case of *ACLU v Ashcroft*, n° 00-1293).

(13) That is to say, essentially, compliance with the rights of the defence.

(14) The dispute has no clear connection with the Court to which it is referred but rather to another Court in whose jurisdiction, for example, the evidence, place of damage etc. is located.

(15) Such as Idaho, Ohio and Texas.

(16) See *Matusevitch v Telnikoff*, 877 F.Supp. 1 (DCC 195); *Bachchan v Indian Abroad Publications Inc.*, 154 Misc.2d 228 (NY Sup Ct 1992); *Reno v ACLU*, 924 F Supp 1, (US Sup.Ct 1997).

Correlatively, in Europe, there is a great deal of reticence when receiving American decisions that concern freedom of speech (17) or tortious proceedings, since North American judges are usually more generous in awarding damages (18).

II. – Advisability
and initiatives for harmonisation

The application of the national rules of indirect jurisdiction for judgments relating to the Internet seems to be inappropriate in that both the location of legal relationships and significant conceptual differences seem to hinder an effective circulation of judgments.

In those circumstances, one has to question the advisability and procedures for the international harmonisation of the conditions for recognition and enforcement of such judgments (A). We should take into account the example of the bodies approved by ICANN (B). Although it is only for domain names, it is an innovative and remarkable illustration. We should also examine the various discussion projects (C) aimed at the transnational harmonisation of the rules on jurisdiction, in particular, those of the Hague Conference and the American Bar Association.

A. – THE ADVISABILITY
OF HARMONISING THE CONDITIONS FOR RECOGNITION
AND ENFORCEMENT OF INTERNET JUDGMENTS

1. – *The specific nature of the Internet*

The characteristics of the Internet are the source of the legal problems encountered by anyone who tries to grasp the phenomenon as a whole : speed, virtual reality, global availability of information and minimal costs combine within this medium.

In private international law, these characteristics manifest themselves in major problems in locating the litigious situation.

---

(17) See, in particular, the French and English examples.

(18) There are numerous other subjects in which differences in point of view between Europe and the United States create problems at the stage of recognition of judgments; including, for example, intellectual property and, in particular, non-pecuniary rights of an author.

Accordingly, for example, when a piece of information is placed online, its author can only be identified by the details he agrees to pass on to the domain name registration body, which can therefore prove to be false. Similarly, its host can very easily change (19). In those circumstances, pinpointing the legal relationship can prove to be extremely complex both in contractual and tortious proceedings.

It would therefore seem advisable that in addition to these insurmountable difficulties linked to the very existence of the network, differences in national concepts should not complicate matters further.

2. – *The lack of international uniformity*

One of the fundamental arguments that governs the establishment of any rule of private international law is particularly appropriate here : compliance with the parties' expectations. E-commerce will only take off when consumers and businesses have confidence in this new means of acquiring information and entering into contracts. However, that confidence resides primarily in the certainty that a precise body of legal rules is applicable and that a judgment obtained in one country can actually be enforced in another country.

B. – EXAMPLES OF WORK IN PROGRESS

1. – *The preliminary draft Hague Convention on the authority of foreign judgments in civil and commercial proceedings*

Since 1998, the concerns about the legal security of cyberspace actors have been central to the work of the Hague Conference on private international law. Accordingly, a preliminary draft convention on jurisdiction and foreign judgments in civil and commercial

---

(19) This situation is far from being an academic hypothesis as is borne out by a recent case involving an association and the most important Internet access suppliers : Paris, provisional order., 12 July 2001, *J'accuse* / Association of Access suppliers and others.

matters was drawn up on 18 June 1999 and revised on 30 October 1999 (20).

In general, it can be confirmed that this preliminary draft drew inspiration largely from the solutions identified by the Brussels Convention of 1968 and reiterated in its modernised version – Regulation n° 44-2001 (21).

The driving principle is that of the virtually automatic recognition of rulings within contracting States. Article 25 of the preliminary draft provides :

1. *A judgement based on a ground of jurisdiction provided for in Articles 3 to 13, or which is consistent with any such ground, shall be recognised or enforced under this Chapter.*
2. *In order to be recognised, a judgment referred to in paragraph 1 must have the effect of res judicata in the State of origin.*
3. *In order to be enforceable, a judgment referred to in paragraph 1 must be enforceable in the State of origin.*
4. *However, recognition or enforcement may be postponed if the judgment is the subject of review in the State of origin or if the time limit for seeking a review has not expired.*

It can therefore be seen that the authority of *res judicata* or enforceability recognised in the judgment's country of origin is sufficient for the judgment to be recognised or enforced in the country in which it is received.

Accordingly, it follows correlatively that the grounds of refusal of recognition or enforcement should be strictly circumscribed. Articles 27 and 28 provide that once the jurisdiction of the original judge is verified – it must be consistent with the criteria of the Convention – only certain grounds can impede acceptance of the foreign judgment. There are six of these grounds and they broadly reiterate those laid down by the legal systems previously analysed in (I), pointing out that at no time may the judge review the substance of the foreign judgment (Article 28 *in fine*).

Accordingly, it provides that :

(20) The Hague conference on private international law, preliminary draft convention on jurisdiction and foreign judgments in civil and commercial proceedings adopted by the Special Commission on 30 October 1999; available online : http://www/hcch.net/f/conventions/draft36f.html.

(21) Council Regulation (EC) n° 44/2001, 22 December 2000 on jurisdiction, recognition and enforcement of judgments in civil and commercial proceedings, *OJEC*, L 012 of 16/01/2001, p. 1.

1. *proceedings between the same parties and having the same subject matter are pending before a court of the State addressed, if first seized in accordance with article 21;*
2. *the judgment is inconsistent with a judgment rendered, either in the State addressed or in another State, provided that in the latter case, the judgment is capable of being recognised or enforced in the State addressed;*
3. *the judgment results from proceedings that are incompatible with the fundamental principles of procedure of the State addressed, including the right of each party to be heard by an impartial and independent court;*
4. *the document which instituted the proceedings or an equivalent document containing the essential elements of the claim was not notified to the defendant in sufficient time and in such a way as to enable him to arrange for his defence;*
5. *the judgment was obtained by fraud in connection with a matter of procedure;*
6. *recognition or enforcement would be manifestly incompatible with the public policy of the State addressed.*

One can detect very clearly here both the requirements of American and of French law (subject to the relationship between principle and exceptions that we saw above) and the provisions of Article 34 of Regulation n° 44/2001 (22), the main difference being the lack of a regulatory court to enable the future Convention to be applied uniformly – despite Article 38 which indulges in wishful thinking to that effect.

So far as concerns one of the major reasons for dissension between Europe and the United States, that is to say the excessive amount of damages awarded by American judges, Article 33 of the preliminary draft attempts to offer a solution by providing that :

1. *Insofar as a judgment awards non-compensatory, including exemplary or punitive damages, it shall be recognised, at least to the extent that similar or comparable damages could have been awarded in the State addressed.*
2. *Where the debtor, after proceedings in which the creditor has the opportunity to be heard, satisfies the court addressed that in the cir-*

---

(22) The relationship between the future Convention and Regulation n° 44/2001 is provided by Article 41 of the preliminary draft which gives some precedence of the Community Regulation over the instrument currently being drafted.

*cumstances, including those existing in the State of origin, grossly
excessive damages have been awarded, recognition may be
limited to a lesser amount.*

3. *In no circumstances shall the court addressed recognise the judgment
for an amount that is less than that which could have been awarded
in the State addressed in the same circumstances, including those
existing in the State of origin.*

4. *In applying paragraph 1 or 2, the court addressed shall take into
account whether and to what extent the damages awarded by the
court of origin serve to cover costs and expenses relating to the
proceedings.*

This provision clearly shows that American law « Punitive
damages » are expressly covered. Therefore, – and this is not
without reminding the French legal expert of Article 1152 of the
Civil Code relating to the criminal clause – if the judge before whom
the case is brought considers the amount of damages awarded by
the foreign judge to be excessive, he can reduce that amount but
he may not award a sum that is less than the amount which he himself would award in similar circumstances. One of the main
obstacles to recognition of American judgments in France could
therefore be removed if the United States would agree to have their
judgments reduced in this way.

With regard, more specifically, to the recognition and enforcement of « Internet » rulings, a meeting of experts was held in
Ottawa between 28 February and 1st March 2000 to examine the
suitability of the preliminary draft Convention on cyberspace (23).
Observations were made with regard to direct jurisdiction,
emphasising, in particular, the importance that should be placed on
the intention of the parties in connection with locating the legal
relationship and the special attention that should be paid to contracts entered into with consumers. Much discussion was also given
over to the jurisdiction of the judge in tortious proceedings.

---

(23) The Hague conference on private international law, « E-Commerce and international
jurisdiction », Ottawa, 28 February - 1st March 2000, preliminary document n° 12; available
online : http://www.hcch.net/f/workprog/jdgm/html.

2. – *The work of the International Chamber of Commerce (ICC)*

The ICC has responded to the concerns of the economic community with regard to the uncertainty surrounding jurisdiction and applicable law in e-commerce between business and consumer. On 6 June 2001, an ICC committee responsible for dealing with issues of jurisdiction and the applicable law in e-commerce, published a general policy statement on jurisdiction and the applicable law in e-commerce (24). Without adopting any specific position or laying down rules relating to the recognition and enforcement of foreign judgments, in this statement, the ICC observed that the current international laws and treaties « *do not routinely provide for effective enforcement options for judgments obtained in a consumer's country of residence against a merchant in a foreign jurisdiction* ».

The ICC considers that there are some principles and strategies which could help legislators, supervisory bodies and the courts to rule on the question of recognition and enforcement of foreign judgments, jurisdiction and the applicable law in e-commerce. That is why the ICC laid down recommendations on the most appropriate way to proceed in the handling of these complex issues. In that respect, it suggests a three-tier procedure for settling disputes between business and consumers arising from online transactions : (i) use the business's internal mechanisms; (ii) rely on alternative dispute resolution (ADR); (iii) and, as a last resort, go to court.

In the latter case, the ICC recommends adopting the following basic principles so as to avoid substantial jurisdiction claims :

i) *Party autonomy* : the ICC takes the view that freedom of contract must be respected as a general principle;

ii) « *Country of origin* » : the ICC considers that the application of the principle of the « country of origin » is the easiest solution to put into practice and therefore should be the preferred method;

---

(24) Http://www.iccwbo.org/home/statements–rules/statements/2001/French–translations/competence–et–loi–applicable.asp.

iii) *Allow self-regulation to demonstrate its efficacy* : The ICC recommends using mechanisms for dispute resolution (Arbitration (25) and ADR (26)).

On this view, the ICC has undertaken to consider a global mechanism that would make the settlement of online disputes easier.

3. – *The work of the American Bar Association*

In 1998, the American Bar Association created a committee that specialises in cyberspace law in order to draft an international legislation that would strengthen the legal security of Internet actors. The ABA's initiative is interesting in that the precondition for drawing up a uniform legislation consists of a specific analysis of the private international law systems of various States, in civil and commercial as well as criminal proceedings. Accordingly, it is envisaged that the practices of the American, European and Pacific Asian regions should be identified in the first stage to allow their impact on business life to be assessed. Based on this finding, the ABA envisages issuing recommendations that include, *inter alia,* uniform rules for jurisdiction.

Currently, the work completed has led to the drafting of two reports concerning the state of the applicable law and jurisdiction

---

(25) Founded in 1923, the ICC's international arbitration Court (« the Court ») is the main world institution that specialises in the settlement of international commercial disputes (http://www.iccwbo.org/court/french/intro-cour/introduction.asp). Its task is to ensure that the ICC's arbitration rules are applied. The ICC's court supervises all the arbitration proceedings, from the initial application to the final sentence. The benefits of arbitration are its flexible procedure and the taking into account of the parties' wishes. Any sentence given is compulsory. Arbitration enjoys better international recognition than national court rulings. Some 120 States have signed up to the 1958 United Nations Convention for the recognition and enforcement of foreign arbitration rulings, known as the « New York Convention ». It facilitates the enforcement of rulings in all the signatory countries.

(26) The ICC has drawn up a new Regulation for the amicable settlement of disputes (ADR Regulation) which came into force on 1st July 2001. The ADR Regulation is for use by parties who wish their disputes or disagreements to be resolved amicably with the help of a third party, in accordance with a structured procedure. This Regulation allows the parties to freely choose the formula for settling their dispute which they consider to be most appropriate, for example, mediation, a « mini-trial », or the search for a solution that is acceptable to all parties, or a combination of the various formulae. The main benefits of the ICC's ADR are its flexibility, the freedom of choice available to the parties, savings in terms of time and expense and its confidentiality (http://www.iccwbo.org/drs/french/adr/all-topics.asp). The ICC's ADR does not lead to an enforceable ruling or decision by a third party. It relies entirely on the goodwill of the parties who may choose to agree or not in writing and to comply with any recommendation or decision made by the third party. They will then be bound by that agreement in accordance with the law applicable to them.

in Europe and in the United States (27). However, these are only concerned with the Brussels Convention and the internal jurisdiction rules of American law.

III. – Assessment and proposal

The transnational nature of the Internet allows potential access in one country to information placed online in another country. Accordingly, it allows each individual to behave as a veritable actor in the international legal system (28).

Against that background, disputes, which are characteristic of any human society, are increasingly becoming international. Although nowadays national judges are more inclined to treat an international dispute as such (and not by routinely applying *lex fori*), nevertheless, ultimately it will often be necessary to get the judgment made against the persons liable recognised and/or enforced abroad. However, enforcing court judgments is not always a simple matter.

A. – THE ISSUES

Generally speaking, States have a different understanding of the concept of freedom of speech. Therefore, there is not *one* freedom of speech but *many* freedoms of speech.

To be persuaded of that, one only has to observe the variety of approaches to sexual morality. Similarly, speeches inciting racial hatred are prohibited in one country as an offence against human dignity and completely tolerated in another, often in the name of freedom of speech. Accordingly, the same goes for pornography, which is banned in Ireland and completely accepted in Sweden.

Therefore, any victim is likely to be faced with the following problem : although the national judge considers that where citizens

---

(27) American Bar Association, Committee on Cyberspace Law, « Jurisdiction On The Internet – The European Perspective – An Analysis Of Conventions, Statutes And Case Law » et « Litigation In Cyberspace : Jurisdiction And Choice Of Law – A United States Perspective », 1997.

(28) International public policy is understood as meaning a set of principles, whether or not in writing, which, at the time of argument, are deemed in one legal system to be fundamental and which, for that reason, require that not only the private intentions (Art. 6 of the French Civil Code) but also foreign laws and acts of foreign authorities shall have no effect in that legal system.

have access to content that is unlawful in the eyes of his own national laws, there has been an offence against international public policy of that State, the foreign judge who is asked to enforce the decision, (i.e. the judge in the State from which the content at issue emanated) might consider, nonetheless, that there has been no breach of his own international public policy and the application for enforcement will then be refused.

In fact, as a condition for recognition and enforcement of a foreign judgment, both ordinary law and the relevant international conventions applicable require verification that such judgment does not conflict with the international public policy of the State in which enforcement is sought (29). The preliminary draft Hague Convention on jurisdiction and foreign judgments in civil and commercial proceedings (30), designed to take into consideration the specific nature of the Internet, also upholds that condition.

Accordingly, it should be noted, especially in the context of relations between Europe and the United States, that there are numerous obstacles to the recognition and enforcement of foreign judgments where freedom of speech is concerned. Moreover, such judgments are not covered by the Brussels Convention, whose conditions for recognition and enforcement are more flexible than in ordinary law.

In fact, the First Amendment of the American Constitution is used to create an obstacle to foreign judgments that restrict that freedom, notably via sentences for defamation or unlawful content.

The best recent illustration of this fundamental difference between Europe and the United States is definitely the Yahoo! case. Initially, as an interim measure, Yahoo Inc was ordered to introduce a filtering device for certain web pages so as to prevent French Internet users from having access to the unlawful content accessible via the portal www.yahoo.com (31).

For its part, the Californian Court, which was asked to rule on the recognition and enforcement of the order against Yahoo Inc., held that this judgment was manifestly contrary to its public

---

(29) Case-law of the French Court of Cassation; Art. 32 *et seq.* of Regulation 44/2001 amending the Brussels Convention of 27 September 1968; in the United States, the Uniform Foreign Money-Judgments Recognition Act which provides, *inter alia*, as a ground of objection to the application for enforcement, a breach of American international public policy.

(30) Last negotiations in June 2001.

(31) Paris, provisional order, *Yahoo! | LICRA and UEJF*, 22 May 2000.

policy, given concrete expression here in the First Amendment of the American Constitution.

This example shows how difficult it is to extricate the recognition of a court ruling from the legal system of the judge who has to pronounce the enforcement. The debate – which should only be procedural – is rapidly encroaching into the area of substance.

Thanks to this case, it is easy to understand that in some types of dispute, the differences can give rise to a real impasse and eliminate any efforts to regulate the Internet.

This situation explains why the debate very soon focussed on the issue of the liability of the service providers and, in this type of international dispute, more specifically on access providers because it is precisely their infrastructure that allows such disputed content to be disseminated throughout the whole world.

However, as a widely reported case in France recently illustrated, in which approximately ten access providers had been sued by anti-racism and anti-revisionist associations, their action to hold them liable proved unsuccessful since the national laws restricted their liability which could only have related to transferring content disseminated on the Internet and not to the very nature of such content.

Accordingly, we need to re-examine this fundamental question, that is to say, how can a court ruling made in one State against content providers or hosts located in another State be enforced?

B. – Proposal

With the benefit of these initial observations, it would seem that there are only two options.

The first is of technical nature, as it is a question of installing a filtering device upstream for the purposes of censure. In my view, this radical solution does not appear to be compatible with our democratic values.

The second option that I shall try to set out in the following arguments is not at all technical but legal. It leads to a derogation from the traditional rules of private international law.

Where a judge is faced with the following three conditions :

i) an offence committed via an Internet site,

ii) such offence manifestly breaches his State's international public policy,

iii) such an offence is punished by a court ruling,

the principle would then be that in addition to the existing requirements as to form laid down by international agreements and ordinary law, the foreign judge who is asked to make an enforcement order would only have to verify that these three conditions are fulfilled in order to grant it and, accordingly, require that both the content provider in question and its host (the only natural persons or legal entities that have a real control over the dissemination of content via the Internet) introduce every means necessary, particularly of a technical nature, to prevent access to the content at issue in the territory of the State whose international public policy has been breached.

Obviously, the implementation of that principle would require bilateral agreements between States to be made beforehand that would allow the condition for compliance with the international public policy of the State in which the order for enforcement is sought to be replaced by these three conditions.

It could also be the subject of an international agreement.

Let us remember that on 8 November last, the 43 Member States of the Council of Europe adopted the Convention on cybercrime, the first international piece of legislation that harmonises national legislation with regard to criminal offences committed via the Internet and other computer networks. (32) However, although consensus on the harmonisation of a number of criminal offences such as child pornography, spreading viruses, the falsification of data, infringements of copyright, etc. was reached between all these States, other criminal offences still remain outside the scope of this vast harmonisation initiative that began four years ago. In particular, the Europeans were unable to include in this legislation making it an offence for sites to publish xenophobic or racist content, because of the categorical refusal of the Americans who invoked freedom of speech. However, plans are now being made to submit a draft additional Protocol to the convention to the Council of Europe. Moreover, it is with that in mind that a Council of

---

(32) The official signing ceremony for this convention will take place on 23 November in Budapest.

Europe working group put to the vote a recommendation to adopt a special protocol that would allow any racist discussion on the Internet to be banned. This difficulty shows that there are still a number of implacable sticking points between States, owing to their different concepts of what freedom of speech should cover.

In that respect, in the Yahoo! case, the American judge himself admitted that at the present time, the absence of international conventions establishing harmonised rules on the subject and the methods for recognising such rules in the context of international disputes, obliged him to enforce his own international public policy, which includes the First Amendment relating to freedom of speech.

It should be emphasised that the purpose of such a proposal is not to force a judge who has to rule on an application for enforcement to renounce the fundamental principles contained in his international public policy but to guarantee effective mutual assistance between all States by helping each State to comply with its own international public policy in a context in which the specific characteristics of the Internet make such compliance particularly difficult.

Accordingly, the mechanism proposed would not really challenge the sovereignty of each State, since :

– authors or hosts of content would continue to fully enjoy the public freedoms that their State guarantees them on national territory. In return, they would still have an overriding obligation to comply with that State's public policy;
– by contrast, they would also have an obligation to introduce the necessary precautions and technical measures to prevent the content that they control from being disseminated in the territory of another State in which it would conflict with the international public policy of that State.

Moreover, a parallel can be drawn in tax-related matters in which bilateral conventions have been drawn up between States in order to prevent the double taxation of citizens. In France, the rule established in public law is that an individual is taxed in relation to the amount of income he receives in his country of residence. By contrast, in the United States, judges interpret the Constitution and its Sixteenth Amendment as justifying the taxation not only of all persons residing in the United States but also of American citizens residing abroad, which resulted in the double taxation of American citizens. This problem has now been circumvented by the implementation of conventions that derogate from the traditional tax rules.

C. – Objections

This proposal is bound to arouse objections including the following :

1. – *This problem is marginal*

The argument is not relevant.

Few people have the resources to incur heavy expenses in proceedings. Moreover, some of them are definitely discouraged by the foreseeable problems of enforcing the court judgement they will obtain in their State abroad. In the *J'accuse* case in particular, the associations admitted that they did not sue the American host first because they knew that it would then invoke the First Amendment of the Constitution and that they would therefore not obtain an order to enforce any judgment made. Accordingly, they preferred to sue the national access providers.

2. – *The technical measures required would be expensive*

The « financial » argument is not relevant either.

Where a content provider takes responsibility for disseminating on the Internet content that is liable to breach the international public policy of other States, it must bear the financial consequences, notably of getting its host provider to introduce filtering devices.

Moreover, these measures concern a relatively limited type of content since the definition of numerous criminal offences has now been harmonised by the adoption of the Convention on Cybercrime.

Accordingly, host providers and States must ensure that offences that are not covered by this Convention are brought to the attention of their customers/citizens so as to enable them to comply with the laws of other States that have mandatory scope (websites in particular).

3. – *This proposal conflicts with the traditional principles of international law*

In numerous areas, both national and international rules have had to be adapted to the specific characteristics of the Internet in order to guarantee that they are not merely notional petitions but that they can also be effective there.

Accordingly, in 2000 in France our traditional concept of evidence, with its roots in our Civil Code, underwent a profound change by extending the concept of « written material » in order, *inter alia,* not to impede e-commerce.

Even apart from the issues surrounding the Internet, our traditional rules have had to evolve when they lost their coherence. The example of bilateral conventions in tax-related matters, which resulted in a profound change in the American concept of the taxation system, shows nevertheless that such changes can prove to be necessary if we want to end up with a fairer system for American citizens.

4. – *Would not such a proposal undermine freedom?*

It is possible to wonder about the harmful effect of such a proposal. In wishing to protect the weakest as far as possible, are we not going to give our support to the strongest?

The example is known and far from being an academic hypothesis.

Let us take the case of a State whose government's culture can described as not being based on democracy, in a word : a totalitarian State.

Clear evidence shows that Internet sites that promote freedom, human rights, the emancipation of women and the fight against discrimination will not find favour in the eyes of such a government.

Therefore, such sites will be condemned in such a country by justice by command and these same States will try to get an internal judgment enforced by a foreign judge who has jurisdiction in accordance with the place in which the Internet site is located. Should we allow a foreign totalitarian State directly or via an association that is used as its leading arm to prevent such sites from broadcasting in its country?

That situation will no doubt serve as a reminder of the fight for freedom that occurred several decades ago, via radiophonic waves and which such regimes tried their best to jam.

It is a difficult question because we can see that what conflicted with our democratic values and what we wish to prohibit in their name can also be a path to freedom, challenge and struggle.

But do we have the right, in the name of our certainties, to interfere in another culture ?

We all know that the reply is not a legal but rather a philosophical one : are our humanist values universal ?

THOUGHTS ON THE DEVELOPMENT
OF CASE-LAW

BY

Jean-Jacques GOMEZ

First Vice President of the Paris regional court

President,

I have often had the occasion to say it :

« The Internet has enormous virtues. It is a marvellous means of communication. It is also a fantastic tool and cultural resource. Moreover, it has become the virtually essential medium for the expansion of economic and financial activities. Finally, it gives all its users an impression that they have personal control over things and events way beyond traditional concepts ».

However, as I emphasised during the recent colloquium organised by the CNIL [*Commission Nationale de l'Informatique et des Libertés : organisation dedicated to information technology and civil rights in France*] :

« This feeling of freedom and absolute control over their actions, often encouraged by libertarian ideas, has given some Internet users the idea that the Internet also places them outside the entire body of rules that govern society and which are born of many and necessary compromises ».

Convinced that they were able to behave as they liked on the Internet without any constraints, these Internet users, either through conviction or naivety, gradually settled into an absolute certainty of impunity and in practical terms that very soon manifested itself in infringements of respect for private life, the right of individuals to their image, breaches of intellectual property law, incidences of counterfeiting, parasitic activities, hacking into computer programmes etc.

All these phenomena were magnified by the multiplying and instantaneous nature of actions on the Internet.

However :

« life in society has its demands and constraints in order to ensure respect for basic values and the protection of individuals ». And gradually, as a reaction to this uncivil, deviant or unlawful behaviour, there was a demand for a return to the respect of these values which form the basis of life in society both in all our democratic countries in Europe as well as in the United States. Established case-law on the subject demonstrates that clearly.

We know that in order to cause this search for a democratic regulation of the Internet to fail, some people then thought that by misapplying their purpose and it seems that it was a good idea, they could use the most favourable provisions drawn from the democratic institutions, in particular those relating to freedom of speech by choosing, for example, as a « home base » the country deemed to be the most open and flexible on the subject. That is to say the United States. That has recently been demonstrated to us in all its « legal » coolness in the judgment given by the San José Court on the application from Yahoo Inc seeking a ruling that it is impossible to make the decision known in France as the « Yahoo decision » enforceable in the United States because it would breach the First Amendment of the American Constitution.

Does that mean that we are now completely disarmed and unable to combat infringements against our laws and the rights of those who seek protection from our courts ? A simple reading of the Yahoo decision given in the United States would imply that everyone is afforded wide immunity and accordingly, even those who might transmit messages that breach human rights and offer services that break the laws of other countries, inasmuch as they might invoke the protection of the First Amendment of the American Constitution.

I do not think so because each national State has an obligation to enforce its laws and to offer its inhabitants the legal protection to which they are entitled. And in the much talked about Yahoo case that legal protection was implemented.

Let us briefly summarise the context of this case : Nazi memorabilia were included in one of the lots for sale on YAHOO INC's free auction site. Now, for we Europeans and in particular, we French, not only did such a sale constitute a breach of domestic criminal laws, even though they resulted from a decree, but it offended the collective memory of the country which was deeply hurt by Nazi atrocities. French associations then decided to react, firstly by approaching Yahoo. Then by going to court.

As I have already pointed out during the CNIL colloquium, these associations certainly did not imagine that their application was going to cause such an upheaval in the Internet world and that it was going to upset the very « idea » of the Internet that was current at the time.

Let us remember all those voices that were raised to assert that the Internet was not designed to tolerate any authoritarian regulation whatsoever since the very operation of the network was the global result of a disconcerted action by a multitude of actors and that the dynamic balance that was established derived from the product of those actions and not from a predefined plan, and the arguments that were supposed to justify the refusal of any regulation.

The first argument centred on the very organisation of the network. It was not possible to envisage any authoritarian regulation whatsoever because such regulation, if it were to prove necessary, would come from the network itself. To reiterate one of the expectations of the decision given in the so-called « *J'accuse contre les FAI* » case, I will say that there is no point in hoping for even a minimum self-regulation of the Internet, an enormous network and unfortunately one that is given over to excess and the « all powerful I want » to use one of Alain Finkielkraut's expressions.

The second, which is still one of the main topics of discussion between legal experts the world over consisted of saying that there was no connecting link with France that could justify the jurisdiction of the French courts within the meaning of private international law, as this site was intended for American and not French Internet users. Can we reasonably talk of services reserved for a category of individuals or nationals of certain countries when the Internet offers services to the entire world in real time and instantaneously without any consideration for geographical borders. Should we not therefore reconsider the application of the rules of private international law ?

The third concerned freedom of speech. Any binding decision, especially for filtering, would be an infringement against freedom of speech. However, which freedom of speech are we talking about ?

No doubt that lambasted by Mrs COQUIO when she gave her statement during the proceedings « *J'accuse contre les FAI* », that is to
say this freedom in the expression of which one cannot find « a
shadow of a thought or the shadow of a democratic opinion » and
which only expresses « the provocation and contempt for the other,
mainly, contempt for the victims ». We will never share that view
of freedom of speech. And I think that our American friends understand us more and more and will end up by aligning themselves
with our European concept of a responsible use of freedom of
speech, aware of the danger that they also face from all the deviant
behaviour observed in the use of that freedom.

Finally, the fourth two-pronged argument : users – not technical
service providers – had to be more responsible – but above all, it
was not possible to filter Internet users – yes to the training of
Internet users, yes to the training of the consumer. However, that
is not enough. The technical intermediaries will need to be more
exposed and more committed. If any serious thought is to be given
to this matter, we would then have to be resigned to the idea that
nothing can be done for the « victims » of the abusive use of the
Internet, except the wealthier amongst them would have to resign
themselves to going to the United States in order to exercise their
rights, in the knowledge that they will require a great deal of time
and money. And would that obligation not mean that it is at odds
with the equality of access to justice by citizens ?

Is it really the Internet to which we aspire ? the Internet that we
wish to transfer to our children and share with the greatest number
of people ?

I do not think so. Nevertheless, let us be optimistic. Because
there are some signs that show that we are on the right track.
Accordingly, you might have noticed that since the judgment given
on 20 November 2000 in the Yahoo case and notwithstanding the
media interest surrounding the application brought by the company
of the same name before the Californian court, the company in
question made a significant about-turn by choosing to replace the
free services with paying services, and by saying that henceforth, it
would no longer accept Nazi memorabilia that make reference to
odious or racist undertakings, in its auction sales. The result
obtained exceeded all that could have been envisaged. Let us
remember that the decision of 20 November 2000 had only required

a simple device to filter Internet users operating from French territory and according to experts, such filtering was entirely feasible. Some time later, the E Bay company took the same decision.

How should we interpret the Yahoo Inc. decision ? Should we regard it merely as the introduction of a new commercial strategy ? Let us give it the benefit of the doubt. But no doubt at least part of the *raison d'être* of this new strategy lies in the fact that it observed (an observation that many others are now making) that victims of deviant behaviour on the Internet will no longer tolerate it and there is a danger that permanent harm might be done to its image and brand.

The sudden emergence of ethical funds in economic and financial transactions is not unconnected to the current challenges either.

That is another reason to be optimistic.

Case-law, which is becoming more refined every day, contributes to the evidence of this positive evolution in all areas. Trade mark law faced with domain names and virtual shopping malls and therefore counterfeiting, copyright faced with unlawful representations and use, the right to one's image faced with the multiple manipulations and unlawful uses, to name only these areas, all have been at the centre of numerous proceedings at the end of which the courts have stated that all the legal restrictions were applicable on the Internet...

In conclusion, I shall say that the court cases that have received most media attention, have shown a definite and continuing opposition between the tenants of an uncontrolled and borderless Internet and the tenants of a responsible Internet. The technical argument often invoked by actors of the Internet and, in particular, by technical service providers in terms of the effectiveness and difficulty of filtering devices, should not be underestimated. But now, the question is whether the Internet is for the service of man and his development or whether it should remain the business of technicians and Internet gurus alone. That is one of the challenges of the imminent information society law. Another just as important question : can we and should we continue to judge Internet disputes by reference to principles drawn up in a legal framework which has not been able to grasp (and with good reason) all the issues of the Internet or should we change them to take into account the reality of the Internet based on contradictions and especially numerous and almost daily challenges to human rights that warrant an immediate adaptation of the judicial response. Should we reconsider the judicial response in order to adapt it to the challenges of the Internet ? We must not continue to take refuge in a restricted concept of the application of the rule of law, regardless of the displeasure of those critics and commentators of our decisions who give the impression that they cannot see things changing. The courts are already heavily involved in this necessary change. However, no doubt we should also include this question in connection with the discussions on the Internet Law because our courts must be provided with means to enable them to adapt the judicial response to these new challenges arising from the emergence of the net.

Of course, such discussions should also include acts of legal cooperation, firstly within the European Community and then at international level so that all Internet users can be offered the legal security that they are entitled to expect.

Naturally, the debate is still open.

Thank you.

USING THE INTERNET TO MANAGE COMPLEX CIVIL LITIGATION

BY

Larry M. SMUKLER

Associate Justice, New Hampshire, Superior Court

Introduction

As the world is moving towards electronic document management and Internet data exchange and storage, court systems are lagging. The filing and service of pleadings by the parties and the issuance of orders and notices by the court continues to be accomplished by the printing of paper documents, conventional photocopying and the postal service. The system sags under the weight of heavy dockets. It is particularly unsuitable for multi-district civil litigation involving many parties and complex technical issues. This paper is a case study of how the New Hampshire Court adopted one method of using existing conventional Internet tools to manage several consolidated complex product liability cases. It examines the application of Internet technologies to four consolidated tobacco cases.

I. – The New Hampshire court system

The New Hampshire Superior Court is a statewide general jurisdiction court. The court's 29 justices preside over criminal, civil, equity and marital cases, as well as miscellaneous appeals from the lower courts, municipal and state agencies. The court is also responsible for all of the state's jury trials. There are eleven court locations in the state's ten counties, along with separate administrative offices. The justices may be assigned to any court location on a month-to-month basis.

II. – The tobacco cases

The New Hampshire tobacco cases were initiated in December of 1999. The estates and representatives of four decedents brought wrongful death actions against multiple tobacco companies. The plaintiffs seek damages based on several legal theories, including strict products liability, negligence, fraud, breach of warranty, and a violation of the state's consumer protection act. The cases were brought in two counties. They were consolidated for pre-trial purposes in one of the counties where the cases were brought and assigned to a justice who generally presides in a third county. Thus, the case file is physically maintained at the courthouse in Manchester, New Hampshire, while the presiding justice is generally located in Laconia, New Hampshire–a distance of over an hour by automobile. By March of 2000, the paper involved in preliminary pre-trial skirmishes more than filled a banker's box. All pleadings and orders are required to be copied and served on 33 attorneys. There are two plaintiffs' attorneys in two New Hampshire locations. The remaining attorneys represent the various tobacco company defendants. In addition to local counsel operating from five New Hampshire offices, there are the out-of-state counsel in locations as diverse as Boston, Massachusetts, Cleveland, Ohio, New York City, and Kansas City, Missouri.

A. – THE CONVENTIONAL PROCESS

Every pleading – whether a routine request to admit out-of-state counsel or a lengthy complex motion to dismiss – required many steps.

The party had to copy the pleadings and send them to all others on the service list.

The party must also file the paper with the court in Manchester, either by mail, overnight delivery or physical delivery.

The clerk of the Manchester court makes the appropriate entries in the court's case management system, which is a 1980s vintage DOS based system.

The box containing the file would then be physically transported from Manchester to the presiding justice's location in Laconia.

The presiding justice would examine the file and determine whether a hearing is necessary.

If so, this must be communicated to the clerk of the Manchester court, who would make the appropriate docket entries and send copies of paper hearing notices to the service list.

After the presiding justice wrote an order on the motion, the case file would be transported back to the clerk of the Manchester court, who would then again make the appropriate docket entries, copy and send the order to those on the service list.

The cumbersome nature of the process is manifest from its mere description.

B. – INTERNET SOLUTION

The difficulties in managing complex civil litigation were compounded by the logistical process inherent in conventional paper filing. An Internet solution involving electronic filing would appear to be a natural fit. The presiding justice identified a vendor – Verilaw – who was willing to provide such a solution.

Verilaw offered to establish a web site where the all pleadings could be posted. The web site would be on a Verilaw server physically located in a secure commercial « server farm » facility. The parties and the court were presented with several alternative methods to file pleadings for posting on the site. The first and least complicated method is to upload the document to the Verilaw site through the Internet. Verilaw accepts any conventional electronic format, allowing a party to continue to use an existing word processing system such as MS Word or WordPerfect. Second, the document could be faxed after Verilaw generated a fax cover sheet through its web site. Third, paper documents could be physically delivered to Verilaw either by an overnight delivery service or by conventional post. Under any method, Verilaw would date and time stamp the document and any attached exhibits and convert them to PDF format. The PDF format preserves all formatting and page breaks of an original electronic document or a scanned paper or faxed document and is readable by the freely downloadable ubiquitous Adobe Acrobat Reader.

Within 10 minutes of the filing of a document, the party making the filing would receive an e-mail confirmation. The e-mail would contain a link to the document on the web site. All other parties and the court would simultaneously receive an e-mail notice with a similar link. The vendor offered the option of receiving e-mail notices as documents were being filed or as one bundled message delivered at the end of a day. A party could easily switch between simultaneous or bundled delivery through a « preferences » link on the web site.

The vendor was very interested in undertaking the project and, consequently, was willing to do it at an initial cost of $10,000 plus a fee of $10 per filed pleading. The filing fee applies whether the pleading is a simple procedural request (such as a two-page motion to admit out-of-state counsel) or a dispositive substantive motion consisting of several hundred pages of legal argument and attached exhibits. The filing fee was waived for documents filed by the court.

C. – ADOPTION AND DEPLOYMENT
OF THE INTERNET SOLUTION

Because of political and budget constraints, the Internet solution could not be adopted if there was any cost to the court system. Thus, the parties would be required to pay. The presiding justice was willing to require the parties to pay nominal fees; however, costs of this magnitude must be voluntarily shouldered by the parties. To ascertain whether the parties would accept the Internet Solution, the court scheduled a structuring conference of counsel. Verilaw was invited to make a presentation—first to court administrative and technical personnel and then to the parties.

As with anything that is a departure from the time-honoured procedures, the parties were initially skeptical of the proposed change and, particularly, the requirement that they bear the cost. The scepticism diminished as counsel began to understand the scope of the proposal and the parties agreed to the Internet Solution. There were many reasons favouring the Internet approach that the parties found persuasive, including :

Cost. While the parties incur the initial set-up cost and ongoing filing fees, they save on other costs, such as printing, copying, paying for physical delivery of paper documents to the court and to other parties. The cost analysis is not simple. For example, while the filing party saves copying costs, the remaining parties may pay a new cost of printing an electronic document. The parties' experience indicates that the overall cost is no more than the cost of the conventional paper process and, indeed, the cost savings increase as the number of parties increase. Thus, there may well be an overall cost reduction.

Convenience. The process of communicating formally with the court and with other parties is simpler. Additionally, the attorneys have a little more time to complete their work. This is because the court indicated that a party would be in compliance with a deadline if the Verilaw timestamp showed that it had been filed by 11 :59 PM on the due date. Previously, the document had to be physically delivered to the court before it closed at 4 :30 PM. Filing and service could now be accomplished from an attorney's desktop by a simple click of the « submit » button on the website. The court also provided that it would deem timely any pleading that was late due to any technical difficulties caused by counsel's Internet Service Provider or by Verilaw.

The Technology Itself. Any observer understands that the practice of law will be changing substantially in the near and mid-future. When the parties thought about the inevitability of coming changes and how the Internet solution is consistent with those changes, it appeared to be much less of a « bleeding edge » process. Indeed, the court and the parties embraced the opportunity to get experience with the technology so that the strengths of the process could be enhanced and the weaknesses could be identified and fixed. In addition, the court and the parties recognised that Internet solution was an elegant fit to the paper process logistical difficulties in these particular cases.

After considering the above factors and an opportunity to consult among themselves and their clients, the parties agreed to the Internet solution. The $10,000 initial cost was charged proportionally to all parties, reducing the cost significantly on a per party basis. The parties individually pay the $10 filing fee with every filing–regardless of the size of the documents. The court also undertook the significant effort of scanning all the previously filed paper documents and delivering them to Verilaw. This enhanced the website by allowing the posting of all pleadings from the beginning of the case. Thus, a party or the court has access to the complete case file either via the Internet or by download and storage on a hard disk or CD.

From the court's point of view, the solution is a vast but imperfect improvement. Portions of the process continue to be awkward. First, the tobacco cases are subject to appellate review by the New Hampshire Supreme Court. There can be no certainty about that court's acceptance of an electronic file. Thus, the superior court determined that it would continue to maintain a conventional paper file in Manchester. Additionally, because of the court's outdated case management system, it was senseless to attempt to automate data entry. Last, the court does lag in technology. While the court personnel have e-mail, only the court's administrative office has full Internet access. Such full Internet access has been promised to the presiding justice and to the court clerk in Manchester, but it has not yet happened.

Thus, tobacco case processing using the Internet solution still requires several otherwise unnecessary steps.

When a pleading is filed electronically, both the Manchester clerk and the presiding justice receive immediate e-mail notification.

The presiding justice downloads the pleading by his personal Internet service either at home or by using his dial-up connection at the court. The court's orders are uploaded in the same manner.

The court's administrative office downloads the pleading or the court's order and sends it by e-mail to the Manchester clerk.

The Manchester clerk prints the document, keys the docket information into the court's case management system and binds the document into the court's paper file.

The process should become more streamlined when the court's administrative office is able to provide the anticipated full Internet access to the Manchester clerk and the presiding justice. Until the court deploys a more up-to-date case management system, however, the clerk will continue to be required to key docket information into the system by hand.

D. – PROBLEMS

One benefit of this type of project is the opportunity to solve anticipated problems and to identify and attempt to resolve unanticipated problems that arise during operation. In this case, we encountered one anticipated problem and several surprises.

The anticipated problem pertained to the requirement of attorney's signatures on pleadings. Documents prepared on a word processor and uploaded by Internet do not accommodate handwritten signatures. After consideration, the court did not require attorneys to obtain and use digital signatures. Because an attorney could not log into the website without a user name and password, the court deemed a pleading filed via the website to be authentic. As with many issues, the solution was apparent from an analogy to the paper process. Attorneys filing pleadings by mail or at a counter of the clerk's office do not have to identify themselves. If an attorney claims later that someone fraudulently file a pleading with that attorney's signature (a practically non-existent problem), the court would hold a hearing, make the appropriate finding and grant appropriate relief. The process does not differ for an electronic pleading. If an attorney claims that someone fraudulently logged onto the website with that attorney's user name and password, the court would likewise hold a hearing, make the appropriate finding and grant appropriate relief.

Several problems were not anticipated. First, the ease of filing facilitates sloppiness. Because a document can go directly from a computer to the web, proofreading is more difficult. Some of the pleadings filed by the parties have errors that would be obvious if they had been printed and proofed, sometimes necessitating an otherwise unnecessary filing of amended pleadings. The court is not immune. In the conventional process, a court order is always subject to a second reading before it is issued. A new process that accomplishes the same objective had to be developed now that orders are being directly uploaded from the computer. Second, the website initially did not specify the size of the documents. This works fine for small documents, but some of the uploaded documents contained over 200 pages of scanned exhibits–a PDF file of over 17MB. For users with dial-up connections, an unanticipated download of this size could unduly tie up a computer. When this problem was brought to the attention of Verilaw, it modified the site to include the size of the document, which resolved the problem. Last, the site does not correlate to the document index used by the court in its paper file. Verilaw is looking into modifying the site to accomplish this correlation.

E. – PUBLIC ACCESS

One collateral issue was the question of public access. Court papers are public documents unless sealed by court order. The web site was only available to those who logged in with a user name and password. Because public response to the project would provide useful information, Verilaw agreed to reproduce the case file on a mirrored public site that would not require a user name and password. That has been accomplished. Any member of the public has searchable access to the entire case file via the following URL : http://www.nhtobacco.verilaw.com.

Some of the parties were concerned that the public site would compromise their ability to maintain confidential information. Initially, the court addressed this issue by permitting the parties to file confidential pleadings conventionally, with an accompanying motion to seal. In a request for reconsideration, some parties raised a valid point. While the court's order addressed the situation where a party knew that the pleadings might contain confidential information, it did not address the situation where a party attached documents to a pleading that a different party believed should be kept confidential. The Verilaw solution was to program a 10-day delay between the filing of pleadings on the secure site and their posting on the public site. Even after 10 days, the pleading would not be posted on the public site until the presiding justice specifically approved such posting. The parties can therefore request confidentiality by motion at any time within the 10-day period. The presiding justice authorises or prohibits public posting through access to an administrator's screen created by Verilaw. Verilaw charged $6,000 to program this mechanism–a charge that was voluntarily assumed by the concerned parties.

Public access is an area of increased concern. Indeed, the National Center for State Courts in the United States has created a web based information resource on the issue, which may be accessed at : http://www.ncsc.dni.us/ncsc/tis/tis99/pubacs99/pubaces1.htm

The New Hampshire 10-day delay appears to be the first application of such a mechanism. It is a mechanism that works well on a single-case basis. If used in a general electronic filing system, the mechanism will require modification, perhaps by automating public posting after 10-days unless the judge specifically seals the pleading.

Conclusion

Government decision-making generally involves a process of careful study and deliberative analysis. With the moving target of technology, the model does not work. A decision made under the conventional process would only result in the adoption of outdated solutions. In the technology area, a better slogan is « deploy and fix ». The application of web based case management in the New Hampshire tobacco cases is an example of how modern technology can be quickly applied. It is also an example of how the quick deployment of such a system on a pilot basis provides information so that planners can avoid otherwise unanticipated problems at the time the system is generally applied.

DISCUSSION

Ana Palacio

We can take at least two questions, three if the replies are brief. Who is going to fire first?

Ah, Mrs Rouchaud, I didn't see you Welcome, Mrs Rouchaud. Mrs Rouchaud is one of the authors of the Commission's initial proposals in this vast field of judicial cooperation in civil matters; it was truly pioneering work, I mean, truly pioneering. Mrs Rouchaud.

Anne-Marie Rouchaud

Thank you, Mrs Palacio. We have heard a great deal said over the last two days about the laws applicable to disputes on the Net, and the thoughts we have heard from the participants call for a discussion in which I should like to involve you. It is quite usual, especially within the Community, to pit the method of resolving choice of laws or the law applicable to a dispute on the Internet through private international law, which would be called the traditional method of resolving conflicts of laws, against the law of the country of origin; the latter would be a solution that would run counter to the solution through choice-of laws and which would therefore tend to apply in all cases. This method would be – and I heard you describe it, Mrs Palacio – in fact I do not know whether you used that word but I interpreted it as such, – as a more modern, more Community-orientated method for resolving the problems. The traditional private international law is used to taking into account a number of parameters in order to determine jurisdiction and the applicable law which are, and I say that loosely and non-exhaustively, the socio-professional class of the parties, the closeness of the judge to the court and the dispute and the closeness of the parties to the dispute; all in all, a number of parameters that fulfil the objectives of legislative policy. Then you also said that traditional private international law is a method that presumes mistrust between States, and which also presupposes the existence of borders. You then draw the conclusion that this method would no doubt no longer be usable at intra-Community level. I therefore ask myself a question : in the end is there no longer any legal border at Community level in the absence of total harmonisation? I think that, all the same, we are still a long way from a harmonised Community-wide law. A great many directives and regulations on consumer matters are regulations and directives for minimal harmonisation. I must also say that in my view, harmonisation of the choice-of-law rules is nevertheless aimed at preventing such mistrust and establishing relationships of trust between the States, inviting some to abandon their inordinate choice of rules concerning jurisdiction or law and have confidence, let us say, in the jurisdiction of other States. I should like to move on somewhat from this quarrel of ancient and modern, of private international law as opposed to the rule of the country of origin, which, moreover, in my opinion, when it is interpreted as applying to all relations of private law, does not become any more or less a choice-of-law rule. Regardless of what you call this method, when, you have to choose between two laws that are likely to apply, you are settling a conflict of laws. I therefore think that we must move on from this quarrel and commit ourselves to thinking about the objectives that we wish to protect; in my view, it is still the most effective way of making progress – objectives to protect some of the parties in contracts or in obligations denied by the Net. I am not taking sides one way or the other, that is not my role here. I am simply saying that to choose the law of the country of origin is not impartial. It is not impartial for the service providers – yesterday we heard Mr Cousin from the GBDe, and we know very well that for a long time the GBDe has argued for the law of the country of origin whereas, for its part, the TACD is arguing for the law of the destination country. Accordingly, the choice of law is not impartial in any respect. I therefore think that we need to take the objectives into consideration, that seems to me to be more important than the technique of traditional private international law or that of the law of the country of origin. I believe that we need to know exactly which objectives should be favoured; and at intra-Community level, consumer protection is an objective that has the same legitimacy as the development of the internal market. Thank you.

Ana Palacio

Thank you Mrs Rouchaud. I may perhaps ask Professor Berger, with the option of adding a comment myself.

Professor.

Thank you.

Jean-Sylvestre Bergé

People are always derisory when technology is created for technology. No private internationalist or legal expert will deny that or he is a fool, and therefore, I think that you are right to say that we must not reduce these considerations to technical issues, even though they have their place and their time. What I see, for example is that I took your model of satellites as an analogy and, on the whole, agree with what you say, there are solutions today that concern the rules of private law.

I mean beyond rules of public law and control to find out who may use certain Hertzian waves, which are the regulatory authorities, etc., there are considerations of pure private law which have nevertheless been absorbed by choice-of-law rules which clearly award jurisdiction to the law of the country of emission. When this country of emission is in the Community, there is a whole series of connecting factors that are specified by legislation. Personally, I am very much in favour of these rules, in that they are not neutral and meet a dual concern : to encourage free movement with minimal compliance with the rules we have given ourselves, that is to say that it is permissible to apply other laws provided that such laws meet a minimum threshold of protection. And they even provide exemption clauses, that is to say, hypothetical situations, you know, on the origin, where this jurisdiction of the country of emission is left out because we are making the transition to non-protection thresholds; and that is wholly exceptional in Community law, since in Community law, in principle, one never talks about reciprocity. So, you see that we have come a very long way, including in the creation of exceptions to Community principles. Therefore, I am in total agreement with your arguments; you just need to understand that the debate is still a traditional-modern or modern-traditional debate, you can call it what you like. When you explain – for my part, I am constantly confronted with it in my discussions with colleagues – when you explain to someone the way in which it could operate and someone replies « But where is the Savignian theory in that ? » we are not speaking the same language. It cannot be denied, and it would be a mistake to deny it, i.e. to say « Listen, stay in Savigny (***); we are going to continue to evolve on a higher plane ». Therefore, it is the means of finding the dialogue. And the way of finding the dialogue is not to force reality. The rule of the country of origin, with regard to jurisdiction, is not a choice-of-law rule; that does not make sense. It is a rule that poses the very simple idea that a service provider established in a Member State may, in principle, freely offer his services in the other Member States. And when there are obstacles, it matters little whether they derive from the law of the country of origin or the host country, these obstacles must be justified by overriding reasons of general interest, and then we come to Community approach. We must not say that it is a question of conflict of laws. Let us then draw from that a legislative rule of jurisdiction as has been done with regard to satellites, let it be deduced, as it was to some extent with regard to data. That is intelligent, that is to say that continuity is created between a Community principle and a tradition of private international law. However, the mistake would be to see private international law where there is none. I prefer to say that there is no private international law at this level because we are above it, not in terms of hierarchy but in terms of concerns of private international law and, sooner or later, we are going to ask ourselves the question « Right, yes, does the applicable law have a tortious attitude or does it have a particular type of contract ? »

I am not necessarily replying to your comments because I do not think that we were in opposition, but you are right to provide this information. However, I think that we need to provide it in both directions. Otherwise, it is incomplete.

Ana Palacio

I agree with what Professor Berger said. I think that, obviously, when there is little time, one tends to paint pictures in broad outlines and that always lends itself to caricature. If anything is subtle, it is the law in general, and I should say private international law in particular, it is really the subtlest of the subtlest. That having been said, I honestly believe that there is a simplification of issues of confidence here. I think that if there is a challenge in constructing this area of justice, it is obviously to overcome such mistrust. But what should be put first, the horse or the cart? And there, Mrs Rouchaud, I believe that the debate has always been promising for the construction of Europe. The construction of Europe takes place through similar debates to that which we are having, on the problem that we have had for some time between – I should not say between you and I – but between the Commission and Parliament. And we are seeking solutions to resolve them. It is not that you are wrong or that those who have a more outspoken position – I should not say more modern but rather in the sense of integration – are wrong. That is to say, why has this problem not been encountered with the Catalan civil law which is different from the civil law that applies in Madrid? I mean, this principle is automatically and naturally applied. Why must there be such differences between a product that is sold from Barcelona to Madrid and a product that is sold from Barcelona to Montpellier? Why? I know that there must be some restrictions in the internal market if only, for example, the language, which poses real problems for entering an external jurisdiction. However, having said that, I think that if we do not try and overcome the problems and we wait for trust, we may have to wait a long time! I gave the example of a warrant for arrest. A warrant for arrest is really based on that trust. It is not yet finalised, but let us hope that the Commission's proposal, the legislation that is being debated both in Parliament and in the Council, will be passed; and it is legislation based on this principle. Obviously, we can then make any comments that we like, but that is my position, and I very much respect yours, you know. Another question.

Catherine Kessedjian

If I may, an observation, then a question. I do not think that one it is the opposite. Private international law allows a foreign law to be enforced in France. On the contrary, it is based on trust with regard to foreign laws, on the principle of recognition of foreign judgments and the ability of a French judge to enforce a foreign law, which always surprises students when one begins to teach them private international law at the beginning of the year. It is based on the international harmony of solutions, it is a pity to raise trust and mistrust. I even think that the entire challenge for private international law is to continue to allow foreign laws to be enforced and to continue to use the exemption of public policy in a reasonable way, so that we do not routinely revert to the name of the public policy, the law of the defendant's place of residence, French law when it is a French judge to whom the matter is referred. The question is addressed to Mrs Christiane Féral-Schuhl. The system that you propose is very interesting and obviously, you cannot expand on it in six minutes but are you considering implementing it in the same way according to whether it concerns intra-Community or international relations and according to whether it concerns civil and commercial law and criminal law, since at the end you mentioned the convention on cybercrime? You told us that we need to establish conventions; in the absence of such conventions, how can your system operate?

Ana Palacio

As far as trust and mistrust are concerned, I emphasise, it really is a caricature. I could go into the details, I am prepared to explain to you. However, all the same, I think that for a French legal expert there are still differences between the understanding of the Spanish legal system – where there should be differences – and the understanding by the same legal expert, judge or legal operator in general terms – of a let's say the Moroccan legal system, or that of a non-member country. We must not forget that in Europe we finally have a plan for integration, joined together in one way or another, but a plan for political integration which necessarily must lead to certain conclusions. But we shall speak about that later. Maître Féral-Schuhl.

Maître Christiane Féral-Schuhl

Thank you. You have given me the opportunity to pick up a little on my speech. I had the privilege of pleading before judge Gomez on many occasions, notably in some cases that he referred to a while ago. I think that, in the approach and awareness I have of the problems that have been raised by the applicants, the citizens who have been faced with this problem, I have assessed the dual obstacle that can be created both by the difficulty, quite simply, of instituting proceedings which will be lengthy in the long term, even by an enforcement procedure, and their natural tendency to be directed towards intermediaries, the access providers, as, on the whole, that has always been the accepted approach. The second characteristic, is that it always involves extremely sensitive issues of public policy, and that is why, in the circumstances I outlined, I did not speak about civil or commercial cases. However, for me, the scope here, or the necessity in all cases to find urgent solutions, is primarily aimed at cases in which public policy is involved. And whoever says public policy is primarily talking about criminal cases, cases in which in all instances there is a criminal law. Revisionism was a magnificent illustration in the past, since there was both the (***) case against Renater and others five years ago and the *J'accuse* case which was mentioned a while ago, in which two cultures that are both democratic have a completely different understanding of these points of view : in the one, the first amendment of the constitution was invoked and in the other country, it was a criminal law. Therefore, to reply to your first question, I would say that in my view, the proposal has no chance of succeeding unless it is extremely limited and confined, and that is why I outlined these three conditions. With regard to the second aspect of your question, which was Community or international related, it seems to me that the difficulty today is based primarily, in any case in the cases that we have heard, on the European approach as opposed to the United States approach. I think that solutions are emerging at European level : particularly with regard to civil, and commercial cases, one can see solutions coming to the fore. Perhaps the solutions will be different but for the moment, it is a global approach; well, at least in all the cases that I wanted to present as being global. As far as objections are concerned, I refer you to my report which is online, only recently but it is online, for help.

Ana Palacio

Well, thank you. And so we shall end this afternoon's first round table.

2. – ALTERNATIVE WAYS OF DEALING WITH CONFLICTS

AN INTRODUCTION
TO ACTIVITIES RELATED TO ONLINE
DISPUTE RESOLUTION
IN THE INFORMATION SOCIETY
AT EU LEVEL (1)

BY

Timothy FENOULHET

Directorate-general information society
European commission

The development of the Information Society and rapid growth in electronic commerce will inevitably give rise to disputes and therefore place new demands on the different parties to settle them. Some of these new demands are already being observed today.

The provision of fair and effective means to settle Information Society disputes is therefore increaslingly important, not least because many of these disputes will arise across geographical and jurisdictional borders and because providing forms of redress that are readily accessible to users will contribute to the creation of a climate of trust and confidence on the Internet, which is essential for the widespread use of e-commerce.

These observations have been acknowledged by the European Union (EU) on repeated occasions, including at the Lisbon Special European Council of March 2000. At Lisbon, the European Council called on « the Commission and the Council to consider how to promote consumer confidence in electronic commerce, in particular through alternative dispute resolution systems ». At the Feira European Council in June 2000, the Commission's eEurope Action Plan was endorsed. A key action within the eEurope Action Plan is « promoting alternative dispute resolution ».

---

(1) Please note that the remarks made in this article represent the personal views of the author and are not necessarily the official position of the European Commission.

In its Communication of 13th March 2001 « eEurope2002 : Impact and Priorities » (2), the Commission took stock of the progress made on the implementation of the eEurope Action Plan and presented a list of priority areas which require further attention. Among these, the Commission underlined that « the rapid development of online dispute settlement systems and codes of conduct for e-commerce in the EU and at global level is a matter of urgency to increase consumer confidence and business predictability ». The Commission announced that it would « made concrete proposals on how to further their development and diffusion ».

It was at the Stockholm European Council of 23 and 24 March 2001 that the Commission announced its « intention to present a Communication promoting online dispute resolution systems », as was recorded in the Presidency Conclusions. This Communication is currently under preparation.

I. – Settling disputes in the information society : the cross-border dimension and alternatives to the court system

Just like in the offline world, we can expect and are already observing various forms of dispute emerging online. These disputes typically occur either between businesses or between businesses and consumers in contractual relationships just as they do offline.

But there are also new forms of dispute that are appearing that are specific to the online world and the Information Society. One notable example is disputes over domain names also known as *cybersquatting*, but we can also expect disputes over the abuse of personal data (privacy), liability for content, defamation, breaches of IPR such as copyright violation of web-content and software.

Another dimension to disputes in the Information Society is that they are increasingly likely to involve parties located across geographical (and jurisdictional) borders. This cross-border dimension is an added complication for the settlement of disputes and entaills extra costs for the parties, legal insecurity and complex and long-winded deliberations about which court or law to apply. The

---

(2) COM(2001)140 final.

impact of resulting business uncertainties on consumer confidence is a major obstacle to the growth of e-commerce in Europe.

Again, in the offline world, in recent years we have observed the increased use by businesses and citizens alike, of alternatives to the judicial system for settling disputes. Typical examples include negotiation, mediation/conciliation and arbitration. These have often been found to be rather effective in bringing parties together to resolve their differences quickly and amicably, without requiring a costly recourse to the courts. These alternative forms of dispute settlement are commonly referred to as alternative dispute resolution or ADR.

Yet with the rise in cross-border transactions, ADR bodies or services, which traditionally require face-to-face contact also need to adapt to the realms of Internet.

A. – ODR MAY BE THE ANSWER

Indeed, with the rising popularity of electronic commerce and the resulting growth in cross-border transactions – which are likely to increase yet further in the EU with the introduction of the Euro and the functioning of the Internal Market – there has been a new interest in using ICT technologies to provide online dispute resolution (ODR) services, particularly for settling cross-border disputes which arise on the Internet. Moreover, ODR can also be helpful in settling cross-border disputes which result offline – especially in the Internal Market – thus easing the tasks of various ADR bodies especially in the self-regulated industries such as financial services.

This potential has been underlined, in particular, in the course of the difficult debate about jurisdiction and applicable law on the Internet, notably at the time of the adoption of the « Brussels Regulation » (3). An international convention, the Hague Convention, is currently in the course of being drafted (4). ODR is seen as being a possible solution for a) preventing the potential exposure of online businesses to the jurisdictions of a range of foreign countries from which a consumer can access their website (country of destination), and b) avoiding obliging consumers to seek redress in a court

---

(3) Http://www.europa.eu.int/eur-lex/en/lif/dat/2001/en–301R0044.html
(4) Http://www.europa.eu.int/comm/justice–home/unit/civil/audition10–01/en/resume–juin–2001.pdf

in a foreign country – the country of the supplier (country of origin). In other words, ODR affords the possibility of avoiding going to court (especially in a foreign country). However, should one of the parties so choose, or should the ADR process break down without an agreement, the court option is always left open.

B. – What is ODR ?

ICTs, and notably web-based technologies are already being used, mainly in North America, as a vehicle to allow companies and consumers to resolve their disputes through online contact (via a website, e-mail, video-conferencing, etc.) with a mediator or arbitrator. These systems typically provide a confidential web space in which the case can be handled and through which a remotely located mediator can facilitate reaching a compromise solution on the basis of the end goals and the evidence provided by the disputing parties. Examples include : insurance claims, refunds on unsatisfactory goods, online auctions etc.

These ODR systems vary in their sophistication (some may just use e-mail, whilst others have sophisticated web-based platforms), but offer both advantages and disadvantages. Among the advantages are speed, efficiency, low cost, and their capacity to bring parties located in different countries or at some distance together (i.e. virtual collocation). Among the disadvantages are the challenge to mediators and to disputing parties to settle a dispute without face-to-face contact (though video-conferencing may help) and the need for specific ICT training for mediators. Other more technical challenges include document processing, ensuring confidentiality and ensuring that such services are available in different languages. Authentication of the identity of the parties and accreditation of mediators will also need some attention. The issue of commercial viability of such systems should not be underestimated. It may be difficult to find appropriate business models for such expensive and sophisticated systems particularly if they are to be provided free of charge to consumers by private organisations. Finally, there is one remaining important difficulty – the enforcement of ODR settlements.

C. – COMMISSION ACTIVITIES :
THE STORY SO FAR...

The Commission has been actively working to promote the use of ADR – especially for settling consumer disputes. So far as concerns using ADR to settle disputes specifically involving consumers, the Commission has adopted two recommendations (98/257/CE and 2001/310/EC (5)) which set out guidelines for ADR bodies to ensure that consumers are adequately protected. The Recommendations establish a system of notification through which Member States have notified the Commission of those ADR bodies that meet the recommended standards. These bodies are being linked through a network of clearing houses in the Member States : the European Extra-Judicial Network (EEJ-Net) (6), which will be supported by an ICT infrastructure to facilitate communication between the clearing houses and to improve access for consumers. This network is currently composed of existing ADR bodies that have no online mediation facilities. The Commission also recently launched an ADR network with the EU Member States specifically for settling disputes in the financial sector (FINNET) (7). Initiatives are also underway at international level, notably in the Global Business Dialogue on electronic commerce (GBDe), which, in September 2000, adopted a comprehensive set of guidelines for ADR (8). Other international initiatives include WIPO's ADR mechanism for settling domain name disputes, the ICC's clearing house, and work is also underway within Consumer International (CI).

The Commission has also been undertaking some technical work in the field of online dispute resolution (ODR), notably through the organisation of a series of workshops (9). The aim has been to examine the technical requirements necessary to ensure that policy and legal issues are effectively implemented by the technological means. The research has also been examining the various business models which may develop in the field of ODR.

---

(5) Http://www.europa.eu.int/comm/consumers/policy/developments/acce–just/acce–just02–en.html and http://www.europa.eu.int/comm/consumers/policy/developments/acce–just/acce–just12–en.pdf

(6) Http://www.europa.eu.int/comm/consumers/policy/developments/acce–just/acce–just07–en.html

(7) Http://www.europa.eu.int/comm/internal–market/en/finances/consumer/adr.htm

(8) Http://consumerconfidence.gbde.org/adr–rec.html

(9) Http://econfidence.jrc.it

II. – Why a communication on ODR?

A. – Objectives

The purpose of the Communication will be to bring together the results of some of the more technical work that has been undertaken to date by the Commission specifically in the field of ONLINE dispute resolution. It also aims to promote their widespread development in the EU as an important component of the rapidly emerging Information Society and eEurope. The Communication will seek to emphasise the importance of ODR in settling the increasing number of cross-border disputes in the Internal Market and beyond and to underline their potential for settling a wide variety of disputes arising specifically in the Information Society context. Moreover ODR can be considered as a tool for the empowerment of consumers in upholding their rights to fair redress.

B. – Scope

The Communication will therefore focus specifically on *ONLINE* dispute resolution involving *mediation* (i.e. settlement by consensus – see definition in Commission Recommendation 2001/310/EC (10)), and is *not* restricted to disputes involving consumers. It will emphasise the potential of ODR systems and services to help settle commercial disputes between businesses (B2B), between business and consumers as well as between consumers (B2C or C2C). Also the emerging eGovernment sector (G2C) will be considered. It will outline a range of areas, backed up with examples, where ODR may have potential (e.g. settling disputes involving abuse of personal data, copyright infringements, domain names, liability). The Communication will discuss a range of technical issues and requirements and the various possible business models, as well as commercial viability and training needs. These technical matters will be illustrated using existing case studies and examples. Reference will also be made to activities and funding possibilities within the Community IST and Ten-Telecom Programmes.

---

(10) Http://www.europa.eu.int/comm/consumers/policy/developments/acce–just/acce–just12–en.pdf

C. – Policy Conclusions and Follow Up

Finally, the Communication will set these activities and issues within both the policy context of the EU and notably the ongoing work in the area of confidence-building (« eConfidence » – see website : http://econfidence.jrc.it) on the Internet and eEurope, as well as the legal context, notably the Brussels Regulation.

In terms of policy conclusions, the role of public administrations in the governance of ODR will be highlighted, both in terms of the legal framework for ODR and of achieving a balance of incentives (« carrots and sticks ») for ODR providers and users. In particular, the Communication will point out that, especially in the consumer field, there is currently a « catch-22 » situation in which ODR services are slow to develop and eConfidence is still rather low. Indeed the public awareness of ADR/ODR is quite low. Hence, demand for ODR is still rather weak. The Communication will conclude that public policy can play a role in encouraging and facilitating the development of ODR, notably :

(*i*) By supporting the standardisation process (i.e. technical requirements, demonstrator projects, pilots, etc.);

(*ii*) By providing clarity in relation to the legal environment;

(*iii*) By helping to raise the awareness of businesses and consumers about the merits of ODR.

In the coming years, it will also be important to take into account the effective and widespread diffusion of ODR mechanisms when examining the legal framework.

ARBITRATION
AND E-COMMERCE RELATED DISPUTES :
LEGAL BARRIERS AND CHALLENGES

BY

ANDRÉS MONCAYO VON HASE

PROFESSOR, UNIVERSITY OF BUENOS-AIRES, ARGENTINA

Introduction

The peculiar context in which private situations and transactions take place on the Internet, that is : (*i*) inherently international in nature, (*ii*) likely to link individuals, merchants and entities from diverse cultures and distant geographical locations, (*iii*) frequently involving disputes over small amounts or conditioned by certain technical aspects or peculiarities of the online world that call for quick remedies and enforcement mechanisms, determines the need to promote alternative dispute resolution mechanisms, like online arbitration. Nevertheless, arbitration is currently confronted with a situation in which many legal instruments that are used to promote and facilitate traditional international commercial arbitration are ill-suited for the development of online arbitration and the underlying characteristics of transactions made by electronic means through the Internet. Legal texts lag behind technology and need to be updated in order to increase merchants' and consumers' confidence in the use of an open network like the Internet to engage in business and settle the disputes that may arise therefrom using the advantages that technological advances offer.

Part I of this report is intended to give an overall picture of the peculiarities of Internet transactions and the legal environment in which international commercial arbitration shall be resorted to and even promoted. *Part II* focuses specifically on online arbitration and the legal barriers that may still exist in international arbitration conventions or domestic arbitration regulations for the use of electronic means to settle conflicts through arbitration. A brief mention will be made of experiences in online arbitration. *Part III* includes a reference to the actions that are still needed to foster international commercial arbitration to settle electronic commerce related disputes.

I. – The legal environment of electronic commerce

A. – FORMS
OF ELECTRONIC COMMERCE AND TRANSACTIONS

Commercial use of the Internet takes place in many different ways. A distinction which is already commonplace in the marketplace but is also legally relevant may be drawn, depending on the nature of the entities or persons involved in a transaction, namely : (*i*) B2B (business to business transactions), and (*ii*) B2C (business to consumer transactions). The first group normally includes online transactions between enterprises or two business as well as broader functions served by aggregators, auctions and exchanges. The second group constitutes probably the most visible manifestation of electronic commerce. It offers traditional business a new channel through which to sell the same things to consumers at lower costs or facilitates new opportunities for small and medium enterprises and allows, for instance, the digital download market of books, videos and music at lower distribution costs. The distinction between B2B and B2C transactions is not devoid of legal consequences as far as e-commerce in general is concerned, as well as, when it comes to arbitration, particularly, with regard to (*i*) the parties' autonomy to chose the applicable law and to adjudicate a dispute to a foreign tribunal, and (*ii*) the enforcement of awards.

B. – THE REASONS THAT MAY JUSTIFY
THE DEVELOPMENT AND PROMOTION OF ONLINE
ARBITRATION IN INTERNET RELATED DISPUTES

1. – *Disparities among national laws*
The application of traditional conflict of law rules to e-commerce related disputes

Most of the countries do not have rules on international jurisdiction that are specially suited to the peculiar features of electronic commerce and transactions taking place on the Internet. In addition, there is no universal convention containing such rules either. In any event, the outcome of any choice-of-law analysis will often depend on where a lawsuit is filed – that is, in the forum in which the dispute is first raised. Due to the fact that each jurisdiction has its own conflict of law rules to determine the substantive rules in the absence of special rules (e.g., an international convention), the parties' control over selecting a jurisdiction (and even the applicable law) is of utmost importance. Courts vary widely over the extent to which they honour parties' contractual choice-of-forum provisions.

Legal rules that tend to replace or disregard private parties' freely negotiated choice of-forum or choice-of-law clauses are deemed to harm international trade in general and electronic commerce in particular. However, the extension to choice-of-forum clauses to consumer transactions is strongly contested in certain countries. In some of them, protective consumer laws restrict such a possibility. This controversial issue has been present in negotiations relating to the European Union's Directive on E-Commerce (1) and the Hague Conference's draft Convention on Jurisdiction and Foreign Judgements in Civil and Commercial Matters (2). All these instruments exclude or limit the free choice-of-forum clauses in consumer contracts under certain circumstances (e.g., business or professional activities of the seller or defendant in or directed to the consumer's home country, business solicitations by means of publicity, etc.). The same applies, in many instances, with respect to the imperative rules of the home country of the consumer (as referred to in Part II, Section A.2). Therefore, while party autonomy is clearly effective in B2B transactions, this is not the case with regard to B2C contracts as stressed earlier.

---

(1) European Parliament and Council Directive on Certain Legal Aspects of Electronic Commerce in the Internal Market (Directive 2000/31, June 8, 2000).

(2) See, http://www.hcch.net/e/conventions/draft36e.html, The Hague Conference on Private International Law, Preliminary Draft Convention on Jurisdiction and Foreign Judgements in Civil and Commercial Matters, 30 October 1999 where the interaction of Article 4.3 and 7 establish the limits to the free choice of the forum by private parties with regard to consumer contracts (i.e., excluding such contracts from the freedom of choice rules and providing for jurisdiction to the courts where the consumer has its habitual residence under certain conditions, namely (i) if the conclusion of the contract on which the claim is based is related to trade or professional activities that the defendant has engaged in or directed to that State, in particular in soliciting business through means of publicity, and (ii) the consumer has taken the steps necessary for the conclusion of the contract in that State).

2. – *The important*
but limited application of the 1980 Vienna Convention
to international e-commerce transactions

The inherently global nature of electronic commerce, inevitably raises the question as to what should be the law applicable to contracts that are made and formed online. Is it the United Nations Convention on the International Sales of Goods of 1980 « CISG »)? The Convention is currently in force in some 60 states. It is a treaty that standardises the substantive rules of law applicable to international sales contracts. It is probably destined to become as widely applicable as the 1958 New Convention on the Recognition and Enforcement of Arbitration Awards. It has even been contended that international traders are increasingly abandoning the right afforded to them by the Convention of excluding its application (article 6). The CISG applies to (*i*) contracts of sales of goods between parties whose place of business are in different states, (*ii*) where the normal private international law rules lead to the application of the law of a contracting state, or (*iii*) where parties directly or indirectly choose its application. The Convention provides a body of flexible substantive rules on the formation of contracts, general provisions dealing with communications between the parties and obligations of sellers and buyers, which may help to facilitate B2B transactions. Another advantage of CISG is that it establishes the freedom of forms as a general rule. The new forms of communication do not hamper the likely application of the CISG to an important segment of online contracts. The Convention is deemed suitable to deal with the new challenges posed by the new means of communication such as the Internet. Furthermore, in the absence of an express choice of law by the parties, modern arbitration, especially in institutional arbitration increasingly allows arbitrators to apply the rules of law that it determines to be appropriate (e.g., Article 17(1) of the 1998 ICC Rules of Arbitration). In this context, there has been a significant increase in arbitration decisions applying the CISG (3). Consequently, the importance of this Convention as one of the potentially global instruments that may be used in electronic commerce transactions

---

(3) H. Van Houtte, « The Vienna Convention in ICC Arbitration Practice », *ICC International Court of Arbitration Bulletin*, Vol. 11, n° 2, 2000, pp. 22-33.

should not be disregarded. However, there are some restrictions that limit its scope of application.

First of all, the Convention does not cover the entire constellation of online transactions that regularly take place in or through the Internet. It excludes sales of goods bought for personal, family or household and is therefore not applicable to B2C transactions. Since it covers only the sales of « goods », service agreements, which are a relevant part of B2B transactions, are also outside the CISG's scope. Secondly, doubts arise as to whether the Convention may apply to agreements not only made in electronic form but also which are entirely performed online. Many transactions take place online in the form of a « delivery » of information, data and software. Some restrictive interpretations of the term « good » (*merchandises*) exclude the sale and delivery of the above mentioned « digital goods » via the Internet from the scope of the CISG and equate the concept of goods with objects or movable or corporal things. However, a broad interpretation of the term « goods » so as to cover all movable things and not just corporeal things is favoured by an increasing number of commentators. Therefore, the sale or delivery of standard software and even of an individual or customised software (e.g., a work made for hire) through the Internet may be deemed to be covered by the Convention. Thirdly, several State parties to the Convention, mainly former socialist countries and Latin American countries made a reservation that considerably limits the application of the Convention to electronic commerce and thus online arbitration. A contracting State whose legislation requires contracts of sale to be concluded in or evidenced by writing may at any time make a declaration that any provision (including those relating to the formation of contracts) « *that allows a contract of sale or its modification or termination by agreement or any offer, acceptance, or other indication of intention to be made in any other form other than writing, does not apply where a party has his place of business in that State* » (Article 96 of the CISG).

3. – *The lack of international comprehensive regulations on e-commerce : an incentive for « virtual arbitration » ?*

It follows from the previous sections that there is no uniform, unique and common Internetlaw. Electronic commerce is composed or governed by different national laws which often overlap or even contradict each other. Legal uncertainty in the context of the Internet affects both sellers and consumers but may be substantially overcome by means of a common body of rules or a kind of international code of conduct (4). Such a common set of rules does not exist at a universal level and States seem far from being prepared to reach a comprehensive international agreement on such questions. However, given the disparities among national e-commerce related legislation and the drawbacks associated with the traditional conflict of law rules, there seem to be much room for the development of line arbitration. In such a context, parties could on a voluntary basis resort to « virtual arbitrators » which would replace the territorial judges and would be committed to fulfil the mission entrusted to them by the parties and their expectations therefrom, but unlike a state court would not be bound – at least to such an extent – to conflicting national conflict of law rules. However, attention should be paid to peculiarities of Internet and the impact of that the traditional legal framework may have on online arbitration.

II. – Online arbitration

A. – THE IMPACT OF THE TRADITIONAL LEGAL FRAMEWORK FOR ARBITRATION IN THE LIGHT OF THE SPECIFIC FEATURES OF E-COMMERCE

Although many of the national laws on arbitration and important conventions on international arbitration are intended to facilitate and promote international arbitration, such hospitality does not at present automatically extend to online arbitration. In general, national arbitration acts and international conventions on international commercial arbitration still focus mainly on traditional arbitration, that is, proceedings in which the physical presence or contact of the parties or its counsels may at some stages or instances be necessary and where arbitration agreements, parties' submissions and awards must be mainly conceived in written form. Online arbitration is considered to be more beneficial than traditional

---

(4) V. BOEHME-NESSLER, « Internetrecht.com », Berlin, Beck, 2001, p. 85.

arbitration mechanisms mainly because of two important reasons : 1) parties would not be required to travel to an arbitration tribunal located in a distant foreign country, and, 2) proceedings may be accelerated since documents and evidence can be exchanged almost instantaneously through electronic mail or interactive electronic means.

1. – *The form of the arbitration agreements*

Arbitration clauses and arbitration, are an instrument of utmost importance for channelling disputes arising in international trade. Nevertheless, attention should be paid to the requirement that arbitration agreements be written and that the original arbitration agreement or a duly certified copy thereof be presented to the state court before which enforcement of the award is sought.

There is no unanimous consensus as to whether or not an arbitration agreement should be in writing according to other international instruments having a far more reaching impact on international business on the international level, including the 1958 New York Convention on the Recognition and Enforcement of Foreign Awards (the « New York Convention ») (Article II.1) which seems to require that an arbitration agreement be made in writing (5). However, the Convention is ready to accept situations in which the arbitration agreement is neither the result of a signature or a simultaneous consent but is a consequence of an exchange of documents (i.e., letters or telegrams according to Article II.2)). The purpose of the convention seems to adopt a uniform common standard to validate arbitration agreements from a formal point of view, namely that the consent of the parties be clear, that is to say, that it be the result of an expressed will (be it simultaneous in a written agreement signed by the parties or differed as a result of an exchange of documents like letters or telegrams) (6).

In fact, at the time of the said Convention, the signatory States could not envisage that consent to arbitrate could be expressed by

---

(5) H. VERBIST & Ch. IMHOOS, « Arbitartion, Telecommunications and Electronic Commerce », *ICC International Court Bulletin*, Vol. 10, n° 2, Fall 1999, p. 22 ; R. SANTOS BELANDRO, *Arbitraje Comercial Internacional*, Tercera Edición, Okford, Mexico, 2000, pp. 60 and P. MANKOWSKI, « Internazionale Zuständichkeit », in SPINDLER/WIEBE, *Internet – Auktionen. Rechtliche Ramhenbedingungen*, München, Beck Verlag, 2001, pp. 224-225.

(6) R. SANTOS BELANDRO, *supra,* note 5, pp. 60-62.

means of a fax or by electronic mail but mention was made to the then most frequent means and technologies (e.g., mail and telegrams). Conceptually, Article II(2) of the New York Convention is prepared to acknowledge the use of the newest technological advances to express the consent of the parties. Consequently, reference made by the Convention to arbitration clauses or agreements « contained in an exchange of letters or telegrams » may be construed so as to encompass any arbitration agreement resulting from an exchange of electronic mails or electronic means. The same conclusion could be applied – normally in the framework of B2B transactions, to the acceptance of an offer which includes an arbitration clause by means of an interactive contact with a web page to the extent that a similar exchange of information takes place as in the case of exchange of electronic mails (7). In any event, differences in national arbitration laws as to the requirement that arbitration agreements be written and the likely divergent judicial interpretations as to the extent and scope of the international rules on the matter by the state courts in the different countries may warrant some precautions (e.g., the confirmation of arbitration agreement made electronically by means of an exchange of faxes) (8). In any case, the prove of an arbitration agreement made in electronic form in a court or arbitration proceeding will be possible and the formal requirement that arbitration agreements be written will be met, to the extent that the countries concerned regulate the effects of electronic signatures and place them on the same foot as handwritten signatures.

The requirement that the arbitration agreement be written is, as already mentioned, aimed at avoiding that a party is unaware that an arbitration agreement or clause exists. Very often arbitration clauses are part of the general terms of a contract which are predisposed and incorporated to a range of contracts or a series of contractual matters in advance by one of the parties. In B2B trans-

---

(7) P.A. DE MIGUEL ASENSIO, *Derecho Privado de Internet*, Segunda Edición, Madrid Civitas, 2001, p. 451. A dynamic interpretation of the 1958 New York Convention may be supported by the 1985 United Nations Commission on International Trade Law (UNCITRAL) Model Law on International Commercial Arbitration which has served as guide for the most modern arbitration laws of the World. Thus, article 7 (2) of the UNCITRAL Model Law seem to admit that an arbitration agreement be made electronically, on condition, however, that evidence of such agreement can be provided. Similar provisions are to be found in the 1961 Geneva European Convention on International Arbitration and some modern arbitration laws.

(8) P.A. DE MIGUEL ASENSIO, *supra*, note 7, p. 451 and P. MANKOWSKI, *supra*, note 5, p. 225.

actions such written requirement may be met if the documents exchanged by the parties electronically contain an express reference to the general conditions governing the contract and such general conditions contain an arbitration agreement or clause, provided, however, that such reference to the general conditions and the arbitration agreement may be verified by any of the parties. In the online world this would mean that any of the parties be capable of viewing those conditions and the arbitration agreement on the screen and reproduce or print them in paper form (9). In any event, in order to avoid evidential problems with respect to the question of whether or not parties consented to arbitration online, it will be in the interest of parties to provide for confirmation of the acceptance by a second click on an icon or by some other equivalent procedure.

2. – *Arbitration involving Consumers*

Special attention should be paid when one of the parties to an arbitration Agreement or clause is a consumer. If that is the case, it is likely that the validity of the consent to an agreement to arbitrate will be assessed more strictly, especially if the arbitration agreement is made by reference.

However, it must be noticed that Article II of the 1958 New York Convention requiring that the arbitration agreement be written or be the result of an exchange of letters or telegrams is supposed to supersede any other additional formal conditions set forth by local procedural regulations. The Convention has been originally conceived to cover civil as well as commercial matters. No distinction is thus made in the Convention as to whether an arbitration agreement is made in the context of a business relationship between merchants or between enterprises and consumers.

Nevertheless, the scope of the Convention may be reduced by the contracting States, namely because the Convention allows them – when signing, ratifying or acceding to the Convention, to make a reservation in order to apply the Convention only to differences arising out of legal relationships whether contractual or not, which are considered as commercial under the national law of the State making such declaration (Article I (3)). Therefore, it is to those

---

(9) M. DE ASENCIO, *supra*, note 7, pp. 452-453.

States to make clear what constitutes a commercial matter and whether or not the Convention applies to consumer contracts. In fact, many countries have restrictive legislation trying to avoid that consumers using new technologies including electronic mail or means to contract (*i*) be obliged to refer their claims to distant jurisdictions and thereby generally giving up certain basic protective rights that the law of their domicile acknowledges them, or (*ii*) that they be deprived of judicial legal actions due to arbitration clauses providing for exclusive binding arbitration. Such strict provisions are based on the fact that consumers very often may not know or lack information about the web site with which they are contracting or the enterprise operating it.

However, there is a growing consensus that barriers should be removed to enable the development of suitable, rapid and efficient online dispute resolution mechanisms for the settlement of many high volume and low value dispute involving consumers. Paradoxically, consumer protective regulation having the effect of limiting the scope for cross border arbitration involving consumers may have a negative effects since many consumers would be in fact deterred from resorting to a long and formal procedure before the state court of it domicile for a small amount dispute involving a foreign web page owner or service provider. One possible way to satisfy the above mentioned public policy concerns is to make the arbitration award binding only on the seller or to have a process in which there is an arbitrator or administrative procedure but the decision is not binding. Along these lines, an interesting scheme could be a conditional binding arbitration, whereby the business agrees in advance to arbitrate disputes online at the consumer's request. The arbitrator's decision is not binding on either party unless the consumer formally accepts the decision. Once accepted the decision becomes binding on both the company and the consumer. For such consumer related arbitration mechanisms to work at a cross-border level on a contractual pre-agreed basis, a minimum common set of principles or standards on consumer protection – directly or indirectly endorsed by governments at an international level to somehow coordinate public policy visions, may be necessary. This would facilitate the success of any online arbitration because an international arbitrator does not have, as a state judge does, a system of conflict of laws to support them. Generally, the notions of *lex fori* and foreign laws are alien to him. From this point of view, arbitration proceedings are less protected than court proceedings by a set of legal provisions. Therefore, the relationship of the arbitrator to public policy is more difficult since, among the various public policies, the one to be applied must be identified (10). Consumer protection is seen, depending on the countries and legal tradition, as deserving protection either through imperative domestic rules, *loi des policies* or public policy. The latter is in any case a ground for refusal of recognition of foreign or international arbitration awards under the 1958 New York Convention.

3. – *Electronics and arbitration proceedings*

Particular problems for online arbitration are likely to arise in (*i*) the proceedings, and (*ii*) the award. Although many arbitration laws, rules of procedures of institutional arbitration bodies and even international conventions on arbitration are to some extent open or prepared to the use of new technologies to carry out arbitration procedures, they still are, to a certain point, based on some of the basic features underlying traditional proceedings where the signature of the parties is required or the terms of reference or submissions shall be in written form. Likewise, some arbitration acts or rules of procedure of institutional arbitration require a « copy » of the arbitration agreement to file a request for arbitration. They do not provide a detailed description on how the notices will be served during the procedure and how the time periods are to be calculated which are fundamental questions to ensure that the due process requirement be undoubtedly met. In addition, sometimes rules are not flexible enough and cast doubts as to whether hearings – if required by the parties, may be carried out electronically.

In this context and taking into account the particularities of the online environment some institutional arbitration bodies have started the move towards the elaboration of specific supplementary rules to reflect the needed interaction between procedural rules, due process concerns and the use of electronic means to carry out arbitration proceedings. A case in point are the Supplementary Procedures for Online Arbitration launched in July 2001 by the *American Arbitration Association* which are conceived to enable par-

---

(10) M. RUBINO-SAMMARTANO, *supra*, note 27, p. 507.

ties that have agreed to arbitration under such Supplementary Procedures, « *arbitration proceedings to be conducted and resolved exclusively via the Internet* » (11).

4. – *The enforcement of awards and the place of arbitration : is delocalised or nationless arbitration possible ?*

First of all, the writing and signature requirements discussed in section A.1) with respect to arbitration agreements pose similar problems with respect to the awards and their enforcement. The 1958 requires a party applying for recognition and enforcement of an award to provide before the courts in which enforcement is sought (*i*) the duly authenticated original award or a duly certified copy thereof; and (*ii*) the original arbitration agreement or a duly certified copy thereof. Likewise, Article 35 (2) of the UNCITRAL Model Law on Arbitration imposes the same requirements. For this purposes, however, UNCITRAL Model Law on Electronic Commerce may be of help by providing that a document may be considered as an original if two conditions are met, namely that there exists a reliable assurance as to the integrity of the information and that such information is capable of being displayed to the person to whom it is presented. However, it remains uncertain whether a state court would always be prepared, on such a basis, to admit a document so transmitted as an original of the computer based document.

Secondly, it is interesting to note that in some of the online arbitration projects and experiments that are discussed in Part II, most of the procedure are carried out online according to a special set of rules which do not bear, in principle, any relationship with a specific seat or place. There is, therefore, no predetermined place or seat of the arbitration. This fact has lead some commentators to consider that a sort of *lex electronica* (a sort of new category of the *lex mercatoria*) would govern or underly the proceedings of the arbitration tribunal (12). The parties are in fact free to choose the law applicable to the procedure as well as to the merits of a dispute

---

(11) Supplementary Procedures for Online Arbitration, American Arbitration Association, http://www.adr.org/rules/commercial/online-arbitartion.html.

(12) M. DE ASENCIO, *supra*, note 7, p. 457.

and nothing prevents them to do so under the New York Convention which regulates only the consequences of invalid arbitration agreements or awards under certain laws. Some national laws and arbitration rules of institutional arbitration bodies do not generally dictate the procedural law which is applicable in the absence of a choice by the parties. It is very often admitted that where the procedural rules chosen by the parties are silent and the parties have not agreed otherwise, the arbitration tribunal may have the power to decide on any additional procedural rules to be applied. However, the denationalisation of arbitration proceedings, even before the emergence of Internet, has given rise to some concern; i.e., that it would lead to arbitration no longer subject to a precise law, and which would therefore be « *floating* ». *Arbitration* proceedings that would find themselves in a sort of legal desert, would hardly seem to be compatible under the New York Convention (13). Therefore, even if proceedings may be delocalised, they may not be completely detached from the procedural legal system of the place of arbitration; arbitrators must always consider the procedural law of the place of arbitration, when checking the extent of their freedom to choose procedural law (14). When arbitration is conducted online, it may be extremely difficult to determine the place of the arbitration if the parties failed to do so (15). The place of the arbitration could coincide with the geographical location of the servers used to arbitrate a dispute (*lex loci server*). Nevertheless, the connection underlying the choice of law may appear to be artificial to the extent that different servers located in diverse countries are used in the proceedings. If online arbitration is to be deemed completely delocalised in nature as some advocate it will be difficult to courts to admit such view under the New York Convention. In such context, it is considered that the least artificial solution – in the framework of the freedom to contract, is that the parties should also be free to determine the place of arbitration albeit fic-

---

(13) H. VERBIST & Chr. IMHOOS, *supra*, note 5, p. 24.

(14) M. RUBINO-SAMMARTANO, *supra*, note 10, p. 485 and R. SANTOS BELANDRO, *supra*, note 5, p. 37.

(15) In any case, non-cooperation by a party bound to online arbitration (e.g., non-appointment of the arbitrator) could be addressed by national laws by entrusting a leading arbitration center (be it a national or international entity) with the task of appointing the arbitrator or supervising online proceedings in general to confer legal security and reliability to the system in the eyes of both national courts and users.

titious (16). Such a solution has been adopted in some of the newest online alternative disputes resolution mechanisms.

The traditional enforcement machinery in the context of cross-border B2C transactions raises additional problems. Account should be taken that many of the controversies involving consumers in Internet are small amount disputes where traditional enforcement may prove elusive or illusory given its sophistication and high costs as compared to the low amounts usually involved in the dispute and the dynamics of electronic commerce where consumers expect to have quicker answers than in the « brick and mortar » world.

5. – *The need for special precautions
in online arbitration*

It is generally admitted that, as far as information technologies are concerned, the content and form of documents can be easily altered either accidentally or fraudulently without leaving any traces. For that reason, electronic documents or contracts have not yet been placed into the same evidentiary position as any other documents or contracts usually employed in the « off-line world ». However, an increasing number of other countries' legislation makes presumptively valid electronic records or signatures which meet certain minimum technological standards and international recommendation on the matter. In addition, the UNCITRAL Model Law on Electronic Commerce tackles that problem by providing that Information in the form of a data message shall be given due evidential weight and establishing a useful guidance as to how the evidential value of a data message should be assessed (17).

In any case, it is not entirely easy to ensure security as to both the integrity of the electronic message and the will of the originator. Certainly, the risks diminish to a great extend through digital signatures and the use of cryptography or encryption which allows secret codes to be applied. The *arbitration* institution chosen by the parties may administer and centralise the exchange of communica-

---

(16) M. DE ASENCIO, *supra,* note 7, p. 458 and H. VERBIST & Chr. IMHOOS, *supra,* note 5, p. 23.

(17) Article 9 (2) of the UNCITRAL Model Law on Electronic Commerce states that : « regard shall be had to the reliability of the manner in which the data message was generated, stored or communicated, to the reliability of the manner in which the integrity of the information was maintained, to the manner in which its originator was identified, and to any other relevant factor ».

tions between the parties and the acknowledgement of their receipt that could be channeled through a controlled server or special site used for the case. In this context, the *arbitration* institution would act as an authenticating party (18).

B. – ONLINE ARBITRATION EXPERIENCES AND PROJECTS

Two important existing initiatives will mainly be discussed in this Section B, namely : (*i*) the Virtual Magistrate arbitration program and (*ii*) the Uniform Dispute Resolution Policy (the « UDRP ») of the Internet Corporation for Assigned Names and Numbers (« ICANN »). Both mechanisms have a different scope of application and history but intend to cover a universe of conflictive situations that commonly arise in the online world.

1. – *The Virtual Magistrate arbitration program*

The Virtual Magistrate arbitration program has been conceived to offer arbitration for rapid, interim resolution of disputes which are very common in the online world, namely conflicts involving (*i*) users of online systems, (*ii*) those who claim to be harmed by wrongful messages, postings, or files, (including, intellectual property infringements), and (*iii*) systems operators (to the extent that such complaints or request for remedies are addressed to the system operators). Cases are to be handled by one single arbitrator who shall render a decision in seventy-two hours.

A listserv/newsgroup (« grist ») will be established for each case, and participants will be directed to post messages to the grist. Messages posted to the grist will automatically be sent to all participants. The address will be included in the initial notification letter. Participants will be provided with password access to the grist, allowing all messages to be reviewed. Each decision, will be posted to the grist (19). Any procedural matters that are not addressed by these rules or in other Virtual Magistrate arbitration program documents will be resolved in accordance with the American Arbitration Association's Commercial Arbitration Rules.

---

(18) H. VERBIST & Chr. IMHOOS, *supra*, note 5, p. 24.
(19) Basic Rules in http://www.vmag.org/docs/concept.html.

The Virtual Magistrate is not a real court, but it attempts to function like one on the Internet. There is no previous arbitration agreement or clause which opens the way to arbitration. Submission proceeds on a case by case basis for those willing to participate in such a mechanism.

The reason why such a project is not as active as expected is apparently the lack of an overall structure or contractual network that mandates parties in advance to resort to arbitration as it is the case with ICANN's Uniform Dispute Resolution Policy that will be discussed in the next Section. A lesson to be drawn from the Project may be that it is difficult to persuade a respondent (or a potential defendant) to participate in an arbitration procedure if there is no prior agreement to do so (20). In addition, an Internet service provider that does not need to negotiate the terms of their service agreements with its subscribers may not have any reason or incentive to agree in advance to go to arbitration if a dispute arises in such a context.

2. – The case of ICANN and the application of the Uniform Domain Name Dispute Resolution Policy (the « UDRP ») : a model to be expanded?

The Internet Corporation for Assigned Names and Numbers (« ICANN ») is one example of a new forms of hybrid forms of governance in which private and public interest intermingles in sophisticated manner. The domain name system was originally managed partly by the United States government and hybrid entities In 1998, management and supervision of the domain name system was turned over to ICANN a non profit corporation established solely for the purpose of managing the domain name system. The domain name system (« DNS ») emerged from technical circles with little concern about the disputes that might be caused by its management simply because it was not necessary. Domain names had little value before the Internet began to be used for commercial purposes. At present, a domain name registration may give a global presence which makes the corresponding online address (e.g., the domain name) accessible from anywhere.

---

(20) E. KATSH and J. RIFKIN, *Online Dispute Resolution. Resolving Conflicts in Cyberspace*, Jossey-Bass, San Francisco, 2001, p. 56.

In such a context, many companies and celebrities had to witness the registering of their trademarks and personal names as domain names by third parties having no legitimate interest. The effects of the « first to come first to serve » rule had to be counterbalanced by an effective and low cost dispute settlement mechanism that could enable trademark holders to protect their rights. For that reasons, ICANN, following the recommendations of WIPO, put in place a process for resolving domain name disputes known as the ICANN Uniform Dispute Resolution Policy (the « UDRP ») which is aimed at providing trademark holders with a process which is faster and less formal and expensive than judicial proceedings. Such policy is in effect since January 3, 2000 and has served as a basis to settle more that 3000 cases involving mostly conflicts between domain names identical or confusingly similar to trademarks which were either in use, registered or well known before the registration of the questioned domain names. The UDRP applies to the administrative procedure that may only be conducted before one of the four administrative-dispute-resolution service providers approved by ICANN (e.g. the WIPO Center on Mediation and Arbitration, e-Resolution, etc.).

The administrative procedures take place essentially online. They apply to trademark-based domain names disputes arising in connection with all the top level domains (« TLDs ») like .com, .net and .org., but are confined to cases involving bad faith or abusive registrations of domain names by third parties having no legitimate interest, that is to say, the so-called « cybersquatting » (21).

The UDRP represents a contractually based system for the implementation of an intellectual property policy specifically aimed at protecting trademarks in the DNS. Intellectual property policy, as expressed in the UDRP, is implemented through registrar

---

(21) It is interesting to note, however, that some experts have extensively applied the UDRP in proceedings involving domain name registrations conflicting with personal names of well known persons or celebrities assimilating such names to unregistered trademarks (e.g., common law marks) deserving protection against cybersquatting. Only trademark rights may be in principle invoked against cybersquatting which means that holders of other intellectual property rights like trade names, copyright, geographical indications or even personality rights may not resort to an administrative panel to settle a conflict arising between a domain name registration and any of such rights. However, the success of the application of the UDRP may determine its gradual extension to some of these categories. See, World Intellectual Property Organisation, Second WIPO Internet Process Domain Name Process, Final Report on « The Recognition of rights and the Use of Names in the Internet Domain Name System », September 3, 2001, in http://wipo2.wipo.int.

accreditation agreements (i.e., between the accredited domain names registrars approved by ICANN) with ICANN and through the contract between the applicant for a domain name registration (e.g., the registration agreement) and the registrar under which the holder of the domain name registration agrees to submit to the UDRP if such registration is challenged by a third party (e.g., normally a holder of a previously registered or well-known trademark). The remedies available to a complainant are limited to what may be technically achieved in the DNS, that is, the cancellation or the transfer of the domain name registration to the complainant itself as decided by the panel. It is then to ICANN Registrar to block the domain name concerned and, as the case may be, implement its transfer to the successful claimant (e.g., normally the trademark holder).

The submission of a domain name applicant or owner to the administrative arbitration procedure is mandatory since the UDRP is incorporated by reference to the registration agreement that the applicant must conclude in advance in order to be able to register a domain name. Such mandatory submission to an administrative procedure before a dispute arises and the incorporation of the UDRP by reference may be questionable under the imperative rules, public policy or *lois de police* aimed at protecting consumers in many countries as described earlier (Section A.2 of Part I) (22). To counterbalance the effect of a mandatory « arbitration clause » by reference in registration agreements which are probably never read, ICANN determined that the application of the UDRP does not preclude any of the parties to initiate judicial proceedings before, during or after the administrative proceedings. If such a circumstance arises during the pendency of the administrative procedure then the panel has the discretion to decide whether to suspend or terminate the administrative proceeding, or to proceed to a decision. The implication of this is that panel decisions of this nature, unlike traditional arbitration decisions, cannot be enforced in a state court. To the contrary, the loosing party can resort to a judicial court and start from the scratch. The legal nature of such mandatory administrative procedures is thus uncertain. Since judi-

---

(22) See, O. ITENEAU, « L'UDRP, le début de la fin de l'action judiciare ? », *Droit des technologies avancées*, vol. 8, n° 1/2001, pp. 122 and 125 who quotes article L 132-1 of the French Consume Code.

cial remedies are available at any time for any of the parties, the administrative procedure has been characterised as a « non-binding arbitration », that may become a popular form of online dispute resolution mechanism in the future in other areas of Internet (23).

III. – Conclusions
Future challenges and proposals

The law of arbitration both at a national and international level lag behind the technological advances. Given the disparities among countries described in Part I there seem to be much room for the development of online arbitration. However, attention should be paid to peculiarities of Internet and the impact of the traditional legal framework may have on online arbitration as discussed in Part I and Part II of this Report. States may, therefore, contribute to the development of online arbitration in direct and indirect ways, be it through unilateral initiatives or in conjunction with other states, industry and consumer associations, as follows :

1) States may contribute to enhance merchants and consumers confidence in electronic commerce and online resolution by pursuing the development of the infrastructure needed for the implementation of digital signature and to ensure information security. This would not only respond to the need to determine the *identity* of the parties and to ensure the *integrity* of a message in the framework of online transactions in a given country but would also satisfy such concerns in online arbitration proceedings allowing parties to a dispute, as well as the tribunal, to exchange communications and evaluate evidence on safe grounds.

2) States parties to the 1980 Vienna Convention that apply it only to written contracts in the traditional sense by virtue of the reservation made under Article 96, should withdraw such declaration. This would remove an important obstacle, namely that formal requirements under national law prevent electronic international

---

(23) E. KATSH and J. RIFKIN, *supra,* note 20, pp. 108-109. On the other hand, its non jurisdictional character and the fact that the parties to the procedure were not bound in advanced by an arbitration agreement before the initiation of the proceedings means that it is not in fact an arbitration but a purely administrative procedure in which experts are called to carry out technical functions in order to settle a specific conflict. See, O. ITENEAU, *supra,* note 22, p. 125.

sales contracts (that include arbitration clauses) from being upheld valid only because they lack the traditional handwritten signature.

3) States parties to the 1958 New York Convention on the Recognition and Enforcement of *Arbitration* Awards (the « New York Convention ») that limit their application to « commercial matters » by virtue of the declaration made under Article I (3) of the New York Convention should withdraw such a reservation (or give express indication as to the precise meaning of what constitutes « a commercial matter ») in order to avoid uncertainties as to the precise scope of application of the New York Convention and facilitate the application of the Convention to the recognition and enforcement of awards involving both B2B and B2C transactions (including, awards regarding voluntary arbitration relating to intellectual property infringements, distribution of illegal content, licensing agreements, etc.). However, many of the controversies involving consumers in Internet are low-value disputes where the traditional enforcement machinery may prove elusive or illusory given its sophistication and high costs as compared to the low amounts of B2C disputes. Therefore, additional or alternative enforcement mechanisms shall be applied and explored with respect to cross-border online disputes involving consumers that could be implemented in the framework of self-regulation mechanisms.

4) Many arbitration laws, rules of procedures of institutional arbitration bodies and even international conventions are still based on some of the basic features underlying traditional proceedings where the signature of the parties or the written form is required with regard to arbitration agreement, the terms of reference, the submissions of the parties or the awards and do not provide detailed rules on notices and how the period of time be calculated. Thus, consideration must be given to amending the fundamental texts of international arbitration in order to allow online arbitration to further develop.

5) If amendments to international conventions happens to be a long-lasting or burdensome process, works on the adaptation of the legal framework of traditional arbitration to the peculiarities of the online environment could be pursued and coordinated through the United Nations Commission on International Trade Law (UNCITRAL). This could be done by adding new provisions to the

Model Law on International Commercial Arbitration or preparing new separate or supplementary rules.

6) Lessons may be drawn from some of the online arbitration experiences and projects like the Virtual Magistrate Project and the application of ICANN's Uniform Dispute Settlement Policy (UDRP) referred to in Part II (Section B). The former shows the difficulties of attracting services providers to arbitration. The administrative procedure of the UDRP has been regarded as a sort of « non-binding arbitration » suitable for the online world since it may give disputants an opportunity to present their arguments in front of a neutral third party and settle conflicts in a quick manner using online technologies for those purposes. If such parties are satisfied with the quality of the third party and believe that they received a fair hearing, they often will not take the case to court even when the arbitrator has ruled against them. The implications of the application of ICANNs matrix may serve as an interest and original precedent of law creating process in other areas of Internet where there might be also international consensus as it was the case with the protection of trademarks against cybersquatting.

7) Finally, coordination between States, consumer associations and industry could be helpful to set forth a single set that of common minimum international rules on consumer protection that could guide online arbitration proceedings in a way that : (*i*) may address in a creative way the policy concerns reflected in national laws as referred to in Part II (Section A.2) and (*ii*) pave the way for the implementation of online arbitration (or other previous alternatives like mediation) to provide both industry and consumers with quick and efficient responses to their conflicts.

ARBITRATION BOARDS
AND E-COMMERCE

BY

Maurice SCHELLEKENS

Centre for law,
Public administration and computerisation
Faculty of law, Tilburg University

Introduction

Disputes with an international component are difficult to resolve. Transnational players have long since acknowledged arbitration as an important tool for resolving conflicts because of its accessibility, flexibility, speed and cost advantages. It is only natural to assume that arbitration will also be able to assist in the resolution of conflicts that arise in the e-commerce-context. Moreover, in the e-commerce context, arbitration boards can go a step further and provide for online resolution. Certain arbitration providers have already opened the possibility to perform arbitration procedures online. This report aims to provide an overview of the arbitration initiatives that have geared up to solve disputes online and of the legal that might be encountered on the way to online resolution. For the analysis of legal obstacles, the New York Convention of 1958 is taken as a starting point because of its central position in the recognition and enforcement of foreign *arbitration* awards.

I. – Arbitration boards
and online arbitration proceedings

There is a rather large contingent of ADR providers that offer arbitration services for a wide variety of disputes, often e-commerce disputes included. Some providers are well known, e.g. : WIPO, eResolution, ICC and the American Arbitration Association (1). Others, exploring the potential of the Internet for dispute resolution by arbitration, are relatively unknown, e.g. : I-courthouse, Virtual Magistrate, Cybercourt, Online Resolution and IntelliCOURT (2). They will not all be dealt with here. I will confine myself to the most prominent providers that have made an effort to adapt their procedure to the online environment and that have geared up to solve commercial disputes.

A. – AMERICAN ARBITRATION ASSOCIATION (HEREINAFTER : AAA)

The AAA, founded in 1926, offers mediation, arbitration and other ADR services. Here, only the arbitration services and, more specifically, the AAA's procedural rules for online *arbitration* proceedings will be dealt with : the Supplementary Procedures for Online Arbitration (3). The purpose of these rules is to permit *arbitration* proceedings to be conducted and resolved exclusively online. With respect to the online arbitration according to the Procedural Rules, the so-called Case Site is a core concept. For each dispute a new Case Site is established. All case files and submissions by the parties are stored therein. Only the AAA, the parties and the Arbitrator have access to the information in the Case Site.

If a party wants to resolve a dispute through arbitration, it can submit its claim to the AAA's Administrative Site. If the claim contains all the necessary information for an *arbitration* procedure to proceed and the claimant has paid his fee, the AAA establishes a Case Site on which the claim is made available. Both parties are notified of the address of the Case Site. In order to notify the respondent, the AAA uses the respondent's e-mail address that has been provided by the claimant. If it appears that the respondent cannot be reached via e-mail, the AAA may decide that the case cannot be handled online and this decision is reported to the claimant. In general the AAA may decide that arbitration will not be

---

(1) See respectively: http://arbiter.wipo.int/center/index.html, http://www.eresolution.com/, http://www.iccwbo.org/index—court.asp and http://www.adr.org/, visited October 2001.

(2) See respectively http://www.i-courthouse.com/, http://www.vmag.org/, http://www.cyber-court.de, http://www.onlineresolution.com and http://www.intellicourt.com (visited, October 2001).

(3) See http://www.adr.org/rules/commercial/online–arbitration.html, visited September 2001.

done online if a party lacks the capacity to participate in online arbitration or if the AAA otherwise finds in its discretion that arbitration should not be conducted online. Thus, it is the arbitration provider – the AAA – that can decide that the proceedings do not take place online, but in the traditional way. If the notification via e-mail is successful, the arbitration commences on the date on which the Case Site is established. The respondent submits a response to the Case Site. Apart from the actual response to the claim and the arguments and evidence supporting it, this response contains any objection to the arbitration, the e-mail address that the respondent shall be using for communication with the Case Site and possibly a counterclaim. If a counterclaim is submitted, the claimant submits a response within thirty days. In principle, the arbitrator makes his award solely on the basis of the submissions, without a hearing. A hearing only takes place if one of the parties or both request one. A hearing is a meeting of the parties before the arbitrator. It may be conducted in-person or by telephone, videoconference or other means. The arbitrator decides on the place of the award and indicates the place in the award. If the parties agree in writing upon the place of the award, the arbitrator will indicate this place in the award. The term « writing » here also comprises an « electronic record » as defined in the Uniform Electronic Transactions Act par. 2 (4). The arbitrator submits the award to the Case Site and the parties are notified of this submission by e-mail.

B. – WIPO

The WIPO Arbitration and Mediation Centre offers a wide variety of ADR services, including arbitration and domain name dispute resolution. Arbitration cannot yet be performed online but the Arbitration and Mediation Centre is currently developing an online, Internet-based system for administering disputes (5). The

---

(4) UETA (art. 2, section 7) defines electronic record as follows : « Electronic record » means a record created, generated, sent, communicated, received, or stored by electronic means. A « record » is defined in art. 2, section 13 UETA as follows : « Record » means information that is inscribed on a tangible medium or that is stored in an electronic or other medium and is retrievable in perceivable form. Art. 2, section 5 UETA defines the word « electronic » : « Electronic » means relating to technology having electrical, digital, magnetic, wireless, optical, electromagnetic, or similar capabilities.

(5) See http://arbiter.wipo.int/arbitration/online/, visited October 2001.

online dispute resolution facility developed for Internet domain name disputes serves as a model for the online settlement of commercial disputes. At the same time, the arbitration rules are adapted to accommodate the online character of the procedure. This will result in the so-called WIPO Online Expedited Arbitration Rules. Since these plans concerning online arbitration have not yet materialised at the time of writing this text, I shall focus on the procedure for domain name dispute resolution that has been up and running for several years.

In 1999, the Internet Corporation for Assigned Names and Numbers (hereinafter : ICANN) created an arbitration-like procedure for resolving certain domain name (6) disputes : the Uniform Domain name dispute Resolution Policy (hereinafter : UDRP) (7). The procedure is meant for relatively « simple » disputes, in which the respondent has no rights or legitimate interests in respect of the domain name. The interests of the domain name holder thus do not have to be weighed against the interests of the complainant (8). The actual dispute resolution is performed by one of the dispute resolution providers that is approved by ICANN (9). The WIPO Arbitration and Mediation Centre is the most prominent amongst these providers, taking the lion's share of the cases. The procedure before a panel – i.e. the « arbitrator(s) » – is governed by the aforementioned UDRP, the Rules for Uniform Domain name dispute Resolution Policy (hereinafter : UDRP-Rules) and the Supplementary Rules of the provider (10).

Submissions may be made in any of several forms : by telecopy or facsimile transmission, by postal or courier service or electronically. The Centre has established an Internet-based case filing and administration system in order to facilitate electronic communica-

---

(6) Dispute resolution under UDRP is available with respect to domain names in the .com, .net and .org TLD's. In addition dispute resolution can also be performed with respect to some country code TLD's and will be available for « new » gTLD's, such as : .biz, .name and .info.

(7) See http://www.icann.org/udrp/udrp-policy-24oct99.htm, visited October 2001.

(8) It seems however that UDRP arbitrators steadily enlarge their jurisdiction. See, I.L. STEWART, « The Best Laid Plans : How Unrestrained Arbitration Decisions Have Corrupted the Uniform Domain Name Dispute Resolution Policy », *Federal Communications Law Journal*, Vol. 53, Number 3, pp. 509-532.

(9) At the present time, four dispute resolution providers have been accredited by ICANN. See http://www.icann.org/udrp/approved-providers.htm, visited October 2001.

(10) For the UDRP-Rules, see : http://www.icann.org/udrp/udrp-rules-24oct99.htm. For the Supplementary Rules of the WIPO Arbitration and Mediation Center, see : http://arbiter.wipo.int/domains/rules/supplemental.html, visited October 2001.

tion. In principle no in-person hearings take place, unless the panel decides, at its sole discretion, that a hearing is necessary to decide the case. The panel sends its decision concerning the dispute to all parties, ICANN and the so-called Registrar, i.e. the entity with which the respondent has registered its domain name. If the panel has so decided, the Registrar will transfer or cancel the domain name registration, unless the (former) respondent initiates a lawsuit in a competent court against the (former) complainant and notifies this fact to the Registrar (11). In principle, the panel's decision will be published in full on the Internet.

C. – eRESOLUTION

The Canadian eResolution offers mediation and arbitration services. It is also one of the administrative panels accredited by ICANN to resolve domain name disputes under the UDRP. Here, I merely deal with eResolution's online arbitration services. The « Arbitration Rules for Canadian SME's » – as in force from 15 September 2001 – take online resolution as a starting point (12). For every case, a Case Site is established. The Case Site is a secure environment that is only accessible by the parties, the assigned arbitrator and eResolution's secretariat. All written communications and notifications are sent through the Case Site messaging system (13). Also, evidence may be submitted in electronic form. However, at any time during the proceedings, the secretariat or the *arbitration* tribunal may request the original paper format (if existent) of documents submitted in electronic format. The testimony of a party or a witness is given using means of distant communication, unless the tribunal decides otherwise. Optionally, a hearing can take place at a physical location. The *Arbitration* Tribunal will apply to the substance of the dispute the rules of law that parties have agreed upon. Failing such choice by the parties, the tribunal applies the rules of law it deems appropriate, having regard to the circumstances of the case. Where possible, it takes into account prevailing e-commerce and trade practices. After closure of the

---

(11) For details, see art. 4.k UDRP.

(12) See http://www.eresolution.bellzinc.ca/arb–rules.html, visited, October 2001.

(13) The confidentiality of the information, while in transit, and the authenticity of the server (Case Site) to which the data are sent to or from which data are received, is guaranteed through a Secure Socket Layer.

proceedings, the tribunal gives its award within thirty-five days. The award is posted on the Case Site. Arbitration awards reached through eResolution's service are kept confidential, unless the parties indicate otherwise.

II. – Issues raised by online arbitration

The online performance of *arbitration* proceedings may encounter a number of stumbling blocks or legal questions on its way. Here, I will focus on formal requirements and the question of the seat of online arbitration.

A. – FORMAL REQUIREMENTS

Is online arbitration hampered by formal requirements ? Formal requirements may come in various guises : the requirement of written material, the requirement of signatures and the requirement of an original. In answering this question, I shall take the New York Convention as a starting point. The formal requirements in the New York Convention mainly concern : 1. the arbitration agreement, and 2. the *arbitration* award.

1. – *The arbitration agreement*

Is it possible to agree on arbitration through electronic means, such as e-mail or by assenting to an offer on a website ? As far as national legislation is concerned, the European Directive on E-Commerce obliges Member States to adapt their legislation in order to remove formal obstacles to electronic contracting (14). Therefore in Europe, little problems are to be expected with regard to national legislation on arbitration. However, this does not remove possible obstacles in the New York Convention (15). The Convention

---

(14) Article 9.1 Directive on e-Commerce : Member States shall ensure that their legal system allows contracts to be concluded by electronic means. Member States shall, in particular, ensure that the legal requirements applicable to the contractual process neither create obstacles for the use of electronic contracts nor result in such contracts being deprived of legal effectiveness and validity on account of their having been made by electronic means.

(15) By virtue of the more-favourable-right provision of Art. VII.1 NYC, a party seeking enforcement of a foreign award is not obliged to base its enforcement on the New York Convention. It may choose to base the enforcement on another treaty or national law (e.g. art. 1076 Dutch Code of Civil Procedure).

requires an « agreement in writing », which, according to Art. II.2 NYC includes an *arbitration* clause in a contract or an arbitration agreement, signed by the parties or contained in an exchange of letters or telegrams. This definition is considered to be a uniform rule which prevails over municipal law regarding the form of the arbitration agreement (16). The question is whether the provision can be interpreted in such a way that online arbitration agreements are covered by it. The exchange of letters and telegrams was added in 1958 to make sure that arbitration could be agreed upon using the most modern means of communication. Therefore, the Convention does take into account the needs of legal practice. Electronic means such as e-mail and website communication may very well be seen as the modern functional equivalents of the traditional telegram (17). Just like telegrams, an e-mail message is a means of personal communication that is in « text form » and provides an (admittedly electronic) record. Furthermore, newer codifications of arbitration law have a more extensive catalogue of technologies : Art. 7 of the Uncitral Arbitration Rules provides, for instance, for « other means of telecommunication which provide a record » (18). Therefore, I think that a reasonable, contemporary interpretation of the New York Convention includes the electronic records in the concept of « writing ».

If enforcement is sought in a court, according to Art. IV NYC, the party must provide the original arbitration agreement or a certified copy of it. Here however, a slight mismatch between the Articles II and IV of the New York Convention surfaces. If the arbitration agreement is contained in an exchange of letters or telegrams, no signatures are required (art. II.2 NYC). The lack of signatures begs the question as to how originality (required by art. IV NYC) is to be determined. From this point on, two lines of reasoning can be followed. In the first place, it can be argued that without a signature, there is no original. A reasonable interpretation of Art. IV.1 NYC would then be that the requirement of an original only needs to be met if the manner in which arbitration was

---

(16) See A.J. VAN DEN BERG, *The New York Arbitration Convention of 1958* (diss. Rotterdam), Deventer : Kluwer 1980, p. 173.

(17) For an extensive analysis of the functional equivalence, see : R. HILL, « Online Arbitration : Issues and Solutions », *Arbitration International* 1999. Also available online : http:// www.umass.edu/dispute/hill.htm, visited October 2001.

(18) See also J. ARSIC, « International Commercial Arbitration on the Internet : Has the future come too early ? », *Journal of International Arbitration*, Vol. 14 (Issue 3), 1997, pp. 209-222.

agreed upon yields « a signed (= original) copy » of the agreement. This would mean that the requirement of an original need not be met if arbitration is agreed upon online. Proof of the existence of the arbitration agreement would of course still be required. The second line of reasoning would be the following : there can be originals, even though they do not bear signatures. An original would then be something like the first and exact transcript of the (conversion into letters of the) signals by the telegrapher. If this is considered to be an original under art. IV NYC, then the step to considering the printout of an e-mail message (or an other electronic record) as an original has become very small indeed. Whatever line of reasoning is followed, proof of the arbitration agreement by printouts of electronic records must, in my view, be possible under Art. IV NYC. My preference lies with the first alternative as the second alternative builds on a weak definition of originals.

2. – The arbitration award

A party seeking enforcement should furnish the duly authenticated original award or a duly certified copy thereof (Art. IV.1 NYC) (19). The question is whether these requirements are obstacles to the application of online arbitration. Compared with the arbitration *agreement*, the New York Convention here imposes an extra requirement : the award has to be *duly authenticated*. This means that the signature of the arbitrator has to be authenticated by a trusted third party, such as a diplomatic or consular agent (20). The extra requirement of authentication makes sense, because the « signatory » of the award (the arbitrator) is neither present, nor a party in the enforcement proceedings. For this reason, I doubt whether an electronic record of the award is sufficient to satisfy Art. IV NYC. Online international arbitration will thus still have to result in a paper award. From a practical perspective, this may not constitute a very large obstacle to online arbitration : it is probably not that burdensome if the arbitrator sends a paper version of the award to the parties. However, through the use of digital signatures reliable electronic authentication comes within technological reach.

---

(19) National arbitration statutes often have similar requirements; see e.g. Art. 1075 jo. 986 Dutch Code of Civil Procedure.

(20) See A.J. VAN DEN BERG, *The New York Arbitration Convention of 1958* (diss. Rotterdam), Deventer : Kluwer 1980, p. 253.

It would be desirable if the convention would place beyond doubt that awards signed with digital signatures (possibly subject to some qualification) would be in accordance with the Convention.

B. – The seat of arbitration

In a number of respects, the seat of arbitration is relevant. If parties do not choose a law that is applicable to the procedure or if the (chosen) autonomous rules of procedure exhibit gaps, the law of the seat of arbitration is applicable. The seat of arbitration is also decisive for the jurisdiction of the courts that can set an *arbitration* award aside or intervene. If arbitration is conducted online the seat of arbitration may not be determinable, as the traditional leads for determining the seat may not yield an unambiguous answer. Arbitrators may travel around in the period during which the arbitration process takes place. Perhaps the place of the servers could be used as a lead. There may however be several servers in as many different jurisdictions involved in the arbitration process. In Arbitration Rules that have been adapted to the online environment, the « seat » problem has been solved by allowing the parties to decide on the seat of arbitration. If they do not do so, the arbitrator decides on the seat (21). eResolution's Rules stipulate that in the latter case, the *arbitration* tribunal pays regard to the circumstances of the case and the contentions of the parties. This solution to the « seat problem » is attractive, as it is a simple means to *unambiguously* determine the « seat » of the arbitration. It also fits in with the freedom of the parties to choose the applicable procedural law. However, the solution may mean that parties choose a seat that has no connection with the dispute or with the arbitration. This might conceivably be a problem if a « strong » party secures an advantage over its opposing party in this way. However, this drawback seems for the moment to be only hypothetical. Another uncertainty might be that courts will not accept the chosen seat. Parties may however reduce this risk by choosing a seat that is « acceptable » in the context of « traditional » leads for determining the seat. In short, I think that the solution found in the arbitration rules may very well be working in practice

---

(21) See Art. 14 eResolution's Arbitration Rules for Canadian SME's and art. 10 AAA's Supplementary Procedures for Online Arbitration.

and that it deserves a chance to prove itself. In my view, an adaptation of the New York Convention in this respect is not desirable at the present time.

Conclusion

The first part or this report gives a brief overview of the initiatives that have been taken to provide for online arbitration. The main proponents of online arbitration are the AAA and eResolution. The WIPO Arbitration and Mediation Centre is working on online arbitration and builds on its experience as a domain name dispute resolver, accredited by ICANN. Furthermore, many other providers are active in the field.

The second part of this report focuses on the legal obstacles that might be encountered when performing arbitration online. The legal analysis is based on the New York Convention, because of its central role in recognition and enforcement in international arbitration. The main (potential) obstacles to online arbitration dealt with, are form requirements (such as the requirement of written material, signatures and originals) and the determination of the seat of arbitration. The main stance taken is that generally speaking, arbitration takes well to the online environment. The legal issues that were dealt with here do not constitute insurmountable obstacles to the application of online arbitration within the context of the New York Convention. The increase in providers of online arbitration seems to reflect this. However, some uncertainties remain. Some of them may be easily resolved. They only need « clarification », certain facts (acceptance of digital signatures as a valid means of authentication) merely need to be placed beyond doubt. Other issues are more complicated. I am thinking here mainly of the determination of the seat of arbitration. In arbitration rules that have been adapted to the online environment, a practical solution is found to the problem of determining the seat of arbitration : the choice of the seat is left to the parties and, absent their choice, to the arbitrator(s). This « practical » solution might very well work, but some doubts as to the desirability of the solution remain : whether an unconstrained possibility of choice is acceptable, is a complicated matter and difficult to ascertain. Here, lies a question that may not be answered without discussion. Nonetheless, for the time being, I would like to give the practical solution a chance to prove itself. Even more so, because there seems to be no simple legislative answer to the issue either.

THE ONLINE SETTLEMENT
OF SMALL CONSUMER DISPUTES

BY

Isabelle DE LAMBERTERIE

Director of Research – CNRS-CECOJI

Introduction

A. – Alternative methods
and consumer disputes

As Loïc Cadiet pointed out, « alternative methods for dispute resolution have become a standalone part of the system of legal regulation » (1). More than ever – and not just for some major international disputes – regulation must now take into account these new methods not only in North America or in countries where this type of process is part of the tradition but also in France and in most European countries.

What is the situation regarding consumer conflicts ? More than other types of dispute, alternative methods can find a solution whose flexibility better meets the needs of consumers and professionals. In fact, these disputes are characterised by a disproportion between the amount involved in the dispute and the cost and duration that a judicial settlement might entail. More often than not, because there is no suitable solution, nothing is done which can cause frustration or even damage the commercial image of the supplier. Although alternative methods might appear to be an economic palliative (low cost, rapidity), they must not be an opportunity of not affording consumers the same guarantees as those they are entitled to expect from traditional justice.

---

(1) Loïc Cadiet, « Les modes alternatifs de règlement des conflits et le droit » (« Alternative methods of settling disputes and the law ») – conclusion of the study day on alternative methods of dispute resolution organised on 18 June 2001 by the *Mission for Research Law and Justice*.

Continuing his demonstration, Loïc Cadiet reminds us that this need did not arise yesterday. Did the Civil Code not make compromise settlements subject to certain conditions? (2)

How can we develop these out-of-court methods so as to provide consumers with the guarantees that their fundamental rights will be respected? The reply is not obvious and despite their undeniable advantages, out-of-court procedures do not all offer sufficient guarantees. That is why both the European Commission and the OECD have made that one of their aims. Since 1998, the European Commission considered it necessary to adopt a recommendation « on the principles applicable to bodies responsible for the out-of-court settlement of consumer disputes » (3). Quite recently, on 4 April 2001, this initial recommendation was supplemented by a new provision « on the principles for out-of-court bodies involved in the consensual resolution of consumer disputes » (4). Both these recommendations form part of a set of Community initiatives to make it easier to resolve consumer disputes – including cross-border disputes – out-of-court. On 16 October last, the commissioner David Byrne opened the conference for launching the pilot project for a new European network (the EJE network – *Extra Judiciaire Européen*) the purpose of which is to help consumers resolve cross-border disputes without having to go to court.

B. – ALTERNATIVE METHODS
IN THE INFORMATION SOCIETY

The OECD also contributed by organising a conference with the International Chamber of Commerce (in February 2001 in The Hague) on the issue of confidence in the digital environment through the resolution of disputes between professionals and consumers. Of course, the out-of-court instruments have a place in the Information Society.

Again on 4 April 2001, the Commission published a communication « on widening consumer access to alternative dispute resolution » (5) and stated that the « new communication technologies have an important role to play ». The Internet is to be taken into

---

(2) Art. 2044 *et seq.* of the Civil Code
(3) 98/257/EC, *OJ* L 115 of 17/4/1998, p. 31.
(4) Notified under number C(2001) 1016, *OJ*, L 109/56 of 19/4/2001.
(5) 4/04/2001, COM (2001) 161 final.

account in two respects in a survey of alternative methods of consumer disputes. Firstly, more than other disputes, disputes arising from electronic commerce raise more problems in finding an outcome that is compatible with the respective interests of the contracting parties. Alternative methods of dispute resolution are therefore an issue encouraged by the European Directive of 8 June 2000 concerning certain aspects of the Information Society and in particular electronic commerce. However, this encouragement is accompanied by recommendations : the appropriate procedural guarantees must be afforded to the parties concerned.

Secondly, in North America (United States and, Canada (6)) for some time now and more recently in Europe (7), the Internet medium appeared to be a means of making it easier to seek a solution to disputes whether or not they related to electronic commerce (putting the parties in touch, possibility of expressing oneself in real time, reciprocal information etc.) Such facilitation is a « plus » added to the traditional methods of resolving disputes. Whilst benefiting from the experience gained in methods of traditional communication, the establishment of the out-of-court process in the electronic environment can give wider access, increased rapidity and sometimes even a better follow-up and monitoring of the procedures. The advantages of using the medium should not be obtained without complying with the same essential guarantees expected from an alternative process, whatever it may be.

We shall therefore study the way in which these guarantees are implemented by the bodies that propose alternative out-of-court methods for resolving consumer disputes (II) after having tried to establish a classification of existing alternative methods whether they use the Internet or not (I).

---

(6) E resolution.

(7) Amongst the European experiments (Webtrader, cybercourt....,) the ECODIR project is the result of research conducted by a European consortium with Canadian involvement to study the feasibility of a B/C online ADR and the establishment of a European platform operating with the rules of procedures and guarantees laid down in the recommendations of the Commission. The author of these lines is a member of the consortium and in charge of the feasibility study, the first phase of the project. The following developments are to a great extent based on the initial results of the ECODIR project and the work of the forum of Internet laws.

I. – Attempt to classify
existing alternative out-of-court methods
that can be used in consumer disputes

Once we have looked at the meaning of alternative, we shall examine the various methods, taking into account whether or not it is necessary to use an intervening third party. Another approach would be to examine the purpose of some processes introduced : preventative or curative.

A. – THE MEANING OF « ALTERNATIVE »

Whether it is a question of ADR (alternative dispute resolution, ODR (online dispute resolution), MARL (*mode alternatif de résolution des disputes*), MARC (8) (*mode alternatif de résolution des conflits*), des MARCEL (9) (*mode alternatif de résolution des conflits en ligne*), behind these acronyms, are very different methods which are all alternative, without knowing what meaning should be given to that adjective.

What meaning do we give to alternative ? Alternative compared to what ? Does it still leave access to the appropriate courts open ?

More often than not, the word alternative is understood in relation to traditional justice. However, the so-called alternative methods are not a substitute for judicial settlement even if their success enables court proceedings to be avoided. The aim is not to empty the courts but to create another type of relationship between the parties in order to find a solution to the dispute in which they are involved.

The question which should then be asked as far as concerns consumer disputesare concerned is whether or not one can take into consideration certain alternative methods which – like arbitration – replace a court settlement.

Opinion is divided on that point. Is not the fact that a consumer can apply to court at any time a fundamental guarantee ? Can he surrender it ? The recommendation of the April 2001 commission states in one of its recitals that « in accordance with Article 6 of the

---

(8) Acronym used in the Internet Laws Forum.
(9) Acronym suggested by Karim Benyklef (Eresolution) as a French alternative to online ADR.

European Human Rights Convention, access to the courts is a fundamental right » and that the use of alternative methods « may not deprive consumers of their right to bring the matter before the courts ». However, the recommendation also adds that the consumer may expressly agree « in full awareness of the facts and only after the dispute has materialised » to waive his right of access. Moreover, in arbitration, the parties still have means of obtaining redress : appeal against the arbitration award or an application to set aside (10).

It would be more for financial reasons that we leave out arbitration. In fact, our subject relates to small disputes and it is difficult to see how they would fall within the scope of a traditional arbitration process which is not suited to consumer disputes.

Accordingly, « Alternative » will be understood here as leaving open recourse to court proceedings at any time. For consumers, it is also the best interpretation to guarantee their rights. Is it not a suitable, appropriate method, as Catherine Kessedjian pointed out during the ECODIR conference a few weeks ago (11).

B. – With or without independent intervening third parties (12) ?

Most of the alternative methods are characterised by the involvement of a third party who assists the parties and helps them find a solution. However, there are situations where solutions can be sought without the involvement of a third party. The principle is that of the independence and impartiality of the third party.

If one goes by the European recommendation, alternative methods do not include *consumer claims services* run by the business or even the process which involves a third person who provides this service for the business or in its name (13).

The search for an amicable solution between the customer and the business is not a procedure within the strict sense but an attempt to handle a dispute that might involve a department of the business and the unhappy consumer, internally. In some cases one

---

(10) Art. 1486 *et seq.* of the New Code of Civil Procedure.

(11) Online dispute resolution conference, Brussels 26 October 2001.

(12) The words « third party interveners » do not cover the « bodies » that offer alternative mechanisms. Their role will be considered in the second part.

(13) Recital 9 of the recommendation of 4/4/2001.

can see the involvement of a new agent of the business, (who is higher up on the hierarchical scale) who intervenes to try and settle the dispute between the customer and its subordinate on its behalf. The same applies for attempts to negotiate within an internal structure of the business (consumer services) which, although separate from the party to the dispute, is nevertheless not independent.

What can one say about *institutional mediation within the business*? In order to settle a dispute, the business proposes using not a structure but a person – often a well-known person – who, although being internal to the institution is completely independent in relation to the various departments of the business. Generally speaking, that person reports to general management. In theory, he plays the role of mediator in the traditional meaning of the word, that is to say he is completely impartial in relation to the interests of the company. As examples I can cite the mediators of *La Poste*, the *SNCF*, the *RATP*, *Société Générale* in France... The ombudsman, who exists in some north European businesses, can be compared to this kind of mediation. His task is comparable to that of the company mediator. Although the impartiality of these mediators – and more often than not their independence – cannot be called into question, the service they provide does not seem to be like that of « out-of-court bodies » within the meaning of the Commission's recommendation, in that this service is provided on behalf of the company.

Would the same apply to mediation services provided by professional groups ?

This type of « *sectorial mediation* » is now well developed and the mediators are appointed and paid by the professional organisations that correspond to the sector of activity : mediator for the French federation of insurance companies, the association of financial companies... Unlike company mediators and although there is nothing to call into question the independence and impartiality of intervening third parties, it would seem that sectorial mediation can be regarded as falling within the category of out-of-court processes that the Commission is referring to.

This latter process can be compared to that of the *independent ombudsman*, familiar in various European countries. This is a person with an official task (which is assigned to him by the State or by a parliamentary institution). He may be responsible for special types of disputes such as consumer disputes (eg. Sweden) or disputes relating to a professional branch (bank, insurance, telecommunications, health service). He is distinguished by his total independence towards the institutional actors (or private) and by his recommendations to prevent the malfunctions found.

In order to guarantee independence and impartiality, it might be effective to form *joint committees* with representatives of the various protagonists (representatives of the business sector of companies and representatives of consumer associations).

Although that is not the case in France, some Member States of the European Union have also chosen formulae which, depending on the country, are imposed (Spain) or not imposed on consumers (Portugal, Germany). These are *Arbitration Centres for consumer disputes*, a body specifically dedicated to resolving consumer disputes, whose procedure is more supple and flexible than judicial procedures. In Portugal, referral is voluntary but like all *arbitration* awards, the decision is imposed on the parties. Germany also has arbitration bodies but neither its use nor the decision are imposed on the parties. In the latter case, the word « arbitration » should be defined. Only Portugal has an arbitration system in the strict sense. In Germany's case, in actual fact it is conciliation as the resolution body only provides recommendations with a view to encouraging an agreement between the parties.

The use of an intervening third party may be proposed during court proceedings. We then talk about a *judicial conciliator* or *mediator*. When the cases are called (especially before district courts), the judge invites the parties to seek an attempt at conciliation. Although the process is virtually identical, a distinction must be drawn between judicial conciliators who are voluntary workers (the attempt at conciliation is free of charge) and judicial mediation where the mediator is paid by the parties. This latter type of alternative method may appear to be purely theoretical for small consumer disputes but remains one possibility where there is an appeal against a judgement at first instance. In all cases, if the mediation or conciliation succeeds, the parties will sign an agreement. If they are not successful, the parties return to the court room and the dispute is settled by the standard judicial procedure.

As we have just seen, the mechanisms for resolving consumer disputes can range from seeking an agreement between the parties to a binding decision with recommendation in between.

Is it not a question, in many cases, of not only resolving a dispute but on a more positive note, of improving communication between consumers and professionals ?

C. – The role
of the intervening third parties :
curative or preventative

Above all, it is the qualities of people asked to play the role of third party that is one of the points most often raised : the conciliator or mediator must be impartial third parties, trained, skilled and they must comply with a professional code that commits them to respecting confidentiality and secrecy.

These intervening third parties can enable the parties to express themselves and listen to each other, to find a solution to the disagreements and to prevent further disputes :

Enable the parties to express themselves and listen to each other

A climate of confidence must be established and the two protagonists must be aware that they have a problem to resolve. They must also be given the chance to express their position on the problem and explain their grievance.

Find a solution to disputes

Different attitudes characterise the role of the intervening « third party » in finding a way out of the dispute. When it is mediation, a distinction should be drawn between the « facilitator » mediator and the « advisor » mediator.

A « facilitator » is a neutral mediator who does not make a proposal. It is the parties who find the solution. The mediator encourages communication and exchanges between the parties and, using a special technique for listening, formulating and creative search for solutions, leads them to find their own agreement to put an end to the dispute. He is then a negotiation and decision-making « facilitator ».

An « advisor » is an intervening third party who enlightens the consumer as to his rights and the company as to its duties (or reciprocally). He also makes concrete proposals to the parties that they may or may not accept.

Prevent further disputes

I shall talk about the power of more general proposals to prevent disputes (eg. removing an ambiguous clause) that some intervening third parties have. This power to make proposals is explicitly defined as falling within the remit of sectorial mediation structures, joint committees and the ombudsman. Through the complaints that they receive, they are privileged witnesses to malfunctions. Part of their task is to inform professionals or the public authorities about them. They do this, on a case to case basis or, more generally, in their annual report.

Another method of preventative treatment can be found in the development of a policy of informing and directing the consumer. Interfaces such as the « EJE » network or the Ecodir portal can fulfil that task.

Seals of approval and insurance

Is not the purpose of alternative methods also to maintain consumer confidence ? That is why some seals of approval or certification initiatives associated with insurance services deserve to be examined for the role they play upstream of the dispute. This type of « service » – which is not new – meets a real need in electronic commerce (14). Private or public organisations offer trading sites a seal of approval, which is granted following a legal, technical and economic audit, (does the concerned trading site offer the guarantees that consumers are entitled to demand ?).

Furthermore, if something goes wrong, both the consumer and the trader have assurance that everything will be done to find a solution : for example, reimbursement if delivery is impossible within 7 days after the consumer's complaint.

---

(14) See the example of Trusted Shops which are developing in Germany and Great Britain with the support of a group of German insurers. In France, Juridica, a subsidiary of AXA offers a legal assistance service which includes information and advice services that can extend to seeking conciliation or mediation.

Is not encouraging and facilitating the resolution of disputes at the earliest possible stage a means of ensuring « a high level of consumer protection and promoting consumer confidence » ? (15) The Commission invites Member States to ensure that this is the case and for that it recommends compliance with a number of rules that are common to the variety of mechanisms offered to settle or prevent minor consumer disputes.

II. – The guarantees provided by alternative out-of-court settlement of consumer disputes

First of all, I shall examine the principles that should be applied by the bodies that implement alternative processes (out of court) for settling consumer disputes and I will then look at how these principles are implemented with the use of the Internet.

A. – THE PRINCIPLES RECOMMENDED

The first of these principles, that is to say independence and impartiality of the intervening third parties, has served as a criterion for determining the alternative methods that are likely or not to fall within the scope of the European recommendation. It is now appropriate to examine which measures guarantee that independence and impartiality.

Other principles concern the operation of procedures and mechanisms introduced. Finally, I shall examine the delicate question of ensuring that the solution found complies with consumers' rights.

Independence and impartiality

A change of vocabulary can be noted. In the 1998 recommendation, the independence of the body or intervening third parties had to be such as to guarantee that the measures they took were impartial. The 2001 recommendation speaks only of impartiality but it refers to the same concepts. It is a question of guaranteeing the *skill*

---

(15) Recital 1 of the aforementioned recommendation of 4 April 2001.

of the intervening third parties (16), of ensuring that there is no *conflict of interests* (alleged or real) with one of the parties. Finally, in order to be able to *act quite independently,* the persons appointed to intervene in the process of finding a solution must have sufficient time (an indefinite period) in which they cannot be dismissed without good reason.

Operation of the procedures

Transparency and effectiveness must be guaranteed. By transparency, naturally I mean a general obligation to provide information which is to be applied throughout the whole process. « Effectiveness » refers to the methods of the procedure facilitating access to it and allowing it to take place in conditions that are beneficial to the consumer. We shall see later how the medium can strengthen effectiveness.

Transparency and information

The parties must be able to choose to use an alternative method in full knowledge of the facts. It is therefore essential that before doing so, they have information about the types of disputes that can be referred. They must also know how the procedure works and the basic rules (legal framework, codes of conduct or good practice etc.) and the form governing that procedure (timetable, potential cost and for cross-border disputes, the languages in which the parties can express themselves...) (17), not forgetting information about the impartiality and skill of intervening third parties (18). The parties must also be informed of their right to refuse to take part in an alternative mechanism, to withdraw from it at any time or to be able to access the judicial systems or other means of out-or-court redress (19). Finally, the consumer must be informed in clear, intelligible terms that he is free to accept or refuse the solution proposed (20).

---

(16) The 1998 recommendation talks of capability and experience – particularly with regard to legal matters – required to fulfil the role.
(17) Art. II B (3) of the recommendation of 4 April 2001.
(18) Art. II A (c)
(19) Art. II D 1 a)
(20) Art. II D 2 a)

You might be surprised not to find in this list of information to be provided any reference to the situation in which the consumer could expressly renounce his right of access to the courts, in full knowledge of the facts (21). This opportunity mentioned in the recitals of the 2001 Commission recommendation, is not repeated in the text itself. We must hope that this delicate issue will be clarified in the near future.

The « effectiveness » of the procedure

The main obstacles to be removed in order to facilitate access to alternative methods are firstly, the « cost » and « time » factors and secondly, the assistance that the parties might receive both from a lawyer or legal representative and from the agency in charge of managing the procedure. It will be noted that the cost to the consumer must be nil or low (at least in proportion with the dispute). That means that the other party, or the public authorities, might have to bear the cost of the procedure.

The brevity of the time-limits, which is one of the principles, must be assessed in accordance with the nature of the dispute. The text of the recommendation talks of appropriate diligence. The interpretation of those words must rely on the experience of those who have practised alternative methods for a long time. As S. Bensimon the philosopher and professional mediator said, it is important that the mediator makes the parties aware that there is a dispute. The mediator must make the parties understand that they both have a problem to resolve. Accordingly, he must be able to let the process unfold in order that it is fully effective, without going too fast and skipping essential stages in seeking a solution.

Compliance with consumer rights and fair solutions

Whereas the 98 legislation spoke only of the principle of legality (the consumer could not be deprived of the protection afforded to him by the overriding provisions of the State in which he resides) the 2001 recommendation has one foot in the camp of consumer

---

(21) See above the comments on recital 14 which allows arbitration to be included in the alternative methods that provide the guarantees expected by consumers.

rights in order to implement the alternative mechanism and one in the possibility of an equitable solution.

Accordingly, first and foremost, equity must be ensured throughout the whole procedure whilst complying with consumer rights : freedom to take part or not, compliance with the principle of listening to the argument of both parties or the right to information or the confidentiality of information that might have been transmitted as well as the possibility – at any time – to fall back on court proceedings. However, secondly, the solution proposed, whilst attempting to be fair cannot be exactly a solution having its basis – « in law ». Although a judge is obliged to apply the law, the same cannot be said of a mediator or intervening third party who assesses the situation on equitable principles. The wording of the recommendation even explicitly acknowledges the possibility that the outcome might be less favourable – to one of the parties – than that which he might have been obtained before a court.

Effectiveness ?

The parties must agree on the solution proposed and on the outcome of the dispute. Are we not now on familiar territory of the law – a contract, a compromise settlement ? In the eyes of the law, the parties are committed and if one of them fails to fulfil its undertakings, the other can apply to the court to seek redress. How many small disputes will go before the courts ? Businesses assess referral to the courts after failure of an alternative method of dispute resolution at 10 %. And the others ? Each must find its advantage in the solution proposed and in order to generate this confidence it is important that the undertakings are fulfilled.

Although the out-of-court framework does not offer any means of coercion to oblige the parties to perform, can one envisage other means of pressure, apart from court proceedings, to make the parties – and especially professionals – fulfil their undertakings ? It can be achieved indirectly through rules specific to certain professions. The example of sectorial mediators shows that the effectiveness of mediation depends on the ability of the professional group to take action with one of its members when he/she does not comply with his/her undertakings nor with the professional charter. Penalties may then be applied to him/her which ultimately can be exclusion.

And the Internet?

In order to assess the notable role that the Internet can play in the online resolution of consumer disputes, we need to start with dispute resolution processes that use traditional means to get the parties to the dispute to talk. One is bound to note that more often than not in consumer disputes, exchanges only take place at a distance, without the physical presence of the parties. Accordingly, one can measure the part played by the Internet which can make communication easier, especially when the parties are in different countries or even different continents. The implementation of the principles recommended can then be facilitated whether it is a question of transparency of the procedure or the provision of information required, the effectiveness of the process (reduced time-limits, even instantaneous for contacts between two or three – and the intervening third party). Similarly, the confidentiality of exchanges can be guaranteed – not only by the body managing the alternative method or even the intervening parties but also by the use of a »tool« that fulfils objective security criteria.

By way of a conclusion some general thoughts...

Firstly, as we have seen, in order to tackle online disputes, firstly, we had to deal with alternative methods regardless of the medium used. Once again regulation of the Information Society follows the same lines as of regulation of Society. Use of the Internet medium in no way changes the balances to be sought and complied with.

Secondly, to encourage the development of alternative methods is also to help re-establish the social links. As for the Internet, if access to it becomes more commonplace and is not reserved for the privileged, it also can contribute to this same objective : it can facilitate access to information, help to make exchanges effective and open up new ways of marketing – particularly in emerging countries.

Georges Chatillon

Unfortunately, we have no more time left and we must move on to Mrs Kessedjian's general report before hearing Mr Dan Eliasson and Mrs Marylise Lebranchu.

GENERAL REPORT

Catherine KESSEDJIAN

PROFESSOR AT THE UNIVERSITY OF PANTHÉON-ASSAS PARIS II

By way of closing this afternoon's discussions devoted to dispute resolution, I should like to take up some key points and outline some avenues for future discussions and work. In order to do so, I am going to lead you through each essential stage of a dispute and its resolution.

The starting point is the computer that we all have in front of us as we are now all seasoned Internet users. We are in the hypothetical situation in which the Internet user accesses a commercial site because when he accesses a completely open site that offers information free of charge, the issue of a potential loss caused by that free information appears to be much more theoretical. Before entering into a contract, the Internet user must ask himself what method his future co-contracting party is offering for settling disputes. In view of the right to access to justice, a fundamental right whose existence we have just been reminded of, it is essential that commercial sites offer their customers a dispute resolution clause and the applicable law in a clear, intelligible and easily accessible manner. Admittedly, the validity of such clauses might be tested subsequently, especially if the Internet user is a consumer. However, one can argue without too much risk of being mistaken, that the structure of this fundamental right to access to justice is undergoing a change, thereby favouring all the alternative methods of dispute resolution including online methods.

This right to access to justice is undergoing a transformation because the right changes under the influence of what consensus calls legal pluralism but also thanks to a mechanism that is well-known, especially to specialists of private international law, which is the principle of contractual autonomy. Pushed to the extreme, this principle leads to what has been referred to during our two days of discussion by an expression that is dear to me and which I have been using for some time : « contractualisation » of the law. In my view, it cannot be denied that the Internet obliges greater consideration to be paid to contractual autonomy and a greater awareness by the partners, including consumers or « weak partners » in general, of the implication of contractual autonomy. In that respect, one might think that the Internet does not really offer anything new but crystalises the need, which is even greater than for analogue transactions, to check the terms and conditions of the contract and their implications. However, somewhat paradoxically, the Internet allows even less discussion than analogue transactions. A site is structured in such a way that the Internet user's only « choice » is to reply « yes » or « no ». If he agrees to enter into the contract under the terms and conditions offered by the partner, can he then argue that the latter can invoke the dispute resolution clause included in the terms and conditions of the contract against him ? It is on this delicate exercise that the national courts are invited to rule since the law on this subject is still evolving.

The link between electronic transactions and access to justice automatically encourages taking an interest in international cooperation. It is not by chance that we find that the people who have been active in the preparation of this colloquium, within the Scientific Committee or otherwise, are themselves members of a number of international cooperation networks : judicial cooperation or extra-judicial cooperation. This aspect is vital. For many years now it has been recognised that without international cooperation, without a definition of the rules applicable at supra-national level, the Internet had little chance of developing and providing all the services we might expect from it.

However, this afternoon you and I heard someone speak about « mistrust » and say, in particular, that private international law is based on the mutual mistrust that States have of their legal and judicial systems. That view seems to me to be deeply flawed and based on a premise on which it is impossible to build. On the contrary, private international law offers rules of tolerance, tolerance towards different cultures and legal and judicial systems that offer solutions that are substantially different but which cannot be judged *a priori* to be bad unless they breach the few major fundamental principles dictated by a universal notion of human rights.

Thinking along the same lines, it seemed worrying to me that the two speakers who have come from a long way geographically and have been so kind as to travel in order to take part in our proceedings, told us that they were waiting to see what the negotiations between the United States and Europe would bring. Admittedly, the transatlantic consensus that we hope for is important. Admittedly, the dialogue between the United States and Europe can offer original solutions and test issues that would not necessarily arise in another context. However, just as equality of the parties is important in contractual matters, such equality is crucial in international cooperation and the ongoing negotiations. All the States, or at least the majority of them must be involved in these negotiations in order that their values might be taken into consideration and that they do not allow solutions put forward by a minority of States to be imposed on them.

We have mentioned international cooperation but another aspect of internationality is important : what criterion are we going to use to find out if we are dealing with an international or transnational dispute ? Traditionally, the economic criterion is favoured in France (cross-border flow) to the detriment of a purely legal criterion (nationality or establishment of the parties, in particular) which is used in a number of countries and international legislation. Traditionally also, the consumer contract is not an international contract. In fact, whenever a consumer travelled abroad to enter into a transaction, he was no longer considered to be a consumer. Nowadays, the Internet obliges us to re-examine those traditional principles. For example, we must ask ourselves whether a new criterion should not be used. Can we say, for example, that a contract that is entered into or enforced via the Internet contains characteristics that mean that it should be treated as if it were an international contract. This presumption could be a simple presumption which would disappear if it were shown that all the aspects of the transaction are located in one and the same State. The question remains. We have not provided any answers during our discussions.

The personality of the parties must also be taken into account. So far as concerns international disputes, we are used to separating relations between professionals (a relationship which is deemed to take place between equal partners) and relations between a professional and a non-professional or consumer a (relationship that is deemed to be unequal, in which one of the parties – the consumer – must be protected). Depending on the method of dispute resolution in question, the inequality of the parties can be a handicap, not to say an obstacle that precludes its use. What methods are available ?

Nowadays, it is essential that operators and Internet users are offered a full range of various methods of dispute resolution. We must not set the various methods of settlement against each other. I would remind you, although we have spoken about it several times this afternoon, that its range is quite enormous. The following list is in order of the least binding to the most binding :

– After-Sales Service : the establishment of alternative methods of dispute resolution must not be a way for companies to provide an « external resource », when ultimately it is their duty as a company and operator to offer their customers a means of preventing disputes by a an effective After-Sales Service which is wholly designed to prevent disputes.

– Mediation : One expects the intervention of a third party but he is not there to find a solution between the parties. The role of the mediator is to gradually lead the parties towards finding their own solution. The mediator is not too much of an interventionist. It is for the parties to find the solution to their problems.

– By contrast, in conciliation, the third party plays a greater role. In fact he can propose solutions and allow the parties to reach a compromise settlement. However, mediation and conciliation are often confused.

– Then there is arbitration and referral to the courts. Both of these correspond to a unique method, a judicial method in which the arbitrator or judge take a decision that is binding on the parties. This parallel is not always necessarily understood by legal experts who deal with online dispute resolution. Especially when reference is made to a supposed « non-binding arbitration ».

Where do methods of online dispute resolution fall in this list ?

If one examines the ICANN rules for settling disputes arising from the use of domain names, one cannot help but think that we are dealing with a sui generis method of settlement which borrows both from an administrative procedure and from arbitration. I am not convinced that this procedure can serve as a model for online settlements, owing, in particular, to the uniqueness of the disputes it is designed to settle as opposed to the great variety of disputes that can arise from the use of the commercial Internet.

The relationship between these different methods of settlement is not competitive but complementary. And the essential avenue to be explored appears to be that of complementarity and the establishment of the necessary bridges between each method of settlement. That reminds me a little of what I wrote elsewhere about the « multi-door court house ».

Finally, four questions arise when one examines international litigation.

Which jurisdiction?

This question is only relevant if the dispute is brought before the national courts. Nowadays it is difficult to establish such jurisdiction from an international point of view. There are discussions underway that give rise to deadlocks, either because there is fear that the « market » for online dispute resolution has not yet grown sufficiently. Pressure groups are acting in a way that will not restrain the emergence of this « market » by a series of rules that are too fixed or that they consider to be unfavourable. Moreover, what happens in the States is often profoundly different on this issue and there is a very wide range between very flexible criteria on the one hand and fixed criteria on the other. The balance that was thought to have been found in 1999 has been disputed so that the negotiations are still ongoing and nowadays there is insufficient transparency to know exactly where these negotiations are leading.

Which procedure?

It is especially important not to tack strict rules inherited from court disputes onto supple and flexible dispute resolution methods such as mediation or conciliation. It would be a grave mistake. The aggressiveness that we are currently seeing in arbitration proceedings for international commerce, when this method was usually less aggressive than judicial proceedings, augurs badly for the future. In any event, this aggressiveness must not creep into mediation or conciliation.

As for the rules of transnational proceedings that Unidroit and the ILA have adopted in an attempt to put forward uniform principles, they are not relevant (not yet?) to the potential adaptations required for online settlements. The pioneer work which was done by E-Resolution (now in liquidation) and the projects of the Paris Chamber of Commerce and Industry or the European project ECODIR have shown the way for rules adapted to the online settlement of disputes arising from the Internet.

Which law is applicable?

This is one of the greatest debates currently raging in Europe, with the transformation into regulations of the 1980 Convention of Rome on the law applicable to contractual obligations and the drafting of another regulation on the law applicable to obligations in tort. However, in view of the integration of markets in the territory of Member States of the European Union, thanks to the four major freedoms of movement, some people argue that only the law of the country of origin is capable of settling all questions without relying on any other choice-of-law rule whatsoever. Moreover, codes of conduct or self-regulation are often brandished as the only possible solution to the question of applicable law. In my view, there again, it would be harmful to oppose the two methods as if they are in competition when both categories of rules must be able to function together.

How effective is the decision?

We are all aware that it is difficult to ensure that decisions are enforced in other countries in a world in which there are many parties (victims or perpetrators of offences) who might be affected by the medium that we are using, the Internet or Web.

There again, it is complementarity that must be the rule. We must continue to negotiate internationally on compulsory methods of enforcing decisions but we must not forget that nowadays companies are working on a principle of effectiveness that is not new,

« *naming and shaming* ». I am surprised that no-one has mentioned it this afternoon. It is a fundamental means of making the decision effective. When a company decides to adopt a code of conduct and it is found to be in breach of it, the market, operators and actors must definitely know that this company is in breach of this code of conduct.

In conclusion, we must work on a code of « *best practices* », in which the best clauses for dispute resolution should be listed, according to the type of disputes in question; the best procedures according to the method of settlement; the most effective codes of conduct, etc. The *best practices* system is the positive side of *naming and shaming* and « blacklists ».

ADDRESS
TO THE INTERNATIONAL COLLOQUIUM ON INTERNET LAW – EUROPEAN AND INTERNATIONAL APPROACHES

BY

Dan ELIASSON

State Secretary
Ministry of Justice, Sweden

Ladies and gentlemen,

There is no need for new legislation to regulate activities in the new technology – old rules on civil law and criminal law can be applied in the online environment, just as they have been in the offline environment.

This is a fictitious quote but one that summarises many reactions I have heard and that I am still hearing when it comes to IT-law or rather : law applicable in the IT-environment.

But in this auspicious gathering I feel confident that you all share my view when I say that it isn't as easy as that. In fact, this colloquium taking place is clear evidence of that.

Let me give you some examples to support this. Look at how the new technology has changed the way that the very basic principles of market economy operates. The market used to be a physical place to which you took commodities and services, a place where comparison and negotiations took place and a place you actually had to go to before you had any chance – or risk – of becoming engaged in its mechanisms. Today the market comes to you, whether you like it or not, as soon as you enter the cyber environment.

We all have consumer protection rules in place to protect the weaker players on the market, normally constructed for situations where the market comes looking for the consumer by selling goods at the door, or when the consumer goes to the market and buys goods. In the new market, the consumer is in the market place as soon as he surfs to the weather report.

The concept of intellectual property is not old, historically speaking, in « offline law » and, on an international level, it still encounters problems of global agreement. This is why the World Trade Organisation still has to negotiate global rules on Trade in Intellectual Property. Applied to the Internet, intellectual property presents an even bigger challenge – here the intangible rights are even more intangible, in addition to a general perception of free access to *all* information. Any regulatory regime will be more or less imperfect, but we – the Governments – cannot abdicate from our role as legislators, and let the market find the proper mechanisms to defend its interests. The Napster-case shows us that, yes, solutions can be found, control mechanisms can be introduced on the transmission of certain services. But this puts the protection against abuse in the hands of those that can pay for it – it may protect the multinational entertainment industry but it will not protect « Joe's Garage Records ».

This colloquium has penetrated a variety of aspects of Internet law. It has examined the standards applicable to the Internet and the ways of regulating the net. In the course of these two days, you have moved ahead to address the challenges of implementing Internet laws.

But leaving the civil law aspects aside, I will now mainly focus on penal aspects of the IT-environment, and in particular the challenges we face in Europe and the European Union.

Ladies and gentlemen,

I would like to extend my warmest compliments to the organisers of this conference, and in particular to Mr Chatillon, who has been the prime mover of the event. It is certainly timely and highly relevant. But I would imagine that when this conference was initially planned, there was little evidence suggesting that the month of November 2001 would be such a crucial month in the history of European IT-law as far as criminal law is concerned.

First of all, we are all still adjusting ourselves to the post September 11th-topography – what was previously planning for events that we all hoped would never take place has suddenly become raising our guard against an enemy we know is out there, although we do not see him. This is as relevant in the field of IT-security as in any other field of law that contributes our own counter-terrorism efforts.

Secondly, all EU Member States will soon embark upon a legislative road of implementing far-reaching provisions on data protection related to telecommunications – a road whose final destination we cannot see but a road we all know will lead to 15 different destinations unless we join forces and coordinate our implementation efforts. The danger that I see lies in the risk of authorities and companies having limited or no access to traffic data in the future. Should that be the case, we will have tied both hands behind our back in the fight against cyber crime.

Let me make this very clear : in this context, we should not equate data protection with human rights and fundamental freedoms. Data protection must not be permitted to erode the security Governments provide their citizens.

Thirdly, next week we will see the first inaugural meeting of the EU Forum on Cyber Crime in Brussels – a forum that strives to meet the just demand for dialogue between government, industry and organisations representing the users of the Internet, to discuss common concerns as regards the safety of the IT-environment.

Fourthly, on Friday this week we will witness the signing ceremony of the Council of Europe Cybercrime Convention – a Convention establishing common definitions of crimes in the new environment, establishing co-operation facilities between the participating states to improve their fight against cyber crimes.

As Mr Guy de Vel from the Council of Europe pointed out yesterday, cyber crime is an increasing problem around the world. It covers traditional forms of crime committed in the new environment but also completely new forms of crime, such as hacking and denial-of-service-attacks – crimes for which there are few counterparts in the « real world ». It is a form of criminality which is often transnational and requires a transnational response. An effective and well-functioning system of international co-operation is therefore of vital importance in the fight against such criminality.

One of the most important aims of the Council of Europe Cyber Crime Convention is to set up a rapid and effective regime of international co-operation in the field of cyber crime. However, the convention is not limited to computer crimes and computer related crimes but is also applicable to the collecting of evidence in electronic form of any criminal offence. This gives the convention a wide field application, which we should welcome.

When I say that the problem of cyber crime is transnational I mean that it is truly global. I think it is very important to point out that the Cyber Crime Convention is also open to states that are not members of the Council of Europe – it is the first global instrument in the field of cyber crime and it is of course my government's wish that as many countries as possible will be able to sign and ratify the convention in a near future.

These four challenges stand before us, and I dare say that the conference organisers were either clairvoyant or extremely lucky when they decided to hold this conference at this moment in time.

Ladies and gentlemen,

At the outset of my presentation I quoted those with doubts over all the legislative activity that we see in the field of Internet law, and I hope I have convinced you that I am not among the doubters. In fact, my Government made an effort during our Presidency of the European Union earlier this year to keep the issue of fighting high-tech crimes on the political agenda. An example of this is that the EU Ministers for Justice and Home Affairs met in the Council of the EU and confirmed this ambition and confirmed it again by adopting a Recommendation to the EU Member States that they should all participate in the Network for Combating High-tech Crime – the so-called 24hours-7days-a-week-network, originally set up by the G8. By doing this, we ensured that our fight does not stay a European fight against a global problem, but a joint global effort.

The fact that we address this issue in this international colloquium underlines that regardless of whether we tackle the challenges of civil law or criminal law aspects of Internet law, broad international agreement and cooperation is the only way forward. To imagine that these challenges can be met successfully at a national level is as optimistic as suggesting that national defence is best provided by the municipal level of our societies, and we would not like to ask our municipalities to defend our territories, would we?

Thank you

CLOSING SPEECH

BY

Marylise LEBRANCHU

Ministre of Justice,
Garde des Sceaux, France

Madam Chairman, Minister, Ladies and Gentlemen,

The colloquium that has just been held on the subject of European and international approaches to Internet law is an important moment for reflecting on this new world of networks and their regulation.

Over two days, at the instigation of the Minister for Justice, the Association for the Renewal and Promotion of Legal Exchanges (ARPEJE) and the University of Paris I, meetings and discussions have led you to reflect and share your experience on the fundamental issues facing our society.

The summary reports reflect the quality of the work carried out, the richness of the exchanges and the value of comparing the various national legal systems.

I should especially like to pay tribute to the attendance of the numerous representatives from foreign countries who agreed to come to France in order to consider adapting international law to developments in information and communication technologies.

The network of networks has a dual aspect : on the one hand a tool for freedom, on the other a vehicle for unlawful or criminal messages.

The Internet is primarily a fantastic tool for mutual knowledge and exchange. Its development can help to improve the living conditions of our fellow citizens and economic growth. The Internet can also help to boost freedom of expression and communication, as is borne out by the fear it engenders in totalitarian regimes.

However, the Internet also carries with it very real deviations and threats as the international dimension of the network multiplies the dangers of some human activities tenfold by allowing them to be deployed on a worldwide scale. The tragedy of 11 September was a cruel reminder. It is very likely that those responsible for these terrible attacks used the resources of the web to exchange information and foment their actions. The Internet can also be used to commit unlawful acts, to circulate racist or xenophobic messages or to launder dirty money. It increases the risk that personal data circulating on the network will be used inappropriately.

These new challenges call for a suitable legal response that reconciles the requirements for security and protection of human rights with the need to preserve freedom of expression and communication.

Your colloquium has outlined solutions that will be particularly useful to national legislators.

Allow me to return to the two main subjects it covered :

– establishing the law applicable to the networks,
– implementing Internetlaws.

I. – Establishing the law
applicable to the networks

A. – The Internet is not an unregulated area

Since the publication of the report of the *Conseil d'Etat* on the Internet and digital networks in July 1998, few people seriously dispute that the Internet should not be an unregulated area.

Subjecting the Internet to the law dashed the hopes of those who, believing in the natural ability of the network to serve the ideals of freedom and equality, thought there was no need for regulation. In fact, the virtual world must comply with the law. However, in exchange, it is protected by the law.

The Internet is subject to the principles of our law. A racist message circulated on the web must be regarded as a criminal act just as it would be in a magazine or on the radio.

However, the Internet is also protected by the law. According to the authorities, correspondence exchanged via e-mail will be protected by privacy just like a letter sent by post.

However, owing to the transnational nature of the Internet and the transience and volatility of its content, it is vital that our legal rulesshould be adapted.

In particular, the transnational nature of the network obliges us to question the territorial jurisdiction of the judge and the applicable law. The courts, especially French courts, tend to award themselves jurisdiction when the Internet site at issue was accessible from their national territory.

The case in France between LICRA (the International League against racism and anti-semitism) and the American company Yahoo is a remarkable illustration of that. Although in the United States, the decision of the French judge came up against the First Amendment of the American Constitution protecting freedom of expression, we all, I think, noted with satisfaction that Yahoo had in fact given up selling Nazi memorabilia by auction.

The transient nature and volatility of content conveyed on the Internet also invite us to consider whether our law is adapted. In criminal matters, they make it more difficult to report an offence and to identify the person responsible for it.

In civil matters, they question the traditional rules of evidence of transactions that are based on the supremacy of the paper medium.

Your colloquium was an opportunity to show that not only does the Internet call into question national law but it also invites us to replace the traditional views of international law which nevertheless appears to be so well suited to a globalised cyberspace.

How can we adapt the law to this new reality or virtuality ? How can we meet the new requirements for legal security arising from the network boom ?

B. – THE REPLY TO THESE QUESTIONS CANNOT BE FOUND BY ESTABLISHING A NEW INTERNATIONAL LEGAL SYSTEM, TRANSCENDING BOTH NATIONAL LAWS AND THE CURRENT INTERNATIONAL LAW

The introduction of a *lex electronica@*, a global uniform law for the Internet, which would replace the diversity of national laws and be implemented on line by cyberjudges@ who themselves would be endowed with universal jurisdiction, is manifestly not an adequate response.

On the contrary, such a view engenders real anxiety because the resulting standardisation of the law would merely be the expression of a parallel standardisation of behaviour, thoughts and cultures. In the best of Internet worlds, the single universal law could only be the law of the strongest.

Answers must be found by adapting national legislation, inventing new ways of regulating and stepping up international cooperation.

C. – ADAPTING NATIONAL LEGISLATION

You know that the French government has decided to set up a huge programme to adapt the legislative and regulatory framework to the information society. Under the government's action plan for the information society (PAGSI), launched in January 1998 by the Prime Minister, various initiatives have been taken in that direction.

Firstly, there is the recent law of 13 March 2000. Followed by the implementing decree of 30 March 2001, it adapts the mode of proof to the requirements of the virtual world, by recognising the legal value of electronic written material and signatures. This law is a perfect illustration of the government's approach : the existing rule is adapted in order to ensure the legal security and efficiency of the rule of law, without calling into question the principles that govern the burden or means of proof or those applicable to obtaining consent.

Then there is the information societybill. This bill, which brings together the adjustments that would appear to be necessary or wise in view of the development of the Internet, contains, *inter alia,* provisions which make it easier for citizens to access information in digital form, sets out the legal framework for electronic commerce, outlines the responsibilities of the technical intermediaries, encourages the development of digital networks and strengthens the means of combating cybercrime.

The bill's provisions concerning the means allowing the administrative and legal authorities to decipher encoded messages and to retain connection data were reiterated in the law on everyday security, which was finally adopted by Parliament on 31 October last.

D. – INVENTING NEW FORMS OF REGULATION

As the Internet develops, as its consequences on economic and social life increase, as its users become more diverse, everyone is aware that the traditional methods of public regulation can no longer cope with the new power issues thus created and we must devise original methods of regulation.

Following the report presented by Mr Christian Paul, the then deputy, a Forum of Internet laws was created in the form of a 1901 law association, whose aim is to inform the public and to be involved in co-regulating the Internet through harmonising actions between public and private partners. An initial report of the actions of this Forum was presented to you yesterday by Mrs Isabelle FAL-QUE-PIERROTIN.

E. – STEP UP INTERNATIONAL COOPERATION

Your colloquium has demonstrated it well : the most appropriate solutions to the questions raised by the development of the networks can only be international.

In that respect, I should like to emphasise the fact that international negotiations take place with the intention of encouraging the Internet boom but also with the strong conviction that the Internet must carry the values chosen by our democracy and not water them down.

In that respect, the Council of Europe Convention on cybercrime is the first international treaty on criminal offences committed against computer networks or with their help. France intends to sign this international agreement which is a definite move forward, notably by incorporating provisions concerning the fight against child pornography. Furthermore, this convention will be supplemented by an additional protocol on racist or xenophobic propaganda circulated via the networks.

The European Union is certainly not absent from this debate. Apart from the proliferation of initiatives aimed at adapting national laws to the Internet in order to encourage the internal market, as illustrated by the decision of 24 January 1999 adopting a multiannual action plan to promote safer use of the Internet as well as the decision of 29 May 2000 on the fight against child pornography on the network.

This flood of legislation governing the network raises the problem of enforcing it effectively and implementing Internet.laws.

II. – Implementing internet laws

The issues raised today in the meetings and discussions are fundamental. Since my arrival at the Ministry of Justice, one of my prime concerns is improving the means of justice to ensure that the law is fully effective.

These issues take on a totally new dimension with the advances in information and communication technologies. How can we ensure that personal data are protected on the network? How can we guarantee the protection of copyright? How can we make access to justice and the enforcement of decisions easier?

Some replies were outlined throughout the day.

Without going back over all the proposals made, I should like to emphasise three points :

A. – WE MUST PROMOTE ALTERNATIVE PROCEDURES FOR DISPUTE RESOLUTION WITHOUT CALLING INTO QUESTION THE BASIC PRINCIPLES OF THE RIGHT TO A FAIR TRIAL AND THE RIGHT TO HAVE ACCESS TO A JUDGE

You know how much importance I place on access to justice and a diversified response to dispute resolution, which is not limited merely to taking action in the courts.

Mediation, conciliation or arbitration seem to be particularly well-suited to the international aspect of Internet disputes and the need to respond quickly.

In the context of the European Union, various initiatives have been taken to develop out-of-court settlement of disputes. I intend to support them, on the understanding that this measure presupposes complying with certain procedural guarantees and the right of access to a judge protected by the European Convention for the Protection of Human Rights. It is only in these circumstances that alternative methods of dispute resolution can be developed.

B. – Promoting alternative methods of dispute resolution must go hand in hand with strengthening the means given to national courts to respond to the new challenges of the information society

We must get beyond the too facile image of a national justice that is restive and indifferent to resolving virtual disputes and put off by the technical nature of the subject. On the contrary, case-law, especially French case-law, attests to the will and ability of courts at all levels to take on virtual disputes and provide appropriate solutions.

On a Community level, the Tampere European Council, pursuing the aim of creating a European space of justice, freedom and security, proposed giving judges in the European Union specific legal instruments that are able to meet the new requirements arising from the transnational nature of disputes. This concern to make justice more effective is shown in both civil and criminal matters.

These measures were relayed internally by various initiatives which significantly reinforce the courts' resources. In order to give the police and the courts the means of conducting enquiries in the virtual world as they do in the real world, the law on everyday security establishes the circumstances in which connection data must be retained by telecommunications operators for use in criminal matters. Furthermore, it establishes the circumstances in which encrypted messages can be decoded in a way that is legally safe, in the context of criminal proceedings.

C. – Finally, we must guarantee the effective implementation of fundamental rights and freedoms on the Internet

It is important to ensure that the technical possibilities of data interconnection, of identifying people, building behaviour profiles or copying content of all kinds do not interfere with the rights of people and property.

The issues of data protection and respect for private life are a recurrent concern in democratic societies. In this field, changes in technology led to an amendment of the Computer and Freedom@ law of 6 January 1978 under the transposition of the European Directive of 24 October 1995, whilst strengthening the fundamental principles laid down by the 1978 legislator.

The bill put forward by the Government thus extends the obligations on those responsible for processing, makes the right of individuals to appeal discretionary. It also reinforces the authority of the CNIL (French organisation dedicated to information technology and civil rights) by conferring on it new powers of control and a bigger role in self-regulation procedures. As far as the protection of literary and artistic property rights is concerned, the Directive of 22 May 2001, which is in the process of being transposed, will provide an initial response to the issues that making use of a work on the networks might raise.

The virtual community must be made to comply with the values which form the basis of human rights and protection of freedoms.

Technology is only a tool. Regulation of the Internet must be based on rules which rely on a political view that derives from ideals of democracy.

Let us stop arguing from a purely defensive point of view, as if the development of the Internet could only result in a decline in rights and freedoms. Let us instead be determined and imaginative so that the adaptation made necessary by advances in technology helps the law to move forward.

In this respect, I must praise your discussions which have contributed to this. Thank you.

INDEX

A

AAA : 602, 609, 610.

ACLU : 426, 528, 529.

Actors : 7, 10, 17, 20, 21, 85, 87, 88, 89, 90, 91, 92, 99, 171, 175, 183, 191, 195, 202, 269, 281, 289, 293, 294, 300, 317, 320, 323, 327, 328, 361, 362, 363, 364, 366, 422, 423, 445, 470, 471, 531, 536, 547, 549, 619, 633.

ADPIC provisions : 26.

ADSL : 249.

AFNIC : 292.

Agreement : 12, 47, 60, 72, 97, 105, 119, 126, 182, 193, 196, 198, 203, 268, 299, 310, 312, 350, 354, 357, 366, 392, 393, 404, 424, 435, 442, 450, 469, 470, 474, 517, 529, 536, 540, 563, 574, 583, 584, 585, 586, 587, 589, 590, 594, 596, 597, 598, 606, 607, 608, 619, 620, 638, 643.

Agreements : 7, 8, 35, 48, 58, 72, 88, 96, 218, 219, 267, 268, 269, 349, 350, 351, 358, 359, 372, 469, 470, 520, 524, 540, 583, 586, 594, 596, 598, 607.

Alcatel : 34, 38, 296, 318.

Alternative Dispute Resolution (ADR) procedures : 302.

Alternative methods of dispute resolution : 30, 274, 362, 365, 366, 471, 472, 613, 627, 630, 645.

American Arbitration Association : 589, 590, 593, 602.

American Bar Association : 406, 412, 519, 530, 536, 537.

American model : 132, 476.

American State : 98.

Anonymiser : 99.

Anonymisers : 100.

AOL : 296.

APEC : 194, 301, 496.

APNIC : 316.

Applicable law : 10, 55, 56, 60, 64, 65, 67, 68, 72, 73, 75, 106, 107, 108, 109, 175, 181, 188, 268, 302, 346, 364, 365, 366, 468, 486, 506, 508, 509, 511, 535, 536, 561, 564, 573, 580, 581, 627, 632, 641.

Arbitration : 7, 30, 31, 57, 60, 64, 67, 115, 157, 268, 289, 389, 435, 488, 529, 536, 573, 579, 580, 582, 583, 584, 585, 586, 587, 588, 589, 590, 591, 593, 594, 596, 597, 598, 599, 601, 602, 603, 604, 605, 606, 607, 608, 609, 610, 616, 617, 619, 624, 630, 631, 644.

D

E

R

Receipt : 8, 77, 78, 130, 143, 593.

Recommendations : 18, 19, 58, 59, 125, 140, 142, 144, 147, 158, 159, 160, 268, 273, 276, 277, 278, 282, 296, 301, 302, 303, 307, 321, 449, 535, 536, 575, 595, 614, 615, 619.

Regulation : 11, 17, 18, 19, 21, 29, 32, 34, 47, 53, 55, 58, 64, 65, 66, 84, 85, 86, 88, 89, 91, 97, 105, 106, 107, 108, 111, 123, 124, 132, 133, 135, 139, 142, 145, 148, 152, 153, 154, 156, 157, 158, 159, 160, 163, 165, 167, 168, 169, 172, 175, 176, 177, 178, 207, 214, 216, 265, 266, 268, 269, 271, 272, 279, 280, 281, 282, 283, 285, 286, 287, 288, 289, 291, 292, 293, 295, 296, 299, 317, 318, 320, 322, 327, 328, 350, 351, 353, 358, 362, 363, 373, 374, 402, 408, 409, 411, 423, 425, 427, 467, 471, 474, 476, 481, 485, 488, 493, 536, 546, 547, 588, 598, 613, 632, 639, 640, 643, 646.

RFCs : 90.

Right of communication to the public : 436.

Right to copy : 447, 449.

Right to information : 35, 424, 625.

RIPE : 316.

Rome 2 : 109.

Rules : 7, 8, 9, 10, 11, 12, 14, 15, 21, 23, 24, 26, 28, 29, 32, 34, 35, 36, 49, 53, 54, 55, 56, 57, 58, 59, 60, 61, 62, 65, 67, 68, 71, 72, 73, 75, 76, 77, 81, 82, 83, 84, 85, 86, 87, 88, 89, 91, 92, 93, 95, 96, 97, 98, 99, 101, 107, 108, 111, 113, 120, 125, 130, 137, 138, 139, 140, 151, 152, 154, 155, 158, 159, 160, 164, 165, 168, 169, 170, 171, 174, 175, 176, 177, 180, 183, 184, 185, 189, 193, 194, 195, 196, 199, 204, 208, 229, 241, 260, 267, 272, 281, 285, 288, 291, 294, 300, 302, 327, 329, 330, 331, 337, 339, 341, 350, 351, 354, 361, 362, 365, 366, 367, 368, 369, 370, 371, 372, 373, 375, 376, 378, 379, 384, 389, 391, 395, 402, 403, 404, 405, 406, 406, 407, 409, 410, 418, 423, 425, 429, 432, 440, 442, 453, 457, 468, 469, 472, 475, 481, 485, 486, 501, 502, 503, 504, 505, 506, 507, 508, 509, 510, 511, 514, 517, 518, 519, 520, 521, 523, 524, 525, 526, 527, 530, 531, 535, 536, 537, 539, 541, 542, 543, 545, 547, 562, 563, 580, 581, 582, 584, 586, 589, 590, 593, 596, 598, 599, 602, 604, 605, 609, 610, 615, 622, 623, 625, 628, 630, 631, 632, 635, 636, 641, 646.

Rules of law : 85, 86, 87, 89, 97, 99, 137, 151, 164, 170, 351, 373, 375, 403, 582, 605.

S

Safe Harbor : 48, 177, 363.

Safe Harbour Principles : 13, 152, 164, 182.

Savigny-type system : 27, 499.

Secret services : 150.

Security : 16, 17, 19, 22, 48, 68, 71, 78, 109, 124, 131, 133, 134, 151, 158, 161, 175, 176, 180, 184, 195, 207, 228, 235, 236, 237, 239, 240, 242, 243, 247, 249, 253, 255, 258, 261, 265, 266, 279, 289, 293, 294, 302, 307, 313, 325, 326, 337, 339, 345, 362, 363, 368, 371, 381, 387, 392, 393, 394, 404, 405, 423, 426, 428, 432, 471, 475, 481, 494, 495, 510, 531, 536, 550, 591, 592, 597, 626, 636, 637, 640, 641, 642, 643, 645.

TABLE DES MATIÈRES

IMPRIMÉ EN BELGIQUE .

ÉTABLISSEMENTS EMILE BRUYLANT, société anonyme, Bruxelles
Prés.-Dir. gén. : JEAN VANDEVELD, av. W. Churchill, 221, 1180 Bruxelles